AF183966

# THE EUROPEAN COURT OF JUSTICE AND THE AUTONOMY OF THE MEMBER STATES

# THE EUROPEAN COURT OF JUSTICE AND THE AUTONOMY OF THE MEMBER STATES

Hans-W. Micklitz
Bruno De Witte
(editors)

intersentia
Cambridge – Antwerp – Portland

Intersentia Publishing Ltd.
Trinity House | Cambridge Business Park | Cowley Road
Cambridge | CB4 0WZ | United Kingdom
tel.: +44 1223 393 753 | email: mail@intersentia.co.uk

*Distribution for the UK:*
Hart Publishing Ltd.
16C Worcester Place
Oxford OX1 2JW
UK
Tel.: +44 1865 51 75 30
Email: mail@hartpub.co.uk

*Distribution for the USA and Canada:*
International Specialized Book Services
920 NE 58th Ave Suite 300
Portland, OR 97213
USA
Tel.: +1 800 944 6190 (toll free)
Email: info@isbs.com

*Distribution for Austria:*
Neuer Wissenschaftlicher Verlag
Argentinierstraße 42/6
1040 Wien
Austria
Tel.: +43 1 535 61 03 24
Email: office@nwv.at

*Distribution for other countries:*
Intersentia Publishing nv
Groenstraat 31
2640 Mortsel
Belgium
Tel.: +32 3 680 15 50
Email: mail@intersentia.be

The European Court of Justice and the Autonomy of the Member States
Hans-W. Micklitz and Bruno De Witte (eds.)



ISBN 978–1–78068–113–9
NUR 828

British Library Cataloguing in Publication Data. A catalogue record for this book is available from the British Library.

# FOREWORD

The Lisbon Treaty has, once again, extended the jurisdiction of the Court of Justice of the European Union to new areas of EU law. The field of criminal justice and police cooperation, covered by the former 'third pillar' of the European Union, will from now on be subject to the full review and interpretation powers of the Court of Justice. In the field of immigration law, lower national courts are now entitled to engage with the Court of Justice through the preliminary reference mechanism, and they have started to make active use of that new possibility. The EU Charter of Rights has now the same legal value as the Treaties themselves, thus opening up yet another field for active intervention by the Court of Justice. We find ourselves in front of a seeming paradox: whereas *individual* Member State governments occasionally complain about judgments of the Court of Justice, especially when those judgments curtail that state's policy autonomy in a sensitive domain, the *collectivity* of the Member State governments have agreed, in each treaty revision so far, to confirm and extend the far-reaching powers which the Court of Justice possesses for enforcing EU law. The explanation of the paradox can only be that, deep down, the Member States of the EU remain convinced that an effective Court of Justice with strong enforcement powers is one of the salient features of European Community law which have stood the test of time, and feel no inclination to clip the wings of that Court for fear that this would affect the effectiveness of the European integration process. Nevertheless, the grumblings about single judgments, or about the consistency and direction of the Court in particular policy fields, have never ceased, and indeed have become more audible in recent years. One overall theme in this respect is the perception that the Court of Justice, quite often, does not leave sufficient autonomy to the Member States in developing their own legal and policy choices in areas where European and national competences overlap.

This overall theme was explored at a conference organised at the European University Institute in Florence in 2009, and was later elaborated in the chapters of this volume. The editors of the volume would like to express their gratitude to the generous sponsors of the conference, namely the Academy of European Law of the EUI, and the European Union Democracy Observatory programme, also based at the EUI. They are grateful for the friendly, patient and efficient cooperation of Intersentia publishers. This book owes a great debt to Hanna

Schebesta, doctoral researcher at the EUI, who played a crucial role during the editing stage of this volume.

Hans Micklitz and Bruno De Witte
Florence/Maastricht, October 2011.

# CONTENTS

*Foreword*.......... v

PART I.
INTRODUCTION

Judge-Made Integration?
Hans-W. Micklitz and Hanna Schebesta .......... 3

1. Introduction .......... 3
2. Introducing the Authors' Contributions.......... 4

PART II.
THE GENERAL SHAPE OF MEMBER STATE AUTONOMY
IN THE COURT'S CASE LAW

Competence and Member State Autonomy: Causality, Consequence and Legitimacy
Paul Craig .......... 11

1. Competence: The 'Allure of the Simple' and the 'Complexity of Reality'... 11
2. Competence and Member State Autonomy: Four Factors in Temporal Perspective .......... 12
   2.1. From Rome to the SEA.......... 12
   2.2. From the SEA to the Treaty on European Union .......... 16
   2.3. From Maastricht to Nice .......... 18
   2.4. Post Nice.......... 21
   2.5. Conclusion.......... 25
3. Member State Autonomy: Choice, Consequences and Legitimacy.......... 25
   3.1. The Logic of Collective Action.......... 26
   3.2. Output Legitimacy: Peace and Prosperity.......... 26
   3.3. Output Legitimacy: Externalities .......... 27
   3.4. Output Legitimacy: 'Tension' and 'Resolution' .......... 28
   3.5. Output Legitimacy: Questioning the Premise.......... 29
   3.6. Output Legitimacy: the Balance between the Economic and the Social .......... 30

3.7. Input Legitimacy: the Rationales for the Shift ........ 31
4. Conclusion ........ 34

The European Court of Justice's Approach to Primacy and European Constitutionalism – Preserving the European Constitutional Order?
Fabian AMTENBRINK ........ 35

1. Introductory Remarks ........ 35
2. European Constitutionalism ........ 38
2.1. Terminology ........ 39
2.2. The National and European (Constitutional) Legal Orders: Companions in Fate ........ 42
3. The ECJ's Principled Approach to Primacy: a Claim of Absolute Sovereignty in Disguise? ........ 52
3.1. On the ECJ's Concept of Primacy ........ 53
3.2. Recognizing Member State's Common (Constitutional) Legal Traditions ........ 56
3.3. Recognition of National (Constitutional) Legal Standards ........ 60
4. Concluding Remarks ........ 62

The Judge's Role in European Integration – The Court of Justice and Its Critics
Jürgen BASEDOW ........ 65

1. Challenges to the Legality of the European Court's Practice ........ 65
2. Centrifugal Forces and the Functions of the Court ........ 66
2.1. The Legal Framework ........ 66
2.2. Centrifugal Forces in the Member States ........ 67
2.3. Three Functions of the Court of Justice ........ 69
3. The Review Function ........ 70
3.1. Infringement Proceedings against Member States ........ 70
3.2. Legal Doctrines Furthering the Review Function ........ 71
4. The Impulse Function ........ 72
4.1. The Synchrony of Political and Legal Action ........ 72
4.2. Example 1: Admission of Foreign Students to Austrian Universities . 73
4.3. Example 2: Opening National Insurance Markets ........ 73
4.4. Example 3: Free Movement for Companies ........ 74
4.5. Summary: Legal Contributions to the Community's Mission ........ 75
5. The Uniformity Function ........ 76
5.1. The Court Confronted with a Growing Body of Fragmentary Legislation ........ 76
5.2. Underperformance ........ 76
5.3. Overperformance ........ 78

5.4. The Court's Insecurity .......... 78
6. Conclusion .......... 79

PART III.
INTERNAL MARKET, CITIZENSHIP AND MIGRATION

How Proportionate is the Proportionality Principle? Some critical remarks on the use and methodology of the proportionality principle in the internal market case law of the ECJ
Norbert Reich .......... 83

1. From Admiration to Frustration? .......... 83
2. Widening the Scope of Application of the Fundamental Freedoms Beyond Market Access – How Wide? .......... 85
2.1. Beyond Market Access .......... 86
2.2. No "Reserved" or "Exempted" Areas .......... 90
2.3. A Broad and at the Same Time a Narrow Reading of "Public Interest" Justifications .......... 91
3. The Proportionality Principle as the "Super-Norm"? .......... 94
3.1. Some Preliminary Methodological Reflections .......... 94
3.2. The Origin in the Early Case Law of the ECJ .......... 95
3.3. Possible Methodological Sophistication or Aberration? The Different and Sometimes Incoherent Tests of the ECJ .......... 97
3.3.1. Examples for the "autonomous balancing" approach .......... 98
3.3.2. Examples for the "state margin of appreciation" approach ... 100
3.3.3. Examples for the – rather ambivalent – "fundamental rights approach" .......... 103
3.3.4. Examples for the "quasi-legislative approach" .......... 105
4. Where Are We Now – A Plea for Judicial Restraint .......... 108

Judicial Activism or Constitutional Interaction? Policymaking by the ECJ in the Field of Union Citizenship
Michael Dougan .......... 113

1. Introduction .......... 113
2. Some Preliminary Remarks on "Judicial Activism" .......... 114
3. A Critical Reading of the Citizenship Case Law from 1998–2008 .......... 122
4. Developments in the Citizenship Case Law since 2008 .......... 131
5. A More Constructive Reading of the Citizenship Case Law? .......... 139

6. Concluding Remarks ........ 146

"Reserved Areas" of the Member States and the ECJ: the Case of Higher Education
Dragana DAMJANOVIC ........ 149

1. Introduction ........ 149
1.1. Article 165 TFEU (ex Article 149 ECT): Education as a "Reserved Area" of the Member States and the Bologna Process ........ 149
1.2. The 'Implied Powers Doctrine' as the Basis of EU Legal Integration within Higher Education ........ 152
1.3. Aim of This Paper ........ 153
2. The Various Strands of ECJ Case Law in Higher Education ........ 153
2.1. Professional Recognition ........ 153
2.2. Student Mobility: Cross-Border Access to Higher Education Courses ........ 155
2.2.1. The issue of student mobility within the triangle of EU case law, EU hard law and European soft law (in particular, the Bologna process) ........ 155
2.2.2. The Austria *v* Commission and Belgium *v* Commission 'student mobility' cases ........ 157
2.2.3. Criticism against the Court ........ 158
2.2.4. Reaction to the Court's judgments: a quota regulation system for medical studies ........ 163
2.2.5. The Bressol judgment ........ 163
2.2.6. Conclusion ........ 166
2.3. Student Mobility: Cross-Border Access to Financial Support for Education ........ 166
2.4. Building the EU Internal Market Based on Free Competition for Higher Education ........ 169
3. Conclusion ........ 171
References ........ 172

The European Court of Justice, Member State Autonomy and European Union Citizenship: Conjunctions and Disjunctions
Dora KOSTAKOPOULOU ........ 175

1. Introduction ........ 175
2. European Union Citizenship as an Experimental Institution ........ 177
2.1. EU Citizenship as a Fundamental Status ........ 180
2.2. Family Reunification ........ 186
2.3. Non-Discriminatory Restrictions ........ 190

2.4. Increased Protection of Union Citizens in the Member State of Residence ... 192
3. EU Citizenship and Member State Nationality: Rethinking the Link? ... 195
4. Conclusion ... 202

PART IV.
FUNDAMENTAL RIGHTS

The Case of Fundamental Rights: a State of Ambivalence
Loïc AZOULAI ... 207

1. Introduction. The Question has Changed ... 207
2. Playing with the Scope of the Protection: the Liberty of the State ... 208
3. Designing the Constraints: the Independence of the State ... 211
4. Conceptualising the Rights: the Identity of the State ... 214
5. Conclusion ... 217

Fundamental Rights Jurisprudence Between Member States' Prerogatives and Citizens' Autonomy
Dagmar SCHIEK ... 219

1. Introduction ... 219
2. The Notion of Fundamental Rights – Autonomy of Human Beings ... 220
3. The Multi-Layered Context of Fundamental Rights in the European Union ... 222
3.1. Protecting Fundamental Rights Alongside Economic Integration ... 223
3.2. Functions of the Court's Fundamental Rights Protection ... 225
3.3. Multi-Polar Dilemmas Underlying the Court's Fundamental Rights Case Law ... 227
4. Recent ECJ Case Law Between EU, Citizens and Member States ... 228
4.1. A Quantitative Appetizer ... 228
4.2. Substantive Assessment of Some Neuralgic Fields ... 229
4.2.1. Assumptions and adequate fields ... 229
4.2.2. Non-discrimination and equality ... 231
4.2.3. Collective labour rights between fundamental freedoms and fundamental rights ... 236
5. Conclusion ... 242
Annex: List of Cases Evaluated ... 244

A Pluralistic Europe of Rights
Marta CARTABIA ... 259

1. Introduction ... 259

2. The New Millennium and the Flourishing of a 'Europe of Rights'....... 262
2.1. The *Tanja Kreil* Case ........ 263
2.2. The *Schmidberger* and *Omega* Cases........ 264
2.3. *K.B.*, *Richards* and *Tadao Maruko* Cases........ 265
2.4. Cases on Terrorism ........ 268
2.5. A Panoramic Overview ........ 269
3. ... and of a 'European Court of Rights' ........ 270
4. 'United in Diversity' at Risk........ 272
5. Looking for an Antidote ........ 275

PART V.
PROCEDURAL AUTONOMY OF THE STATES

The "Procedural Autonomy" of Member States and the Constraints Stemming from the ECJ's Case Law: Is Judicial Activism Still Necessary?
Adelina ADINOLFI ........ 281

1. Introduction........ 281
2. The Constraints on "Procedural Autonomy" of the Member States: the extent of the discretionary power of the Court in the assessment of the adequacy of national procedures........ 284
3. The Critical Reactions Caused by the Judicial Limitation of "Procedural Autonomy" of Member States ........ 286
4. Why Limit the "Procedural Autonomy" of Member States?........ 291
4.1. Supremacy of EU law ........ 291
4.2. Uniform Application of EU law........ 294
4.3. The Fundamental Right to Obtain Judicial Protection ........ 296
5. A Tentative Paradigm to Explain the Court's Unsteady Approach in Assessing Adequacy of National Procedural Law ........ 299
6. Conclusion ........ 302

Why There is No Principle of "Procedural Autonomy" of the Member States
Michal BOBEK........ 305

1. Introduction........ 305
2. The Orthodoxy........ 305
3. The Cases........ 307
4. The Theories ........ 309
5. The Requirements........ 312
5.1. Equivalence ........ 312
5.2. Effectiveness ........ 316
5.3. Their Relationship ........ 317

6. The Misunderstanding ... 319
7. Conclusion ... 322

National Voice and European Loyalty. Member State Autonomy, European Remedies and Constitutional Pluralism in EU Law
Daniel SARMIENTO ... 325

1. Exit, Voice, Loyalty and the Legitimacy of the European Court of Justice ... 326
2. Member State Voice ... 327
   2.1. Judicial Review of National Legislation ... 327
   2.2. Judicial Review of National Judicial Action ... 330
   2.3. Judicial Review of the Pouvoir Constituant ... 336
   2.4. Constitutional Voice and Non-Constitutional Claims ... 338
3. Individual Voice ... 339
4. Autonomy through Pluralism ... 342

PART VI.
CONCLUDING REMARKS – THE RIGHT'S DIMENSION

The ECJ Between the Individual Citizen and the Member States – A Plea for a Judge-Made European Law on Remedies
Hans-W. MICKLITZ ... 349

1. The ECJ Between the Individual Citizen and the Autonomy of the Member States ... 349
2. RRP in a 'New' European Legal Order Having Its 'Own' Legal System ... 351
   2.1. The EU Legal Order Autonomous and/or Integrated ... 352
   2.2. Three European Legal Orders – Economic, Social and Citizen? ... 356
   2.3. A Rights Based Order – Economic, Fundamental, Social, Human, Citizen Rights ... 360
3. RRP – First, Second, Third ... How Many Generations? ... 364
   3.1. The Ambiguities of the Concept of Conferred or Attributed Competences ... 364
   3.2. A Shaky Consensus – The Competence Divide in RRPs ... 366
   3.3. Beyond Consensus – The Horizontal Implications of RRPs ... 369
4. The Institutional Framework of Judge-Made European Law on Remedies ... 373
   4.1. The Parameters: Judicial Co-operation, Organised Law Enforcement and Legitimacy in RRPs ... 374
   4.2. Is the Concept of Subjective Rights a Procrustean Bed? ... 376
      4.2.1. Prevalence of EU economic rights over social rights ... 377
      4.2.2. The missing EU collective rights ... 380

4.3. Competence (Constitutional) Boundaries in the Development of an EU Law on Remedies . . . . . . 383
4.3.1. The impact of the distinction between primary *vs.* secondary EU law on RRPs . . . . . . 385
4.3.2. The line between constitutional and non-constitutional RRPs . . . . . . 388
5. Thoughts on the Future for the EU Law on Remedies *De Lege Lata* . . . . . . 392
5.1. Constitutional Implications: a Right to Access in the Preliminary Reference Procedure . . . . . . 393
5.2. Substantive Implications: RRPs to Counterbalance the European Economic Order . . . . . . 395
5.2.1. From uniform application to uniform enforcement . . . . . . 395
5.2.2. The principle of effectiveness and the doctrine of economic efficiency . . . . . . 397
5.2.3. Materialising the principle of equivalence . . . . . . 399

*Index* . . . . . . 401

# PART I

# INTRODUCTION

# JUDGE-MADE INTEGRATION?

Hans-W. Micklitz and Hanna Schebesta

## 1. INTRODUCTION

European integration has for a long time been perceived as a process rather than a condition. After the big bang and the strong expansive and deepening dynamic that followed, European integration is a concept in need of direction.

While the EU has had to overcome many crises already, there is a persistent narrative of integration through law, telling a tale of a reliable and continuous motor – the Court of Justice – which, for example, in the midst of the de Gaulle empty chair crisis continued to issue landmark pro-integration judgments. In Europe crises seemed confined to the political arena, without affecting the legal one.

The nature of European integration has changed and reveals new complexities: With the internal market task being close to fulfilled, the question of the desired nature and finality of the EU's internal dimension is drawing closer. The challenge as it stands today, is to define the *limits* of European integration inward looking. Cases that reach the CJEU are becoming increasingly political and the Court finds itself confronted with significant value judgments, for example on national and European identity (citizenship) or public interest evaluations (proportionality).

The problematic of the limits to integration, and the Member States' increasingly widespread defence of autonomy, is a general one, which confronts the EU as a whole, affecting its institutions, national institutions and constituencies. Yet, it poses specific questions to the legitimacy of the Court to take decisions which define the path of European integration. The CJEU is increasingly met with criticism – on two accounts: First that of institutional balance, and secondly the appropriate decision making instance as between the legislative and the judiciary. At the same time, a constitutional dimension is being raised, specifically that of the European and Member State relationship. Emblematic for this is the article entitled 'Stop the European Court of Justice' which has become so widely cited because it is seen as lending voice to a strong and widely held sentiment of disapproval on the Court.

Most commonly this criticism is delivered in terms of limits to competence and legitimacy. The EU judicial system – the application of EU law by Member State courts, supported by the preliminary reference mechanism and then

EU enforcement – are rarely questioned. Criticism tends to target the Court's interpretations on a substantive level, but much less so the Court as an institution. The few proposals for institutional reform of the EU judicial structure focus on a truly EU constitutional court to settle questions of competence.

Legally speaking, it was widely thought that EU integration was a project strictly headed one way; towards deeper, and more intense legal harmonization. This paradigm may no longer hold, necessitating an inquiry into the recent role of the European Court of Justice and the Autonomy of the Member States.

## 2. INTRODUCING THE AUTHORS' CONTRIBUTIONS

The present compendium presents a collection of contributions which take stock of the CJEU direction in four different clusters: Member State Autonomy as a competence question; Internal Market, Citizenship and Migration; Fundamental Rights; and Procedural Autonomy – the conclusion presenting a synthesis from a rights-based point of view. In the following we briefly present the individual articles:

*Member State Autonomy as a competence question*

The first part presents Member State autonomy largely from the point of view of competence, helping to convey the message that competence requires a holistic reading of the praxis of EU law.

Craig surveys the changes in the balance of EU competence and Member State autonomy from a historical perspective with the help of four factors – arguing that "the reality of EU competence" is the result of the "symbiotic interaction" of Member State choice as to competence in Treaty and revisions, acceptance of legislation, jurisprudence, and the praxis of institutions regarding EU law. He then proceeds to discuss the question of legitimacy. The ECJ is one variable that shapes the "reality of EU competence" in the midst of a general shift from European integration being seen as a solution to the realization that integration itself may constitute problems.

In his contribution, Ambtenbrink discusses the notions of primacy and European constitutionalism, stressing the "crucial integrative function" of national constitutional orders. The author notes the potential for conflict between the CJEU on the one hand and national constitutional orders on the other. While drawing attention to the fact that the EU narrative of primacy is not matched in practice with an acceptance thereof in constitutional orders, he provides a positive interpretation of constitutional identities which perform such integrative function.

Basedow presents voices of criticism on the CJEU, and distinguishes three different functions of the Court: The review function, the impulse function, and the uniformity function. He criticizes the competence dimension as an "insufficient and inappropriate yardstick" against which to measure the Court's practice in many areas of law, for example private law that would rather require a balance of parties' interests.

Reading the contributions together, competence extends beyond the jurisprudence of the CJEU, the interplay of which has historically varied. The functions performed by the CJEU's jurisprudence in European integration lies in reviewing national laws, giving impulses to political action, and assuring uniformity in the national EU law. National constitutional orders – which continue, at least in praxis, to retain elements of autonomy – do not necessarily constitute an obstacle or a source of resistance to European integration, but rather can be read as being an active part of European integration.

*Internal Market, Citizenship and Migration*

The second part approaches Member State autonomy on substantive grounds: 'The Internal Market, Citizenship and Migration' combines articles which deal with the methodology of the Court regarding, for example, the proportionality test in the Internal Market, the impact of Union Citizenship, and the workings of both in a case study of an area of exclusive competence.

Reich discusses the use and methodology of the proportionality principle in the internal market case law of the ECJ. Analytically, he distinguishes an approach in which the Court conducts the balancing autonomously, or uses a margin of discretion, a fundamental rights balancing exercise, and lastly a quasi-legislative approach. Reich ends with a plea for judicial restraint in applying the proportionality test, particularly in areas of important Member State interests. Here, proportionality is presented as an example of a principle through which the ECJ encroaches (to varying degree) on Member State autonomy.

Dougan examines judicial activism in light of the Union Citizenship case-law. From 2008 onwards, he observes a different approach being taken by the Court which "might well suggest a new mood of uncertainty" about judicial policymaking and its constitutional relationship with the Union's political institutions. The author recommends reading the judicial transformation as having taken place "within a long-term process of constitutional dialogue". Dougan expects the technique of judicial review to become more muted, and the proportionality principle to accommodate national choices in sensitive policy fields – thus becoming more protective of Member State autonomy.

Damjanovic provides a case study on higher education as one of the reserved areas of Member States. Dealing with a particular policy field, she is able to shed specific light on the combined dynamics of both competence questions and the proportionality principle therein. The example clearly illustrates the intense pressure that EU law brings to bear on national models of higher education – the consequence of the CJEU's rulings being that the financial capacity of Member States to retain an autonomous education policy is demonstrably diminished.

The contribution by Kostakopoulou traces the developments of the material and personal scopes of Union citizenship. Furthermore, she discusses the autonomy of national citizenship vis-à-vis the European equivalent, and the currently open link between the two. The article concludes that EU citizenship is an "evolving, experimental institution" – leaving the CJEU with considerable room to manoeuvre.

Regarding the balancing exercise which the Court performs, all the contributions identify scales of intrusiveness of the Court – and therefore as a test which has not yet reached a point of rigid doctrinal predictability. Rather, proportionality remains a mechanism which needs to mature, and by means of which the Court may both prove itself to be self-restrained or intrusive. The same holds true for Union Citizenship which currently represents one of the major potential doctrinal gateways into areas which were previously regarded as clearly belonging to the Member States' realm. In the hands of a pro-active Court, they are very potent tools which may, for example, overturn the reverse discrimination doctrine in the near future. The fact that the Court's judgments are neither mere abstract rulings, nor individual cases with no bearing on the reality of Member States' policy making is made strongly for the field of higher education. At the same time, the case study illustrates the deep impact which judicially developed case law under these doctrines already has on Member State to date. What resounds implicitly in each of the contributions is an understanding of the instruments of both proportionality and citizenship that must be informed and differentiated according to the nature and sensitivity of the national interests at stake.

*Fundamental Rights*

The third part scrutinizes the role that the Court plays in relation to Fundamental Rights and their constitutional dimension with regard to Member State Autonomy.

Azoulai notes the absence of a set of justifications for the constraints imposed on the Member States, and appreciates fundamental rights as both "reducers and vectors" of Member States' autonomy, distinguished along three dimensions: The state's liberty to be free from European control, its independent power to act as authority, and identity. Justifications then serve to allow a better assessment of the desirability of alleged encroachments on Member States' autonomy.

Schiek examines the use of fundamental rights by the Court of Justice and the reasoning it provides, including balancing exercises with a distinction of the different rights involved, finding that it will more often enhance the substantive autonomy of citizens at the expense of Member States' prerogatives than at the expense of EU prerogatives – possibly exhibiting a slight prevalence of rights supported by EU law in a given field. In terms of autonomy this raises the question of who is the prime enforcer of fundamental rights, the State or the EU.

Cartabia conceives 'A Pluralistic Europe of Rights', sketching the activity of the CJEU related to fundamental rights which gradually creates a "European" understanding thereof. She traces the "new dynasty of constitutional cases" – specifically the expanding importance of the Charter of Fundamental Rights – and finds that it has strengthened the position of the CJEU through both a legitimizing and a hermeneutical effect. All the same, she is cautious towards the ambivalent nature of fundamental rights which, despite a longing for universality, are fed by particularity and pluralism.

The constitutional nature of fundamental rights is clearly one which must be read in light not only of the activity of the CJEU, but also of the development of legal instruments such as the Lisbon Treaty, and specifically the Charter of Fundamental Rights. These politically induced changes provide a certain legitimacy and foreseeability to a reconceived attitude on behalf of the Court when dealing with cases involving fundamental rights. Clearly, the use and balancing of fundamental rights in horizontal relations can be identified as one of the flashpoint areas, in which the Court will have the most challenges and questions of legal doctrine in the future.

*Procedural Autonomy of the Member States*

The last part addresses the judicial doctrine of Procedural Autonomy and the role it may play with regard to the autonomy of procedural law of the Member States.

Adinolfi explains the non-uniform approach which the CJEU has taken towards procedural rules of the Member States through the different ratios deployed. She characterizes the Court's approach as shaped by the degree of substantive harmonization, with the Court being more rigorous where the supremacy of EU law is at stake. The fundamental right of judicial protection thus sometimes becomes an instrument for containing Member States, rather than "enhancing citizens' rights". Overall, this leads to a minimum level of indirect harmonization. The author observes that the Court more frequently leaves the assessment of a procedural rule to the national Court, which could be regarded as "an attitude of judicial self-restraint by the Court".

Bobek offers a critical analysis of the dual requirements of equivalence and effectiveness and the notion of 'procedural autonomy', observing the uncertainty of the current tests. He argues that the Court ought to reconsider its conceptualization as it leads to legal uncertainty – drawing the conclusion that there is no principle of 'procedural autonomy' in the current state of EU law.

Sarmiento advances a new conception of Member State 'Voice', which stresses the active role of the individual. After surveying the areas of national legislative provisions, last instance decisions and constitutional norms, the author proposes to combine 'Voice' and 'Loyalty' in a context of constitutional pluralism as a normative foundation. This would entail "a European-oriented interpretation of conflicting scenarios" for national courts, and at the same time a European Court that engages in "national-oriented interpretations".

The previous parts largely highlighted the potential of legal doctrine to encroach upon Member States' autonomy, with procedural autonomy being portrayed as possibly the first judicially created brake to European integration. At the same time, like other doctrines, it is characterized by inconsistencies in the case law. While the CJEU so far has not followed national courts' calls for it to place greater emphasis on the principle of subsidiarity as a judicial technique, procedural autonomy might take on precisely that function.

The book is completed by a concluding and synthesizing article by Micklitz that sketches a place for the CJEU between the individual citizen and the Member States in a plea for a judge-made European law on remedies. Taking the other contributions as points of reference, the author analyses rights, remedies and procedure in their constitutional dimension and finds a difference between primary/secondary and negative/positive effectiveness. The reconceptualised understanding of the CJEU's function in rights, remedies and procedure leads the author to call for a right to access in the preliminary reference procedure, and for a renewed understanding which acts as a substantive counterbalance to the economic European bias.

The contributions read individually are certainly very rich and provide highly valuable insights into the numerous and specific issues chosen. However, the articles also inform each other, and the reader will find that a joint reading provides an all-encompassing overview of the different sets of burning issues which the CJEU will be confronted with in the near future. They foretell the impending arrival of several highly decisive interpretations of the reach of EU law, the answer to which will greatly define the future of European integration.

Against a background which is relatively hostile to deeper European integration, a picture of a rather self-conscious Court emerges. In its hands are the powerful tools of the proportionality methodology, European citizenship and politically constitutionalized fundamental rights, yet these same hands seem to be suspended in the air. Before deciding whether and how to use them, the CJEU (or rather, the body of judges issuing the judgments) seems to be very receptive to outside voices and context in a feedback process. Most likely, rather than one-off event landmark judgments, we are in for a trickle-down process of gradual change through case law, which do not leave an absolute sphere for Member State autonomy, but which strives to create a shared understanding.

# PART II

# THE GENERAL SHAPE OF MEMBER STATE AUTONOMY IN THE COURT'S CASE LAW

# COMPETENCE AND MEMBER STATE AUTONOMY: CAUSALITY, CONSEQUENCE AND LEGITIMACY

Paul Craig*

The scope of EU competence and the limits on Member State autonomy can validly be analysed from a variety of perspectives.[1] This chapter considers one such perspective, the prevailing concern about the scope and exercise of EU competence, which is of especial significance given the focus of this book. This concern is often based on the premise that some reified entity called the EU has increasingly arrogated power, with a consequent diminution of national autonomy that the Member States have been unable to resist, and the ECJ is frequently regarded as bearing primary responsibility.

It will, however, be argued in the first half of this chapter that the Community courts were but one factor out of four responsible for the expansion of EU power over time, and that the Member States themselves were equally important. This in turn raises interesting questions as to why Member States accepted and contributed to the expansion of EU competence, which is addressed in the second half of the chapter.

## 1. COMPETENCE: THE 'ALLURE OF THE SIMPLE' AND THE 'COMPLEXITY OF REALITY'

Simple propositions are tempting, but are nonetheless apt to mislead. The 'simple proposition' is that the Community courts, driven by the teleological imperative of market and political integration, have been the principal vehicle for the expansion of EU competence, with a corresponding diminution of Member State

* Professor of English Law, St John's College and the University of Oxford. I am grateful for comments on an earlier version of this paper in a seminar held at the EUI. Because this chapter deals with the evolution in time of the Court's case law, references to Treaty articles come with their pre-Lisbon numbers.

1 See, eg, R. Schutze, *From Dual to Cooperative Federalism, The Changing Structure of European Law*, Oxford University Press, Oxford, 2009.

autonomy. The premise is that the shift in power upward towards the EU has been the result primarily of arrogation of power by the Community courts to the detriment of states' rights, which Article 5 EC has been powerless to prevent.

The truth is however more complex and nuanced. The reality of EU competence has resulted from the symbiotic interaction of four variables: Member State choice as to the scope of EU competence, as expressed in Treaty revisions; Member State, and since the SEA, EP acceptance of legislation that has fleshed out the Treaty articles; the jurisprudence of the Community courts; and decisions taken by the institutions as to how to interpret, deploy and prioritize the power accorded to the EU.

Thus, the judicial contribution to the expansion of competence is but one factor in the distribution of power between Member States and the EU. Political choice by the Member States to grant the EU competence in areas such as the environment, culture, health, consumer protection, employment, and vocational training expressed through Treaty revision after extensive discussion in successive IGCs has been equally important, so too has political choice embodied in Community legislation, accepted by the Member States in the Council and in many instances after the SEA also by the EP. The action of Community institutions in deciding how to use the power formally accorded to them is also of real significance. Space precludes detailed elaboration of this thesis since the inception of the EEC, since this would occupy a book in itself. The nature of the argument can nonetheless be exemplified in temporal sequence.

## 2. COMPETENCE AND MEMBER STATE AUTONOMY: FOUR FACTORS IN TEMPORAL PERSPECTIVE

### 2.1. FROM ROME TO THE SEA

The Rome Treaty, the result of conscious Member State choice, established a common market that went beyond a customs union by providing for free movement of factors of production in order to facilitate the optimal allocation of resources. It embodied what might be termed 'flanking policies' designed to prevent either the state or private parties impeding the creation of a level playing field, as exemplified by the prohibition on state aids, and the rules on competition. The Treaty provisions on negative integration were complemented by those to enhance positive integration, most notably through harmonization of laws.

Community legislation built on these Treaty foundations. It embodied conscious political choice or acceptance by the Member States. The legislation varied in nature. Some provisions laid down substantive guidance concerning free movement of goods,[2] establishment[3] and services.[4] Other legislation established detailed substantive[5] and procedural[6] rights associated with free movement, and limited Member State discretion.[7] The quantity of legislation adopted to make negative integration a reality should not be forgotten. There were, for example, approximately fifty such measures enacted from 1962–82, pursuant to the general programmes for the abolition of restrictions on freedom of establishment and the provision of services. Progress was nonetheless slow in relation to positive integration through Community harmonization, since Article 94 required unanimity, and prior to the Single European Act 1986 directives normally demanded Member State agreement on a detailed measure that was difficult to attain.

The judicial contribution was equally important, as exemplified by *Cassis de Dijon*.[8] The ECJ held that Article 28 could apply to national trade rules that did not discriminate against imported products, but which nonetheless inhibited trade because they differed from those applicable in the country of origin. When goods had been lawfully marketed in one Member State, they should be admitted into any other state, unless the state of import could successfully invoke a mandatory requirement. The judgment therefore encapsulated a principle of mutual recognition. It had a marked impact on the scope of Article 28, and caused a major re-orientation in the Commission's regulatory strategy.

The ECJ moreover signalled in cases such as *Reyners*[9] that it was willing to act as a 'legislative catalyst'. It made clear that the principles embodied in the Treaty would be judicially applied through direct effect, even if the Treaty article had not yet been fleshed out by Community legislation in the manner envisaged by the Treaty. Thus the absence of such legislation pursuant to Article 43 EC

2 Commission Directive 70/50/EEC of 22 December 1969 on the abolition of measures which have an effect equivalent to quantitative restrictions on imports and are not covered by other provisions adopted in pursuance of the EEC Treaty, OJ Sp Ed, 1970, I, 17.

3 General Programme for the abolition of restrictions on freedom of establishment, OJ Sp Ed, 2nd Series, IX, 7.

4 General Programmes for the abolition of restrictions on freedom to provide services, OJ Sp Ed, 2nd Series, IX, 3.

5 Regulation (EEC) No 1612/68 of the Council of 15 October 1968 on freedom of movement for workers within the Community, OJ 1968 257/2.

6 Council Directive 68/360/EEC of 15 October 1968 on the abolition of restrictions on movement and residence within the Community for workers of Member States and their families, OJ 1968 L257/13; Council Directive 73/148/EEC of 21 May 1973 on the abolition of restrictions on movement and residence within the Community for nationals of Member States with regard to establishment and the provision of services, OJ 1973 L172/14.

7 Council Directive 64/221/EEC of 25 February 1964 on the co-ordination of special measures concerning the movement and residence of foreign nationals which are justified on grounds of public policy, public security or public health, OJ Sp. Ed., 1963–64, 117.

8 ECJ 20 February 1979, Case 120/78, *Rewe-Zentrale AG v Bundesmonopolverwaltung für Branntwein* [1979] ECR 649.

9 ECJ 21 June 1974, Case 2/74, *Reyners v Belgian State* [1974] ECR 631. See also, ECJ 3 December 1974, Case 33/74, *Van Binsbergen v Bestuur van de Bedrijfsvereniging voor de Metaalnijverheid* [1974] ECR 1299.

did not preclude it from having direct effect, and the ECJ delicately ignored the objection raised by some Member States that it was not for the 'court to exercise a discretionary power reserved to the legislative institutions of the Community and the Member States'.[10] The Court accorded primacy to the prohibition of discrimination within Article 43, and treated the further legislation as a way of effectuating this goal. The Community legislation had not been promulgated within the requisite period because of Member State unwillingness in the Council to make the necessary compromises to allow it through. This was the period of legislative malaise in which getting things done in the Council operating under the shadow of the veto was problematic. The ECJ signalled that it was not willing to allow Article 43 to atrophy. The Court would develop Article 43 through adjudication should the detailed legislation not be forthcoming. The decision therefore constitutes a prime example of normative supranationalism being used to overcome the deficiencies of decisional supranationalism:[11] the Court would use the former via direct effect to overcome the deficiencies in the latter through the logjam in the legislative process.

The judicial contribution to the broadening of Community competence was also manifest in the ECJ's purposive interpretation of the Treaty and Community legislation. Thus, for example, it gave: a broad interpretation to the term 'charges having an equivalent effect';[12] a wide meaning to tax discrimination;[13] an autonomous, broad meaning to the concept[14] and rights of[15] workers; a narrow interpretation to the public service exception;[16] a construction to Community legislation to ensure that procedural requirements therein did not undermine the primary Treaty article;[17] and a narrow interpretation to exceptions to free movement.[18]

---

10 *Ibid.* at [7]. Council Directive 64/221/EEC of 25 February 1964 on the co-ordination of special measures concerning the movement and residence of foreign nationals which are justified on grounds of public policy, public security or public health, OJ Sp. Ed., 1963–64, 117.

11 J. Weiler, 'The Community System: the Dual Character of Supranationalism', (1981) 1 *YBEL (Yearbook of European Law)* 267.

12 ECJ 1 July 1969, Case 24/68, *Commission v Italy* [1969] ECR 193; ECJ 1 July 1969, Cases 2 and 3/69, *Social Fonds voor de Diamantarbeiders v SA Ch. Brachfeld & Sons* [1969] ECR 211.

13 ECJ 9 May 1985, Case 112/84, *Humblot v Directeur des Services Fiscaux* [1985] ECR 1367; ECJ 27 February 1980, Case 168/78, *Commission v France* [1980] ECR 347; ECJ 12 July 1983, Case 170/78, *Commission v United Kingdom* [1983] ECR 2265.

14 ECJ 19 March 1964, Case 75/63, *Hoekstra (nee Unger) v Bestuur der Bedrijfsvereniging voor Detailhandel en Ambachten* [1964] ECR 177; ECJ 23 March 1982, Case 53/81, *Levin v Staatssecretaris van Justitie* [1982] ECR 1035; ECJ 3 June 1986, Case 139/85, *Kempf v Staatssecretaris van Justitie* [1986] ECR 1741.

15 ECJ 30 September 1975, Case 32/75, *Fiorini (nee) Cristini v SNCF* [1975] ECR 1085; ECJ 16 December 1976, Case 63/76, *Inzirillo v Caisse d'Allocations Familiales de l'Arrondissement de Lyon* [1976] ECR 2057; ECJ 14 January 1982, Case 65/81, *Reina v Landeskreditbank Baden-Württemberg* [1982] ECR 33.

16 ECJ 26 May 1982, Case 149/79, *Commission v Belgium* [1980] ECR 3881.

17 ECJ 8 April 1976, Case 48/75, *Royer* [1976] ECR 497; ECJ 7 July 1976, Case 118/75, *Watson and Belmann* [1976] ECR 1185.

18 P Craig and G de Burca, *EU Law, Text, Cases and Materials,* Oxford University Press, Oxford, 4th ed, 2007, 783–788.

It was argued above that four factors contributed to the balance between EU competence and Member State autonomy. We have thus far considered in outline three of these, and we now turn to the fourth, the contribution of the Community institutions, most notably the Commission, which was both proactive and reactive.

It was proactive in promoting regulations and directives to breathe life into the bare bones of the Treaty articles. The Commission was also reactive, responding to developments in the wider political forum. This is exemplified by the Communication[19] addressed to the Council in response to the *Reyners* decision.[20] The Commission drew out the implications of the decision, making clear to the Council that if it continued to delay passage of directives to effectuate Article 43 then recourse might be had to the ECJ, since such delaying tactics constituted derogation from the unconditional rule in Article 43.[21] Directives designed solely to abolish restrictions based on nationality were unnecessary in the light of the *Reyners* case.[22] The Council should, however, continue work on directives relating to Article 47 EC[23] and the mutual recognition of diplomas.[24]

The Commission therefore reinforced the Court's ruling. The principles in Article 43 could not be avoided, because of Member States' unwillingness to agree on implementing provisions. If the Member States continued to be tardy then the Court would fill out the more detailed meaning of the Treaty Article. The resulting norms might not be those which the Member States would have chosen in Community legislation. If the Member States delayed in promulgating these legislative norms to ensure that they accorded with their interests, they might then have little say in the rules developed by the Court.

The decision in *Reyners*, and the Commission's Communication, did not suddenly lead to a positive surge of legislative activity. The Council did however pass a Resolution[25] acknowledging the importance of mutual recognition of diplomas and harmonization directives were enacted covering particular economic sectors. In the absence of more general provisions the ECJ developed its jurisprudence, limiting the ability of Member States to refuse entry to the host state where the applicant possessed the relevant qualifications in her home state.[26]

---

19 Commission Communication to the Council on the consequences of the judgment of the Court of Justice of June 21 1974, in Case 2/74 (Reyners and the Belgian State) on the proposals for Directives concerning the right of establishment and freedom to provide services at present before the Council, SEC (74) 4024 final.

20 Case 2/74, *Reyners*, fn 9.

21 SEC (74) 4024 final, fn 19, at [I.2–3].

22 *Ibid.* at [II].

23 Ex Art 57 EEC.

24 Fn 19, at [III].

25 Council Resolution on the Mutual Recognition of Diplomas, Certificates and Other Evidence of Formal Qualifications [1974] OJ C98/1.

26 ECJ 7 May 1991, Case 340/89, *Vlassopoulou v Ministerium fur Justiz, Bundes- und Europa-angelegenheiten Baden-Württemberg* [1991] ECR 2357.

## 2.2. FROM THE SEA TO THE TREATY ON EUROPEAN UNION

The same four factors operating symbiotically forged the balance between EU competence and Member State autonomy in the period between the SEA and TEU.

In terms of Treaty amendments, there is continuing debate as to whether the SEA is best perceived in terms of elite bargain made with the Commission's influence,[27] or through the lens of liberal intergovernmentalism.[28] The institutionalist view espoused by Armstrong and Bulmer is perhaps closest to the truth:[29] thus while the Member States were the key players within the European Council, this body 'provided an institutional opportunity for the European Commission to make an input into shaping the guidelines of integration'.[30] Whichever view one subscribes to it was clear that by the early 1980s much remained to be done notwithstanding the efforts of the Commission and the Court. The fact that the Community was falling behind its agenda generated the pessimism of the late 1970s and early 1980s, since the reality of single-market integration appeared to be as far away as ever.

The SEA sought to remedy this malaise. It enhanced the legitimacy of Community decision-making through Article 252 EC, the co-operation procedure, which brought the EP properly into the legislative process for the first time. It improved the efficacy of decision-making by shifting from unanimity to qualified majority decision-making in certain areas. The practice of delegation subject to committee oversight was formalized through amendment of Article 202 EC.[31] There were significant amendments for the single market project, notably Article 14 and Article 95 EC. The latter was especially important since it allowed the passage of harmonization measures by qualified majority, rather than unanimity. The *quid pro quo* for the market liberalizing measures in the SEA was the inclusion of Treaty provisions to strengthen social policy, such as what was Article 118A, concerned with health and safety of workers, and the introduction of social dialogue between employers and employees via what was Article 118B. The new title on economic and social cohesion, designed to reduce the disparities between the regions of the Community, was equally important.

The legal reality of Community competence was also markedly affected by legislative activity, which was framed by the Commission's White Paper,

---

27 W. Sandholtz and J. Zysman, '1992: Recasting the European Bargain', (1989) 42 *World Politics* 95.

28 A. Moravcsik, 'Negotiating the Single European Act: National Interests and Conventional Statecraft in the European Community', (1991) 45 *International Organization* 19.

29 K. Armstrong and S. Bulmer, *The Governance of the Single European Market*, Manchester University Press, Manchester, 1998, Chap 1.

30 *Ibid.* 18–19.

31 Ex Art. 145.

*Completing the Internal Market.*[32] It provided the blueprint for Community regulatory activity. The Commission moved away from the previous concept of harmonization towards that of mutual recognition and equivalence[33] by building on the *Cassis* jurisprudence.[34] For the future, harmonization would generally only be used for trade barriers that survived scrutiny under the *Cassis* test, where the Member State advanced a plausible claim that the restriction was necessary on one of the mandatory grounds of public health, fiscal supervision etc.[35] Article 95 was the principal Treaty foundation for the passage of legislation. The new approach to harmonization took hold.[36]

The ECJ contributed towards expansion of EC competence through the purposive approach to interpretation it had developed prior to the SEA. It expanded on its rulings in *Reyners*[37] and *Thieffry*[38] and used direct effect to foster the single market by breaking down barriers to free movement. National authorities could not, for example, refuse, without explanation, to allow nationals from another Member State to practise their profession on the ground that their qualifications were not equivalent to the corresponding national qualification. The national authorities had to make an objective assessment of the equivalence of the relevant regulations, even where there was no Community measure providing for equivalence.[39] The difficulties of securing agreement within the Community legislature would not, therefore, be allowed to hinder realization of fundamental Community goals. The ECJ also grappled with the 'burdens of success'. The very success of mutual recognition as articulated in *Cassis* led to the difficulty of drawing the boundary lines of Article 28, an issue that still plagues the case law.[40]

The fourth factor that significantly affected the institutional balance between EU competence and Member State autonomy was the focus of the Community institutions, most notably the Commission. It used its regulatory resources to institutionalize and enforce the new approach to harmonization, premised on *Cassis de Dijon*. A product lawfully manufactured in a Member State could be sold in any other Member State. Mutual recognition should be the norm. No harmonization was required for national measures condemned under the *Cassis* reasoning. They would be invalid, unless they came within the mandatory requirements. This strategy was reinforced by Member States' obligation to

32 COM(85)310, 14 June 1985.
33 *Ibid.* at [13].
34 Case 120/78, *Rewe-Zentrale*, fn 8.
35 COM(85)310, n 32, at [65].
36 www.newapproach.eu/.
37 *Reyners*, fn 9.
38 ECJ 28 April 1977, Case 71/76, *Thieffry v Conseil de l'ordre des avocats à la cour de Paris* [1977] ECR 765.
39 ECJ 15 October 1987, Case 222/86, *UNECTEF v Heylens* [1987] ECR 4097; ECJ 7 May 1991, Case 340/89, *Vlassopoulou v Ministerium fur Justiz, Budes- und Europaangelegenheiten Baden-Württemberg* [1991] ECR 2357.
40 P. Craig and G. de Burca, fn 18, Chap 19.

provide information to the Commission before adopting technical standards.[41] Legislative harmonization was restricted to laying down essential health and safety standards, and European standardization was promoted.[42] The advantages of the new approach to harmonization were considerable, since directives could be drafted more easily and made applicable to a variety of goods.

## 2.3. FROM MAASTRICHT TO NICE

The balance between EU competence and Member State autonomy continued to be affected by the interplay between the four variables in the period between the TEU and the Nice Treaty.

In institutional terms, the TEU increased the legitimacy of Community decision-making by further enhancing the power of the EP, through the co-decision procedure, Article 251 EC, which applied, *inter alia*, to harmonization under Article 95 EC. This latter Article was itself modified by the Amsterdam Treaty, so as to increase central power over those parts of Article 95 that accord the Member States room for manoeuvre in relation to harmonization measures. The TEU also introduced subsidiarity, which had some impact on the volume and nature of rules to implement the single market.[43]

In substantive terms, Member State agreement on the provisions concerning economic and monetary union was the main innovation to the Community Pillar in the Maastricht Treaty. It should also be remembered that the Member States, through amendments in the Maastricht Treaty and Amsterdam Treaty, accorded the Community competence in other areas, including: citizenship, Articles 17–21; consumer policy, Article 153; social policy, Articles 136–145; employment, Articles 125–130 EC; public health, Article 152 EC. The Member States were in addition willing in the TEU to grant competence over Common Foreign and Security Policy, and Justice and Home Affairs, albeit retaining the reins of power more firmly in their own hands in these areas. It was but a few years later in the Amsterdam Treaty that the rules relating to visas, asylum, immigration, and judicial co-operation in civil matters were transferred from the Third Pillar to the Community Pillar.

Community legislation continued to affect the degree of Member State autonomy. Much legislation concerned the single market, which is unsurprising, given that the single market project did not come magically to an end in 1992. This legislation was in part procedural, concerned with the provision of information. The Member States' obligations to inform the Commission of proposed technical

---

41 Council Directive 83/189/EEC of 28 March 1983 laying down a procedure for the provision of information in the field of technical standards and regulations, OJ 1983 L109/8.

42 http://ec.europa.eu/enterprise/newapproach/legislation/guide/index.htm.

43 K. Armstrong and S. Bulmer, fn 29, 292–296.

standards were consolidated and extended to services.[44] This was complemented by an obligation to provide information on national measures derogating from free movement of goods.[45] There was also a large volume of substantive legislation, concerning, *inter alia*:[46] health and safety in relation to goods; public procurement; the environment, and services, such as banking, investment services, insurance, credit institutions and the like.[47] Minimum harmonization clauses were common in these directives.[48] There was increased recourse to legislative and non-legislative measures to achieve an objective, which is common in many legal orders. The difference in the late 1990s is that this was positively lauded in the Community, rather than seen as a cause for apology.[49]

The scope of EC competence and Member State autonomy continued to be affected by the ECJ's jurisprudence. Thus this period saw the redefinition of Community competence in relation to goods, *Keck*,[50] and the limitation of Community regulatory competence in the *Tobacco* judgment,[51] although the former case gave rise to significant problems, and the latter has largely been overtaken by subsequent case law. It would however be wrong to present all case

44 Directive 98/34/EC of the European Parliament and of the Council of 22 June 1998 laying down a procedure for the provision of information in the field of technical standards and regulations, OJ 1998 L204/37; Directive 98/48/EC of the European Parliament and of the Council of 20 July 1998 amending Directive 98/34/EC laying down a procedure for the provision of information in the field of technical standards and regulations, OJ 1998 L217/18, extending this to services.

45 Decision 3052/95/EC of the European Parliament and of the Council of 13 December 1995 establishing a procedure for the exchange of information on national measures derogating from the principle of the free movement of goods within the Community, OJ 1995 L321/1.

46 See, e.g., Decision 283/1999/EC of the European Parliament and of the Council of 25 January 1999 establishing a general framework for Community activities in favour of consumers, OJ 1999 L34/1; Directive 96/92/EC of the European Parliament and of the Council of 19 December 1996 concerning common rules for the internal market in electricity, OJ 1997 L27/20; Regulation (EC) 1980/2000 of the European Parliament and of the Council of 17 July 2000 on a revised Community eco-label award scheme, OJ 2000 L237/1; Directive 1999/93/EC of the European Parliament and of the Council of 13 December 1999 on a Community framework for electronic signatures, OJ 2000 L13/12; Directive 2000/31/EC of the European Parliament and of the Council of 8 June 2000 on certain legal aspects of information society services, in particular electronic commerce, in the Internal Market ('Directive on electronic commerce'), OJ 2000 L178/1.

47 See, e.g., Council Directive 92/96/EEC of 10 November 1992 on the coordination of laws, regulations and administrative provisions relating to direct life assurance, OJ 1992 L360/1; Council Directive 92/49/EEC of 18 June 1992 on the coordination of laws, regulations and administrative provisions relating to direct insurance other than life assurance and amending Directives 73/239/EEC and 88/357/EEC (third non-life insurance Directive), OJ 1992 L228/1; Council Directive 93/6/EEC of 15 March 1993 on the capital adequacy of investments firms and credit institutions, OJ 1993 L141/1.

48 M. Dougan, 'Minimum Harmonization and the Internal Market' (2000) 37 *CMLR (Common Market Law Review)* 853, at 855–856.

49 See, eg, Commission in its 2000 Review of the Internal Market Strategy, COM(2000) 257 final; Nice European Council, 7–9 December 2000, Annex 1, at [28].

50 ECJ 24 November 1993, Cases C-267 and 268/91, *Criminal Proceedings against Keck and Mithouard* [1993] ECR I-6097.

51 ECJ 5 October 2000, Case C-376/98, *Germany v European Parliament and Council* [2000] ECR I-08419.

law as restrictive of Community competence. The picture was more subtle.[52] The Court shifted its activism from free movement of goods to the other freedoms, such as establishment, services[53] and persons.[54]

The real picture concerning the balance between EU competence and Member State autonomy was also markedly influenced by the fourth factor, the use made by the Community institutions of its powers.

Thus the Commission became increasingly concerned that mutual recognition, which was central to the single market project, was not functioning properly, because of lack of awareness and/or application by national officials at ground level.[55] It pressed for practical measures to increase the efficacy of EC law, such as the inclusion of mutual recognition clauses in national legislation, an argument accepted by the ECJ.[56]

The Commission and the European Council also consciously conceptualized the single market in a broader, more holistic, manner. Consumer welfare, social policy, and environmental policy were regarded as important facets of the internal market strategy.[57] The Lisbon European Council constituted an important stage in the reconfiguration of the internal market agenda. The meeting focused on employment, economic reform and social cohesion. It set a 'new' strategic goal: the Union was to become 'the most competitive and dynamic knowledge-based economy in the world, capable of sustainable economic growth with more and better jobs and greater social cohesion'.[58] Completion of the internal market was one way of achieving this strategy.[59] The modernisation of the European social model through the building of an active welfare state was to be another. This was crucial to ensure that 'the emergence of this new economy does not compound the existing social problems of unemployment, social exclusion and poverty'.[60] This objective was further particularised in terms of better education, an active employment policy, modernising social protection and promoting social inclusion.[61] These commitments were reiterated at the Feira and Nice

52 M. P. Maduro, *We the Court, The European Court of Justice & the European Economic Constitution*, Hart, Oxford, 1998, 100–102; E. Johnson and D. O' Keefe, 'From Discrimination to Obstacles to Free Movement: Recent Developments Concerning the Free Movement of Workers 1989–1994', (1994) 31 *CMLR* 1313.

53 ECJ 10 May 1995, Case C-384/93, *Alpine Investments v Minister van Financiën* [1995] ECR I-1141.

54 ECJ 15 December 1995, Case C-415/93, *Bosman* [1995] ECR I-4921.

55 Commission Communication to the European Parliament and the Council, Mutual Recognition in the Context of the Follow-up to the Action Plan for the Single Market, 16 June 1999.

56 ECJ 22 October 1998, Case C-184/96, *Commission v France* [1998] ECR I-6197.

57 See, eg, *Single Market Action Plan sets Agenda*, 18 June 1997, 2; *Action Plan*, 9–11.

58 Lisbon European Council, 23–24 March 2000, at [5].

59 *Ibid.* at [5], [16]-[21].

60 *Ibid.* at [24].

61 *Ibid.* at [25]-[34].

European Councils.[62] The latter meeting approved the Commission's European Social Agenda, endorsed by the European Parliament, which was characterised by the 'indissoluble link between economic performance and social progress'.[63] A high level of social protection, coupled with services of general interest vital for social cohesion, constituted the common core of values for the Community: economic growth and social cohesion were seen as mutually reinforcing.[64] The Stockholm European Council echoed the same idea, with 'full agreement that economic reform, employment and social policies were mutually reinforcing'.[65] The principal Commission reports concerning the internal market developed the ideas articulated by the European Council.[66]

## 2.4. POST NICE

The symbiotic interaction between the four factors continued to determine the legal and political reality of EU competence in the new millennium.

In terms of Treaty amendments, the decade post the Nice Treaty has been dominated by attempts at 'comprehensive' Treaty reform in the Constitutional Treaty,[67] and thereafter in the Lisbon Treaty.[68] They included provisions expressly dealing with the delineation of competence between the EU and Member States, which have been examined in detail elsewhere.[69] Suffice it to say for present purposes that while these provisions will frame the competence issue if the Lisbon Treaty is ratified, the four factors considered in this paper will continue to determine the legal and political reality of competence between the EU and the Member States. Thus in relation to, for example, the many areas that fall under the category of shared competence in the Lisbon Treaty, the more precise nature of this sharing will be determined by an admixture of: the detailed Treaty articles that govern the particular area; the EU legislation enacted pursuant to such Treaty articles; judicial interpretation by the ECJ; and decisions made by the EU institutions as to how such powers should be prioritized and deployed.

The problems of comprehensive Treaty reform did not however slow the passage of legislation in the last decade. A mere flavour of the plethora of legislation enacted during this period can be conveyed here. There has been much legislative

62 Feira European Council, 19–20 June 2000, at [19]-[39], [44]-[49]; Nice European Council, 7–9 December 2000.

63 Nice European Council, n 62, at [15]; Annex 1, at [8]-[9].

64 *Ibid.* Annex 1, at [9], [11].

65 Stockholm European Council, at [2].

66 2000 Review of the Internal Market Strategy, COM(2000) 257 final; Economic Reform: Report on the Functioning of Community Capital and Product Markets, COM(2000) 881 final.

67 Treaty Establishing a Constitution for Europe, OJ 2004 C310/1.

68 Treaty of Lisbon, OJ 2007 C306/1.

69 P. Craig, 'Competence: Clarity, Conferral, Containment and Consideration' (2004) 29 *ELR (European Law Review)* 323.

activity concerned with justice, freedom and security, dealing with topics such as the fight against organized crime and terrorism, drugs, human trafficking, asylum and immigration, and police and customs cooperation.[70] Legislative attention has also been focused on the internal market, and in particular on services, this being reflective of its economic importance, given that it constitutes 70% of Member State economic activity. The passage of such legislation has not always been easy, as exemplified by opposition from the European Parliament to Commission proposals for the Services Directive, the final version of which was less far-reaching.[71] This should not mask the fact that the Community has pressed ahead with a plethora of important legislation relating to services, concerning banking,[72] financial services,[73] insurance,[74] and securities.[75] There was major legislation relating to goods, most notably through the long awaited REACH regulation,[76] but also in areas such as pharmaceuticals,[77] and technical harmonization.[78] The Community legislature has been active in other core areas, such as customs, enacting a modernized customs code,[79] taxation,[80] and regional policy.[81] It should be emphasized that the preceding are but examples of legislative activity in the last decade, and the reality is that important primary legislation, accompanied by more numerous secondary Comitology regulations, is evident in all areas of Community activity.

---

70 http://europa.eu/legislation_summaries/justice_freedom_security/index_en.htm.

71 Directive 2006/123/EC of the European Parliament and of the Council of 12 December 2006 on services in the internal market, OJ 2006 L376/36.

72 Legislation relating to matters such as: the reorganization of credit institutions, capital adequacy of investment firms, the taking up and pursuit of business of credit institutions, supervision of credit institutions, electronic money institutions, combating fraud in relation to payments, payment services in the internal market, http://europa.eu/legislation_summaries/internal_market/single_market_services/financial_services_banking/index_en.htm.

73 Legislation relating to, *inter alia*, distance contracts for financial services, supervision, and markets in financial instruments, http://europa.eu/legislation_summaries/internal_market/single_market_services/financial_services_general_framework/index_en.htm.

74 Legislation relating to, for example, supervision, solvency, accounts, http://europa.eu/legislation_summaries/internal_market/single_market_services/financial_services_insurance/index_en.htm.

75 Legislation on shareholders' rights in listed companies, transparency, insider dealing, http://europa.eu/legislation_summaries/internal_market/single_market_services/financial_services_transactions_in_securities/l24035_en.htm.

76 Regulation (EC) No 1907/2006 of the European Parliament and of the Council of 18 December 2006 concerning the Registration, Evaluation, Authorisation and Restriction of Chemicals (REACH), establishing a European Chemicals Agency, OJ 2006 L396/1.

77 http://europa.eu/legislation_summaries/internal_market/single_market_for_goods/pharmaceutical_and_cosmetic_products/index_en.htm.

78 http://europa.eu/legislation_summaries/internal_market/single_market_for_goods/technical_harmonisation/index_en.htm.

79 Regulation (EC) 450/2008 of the European Parliament and of the Council of 23 April 2008 laying down the Community Customs Code (Modernised Customs Code), OJ 2008 L145/1.

80 See, e.g., Council Directive 2006/112/EC of 28 November 2006 on the common system of value added tax, OJ 2006 L347/1.

81 Council Regulation (EC) 1083/2006 of 11 July 2006 laying down general provisions on the European Regional Development Fund, the European Social Fund and the Cohesion Fund and repealing Regulation (EC) 1260/1999, OJ 2006 L210/25.

The ECJ's case law continued to play an important role in relation to Community competence and Member State autonomy during this period. This is apparent in many spheres of Community activity. It can be exemplified by the jurisprudence on citizenship, and services.

In relation to citizenship, the ECJ gave an expansive reading to Articles 12 and 17 EC, and a narrow reading to Article 18(1) EC, insofar as it limited the citizen's right to move freely within the EU by conditions laid down in the Treaty and in measures adopted pursuant thereto. The judicial statement that 'union citizenship is destined to be the fundamental status of nationals of the Member States, enabling those who find themselves in the same situation to enjoy the same treatment in law irrespective of their nationality, subject to such exceptions as are expressly provided for',[82] rapidly became the ECJ's guiding principle. Thus the ECJ applied Union citizenship to situations where the citizen was lawfully resident within the Member State and hence was said to benefit from Article 17 and Article 12, provided that the subject matter was within the scope of the Treaty *ratione personae* and *ratione materiae*,[83] notwithstanding that the applicant did not satisfy the conditions laid down by other Treaty Articles or Community legislation, and could not therefore rely on Article 18. The ECJ also gave an expansive interpretation to the right to move and reside within Article 18 and interpreted the qualification to this right, that it is subject to limits and conditions laid down in the Treaty and in Community legislation, narrowly, thereby enabling applicants to benefit from Article 18 and Article 12.[84] The Court in addition used the introduction of the citizenship provisions as a reason for expanding the interpretation of other Treaty Articles or Community legislation, thereby expanding the scope of equal treatment and Article 12.[85] The citizenship jurisprudence generated, unsurprisingly, considerable academic commentary concerning the Court's reading of the Treaty provisions and the financial consequences for the Member States.[86]

In relation to services, this period saw an expansive jurisprudence in which the Community courts defined commercial services broadly, and applied this

---

82 ECJ 20 September 2001, Case C-184/99, *Rudy Grzelczyk v Centre Public D'Aide Sociale d'Ottignes-Louvain-la-Neuve (CPAS)*, [2001] ECR I-6193, at [31].

83 ECJ 12 May 1998, Case C-85/96, *Maria Martinez Sala v Freistaat Bayern*, [1998] ECR I-2691; ECJ 7 September 2004, Case C-456/02, *Trojani v Centre Public D'Aide Sociale de Bruxelles (CPAS)* [2004] ECR I-7573.

84 Case C-184/99 *Rudy Grzelczyk*, fn 82; ECJ 15 March 2005, Case C-209/03, *The Queen (on the application of Bidar) v London Borough of Ealing and Secretary of State for Education* [2005] ECR I-2119.

85 ECJ 23 March 2004, Case C-138/02, *Collins v Secretary of State for Work and Pensions* [2004] ECR I-2703; Case C-209/03 *Bidar*, fn 84.

86 M. Dougan, 'Fees, Grants, Loans and Dole Cheques: Who Covers the Costs of Migrant Education within the EU', (2005) 42 *CMLR* 943; J. Mather, 'The Court of Justice and the Union Citizen' (2005) 11 *ELJ* 722; K. Hailbronner, 'Union Citizenship and Access to Social Benefits', (2005) 42 *CMLR* 1245; M. Dougan, 'The Constitutional Dimension to the case law on Union Citizenship', (2006) 31 *ELR* 613.

to cases concerning cross-border access to medical and health-care services, which had significant implications for national welfare systems.[87] Thus the ECJ held that health care regimes requiring authorization before treatment could be obtained in another Member State were caught by Articles 49–50 EC,[88] and this was so even though the home Member State's health regime was tax funded as opposed to insurance based, and even though there was no fund for payment of health care in another state, and no obligation to pay for private health care in the home Member State.[89] The ECJ acknowledged the importance of stable financing of national social-insurance systems and the need for measures to maintain a manageable national health-care system, but nonetheless subjected certain core aspects of national welfare systems to the Treaty rules on free movement.[90]

Institutional choice as to how to deploy and prioritize the power accorded to the EU, the fourth factor that has influenced the reality of EU competence, has been as important in this period as hitherto. It is manifest at the turn of the millennium in the choices made by the European Council in Lisbon, Nice, and Stockholm as to the overall balance of the social and the economic within the EU. It is evident once again in the Commission's choice to move away from minimum harmonization in the proposed consumer rights directive, and embrace full harmonization.[91] It is apparent moreover in the 'rise and rise' of Commission action plans. Now to be sure these have always been part of the political landscape. The Commission has nonetheless made ever more extensive use of such plans in areas as diverse as regional policy, culture, customs, financial services, energy, health, environment, entrepreneurship, and education. There is of course nothing untoward about planning, quite the contrary. Such plans nonetheless affect the legal and political reality of competence. They enhance the Commission's ability to frame Community thinking, set the agenda and decide how to use broadly defined Treaty powers.

---

87 ECJ 28 April 1998, Case C–158/96, *Kohll v Union des Caisses de Maladie,* [1998] ECR I–1931; ECJ 12 July 2001, Case C–368/98, *Vanbraekel v ANMC,* [2001] ECR I–5363; ECJ 12 July 2001, Case C–157/99, *Geraets-Smits* and *Peerbooms,* [2001] ECR I–5473, ECJ 13 May 2003, Case C-385/99, *Müller-Fauré,* [2003] ECR I-4509; ECJ 23 October 2003, Case C-56/01, *Inizan v Caisse primaire d'assurance maladie des Hauts-de-Seine,* [2003] ECR I-12403; ECJ 16 May 2006, Case C-372/04, *Watts v Bedford Primary Care Trust,* [2006] ECR I-4325; ECJ 19 April 2007, Case C-444/05, *Stamatelaki v OAEE,* [2007] ECR I-3185.

88 ECJ 12 July 2001, Case C–157/99, *Geraets-Smits* and *Peerbooms,* fn 87.

89 Case C-372/04, *Watts,* fn 87.

90 G. Davies, 'Welfare as a Service', (2002) 29 *LIEI (Legal Issues of Economic Integration)* 27; P. van Nuffel, 'Patients' Free Movement Rights and Cross-border Access to Health-Care', (2005) 12 *MJ (Maastricht Journal)* 253; C. Newdick, 'Citizenship, Free Movement and Health Care: Cementing Individual Rights by Corroding Social Solidarity', (2006) 43 *CMLR* 1645.

91 Proposal for a Directive of the European Parliament and of the Council on consumer rights, COM(2008) 614 final.

## 2.5. CONCLUSION

Lawyers tend to like cases more than legislation. This is, like all generalizations, false, but it nonetheless contains a kernel of truth, and serves to explain in part at least the emphasis placed on the Community courts when discussing competence. The preceding analysis does not deny the importance of the judicial role in this respect, but sees it as but one of four factors that have been central to competence, de jure and de facto, over time. The reality is that Member State choice whether in the form of Treaty amendment, or in assent to Community legislation, has been central to where we are now, and that institutional choice as to how to deploy and prioritize Community power has also been a powerful factor.

It is important also to highlight a point made in the preceding analysis, which is the symbiotic interaction of these four factors in determining the reality of Community competence. It should not be thought that this interaction is merely in one direction, or that one of the four factors will always be dominant. The reality is more complex. Thus on some occasions the Commission will seek to enshrine judicial doctrine in legislation, as exemplified by the proposals for legislation on cross-border medical treatment,[92] but as is shown by the story of the Services Directive the Community legislature may not be willing to enact the Commission's vision of the legal status quo. There are other instances, such as with proposed legislation on mutual recognition,[93] where the Commission seeks to render judicial doctrine more efficacious through legislation. There are moreover the great many instances where Community legislation gives detailed substance to the general precepts in a Treaty article, going beyond what can be or has been achieved through ad hoc case law, and thereby sharpens the legal reality of Community competence within that area. The nature of that legal reality, and how much choice is left to Member States, will perforce vary markedly even within areas that may in a general sense be regarded as instances of co-operative federalism.

# 3. MEMBER STATE AUTONOMY: CHOICE, CONSEQUENCES AND LEGITIMACY

The discussion thus far has focused on the factors that have shaped the EU's competence and the consequences for Member State autonomy. It is nonetheless interesting to inquire further as to the meaning of Member State autonomy that underlies the preceding discussion, more especially because little is normally said

[92] http://europa.eu/legislation_summaries/public_health/european_health_strategy/sp0002_en.htm.

[93] Proposal for a Regulation of the European Parliament and of the Council, of 14 February 2007, laying down procedures relating to the application of certain national technical rules to products lawfully marketed in another Member State, COM(2007) 36 final.

about it, other than the bare fact that it increases or decreases in inverse relationship with the EU's competence. It is fitting to build from basic principles.

## 3.1. THE LOGIC OF COLLECTIVE ACTION

It is axiomatic that any form of collective action will entail some loss of autonomy.[94] Collective action entails both direct costs of organizing the group and indirect costs because some individual autonomy is foregone, since the group's choice will often be expressed through majority voting. Collective action also has benefits. The group will often be more powerful than any individual; it will bring together expertise; it will spread the workload; it will normally have greater resources than any individual; and it can facilitate attainment of goals that could not have been otherwise achieved. Collective action will be the preferred option when the benefits outweigh the costs, which is increasingly the case in modern society.

## 3.2. OUTPUT LEGITIMACY: PEACE AND PROSPERITY

The rationale for collective action serves to explain in part the Member State's willingness to sacrifice some autonomy by joining the EU.[95] The giving up of some individual decision-making power by the Member States was initially perceived in terms of outcomes, the justification flowing from the peace and prosperity by being part of the club. Legitimacy was thus conceived of largely in terms of output, and increase in aggregate output was felt to justify diminution in Member State autonomy.

This conception of legitimacy was prominent in the thinking of those who shaped the EEC. For Monnet and kindred spirit the legitimacy of the Community was to be secured through outcomes, peace and prosperity. The ECSC was established in part to render a third European war impossible. The founders of the EEC hoped it would lead to further political integration, but were mindful of the economic benefits of a common market. Peace and prosperity were the potent benefits for the people of Europe after war and economic protectionism. These benefits were to be secured through technocratic elite-led guidance. Democracy was, by way of contrast, a secondary consideration, hence the limited powers accorded to the Assembly. When attention was directed towards the 'people' the notion of democracy was attenuated. The focus was on the way in which the

[94] J. Buchanan and G. Tullock, *The Calculus of Consent: Logical Foundations of Constitutional Democracy*, University of Michigan Press, Ann Arbor, 1962; M. Olson, *The Logic of Collective Action: Public Goods and the Theory of Groups*, Harvard University Press, Cambridge, 1965.

[95] A. Moravcsik, 'Preferences and Power in the European Community: A Liberal Intergovernmentalist Approach', (1993) 31 *JCMS (Journal of Common Market Studies)* 473, at 480–481.

success of the EEC, measured in terms of outcomes, would generate loyalty to, and acceptance of, the Community institutions. It was not directed towards the issue of whether normal democratic controls should form an important part of the Community order.

The same patterns of thought were central to the work of the neofunctionalists.[96] Legitimacy was conceived largely in terms of outcomes, more specifically increased prosperity, to be secured through gains made possible by technocracy. Discussion of democracy was directed towards the loyalty which people might display towards the Community, and to the 'permissive consensus' necessary to enable the technocratic elite to perform their tasks. Standard democratic controls were perceived as important only where governmental changes led to significant alteration in policy, with consequential deprivations or rewards to particular groups. It was felt, by way of contrast, that an agreed aim of wealth maximization would sublimate social cleavage, and dissolve political conflict. The attainment of this objective was to be entrusted to the experts, the technocrats.

## 3.3. OUTPUT LEGITIMACY: EXTERNALITIES

The Member State's willingness to sacrifice autonomy by joining the EU was also influenced by the need to deal with externalities. An enduring insight from integration theory is that cross-border flows of goods create international policy externalities, which in turn create incentives for policy co-ordination.[97] The key issue then becomes not whether States interact, but how. They can do so by *ad hoc* international agreements. Some more permanent form of international co-operation may be preferred to reduce the transaction costs of *ad hoc* co-ordination. This is especially so when the number of parties becomes larger, and the issues on which they seek to co-ordinate become broader. Delegation of power to supranational institutions can moreover lend credibility to Member State bargains.

---

96 E. Haas, *The Uniting of Europe: Political, Social and Economic Forces 1950–1957*, Stanford University Press, Stanford, 1958; L. Lindberg, *The Political Dynamics of European Economic Integration*, Stanford University Press, Stanford, 1963; L. Lindberg and S. Scheingold, *Europe's Would-Be Polity: Patterns of Change in the European Community*, Prentice-Hall, Englewood Cliffs, 1970; L. Lindberg and S. Scheingold, *Regional Integration*, Harvard University Press, Cambridge, 1970.

97 A. Moravcsik, 'Preferences', fn 95, 485; W. Wessels, 'The Modern West-European State and the European Union: Democratic Erosion or a New Kind of Polity?', in S. Andersen and K. Eliassen (eds) *The European Union: How Democratic Is It?*, Sage, London, 1996, Chap 4; G. Majone, 'The European Community Between Social Policy and Social Regulation' (1993) 31 *JCMS* 153 and 'The Rise of the Regulatory State in Europe' (1994) *West European Politics* 1; P. Craig, 'The Nature of the Community: Integration, Democracy and Legitimacy', in P. Craig, and G. de Burca eds., *The Evolution of EU Law*, Oxford University Press, Oxford, 1999, Chap 1.

## 3.4. OUTPUT LEGITIMACY: 'TENSION' AND 'RESOLUTION'

The Rome Treaty was structured so as to lay down the principles governing core concepts such as free movement, with the stipulation that regulations and directives should be enacted to make these principles a reality. The passage of these legislative initiatives became increasingly difficult during the 1970s and early part of the 1980s, leading to what Middlemas termed a 'condition of immobility'.[98] The Council rejected social measures, such as directives on co-determination and worker consultation, and many others were stalled, awaiting a Council decision. There was growing concern that the Community's objectives were not being fulfilled.

The corollary was equally important. If the Community's legitimacy was to be judged in terms of outcomes, the prosperity that would accompany a single market, then falling short in this respect could threaten the entire Community project. The period from the early 1970s to the early 1980s has been characterised as the 'dark ages' for the Community.[99] Dankert, the President of the European Parliament, bemoaned the jungle of half-implemented treaties, and neglected Treaty articles, and spoke of institutions, such as the European Council, that owed their existence to a press release.[100] Wallace concluded that the Community had moved beyond other international regimes, but that it could drift towards them as 'recession at home and uncertainty abroad progressively undermine its authority'.[101]

It is therefore unsurprising that reform to facilitate completion of the internal market was the prominent feature of the SEA. The ideal of increased prosperity from a common market, freed from tariffs and quotas, in which goods and factors of production could move freely, was re-launched after the disappointment of the previous decade. This very re-launch served however to increase the powers of the Community, most especially via Article 95, and hence to intrude further on Member State autonomy, in order to deliver the economic gains that were promised from the club.

---

98 K. Middlemas, *Orchestrating Europe, The Informal Politics of the European Union 1973–1995* (Fontana, 1995), 90.

99 J. Caporaso and J. Keeler, 'The European Union and Regional Integration Theory', in C. Rhodes and S. Mazey (eds.), *The State of the European Union, Building a European Polity?*, Longman, London, 1995, 37; S. George and I. Bache, *Politics in the European Union*, Oxford University Press, Oxford, 2001, Chap 9.

100 See, e.g., P. Dankert, 'The European Community – Past, Present and Future', in L. Tsoukalis (ed), *The European Community, Past Present and Future*, Basil Blackwell, Oxford, 1983, 8.

101 W. Wallace, 'Europe as Confederation: The Community and the Nation State', in *The European Community, Past Present and Future*, fn 100, 68.

## 3.5. OUTPUT LEGITIMACY: QUESTIONING THE PREMISE

The very need to increase the Community's powers to deliver the promised economic goals led to questions about the nature of 'market freedom' and the limits on Member State autonomy that were deemed necessary to attain this goal.

Some commentators such as Streit and Mussler[102] defended the market orientation in the Rome Treaty, viewing it as a mechanism through which autonomous economic agents expressed their utility preferences across a European-wide market. The normative underpinnings of their view were explicitly Hayekian. They acknowledged that the original Treaty contained non-market elements, principally in the common policies for agriculture, iron and steel and the like, but they deprecated such interventions in the market order, which they regard as a failure. For Streit and Mussler it has been all down hill since then. The non-market elements had been strengthened through successive Treaty amendments. Community power over industrial policy, employment, economic and social cohesion all offered a 'considerable number of opportunities for the EC authorities to apply discretionary policies incompatible with the principle of undistorted competition'.[103] In their view the Treaty now 'allows for a broadly based policy of protecting the losers and of trying to pick the winners'.[104] It was, they believed, a rent seeking Community, using that phrase with all the opprobrium of the public choice school.[105]

Many other commentators, however, increasingly questioned the conception of market freedom that underpinned the Community. The 'completion' of the internal market threw this issue into sharp relief. Thus Heller responded to Streit and Mussler by noting the need for intervention to combat market failure, the fact that public intervention can be welfare enhancing, and that it would be 'shocking if the contemporary nation states of Europe which have spent so much political blood and effort in the development of sophisticated modes of organizing the labour, capital and transfer markets of mass industrial economies, were now to abandon that path in the embrace of the liberal constitution'.[106] These concerns were echoed by Weiler who emphasized that completion of the single market went beyond the mere removal of technocratic obstacles to trade. It embraced, as Weiler noted,[107] 'a highly politicized choice of ethos, ideology and political culture: the culture of "the market"'. The removal of barriers to free movement was a means to

102 M. Streit and W. Mussler, 'The Economic Constitution of the European Community—From Rome to Maastricht', in F. Snyder (ed), *Constitutional Dimensions of European Economic Integration*, Kluwer Law International, The Hague, 1996, 109–149.

103 *Ibid.* 132.

104 *Ibid.* 134.

105 *Ibid.* 136–137.

106 T. Heller, 'Comments by Thomas Heller' in *Constitutional Dimensions of European Economic Integration*, fn 102, 161.

107 J. Weiler, 'The Transformation of Europe', (1991) 100 *Yale Law Journal* 2403, 2478.

maximize utility, premised on the assumption of formal equality of individuals, in which market efficiency was prized above other competing values.[108] Scharpf voiced the same concern, speaking of the 'zealots of undistorted competition',[109] and the need for liberation from 'the tyranny of regulatory competition'.[110]

## 3.6. OUTPUT LEGITIMACY: THE BALANCE BETWEEN THE ECONOMIC AND THE SOCIAL

The concerns expressed in the previous section generated debate about the balance between the economic and social dimensions of the Community. This in turn led, whether paradoxically or not, to increase in the Community's powers so as to accord it some degree of competence in areas of social policy, and hence alleviate such concerns, even if the 'price' of doing so was to limit Member State autonomy further than hitherto. The Member States were, as seen above, central to this process, since they debated and agreed such revisions in Treaty amendments. This does not alter the fact that the need to redress the perceived imbalance between the economic and social order led to a net increase in Community power compared with the status quo ante. The fact that the Community's powers were limited in some such areas, and the fact that 'co-operative federalism' might well be the modus vivendi, is relevant but does not alter the force of the basic point being made here.

This is exemplified by the inclusion in the 'SEA package' of reinforced provisions concerning the Structural Funds, in order to quieten fears of the weaker economic Member States that they would suffer inordinately from market liberalization. It is exemplified more generally by the greater contestability as to the outcomes that the Community ought to be striving for. There were concerns voiced about the balance between consumer and trade interests, more especially because of the deregulatory impact of the ECJ's jurisprudence.[111] Commentators spoke of the need for a strong regional policy to balance the effect of market integration on the weaker economies.[112] Political leaders, and Delors, came to see the necessity for an increase in European social policy in order to retain

---

108 *Ibid.* 2478.

109 F. Scharpf, *Governing in Europe: Effective and Democratic?*, Oxford University Press, Oxford, 1999, 167.

110 *Ibid.* 180.

111 A. McGee and S. Weatherill, 'The Evolution of the Single Market-Harmonisation or Liberalisation' (1990) 53 *MLR (Modern Law Review)* 578; N. Reich, 'Protection of Diffuse Interests in the EEC and the Perspective of Progressively Establishing an Internal Market', (1988) 11 *JCP (Journal of Consumer Policy)* 395.

112 R. Dehousse, 'Completing the Internal Market: Institutional Constraints and Challenges', in R. Bieber, R. Dehousse, J. Pinder, J. Weiler (eds), *1992: One European Market?*, Nomos, Baden-Baden, 1988, 336.

the support of workers.[113] The amendments in the Maastricht and Amsterdam Treaties that created new heads of social competence, or modified those existing hitherto, were in no small measure the result of the perceived need to re-balance the economic and social orders within the EU, even if this required some net increase in Community competence, and some net diminution in Member State autonomy. Nor is it fortuitous that during this period the Community political organs, as we have seen, consciously re-conceptualized the internal market in more holistic terms, to embrace not only the traditional economic sphere, but also a wider range of social, environmental and consumer concerns.[114]

## 3.7. INPUT LEGITIMACY: THE RATIONALES FOR THE SHIFT

The very fact that the Community had power over an increasing variety of subject matter fuelled the change whereby legitimacy was conceived not only in terms of output, but also in terms of input. This was in part because discourse concerning output legitimacy made less sense when applied to the social realm than it did in the economic context. It was in part reflective of the very fact that the increased array of Community power naturally led to greater focus on the Community decision-making process whereby such powers were exercised.

It would be mistaken to imagine that the debate concerning legitimacy, input and democracy within the Community only began after the SEA. It did not. There were earlier concerns voiced about these issues.[115] These issues did however come to the fore from the mid-1980s onwards. This is readily apparent in the rich vein of academic literature published during this period.[116] It is evident in the

113 M. Kleinman, *A European Welfare State? European Union Social Policy in Context,* Palgrave, Basingstoke, 2002, 82–3, 86–7.

114 See ns 55–66.

115 W. Wallace and J. Smith, 'Democracy or Technocracy? European Integration and the Problem of Popular Consent', in J. Hayward (ed), *The Crisis of Representation in Europe,* Frank Cass, London, 1995.

116 See, e. g., J. Hayward (ed), *The Crisis of Representation in Europe,* Frank Cass, London, 1995; R. Bellamy, V. Bufacchi, and D. Castiglione (eds), *Democracy and Constitutional Culture in the Union of Europe,* Lothian Foundation Press, London, 1995; S. Andersen and K. Eliassen (eds), *The European Union: How Democratic Is It?,* Sage, London, 1996; R. Bellamy and D. Castiglione (eds), *Constitutionalism in Transformation: European and Theoretical Perspectives,* Blackwell, Oxford, 1996; F. Snyder (ed), *Constitutional Dimensions of European Economic Integration,* Kluwer Law International, The Hague, 1996; R. Dehousse (ed), *Europe: The Impossible Status Quo,* Macmillan, London, 1997; D. Curtin, *Postnational Democracy, The European Union in Search of a Political Philosophy,* Kluwer, The Hague, 1997; J. Weiler, *The Constitution of Europe,* Cambridge University Press, Cambridge, 1999; P. Craig, and G. de Burca (eds), *The Evolution of EU Law,* Oxford University Press, Oxford, 1999; F. Scharpf, *Governing in Europe: Effective and Democratic?,* Oxford University Press, Oxford, 1999; C. Hoskyns and M. Newman (eds), *Democratizing the European Union,* Manchester University Press, Manchester, 2000; F. Mancini, *Democracy and Constitutionalism in the European Union,* Hart Publishing, Oxford, 2000; K. Neunreither and A. Wiener (eds), *European Integration*

institutional submissions that led to the Treaty of Amsterdam in 1996.[117] There is a certain paradox in this shift in emphasis, given that it occurred at the very time that the European Parliament was being granted a measure of real power in the legislative process. There are nonetheless a number of reasons why these matters came to occupy centre stage in debates about the Community.

First, the shift to qualified majority voting in the SEA, the decline in use of the Luxembourg Accords and the increase in the EP's legislative power, provide one explanation. The Rome Treaty did provide for qualified majority voting in many areas, prior to the SEA. The applicability of these provisions was however weakened by the de facto veto of the Luxembourg Accords. The application of qualified majority voting to Article 95, under which most harmonization measures were enacted, combined with the 'political decline' in the veto power, altered the dynamics of the legislative process. Decision-making in the Council continued to be dominated by the search for consensus. There was nonetheless the possibility that Member States could truly be outvoted. The EP's involvement, through the co-operation procedure and then co-decision, meant that the content of any measure was not solely in the hands of the Council. These changes led many to reflect on the nature of the Community's legislative process, and the extent of its democratic pedigree.

A second rationale was that the EP, post the SEA, sought to increase its limited power and to keep the 'democracy issue' on the agenda in subsequent Treaty reforms. Prior to the SEA the EP had very limited input into the legislative process. It had sought wide-ranging Treaty reform in the discussions leading to the SEA. These efforts were unsuccessful, but it was given the co-operation procedure. The EP's strategy thereafter was predictable. It sought to extend this power to new areas, and to gain more extensive powers in the legislative process. The advent of the co-decision procedure in the Maastricht Treaty, the strengthening of this procedure in the Treaty of Amsterdam and its extension to other substantive areas in the Amsterdam and Nice Treaties, were the results of this strategy.

Thirdly, the successful passage of Community legislation post the SEA provides a further explanation for the focus on input and democracy. The very fact that the Community legislative process was used successfully to enact the plethora of measures designed to complete the single market led to increased attention being focused on the nature of the legislative procedure itself. It placed the Community's decision-making under the spotlight.

---

*after Amsterdam, Institutional Dynamics and Prospects for Democracy,* Oxford University Press, Oxford, 2000; R. Prodi, *Europe As I See It,* Polity, Cambridge, 2000; P. Schmitter, *How to Democratize the European Union ... and why bother?,* Rowman and Littlefield, Lanham, 2000; L. Siedentop, *Democracy in Europe,* Penguin, London, 2001.

117 P. Craig, 'Democracy and Rule-Making within the EC: An Empirical and Normative Assessment', (1997) 3 *ELJ* 105; G. de Burca, 'The Quest for Legitimacy in the European Union', (1996) 59 *MLR* 349.

Fourthly, this tendency was fuelled by the increase in the scope of Community competence. Successive Treaty revisions, beginning with the SEA, added further chapters or titles to Community competence. Areas such as the environment, consumer protection, economic and monetary union, health, culture, employment, and industrial policy were brought, albeit to varying degrees, within the scope of the Community. It was unsurprising that this should lead to increased questioning about the way in which policy was made in these areas. This was more especially so given that some of these issues, such as economic and monetary union, touched the very core of national sovereignty, and constrained national macro-economic policy. The fact that some of these policy issues were 'taken from' national regional bodies, which had only very limited input into decision-making at Community level, created a 'constituency' eager to voice the democratic shortcomings of this shift of competence.

Fifthly, the increased attention accorded to democracy is also related to more general concerns as to the health of democracy at national level, which were replicated within the EU. The 'new right' initiated the revolution in government of the 1980s. Privatization, contracting-out, and the preference for market-based solutions were the familiar features of this form of governance. For some, such as Siedentop, these developments provoked concerns about the dominance of economics, and the withering of politics. The EU was seen as reflecting and exacerbating this trend. The dominance of economic outcomes, combined with French *etatisme*, was said to diminish yet further the realm of the political.[118]

Finally, there was a deeper reason for the increased attention accorded to legitimacy and democracy in the Community. This was the shift in perception of the Community as being part of the solution to being part of the problem. Weiler skilfully captures this point.[119] He points out that the Community was, in its foundational period, 'perceived as part of a moral imperative in dealing with the heritage of World War II'.[120] By removing the possibility of war in Europe, so too was the moral imperative, the mantle of ideals, removed, leaving us with politics as usual, with the twist that it was much less easy to change the political status quo.[121] The concerns of modernity, such as the increased bureaucratization of life, the depersonalization of the market, and the centralization of power, became concerns voiced about the Community itself. The values of integration, as exemplified by the breaking down of local markets, and the insertion of universal norms into domestic cultures, were also 'part of the deep modern and post-

118 L. Siedentop, n. 116, 35–36, 216–217, 226.

119 J. Weiler, 'The European Court of Justice: Beyond "Beyond Doctrine" or the Legitimacy Crisis of European Constitutionalism', in A.-M. Slaughter, A. Stone Sweet and J.H.H. Weiler (eds), *The European Courts and National Courts, Doctrine and Jurisprudence*, Hart, Oxford, 1998, 365, 368–371.

120 *Ibid.* 368.

121 *Ibid.* 368–369.

modern anxiety of European belongingness and part of the roots of European angst and alienation'.[122]

## 4. CONCLUSION

Hindsight is a wonderful thing. It is tempting when looking back to see that the original 'bargain' encapsulated in the Rome Treaty would always prove 'incomplete'. The initial idea of output legitimacy embodied a quid pro quo: Member States sacrificed some autonomy by according power to the EEC where the resulting benefit was increase in aggregate peace and prosperity.

The need to augment the Community's powers over the economic sphere then became apparent when the Community's political decision-making structures led to the malaise in the 1970s, and early 1980s. The very rejuvenation of the single market project made possible by greater constraints on Member State autonomy introduced by the SEA, created, when combined with the ECJ's activist jurisprudence, concerns as to the nature of the market freedom that underpinned the Community, and the balance between it and social policy that had hitherto resided largely with Member States.

This led, as we have seen, to transfer of some greater powers over the social sphere to the Community, even though such transfers were conditional and limited. The transfer of economic power from Member State to Community was always likely to lead to some assumption of central responsibility for matters such as social, industrial, environmental policy and the like. This was so irrespective of whether one believes in the dictates of neo-functionalist reasoning or not. Given that this was so, it was natural for the debates about the balance between market and non-market strategies which are so common within Member States to surface within the Community.

The very increase in the powers accorded to the Community, combined with the complexity of the types of competence possessed by the EU, contributed towards the greater emphasis placed on input legitimacy than hitherto. The limitation of Member State autonomy could no longer be rationalized purely in terms of the quid pro quo adumbrated above, premised as it was on output legitimacy. This conception of legitimacy continued to be important, but it was complemented by concern over input legitimacy and the nature of the Community's decision-making process.

---

[122] *Ibid.* 371.

# THE EUROPEAN COURT OF JUSTICE'S APPROACH TO PRIMACY AND EUROPEAN CONSTITUTIONALISM – PRESERVING THE EUROPEAN CONSTITUTIONAL ORDER?

Fabian AMTENBRINK*

## 1. INTRODUCTORY REMARKS

European integration stands for the assimilation of partially divergent legal systems that previously were conceptualised as autonomous. Courts at national and European, but also at the international level were and still are faced with the challenge of deciphering how the various legal systems inter relate. Perhaps more importantly, they have to decide on their mutual inter-relationships as appliers and interpreters of the law.[1]

In the European context, it is a well-documented fact that the Court of Justice of the European Union (ECJ) has been essential for the rapid development of the newly created legal order as laid down primarily in the founding Treaties of what is now referred to as the European Union (EU). By foreseeing in vague and open norms and by creating an institution on the European level charged with ensuring that in the interpretation and application of the Treaties the law is observed,[2] the drafters of primary European law have effectively created a dynamic legal system open to development through judicial process. The continual evolving of the relationship between the constitutional legal orders of the Member States and the newly established European legal order also had its impact on the allocation of tasks between the national and European judiciary.

* Professor of European Union Law at the Erasmus School of Law, Erasmus University Rotterdam. Visiting Professor at the College of Europe (Bruges). The author wishes to express his gratitude to Dr. P.A.J. van den Berg and the participants of the conference 'The ECJ and the autonomy of the Member States' held on 20–21 April 2009, at the Europa University Institute for inspiring discussions on the topic of this contribution. The usual disclaimer applies.

1. This applies not only to the relationship between the national courts and tribunals and the Court of Justice of the European Union discussed hereafter, but also, for example, to the European Court of Human Rights and the WTO dispute settlement system.
2. Article 164 of the original Treaty establishing a European Economic Community.

From the outset the ECJ has firmly anchored the new legal order in the constitutional legal orders of the Member States, by defining the position of the individual as a bearer of rights and obligations deriving directly from the European legal order and by determining that this position must be given effect by the courts and tribunals of the Member States as an integral part of the domestic legal order. This is not to say however that the European legal order has necessarily been put on an equal footing with its national counterparts. As will be observed in more detail hereafter, based on the ECJ's doctrines of primacy and direct effect, Union law is in principle considered to take precedence over any national legal act including (unwritten) constitutional provisions and principles.[3]

With this said, however, rather than replacing them, the European legal order has effectively been created alongside the national constitutional legal orders of the Member States. Consequently, the national judiciary and namely the highest (constitutional) courts of the Member States have not lost their function as a result of the establishment of the European legal order with its own system of judicial review. As the mandate of the ECJ is *de jure* limited to ensuring that in the interpretation and application of the Treaties the law is observed, it is for the courts of the Member States to enforce European law in the national legal order.[4] While both the ECJ and, in the last instance, the highest national (constitutional) courts thus '*have adjudicatory responsibility of their own for the success of the European legal community*',[5] the interwoven relationship that exists between the European and the national legal orders of the Member States excludes the functioning and indeed studying of these systems in isolation.

The ECJ, in deciding on the compatibility with Union law of national laws, legally binding measures and practices, effectively casts its shadow over the national legal order. National highest (constitutional) courts find themselves in a situation in which challenges to the constitutional legal order not only arise in the domestic legal sphere but also derive from the supranational, European law. These courts are faced with potentially conflicting tasks. First and foremost, they have to ensure in last instance that the constitutional legal order is observed on the territory of the state. Constitutional courts may also be entrusted with ensuring that the reach of Union law stays within the margins of the constitutional empowerment to voluntarily limit sovereign power for the benefit of the European legal order and, moreover, that the Union institutions themselves exercise public power within the framework of what has been agreed upon in the Treaty on European Union (TEU) and the Treaty on the Functioning of the European Union (TFEU)

---

3 Generally, with regard to these principles see P. Craig and G. de Búrca, *EU Law. Text, Cases and Materials*, 4th ed, OUP, Oxford, 2008, chapters 8 and 10, with further references.

4 Article 19(1) TFEU.

5 P. Kirchhof, 'The Balance of Powers between National and European Institutions', (1999) 5 *(ELJ) European Law Journal* 225–242, at p 241.

(primary Union law).[6] At the same time, national courts, including the highest (constitutional) courts, are expected to ensure that Union law is observed on the territory of the state under the conditions dictated by the European legal order itself. It is this allocation of tasks, which very much reflects the current nature of the EU, which bears the potential for conflict and has arguably formed the basis for stylised struggles between some national highest (constitutional) courts and the ECJ concerning the locus of the judicial *Kompetenz-Kompetenz*. Returning to this issue may seem redundant, as numerous academic publications have accompanied the judgments by national courts questioning the primacy of Union law in cases of conflict with the national constitutional legal orders.[7] In particular the well-known *Solange*-jurisprudence of the German Federal Constitutional Court (*Bundesverfassungsgericht*) linked to the protection of fundamental rights under the German Basic Law (*Grundgesetz*) and the accompanying debate has found its way into standard textbooks on European Union law.[8]

However, coinciding with a more responsive approach by national highest (constitutional) courts to the position of the European legal order, in particular in the area of fundamental rights protection in recent times, as well as an increased understanding of the complex character of the relationship between the different (constitutional) legal orders, the focus in the debate has somewhat shifted. Rather than focusing on the competing and possibly even conflicting objectives of national and European courts, attention has moved to issues such as the division of labor, mutual cooperation and dialogue between the courts. In this perspective, the relationship of national constitutional courts with the European legal order and the ECJ should not be defined in antagonistic terms. Reference is made to '*a system of balance and co-operation' that cannot be defined in hierarchical terms*'.[9] Moreover, the constitutional reservations which some national courts continue to voice – albeit on a somewhat less-shrill tone than in the past – with regard to the primacy of the European legal order should not be perceived as a threat directed

6 J. Limbach, '50 Jahre Deutsche Verfassung in Europa', Vortrag anlässlich des 50jährigen Bestehens des Europa-Instituts der Universität des Saarlandes am 15. Juni 2001 in Saarbrücken, available online at http://archiv.jura.uni-saarland.de/projekte/Bibliothek/text.php?id=200 (accessed 20 October 2010).

7 See for example: T. Schilling, 'The Autonomy of the Community Legal Order – An Analysis of Possible Foundations', (1996) 37 *Harvard International Law Review* 389. And the response by J.H.H. Weiler, 'The State "Über Alles": Demos, Telos and the German Maastricht Decision', in Ole Due et al (eds), *Festschrift für Ulrich Everling*, (No.2) Nomos, Baden-Baden, 1995, 1651, with further references.

8 See e.g. P. Craig and G. de Búrca, *EU Law. Text, Cases and Materials*, 4th ed, OUP, Oxford, 2008, chapter 10; C.W.A. Timmermans, General Aspects of the European Union and the European Community', in Kapteyn & VerLoren van Themaat, *The Law of the European Union and the European Communities*, 4th ed, Kluwer Law International, Austin et al, 2008, section 3.3; D. Chalmers, C. Hadjiemmanuil, G. Monti and A. Tomkins, *European Union Law*, Cambridge University Press, Cambridge, 2006, chapter 5; R. Streinz, *Europarecht*, 6th ed, C.H. Müller, Heidelberg, 2003, § 3 VII.

9 P. Kirchhof, 'The Balance of Powers between National and European Institutions', (1999) 5 *ELJ*, at 241–242.

towards the ECJ, but rather as '*an expression of the normative idea, common to modern democratic constitutions, that all public power is bound by human rights and civic rights*'.[10]

What is argued hereafter is that national highest (constitutional) courts have an important role to play in safeguarding the European constitutional order as a whole of which the national constitutional orders of the Member States form an integral, and by no means in all regards subordinated part. More recent decisions in the national sphere suggest that at least some highest national (constitutional) courts are prepared to question the preeminence of the European legal order on a wider range of constitutional issues than has previously been the case. Some of these can be linked to what is hereafter explained as the integrative function of national constitutional legal orders. At the same time, it is questionable whether the ECJ's fundamental case-law on the relationship between the European and national legal orders sufficiently recognises the current state of constitutionalism in the EU and the role that national highest (constitutional) courts play in this regard. Put differently, does the ECJ's approach to primacy and direct effect put into question the integrative function of national constitutions and with it, the integrative function of the European constitutional legal order as a whole?

Exploring this issue calls for a critical reconstruction of the ECJ's approach to these fundamental concepts of European law against the background of a characterisation of the European constitutional legal order. In this context, a distinction is made between the organisational and integrative functions of constitutional legal orders. Moreover, as a case in point, several recent judgments by highest national (constitutional) courts are explored with regard to their approach to the issue of primacy and the position of the national constitutional legal orders. Rather than simply dissecting the disparities in approaches of the ECJ and the national highest (constitutional) courts namely, but certainly not exclusively, linked to fundamental rights protection, this contribution seeks to develop a more general (European) constitutional argument, placing the ECJ's approach to primacy in a new light.

## 2. EUROPEAN CONSTITUTIONALISM

The relationship between the legal systems of the Member States and the European Union legal order that lies at the heart of today's complex system of government

---

[10] J. Limbach, '50 Jahre Deutsche Verfassung in Europa', Vortrag anlässlich des 50jährigen Bestehens des Europa-Instituts der Universität des Saarlandes am 15. Juni 2001 in Saarbrücken, available online at http://archiv.jura.uni-saarland.de/projekte/Bibliothek/text.php?id=200 (accessed 20 October 2010), with regard to the position of the *Bundesverfassungsgericht*: '*Die vom Bundesverfassungsgericht behauptete – sehr theoretische – Reservekompetenz ist keine Drohung gegenüber dem EuGH. Sie unterstreicht nur die – den modernen demokratischen Verfassungen gemeinsame – normative Idee, dass jede öffentliche Gewalt durch die Menschen- und Bürgerrechte gebunden ist.*'

and governance can neither be easily defined by way of adaptation from national constitutional and public international law jargon, nor by reference to a hierarchical relationship between the national and European legal orders. Yet, this is not to say that describing the current state of European integration in terms of constitutionalism is misplaced.

## 2.1. TERMINOLOGY

Broadly speaking, constitutionalism can be linked to the notion of the creation and thereafter limitation of public power by law. This includes the defining of restraints on the exercise of public power both through the vesting of powers in more than one institution (separation of powers), by providing for rules which govern the exercise of that power and to which the institutions are subjected (rule of law), and by vesting rights in individuals (fundamental rights) which they can invoke against the exercise of public power (procedural safeguards). Constitutions, whether written or unwritten, thus constitute and organise the exercise of public power by state institutions. Constitutional legal orders define the scope of public power and the procedure for its application. Yet, to the extent that they contribute to popular faith in democracy and in public authority exercised by institutions,[11] these arrangements also serve a second, broader purpose that is referred to hereafter as the integrative function of constitutional legal orders.

Constitutional legal orders have been instrumental in the identification of the citizen '*with the (democratic) political order and the constitutional principles or with the achievements of democracy*'.[12] Political decision-formation and decision-making processes must ensure the balancing of the diverse opinions, interests and aims of modern pluralistic societies. For Hesse, the political unity (*politische Handlungseinheit*) of a state rests on this integrative function.[13] Yet, the integrative function of constitutional legal orders also extents to the social acceptance of a given system. They provide the fundament for '*the basis for partisanship beyond ethnical and cultural commonalities in the absence of a plausible or acceptable "transcendental past"*' and moreover '*offer stability and security, primarily on the basis of universal principles enshrined in the constitution, in what has been*

11 Written constitutions may also emphasise the fundamental importance of some basic choices that are being made by excluding the amendment of some of its contents or by making it subject to special procedural requirements (constitutional entrenchment). See e.g. Art. 79(3) of the German Basic Law (Grundgesetz).

12 C. Closa, 'Deliberative Constitutional Politics and the EU Value-Based Constitution', in C. Closa and E. Fossum (eds.), *Deliberative Constitutional Politics in the EU*, ARENA and Universidad de Zaragoza, Oslo and Zaragoza, 2004, 21–52, at p 30.

13 K. Hesse, '§ 1 Verfassung und Verfassungsrecht', in E. Benda, W. Maihofer, H.-J. Vogel, *Handbuch des Verfassungsrechts der Bundesrepublik Deutschland*, Teil 1, 2nd ed, Walter de Gruyter, Berlin, N.Y., 1995, at p 5.

*referred to as "constitutional patriotism"*'.[14] Constitutional legal orders facilitate identification with and attachment to the polity to which they relate, thereby creating a sense of membership. Common values with which the individual can identify with and which are shared by the members of the polity find their expression not only in fundamental rights, but also in other legal principles and values enshrined in the constitutional legal order. The fact that such principles and values are often rather elusive and thus difficult to employ in practice[15] does not diminish their integrative function. Rather, they are primarily reflected in the fundamental choices that are made in the organisation of the polity.

With Hurrelmann, it can be observed that social acceptance of a political system differs from normative legitimation in that it refers to a '*factual acceptance in the citizenry—which is not necessarily based on democratic standards.*'[16] This coincides with Snyder's concept of a constitution in the subjective sense, which stands for '*the people's subjective orientation: that is, to use Weber's terms, whether people are subjectively oriented to the constitution in a substantive sense as if it were their fundamental legal act.*'[17] What both approaches have in common is the recognition of a function of constitutional legal, that does not (primarily) refer to deliberative processes.

Constitutional legal orders can maintain an integrative force by bringing about of a sense of order and coherence, a sense of belonging and collective identity and ownership of policies and decisions-making. Trust and coherence is not only created through procedural and substantive elements but also through the recognition of fundamental principles such as democracy, the rule of law and individual rights. Factual circumstances, such as general welfare and education, are equally vital for societal acceptance. A constitutional legal system can create the conditions in which they can flourish, such as by a commitment to social market economy,[18] thereby creating and maintaining social structure.

---

14 Footnotes omitted. See F. Amtenbrink and P.A.J. van den Berg, 'Lost in Translation? On the Role of National Constitutions in the European Constitutional Order', in F. Amtenbrink and P.A.J. van den Berg, *The Constitutional Integrity of the European Union*, T.M.C. Asser Press, The Hague, 2010, 1–12, at p 2, with reference to C. Closa, 'Deliberative Constitutional Politics and the EU Value-Based Constitution', in C. Closa and E. Fossum, eds., *Deliberative Constitutional Politics in the EU*, ARENA and Universidad de Zaragoza, Oslo and Zaragoza, 2004, pp. 21–52, and J.-W. Müller and K.L. Scheppele, 'Constitutional patriotism: An introduction', (2008) 6 *Int J Constitutional Law* 67–71.

15 P. Kirchhof, 'The Balance of Powers between National and European Institutions', (1999) 5 *ELJ*, 225–242, at p 235, in the context of the German Basic Law refers to objectives which are 'vague and accordingly almost without dispositive power in judicial terms'.

16 A. Hurrelmann, 'European Democracy, the 'Permissive Consensus' and the Collapse of the EU Constitution', (2007) 13 *ELJ* 343–359, at p 346.

17 F. Snyder, 'The unfinished constitution of the European Union: principles, processes and culture', in J.H.H. Weiler and M. Wind, *European Constitutionalism Beyond the State*, Cambridge University Press, Cambridge, 2003, 55–73, at p 56.

18 Art. 20(1) of the German Basic Law of 23 May 1949 refers to a 'democratic and social federal state' (*demokratischer und sozialer Bundesstaat*).

The recognition of legal systems beyond the national sphere and the shift of public power that has come with it challenges the national constitutional legal orders both with regard to their organisational and integrative functions and raises the question of the constitutional quality of the new European legal order as an adequate substitute.[19] While the failure of the Treaty establishing a Constitution for Europe may or may not have been the collapse of a 'constitutional moment',[20] this perceived low-point in the history of European integration neither marks the beginning nor the end of what is presently referred to as European constitutionalism.[21] In fact, long before that the ECJ, itself a creature of the new legal order, had effectively advanced a doctrine of 'European constitutionality'[22] through its interpretation of the nature of the European legal order and the fundamental institutional and procedural principles which it introduces.[23] The ECJ's recurring qualification of the former Treaty establishing the European Community as the 'basic constitutional charter' can be interpreted as a logical extension of this approach.[24]

To be sure, attempts to capture the nature of European integration by applying national constitutional law and public international law jargon have delivered little insights into the actual working of this unique system,[25] revealing

---

19 F. Amtenbrink and P.A.J. van den Berg, 'The Constitutional Integrity of the European Union. An Introduction', in F.Amtenbrink and P.A.J. van den Berg, *The Constitutional Integrity of the European Union*, T.M.C. Asser Press/Springer, The Hague/Berlin, 2010.

20 A phrase borrowed from I. Pernice, 'The Draft Constitution of the European Union: A Constitutional Treaty at a Constitutional Moment?' in I. Pernice and M. Poiares Maduro, *A Constitution for the European Union: First Comments on the 2003-draft of the European Convention*, Nomos, Baden-Baden, 2003, 13–21. See also T. Eijsbouts, 'Lisbon and the Quest for the European Public: Let Elections do some of the Work', in I. Pernice and E. Tanchev (eds.), *Ceci n'est pas une Constitution – Constitutionalisation without a Constitution?*, Nomos, Baden-Baden, 2009, 203–211.

21 As J. Kokott and A. Rüth, 'The European Convention and its Draft Treaty establishing a Constitution for Europe: Appropriate Answers to the Laeken Questions?', (2003) 40 *CMLR* 1315–1345, at 1320 observe: 'The establishment of the Constitution [...] was [...] not an exercise of constitutionalization, but of constitutional rewriting and formalisation.' Brackets added.

22 A term borrowed from S. Douglas-Scott, *Constitutional Law of the European Union*, Longman, Harlow etc., 2002, at p 517.

23 See e.g. also E. Tanchev, 'The Lisbon Treaty within and without Constitutional Orthodoxy, in I. Pernice and E. Tanchev (eds.), *Ceci n'est pas une Constitution – Constitutionalisation without a Constitution?*, Nomos, Baden-Baden, 2009, 22–43, at 29, who refers to constitutionalisation through the ECJ's jurisprudence.

24 ECJ 26 September 1984, Case 295/83, *Parti écologiste "Les Verts"* [1986] ECR 1339; ECJ 10 July 2003, Case C-15/00, *Commission v European Investment Bank* [2003] ECR I-7281. See also more recently ECJ 3 September 2008, Joined Cases C-402/05 P and C-415/05 P, *Kadi* [2008] ECR I-6351, para 81.

25 The attempt by the *Bundesverfassungsgericht* (BVerfGE 89, 155) may be recalled here, which referred to a '*Staatenverbund*' (a sort of hybrid between a confederation and a federation). See also J.H.H. Weiler, 'Federalism and Constitutionalism: Europe's *Sonderweg*', NYU Jean Monnet Working Papers No. 10/00, available online at www.jeanmonnetprogram.org/papers/papers00.html (accessed 20 October 2010). For a brief and informative account of the different (German) views, M. Schweitzer and W. Hummer, *Europarecht*, Metzner/Luchterhand, 1993, p 207 et seq.

the absence of a theoretical normative concept that could form the base of the European legal order.[26] It has been observed by Ley that in the past European integration scholars may have adopted constitutional (law) jargon mainly so as to emphasise the difference in character of the European legal order from classic public international law.[27] It is indeed difficult to capture what amounts to an intricate and in some regards cluttered multiple of legal systems, the result of a more or less organic development over more than five decades, in a single phrase.[28] As the European 'constitutional charter' does not constitute a written and unwritten body of law or practices which lay down the organisational system of a state,[29] in constitutional law terms its significance can only be adequately assessed once the term constitution is separated from the notion of statehood.[30] In the context of European integration, constitutionalism until now primarily stands for *'the idea of a legal and institutional framework in which the exercise of public power beyond the state [...] are emulated in conditions which ensure – as central features – a sufficient degree of democratic legitimacy and accountability.'*[31]

## 2.2. THE NATIONAL AND EUROPEAN (CONSTITUTIONAL) LEGAL ORDERS: COMPANIONS IN FATE

The question that arises from the observations on the European legal order in the previous section is whether and to what extent the constitutionalisation of the European legal order has resulted in the substitution of the organisational and integrative functions of the constitutional legal orders of the Member States?

26 F. Amtenbrink, 'The Multidimensional Constitutional Legal Order of the European Union – A Successful Case of Cosmopolitan Constitution-Building?', (2009) 40 *Netherlands Yearbook of International Law*, 3–68, at 44.

27 I. Ley, 'Kant versus Locke: Europarechtliche und völkerrechtlicher Konstitutionalismus im Vergleich' (2009) 69 *ZaöRV*, 317–345, at 32–321, with reference to early contributions by – among others – E. Stein, 'Laywers, Judges, and the Making of a Transnational Constitution' (1981) 75 *American Journal of International Law* 1; G.F. Mancini, 'The Making of a Constitution for Europe', (1989) 26 *CMLR* 595.

28 J.-P. Jacqué, 'The Principle of Institutional Balance', (2004) 41 *CMLR* 383–391, at 387, observes: '*The Community lacked an architect with an overall vision of the building that was constructed by means of the successive additions.*'

29 J.-C. Piris, 'Does the European Union have a Constitution? Does it need one?', NYU Jean Monnet Working Paper No. 5/00, available online at www.jeanmonnetprogram.org/papers/00/000501.html (accessed 31 March 2010).

30 See already A. Albi, 'The EU Constitution, National Constitutions and Sovereignty: An Assessment of a European Constitutional Order', (2004) 29 *ELR* 741, at 747 et seq. with regard to the Treaty establishing a Constitution for Europe.

31 Brackets added. F. Amtenbrink, 'The Multidimensional Constitutional Legal Order of the European Union – A Successful Case of Cosmopolitan Constitution-Building?', (2009) 40 *Netherlands Yearbook of International Law* 3–68, at 19, where a similar definition is developed in the context of the debate on the constitutionalisation of cosmopolitan law. Note how the above mentioned integrative function is missing in this definition.

The European legal order does not necessarily have to be perceived as consisting of multiple (constitutional) legal systems that are in competition with one another, but rather as a set of (constitutional) legal orders that are intertwined and complementary. The EU has multiple sources of government and tools '*for dealing with a broad range of problems and conflicts in which actors regularly arrive at mutually satisfactory and binding decisions by negotiating and deliberating with one another and cooperating in the implementation of the decisions.*'[32] Both the constitutional legal orders of the Member States and the European legal order define and limit the exercise of public power and vest rights in individuals. Both legal sources thus legitimise public power in the EU. Consequently, these systems can neither be studied in isolation nor can their relationship be simply characterised in hierarchical terms. In fact it has even been suggested that references to the EU as a multi-level or multi-layered constitutional system of governance[33] may be misleading to the extent that this implies the existence of such a clear hierarchical order.[34] While the validity of this criticism rests entirely on the definition of terminology, an alternative approach to the relationship between the national (constitutional) legal orders of the Member States and the European legal order may be to view them as mutually dependent in the process of European integration both with regard to their organizational and integrative functions. As such they may be considered as companions in fate.

With regard to the organizational function of a constitutional legal order, the European legal order has to provide legitimacy at the national level where Union law is directly enforced. At the same time, the national constitutional legal orders of the Member States form an indispensable source of legitimacy. This is not limited to the initial transfer of sovereign power from the national to the European level, but moreover in a broad sense also includes the *continuous* exercise of public power at the European level.[35] In the most recognisable way this is the case for the input legitimacy provided by the democratic system of the Member States as organised by their respective constitutional legal orders, namely through the involvement of democratic elected institutions in the implementation of Union

32 P.C. Schmitter, 'Democracy in Europe and Europe's Democratization', 14 *Journal of Democracy* (2003), 71–85, at p 74, who uses this as the definition of the term 'governance'.

33 See e.g. I. Pernice, 'Multilevel constitutionalism and the Treaty of Amsterdam: European Constitution-Making Revisited?', (1999) 36 *CMLR* 703–750; and by the same author: 'Rethinking the Methods of Dividing and Controlling the Competencies in the Union' Walter-Hallstein-Institut, Paper 6/01; and, also by the same author: 'Introduction: Multilevel Constitutionalism in Action', in I. Pernice and E. Tanchev (eds.), *Ceci n'est pas une Constitution – Constitutionalisation without a Constitution?*, Nomos, Baden-Baden, 2009, 12–20.

34 Critically e.g. L.F.M. Besselink, *Een samengestelde Europese Constitutie*, Europa Law Publishing, Groningen, 2007. See also L.J. Brinkhorst, *Europese Unie en nationale soevereiniteit*, Inaugural lecture, Universiteit Leiden, 2008.

35 By emphasising the need for continuous legitimation of the exercise of public power on the European level it becomes clear that the act of transfer of competences by the Member States is not sufficient in this regard.

law and their direct or indirect participation in the decision-formation and decision-making process on the European level. What becomes clear from this is that with the transfer of public power to the European level some but not all of the organisational functions of national constitutional legal orders are taken over by the European legal order. The latter has not fully replaced those of the Member States. Instead, both systems mutually rely on the existence and effectiveness of the instruments foreseen in the respective other system.

It is doubtful whether the same can be said for the more elusive integrative function of national constitutional legal orders. Indeed, European integration, for a large part, has been an economically-driven process authored by states and featuring decision-making mechanisms that are increasingly democratically legitimised, while falling short of providing for processes of social transformation that allow for the creation of integrative forces beyond the state.[36] Integration has amounted to what Curtin has described as '*constitutionalisation without a Constitution*'.[37] In fact, the European legal order in principle '*respect[s] the allegiance to particular communities – the nation-state*'.[38] While an extensive legal framework, concrete rights and even some common values have been created on the basis of which citizens should at least to some extent be able to '*articulate their discourses and, from these, [...] can develop feelings of attachment and allegiance*',[39] neither the development of economic and social rights in the context of the internal market, nor the creation of a European citizenship[40] and the introduction of a common European currency have resulted in the integration of '*plural national identities into a larger polity.*'[41]. What is missing is a real 'pluralisation of identities'[42] in line with the current multiple constitutional

---

36 Nevertheless there seems to be a tendency in social science to emphasize the latter. See C. Rumford, 'Cosmopolitanism and Europe. Towards a new EU studies agenda?', (2005) 18 *Innovation* 1, at 2.

37 D. Curtin, The Sedimentary European Constitution – The Future of 'Constitutionalisation' without a Constitution', in I. Pernice and E. Tanchev (eds.), *Ceci n'est pas une Constitution – Constitutionalisation without a Constitution?*, Nomos, Baden-Baden, 2009, 76–85, who argues at p 78: 'In Europe we do have a constitution in an empirical sense and in a material sense but not a political or democratic Constitution.'

38 Brackets added. E.O. Eriksen, 'Towards a Cosmopolitan EU?', Arena Working Paper no. 9, February 2005, available online at www.arena.uio.no/cidel/wp05_09.pdf (accessed 20 October 2010), at p 29.

39 Brackets added. C. Closa, 'Deliberative Constitutional Politics and the EU Value-Based Constitution', in C. Closa and E. Fossum (eds.), *Deliberative Constitutional Politics in the EU*, ARENA and Universidad de Zaragoza, Oslo and Zaragoza, 2004, at p 33. See in particular Art. 2 TEU.

40 On the point of EU citizenship see: F.G. Jacobs, 'Citizenship of the European Union – A Legal Analysis', (2007) 13 *ELJ* 591–610, for whom EU citizenship adds to national citizenship. See also section 3.3.

41 R. Bauböck, 'Political Community Beyond the Sovereign State, Supranational Federalism, and Transnational Minorities', in S. Vertovec and R. Cohen (eds.), *Conceiving Cosmopolitanism. Theory, Context, and Practice*, OUP, Oxford, 2002, 110–136, at p 127.

42 A term borrowed from D. Held, 'Culture and Political Community: National, Global, and Cosmopolitan', in in S. Vertovec and R. Cohen (eds.), *Conceiving Cosmopolitanism. Theory,*

legal system of the EU. Whether considered desirable or not, what European integration has not in practice (yet) achieved is to create the conditions that allow for the emergence of what may be referred to as a European constitutional patriotism.[43] Article 4(2) TEU, according to which the Union must respect the national identities of Member States, inherent in their fundamental structures, political and constitutional, inclusive of regional and local self-government, may be interpreted as a recognition of this European constitutional reality, as does the failed attempt of the injection of European constitutional symbolism by the Treaty on the establishment of a Constitution for Europe.

The constitutional legal orders of the Member States currently provide the main source of social acceptance of European integration. They are largely perceived to offer the normative patterns on which societies in the Member States are organised. The 'permissive consensus'[44] on which acceptance of European integration has been built has its roots in the societal acceptance of political decisions and political order by the citizens of the Member States resulting from the stability and durability of the constitutional legal orders of their own national constitutional systems.[45] As Kirchhof has observed: '*European law would lose its roots and its powers to grow by being made autonomous and separate from the Member States, whereas in the close interweaving with Member State's constitutions it gains its identity in a unitary origin and a unitary future*'.[46] The gradual deterioration of the consent by silence on which European integration has at least partly been built, and which finds its expression in the rejection of large European integrationist projects, may be explained by the, in parts actual and in parts perceived, erosion of the constitutional legal orders of the Member States resulting from a progressive Europeanisation – whether or not by stealth[47] – that has not (fully) succeeded in taking over the integrative functions of the

*Context, and Practice*, Oxford, OUP, 2002, 48–58, at p 56, who refers somewhat more narrowly to a 'pluralisation of political identities'.

43 On this notion e.g. J. Lacroix, 'For a European Constitutional Patriotism', (2002) 50 *Political Studies* 944–958. See also the response by R. Bellamy and D. Castiglione, 'Lacroix's European Constitutional Patriotism: A Response' (2004) 52 *Political Studies* 187–193. Also: J.W. Müller, *Constitutional Patriotism*, Princeton University Press, Princeton, N.J., 2007.

44 With regard to this concept and its origin see A. Hurrelmann, 'European Democracy, the "Permissive Consensus" and the Collapse of the EU Constitution', (2007) 13 *ELJ* 343–359, at p 346. See also F. Amtenbrink, *Continuation or Reorientation. What Future For European Integration?* Erasmus Law Lectures (9), Boom Juridische uitgevers, Den Haag, 2008.

45 M. Zürn, 'Global Governance and Legitimacy', in D. Held and M. Koenig-Archibugi, *Global Governance and Public Accountability*, Blackwell, Malden MA, 2005, 136–163, at p 136, observes that the lack of normative legitimacy results in an erosion of societal acceptance of international institutions.

46 P. Kirchhof, 'The Balance of Powers between National and European Institutions', (1999) 5 *ELJ* 225–242, at p 230.

47 See G. Majone, *Dilemmas of European Integration: The Ambiguities and Pitfalls of Integration by Stealth*, Oxford, OUP, 2005.

national constitutional legal orders and namely the legitimating function for the redistributive effects of policies.[48]

If the observation is indeed correct that the constitutional legal orders of the Member States and the supranational European legal order complement each other in forming what Pernice has referred to as a '*Verfassungsverbund*', or, as De Wet has put it, '*Verfassungskonglomerat*',[49] the glue that holds this 'composite constitution'[50] together is not, or at least not exclusively, a common *European* constitutional law (*gemeineuropäisches Verfassungsrecht*),[51] but also the separate constitutional legal orders of the Member States. As such, in preserving the constitutional integrity of the EU not only the European legal order, but also the constitutional legal orders of the Member States must be observed to the extent that they constitute a *conditio sine qua non* for the being of the EU. Indeed, as Maduro has pointed out: '*Whatever limits European integration has imposed on the performance of the traditional functions at the national level, it has not envisaged the EU taking over those functions. The Union, as yet, neither fulfills the conditions nor has the capacity to perform those functions.*'[52]

Considering the current state of European constitutionalism it is evident that the courts of the Member States and namely the highest (constitutional) courts continue to play a vital role in maintaining the constitutional legal order of their respective country. To the extent that this also includes integrative functions of national constitutional legal orders, it may be argued that these courts fulfil an important function for the European constitutional legal order as a whole. This permits the role of national courts, as decentralised Union courts, and the approach by some of national highest (constitutional) courts to the issue of primacy of the European legal order to appear in a somewhat different light.[53]

In fact, primacy is not only reflected upon by courts in the well-known and much discussed area of fundamental rights as perceived in the national constitutional legal order, but is notably increasingly linked to broader constitutional principles

48 Generally on this issue M. Poiares Maduro, 'The importance of being called a constitution: Constitutional authority and the authority of constitutionalism', 3 *International Journal of Constitutional Law* (2005) 332–356.

49 I. Pernice, Kompetenzabgrenzung im Europäischen Verfassungsverbund', Antrittsvorlesung, Humboldt-Universität zu Berlin, 6. Juli 2000; E. de Wet, *The International Constitutional Order*, Vossiuspers UvA, Amsterdam, 2005, at p 6–7.

50 A term used by L.F.M. Besselink, *Een samengestelde Europese Constitutie*, Europa Law Publishing, Groningen, 2007.

51 P. Häberle, 'Europa als werdende Verfassungsgemeinschaft', (2000) *Deutsches Verwaltungsblatt* 840; by the same author: 'Gemeineuropäisches Verfassungsrecht', (1991) *Europäische Grundrechte Zeitschrift* 261; M. Heintzen, 'Gemeineuropäisches Verfassungsrecht in der Europäischen Union', (1997) *Europarecht* 1.

52 M. Poiares Maduro, 'The importance of being called a constitution: Constitutional authority and the authority of constitutionalism', (2005) 3 *International Journal of Constitutional Law* 332–356, at 345.

53 See also Lord Slynn of Hadley, 'What is a European Community Law judge?', (1993) 52 *Cambridge Law Journal* 234–244, who differentiates between two groups of 'European law judges'.

and values. Put differently, national highest (constitutional) courts may not only perceive themselves as the ultimate guardian of fundamental rights, but increasingly and more broadly as defenders of a broader constitutional identity. The latter is linked both to the organisational and integrative functions of national constitutional legal orders.

The judgment of the *Bundesverfassungsgericht* on the act of parliament ratifying the Maastricht Treaty, in which the Court indirectly reviewed the compatibility of this Treaty with the principle of democracy as laid down in the German Basic Law, may serve as a classic example here.[54] To be clear, in this decision the Court accepted the binding effect of decisions taken in the context of the European (legal) Community as compatible with the general preference towards integration expressed in the Basic Law and the openness of the latter towards participation in the establishment of an international legal order. Yet by emphasising the principle of democracy it implicitly also underlined the importance of an organisational and, to the extent that democracy also contributes to popular faith in a political system as a whole, integrative function of the national constitutional legal order.[55]

Evidence from more recent case law by some national highest (constitutional) courts further suggests that these courts consider themselves to be more than a simple defender of national fundamental rights. In the decision of the French Constitution Council (*Conseil Constitutionnel*) reviewing the constitutionality of the French Act pertaining to copyright and related rights in the information society (transforming Directive 2001/29/EC),[56] the Constitutional Council states that '*the transposition of a Directive cannot run counter to a rule or principle inherent to the constitutional identity of France, except when the constituting power consents thereto;*'[57] Rather than accepting the primacy of the European legal order deriving from its legal nature per se, as Charpy observes, the Constitutional Council interprets this primacy as an act of toleration by the French Constitution of 1958. In the words of the same author '*it is the Community legal order which is integrated into the national order, and not the other way around.*'[58] This approach also seems to be taken to the effects of primary Union law. In its decision concerning the question whether authorisation to ratify the Treaty establishing

54 BVerfGE 89, 155. See generally on this decision M. Herdegen, 'Maastricht and the German Constitutional Court: Constitutional Restraint for an "Ever Closer Union"', (1994) 31 *CMLR* 235–249; D. Grimm, The European Court of Justice and the National Courts: The German Constitutional Perspective after the (1996–1997) *Maastricht Decision*' 3 *Colum.J.Eur.L.*, 229–242.

55 See above section 2.1.

56 Directive 2001/29/EC of the European Parliament and of the Council of 22 May 2001 on the harmonisation of certain aspects of copyright and related rights in the information society (OJ 2001 L167/10).

57 2006–540 DC. para 19.

58 C. Charpy, 'The Status of (Secondary) Community Law in the French Internal Order: the Recent Case-Law of the *Conseil Constitutionnel* and the *Conseil d'Etat*', (2007) 3 *EuConst* 436–462, at p 459.

a Constitution for Europe requires prior revision of the French Constitution, the Constitutional Council points out first of all that '*The name given to this new Treaty does not require as such any ruling as to its constitutionality; Article I-5 thereof, pertaining to the relations between the European Union and the Member States thereof, shows that the title of said treaty has no effect upon the existence of the French Constitution and the place of the latter at the summit of the domestic legal order*'[59] With reference to Article 88–1 of the French Constitution, allowing for the participation of France in the European Union, the Constitutional Council argues '*that the drafters of this provision thus formally acknowledged the existence of a Community legal order integrated into the domestic legal order and distinct from the international legal order*'.[60]

Certainly the reference to a constitutional identity of France suggests that the primacy of the European legal order would not be considered acceptable in a situation in which this would run contrary to the basic constitutional structure as laid down in Article 1 of the French Constitution. This provision refers *inter alia* to France being a secular, democratic and social Republic, organised on a decentralised basis.

To the extent that these decisions can thus be interpreted as an expression of the determination of national courts to preserve the organisational and integrative functions of national constitutional legal orders, the controversial court decisions on primacy from some of the Central and Eastern European Member States should not be easily dismissed as childhood illnesses and signs of a national judiciary that has yet to overcome the initial phase of denial.[61] Instead, it may be that due to the fact that these countries have just (re-)gained their sovereignty after the collapse of the Soviet Union and have (re-) established democracy and the rule of law that their courts define their role in terms of the building of the stability and durability of the national constitutional legal order and the promotion of the identification of the citizens with this order.

The Polish Constitutional Tribunal's decision on the constitutionality of the Treaty of Accession to the EU is very informative in this regard. The Tribunal states in this decision that '*The accession of Poland to the European Union did not undermine the primacy of the Constitution over the whole legal order within the field of sovereignty of the Republic of Poland. The norms of the Constitution, being the supreme act which is an expression of the Nation's will, would not lose their binding force or change their content by the mere fact of an irreconcilable inconsistency between these norms and any Community provision. In such a situation, the autonomous decision as regards the appropriate manner of resolving*

59 2004–505 DC, para 10.

60 Ibid, para 11.

61 Generally on the situation in those countries, see J. Zemánek, 'The Constitutional Courts in the New Member States and the Uniform Application of European Law', available online at www.ecln.net/elements/conferences/book_berlin/zemanek.pdf (accessed 20 October 2010).

*that inconsistency, including the expediency of a revision of the Constitution, belongs to the Polish constitutional legislator.*'[62]

The Polish Constitutional Tribunal goes on to argue that: '*The principle of interpreting domestic law in a manner "sympathetic to European law", as formulated within the Constitutional Tribunal's jurisprudence, has its limits. In no event may it lead to results contradicting the explicit wording of constitutional norms or being irreconcilable with the minimum guarantee functions realised by the Constitution. In particular, the norms of the Constitution within the field of individual rights and freedoms indicate a minimum and unsurpassable threshold which may not be lowered or questioned as a result of the introduction of Community provisions.*'[63]

Finally, on the role of the ECJ the Polish Constitutional Tribunal concludes that '*The Court of Justice of the European Communities (ECJ) is the primary, but not the sole, depositary of powers as regards application of the Treaties within the legal system of the Communities and Union. The interpretation of Community law performed by the ECJ should fall within the scope of functions and competences delegated to the Communities by its Member States. It should also remain in correlation with the principle of subsidiarity. Furthermore, this interpretation should be based upon the assumption of mutual loyalty between the Community/Union institutions and the Member States. This assumption generates a duty for the ECJ to be sympathetically disposed towards the national legal systems and a duty for the Member States to show the highest standard of respect for Community norms*'[64]

The reference by the Polish Constitutional Tribunal to the duty of the ECJ to assume a positive inclination towards the national constitutional legal order may be no more than a reminder of the principle of sincere cooperation now laid down in Article 4(3) TEU, which also includes cooperation between Union institutions and the national judicial authorities.[65] But it can also be interpreted as an implicit warning that judicial cooperation is not a one-way street and that the discounting of this principle by the ECJ may result in a reassessment by the Polish Constitutional Tribunal of the position of the European legal order in the Polish constitutional legal order.

Arguably the most direct reference to what in the present contribution has been referred to as the integrative functions of national constitutional legal orders can be found in the 2009 decision by the *Bundesverfassungsgericht* on the constitutionality of the German Act approving the Treaty of Lisbon.[66] The Court first of all builds on its above mentioned Maastricht-decision in reference

62 Judgment of 11th May 2005, K18/04, para 1.
63 Ibid, para 14.
64 Ibid, para 16.
65 See Order of 13 July 1990, Case C-2/88, *Imm* [1990] ECR I-3365, paras 17–18.
66 BVerfG, 2 BvE 2/08 of 30 June 2009. An English language version is available at www.bundesverfassungsgericht.de/entscheidungen/es20090630_2bve000208en.html (accessed 20 October 2010). See also 'Karlsruhe has spoken: Yes to the Lisbon Treaty, but…' Editorial Comments, (2009) 46 *CMLR* 1023–1033; D. Thym, 'In the Name of Sovereign Statehood: A Critical

to the democracy principle by pointing out that '*A permanent responsibility for integration is incumbent upon the German constitutional bodies. It is aimed at ensuring, as regards the transfer of sovereign powers and the elaboration of the European decision-making procedures, that in an overall view, the political system of the Federal Republic of Germany as well as that of the European Union comply with democratic principles within the meaning of Article 20.1 and 20.2 in conjunction with Article 79.3 of the Basic Law.*'[67]

In the view of the *Bundesverfassungsgericht* '*the principle of conferral under European law and the duty, under European law, to respect identity, are the expression of the foundation of Union authority in the constitutional law of the Member States.*'[68] On the one hand the Court emphasizes that '*The safeguarding of sovereignty, demanded by the principle of democracy in the valid constitutional system, in the manner prescribed by the Basic Law, i.e. in a manner that is open to integration and to international law, does not mean per se that a number of sovereign powers which can be determined from the outset or specific types of sovereign powers must remain in the hands of the state*'. On the other hand, the Court also points out the limits of this integration by stating that '*European unification on the basis of a union of sovereign states under the Treaties may not be realised in such a way that the Member States do not retain sufficient room for the political formation of the economic, cultural and social circumstances of life. This applies in particular to areas which shape the citizens' circumstances of life, in particular the private space of their own responsibility and of political and social security, which is protected by the fundamental rights, and to political decisions that particularly depend on previous understanding as regards culture, history and language and which unfold in discourses in the space of a political public that is organised by party politics and Parliament.*'[69]

It has to be admitted that in making these observations the German Constitutional Court is clearly concerned with the scope of the principle of democracy and thus mainly organisational aspects of the national constitutional legal order. Yet, one particular passage of the decision may be interpreted as hinting towards a deeper concern in relation to the lack of an integrative function of the European legal order. The Court argues that '*Even if due to the great successes of European integration, a joint European public that engages in an issue-related cooperation in the rooms of resonance of their respective states is evidently growing, it cannot be overlooked, however, that the public perception of factual issues and of political leaders remains connected to a considerable extent to patterns of identification which are related to the nation-state, language, history*

Introduction to the *Lisbon* Judgment of the German Constitutional Court', (2009) 46 *CMLR* 1795–1822.

67 Ibid, para 245.

68 Ibid, para 234.

69 Ibid, para 249.

*and culture.'*[70] Language, history and culture may all be considered to have an integrative function for a polity without however necessarily all being linked to the principle of democracy and thus mainly to an organizational function.

The *Bundesverfassungsgericht* had to decide whether the reference in the Treaty of Lisbon to a *'competition oriented "open market economy"'*[71] is compatible with the principle of the social state as laid down in the German Basic Law. Referring to Article 23 German Basic Law, which allows for the participation in and development of the EU that is committed to several (quasi-)constitutional principles enumerated in this provision,[72] the Court emphasizes that *'Germany's participation in the process of integration depends, inter alia, on the European Union's commitment to social principles. Accordingly the Basic Law not only safeguards social tasks for the German state union against supranational demands in a defensive manner but wants to commit the European public authority to social responsibility in the spectrum of tasks accorded to it'.*[73]

The Court makes clear that *'the essential decisions in social policy must be made by the German legislative bodies on their own responsibility. In particular the securing of the individual's livelihood, which is a responsibility of the state that is based not only on the principle of the social state but also on Article 1.1 of the Basic Law, must remain a primary task of the Member States, even if coordination which goes as far as gradual approximation is not ruled out. This corresponds to the legally and factually limited possibilities of the European Union for shaping structures of a social state.'*[74]

These statements can be interpreted as the recognition of the autonomous identity which the national constitutional legal order still provides in the view of the *Bundesverfassungsgericht*, corresponding with the above-argued concept of the integrative function of national constitutional legal orders. It has been rightly observed in this context that, if followed by highest (constitutional) courts in other Member States, *'divergent views as to what amounts to the identity of the relevant Member State'* could emerge resulting in *'competence clashes in an unforeseen dimension.'*[75]

What becomes clear from these few examples is that some national courts can be seen defining their roles as guardians of the national constitutional order *within* the overall European constitutional legal order. Rather than to

---

[70] Ibid, para 251. Brackets omitted.

[71] Ibid, para 116 and 117.

[72] Article 23(1) German Basic Law refers to *'democratic, social, and federal principles, to the rule of law, and to the principle of subsidiarity, and that guarantees a level of protection of basic rights essentially comparable to that afforded by this Basic Law'.*

[73] BVerfG, 2 BvE 2/08 of 30 June 2009, para 258.

[74] Ibid, para 259.

[75] 'Karlsruhe has spoken: Yes to the Lisbon Treaty, but...' Editorial Comments, (2009) 46 *CMLR* 1023–1033, at 1031. But see D. Thym, 'In the Name of Sovereign Statehood: A Critical Introduction to the *Lisbon* Judgment of the German Constitutional Court', (2009) 46 *CMLR* 1795–1822, at 1810–1811.

unconditionally accept the primacy of the European legal order, some highest (constitutional) courts seem to be set to guard national constitutional identity. The *Bundesverfassungsgericht* appears to be at the forefront of this movement by maintaining that an inviolable core of competences has to remain at the national level and by effectively exercising an identity review.[76] The 'constitutional tolerance', that what Weiler has described as the willingness of constitutional actors in the Member States to accept the 'European constitutional discipline' '*as an autonomous voluntary act, endlessly renewed on each occasion of subordination, in the discrete area governed by Europe, to a norm which is the aggregate expression of other wills, other political identities, other political communities*' is clearly not infinite.[77]

## 3. THE ECJ'S PRINCIPLED APPROACH TO PRIMACY: A CLAIM OF ABSOLUTE SOVEREIGNTY IN DISGUISE?

The question here revolves around whether the ECJ's approach reflects the current state of European constitutionalism sketched in the previous sections?

Undoubtedly the democratically elected governments of the Member States have willingly curtailed their constitutionally defined powers by signing up to international obligations, thereby challenging the traditional approach to the sovereignty of states and thus the very essence of the Westphalian order. Yet, in the absence of an explicit primacy clause in the founding Treaties and given the rather ambiguous vertical allocation of competences, it was really left to the ECJ to address the legal implications of this unprecedented extent of transfer of public power from the state level. It is very telling in this regard that while the abolished Treaty on the establishing of a Constitution for Europe included an explicit provision on primacy, in the Treaty of Lisbon it has only found its way into a Declaration on primacy annexed to the Treaty.[78]

---

76 The term is borrowed from D. Thym, 'In the Name of Sovereign Statehood: A Critical Introduction to the *Lisbon* Judgment of the German Constitutional Court', (2009) 46 *CMLR* 1795–1822.

77 J.H.H. Weiler, 'In defense of the status quo: Europe's constitutional *Sonderweg*', in J.H.H. Weiler and M. Wind, *European Constitutionalism Beyond the State*, Cambridge University Press, Cambridge, 2003, 7–23, at p 21. See also already J.H.H. Weiler, 'A Constitution for Europe? Some Hard Choices', (2002) 40 *JCMS* 563–580.

78 Declaration No. 17, according to which '*The Conference recalls that, in accordance with well settled case law of the Court of Justice of the European Union, the Treaties and the law adopted by the Union on the basis of the Treaties have primacy over the law of Member States, under the conditions laid down by the said case law.*'

## 3.1. ON THE ECJ'S CONCEPT OF PRIMACY

The ECJ has described the European Communities (now European Union) as a new, legal order for the benefit of which Member States have limited their sovereign rights within limited fields. This legal order is distinct from public international law in that the states, but also their nationals, are its subjects and in that it creates rights and obligations for both.[79] As opposed to the conception in public international law '*which leaves the regulation of internal effect of rules of international law to national constitutional law*', the ECJ made clear at an early stage that primary and secondary Community law (now Union law), penetrates the national legal systems of the Member States directly, as they are directly applicable and can produce – upon the fulfilment of certain conditions – direct effect.[80] European law is considered an integral part of the legal systems of the Member States, and national courts are expected to apply Union law accordingly.[81]

The European legal order is understood to exist independently of the legislation of the Member States.[82] Despite the absence of a clear definition of the source of primacy,[83] the ECJ has maintained that European law "*cannot be overridden by rules of national law, however framed, without being deprived of its character as Community law and without the legal basis of the Community itself being called in question. Therefore the validity of a Community measure or its effect within a Member States cannot be affected by allegations that it runs counter to either fundamental rights as formulated by the constitution of state or the principles of its constitutional structure.*"[84] Consequently, any national law and any legislative, administrative or judicial practice that can impair the effectiveness of Union law is considered '*incompatible with the requirements which are inherent in the very nature of [Union] law.*'[85] National courts, including the highest ones, must interpret and apply national law in accordance with Union law and "*to the extent that such an interpretation is not possible in relation to the Treaty provisions conferring rights on individuals which are enforceable by them and which the*

79 ECJ 5 February 1963, Case C-26/62, *Van Gend & Loos* [1963] ECR 1.

80 Emphasizing this difference with public international law: C.W.A. Timmermans, General Aspects of the European Union and the European Community', in Kapteyn & VerLoren van Themaat, *The Law of the European Union and the European Communities*, 4th ed, Kluwer Law International, Austin et al, 2008, at p 75 et seq.

81 ECJ 15 July 1964, Case 6/64, *Costa v E.N.E.L* [1964] ECR 585.

82 ECJ 3 April 1968, Case 28–67, *Molkerei-Zentrale Westfalen/Lippe* [1968] ECR 211.

83 As rightly pointed out by F. Mayer, 'The European Constitution and the Courts. Adjudicating European constitutional law in a multilevel system', Jean Monnet Working Paper 9/03, at p 17.

84 ECJ 17 December 1970, Case 11/70, *Internationale Handelsgesellschaft* [1970] ECR 1125, para 3. Also ECJ 17 October 1989, Joined Cases 97/87 et al., *Dow Chemical Ibérica, SA* [1989] ECR 3165, para 38.

85 Brackets added. ECJ 19 June 1990, Case C-213/89, *Factortame* [1990] ECR I-2433.

*national courts must protect, [...] disapply any provision of domestic law which is contrary to those provisions.*"[86]

The ECJ has emphasized that not only the new legal order, but also its relationship with the legal orders of the Member States is governed by the rule of law, that is, the *European* rule of law.[87] While the ECJ may not have the jurisdiction to directly order national courts to give European law precedence in the face of national law as the latter is interpreted in the national legal order,[88] the non-application of Union law by national courts, including the highest one, can become the subject of an infringement procedure before the ECJ or an action for state liability before the competent national court.[89]

On an abstract level, the ECJ takes a rather rigorous approach to defining the relationship between the national (constitutional) and the European legal order. From a purely European perspective this may make perfect sense in the light of effectiveness, as a recourse to national law of any of the Member States would adversely upset the uniformity and efficacy of Union law and thus, in the view of the ECJ, the fundament of the supranational legal order.[90] Moreover, in reference to the early landmark decisions in the cases *Van Gend en Loos* and *Costa v E.N.E.L.*, this approach can be best understood when placed in a historical context, taking into account the development of the rich meaning of these judgments over time.[91] Taking a rather more normative approach, Timmermans argues that it is the permanent limitation of sovereignty in favour of the European legal order that results in European law falling outside the scope of national constitutional rules governing the internal effect and the internal order of priority of rules of international law, as these rules can only apply within the limits of sovereignty.[92] Yet, one may wonder, exactly what the limits of *European* sovereignty are then?

86 Brackets added. ECJ 11 January 2007, Case C-208/05, *ITC Innovation Technology Center GmbH* [2007] ECR I-181, paras 68–69, with further references.

87 See ECJ 23 April 1986, Case 294/83, *Parti écologiste "Les verts"* [1986] ECR 1339, para 23, where the ECJ states that the "*Community is based on the rule of law, inasmuch as neither its Member States nor its institutions can avoid a review of the question whether the measures adopted by them are in conformity with the basic constitutional charter, the Treaty*".

88 A point made by C.W.A. Timmermans, General Aspects of the European Union and the European Community', in Kapteyn & VerLoren van Themaat, *The Law of the European Union and the European Communities*, 4th ed, Kluwer Law International, Austin et al, 2008, at p 78.

89 ECJ 30 September 2003, Case C-224/01, *Köbler* [2003] ECR I-10239; ECJ 13 June 2006, Case C-173/03, *Traghetti* [2006] ECR I-5177.

90 ECJ 17 December 1970, Case 11/70, *Internationale Handelsgesellschaft* [1970] ECR 1125, para 3; ECJ 9 March 1978, Case 106/77, *Simmenthal* [1978] ECR 629, para 18. See also ECJ 21 February 1991, Joined Cases C-143/88 and C-92/89, *Zuckerfabrik Süderdithmarschen and Zuckerfabrik Soest* [1991] ECR I-415, para 26.

91 A. Vauchez, 'The transnational politics of judicialisation. *Van Gend en Loos* and the making of EU polity', (2010) 16 *ELJ*, 1–28.

92 C.W.A. Timmermans, General Aspects of the European Union and the European Community', in Kapteyn & VerLoren van Themaat, *The Law of the European Union and the European Communities*, 4th ed, Austin et al, Kluwer Law International, 2008, at p 78.

The textbook answer to this question seems easy enough. The limitations derive first and foremost from the principles of conferral, subsidiarity and proportionality articulated in Article 5(1) TEU. On a more substantive level, limitations may also stem from the possibility provided by the TFEU and the mandatory-requirements doctrine of the ECJ for the justification of national rules or practices directly or indirectly, actually or potentially in conflict with the (fundamental) free movement rights.[93] Yet, the stringency of these boundaries is questionable. Much more than the absence of an explicit competence catalogue, it is the presence of broad legal bases in primary Union law,[94] paired with general principles and prohibitory provisions, which essentially determined the tolerability of the national constitutional legal orders, that have undermined the emergence of a clear delineation of competences.[95] Thus, for example, the absence of any authorisation on the part of Member States for the Union to take large-scale harmonisation measures in the area of public health does not also signify the absence of any scrutiny, namely by national courts and tribunals acting as decentralised Union courts, and, ultimately by the ECJ itself in the context of the preliminary reference procedure under Article 267 TFEU. National legislative measures relating to public health and public health policy can become subject to review under the internal market's free movement provisions and European competition rules, as well as the general principle of non-discrimination. The consequences of this approach are potentially far-reaching as Member States may actually be forced to reorganise their welfare systems.[96] What is more, the principle of subsidiarity is believed not to function as restraint, partly because the ECJ has been rather cautious in applying this principle.[97] The newly introduced Part One Title I of the TFEU on categories and areas of Union competences is unlikely to change this picture substantially given its close resemblance to the competence system *de facto* existing prior to the Treaty of Lisbon and the limited conclusiveness of an explicit catalogue of competences in the light of the broad application of the internal market rules.[98]

---

93 This point will be returned to hereafter in section 3.3.

94 In particular former Article 95 EC (now Article 114 TFEU) and former Article 308 EC (now Article 352 TFEU).

95 B. de Witte, 'Droit communautaire et valeurs constitutionnelles nationales', (1991) 14 *Droits* 87–96, at 88, notes: '*Le problème principal, cependant, réside dans la nature dynamique de la construction communautaire.*'. See also R. Barents, 'The internal market unlimited: Some observations on the legal basis of Community legislation', (1993) *CMLR* 30, 85–109; S.R. Weatherill, 'Competence creep and competence control' (2004) 23 *YEL*, 1–55.

96 See e.g. G.T. Davies, 'The Process and Side-Effects of Harmonisation of European Welfare States, Jean Monnet Working Paper No. 02/06. Available at http://papers.ssrn.com/sol3/papers.cfm?abstract_id=900934 (accessed 20 October 2010).

97 For an explanation see G.T. Davies, 'Subsidiarity: The Wrong Idea, In the Wrong Place, At the Wrong Time', (2006) 43 *CMLR* 63–84.

98 See also M. Dougan, 'The Treaty of Lisbon 2007: Winning Minds, Not Hearts', (2008) 45 *CMLR* 617–703, at 656, who observes that most competences existed previously.

The principle of conferral is thus effectively hollowed out. It turns out that by allowing for a system of negative harmonisation in the first place the signatory states have effectively limited their regulatory competences in a rather broad fashion while not in all instances reinstating such competences as part of the supranational legal order. This results in '*policy lacunae, which are eventually filled by the supranational legal order.*'[99] Moreover, it is this openness of the European legal order that has put the ECJ in a decisive position to shape the relationship of the former with the national constitutional legal orders of the Member States. Much more than by means of treaty-making, the supranational legal order has been constructed by 'judicial empowerment', whereby the dividing lines between defining and constructing public power are not always clearly visible.[100]

## 3.2. RECOGNIZING MEMBER STATE'S COMMON (CONSTITUTIONAL) LEGAL TRADITIONS

The ECJ considers that Union law is intended to confer rights on individuals which become 'part of their legal patrimony'.[101] Moreover, European law is considered to form an integral part of the legal orders of the Member States. Does this not imply than that the constitutional legal orders of the Member States forms the other part of the very same legal patrimony that the ECJ is referring to?

Of course it may be argued that the picture of the ECJ that emerges from the observations on the conceptual approach to primacy in the previous section is misleading as no reference was made to the Court's recognition of national constitutional traditions and, moreover, the recognition of national standards.[102] In fact, it could be claimed that in doing so the ECJ is effectively recognising the national legal patrimony. In the past, the Court has upheld fundamental elements of the constitutional legal orders of the Member States. Its approach to the protection of fundamental rights is often propagated as a case in point. Leaving aside the undoubtedly very relevant issue as to what or rather who triggered this course of action by the ECJ,[103] what is interesting to observe in the

---

99 F. AMTENBRINK, 'The Multidimensional Constitutional Legal Order of the European Union – A Successful Case of Cosmopolitan Constitution-Building?' (2009) 40 *Netherlands Yearbook of International Law*, 3–68, at 48.

100 See generally K.J. ALTER, 'The European Court's Political Power', (1996) 19 *West European Politics* 458–487.

101 The phrase is used by the Court in ECJ 19 November 1991, Joined Cases C-6/90 and C-9/90, *Francovich and Bonifaci* [1991] ECR I-5357, para 31.

102 The latter point is discussed hereafter in section 3.3.

103 The standard response, that the ECJ could be seen as effectively diffusing a constitutional standoff with national highest (constitutional) courts (see. e.g. T.C. HARTLEY, *The Foundations of European Community Law*, 5th edition, OUP, Oxford, 2003, at p 136) is contested by U. EVERLING, 'Bundesverfassungsgericht und Gerichtshof der Europäischen Gemeinschaft nach dem Maastricht-Urteil', in A. RANDELZHOFER, R. SCHOLZ und D. WILKE, *Gedächtnisschrift für Eberhard Grabitz*, C.H. Beck, München, 1995, 57–75, at p 62 et seq, with

context of the present contribution is the argumentative artifice which the ECJ applies in recognizing these standards in the first place. In the case of *Stauder*, the Court considered fundamental rights simply to be '*enshrined in the general principles of Community law*' and declared itself competent to protect these rights.[104] In *Internationale Handelsgesellschaft*, while rejecting the idea of a review of Community measures based on fundamental rights or principles formulated by a Member State constitution, the Court argues that '*an examination should be made as to whether or not any analogous guarantee inherent in Community law*' exists.[105] In the same judgment the ECJ makes clear that the protection of such rights is '*inspired by the constitutional traditions common the Member States*'.[106]

In the case of *Nold* the ECJ observes that because it is '*bound to draw inspiration from constitutional traditions common to the Member States, and it cannot therefore uphold measures which are incompatible with fundamental rights recognized and protected by constitutions of those states.*'[107] In this case, the ECJ acknowledges the right of ownership notably referring to the protection of such a right by '*the constitution laws of all the Member States*'[108] Outside the sphere of fundamental rights, the ECJ apparently implicitly takes a similar approach namely in recognising what it refers to as '*fundamental democratic principles*'.[109]

What becomes clear from these and other references to national constitutional traditions is that the ECJ reserves the right for itself to decide on the scope of such rights and the extent to which it seeks inspiration from the national legal orders in the first place. A methodological foundation for the notion 'constitutional traditions' is difficult to bring to light. What seems certain is that in the comparative law approach inherent to this notion the (constitutional) legal

reference to the historic course of events. However, it can hardly be denied that the fundamental rights dimension of the European economic rights was brought to the attention of the ECJ by national courts, see F. Amtenbrink and H.H.B. Vedder, *Recht van de Europese Unie*, 4th ed, Boom Juridische Uitgevers, The Hague, 2008, at p 214.

104 ECJ 12 November 1969, Case 29/69, *Stauder* [1969] ECR 419, para 7.

105 ECJ 17 December 1970, Case 11/70, *Internationale Handelsgesellschaft* [1970] ECR 1125, para 3. To be clear, the ECJ also seeks inspiration from international treaties to which the Member States are signatories. This point is briefly returned to hereafter in the context of the discussion of the case *Mangold*.

106 ECJ 17 December 1970, Case 11/70, *Internationale Handelsgesellschaft* [1970] ECR 1125, para 4.

107 Brackets added. ECJ 14 May 1974, Case 4/73, *Nold v Commission* [1974] ECR 491, para 13.

108 Brackets added. Ibid, para 13.

109 See ECJ 29 October 1980, Case 138/79, *SA Roquette Frères v Council of the European Communities* [1980] ECR 3333; ECJ 11 June 1991, Case 300/89, *Commission v. Council* [1991] ECR I-286. Both judgments refer to a fundamental democratic principle that the people should take part in the exercise of power through the intermediary of a representative assembly. The principle of democracy has also been invoked in the context of the right to information and the right to access documents see e.g. ECJ 30 April 1996, Case C-58/94, *Netherlands v Council* [1996] ECR I-2169. See also GC 17 June 1998, Case T-135/96, *Union Européenne de l'artisanat et des petites et moyennes entreprises (UEAPME) v Council* [1998] ECR II-2335, para 89, with regard to participatory rights in the conclusion of an agreement on social policy, where the Court of First Instance (now General Court) considers the principle of democracy as one of the founding principles of the Union.

tradition of any one Member State is not decisive.[110] Moreover, as opposed to what the above cited consideration by the ECJ in the case of *Nold* may suggest, the ECJ is not limiting the application of this concept to situations in which a particular legal concept can be found in *all* national legal orders. A general case in point is the ECJ's approach in the case of *Brasserie du Pêcheur.*[111] In defending the development of the principle of state liability, the ECJ indirectly suggests that this principle is based on a common legal tradition in the Member States. With regard to the principle of the non-contractual liability of the Community the Court considered that this is '*simply an expression of the general principle familiar to the legal systems of the Member States that an unlawful act or omission gives rise to an obligation to make good the damage caused.*' Yet, at least in the case of one Member State, i.e. Germany, the concept of damages for legislative wrongdoing (*Haftung für 'legislatives Unrecht'*) was considered controversial.[112]

This somewhat liberal comparative law approach by the ECJ can also be observed in areas of law which are more directly linked to fundamental policy choices that Member States make in accordance with their own constitutional legal order. One notable example in this regard is the ECJ's judgment in the case of *Mangold*, with potentially far-reaching consequences for the social and employment policies of the Member States.[113] Based on a rather general reference to the existence of various international instruments and constitutional traditions common to the Member States, the ECJ has constructed a general principle of Community law of non-discrimination on grounds of age.[114] As a consequence of this, a provision in German law on part-time working and fixed-term contracts amending and repealing provisions of employment law, which authorised, in principle without restrictions, the conclusion of fixed-term contracts of employment once the worker had reached the age of 52, was considered incompatible with Community law. At the time of the judgment, the deadline for transposition of the Directive had not yet expired.

This judgment has received much attention, particularly by German legal commentators, for its approach to the establishment of a general principle and the effects which it assigns to a directive prior to the expiry of the deadline for its transposition.[115] It has been pointed out that at the time of the deliberations

---

110 On the use of comparative law by the ECJ see generally K. Lenaerts, 'Le droit comparé dans le travail du juge communautaire', (2001) *Revue trimestrielle de droit européen* 487–528.

111 ECJ 5 March 1996, Joined Cases C-46/93 and C-48/93, *Brasserie du Pêcheur* [1996] ECR I-1029.

112 See R. Streinz, *Europarecht*, 6th ed, C.H. Müller, Heidelberg, 2003, p 152–153 and p 175–176, with further references to relevant literature.

113 ECJ 22 November 2005, Case C-144/04, *Mangold* [2005] ECR I-9981.

114 Ibid, para 74–75. The ECJ in this context simply refers to the preamble of Council Directive 2000/78/EC establishing a general framework for equal treatment in employment and occupation (OJ 2000 L303/16).

115 See e.g. K. Hailbronner, 'Hat der EuGH eine Normverwerfungskompetenz?', (2006) *Neue Zeitschrift für Arbeitsrecht* 811–816; N. Reich, '"Mangold" und kein Ende – oder doch?', (2007) *Europäische Zeitschrift für Wirtschaftsrecht* 198–199; F. Temming, 'Freie Rechtsschöpfung oder nicht: Der Streit um die EuGH-Entscheidung Mangold spitzt sich zu', (2008) *Neue Juristische*

there was no compelling evidence for the existence of international conventions and treaties or legal traditions common to the Member States that would justify the recognition of such a general European principle.[116] It may be somewhat overdrawn to take this judgment as an example of the dangers of a broad, unattached and unrestrained judicial power. Yet, what can be observed is that there is a notable lack of recognition of the potentially far reaching implications of the introduction of such a general principle for the social and employment policies in the Member States. It becomes clear from the more recent decision in the case of *Kücükdeveci* that the ECJ does not seem to have any intention to reconsider this approach,[117] despite the fact that even from within the European judiciary concerns have been voiced with regard to its potential effects. In the case of *Palacios de la Villa,* Advocate General Mazák considers that '*the application of the prohibition of discrimination on grounds of age [...] requires a complex and subtle assessment*'.[118] In view of the approach adopted by the ECJ, the German Constitutional Court may actually be somewhat overoptimistic – something this Court is not often accused of – when it states in its Lisbon-decision that '*there are also no indications justifying the assumption that the Member States are deprived of the right, and the practical possibilities of action, to take conceptual decisions regarding systems of social security and other social policy and labour market policy decisions in their democratic primary areas.*'[119]

To the extent that the ECJ may thus actually be seen developing constitutional principles beyond what can be construed from an interpretation of primary Union law[120] and common national constitutional traditions that may have found their expression in international treaties, the question is who should be the final arbiter in dealing with allegations that the ECJ acts *contra constitutionem*?[121] In light of the conceptual approach to primacy taken by the ECJ, supposedly supported by Article 19(1) TEU and Article 267 TFEU, the answer seems clear from a European law perspective: the ECJ itself.

---

*Wochenschrift* 3404–3406; L. Gerken, V. Riebe, G.H. Roth, T. Stein und R. Streinz, *„Mangold" als ausbrechender Rechtsakt*, München, Sellier. European Law Publishers, 2009.

116 See in particular L. Gerken, V. Riebe, G.H. Roth, T. Stein und R. Streinz, *„Mangold" als ausbrechender Rechtsakt*, München, sellier. european law publishers, 2009, p 19–22. See however M. Schmidt, 'The Principle of Non-discrimination in Respect of Age: Dimensions of the ECJ's *Mangold* Judgment', (2006) 7 *German Law Journal* 505–524, who seems to lean towards a defense of the ECJ's approach.

117 ECJ 19 January 2010, Case C-555/07, *Kücükdeveci* [2010] ECR I-365.

118 Brackets added. Opinion of AG Mazák 15 February 2007, Case C-411/05, *Palacios de la Villa* [2007] ECR I-8531.

119 BVerfG, 2 BvE 2/08 of 30 June 2009, para 399.

120 See e.g. B. de Witte, 'Interpreting the EC Treaty like a constitution: the role of the European Court of Justice in comparative perspective', in R. Bakker, A.W. Heringa and F. Stroink (eds.), *Judicial control. Comparative essays on judicial review*, Maklu, Antwerpen/Apeldoorn, 1995, 133–152, in particular p 148 et seq.

121 Generally with regard to the judicial functionalism of the ECJ and the legal debate on this point see A. Knook, *Europe's Constitutional Court*, PhD, University of Utrecht, 2009, p 67 et seq.

## 3.3. RECOGNITION OF NATIONAL (CONSTITUTIONAL) LEGAL STANDARDS

It has been observed by the *Bundesverfassungsgericht* in its Lisbon-decision that '*In its case-law, the Court of Justice has developed principles which strengthen the social dimension of the European Union*' and moreover that '*The Court of Justice has for instance recognised numerous important social concerns as mandatory requirements of the common good which can justify the restriction of the market freedoms of Community law.*'[122] Undoubtedly, the recognition of standards originating from the constitutional legal orders of the Member States has, to a considerable extent, been channelled through the acceptance of justifications of diverging national standards in the internal market. It is against this background that Thym, by reference *inter alia* to mandatory requirements in the area of fundamental freedoms, has observed that there is '*ample room for a case-specific respect for national constitutional identity*'. In the view of this author, '*Potential areas of conflict may thus appear much less pronounced after closer inspection of the legal material at hand.*'[123]

Leaving aside for the moment the previously mentioned issue of the source of these principles, their development can undoubtedly add to the currently frail integrative function of the European legal order. Indeed, it can be argued that the ECJ's conceptual approach to primacy sketched so far does not extend to the substantive review of the compatibility with Union law of national measures forming (potential) barriers to trade. This is not to say, however, that the ECJ's case-law in this area points towards an unqualified recognition or indeed preservation of national (constitutional) standards.

Both in recognising the legal traditions of the Member States as general principles of Union law, as well as in accepting national barriers to trade in the internal market, the ECJ applies its own policy standards. One possible outcome of this approach is highlighted by the judgments in the much debated cases *Laval*[124] and *Viking*,[125] which interestingly enough are cited by the *Bundesverfassungsgericht* as positive examples of the acknowledgement by the ECJ of the EU's social dimension. In the *Laval* case, the ECJ recognises collective action as a fundamental right in Community law, stating that the protection of this right is '*a legitimate interest which, in principle, justifies a restriction of*

122 BVerfG, 2 BvE 2/08 of 30 June 2009, para 398. In para 399, the Court lists several relevant judgments by the ECJ.

123 D. Thym, 'In the Name of Sovereign Statehood: A Critical Introduction to the *Lisbon* Judgment of the German Constitutional Court', (2009) 46 *CMLR* 1795–1822, at 1811. These comments are made in the context of the statements by the *Bundesverfassungsgericht* on the importance of constitutional identity in its Lisbon-decision. On the status of non-market values in positive harmonisation see B. de Witte, 'Non-market values in internal market legislation', in N. Nic Shuibhne, *Regulating the Internal Market*, Edward Elgar Publishing, Cheltenham, 2006, 61–86.

124 ECJ 18 December 2007, Case C-341/05, *Laval* [2007] ECR I-11767.

125 ECJ 11 December 2007, Case C-438/05, *Viking* [2007] ECR I-10779.

*the obligations imposed by Community law, even under a fundamental freedom guaranteed by the Treaty'*.[126] Yet in the same breath, referring to its judgments in the *Schmidberger* and *Omega* cases,[127] the Court emphasized that *'the exercise of such rights does not fall outside the scope of the provisions of the Treaty and must be reconciled with the requirements relating to rights protected under the Treaty and in accordance with the principle of proportionality.'*[128] In the given cases, the fundamental right is evaluated against the background of the free movement of services and freedom of establishment provisions, now laid down in Articles 56 and 49 TFEU, and the possibility to justify a national restriction of these freedoms. In doing so, the ECJ considers the free movement provisions to be of the same (constitutional) rank as the fundamental rights, as recognised by the ECJ, to strike and take collective action.

In balancing the different policy considerations, the principle of proportionality, according to which a national restriction must be suitable for ensuring the attainment of a legitimate objective pursued by the Member State and must not go beyond what is necessary to achieve that objective, has a decisive role. In the case of *Schmidberger*, the ECJ states that while national authorities enjoy a wide margin of discretion in weighing the free movement provisions against legitimate interests, it is for the Court itself to decide whether the national measures are proportionate in the light of the legitimate objective pursued.[129] In the *Omega* case, the ECJ makes clear that for the consideration of public policy grounds *'It is not indispensable in that respect for the restrictive measure issued by the authorities of a Member State to correspond to a conception shared by all Member States as regards the precise way in which the fundamental right or legitimate interest in question is to be protected.'*[130] The Court goes on to emphasize that *'the need for, and proportionality of, the provisions adopted are not excluded merely because one Member State has chosen a system of protection different from that adopted by another State'*[131] The ECJ explicitly rejects the idea of the need for a legal tradition to be common to all Member States and refrains from formulating *'a general criterion for assessing the proportionality of any national measure which restricts the exercise of an economic activity.'*[132]

In these cases, the ECJ does not seem to apply the same strict conceptual approach to primacy as described above. Yet, the placing on an equal level of national constitutional principles and European legal norms, and the balancing of partially incompatible interests, make the outcome rather uncertain, even, arguably, at times to the expense of what may be called the integrative function

126 ECJ 18 December 2007, Case C-341/05, *Laval* [2007] ECR I-11767, paras 93–94.
127 ECJ 12 June 2003, Case C-112/00, *Schmidberger* [2003] ECR I-5659; ECJ 14 October 2004, Case C-36/02, *Omega* [2004] ECR I-9609.
128 ECJ 18 December 2007, Case C-341/05, *Laval* [2007] ECR I-11767, paras 93–94.
129 ECJ 12 June 2003, Case C-112/00, *Schmidberger* [2003] ECR I-5659, summary No. 2.
130 ECJ 14 October 2004, Case C-36/02, *Omega* [2004] ECR I-9609, para 37.
131 Ibid, para 38.
132 Ibid, para 37.

of national constitutional legal orders. For Reich, commenting on the *Laval* and *Viking* cases, '*This balancing is clearly on the side of free movement and against social rights*'.[133]

## 4. CONCLUDING REMARKS

It has been argued throughout this contribution that, for the time being, the national constitutional orders of the Member States continue to perform an important integrative function both in the national and European legal order and, thus, for the European constitutional legal order as a whole. Therefore, the ECJ's conceptual approach to Union law, as an autonomous legal order that is moreover supreme, is difficult to align with the theoretical evaluation of the current state of European constitutionalism and the role of the national highest courts in this context. The same arguably holds true for the ECJ's rather vague notion of legal traditions common to the Member States. Caught up in its role as Union court and driven by the will to ensure the uniformity and efficacy of the European legal order, the ECJ leaves itself but few options to actually recognise the vital integrative function of the national constitutional legal orders of the Member States. To the extent that the ECJ does draw from the latter, by requiring a legal tradition or principle *common* to the Member States, it neglects the function which each national constitutional legal system has, independently of the constitutional system of another Member State or the European legal order, as building-block for the public acceptance of the system as a whole. In the sphere of the recognition of national standards in the internal market, the ECJ seems to be willing to depart from its strict conceptual approach on a case-to-case basis. Nevertheless, all in all, the ECJ's approach is arguably not fully in tune with the '*multi-centred and heterogeneous nature of European governance*', thereby creating at least the potential for confrontation with highest national (constitutional) courts.[134]

While the European legal order defines and limits the exercise of public power beyond the state, it only provides for the organisational framework required to legitimise the exercise of public power to a limited extent. It does so to an even lesser extent when it comes to the integrative functions of national constitutional legal orders. The constitutionalisation of the European legal order cannot be viewed in isolation from the constitutional legal orders of the Member States and the crucial organisational and integrative functions they continue to perform. National highest (constitutional) courts are undoubtedly decentralised Union courts and as such must cooperate closely with the ECJ. Yet they are also charged with ensuring the coherent application of the constitutional legal order throughout

133 N. Reich, 'Free Movement v. Social Rights in an Enlarged Union – the Laval and Viking Cases before the ECJ', (2008) 9 *German Law Journal* 125–161, at 160.

134 J. Zielonka, 'Plurilateral Governance in the Enlarged European Union', (2005) 45 *JCMS* 187–209, at 199.

the state territory, and to defend and reinforce it in light of changing social realities.[135] Against this background, the position which highest (constitutional) courts in some Member States have taken towards the primacy of the European legal order, can be given a meaning that is somewhat more constructive than to simply point out their unwillingness to accept the consequences of the surrender of state sovereignty and the role of the ECJ in this new legal order. To be clear, it was not the aim of this contribution to construct a '*claim of higher validity for national constitutionalism vis-à-vis European constitutionalism*'.[136] Rather, it should be read as pleading for a reevaluation of the crucial integrative function of the national constitutional legal orders of the Member States for the EU as a whole.

While mutual cooperation and dialogue may be what both national courts and the ECJ strive for, recent judgments suggest that the ECJ's approach to primacy continues to receive wavering approval by national courts. Grimm has observed in this context that '*It is disquieting for lawyers to be confronted with the possibility for jurisdictional conflict that cannot be resolved within the existing legal order*' and, moreover, has pointed out that what is missing in the relationship between European and national law in the case of conflicting provisions is '*a smooth hierarchy*' that '*can only be established if one set of norms is clearly superior to the other*'.[137] In the author's view, this follows from a '*divided sovereignty that is not reconciled under the umbrella of federalism*'.[138] Grimm's conjecture about the cause suggests that the direction which solutions would have to take will be met by resistance in particular, ironically perhaps, by those observers that categorically reject the ECJ's current approach.

---

[135] This is e.g. recognised in the context of the German Basic Law of 1949 and the role of the German Federal Constitutional Court by J. Limbach, '50 Jahre Deutsche Verfassung in Europa', Vortrag anlässlich des 50jährigen Bestehens des Europa-Instituts der Universität des Saarlandes am 15. Juni 2001 in Saarbrücken, available online at http://archiv.jura.uni-saarland.de/projekte/Bibliothek/text.php?id=200 (accessed 20 October 2010).

[136] A criticism raised against some debates on national and European constitutionalism, see M.Poiares Maduro, 'Europe and the constitution: what if this is as good as it gets?' in J.H.H. Weiler and M. Wind, *European Constitutionalism Beyond the State*, Cambridge University Press, Cambridge, 2003, 74–102, at 74.

[137] D. Grimm, The European Court of Justice and the National Courts: The German Constitutional Perspective after the *Maastricht Decision*' (1996–1997) 3 *Colum J Eur L* 229–242, at 241–242.

[138] Ibid, at p 242.

# THE JUDGE'S ROLE IN EUROPEAN INTEGRATION

## The Court of Justice and Its Critics

Jürgen Basedow*

## 1. CHALLENGES TO THE LEGALITY OF THE EUROPEAN COURT'S PRACTICE

On December 31, 2005, the German Newspaper *Süddeutsche Zeitung* published an interview with the then Federal Chancellor of Austria, *Wolfgang Schüssel*, who was about to take over the Presidency of the European Council. Among other subjects he addressed the Court of Justice of the European Union saying that "nobody can creepingly read a centralist note into the case law. However, the Court of Justice has systematically extended European competences in recent years, even in areas where there is definitely no Community law. All of a sudden, judgements about the role of women in the German army or about the admission of foreign students to Austrian universities are handed down – this is clearly national law."[1]

On 24 July 2007, another German newspaper, the *Frankfurter Allgemeine Zeitung*, published an interview with the President of the German Constitutional Court, *Hans-Jürgen Papier*. The highest German judge identified a "not unproblematic inclination of the European Court of Justice to check the compatibility of national acts, even those not implementing mandatory Community law with self-developed general principles of law. This involves the risk that the Community, by virtue of the case law of its Court of Justice, attracts competences which it does not have under the Treaties."[2]

---

* Prof. Dr. Dr. h.c. Jürgen Basedow, LL.M. (Harvard Univ.), Director, Max Planck Institute for Comparative and International Private Law; Professor of law, University of Hamburg.

1 Cited after www.ue2006.at/de/news/speeches_interviews/schuessel_sueddeutsche.html?month=4&day=1 (my translation, J.B.).

2 An electronic version of the interview is published in FAZ.net (my translation, J.B.).

The most drastic criticism has recently been voiced by the former President of the Federal Republic of Germany who, before his appointment to that office, had been President of the German Constitutional Court. In a newspaper article entitled "Stop the European Court of Justice" *Roman Herzog* analysed several judgements of the Court which in his view extended Community competences beyond the limits established by the Treaty and concluded that the Court has "knowingly and systematically ignored central principles of the occidental judicial interpretation of laws, has motivated its decisions in an improper way, has disregarded or even twisted around the legislator's intention and has invented principles of law which could be used as basis in later decisions." He concludes that "the Court of Justice is eroding the rights of Member States even in the core areas of national competences."[3]

Both by tone and content, this harsh critique of leading lawyers and politicians goes far beyond any commentary on the Court of Justice that has ever been made in German-speaking countries since its foundation. Is this a mere coincidence of overreactions to single opinions of the Court? Or is there something wrong with the Court of Justice? My following remarks will try to answer these questions by a functional approach to the Court's position in European integration. They will first identify three different functions of the Court (infra *2.*) and then try to assess some leading opinions in the light of these functions (infra *3.* to *5.*).

## 2. CENTRIFUGAL FORCES AND THE FUNCTIONS OF THE COURT

### 2.1. THE LEGAL FRAMEWORK

The jurisdiction of the Court of Justice is established in a number of articles of the Treaty, see Article 227 seq. EC (now Article 259 TFEU). From a practical point of view the most important types of proceedings are infringement proceedings under Articles 226 seq. EC (now Article 258 TFEU) and in particular reference proceedings under Article 234 EC (now Article 267 TFEU). Much of the above cited criticism draws from opinions of the Court handed down in proceedings of these two types. It is noteworthy that the rules on reference proceedings gave rise to intense debate when the Community was founded.

When the Court of Justice – or rather its predecessor – was established by the Coal and Steel Community Treaty,[4] its powers were more limited than today.

[3] R. Herzog/L. Gerken, Stoppt den Europäischen Gerichtshof, *Frankfurter Allgemeine Zeitung* 8.9.2008, Nr 210, p 8 (my translation, J.B.).

[4] Treaty establishing the European Coal and Steel Community (ECSC) of 18 April 1951, 261 UNTS 140 = BGBl. 1952 II, 447.

Under Article 41 ECSC the Court was only competent to examine the *validity* of the acts of the High Authority, but not to interpret those acts upon a referral by a national court. The *interpretation* of secondary Community law was entrusted to the Court of Justice only by Article 177 EEC, which became Article 234 EC (now Article 267 TFEU).[5] In the early years, this extension of the Court's competence may have appeared as insignificant next to the previously existing power to check the validity of, and strike down, Community acts. But in practice, the preliminary questions addressed to the Court concern the interpretation of Community law much more frequently than its validity.

Moreover, it has been this extension which has increasingly often caused national judges to request a clarification of Community directives and to ask the Court whether national law implementing those directives is compatible with them. When interpreting directives many of which are fragmentary in nature, covering only isolated issues, the Court has often been invited by national judges to take recourse to general principles which allow to put the single rule into a broader framework.

Thus, it can be said at this early stage of our inquiry already that the extension of the Court's powers in referral proceedings by the Treaty of Rome has somehow paved the way for the Court's activities which raised the criticism reported above. This is even more so as the referral proceedings have become the dominant type of procedure over the years.[6] Thus, the referral procedure, dealing with a huge and ever increasing body of fragmentary Community legislation is characterized by an inherent trend towards an extension of Community law as such. This observation does not address the single opinions criticised in recent years, but is meant to point to the institutional framework approved by the Member States that favours the expansion of Community law.

## 2.2. CENTRIFUGAL FORCES IN THE MEMBER STATES

This takes us to a common denominator of recent criticism of the Court of Justice. All critics cited above complain of a usurpation of powers, by the Court of Justice, for the European Community to the detriment of the Member States. The

5 Together with other proposed amendments, it appeared for the first time in a Committee document in January 1957, see R. Schulze/T. Hoeren (eds), *Dokumente zum europäischen Recht*, vol 1, Gründungsverträge, Springer, Heidelberg, 1999, p 1065.

6 The number of referrals to the Court of Justice increased from 1 in 1961 to 37 in 1971, 109 in 1981, 186 in 1991, 237 in 2001 to 265 in 2007; see the statistics reproduced by F. Ferrand, 'Das Vorabentscheidungsverfahren aus französischer Sicht', (2002) 66 *RabelsZ*, 391, 413–415, and for the years 2001 and 2007 the statistics provided in the Annual Report of the European Court of Justice: <http://curia.europa.eu/en/instit/presentationfr/index.htm>. In 2007 the 265 references for a preliminary ruling amounted to 46 percent of all cases before the Court of Justice.

Federal Chancellor's office of Austria has even inspired, and given its support to, a research project conducted at the University of Innsbruck and entitled "The European Court of Justice and the sovereignty of Member States".[7] In their preface the editors of a book resulting from that project point out that „the founding fathers of the European Economic Community most likely did not envisage concepts like those espoused by the Court in *van Gend & Loos* (1963 [direct effect][8]) and *Costa/ENEL* (1964 [priority of Community law][9])".[10]

The editors of that book do not mention that the principles of direct effect and priority of Community law have generally been approved and confirmed by subsequent amendments of the Treaty ratified by national parliaments.[11] They rather conduct research on a single issue: To what extent has the practice of the Court of Justice expanded the powers of the Community beyond the limits drawn by the Treaty ? While this perspective certainly is legitimate, it is definitely too narrow for most areas of the law. Think for example of private law; here, the yardstick for the evaluation of case law is rather the content of decisions and the balancing of interests involved than the national or European identity of judges and policymakers.

Yet, the political criticism and the legal research cited above give evidence of a major change that can be observed in the present perception of European integration. While the Court's contributions to European integration have been cherished for many years and have even brought about its reputation as "the motor of integration", the recent debate points to the increased weight accorded to the preservation of national competences in the Member States. Centrifugal forces seem to gain strength.

---

7 See G. Roth/P. Hilpold (eds), *Der EuGH und die Souveränität der Mitgliedstaaten*, Linde, Vienna, 2008.

8 ECJ 5 February 1963, Case 26/62, *Van Gend en Loos* [1963] ECR 1.

9 ECJ 15 July 1964, Case 6/64, *Costa/ENEL* [1964] ECR 585.

10 See the preface of G. Roth/P. Hilpold (eds), *Der EuGH und die Souveränität der Mitgliedstaaten*, Linde, Vienna, 2008, p 5.

11 It suffices to compare the present wording of the Treaty provisions implementing the basic freedoms with their predecessors, see e.g. Article 39 EC: "Freedom of movement for workers shall be secured within the Community." In the Treaty of Rome of 1957 the predecessor proviso of Article 48 EEC was phrased: "Freedom of movement of workers shall be secured within the Community *by the end of the transitional period at the latest*" (my emphasis, J.B.), thereby suggesting that additional measures had to be taken to attain the goal. When the italicized words were deleted, the Member States made clear that they approved of the Court ruling giving direct effect to the freedom of movement of workers.

## 2.3. THREE FUNCTIONS OF THE COURT OF JUSTICE

The centrifugal forces outlined above lay stress on the Court's primary constitutional function which the critics believe to be the delimitation of national and Community competences. However, this is only one aspect out of the *review function* that the Court exercises over all actors in the framework of Community law (see infra 3).

What is disregarded in most discussions about Community and Member State competences is the fact that the primary content of the Treaty is not the delimitation of competences, but the conferral of instructions upon the Community for the implementation of policies in certain areas identified in the Treaty. The scope of the respective mission determines the Community's competence. In some of these areas the objectives of Community policy are clearly defined in the Treaty, in others the Treaty simply provides for a communitarisation of a given area of policy-making or for support to be given to Member State policies.[12] While those objectives have to be attained by Community legislation, i.e. in the political arena, they also have a certain legal significance which gives rise to another constitutional function of the Court of Justice: the *impulse function*. In many instances the Court has in fact tried to further the progress of Community policies by giving impulses to the political actors, i.e. to the Commission, the Council and the European Parliament (see infra 4).

Finally, the growing body of Community law is of course exposed to an increasing risk of inconsistent interpretation and divergent application in the Member States. In this context, the Court of Justice performs the *uniformity function* of a supreme court that has to ensure the uniform application in the whole territory of the Community (see infra 5).

The three functions listed above are not unknown at the national level. In federal states the review function and the impulse function are sometimes (e.g. in Germany and Spain) entrusted to the constitutional court while the uniformity function is bestowed on one or several superior courts in the country. But there are other states like for example the U.S. where the Supreme Court performs all three functions. Nor are these functions clearly distinct from each other; they sometimes overlap in one and the same case.

---

12 See J. Basedow, 'Zielkonflikte und Zielhierarchien im Vertrag über die Europäische Gemeinschaft', in O. Due/M. Lutter/J. Schwarze (eds.), *Festschrift für Ulrich Everling*, vol 1, Nomos, Baden-Baden, 1995, p 49–60.

# 3. THE REVIEW FUNCTION

## 3.1. INFRINGEMENT PROCEEDINGS AGAINST MEMBER STATES

Under Article 220 EC (now replaced, in substance, by Article 19 TEU) the Court of Justice shall ensure that in the application of the Treaty the law is observed. The application of Community law is *inter alia* incumbent upon the Member States, and the founders of the Community foresaw that Member States might fail to fulfil an obligation arising under the Treaty. That is why infringement proceedings were created which may be initiated both by the Commission and other Member States, see Articles 226 and 227 EC (now 258 and 259 TFEU). Member States usually do not make use of this right of action.[13] They will of course dislike breaches of Community law committed by other Member States and complain of them to the Commission. They also hope that the Commission will eventually go to court in which case they would sometimes support the Commission's claim. But national governments will generally not initiate infringement proceedings against other Member States by themselves, being afraid that litigation will disturb diplomatic life.

As a consequence, many infringement proceedings brought by the Commission are proxy litigations. Take the opening of the national insurance markets for cross-border insurance services by the Court's judgement of 1986.[14] There could not be any doubt that the requirement set forth in German law that a foreign insurer must have an establishment in Germany can by no means be reconciled with the freedom to provide services. Yet, Britain and the Netherlands whose insurance companies were very much interested in the opening of the insurance markets, did not sue Germany, but confined themselves to supporting the complaint brought by the European Commission. And in those proceedings it was alleged by some governments that the matter was political and not legal.

In the more recent case dealing with the discriminatory admission of foreign students to Austrian universities, the main interested Member State was of course Germany which neither sued Austria nor supported the Commission's infringement claim.[15] But of course, many German students were happy about the outcome. However, the Commission was not alone in this case either, having the support of Finland. It is not uncommon indeed that single Member States give their support to the Commission's claim. The views on the Community's competence which have been criticised as expansive or even as a usurpation of powers thus

13 See Borchardt in C. O. Lenz/K.-D. Borchardt, *EU- und EG-Vertrag*, 4th ed, Bundesanzeiger-Verlag, Köln, 2006, art 227 no 1.

14 ECJ 4 December 1986, Case 205/84, *Commission/Germany* [1986] ECR 3755.

15 ECJ 7 July2005, Case C-147/03, *Commission/Austria* [2005] ECR I-5969.

are not only those of the Commission and of the Court, but are apparently shared by some Member States. It follows that, contrary to the assertion of some critics; the conflicts decided in these cases are not political, but legal.

While infringement proceedings directed against single Member States often give rise to tensions between that Member State and the Community, the review function of the Court of Justice is by no means limited to that kind of litigation. The Community institutions themselves are subject to the same review of the legality of their actions or failure to act in proceedings which may be initiated by the Member States or other Community institutions. The common transport policy would not have made much progress had the Court not, in 1985, convicted the Council, at the Parliament's complaint, for its failure to act.[16]

## 3.2. LEGAL DOCTRINES FURTHERING THE REVIEW FUNCTION

The review function of the Court has in practice been extended by the *doctrines of priority of Community law and of the direct effect* of some of its provisions.[17] Where Community provisions which are sufficiently clear and unconditional purport to confer subjective rights on private parties, the two doctrines, taken together, enable every individual favoured by such provisions to challenge any rule of national law that cannot be reconciled with them. Where such conflicts emerge, national courts will therefore usually submit preliminary questions to the Court of Justice. As explained before, however, those key doctrines now form part of primary Community law.[18] While they have considerably enlarged the procedural possibilities of a *de facto* review of national law by the Court of Justice, they have not changed the substantive content of Community law. Their critics therefore appear to imagine a Community where basic freedoms are nothing more than vague guidance for politicians, but do not confer any enforceable rights on the individuals concerned.

Over the years the Court of Justice has developed a number of measures designed to ensure compliance, by Member States, with Community law: the doctrine of *indirect effect*, i.e. the obligation of national institutions to interpret national law in accordance with Community law;[19] the *direct effect* of directives in vertical

---

16 ECJ 22 Mai1985, Case 13/83, *Parliament v Council* [1985] ECR 1513.

17 ECJ 5 February 1963, Case 26/62, *Van Gend en Loos* [1963] ECR 1 and ECJ 15 July 1964, Case 6/64, *Costa/ENEL* [1964] ECR 585.

18 See above at fn 11.

19 ECJ 10 April 1984, Case 14/83, *von Colson and Kamann / Nordrhein-Westfalen*, [1984] ECR 1891; ECJ 13 November 1990, Case C-106/89, *Marleasing SA / La Comercial*, [1990] ECR I-4135.

relations;[20] and the *liability of Member States* for losses caused by the breach of obligations arising under Community law.[21] Whatever criticism may be addressed to this case law, in particular to the liability sanction, it cannot be said to infringe upon the Member States' autonomy. In all cases concerned the Member States have been in breach of Community obligations, i.e. they were no longer autonomous in the respective areas.

# 4. THE IMPULSE FUNCTION

## 4.1. THE SYNCHRONY OF POLITICAL AND LEGAL ACTION

Unlike many national constitutions the European Treaties do not simply create a framework and establish procedures for a political decision-making whose content is left to changing trends and majorities. As pointed out above, the Community has a mission outlined in Articles 2 and 3 EC.[22] According to the preamble the overarching objective is to lay the foundations for an ever closer union among the peoples of Europe. In the light of this mission the framework established by the Treaty has to be seen as dynamic, not as static. Just like the other institutions of the Community, the Court, within the limits of its jurisdiction, has to contribute to the achievement of the goals laid down in the Treaty.

This includes the so-called dynamic interpretation of Community law.[23] The solution of a legal issue in 2010 may be different from the solution that the same issue has received 30 years ago. The commitment of the Court of Justice to the mission of the Community also includes the need to take into account major trends in Community policy. Where the political institutions of the Community give priority to the development of policies in a given area, the Court will often be asked to focus its own attention on legal issues arising in that context and will try to honour its own obligations under the Treaty by contributing to the achievement

---

20 ECJ 4 December 1974, Case 41/74, *van Duyn / Home Office*, [1974] ECR 1337; ECJ 19 January 1982, Case 8/81, *Ursula Becker / Finanzamt Münster-Innenstadt*, [1982] ECR 53; ECJ 14 July 1994, Case C-91/92, *Faccini Dori / Recreb*, [1994] ECR I–3325.

21 ECJ 19 November 1991, Joined Cases C-6/90 and C-9/90, *Francovich / Italian Republic*, [1991] ECR I–3843; ECJ 5 March 1996, Joined Cases C-46/93 and C-48/93, *Brasserie du Pêcheur / Federal Republic of Germany; ex parte Factortame*, [1996] ECR I–1029.

22 Article 2 EC corresponds to Article 3 TFEU; Article 3 EC is now replaced, in substance, by Article 7 TFEU and by Articles 13(1) and 21, paragraph 3, second subparagraph of the TEU.

23 See the early characterization by H.-P. Ipsen, *Europäisches Gemeinschaftsrecht*, Mohr, Tübingen 1972, no 1/12: "Vom Organisationsrecht im Wesentlichen abgesehen, eignet zahlreichen Komplexen des Gemeinschaftsrechts ein Zug motorischer, plan- und zeitbestimmter Impulsivität und eine Tendenz, im nationalen Recht Veränderung und Entwicklung hervorzurufen. Das charakterisiert den Beziehungszustand zwischen Gemeinschaftsrecht und nationalem Recht als einen solchen von Übergängen, von Schwebelagen, von dynamischem Gehalt..."

of those policy goals. The relation between the Court of Justice and the political institutions of the Community sometimes appears as a kind of osmosis or even as a dialogue, a reciprocal exchange of initiatives and comments. In various instances judgements of the Court have helped to increase the consciousness of the political actors for certain problems or to overcome their resistance in the political debate.

## 4.2. EXAMPLE 1: ADMISSION OF FOREIGN STUDENTS TO AUSTRIAN UNIVERSITIES

Among the various examples that give evidence of this process only some can be cited in this context. Think again of the case concerning the admission of foreign students to Austrian universities: The Commission started these proceedings in late 1999, only some months after the so-called Bologna Declaration had been adopted by the European ministers of education.[24] In view of a European area of higher education the Bologna Declaration lay stress, *inter alia,* on the "promotion of mobility by overcoming obstacles in the effective exercise of free movement with particular attention to – for students – access to study and training opportunities and to related services".

In its 2005 opinion the Court of Justice, without mentioning the Bologna Declaration made clear in substance that a political announcement of this kind which had also been signed by defendant Austria cannot remain without consequences. A Member State cannot commit itself to furthering the mobility of students and at the same time discriminate against foreign students. The latent power of Community law was used to provide additional momentum to the political intention of the European countries to open up their systems of higher education.

## 4.3. EXAMPLE 2: OPENING NATIONAL INSURANCE MARKETS

The situation was similar in the insurance case. In the early 1980s, the quest for the implementation of the freedom to provide services in the insurance sector had led to a Commission proposal of what later became the second generation Direc-

24 Joint Declaration of the European Ministers of Education convened in Bologna on the 19th of June 1999, see http://ec.europa.eu/education/policies/educ/bologna/bologna.pdf; on the infringement proceedings leading to the Court's judgement in case C-147/03 see cons 7 seq of that judgement, above at fn 15.

tive on non-life insurance.[25] In the proceedings before the Court of Justice, the Irish government maintained that the case dealt with the same problems as were at issue in the political discussions, concerning the definition of the scope of the freedom to provide services, and considered that the Commission was asking the Court "to perform the task assigned by the Treaty to the Council".

In response to that argument which questioned the admissibility of the proceedings the Court said that it was open to the Commission, in carrying out its tasks under the Treaty, to bring an action under what is Article 226 EC (now 258 TFEU), and that "the mere fact that a proposal for a legislative measure, which if adopted and transposed into national law would terminate the infringements alleged by the Commission, has already been submitted to the Council does not prevent the Commission from bringing such an action".[26] The result of that decision was that some of the previous national requirements could not be enforced any more. This amounted to a kind of new deal for the negotiations in the Council where the previous positions of some Member States could not be maintained. As a result, the Community made a great step forward on its way towards a single insurance market, i.e. an objective laid down in binding provisions of the Treaty.

## 4.4. EXAMPLE 3: FREE MOVEMENT FOR COMPANIES

A third area where such a dialogue between politics and the Court of Justice can be observed relates to company law, in particular to the direct effect of the freedom of establishment for companies under Article 48 EC (now Article 54 TFEU). In the 1980s the operating company of the English newspaper Daily Mail wanted to transfer its seat to the Netherlands, but did not succeed to get the approval of the British government required under British tax law. Invoking the direct effect of the freedom of establishment, Daily Mail plc. went to court. Upon a referral from the English High Court the Court of Justice decided that what is now Article 54 TFEU does *not* confer on companies incorporated under the law of a Member State a right to transfer their central management to another Member State. While the freedom of establishment was explicitly held to be a fundamental principle of the Community also for companies, its implementation was said to be a matter for political decision making under provisions such as Article 44 EC (now Article 50 TFEU) or Article 293 EC (now repealed).[27]

---

25 Second Council Directive of 22 June 1988 on the coordination of laws, regulations and administrative provisions relating to direct insurance other than life assurance and laying down provisions to facilitate the effective exercise of the freedom to provide services and amending Directive 93/239/EEC (88/357/EEC), OJ 1988 L 172/1.

26 ECJ 4 December1986, Case 205/84, *Commission/Germany* [1986] ECR 3755, cons. 6.

27 ECJ 27 September1988, Case 81/87, *Daily Mail* [1988] ECR 5483, cons. 15–24; the decision has recently been confirmed by ECJ 16 December 2008, Case C-210/06, *Cartesio* [2008] ECR I-9641.

More than a decade later, the Court of Justice has handed down a series of judgements which presuppose the direct effect of Article 48 EC (now 54 TFEU). In this context, it is sufficient to mention one of these cases decided under the name *Überseering*. The shares of a Dutch private limited company had been sold to a German buyer who transferred the main office to Germany where the company was involved in a litigation with a German contracting partner. This party alleged that under the rules of German private international law *Überseering* had no legal capacity since it had not been established and registered under the laws of Germany, the country of its management office. A 1968 convention of the EEC Member States providing for the recognition of foreign companies and negotiated under what is now Article 293 EC (now repealed) had never taken effect. Nevertheless, the Court of Justice held that *Überseering* as being validly incorporated in the Netherlands had been entitled under Articles 43 and 48 EC (now 49 and 54 TFEU) to exercise its freedom of establishment in Germany and that its transfer to Germany was of little significance in that regard. The requirement of re-incorporation of the same company in Germany was therefore said to be "tantamount to outright negation of freedom of establishment".[28]

The different lines of case law may be reconciled if Article 48 EC (now Article 54) is interpreted as being directly applicable only in countries of *immigration* of companies which have to accept a foreign legal entity as such, but not in the country of *emigration*. Another interpretation that would focus on the impulse function of the Court of Justice would rather consider the unsuccessful plea of the Daily Mail court for political action to ensure the free movement of companies in the European Union. Since a political compromise between the different approaches to the conflict of laws in company law appeared to be out of reach, the Court, having stressed the importance of the freedom of establishment for companies as early as 1988, saw the need to push the political discussions by providing new guidance after 1999. More recent legislative instruments in the field of company law show the fruitful effect of that new guidance.

## 4.5. SUMMARY: LEGAL CONTRIBUTIONS TO THE COMMUNITY'S MISSION

Further examples could be given in areas such as the prohibition of discrimination on grounds of sex or the private enforcement of EC competition law or the external relations of the area of justice – they would all give evidence of the Court's consciousness of the main lines of policymaking in the Community as defined by its political institutions. This phenomenon cannot sufficiently be explained by a

[28] ECJ 5 November 2002, Case C-208/00, *Überseering B.V. / Nordic Construction Company Baumanagement GmbH* [2002] ECR I-9919, cons. 81.

delimitation of competences, it is much more closely linked to the mission of the Community. The criticism voiced by present and past members of the German Constitutional Court is even more surprising as the German Constitutional Court itself frequently provides input to the political process by its decisions.

## 5. THE UNIFORMITY FUNCTION

### 5.1. THE COURT CONFRONTED WITH A GROWING BODY OF FRAGMENTARY LEGISLATION

Ever since its foundation the legislative machinery of the European Community has been highly productive. The amendments to the Treaty adopted by the Single European Act, the Treaty of Maastricht and the Treaty of Amsterdam have broadened the scope of Community legislation which now covers many areas of private law that generate a high level of litigation at the national level. As a consequence, the number of requests for preliminary rulings of the Court of Justice is growing incessantly.[29] Many of these requests do not raise issues of national or Community competence. The national courts simply want to know more about the interpretation of certain Community rules and concepts. The answers are increasingly difficult for the European Court. Community legislation is not systematic, following an overall legislative program, but fragmentary, responding to particular regulatory needs felt in very specific fact situations. As a consequence, this legislation is far from consistent.

### 5.2. UNDERPERFORMANCE

Take the example of legislative rules on damages and in particular on the compensation of non-material loss. The 2004 Directive on the enforcement of intellectual property rights explicitly refers to moral prejudice caused to the owner of a right by an infringement as an aspect to be taken into account when assessing damages.[30] Quite to the contrary, the products liability Directive leaves the issue of non-material damage to national provisions.[31] Under the package tour Directive the tourist is equally entitled to damages in the case of a breach of obligations by the tour operator, but the Directive is silent on the issue of non-material damages.[32]

29 See the statistical data above in fn 6.

30 See Article 13 para. 2 of Directive 2004/48/EC of the European Parliament and of the Council of 29 April 2004 on the enforcement of intellectual property rights, OJ 2004 L 157/45.

31 See Article 9 last sentence of Council Directive of 25 July 1985 on the approximation of the laws, regulations and administrative provisions of the Member States concerning liability for defective products, OJ 1985 L 210/29.

32 See Article 5 of Council Directive of 13 June 1990 on package travel, package holidays and package tours, OJ 1990 L 158/59.

When the Court of Justice was asked whether tourists could claim compensation for pain and suffering sustained during the tour, and for foregone holidays, the Advocate General *Tizzano* outlined the general development of the law relating to non-material damages in a broad comparative perspective and concluded that non-material damages are included in the respective provision of the package tour Directive. The Court of Justice followed the Advocate General as to the result, but confined its reasoning in a very narrow manner to those arguments that directly flow from the Directive.[33] Thus, it is difficult to draw any inferences from this judgment that relate to a general principle providing for the compensation of non-material losses either in general or in consumer cases or when personal harm or bodily injury is involved.

This decision gives evidence of a certain reluctance of the Court of Justice to provide guidance to the national judiciary in applying secondary private law legislation of the Community. The same impression emerges from the leading case dealing with the Directive on unfair terms in consumer contracts.[34] Under the central provision of that Directive "a contractual term which has not been individually negotiated shall be regarded as unfair if, contrary to the requirement of good faith, it causes a significant imbalance in the parties' rights and obligations arising under the contract, to the detriment of the consumer". While the national provisions implementing this article are invoked in national contract litigation very frequently, the Court has more or less refused to guide the national courts in the interpretation of the above provision pointing out that its application depends on national law which is beyond its jurisdiction.[35] It follows that the harmonisation of laws intended by the European legislature failed because the Court of Justice was unwilling to embark upon the road towards the interpretation of a general clause.[36]

If any criticism of the Court is possible in these cases, it would rather be the complaint that the Court leaves too much latitude or even free hand to the judiciary of the Member States and does not perform the uniformity function entrusted to it.

---

33 ECJ 12 March 2002, Case C-168/00, *Simone Leitner/TUI Deutschland*, [2002] ECR I-2631.

34 Council Directive 93/13/EEC of 5 April 1993 on unfair terms in consumer contracts, OJ 1993 L 95/29.

35 ECJ 1 April 2004, Case C-237/02, *Freiburger Kommunalbauten/Hofstetter* [2004] ECR I-3403.

36 For a closer analysis see J. Basedow, 'Der Europäische Gerichtshof und die Klauselrichtlinie 93/13: der verweigerte Dialog', in G. Müller/E. Osterloh/T. Stein, *Festschrift für Günter Hirsch*, Beck, München, 2008, 51–62.

## 5.3. OVERPERFORMANCE

A certain insecurity of the Court of Justice becomes visible in other cases where the Court did not decide too little, but too much. The most conspicuous case is the *Mangold* decision which has aroused much of the criticism cited above. In a case concerning the discrimination on grounds of age in employment matters the Court was asked for the interpretation of two specific legislative instruments, a framework agreement and one of the anti-discrimination Directives. It held that the national provisions at issue were not contrary to the framework agreement and that the facts giving rise to litigation occurred before the transposition period of the Directive in question had elapsed. In this situation it would have been sufficient to criticise the Member State for having enacted, after the adoption of the Directive, provisions of a transitory nature which in substance could not be reconciled with the Directive. Instead, and without any restrictions relating to the substantive scope, i.e. employment, the Court discovered a principle of non-discrimination on grounds of age as a general principle of Community law which was held to be directly applicable even before the expiration of the transposition period.[37]

Such a principle does not exist, neither in the international conventions which the Court refers to without specification, nor in national law. What is more important in our context than the lack of empirical basis is perhaps that there was no need for giving any impulse to European legislation which had already issued the Directive in question; in the course of its implementation in the Member States that directive would have achieved the harmonisation it was made for. What also strikes the reader of this decision is the Court's lack of sensitivity for the peculiarities of private law. The opinion is drafted as a discussion of a Member State's (potential or actual) failure to comply with obligations under Community law. The Court appeared completely unaware of the effect of its decision as between the employee and the employer. There is not a single word about the latter's potential trust in the validity of national legislation.

## 5.4. THE COURT'S INSECURITY

To summarize our observations it can be said that the Court's practice is characterized by a certain insecurity as far as its uniformity function is concerned. There is partly overperformance and partly underperformance; sometimes the Court is aiming at excessively general principles and sometimes abstaining from

[37] ECJ 22 November 2005, Case C-144/04, *Mangold/Helm*, [2005] ECR I-7917, cons 75; for a closer analysis and criticism see J. Basedow, 'Der Grundsatz der Nichtdiskriminierung im europäischen Privatrecht', (2008) *ZEuP (Zeitschrift für Europäisches Privatrecht)* 230–251.

generalisation whatsoever, sticking to the petty questions asked by the national court. What is needed in this area is a growing consciousness of the Court for the elaboration of principles of medium abstraction. As far as contract law is concerned, the Principles of European Contract Law[38] or the future Common Frame of Reference[39] may help to provide standards for the optimal level of abstraction.

## 6. CONCLUSION

(a) The European Court performs three functions in European integration: the review function, the impulse function, and the uniformity function.
(b) The legal review of Member State laws has in fact been extended beyond what was intended by the founders of the Community, but the extensions were included in the design of the Treaty of Rome and/or later approved by Member States.
(c) The impulse function follows from the mission of the European Community that is laid down in the Treaty and binding upon the Court of Justice, too. It includes what may be called an osmotic relation between the progress of Community policies and the case law of the Court.
(d) The Court has to ensure the uniformity of the application of Community law in the Member States. In this regard its practice is insecure and oscillating between underenforcement, i.e. a reluctance to provide guidance, and overenforcement in terms of excessively broad principles.
(e) While the Court's critics focus on a transgression of Community competences by the Court, the demarcation of Community and Member State competences is an insufficient and inappropriate yardstick for the Court's practice in many areas of the law. In private law in particular the reasonable balancing of the interests of the parties involved is more important. But it appears that the Court is not yet fully aware of the difference in approach that is needed for the various areas of the law.

[38] O. Lando/H. Beale (eds.), *Principles of European Contract Law – Parts I and II*, Nijhoff Publishers, Dordrecht, 2000; O. Lando/E. Clive/A. Prüm/R. Zimmermann, *Principles of European Contract Law* – Part III, Nijhoff Publishers, Dordrecht, 2003.

[39] For a preparatory work see C. von Bar/E. Clive/H. Schulte-Nölke, *Principles, definitions and model rules of European private law – Draft Common Frame of Reference (DCFR)*, Interim outline edition, Munich, 2008.

# PART III

# INTERNAL MARKET, CITIZENSHIP AND MIGRATION

# HOW PROPORTIONATE IS THE PROPORTIONALITY PRINCIPLE?

## Some critical remarks on the use and methodology of the proportionality principle in the internal market case law of the ECJ

Prof. Dr. Dr. h.c. Norbert REICH*

### 1. FROM ADMIRATION TO FRUSTRATION?

In the shaping years of the then EEC, the case law of the ECJ was greatly respected for its contribution to European integration in general, and in particular, to the promotion of the idea of creating a truly single market. Important principles such as "supremacy", "direct effect", "effet utile", "mutual recognition", "effective judicial protection" and even "*Francovich* liability"[1] were usually accepted by Member State legislatures and courts, albeit at times after some hesitation and criticism. The emerging conflicts with Constitutional courts, first of old and later of new member countries, were settled by referring to a specific EU fundamental rights catalogue, based on the common constitutional traditions and the European Convention on Human Rights (ECHR). The continuous "competence creep" of the EU into Member States' "reserved areas" was halted by the well known *tobacco advertising* judgment of 5 October 2000,[2] even though it was somewhat softened by subsequent judgments.[3]

---

* Emeritus, University of Bremen, Faculty of Law, Braudel Senior Fellow, EUI Florence (1.1.-31.5.2009), e-mail n.reich1@gmx.net. Updated paper initially presented at the EUI Workshop "The European Court of Justice (ECJ) and the Autonomy of Member States", Florence 20–21 April 2009.

1 ECJ 19 November 1991, Case C-6 and 9/90, *Andrea Francovich and Danila Bonifaci and others v Italian Republic* [1991] ECR I-5357.

2 ECJ 5 October 2000, Case C-376/98, *Germany v European Parliament and Council* [2000] ECR I-8419.

3 ECJ 12 December 2006, Case C-380/03, *Germany v European Parliament and Council* [2006] ECR I-11573: more recently and also very controversially ECJ 10 February 2009, C-301/06, *Ireland v European Parliament and Council* [2009] ECR I-593 concerning retention of data.

Lately, however, the tide seems to have changed. Some cases like "*Mangold*"[4] (even though recently confirmed by an order of the German Bundesverfassungsgericht[5]), "*Commission v. Austria*"[6] (recently somewhat "softened" by *Bressol*[7]), "*Watts*"[8], "*Viking and Laval*"[9] have become symbols of a seemingly overarching and overstepping European jurisdiction which must be brought into line for not respecting Member States' prerogatives, social models, legal certainty or whatever the critical labels are. Is the ECJ, formerly the engine of integration, now the one-sided "ultra- or neo-liberal" agent of a "turbo-capitalism", acting irresponsibly with regards to respect of societal demands and social policy objectives? This on-going political debate is to some extent dangerous in our time of economic crisis because it may engage in an unhappy marriage with a felt "need" towards protectionism, national seclusion, promotion of national champions etc.

This paper will not go into the political or/and social debate. Nor will it discuss in detail all of the so called "horror cases", only to mention that I have been very critical myself of the *Mangold*[10] and *Viking*[11]judgments (not the *Laval*[12]judgment though, to the regret of some goods friends of mine!). My approach will rather begin with a methodological analysis that permits acknowledgment of the developments in the case law of the internal market (I will not delve into citizenship issues of student mobility like in *Commission v. Austria* and *Bressol* even though the problems are somewhat similar there) while trying to correct some of the so-called "excesses" by reshaping the well-known proportionality principle. The paper will therefore firstly give an overview on how the ECJ, in particular through its case law of the last 10 years, continuously expanded the scope of application of the EU fundamental freedoms – free movement of goods, establishment, services, and capital, thereby gradually intruding into "reserved

For a more general discussion see S. Weatherill, 'Competence and Legitimacy', in: Chr. Barnard/O. Odudu, *The Outer Limits of EU Law*, Hart Publishing, Oxford, 2009, 17, at p 19.

4 ECJ 22 November 2005, Case C-144/04, *Mangold v Helm* [2005] ECR I-9981.

5 2 BvR 2661/06 of 6 July 2010 insisting on a "European law friendly" review towards ECJ judgments by the BVerfG.

6 ECJ 7 July 2005, Case C-147/03, *Commission v Austria* [2005] ECR I-5969.

7 ECJ 13 April 2010, Case C-73/08, *Nicolas Bressol et al v Gouvernement de la Communauté francaise*, 2735, comment P. Hilpold, (2010) *EuZW (Europäische Zeitschrift für Wirtschaftsrecht)*471; I had critically commented on the opinion of AG Sharpston of 25.6.2009, N. Reich, 'Herkunftsprinzip oder Diskriminierung als Maßstab für Studentenfreizügigkeit?', (2009) *EuZW* 637.

8 ECJ 16 May 2006, Case C-372/04, *Yvonne Watts v Bedford Primary Care Trust et al* [2006] I-4325.

9 ECJ 11 December 2007, Case C-438/05, *International Transport Workers Federation (ITF) and Finnish Seaman's Union (FSU) v. Viking Line* [2007] ECR I-10779 and ECJ 18 December 2007, Case C-341/05, *Laval un Partneri Ltd v Bygnadds et al.* [2007] ECR I-11767.

10 N. Reich, comment (2006) *EuZW* 20–22.

11 N. Reich, 'Fundamental Freedoms vs. Fundamental Rights: Did *Viking* get it wrong?', (2008) *Europarättslig Tijdskrift* 851.

12 N. Reich, 'Free Movement v. Social Rights in an Enlarged Union – the Laval and Viking Cases before the ECJ', (2008) 2 *German Law Journal* 125.

areas" of Member States' powers, a process not really halted by the Lisbon Treaty. Even though there is some incoherence, in my opinion the case law as such rests on a firm constitutional basis, which however, may need some modifications. The decisive testing ground will then be on a second, more complex but at the same time more promising level, namely the proportionality principle itself where indeed, as I will try to show, a deeper methodological critique is justified and corrections to the existing case law will be recommended.

## 2. WIDENING THE SCOPE OF APPLICATION OF THE FUNDAMENTAL FREEDOMS BEYOND MARKET ACCESS – HOW WIDE?

Any discussion on the internal market must start with its basic premise, that is, the guarantee of *market access* to economic agents – workers, producers of goods, providers of services, establishment in professional activities or as undertakings, and investors as well as clients in financial and capital markets. That market access is not unlimited, that it can and sometimes must be regulated by secondary law, that Member State limitations to access should be interpreted strictly, and that the ECJ is the guardian on the functioning of the market forces and in carefully monitoring "clandestine protections" under the notion of public interest concerns, should be without doubt at this stage. The "Economic Constitution" of the EU is indeed a market economy where national markets merge, as far as possible, into a single market – this basic objective had already been expressed by the ECJ as early as 1966 in the *Grundig* case concerning competition, and again in the *Schul* case[13] of 1982, specifically regarding the abolition of internal trade restrictions.

So far so good. The problem of today is a remarkable extension of this basic concept of the constitutional structure of the internal market far beyond market access *stricto sensu*. We will briefly analyse this legal evolution pushed forward by the ECJ in three steps:

13 ECJ 13 July 1966, Joined Cases 56 and 58/64, *Établissements Consten S.à.R.L. and Grundig-Verkaufs-GmbH v Commission of the European Economic Community* [1966] ECR 299, at 30; ECJ 5 May 1982, Case 15/81, *Gaston Schul Douane Expediteur BV v Inspecteur der Invoerrechten en Accijnzen, Roosendaal* [1982] ECR 1409 para 33.

## 2.1. BEYOND MARKET ACCESS[14]

The first step concerns the *widening of the scope of the fundamental freedoms* themselves far beyond market access. I will give some examples without even trying to be exhaustive in looking at the rich case law of the ECJ:

- The fundamental freedoms also protect the *recipients* of goods, services, and capital. Already in 1984 in *Louisi and Carbone,*[15] the Court had found that the freedom to provide services also protected potential recipients. At the same time, it liberalised "on its own" payment services, which at that time were still restricted and didn't come under primary law until the Maastricht Treaty. This so-called "passive freedom" was gradually extended to include employers (*Clean-Car*[16]), recipients of health services (*Kohll,*[17] *Watts*), and tourists (*Cowan*[18]).
- The fundamental freedoms are not only concerned with "moving in", but also with economic activities of "*moving out*". This becomes particularly relevant in the case law on citizenship which we will not discuss here. Regarding the freedom to provide services, the early *Alpine Investment* case[19] should be remembered. In company law, one should recall the *Centros* [20] litigation, which was only concerned with companies moving into another jurisdiction. The recent *Cartesio* case,[21] under a very outspoken opinion of AG Poiares Maduro of 17 July 2008, seems to take a similar step with regard to companies moving out of a jurisdiction, even though the consequences of the Court judgment are more restrictively worded and therefore less than clear. *Viking* concerning social action to prevent the re-flagging of a ferry to a country with lower social standards can be read in a similar direction. More important seems to be the recent *Gysbrecht* judgment,[22] applying, for the first time, Article 29 (now Article 35 TFEU) on export restrictions also to national rules

---

14 For a recent critique of this concept see J. Snell, 'The notion of market access: A concept or a slogan?', (2010) 47 *CMLR (Common Market Law Review)* 437; see also G. Bachmann, 'Nationales Privatrecht im Spannungsfeld der Grundfreiheiten', (2010) 210 *AcP (Archiv für die civilistische Praxis)* 424, at 428–438.

15 ECJ 31 January 1984, Joined Cases 286/82 and 26/83, *Luisi & Carbone/Ministerio del Tesoro* [1984] ECR 377.

16 ECJ 18 June 1998, Case C-35/96, *Clean Car Autoservice v Landeshauptmann Wien* [1998] I-2521.

17 ECJ 28 April 1998, Case C-158/96, *Kohll v Union des Caisses de Maladie* [1998] ECR I-1931.

18 ECJ 2 February 1989, Case 186/87, *Ian William Cowan v Trésor public* [1989] ECR 195.

19 ECJ 10 May 1995, Case C-384/93, *Alpine Investments BV v Minister van Financien* [1995] ECR I-1141.

20 ECJ 9 March 1999, Case C-212/97, *Centros Ltd. v Erhvervs og Selskabsstyrelsen* [1999] ECR I-1459.

21 ECJ 16 December 2008, Case C-210/06, *Cartesio Oktató és Szolgátató* [2008] ECR I-9641; comment M. Szydlo, (2009) *CMLR* 703.

22 ECJ 16 December 2008, Case C-205/07, *Lodewijk Gysbrechts and Santurel Inter BVBA* [2008] ECR I-9947; W.-H. Roth comment (2010) 47 *CMLR* 509.

making cross-border payment transactions more difficult. AG Trstenjak, in her opinion of 17 July 2008, even goes further and attempts to put Article 28 (now Article 34 TFEU) – import restrictions and measures of equivalent effect – and Article 29 – measures of equivalent effect as export restrictions – on the same footing, thus implicitly overruling earlier case law (*Groenveld*[23]). The Court did not go quite that far, but there seems to be a tendency to apply Articles 34 and 35 TFEU both for restrictions on market access *and on market exit*, in conformity with the criteria of the earlier *Keck* case[24] law differentiating between "product regulations" and "selling arrangements".

– As a consequence of this development, the traditional "cross-border" element in the free movement case law, thus distinguishing "purely internal situations" where EU law does not apply, from those where at least one element has a link with the internal market, becomes blurred and to some extent obsolete. The "fundamental freedoms" tend to become "*fundamental rights*", at least insofar as EU citizens (including EU-undertakings) are concerned. This is particularly important in the age of the internet, since the traditional distinction between "purely internal" and "cross-border" matters cannot be maintained any more. Take as an example the *Carpenter* case,[25] in which the path to Article 49 (now Article 56 TFEU) was paved by the simple fact that Mr Carpenter, who lived with his Philippine wife in the UK (where the case against her extradition was brought), got part of his business (acquisition of advertising messages for medical journals) from other EU countries. *Parking Brixen*[26] concerned litigation about a concession contract in the town of Brixen where all elements related to Southern Tirol in Northern Italy, *Mobistar*[27] a Belgian local tax regulation imposed on Belgian MP-companies. Most striking have been the "golden share" cases brought by the Commission against several Member countries under the free movement of capital-provisions. In none of the cases, if I am correctly informed, has a distinction been made between "internal capital transactions" and "cross border investments". I am tempted to take a closer look at these cases, particularly with regard to the proportionality criteria used by the ECJ, but space does not allow me to do so. The problem of applying the free movement of capital provisions to the "golden share" cases might have been decided already on the first level based on their scope, as the UK government had proposed in the

23 ECJ 8 November 1979, Case 15/79, *P.B. Groenveld BV v Produktschap voor Vee en Vlees* [1979] ECR 3409.

24 ECJ 24 November 1993, Joined Cases C-267 and 268/91, *Bernhard Keck and Daniel Mithouard* [1993] ECR I-6097.

25 ECJ 11 July 2002, Case C-60/00, *Mary Carpenter v Secretary of State for the Home Department* [2002] ECR I-6279.

26 ECJ 13 October 2005, Case C-458/03, *Parking Brixen v Gemeinde Brixen/Stadtwerke Brixen* [2005] ECR I-8585.

27 ECJ 8 September 2005, Case C-544 and 545/03, *Mobistar et al v Commune de Fleuron* [2005] ECR I-7723 with reference to the *Keck* criteria.

case *Commission v. UK*[28] that concerned the privatisation of the Heathrow Airport which – similar to the concept used in *Keck* on "selling arrangement"- should not be applicable to mere "investment arrangements" not precluding market entry – a proposition flatly rejected by the Court. In the *German VW* litigation,[29] the conflict was really concerned with an internal (unsuccessful!) take-over bid by the German Porsche company, which seemingly was made less attractive by the continuous existence of a blocking minority, equalling 20% in shares held by the Land Niedersachsen under special legislation. Is the case really concerned with "free movement of capital between Member States", as required by Article 56 EC (now Article 63 TFEU), or rather was it purely a German take over case?

- It is also well known and widely debated that the Court extended the protective scope of the fundamental freedoms beyond mere discrimination to a *broad restriction test*. Any Member State rule which is capable of making less attractive or more onerous the use of a fundamental freedom will come under its protective scope. The somewhat more restrictive case law in the area of free movement of goods after *Keck* does not really constitute proof to the contrary because the finely knit distinction between "product regulations" to which Article 34 TFEU applies in full (without detailed discussion of the cross-border element) and "selling arrangements" has become rather blurred in the subsequent case law. Mere "use" restrictions have recently been included in Article 34.[30]
- As a consequence of this broad reading, even *ancillary restrictions* which are not impeding market access as such, but only put some limitations or qualifications on it, come under the scope of the fundamental freedoms. Take as an example the case of *Caixa-Bank,*[31] a French subsidiary of a significant Spanish bank which complained of French regulations forbidding the possibility of offering interest for sight accounts. There was really no impediment to market access because *Caixa* was, under the relevant EU banking legislation, already established in France. It could market its financial products under the same terms as French banks; there was no discrimination inherent in the French regulation because it applied equally to all banks and was not in violation of secondary EC law. Notwithstanding this, the Court found a violation of the establishment rules; it confused, in my opinion, "market access" with "marketing methods", without taking a look at the parallel case law in *Keck,* where market access and freedom of marketing methods where put

[28] ECJ 13 May 2003, Case C-98/01, *Commission v UK* [2003] ECR I-4641 para 45.

[29] ECJ 23 October 2007, Case C-112/05, *Commission v Germany* [2007] ECR I-8995; in the meantime the VW-law was modified still allowing the Land Niedersachsen a blocking minority of 20%. Much ado about nothing?

[30] ECJ 10 February 2009, Case C-110/05, *Commission v Italy* [2009] I-519.

[31] ECJ 5 October 2004, Case C-442/02, *CaixaBank France v Ministère de l'Économie, des Finances et de l'Industrie* [2004] ECR I-8961.

on a different legal footing. Similar methodological problems can be found in *Centros* – a case which did not concern market access as such but a particularly "cheap" form of doing business exclusively in Denmark by registering as a branch of a letter-box company in the UK, a case to which I will return later. Neither did the *"golden share"* cases concern access to capital markets and investment services; they may have made certain types of investment less attractive to (national or foreign) investors, but given transparency, wouldn't the market take care of this impediment by discounting the price of shares?

- Finally, the fundamental freedoms have also moved in the direction of restrictions induced by private associations. The *Bosman* case[32] is well known and has protected workers (as well paid professional football players!) even against restrictions imposed by "collective regulations" of professional football associations registered under private law. This has been extended to similar restrictions regarding establishment and freedom to provide services. The extent of this case law with regard to capital movements limited by company by-laws is not yet clear but will certainly pop up in the future. Most controversial have been the recent *Viking* and *Laval* judgments mentioned above where also social action aiming at collective regulation, i.e. in a collective bargaining agreement under national labour law, was said to come under the scope of application of Articles 43 and 48 EC (now Articles 49, 56 TFEU). While I have defended this approach as a logical consequence of the earlier *Bosman* case law,[33] both cases have aroused strong protest among labour lawyers who considered themselves immune from the EU internal market law up until now.[34] As a result, EU fundamental

32 ECJ 15 December 1995, Case C-415/93, *Union royale belge des sociétés de football association ASBL v Jean-Marc Bosman, Royal club liégeois SA v Jean-Marc Bosman and others and Union des associations européennes de football (UEFA) v Jean-Marc Bosman* [1995] ECR I-4921.

33 N. Reich, supra notes 10 and 11; T. von Danwitz, 'Grundfreiheiten und Kollektivautonomie', (2010) *EuZA (Europäische Zeitschrift für Arbeitsrecht)* 6. Concerning the question of compensation for social action violating the fundamental freedoms see the recent judgment of the Swedish Arbetsdomstolen (Labour Court) of 2.12.2009, in N. Reich, 'Laval "4. Akt"', (2010) *EuZW* 454; U. Bernitz and N. Reich, 'The Laval saga: Do the Treaty Provisions on Free Movement Include a Right to Damages in Relations between Private Parties?' (2011) *CMLR* 603.

34 For an overview see N. Hös, 'The principle of proportionality in the *Viking* and *Laval* cases: An appropriate standard of judicial review?', (2009) 6 *EUI Working Papers Law*. For a detailed critical account see C. Joerges and F. Rödl, 'Von der Entformalisierung europäischer Politik und dem Formalismus europäischer Rechtsprechung im Umgang mit dem "sozialen Defizit" des Integrationsprojekts – Ein Beitrag aus Anlass der Urteile des EuGH in den Rs. *Viking* und *Laval*', (2008) 2 *ZERP-Diskussionspapier*. 'Informal Politics, Formalised Law, and the 'Social Deficit' of European Integration: Reflections after the Judgments of the ECJ in *Viking* and *Laval*', (2009) 15 *ELJ (European Law Journal)* 1; P. Rodière, 'Les arrêts *Viking* et *Laval*, le droit de grève et le droit de négociation collective', (2008) *RTD eur (Revue trimestrielle de droit européen)* 47; E. Kocher, 'Kollektivverhandlungen und Tarifautonomie – welche Rolle spielt das europäische Recht?', (2008) *AuR (Arbeit und Recht)* 13; R. Rebhahn, 'Grundfreiheiten und Arbeitskampf', (2008) *ZESAR (Zeitschrift für europäisches Sozial- und Arbeitsrecht)*109; A.C. L. Davies, 'One Step Forward, Two Steps back? The *Viking* and *Laval* cases in the ECJ', (2008) 37 *ILJ (Industrial Law Journal)* 126; J. Malmberg and T. Sigman, 'Industrial actions and

freedoms have entered – some say intruded – into areas which previously remained subject to the very different social models of the Member States, with little or no legal regulation. In *Raccanelli*,[35] a doctoral student from Italy complained of discrimination on the basis that he only received a stipend as opposed to a regular contract, even though he allegedly carried out work similar to German employees. The case was taken against the private (though publicly financed!) German Max Planck-Gesellschaft. The ECJ extended the scope of the fundamental freedoms contained in Article 45 TFEU also "to (employment, NR) contracts between individuals" (para 45).

## 2.2. NO "RESERVED" OR "EXEMPTED" AREAS

The second step concerns the persistent claim of the ECJ that the Treaty does not recognise any *reserved areas* to Member States where the fundamental freedoms cannot be applied in the broad sense as developed above.

- This concerns specific provisions of the EC Treaty (now TFEU) where secondary legislation is excluded or made subject to unanimity, for instance Article 114(2) TFEU (ex-Article 95(2) EC) on direct taxation, Article 153 (5) TFEU (ex-Article 137(5) EC) on social action, Article 166(4) TFEU (ex-Article 149(4) EC) on education, Article 168(5) TFEU (ex-Article 152(4) EC) on health, Article 345 TFEU (ex-Article 295 EC) on the property regime. The Court uses the standard formula that in areas of limited Community/Union competence the Member States must still, in the exercise of their powers, respect the fundamental freedoms.[36]
- This is also true in areas where secondary law expressly excludes its application to activities which therefore remain in the legislative competence of states. Examples concern the exclusion of gambling from Article 1(2) d) of the E-commerce Dir. 2000/31 and in Article 2(2) h) of the Service Directive

EU economic freedoms: The autonomous collective bargaining model curtailed by the ECJ', (2008) 45 *CMLR* 1115; L. Azoulai, 'The Court of Justice and the social market economy: The emergence of an ideal and the conditions for its realization', (2008) *CMLR* 1335; M. Höpner, *Usurpation statt Delegation – Wie der EuGH die Binnenmarktintegration radikalisiert und warum er politischer Kontrolle bedarf*, Max Planck Institut für Gesellschaftsforschung, DP 08/12; S. Deakin, 'Regulatory Competition after Laval', (2008) 10 *Cambridge Yearbook of European Legal Studies* 581; W. Däubler, 'ITF-Aktionen gegen Billig-Flaggen-Schiffe – im Widerspruch zum EG-Recht?', (2008) *AuR* 409. Critically concerning competence questions under Art. 137 (5)EC (now Art. 153 (5) TFEU) see G. Conway, 'Conflict of competence norms in EU Law and the Legal reasoning of the ECJ', (2010) 11 *GermLJ (German Law Journal)* 966, at 991.

35 ECJ 17 July 2008, Case C-94/07, *Andrea Raccanelli v Max-Planck-Gesellschaft zur Förderung der Wissenschaften eV*, [2009] ECR I-5939.

36 For a recent example see ECJ 19 May 2009, Joined Cases C-171 and 172/07, *Apothekerkammer des Saarlands v Doc Morris* [2009] ECR I-4171, at para 18 concerning social security systems; similar *formulae* can be found in other areas of reserved Member State competences

2006/123.[37] The Court frequently will limit certain reservations contained in secondary law by reference to the fundamental freedoms. An example of this can be seen in Article 22 of (old) Reg. 1408/71,[38] requiring migrants to get prior authorisation from their national social security system before any health treatments are received abroad for reimbursement purposes. *Kohll* and *Watts* practically set aside this requirement by allowing patients to receive health services abroad under certain limited circumstances without the need for prior authorisation, followed by an *ex-lege* right to reimbursement based on similar services at home. Other examples include the extension of the recognition directives on diplomas beyond formal professional qualifications also to certain university diploma. (*Kraus*[39], *Morgenbesser*[40]).

To avoid misunderstandings: I do not object to the Court's approach as such and the results of its case law, but rather to the methodology used which frequently lacks convincing arguments concerning the relationship between primary law – which is only "interpreted" by the Court –, and secondary law providing for a legislative procedure in which Member States can fully participate and make their policy priorities known. This interplay between primary and secondary law should, in my opinion, be respected by the ECJ in the existing system of distribution of powers under Article 5(1) EU Lisbon (ex-Article 5 EC) which binds *all EU institutions.*

## 2.3. A BROAD AND AT THE SAME TIME A NARROW READING OF "PUBLIC INTEREST" JUSTIFICATIONS

In relation to the reading of the public interest justification, we can note seemingly contradictory developments: on the one hand an (almost open-ended) extension of public interest provisos, and on the other, a substantial narrowing-down in the area of only "economic" or/and administrative interests of Member States:

---

37 Directive 2000/31/EC of the EP and of the Council of 8 June 2000 on certain legal aspects of information society services, in particular electronic commerce, in the Internal Market ('Directive on electronic commerce'), OJ L 178, 17 July 2000, 12; Directive 2006/123/EC of the EP and the Council of 12 December 2006 on services in the internal market, OJ L 376, 27 December 2006, 36.

38 Council Regulation (EEC) No 1408/71 of 14 June 1971 on the application of social security schemes to employed persons, to self-employed persons and to members of their families moving within the Community (last amended by Council Regulation (EC) No 592/2008 of 24.7.2008, OJ L 177/1 of 2008); However, case C-211/08, *Commission v Spain* [2010] ECR I-(15.6.2010) limited compensation in case of a temporary stay in another country to the sums due in the home country of the hospitalised person.

39 ECJ 31 March 1993, Case C-19/92, *Kraus v Land Baden-Württemberg* [1993] ECR I-1663.

40 ECJ 13 November 2003, Case C-313/01, *Christine Morgenbesser v Consiglio dell'Ordine degli avvocati di Genova* [2003] ECR I-13467.

- The Treaty had inserted rather limited catalogues of justified restrictions of the free movement provisions in Articles 36, 45 (3/4), 45, 62, 65 TFEU (ex-Articles 30, 39 (3) (4), 46, 55, 58(2) EC) which usually refer to public policy, public security, and public health. This catalogue was interpreted *strictly* by the Court.
- Ever since the seminal *Cassis*-case,[41] the Court extended this *numerus clausus* of justified restrictions to genuine concerns of public interest or public policy like consumer protection (*Cassis*), environmental protection (*Radlberger*[42]), social protection (*Rush Portuguesa*[43]), protection of clients of legal services (*Broede,*[44] */Cipolla*[45]), and road safety (*Commission v. Italy*[46]). Later case law added fundamental rights protection (*Schmidberger*[47]), even if it was a fundamental right recognised only in one Member country (*Omega*[48]*).* Recent case law refers to the EU Charter of Fundamental Rights in order to justify restrictions on free movement (*Dynamic Medien*[49]).
- As a somewhat opposing trend, the Court excluded mere "*economic grounds*" from the scope of the public interest test like business, workplace or job protection, or the shielding of certain professions from competition by "*numerus clausus*" provisions. Surprisingly, " the (prevention of a) diminution or reduction of tax revenue is not one of the grounds listed in Article 46 EC and does not constitute a matter of overriding general interest which may be relied on to justify a restriction on the freedom of establishment or the freedom to provide services" (*Gambelli*[50]*).* Accordingly, mere administrative expediency is not a ground for justifying restrictions on fundamental freedoms. However, restrictive regulations to secure supply of energy in times of crisis by "national champions" were regarded as a justified public interest.[51]
- This approach faced the Court with conceptual problems concerning the financing of health services which may become problematic once patients can

41 ECJ 20 February 1979, Case 120/78, *Rewe-Zentral AG v Bundesmonopolverwaltung für Branntwein (Cassis de Dijon)* [1979] ECR 649; for an overview see Chr. Barnard, Derogations, Justifications, and the Four Freedoms: Is State Interest Really Protected, in: Barnard/Odusu, supra note 3, at p 273.

42 ECJ 11 June 2009, Case C-309/02, *Radlberger Getränkegesellschaft v Land Baden-Württemberg* [2004] ECR I-11763.

43 ECJ 27 March 1990, Case C-113/89, *Rush Portuguesa v Office national d'immigration* [1990] ECR I-1417.

44 ECJ 12 December 1996, Case C-3/95, *Reiseburo Broede v Gerhard Sandker* [1996] ECR I-6511.

45 ECJ 5 December 2006, Joined Cases C-94 and 202/04, *Frederico Cipolla et al v Rosaria Fazari, née Portolese et al* [2006] ECR I-11421.

46 Supra note 30.

47 ECJ 12 June 2003, Case C-112/00, *Eugen Schmidberger v Austria* [2003] ECR I-5659.

48 ECJ 14 October 2004, Case C-36/02, *Omega Spielhallen- und Automatenaufstellungs-GmbH v Oberbürgermeisterin der Bundesstadt Bonn* [2004] ECR I-9609.

49 ECJ 14 February 2008, Case C-244/06, *Dynamic Medien Vertriebs GmbH v Avides Media AG* [2008] ECR I-505.

50 ECJ 6 November 2003, Case C-243/01, *Piergiorgio Gambelli et al* [2003] ECR I-13031, para 61.

51 ECJ 10 July 1984, Case 72/83, *Campus Oil Limited et al v Minister for Industry and Energy* [1984] ECR 2727.

freely choose where to get medical care (whether ambulant or hospital treatment). The Court therefore accepted Article 46, which allows a protection of public health, to be one of the overriding reasons in the general interest that can justify restrictions of the freedom of establishment or provision of services. This includes rules guaranteeing a balanced financing of the public health system, for instance by restrictions on access to certain health services.[52] Surprisingly the Court did not accept a similar argument related to the financing of higher education in the litigation against Austrian restrictions on access to its universities to foreign students who had not complied with the host country's requirements.

This is not the place to evaluate the existing case law. Suffice it to say that the Court, in broadly extending the scope of application of the fundamental freedoms, at the same time must have felt the need to also broaden the scope and extent of justifications. One may wonder whether this judicial extension/retreat is methodologically more promising than a traditional discrimination test which seems to be more in line with the wording of the relevant EU Treaty provisions.[53] But the case law "stands as it stands". It probably cannot be avoided that it be accepted as an attempt to conform the imperatives of the internal market with the prerogatives and regulatory powers of Member States, unless changed by adding a Protocol to the Treaty which seems highly unlikely.

The fine-tuning of this conflicting relationship however must be conducted by using the *flexibility inherent in the proportionality* criteria to which we will turn now. In this context it should be emphasised that the widening of the field of application of the fundamental freedoms put the Court in the difficult position of acting as the final arbiter in cases concerning Member State measures which are usually justified by a public interest test, and which have undergone a political bargaining process subject to their constitutional requirements. In taking a stand for or against a national measure by using the proportionality criteria as described below, the Court necessarily becomes involved in Member State policies. This warrants a *certain caution* on the side of the Court, particularly in areas where either primary or secondary law has clearly stated that the matter in question is a prerogative of Member States.

I will try to show that a proportionality test can serve this objective if it is handled with some care which has not always been the case if looking at the extended jurisprudence of the Court. Very recent case law seems to be somewhat

52 For a recent restatement see ECJ 10 March 2009, Case C-169/07, *Hartlauer Handelsgesellschaft mbH v Wiener Landesregierung and Oberösterreichische Landesregierung* [2009] ECRI-1721, comment L. Hancher and W. Sauter, 'One Step Beyond? From Sodemare to DocMorris: EU's Freedom of Establishment Case Law Concerning Health Care', (2010) 47 *CMLR* 117, at 136.

53 For a discussion see P. Craig and G. de Burca, *EU Law*, Oxford University Press, Oxford, 4th ed, 2008, at 831.

more cautious in this respect – the *autonomy of Member States* becomes reinforced against an earlier "over-activist" Court.

# 3. THE PROPORTIONALITY PRINCIPLE AS THE "SUPER-NORM"?

## 3.1. SOME PRELIMINARY METHODOLOGICAL REFLECTIONS

In an interesting recent article, Harbo[54] shows that the proportionality principle can be interpreted in several ways, depending on the interrelation of a liberal theory of rights with the (supra-) national commitment to a welfare state. He distinguishes a "weak" and a "strong" rights regime within the proportionality principle. At first glance based on the theoretical work of Alexy,[55] the "proportionality principle is a tool in which a balance between individual and group interests, on the one hand, and the public interest, on the other hand, can be struck in the best possible way." Under the second more liberal reading, greatly influenced by a Dworkinian/Habermasian understanding of rights,[56] "there is no room for weighting mechanisms like the one laid down in the proportionality principle."

This theoretical distinction may not always be easy to prove in practice and may appear in more or less combined or "mixed" forms. In a somewhat broader and more theoretical context, it is well known that constitutional doctrine, in many jurisdictions based on democratic principles and the rule of law, extended the proportionality principle to a general and broad instrument to control state powers interfering with individual, constitutionally guaranteed, mostly fundamental rights like liberty, property, and judicial protection.[57] Its basic methodological approach is not an abstract but a concrete and pragmatic one to 'balance' opposing constitutional propositions: "L'objet principal des arguments

[54] T.-I. Harbo, 'The Function of the Proportionality Principle in EU Law', (2010) 16 *ELJ*, 158, at 166–168.

[55] See A. Stone Sweet and J. Mathews, 'Proportionality Balancing and Global Constitutionalism', (2008) 47 *Columbia Journal of Transnational Law* at 76, 93 for a theoretical justification of this balancing test, referring to Alexy's optimisation concept supra note 54, at 44–61; J. Rivers, 'Proportionality, Discretion and the Second law of Balancing' in G. Pavlakos *Law, Rights and Discourse – The Legal Philosophy of Robert Alexy*, Hart Publishing, Oxford, 2007, at 168 referring to "public interests" as principles which may justify a limitation of rights under "optimisation requirements".

[56] R. Dworkin, *Taking Rights Seriously*, Harvard University Press, Cambridge, 1977, 81; J. Habermas, *Between Facts and Norms*, MIT Press, Cambridge, 1998, 259–260 criticising the so-called "value jurisprudence" against the "deontological character of basic rights.. which are withdrawn from such a cost-benfit analyis."

[57] For comparative overviews see E. Ellis (ed.), *The Principle of Proportionality in the Laws of Europe*, Hart Publishing, Oxford, 1999; N. Emiliou, *The principle of proportionality in European Law – A comparative study*, Kluwer Law International, London, 1996.

juridiques est la justification des propositions empiriques avancées au soutien des prétentions concurrentes relatives à la proportionnalité des équilibres".[58] It plays a great role in the case law of the European Court of Human Rights in balancing, on the one hand, the human rights guarantee of the Convention with, on the other hand, the legitimate governmental concerns prescribed therein. Most notably, States enjoy a certain *margin of appreciation* when performing this balancing test which is only limited when the very essence of fundamental rights is at stake.[59]

## 3.2. THE ORIGIN IN THE EARLY CASE LAW OF THE ECJ

The "transplant" of the proportionality principle into the case law of the ECJ has followed a somewhat different path. Its original source: a specific understanding of the dualistic relationship between the state and the individual, had to be transposed on a more complex, *triangular* relationship between the individual (the then EEC "market citizen" - *Marktbürger* - engaged in using the market freedoms under the EEC Treaty), the Member State imposing certain burdens on that individual which may impede his freedom to act in the "Common" and later the "Internal market", and the role of the ECJ to monitor the respect of these "fundamental freedoms" as they were later called. Since this "market citizen", under the theory of "direct effect" of E(E)C law as developed by and after *Van Gend und Loos*,[60] could invoke his market freedoms as subjective rights against the state,[61] and since Member State courts as "European courts" had to ensure the protection of these rights granted under E(E)C law, the ECJ became the *final arbiter* on the extent of these directly applicable market freedoms, either under the reference procedure of Article 267 TFEU (ex-Article 234 EC), or, legally less importantly, by the infringement procedure of the Commission under Article 258 TFEU (ex-Article 226 EC). Conflicts arose both on the administrative and on the legislative level of Member States. The ECJ had to fine tune and balance the scope of the fundamental freedoms as interpreted extensively, against the still allowed restrictions under the broad public interest test. This balancing had to be done by using the ever more important *proportionality principle.*

---

58 L. Tremblay, 'Le fondement normatif du principe de proportionalité en théorie constitutionelle', paper delivered at the EUI, Florence, conference on reasonableness, 8.10.2008.

59 A. Stone Sweet & Mathews, supra note 55, at 145; J. Christoffersen, *Fair Balance – A Study of Proportionality, Subsidiarity and Primarity in the ECHR*, M. Nijhoff Publishers, Leiden, 2009.

60 ECJ 5 February 1963, Case 26/62, *Van Gend en Loos v Nederlandse Administratie van Belastingen* [1963] ECR 1.

61 N. Reich, 'System der subjectiven öffentlichen Rechte' in the Union: A European Constitution for Citizens of Bits and Pieces' in Academy of European Law (ed), *Collected Courses of the Academy of European Law VI/1*, 1995, 157–241.

The methodological origins of this important principle are however modest, particularly if we look again at the seminal *Cassis* case[62] whose legal argumentation looks rather poor from today's perspective, even though it created the very fundamentals of the internal market law.[63] The balancing test,[64] followed up by an "information approach",[65] is the result of the above mentioned search for an equilibrium between the producer or importer invoking his market freedoms, and the state promoting a legitimate public interest, namely consumer protection: both objectives should be adequately attained by information provision without mandatory standard setting. This has been labelled somewhat incorrectly as the *"information" vs. the "regulation"* – approach to protect consumers (or other legitimate interests, where appropriate). At the same time, the use of the proportionality argument can also be justified on economic efficiency grounds[66] even though the Court in this and the many later judgments (mostly concerning so-called "purity laws") hardly referred to it.

It was only in the later *Gebhard* case[67] that the Court set out a more sophisticated approach to the proportionality test to be used in checking Member State restrictions on the fundamental freedoms. Restrictions to establishment (and other fundamental freedoms) must fulfil a four-step test:

- They must be applied in a non-discriminatory manner.
- They must be justified by imperative requirements in the general interest.
- They must be suitable for securing the attainment of the objective which they pursue.
- They must not go beyond what is necessary in order to attain it.

In *Gebhard,* the Court did not mention „proportionality in the narrow sense", known in German Constitutional law as *Übermaßverbot,* as a third stage of the proportionality test.[68] This means that, even if a state measure is *suitable*

---

62 Supra note 41.

63 For an appraisal see N. Reich et al. *Understanding EU Internal Market Law*, Intersentia, Antwerp, 2010, 3rd ed, at paras 1.2, 7.6.

64 H. Unberath and A. Johnston, 'The double-headed approach of the ECJ concerning consumer protection', (2007) 44 *CMLR* 1237, at 1250.

65 J. Stuyck, 'European Consumer Law after the treaty of Amsterdam: Consumer Policy in the Internal Market', (2000) 37 *CMLR* 367, at 384; N. Reich, 'Crisis or Future of European Consumer Law?', (2008/2009) *British Yearbook of Consumer Law* 3, at 6–18; H.-W. Micklitz and N. Reich, 'Crónica de una muerte anunciada:The Commission proposal for a "Directive on consumer rights"' (2009) 46 *CMLR* 471, at 485 criticising the new legislative proposal by the Commission.

66 See the contributions in S. Grundmann, W. Kerber and S. Weatherill, *Part Autonomy and the Role of information in the Internal Market*, Walter de Gruyter, Berlin, 2001.

67 ECJ 30 November 1995, Case C-55/94, *Gebhard v Consiglio dell'Ordine degli Advocati e procuratori di Milano* [1995] ECR I-4165.

68 D. Grimm, *'Proportionality in Canadian and German Constitutional Jurisprudence' (2007) 57 University of Toronto Law Journal 383.*

to attain the given objective (relationship between means and end), and if the chosen measure is *necessary* to achieve the proposed goal, it still should not put an *excessive burden* on the individual, implicitly inherent in the "'less restrictive alternative'" test.[69] A state measure which puts an unreasonable burden on the individual and can easily be substituted by a less intrusive measure capable of attaining the same objective (a financial instead of a criminal sanction) will not be regarded as being "necessary".

## 3.3. POSSIBLE METHODOLOGICAL SOPHISTICATION OR ABERRATION? THE DIFFERENT AND SOMETIMES INCOHERENT TESTS OF THE ECJ

The *Gebhard* test has been used many times in subsequent cases, sometimes with slight variations in the wording which we will not follow up here. With regard to the "imperative requirements in the general interest", I refer to what was said in the preceding section: since the catalogue of these interests is an open-ended one (perhaps with the exception of "purely economic interests" which do not justify restrictions unless they can be upgraded to a "legitimate public interest" as in the case of health care financing systems), Member States will usually be able to find a justified public interest which legitimises restrictions on the exercise of fundamental freedoms by EU market citizens. The debate in the many cases which have been decided under the *Gebhard* or closely related tests will therefore usually concentrate,

- first on the "*adequacy*" of a certain restrictive regulation (is it suitable at all to attain the proclaimed general interest objective?);
- second on its "*necessity*" with regard to its intrusive elements (does it not go beyond what is required to attain this objective, e.g. as in the case of "information" vs. "regulation" to protect consumers or guarantee fair commercial practices).

Obviously the *Gebhard* test is more complex than it looks on paper. It refers to a *balancing* between competing policies, interests, arguments and instruments. The specific structure of proceedings before the ECJ makes this balancing a rather complex process. How will the ECJ as a court of law with very limited information input, in particular in the reference proceedings under Article 267 TFEU where only the parties to the original litigation, the Commission, Member States and eventually the Council and the EFTA surveillance authority, but not independent

[69] T. Tridimas, *The General Principles of Community Law*, Oxford University Press, Oxford, 2nd. Ed, 2006, 193, at pp. 209–220 (Proportionality – review of national measures); T.-I. Harbo, supra note 54.

experts, public interest groups, NGOs, national parliaments responsible for the legislation under scrutiny etc., can submit observations, and where the referring court may only provide little factual information, be able to decide matters of "suitability" and, even more complicated, "necessity" of a regulation said to violate fundamental freedoms? Isn't this really a "*black box procedure*"? And how do we define the interdependence of protected interests and the intensity of State measures to protect them?

In order to allow a more enlightened and at the same time critical methodological discussion, I will scrutinise the abundant case law – which unfortunately cannot be examined in its entirety – as follows. I will distinguish four approaches of the Court:

1. an approach where the Court conducts the balancing act "pro" or "contra" itself;
2. a "margin of discretion" approach, frequently sending the judgment on proportionality back to the referring court;
3. a "fundamental rights" approach within which the freedoms must be balanced against fundamental rights which may lead to rather ambivalent results;
4. a "quasi-legislative" approach where the Court uses the "proportionality" principle to impose measures of a legislative nature on Member States, recently supported by the requirement of "consistency",[70] even though formally the Court is only "interpreting" EU law and thus seemingly not invading the legislative competences of Member States.

The few cases which I mention – no complete case analysis is intended here – are supposed to illustrate the approach chosen and should at the same time allow for an understanding and a critical evaluation of the methodological argument of the Court. This is particularly true with regards to what I call the "quasi-legislative approach".

### *3.3.1. Examples for the "autonomous balancing" approach*

Looking at the many cases decided under the proportionality principle, I submit that the "autonomous balancing" approach, first developed in *Cassis,* is still the dominant one and usually has been accepted more or less enthusiastically by

[70] Case C-169/07, *Hartlauer*, supra note 52, at para 55 writing: "..it must be recalled that national legislation is appropriate for ensuring attainment of the objective pursed (health protection, NR) only if it genuinely reflects a concern to attain it in a consistent and systematic manner…"; also case C-73/08, *Bressol*, supra note 7, at para 71 requiring "solid and consistent" data to support a claim that a restriction of access of foreign students to studies of medicine may lead to "genuine risk to public health"; see the remarks by L. Hancher and W. Sauter supra note 52, at 119.

Member States. It should not serve as a basis for the somewhat diffuse criticism mentioned in the beginning of my paper because it can be found also in the constitutional traditions common to the Member countries. I will refer here to just some examples without going into details, namely *Schindler*[71] concerning restrictions on the cross-border marketing of games of chance, *Überseering*[72] denying standing to a foreign company having transferred its business activity to Germany under the old „seat-theory", *Doc Morris*[73] differentiating between (unjustified) restrictions on cross-border marketing of over the counter (OTC) medicines and (justified) restrictions for prescription drugs, and *Watts*[74] on health-care services utilised by British citizens abroad subject to the authorisation requirement of the NHS.

A good recent example is the *Case X*,[75] which discussed different recovery periods and fines for unpaid wealth taxes in the case of assets held outside the Member State of residence. The relevant EC directive 77/799/EEC sets up an information system between tax authorities, but only on request in particular cases; Member States can invoke bank secrecy provisions to refuse information. Dutch law provided for a 5 year recovery period for undeclared assets held in the Netherlands and 12 years for assets held in another Member country. The Court, in its broad approach to the interpretation of fundamental freedoms concerning services and capital according to Articles 49 and 56 EC, decided first that the Dutch regulations could be regarded as a restriction because it made the provision of cross-border services more difficult, and it dissuaded residents from obtaining loans or making investments in other Member countries (paras 32 & 33). Interestingly, it did not discuss the issue of (direct) discrimination. The case thereby revolved around the justification which the Court found in the need to guarantee the effectiveness of fiscal supervision and the prevention of tax evasion (para 45). The regulation must however, according to the Court, comply with the principle of proportionality. The Court had no problem with the "appropriateness" test, but discussed at length the "necessity" criteria because the extension of the recovery period would not guarantee recovery as such. Due, however, to the weak regulation on information exchange in Dir. 77/799 and the difficulty inherent with information recovery, especially when one considers foreign assets, the provision of a longer period for discovery and recovery of taxable assets does not go beyond what is necessary to guarantee the effectiveness of fiscal supervision and to prevent tax evasion (para 70). An exception was only perceived for cases where the mechanisms of Dir.

71 ECJ 24 March 1994, Case C-275/92, *HM Customs and Excise v Schindler* [1994] ECRI-1039.

72 ECJ 5 November 2002, Case C-208/00, *Überseering BV v Nordic Construction Company Baumanagement GmbH (NCC)* [2002] ECR I-9919.

73 ECJ 11 December 2003, Case C-322/01, *Deutscher Apothekenverband v Doc Morris NV and Jacques Waterval* [2003] ECR I-14887.

74 Supra note 7.

75 ECJ 28 October 2010, Case C-423/09, *X et al v Staatssecretaris van Financien*, nyr.

77/799 could be said to work, e.g. the Member State of residence has evidence of tax evasion and can therefore launch an investigation, provided this is not hampered by issues concerning bank secrecy. Without directly saying so, the Court tries to compensate the weakness of the system of information exchange among tax authorities under Dir. 77/799 by allowing Member States a "second level remedy", thereby indirectly amending Dir. 77/799. This shows the amazing flexibility of the proportionality argument of the Court by allowing it to amend existing (incomplete and ineffective) EC legislation.

### 3.3.2. *Examples for the "state margin of appreciation" approach*

Several cases on proportionality expressly allow Member States a certain "margin of appreciation" or a "discretion" in order to determine whether a measure restricting the free movement of "market citizens" is adequate and necessary. Usually there is a correlation between the relevance of the protected public interest and the extent of the discretion. I just mention some examples without going into details: *Broede*[76] concerned the (legitimate) monopolisation of debt collection services to lawyers. *Cipolla*[77] concerned Italian rules on minimum fees for lawyers which were said to have a negative, restrictive effect on the entry of foreign lawyers into the Italian market, but possibly justified by overriding concerns of the protection of consumers, in particular recipients of legal services, and the safeguarding of the proper administration of justice. This must be decided by the national judge. Health and safety interests have played a similar privileged role in the proportionality case law of the ECJ. The *Gourmet* case[78] concerned a Swedish ban on the advertising of alcoholic drinks. In case C-110/05[79] *Commission v Italy* an Italian regulation forbidding the use of trailers being towed by motorcycles was attacked by the Commission. For the first time, the Court applied Article 28 (now Article 34 TFEU) to invoke use restrictions: Against the opinion of AG Bot of 8 July 2008, this could be justified by concerns of road safety, an area in which Member States enjoy "a margin of appreciation" (para 67). In *Kattner*,[80] the Court had to decide about the conformity of the German compulsory work accident insurance system restricting the freedom of employers to receive services from competing foreign insurance companies. The decisive question revolved around the proportionality of this scheme which the Court basically left to be determined by the national court. It gave some interesting guidance in this direction based on risk assessment. The story was continued by *Apothekerkammer des Saarlands*

76 Supra note. 43.

77 Supra note 44.

78 ECJ 8 March 2001, Case C-405/98, *Konsumentenombudsmanen (KO) v Gourmet International products* [2001] ECR I-1795.

79 Supra note 30.

80 ECJ 28 October 2010, Case C-350, *Kattner Stahlbau v Maschinen- und Maschinenbauberufsgenossenschaft*, [2009] ECR I-1513.

*v Doc Morris.*[81] This case concerned a challenge to the German rule (sanctioned by Constitutional Law) that a pharmacy can only be operated by a pharmacist, not by a company even if that company employs a qualified pharmacist. In a very carefully worded judgment, the Court referred to the importance of health protection as "one of the overriding reasons in the general interest" (para 27) which allows Member States "discretion" (para 19).

Most spectacular has been the recent "clarification" in the case law concerning State imposed restrictions on games of chance marketed via the internet. In *Gambelli,*[82] the Court held that restrictions on the activities of the Italian agencies to take bets for Stanley (UK) constituted obstacles to the freedom of establishment. The prohibition, imposed on Italian customers and sanctioned by criminal law, indeed restricted the possibility to freely receive services from other EU countries. The decisive question therefore concerned the justification for the restrictions, which must meet the criteria set out in *Gebhard.* In the opinion of the Court, the mere collection of revenue for the state does not serve, as such, as a justification. The restriction must rather "reflect a concern to bring about a genuine diminution of gambling opportunities, and the financing of social activities through a levy on the proceeds of authorised games must constitute only an incidental beneficial consequence and not the real justification for the restrictive policy adopted" (para 62). If a Member State follows a policy of inciting betting for revenue purposes, it cannot claim the consumer protection and fraud prevention argument to forbid cross border betting. The rules on licensing must be applied without discrimination, e.g. foreign companies must have access to the national betting market (which was not the case in Italy due to the state monopoly that was in place). This argumentation seems to be convincing at first sight. However, the main problem of the argument seems to be the somewhat *artificial separation* that the Court drew between legitimate Member States' action to combat fraud, including to protect consumers against illegal betting activities, and the seemingly illegitimate collection of revenue via monopolised betting and preventing access to foreign providers, something the Court viewed much more positively in its *Schindler* judgment. The later *Placanica*[83] judgment followed this line of argumentation by critically considering the different elements of the Italian system of betting regulation. The Court insisted that a rule in the national licensing scheme which excluded operators in the form of companies whose shares are quoted on the regulated markets (blanket exclusion), goes

[81] Joined Cases C-171 and 172/07, *Apothekerkammer des Saarlandes and Others (C-171/07) and Helga Neumann-Seiwert (C-172/07) v Saarland and Ministerium für Justiz, Gesundheit und Soziales* [2009] ECR I-4171.

[82] Supra note 50; see C. Barnard, supra note 41, at p. 284.

[83] ECJ 6 March 2007, Joined Cases C-338, 359 and 360/04, *Criminal proceedings against Massimiliano Placanica (C-338/04), Christian Palazzese (C-359/04) and Angelo Sorricchio (C-360/04)* [2007] ECR I-1891.

beyond what is necessary to achieve this objective, vaguely referring to "other ways of monitoring the accounts and activities of operators in the betting and gaming sector which impinge to a lesser extent on the freedom of establishment and the freedom to provide services, one such possibility being the gathering of information on their representatives or their main shareholders" (para 62). Again the question remains: How and wherefrom did the ECJ know that the exclusion of public stock companies (whether registered in Italy or in other EU countries) from penetrating the betting market was not "necessary" to avoid betting fraud? In particular: how can the persons behind a foreign stock company be effectively controlled in case of illegal betting activities, when the country of origin (UK) seemingly imposed rather lax standards of supervision?

The more recent case, the *Santa Casa* judgment of 8 September 2009,[84] was concerned with Portuguese legislation giving the public charity Santa Casa the exclusive right to take bets. It prohibited entry of an operator established in another EU country into the national market for games of chance and of co-operation with sports associations. There was obviously a restriction to the freedom to provide services; the question therefore turned on the proportionality of the justification on the basis of the public interest to combat fraud. The Court insisted that "(t)he Member States are … free to set the objectives of their policy on betting and gambling and, where appropriate, to define in detail the level of protection sought. However, the restrictive measures that they impose must satisfy the conditions laid down in the case-law of the Court as regards their proportionality" (para 59). The Portuguese scheme, as opposed to the Italian one, passed the strict proportionality test because the control of betting by the country of origin was not regarded as being sufficient to prevent fraud, and because the co-operation of the operator with a sporting association may put him "in a position to influence their outcome (of soccer games) directly or indirectly, and thus increase its profits" (para 71). This line of case-law was continued in *Ladbroke*,[85] concerning an exclusive license for internet betting given to a Dutch company and therefore lead to the exclusion of a UK betting service company which was supervised according to UK law. The Court held that the fight against consumer addiction to betting is a justified public interest reason, justifying proportionate restrictions on cross-border services. This would even cover advertising for its activities, unless "it were established that the Kingdom of the Netherlands is pursuing a policy of substantially expanding betting and gaming, by excessively inciting and encouraging consumers to participate in such activities, principally with a view to obtaining funds, and that, for that reason, the financing of social activities through a levy on the proceeds of authorised games of chance

[84] ECJ 8 September 2009, Case C-42/07, *Liga Portuguesa de Futebol Professional & Bwin Int v Departamento de Jugos da Santa Casa da Misericordia de Lisboa* [2009] ECR I-7633.

[85] ECJ 3 June 2010, Case C-258/08, *Ladbrokes Betting & Gaming Lt. et al v Stichting de Nationale Sportstotalisator* nyr para 28.

constitutes not an incidental beneficial consequence but the real justification for the restrictive policy adopted by that Member State..." (para 28), thus putting the *burden of proving proportionality* not on Member States but on UK companies challenging it!

In a most recent series of cases the German state monopoly of lotteries ran foul of its inconsistent implementation which rather incited the public to other forms of games of chance instead of restricting it by truly combating consumer addiction under the proportionality case law of the ECJ.[86] Eventually the referring German courts will have to decide on whether the monopoly complies with EU law.

### 3.3.3. *Examples for the – rather ambivalent – "fundamental rights approach"*

Another development concerns the use of fundamental rights arguments in the free movement case law. I cannot adequately delve into the many aspects of this development. The case law developed in two seemingly contradictory directions:[87] Some cases like *Familiapress,*[88] *Carpenter,*[89] and *Karner*[90] try to combine free movement with fundamental rights to reinforce the position of the individual. Other cases allow Member States to use fundamental rights' concerns to restrict fundamental freedoms and to avoid a unilateral use of the proportionality argument against them. I will only be concerned with the latter cases. The landmark case was and still is *Schmidberger*[91]. It uses a complex "double proportionality" balancing of "free movement" vs. "fundamental rights" under Articles 10 & 11 ECHR in justifying the temporary closure of the Brenner Autobahn by the Austrian regional government to allow an ecological demonstration. *Omega*[92] went even further. It concerned a German regulation prohibiting certain games which involved firing on human targets, considered to be in breach of the fundamental principle of human dignity enshrined in the German Constitution. In *Dynamic Medien,*[93] a German prohibition on distance selling of image store media was at-

---

86 ECJ 8 September 2010, Case C-46/08, *Carmen Media Group v Land Schleswig Holstein* nyr; ECJ 8 September 2010, Joined cases C-316, 358, 359, 360, 409 and 410/07, *Markus Stoß (C-316/07), Avalon Service-Online-Dienste GmbH (C-409/07) and Olaf Amadeus Wilhelm Happel (C-410/07) v Wetteraukreis and Kulpa Automatenservice Asperg GmbH (C-358/07), SOBO Sport & Entertainment GmbH (C-359/07) and Andreas Kunert (C-360/07) v Land Baden-Württemberg* nyr.

87 N. Nic Shuibhne, 'Margins of appreciation: National values, fundamental rights and EC free movement law', (2009) *ELR* 230, at 24–235 distinguishes four groups which in the end boil down to the two mentioned above.

88 ECJ 26 June 1997, Case C-368/95, *Vereinigte Familiapress Zeitungsverlags- und Vertriebs GmbH v Heinrich Bauer Verlag* [1997] ECR I-3689.

89 Supra note 25.

90 ECJ 25 March 2004, Case C-71/02, *Herbert Karner Industrie-Auktionen GmbH v Troostwijk GmbH* [2004] ECR I-3025.

91 Supra note 47.

92 Supra note 48; Comment T. Ackermann, (2005) 42 *CMLR* 1107; critique N. Shuibhne, supra note 87, at 244.

93 Supra note 49.

tacked on the basis that it had not received clearance for children's use by the competent German authority, disregarding prior clearance in another Member country. The restriction was caught by Article 28 EC (now Article 34 TFEU). With regard to justification, the Court pronounced itself in favour of child-protection based on international treaties to which the EU is a member. The Court also referred to the (then non-binding) Charter of Fundamental Rights in the EU. Member States enjoy a "definite margin of discretion" in the field of protecting the rights of the child (para 44).

The most controversial case in this respect is well known to be *Viking*.[94] As previously mentioned, the Court applied the fundamental freedoms in this case to social action which intended to prevent an undertaking – Viking line Finland – to re-flag its ferryboat "Rosella" so that it would yield the Estonian flag, based on the fact that wages were lower there and therefore wage cutting could legitimately be carried out. The rather complex litigation will be examined here for its proportionality aspects only, which the Court surprisingly held to be applicable to social action even though it recognised that the fundamental right to strike was protected also by EU law under Article 6(2) referring to the ECHR and its Article 11, as well as Article 28 of the Charter, thus justifying restrictions on free movement. In its judgment, the Court found it necessary to distinguish between the social action of the Finnish Seaman's Union (FSU) on the one hand, and the call for solidarity action by the International Transport Worker's Federation (ITWF) on the other. With regard to FSU, the Court insisted that the social action must truly service the protection of workers which would not be the case "if it were established that the jobs or conditions of employment at issue were not jeopardised or under serious threat (para 81)", e.g. if the undertaking which takes over the re-flagged vessel would be bound by the prior collective agreement or statutory provisions protecting workers. The action taken by FSU, which is as such a legal means of defending workers' rights, must meet the requirements of proportionality. This must be established by the national court; the ECJ can (only?) give guidance. In particular, the ECJ stressed the *ultima ratio* principle to justify social actions against re-flagging as an infringement of the freedom of establishment. A stricter ruling concerned the boycott and solidarity action by ITWF where it was suggested that it might be disproportionate because it would cover situations where the policy against "flags of convenience" would also hit outsourcing activities, which however, did not deteriorate the social position of workers – a somewhat improbable result where the Court seemed to misunderstand the economic logic of outsourcing. But is the ECJ authorised to second-guess social action by referring to the proportionality principle that may be justified in relation to state action? What is the place of the autonomy concept in social actions of labour unions and their umbrella organisations, protected

[94] Supra note 9.

by the freedom of association provisions of the ECHR and by the EU Charter? Is EC law in general and the ECJ in particular competent to regulate social action unless it pursues clearly illegal objectives, e.g. by enforcing "closed shops", discriminating against certain groups of workers, or segregating job markets as AG Poiares Maduro seemed to suggest in his opinion of 23 May 2007, and as can be deduced from the case law of the ECtHR in the *Gustavson* and *Rasmusen* cases, which insist on the "negative right of association"?[95]

### 3.3.4. *Examples for the "quasi-legislative approach"*

When I refer to a "quasi-legislative approach" of the Court to the application of the proportionality principle, I seem to indicate a point of critique which indeed will be developed further in looking at some problematic cases. This approach is "quasi-legislative" insofar, as certain elements of a state measure may be excessive if seen in isolation, but may still be justified in a complex policy area where different public interests are at stake and choices have to be made respecting democratic procedures which will, however, not be accepted by the Court, for instance on arguments of consistency.[96] The Court has been criticised for substituting the national legislators' evaluation (and solution!) of a certain problem area by its own understanding of the legislative process..

I will try to limit my argument to the methodological elements of a few controversial cases and not be concerned with the underlying or following political debate. Methodologically speaking, most problematic for me always has been and still is the *Centros* case.[97] The facts of the case as well as the final judgment are well known. The case has, as usual, many aspects: Some relate to international company law with regard to different Member State theories known as the "incorporation" or the "real seat theory". The second concerns the autonomy of Member States in defining regimes of companies "as products of law" under their jurisdiction, and the failure of the Community to harmonise company law, both recognised in the earlier *Daily Mail* judgment,[98] allowing Member states to impose restrictions on the free movement of companies, as was recently reaffirmed in *Cartesio*.[99] A new, "dynamic internal market" element

95 *Recueil des Arrêts de la Cour*, 1996-II, 637 paras 44–45; Judgment of 11 January 2006, applications No. 52656 and 52620/99, paras 58. Available at: http://cmiskp.echr.coe.int/tkp197/search.asp?skin=hudoc-en; also ECJ 9 March 2006, Case C-499/04, *Hans Werhof v Freeway Traffic Systems GmbH & Co. KG* [2006] ECR I-2397, para 33. For a more detailed discussion see my paper supra note 11, at 858.

96 See references at supra note 70.

97 Supra note 20.

98 ECJ 27 September 1988, Case 81/87, *R v Treasury and Commissioners of Inland Revenue ex parte Daily Mail and General Trust* [1988] ECR 5483.

99 Supra note 21, para 104. In the meantime, Articles 35–39 of the Commission proposal of a European Private Company of 25 June 2008, COM (2008) 396 contain detailed rules on the transfer of the seat of a company, see S.M. van den Braak in D.F.M.M. Zaman et al (eds),

has been added to cross-border mobility of companies in the interest of "market citizens" to register their business in the least restrictive regime of company law of Member State A (the UK) to do business via a branch in jurisdiction B (Denmark). Can this be justified under a theory of "competition of legal orders" which would allow the parties themselves and not governments to find the best legal regime on "corporate governance", as AG La Pergola suggested in his opinion of 17 June 1998 (para 20)? As a contrasting argument, there is the interest of states to avoid an "opting out" of their jurisdiction by "wholly artificial arrangements", as the Court wrote in the later *Cadbury-Schweppes* judgment,[100] thus trying to avoid an "abuse of EU freedoms". Will the proportionality test help to solve this "mixture" of quasi-legislative legal interests? Yes and no. I think that the Court correctly argued that restrictions on the freedom of establishment which indeed were imposed by Danish legislation on companies registered in country A (the UK) doing business via a branch in Denmark can only be justified under the 4-step *Gebhard* test; the mere reference to international company law under the "real seat theory" does not exclude this restriction, as many company lawyers had argued before, and are still arguing. [101] On the other hand, creditor protection qualifies for a public interest justifying such restrictions, but the measures must be appropriate and necessary, something the Court denied in the case before it. Creditors could be given notice that the company is established under UK law and thereby be warned against certain risks (para 36). Creditor protection could also be achieved by less restrictive means, e.g. guarantees (para 37). But the question remains: where did the Court get its knowledge from? Is the reference to the *Cassis* principle: "information should be preferred to regulation" justified with regard to complex questions of corporate governance? How can unsecured creditors like workers, social security institutions, tax authorities be protected? Is it really justified to put the information burden, concerning the effect of using a foreign company law for business conducted exclusively in the home country, on third parties and not on those which operate the company? Shouldn't the Court also have left the final decision to the Danish court which is much more familiar with the problems of corporate governance and creditor protection than the ECJ?

*Gybrechts*[102] is the most recent case using a quasi-legislative approach of the proportionality argument. It concerned a Belgian regulation, made possible under

---

*European Private Company (SPE): A Critical Analysis of the EU Draft Statute*, Intersentia Publishers, Antwerp, 2010, at 175.

100 ECJ 12 September 2006, Case C-196/04, *Cadbury Schweppes (Overseas) v Commissioners of Inland Revenue* [2006] ECR I-7995; for a general discussion see R. de la Feria, 'Prohibition of Abuse of (Community) Law: The Creation of a New General Principle of EC Law through Tax', (2008) 45 *CMLR* 395.

101 This is the main argument against *Centros* voiced by G. Roth in G. Roth and P. Hilpold, *Der EuGH und die Souveränität der Mitgliedstaaten*, Linde Verlag, Wien, 2008, 427, at 453.

102 Supra note 22.

the minimum harmonisation concept of the distance selling Dir. 97/7/EC,[103] forbidding internet providers from asking for advance payments and requesting the credit card number of the consumer before the withdrawal period had lapsed. Since criminal action was brought against the Belgian internet provider, who had violated the former rule, it first had to be decided whether the prohibition on measures having an equivalent effect as export restrictions under Article 29 EC (now Article 35 TFEU) applied to the case according to the broad interpretation given to fundamental freedoms as mentioned above. The entire debate revolved around the justification under proportionate consumer policy arguments. AG Trstenjak, in her opinion of 17 July 2008, condemned the Belgian regulation for not attaining a fair balance for both the supplier and the consumer concerning advance payments. The AG stated that "absolute consumer protection" resulted in "*summum ius – summa iniuria*" (?).[104] The Court found "that Article 29 EC does not preclude national rules which prohibit a supplier, in cross-border distance selling, from requiring an advance or any payment from a consumer before expiry of the withdrawal period, but Article 29 EC does preclude a prohibition, under those rules, on requesting, before expiry of that period, the number of the consumer's payment card." The first was regarded as being "necessary", the second not: "..the value of the prohibition on a supplier requiring a consumer's payment card number resides only in the fact that it eliminates the risk that the supplier may collect the price before expiry of the period for withdrawal. If, however, that risk materialises, the supplier's action is, in itself, a contravention of the prohibition laid down by the provision at issue in the main proceedings, a prohibition which must be regarded as an appropriate and proportionate measure to attain the objective pursued, ... It must therefore be held that the imposition on a supplier of a prohibition on requiring that a consumer provide his payment card number goes beyond what is necessary to attain the objective pursued" (para 60–62). The "non-necessity"-argument however remains somewhat a myth. Is a criminal or administrative sanction really enough to protect the consumer whose account was debited by the illegal use of the credit card and who may be at odds to get his money back? Isn't it a matter of the Member States, expressly authorised to do so by the relevant directive, to decide on the means of protection for consumers and to avoid undermining the consumer withdrawal right by requesting his credit card number?

103 Directive 97/7/EC of the EP and of the Council of 20 May 1997 on the protection of consumers in respect of distance contracts, OJ L 144, 4.6. 1997, 19.

104 Comment H.-W. Micklitz and Reich, (2008) *VuR (Verbraucher und Recht)* 349–351.

## 4. WHERE ARE WE NOW – A PLEA FOR JUDICIAL RESTRAINT

The paper has hopefully given an overview of the different approaches in the recent ECJ case law on proportionality. There is no doubt about its overarching importance given both the broad interpretation of the fundamental freedoms on the one side, and the public interest justifications on the other. Cases brought to the ECJ, both under the reference procedure and – less frequently but still important – under the infringement proceedings by the Commission, usually have to be decided on the proportionality argument. It is in areas where the Court has developed its own agenda and advances its own methodological "Vorverständnisse" where I deduce four classifications, i.e., "autonomous balancing", "state margin of appreciation" "fundamental rights" ", and "quasi-legislative" approaches. The Court clearly has developed a liberal, individual rights oriented agenda, but has left Member States with a differentiated set of regulatory powers which is sometimes difficult to predict and most restricted in the "quasi-legislative approach" cases where usually one element out of a multitude of different arguments runs foul to the Court's scrutiny, and where States seem to be puzzled on how to comply with rulings of the ECJ. It leads to ambivalent results in the fundamental rights area, if one compares *Schmidberger,* supporting autonomy of ecological actions, vs. *Viking,* severely restricting social action.

To sum up *firstly,* the "autonomous balancing approach" seems to work where on the one hand, a clear public policy choice can be determined, but on the other, some equally justified opposing private interests can be defined. This is quite clear in cases concerning health matters: Member States retain responsibility here, but they must respect new marketing methods insofar as they can be made to conform, on the one hand, to health imperatives like in *Doc Morris,* and on the other hand, allow patients a reasonable choice without overburdening the public finance as in *Watts.* Effective legal protection is another important element which has been integrated into this balancing test, resulting in the Court leaving aside the somewhat artificial German consequences of a transfer of the "real seat" of a company as in *Überseering.*

*Secondly,* the "state margin of appreciation approach" which has its roots in the case law of the European Court of Human Rights seems justified wherever the law and facts do not give a clear answer; the Court in my opinion correctly refers the decision back to Member State courts and instructs them on how the proportionality principle operates in the EU. This approach seems to be most consistent with the multilevel system of judicial governance in the EU, but does not guarantee uniform standards for similar restrictions of fundamental freedoms in the entire EU. After some hesitation and confusion, this seems to be the approach now to evaluate Member State restrictions on cross-border betting activities via the Internet (*Santa Casa, Ladbroke* clarifying *Gambelli/Plancanica*) and rejecting the country-of-origin approach regarding control of such activities. But Member States must follow their policies against betting and games of chance in a consistent and systematic manner, as the Court recently restated with regard to the German monopoly on betting and games of chance.[105]

*Thirdly*, the more recent "fundamental rights approach" to some extent continues this type of division of work between Union and national jurisdictions; it underlines the importance of autonomous fundamental rights protection as in *Schmidberger*, but unfortunately stopped short in *Viking* by not respecting the collective autonomy of labour and management with regard to social action, something which should not be limited by a simple reference to the proportionality principle that was developed for state, not for private (even though collective) action. This approach is however not without problems in cases where no fundamental rights in the traditional sense, such as protecting the individual or a group against public interventions, are at stake, but rather where the state simply veils its (possibly legitimate) "public interest" in terms of fundamental rights as in *Omega* or *Dynamic Medien*. The mere reference to "fundamental rights" therefore does not seem to make the application of the proportionality principle any easier or more predictable; it actually remains rather ambivalent.

*Fourthly*, most problematic in this analysis have been cases where the Court has used a "quasi-legislative approach". It posits, on the one hand a broad public policy objective which Member States may pursue like creditor protection in *Centros*, or consumer protection in *Gysbrechts*, but on the other hand, the ECJ will substantially weaken and water down Member State possibilities to attain these objectives by using adequate and effective instruments within their margin of discretion which are condemned as "disproportionate". Shouldn't it be left to a Member State[106] to organise creditor protection, or guarantee consumer protection against prepayment clauses before a lapse of the withdrawal period? Since there is no "positive" EU policy in this field, is the Court allowed to step in by substituting itself as a *quasi-legislator*?

In this context we should point out a certain paradox. The Court has recognised that "the Community legislature must be allowed a broad discretion in areas which involve political, economic and social choices on its part, and in which it is called upon to undertake complex assessments", even though it is bound by the proportionality principle according to Article 5(2) EU Lisbon (ex-Article 5(2)

---

105 See the judgments of 8 September 2010 supra note 86.

106 In this sense see J. Snell, 'True Proportionality and Free Movement of Goods and Services', (2000) 11 *EBLR (European Business Law Review)* 50, at 54.

EC).[107] Why isn't this "broad discretion" also applied to Member State legislation in areas where it involves complex (and controversial!) choices, particularly in areas under the "quasi-legislative approach". According to Harbo,[108] the Court starts from a "weak rights regime" in controlling Union law measures under the proportionality test by taking a "deferent approach vis-à-vis the legislator", being based on a "very strong substantial bias, namely that of promoting European integration", while it employs much more restrictive language – even though not consistently, as we have tried to show – with regard to Member State measures, allegedly restricting fundamental freedoms in a "non proportionate" way. In an analysis of recent case law focusing on the dichotomy of commercial purposes and social policy of Member States under EU imperatives, Schiek[109] found that, in the opinion of the ECJ, "… markets are portrayed as working better than public institutions. This is not always supported by legal rules, but partly also related as eternal truth".

Two arguments can be added to this critique:

- The very nature of the proceedings before the Court will always result in "negative integration", that is, stating the non-conformity of a national measure with EC law. The "positive integration" may not be a necessary consequence, as follow-up litigation frequently shows, like in the area of gambling where the Court originally had created quite a conundrum in Member States' legislation, only recently "softened" by its more "pro" Member State case law, provided they stick to consistency in their restrictive measures combating the spreading of games of chance.
- The factual input in the above mentioned cases seems rather weak and restricted, particularly in the context of the reference proceedings. I have mentioned the limited number of participants who may submit observations, which does not relate to the widespread effects of the judgments of the Court on third parties like national parliaments, business associations, consumer NGOs and labour unions. In some cases, the Court indeed has used the argument of judicial restraint and conferred the final power to decide on proportionality to Member States' courts by giving interpretative guidelines, while in others, criticised here, it has decided more or less by itself with a different set

107 Case C-376/03, *Germany v EP and Council*, supra note 3, at para 145; ECJ 10 January 2006, C-344/04, *IATA and ELFAA v Department for Transport* [2006] ECR I-403, at para 80, referring to earlier cases like ECJ 12 November 1996, Case C-84/94, *United Kingdom* v *Council* [1996] ECR I-5755, para 58; ECJ 13 May 1997, Case C-233/94, *Germany* v *Parliament and Council* [1997] ECR I-2405, paras 55 and 56; ECJ 5 May 1998, Case C-157/96, *National Farmers' Union and Others* [1998] ECR I-2211, para 61; and ECJ 10 December 2002, Case C-491/01, *British American Tobacco (Investments) and Imperial Tobacco* [2002] ECR I-11453, para 123.

108 Supra note 54, at 166, 172, 177.

109 D. Schiek, 'Is there a social ideal behind the ECJ?' in U. Neergaard et al (eds) *The Role of Courts in developing a European Social Model*, Djoef Publishing, Copenhagen, 2010, 63, at 96.

> of not always transparent and convincing criteria. While in the "autonomous balancing" and the "fundamental rights" cases the Court seemed to take an implicit ranking between the protected public interests in conflict with fundamental freedoms, and the proportionate use to attain a conceptual equilibrium, the "quasi-legislative approach" cases are much less clear and seem to focus on one element exclusively out of a set of possible criteria to condemn substantial parts of a Member State regulation. An overall balancing of the proposed measures might have allowed a more flexible approach respecting the constitutional powers of Member States under the Treaty.

As a frequent result, at least in the "quasi-legislative approach" cases, but also by using some of the other approaches, the Court's understanding of Member State legislation is *not a political one* where complex choices and preferences are decided, but rather a *regulatory one* where the abstract market rationale prevails over the political bargaining process, despite a different rhetoric in the Preamble of the EU Charter, referring to the "respect of the diversity of cultures and traditions of the people of Europe as well as the national identities of Member States". Shouldn't different national identities be taken more seriously in this context without sacrificing them on an overly strict regime of proportionality? In my opinion, it seems advisable for the Court to use *judicial restraint*[110] in areas where important Member State interests are at stake, including the collection of revenue and the protection of employment by non-discriminatory means. In furtherance to this, the Court should take care when extending the proportionality argument beyond its clear methodological boundaries unless supported by sufficient evidence. Some recent cases, all decided in 2009/2010, like *Kattner* on compulsory workplace insurance, the results of the litigations in *Commission vs. Italy* regarding road safety, *Santa Casa* and *Ladbroke* concerning exclusive management of games of chance by national entities, and *Apothekerkammer Saarland* concerning management of pharmacies in Germany, in fact seem to go in this direction.

110 See Roth, supra note 101, at p. 605.

# JUDICIAL ACTIVISM OR CONSTITUTIONAL INTERACTION?

## Policymaking by the ECJ in the Field of Union Citizenship

Michael DOUGAN*

## 1. INTRODUCTION

This chapter examines the debate about judicial activism by the European Court of Justice with specific reference to the case law on the free movement of Union citizens. We begin with some preliminary remarks about the inevitably selective and subjective nature of allegations of judicial activism, particularly within the Union legal order, where there is neither a clear constitutional definition of, nor a common political and intellectual consensus on, the proper functions and limits of judicial power (Section 2). Against that background, we will consider some of the core criticisms levelled against the Court's case law as it developed in the decade following the *Sala* ruling in 1998;[1] specifically, the accusation of unilateral judicial policymaking, especially in the sensitive field of welfare rights and responsibilities, to the detriment of legitimate political choices made by the competent national and/or Union authorities (Section 3). However, consideration of the most recent case law since 2008 (Section 4) should prompt us to re-evaluate that jurisprudence: a longer-term and broader perspective suggests that the Court's relationship to the other Union institutions has been one of continuous

* Liverpool Law School. This chapter is based on the paper I presented at the EUI conference on *The ECJ and the Autonomy of the Member States* in April 2009, as well as presentations at the University of Gothenburg and the University of Birmingham. I am very grateful to participants for their comments and suggestions. I am indebted, as ever, to Eleanor Spaventa for her insightful remarks. The law is stated as on 31 March 2010.

1 ECJ 12 May 1998, Case C-85/96, *María Martínez Sala v Freistaat Bayern*, [1998] ECR I-2691.

dialogue about how best to construct a meaningful yet balanced legal framework for Union citizenship, while at the same time remaining sensitive to the often tumultuous environment of European integration during the constitutional reform process initiated by the European Council at Nice and Laeken (Section 5).[2]

## 2. SOME PRELIMINARY REMARKS ON "JUDICIAL ACTIVISM"

Allegations of judicial activism against the ECJ are hardly anything new. Time and again, the Court has stood accused of (and been defended against) the charge of overstepping its proper judicial function, in particular, by advancing its own pro-integrationist political agenda.[3] Such allegations were once common currency in debates (for example) about the Court's case law on the principles of direct effect and supremacy,[4] its recognition of fundamental rights as general principles of Community (now Union) law,[5] and the jurisprudence on effective judicial protection as regards remedies and procedural rules before the national courts[6] – all doctrines which, even if they are still controversial for other reasons, have nevertheless since been accepted as core, indeed essential, tenets of the Union's constitutional order. Yet the charges of judicial activism persist, sounding the same tone of "integrationist bias", though now more likely to be framed in terms of distorting the federal balance between Union and Member State competences. Indeed, among the themes which this edited collection invited its contributors to explore was precisely the allegation that the ECJ has unduly extended the scope of Union law and overstepped its own jurisdiction, to the detriment of the "reserved competences" or (more broadly) the political autonomy of the Member States.

---

2 Nice European Council Presidency Conclusions of 8 December 2000; Laeken European Council Presidency Conclusions of 14 December 2001.

3 E.g. H. Rasmussen, *On Law and Policy in the European Court of Justice,* Martinus Nijhoff, Dordrecht, 1986; M. Cappelletti, 'Is the European Court of Justice 'Running Wild'?', (1987) 12 *ELR (European Law Review)* 3. Also, e.g. T. Hartley, 'The European Court, Judicial Objectivity and the Constitution of the European Union', (1996) 112 *LQR (Law Quarterly Review)* 95; A. Arnull, 'The European Court and Judicial Objectivity: A Reply to Professor Hartley', (1996) 112 *LQR* 411.

4 See further, e.g. P. Craig, 'Once Upon a Time in the West: Direct Effect and the Federalization of EEC Law', (1992) 12 *OJLS (Oxford Journal of Legal Studies)* 453.

5 See further, e.g. J. Coppel and A. O'Neill, 'The European Court of Justice: Taking Rights Seriously?', (1992) 29 *CMLR (Common Market Law Review)* 669; J. Weiler and N. Lockhart, "Taking Rights Seriously' Seriously: The European Court and its Fundamental Rights Jurisprudence', (1995) 32 *CMLR* 51 and 579.

6 See further, e.g. A. Biondi, 'The European Court of Justice and Certain National Procedural Limitations: Not Such a Tough Relationship', (1999) 36 *CMLR* 1271.

Thus, in some recent rulings, the Court is accused of endorsing an interpretation of the Treaties that fails to offer any meaningful constraint upon the Union institutions' expansionist conception of their own regulatory competences: consider, for example, the *Environmental Crimes* decision which (pre-Lisbon) recognised a derived competence to harmonise various aspects of national criminal law under the Community's First Pillar rather than the Union's Third Pillar powers.[7] In other recent cases, the Court is alleged rather to have pursued its own aggressive construction of Union law, to the cost of sensitive national policy choices: consider, for example, the decision in *Commission v Austria*, forcefully reaffirming the principle of equal treatment on grounds of nationality as regards access to university, despite grave domestic concerns about the (allegedly) exceptional scale and detrimental effects of cross-border educational mobility.[8] Indeed, a whole series of rulings in recent years – such as *Geraerts-Smits and Peerbooms*,[9] *Carpenter*,[10] *Mangold*,[11] *Viking Line* and *Laval un*

[7] ECJ 13 September 2005, Case C-176/03, *Commission v Council* [2005] ECR I-7879. Also: ECJ 23 October 2007, Case C-440/05, *Commission v Council* [2007] ECR I-9097. See now Article 83(2) TFEU. See further, e.g. E. Herlin-Karnell, '*Commission v Council:* Some Reflections on Criminal Law in the First Pillar', (2007) 13 *EPL (European Public Law)* 69; A. Dawes and O. Lynskey, 'The Ever-Longer Arm of EC Law: The Extension of Community Competence Into the Field of Criminal Law', (2008) 45 *CMLR* 131.

[8] ECJ 7 July 2005, Case C-147/03, *Commission v Austria* [2005] ECR I-5969. Cp. Case C-73/08 *Bressol* (Opinion of 25 June 2009; Judgment forthcoming). See further the detailed discussion by D. Damjanovic in this collection.

[9] ECJ 12 July 2001, Case C-157/99, *B.S.M. Geraets-Smits v Stichting Ziekenfonds VGZ and H.T.M. Peerbooms v Stichting CZ Groep Zorgverzekeringen* [2001] ECR I-5473. Cp. Case C-385/99, *Müller-Fauré* [2003] ECR I-4509; ECJ 16 May 2006, Case C-372/04, *The Queen, on the application of Yvonne Watts v Bedford Primary Care Trust and Secretary of State for Health* [2006] ECR I-4325. See further, e.g. J. Montgomery, 'Impact of European Union Law on English Healthcare Law', in M. Dougan and E. Spaventa (eds), *Social Welfare and EU Law*, Hart Publishing, Oxford, 2005; C. Newdick, 'Citizenship, Free Movement and Health Care: Cementing Individual Rights by Corroding Social Solidarity', (2006) 43 *CMLR* 1645.

[10] ECJ 11 July 2002, Case C-60/00, *Mary Carpenter v Secretary of State for the Home Department* [2002] ECR I-6279. See further, e.g. Editorial, 'Freedoms Unlimited? Reflections on *Mary Carpenter v Secretary of State*', (2003) 40 *CMLR* 537; E. Spaventa, 'From *Gebhard* to *Carpenter*: Towards a (non-)Economic European Constitution', (2004) 41 *CMLR* 743.

[11] ECJ 22 November 2005, Case C-144/04, *Werner Mangold v Rüdiger Helm* [2005] ECR I-9981. Cp. ECJ 23 September 2008, Case C-427/06, *Birgit Bartsch v Bosch und Siemens Hausgeräte (BSH) Altersfürsorge GmbH,* [2008] ECR I-7245; ECJ 19 January 2010, Case C-555/07, *Seda Kücükdeveci v Swedex GmbH & Co. KG*, nyr. See further, e.g. E. Muir, 'Enhancing the Effects of Community Law on National Employment Policies: The *Mangold* Case' (2006) 31 *ELR* 879; A. Dashwood, 'From *Van Duyn* to *Mangold* via *Marshall*: Reducing Direct Effect to Absurdity?' (2006–2007) 9 *CYELS (Cambridge Yearbook of European Legal Studies)* 81.

*Partneri*,[12] *Metock*[13] and *Soysal*[14] – have provided fuel for a contemporary critique of judicial activism based upon the nonetheless familiar argument that the ECJ improperly substitutes itself as legislature in place of the competent (national and / or Union) political institutions. The Court, so it goes, is too willing to deliver judgments that are not explicable primarily by hermeneutic techniques, but are the product of subjective preferences as regards deeply contested economic and / or social questions. Furthermore, it is suggested, the Court often appears too ready to frame such policy judgments in terms of the primary Treaty provisions, or the general principles of Union law, in a manner that effectively reduces the capacity of the Member States acting in the exercise of their individual regulatory autonomy, the Council and / or European Parliament performing their legislative functions, or even the Member States exercising constitutional power as "masters of the Treaties", to negotiate and adopt a different policy choice.

Those sympathetic to such criticisms propose various measures to help clip the judicial wings. Consider, for example, the campaign in Germany, led by Herzog and Gerkin, to "Stop the European Court of Justice" – accusing the Court of deliberately and systematically abusing its jurisdiction, and calling for the establishment of a new judicial body with specific responsibility for adjudicating over competence disputes.[15] As other commentators have pointed out, it would be wrong to give too much academic credence to that critique, based as it is upon a reading of the case law by turns misguided and ill-informed, and offering a supposed solution which would in fact create as many problems as it claims to solve.[16] But critics of the Court warn of other self-induced dangers to its judicial authority. On the one hand, there is the threat of open rebellion by disgruntled national courts – a storm cloud which seems to have darkened since the German

---

12 ECJ 11 December 2007, Case C-438/05, *International Transport Workers' Federation and Finnish Seamen's Union v Viking Line ABP and OÜ Viking Line Eesti* [2007] ECR I-10779; ECJ 18 December 2007, Case C-341/05, *Laval un Partneri Ltd v Svenska Byggnadsarbetareförbundet, Svenska Byggnadsarbetareförbundets avdelning 1, Byggettan and Svenska Elektrikerförbundet* [2007] ECR I-11767. Further, e.g. P. Syrpis and T. Novitz, 'Economic and Social Rights in Conflict: Political and Judicial Approaches to their Reconciliation', (2008) 33 *ELR* 411; L. Azoulai, 'The Court of Justice and the Social Market Economy: The Emergence of an Ideal and the Conditions for Its Realisation', (2008) 45 *CMLR* 1335.

13 ECJ 25 July 2008, Case C-127/08, *Blaise Baheten Metock and Others v Minister for Justice, Equality and Law Reform* [2008] ECR I-6241. Cp. ECJ 19 December 2008, Case C-551/07, *Deniz Sahin v Bundesminister für Inneres* [2008] ECR I-10453; ECJ 4 March 2010, Case C-578/08, *Rhimou Chakroun v Minister van Buitenlandse Zaken*, nyr. See further, e.g. S. Currie, 'Accelerated Justice or a Step Too Far? Residence Rights of Non-EU Family members and the Court's Ruling in Metock' (2009) 34 *ELR* 310; C. Costello, '*Metock*: Free Movement and 'Normal Family Life' in the Union', (2009) 46 *CMLR* 587.

14 ECJ 19 February 2009, Case C-228/06, *Soysal* [2009] ECR I-1031. See further, e.g. N. Tezcan/ Idriz, 'Free Movement of Persons between Turkey and the EU: To Move or Not To Move? The Response of the Judiciary', (2009) 46 *CMLR* 1621.

15 Writing in the *Frankfurter Allgemeine Zeitung* (8 September 2008).

16 E.g. Editorial, 'The Court of Justice in the Limelight – Again', (2008) 45 *CMLR* 1571.

Federal Constitutional Court's *Lisbon Ruling* (2009).[17] The latter's signal to undertake a more critical assessment of the ECJ's performance might yet be applied in practice when the FCC delivers its long-awaited ruling in the *Honeywell* dispute concerning the status of the *Mangold* case law within Germany.[18] On the other hand, and potentially just as damaging, would be the possibility that national judiciaries which no longer trust the ECJ to act as an impartial and persuasive judicial authority might begin simply to respond with indifference – preferring to settle even novel issues of Union law for themselves rather than risk being stuck with a preliminary ruling from Luxembourg which (as they might see it) promotes a given political strategy or falls short of compelling legal argumentation.[19]

Against such criticisms, it is important to recall two main points that may well seem trite but remain none the less true. First, any critique of judicial activism is usually built up from a highly selective crop of rulings: as Schmitz has observed, alleged difficulties with the case law invariably concern only a relatively small proportion of the Court's overall output; for its part, each awkward case is usually capable of being explained and defended in its own particular context.[20] Indeed, for every example of "judicial activism", one can usually point to a converse instance of "judicial restraint": the ruling in *UPA*, after all, is as much a product of Luxembourg as the decisions in *Peerbooms* or *Mangold*.[21] Moreover, to draw attention to the various problems implied by certain rulings is not necessarily to subscribe to conspiracy theories about the ECJ's hidden federalist agendas or self-aggrandising motivations. Difficulties are just as likely to arise from poorly articulated (and sometimes simply poor) judicial reasoning, or only an incomplete appreciation of the full consequences of a given line of argumentation, each such weakness being partly attributable to underlying considerations relating to the logistical functioning of the institution itself.[22]

---

17 Judgment of 30 June 2009. See further, e.g. D. Thym, 'In the Name of Sovereign Statehood: A Critical Introduction to the Lisbon Judgment of the German Constitutional Court', (2009) 46 *CMLR* 1795; D. Doukas, 'The Verdict of the German Federal Constitutional Court on the Lisbon Treaty: Not Guilty, But Don't Do It Again!', (2009) 34 *ELR* 866; J. Ziller, 'The German Constitutional Court's Friendliness Towards European Law: On the Judgment of *Bundesverfassungsgericht* over the Ratification of the Treaty of Lisbon', (2010) 16 *EPL* 53.

18 Case 2 BvR 2661/06 (pending).

19 For examples of dubious non-referrals by the UK House of Lords / Supreme Court, see A. Arnull, 'The Law Lords and the European Union: Swimming with the Incoming Tide' (2010) 35 *ELR* 57.

20 T. Schmitz, 'On the Limits of Obedience to the European Courts', and other comments, presented at the conference *The Principle of Accountability in the EU: The European Parliament, National Parliaments and the European Court of Justice* (University of Gothenburg, 26 February 2009).

21 ECJ 25 July 2002, Case C-50/00, *Unión de Pequeños Agricultores v Council of the European Union* [2002] ECR I-6677.

22 See further, e.g. T. Tridimas, 'The Court of Justice and Judicial Activism', (1996) 21 *ELR* 199. For critical analysis of the ECJ's legal reasoning, consider J. Bengoetxea, N. MacCormick and L. Moral Soriano, 'Integration and Integrity in the Legal Reasoning of the European Court of Justice', in G. de Búrca and J. Weiler (eds), *The European Court of Justice*, Oxford University Press, Oxford, 2001; J. Bengoetxea, 'Legal Reasoning and the Hermeneutic Turn

Secondly, any allegation of judicial activism against the Union courts merely begs difficult questions about how one can possibly define what to consider "activist" within a highly idiosyncratic constitutional order. For present purposes, it should suffice to distil only a few relevant observations from the extensive literature exploring the nature and limits of the ECJ's position *qua* "supreme court" for the Union.[23] It is generally accepted that the Treaties enshrine no particular model for the exercise of higher judicial powers: there is neither a clear mandate for, nor express prohibition against, the Court accruing to itself the power to participate actively in, and indeed to pronounce definitively on, matters of substantive economic and social policy based on the Union's primary law (in a manner akin to that often attributed to, say, the US Supreme Court); or, for that matter, the Court acting merely as executor of the legislature's binding will, lacking the competence or authority to pass final judgment upon contested policy issues, and averse to treating its own preferences in economic and social matters as the expression of inalienable constitutional values (a position often adopted, say, by the UK Supreme Court). The existence of such fundamental open questions implies that any accusation of judicial activism against the Court rests upon certain unproven and ultimately unproveable assumptions about the proper nature of the Union's judicial function.

In particular, allegations that the Court is undermining the Union's federal balance by accruing to itself a quasi-legislative power perhaps exploit an important source of constitutional uncertainty within the Union legal order: the complexity and opaqueness of the relationship between the "superior" legal sources – primary Treaty provisions and general principles of Union law – within the Union's hierarchy of norms.[24] Consider especially the interaction between three categories of such superior legal norms: those primary Treaty provisions that are capable of independent application as a source of binding rights and obligations (such as the provisions guaranteeing the free movement of goods, services, capital and persons); those primary Treaty provisions which confer regulatory competences and decision-making discretion upon the Union's political institutions (in fields such as the internal market, agriculture, environmental protection and social policy); and the general principles of Union law recognised and developed by the

in the Law: Remarks on the European Court of Justice', in U. Neergaard, R. Nielsen and L. Roseberry (eds), *The Role of Courts in Developing a European Social Model: Theoretical and Methodological Perspectives*, DJØF Publishing, København, 2010.

23 See further, e.g. A.-M. Slaughter, A. Stone Sweet and J. Weiler (eds), *The European Court and National Courts: Doctrine and Jurisprudence*, Hart Publishing, 1998; G de Búrca and J Weiler (eds), *The European Court of Justice*, Oxford University Press, 2001; A. Arnull, *The European Union and Its Court of Justice*, Oxford University Press, Oxford, 2nd ed, 2006; K. Alter, *The European Court's Political Power*, Oxford University Press, 2009.

24 As opposed to the relationship between the inferior norms (legislative and non-legislative measures, including delegated and implementing acts) dealt with by the Treaty of Lisbon: see Articles 289–291 TFEU.

Union courts in their case law and treated as equivalent to the Treaties themselves (including such familiar principles such as proportionality, legal certainty and legitimate expectations). Despite the fact that the interactions between those three legal sources may have a decisive influence upon our underlying assumptions about when proper "judicial interpretation" melds into more pejorative "judicial activism", the relevant legal and conceptual framework remains surprisingly murky.

For example: when should any given Treaty provision capable of independent application be treated as imposing an absolute standard of conduct, in the sense that the Court's interpretation is binding upon all addressees for all purposes, including also the Union's political institutions in the exercise of their otherwise autonomous decision-making powers? Or when should such Treaty provisions instead be considered more porous in nature, especially as regards their capacity to interact with rather than override the regulatory competences of the other Union institutions, such that the Court's interpretation can indeed be adapted to the actual or potential exercise of its political discretion by the Union legislature?[25] Similar questions arise with regard to the general principles of Union law, insofar as they further articulate the Union's fundamental, albeit unwritten, constitutional values.[26] In fact, determining how far interpretation of the primary Treaty provisions and/or the general principles of Union law should act as a medium for providing judicial solutions to policy problems whose resolution might instead be considered a responsibility of the political institutions is a far from easy task: for example, identifying when judicial interpretation might take precedence over an expression of political will by the Union legislature as regards one and the same subject matter;[27] or replicate certain regulatory choices made by

[25] Consider, e.g. the ECJ's express deference towards the competence of the Union legislature to make alternative provision for dealing with barriers to the cross-border trade in goods evident from its interpretation of ex-Article 28 EC (now Article 34 TFEU) in Case 120/78, *Cassis de Dijon* [1979] ECR 649.

[26] The most obvious and absolute qualification to the exercise of the Union institutions' legislative discretion is respect for fundamental rights as general principles of Union law (e.g. Cases C-402/05 and C-415/05, *Kadi and Al Barakaat* [2008] ECR I-6351); and now also in accordance with the Union's primary law as provided for under Article 6 of the revised TEU and the Charter of Fundamental Rights [2007] OJ C303/1. See further, e.g. K. Lenaerts and P. Van Nuffel, *Constitutional Law of the European Union*, Sweet & Maxwell, London, 2nd ed, 2005; X. Groussot, *General Principles of Community Law*, Europa Law Publishing, Groningen, 2006; T. Tridimas, *The General Principles of EU Law*, Oxford University Press, Oxford, 2nd ed, 2006; U. Bernitz, J. Nergelius and C. Cardner (eds), *General Principles of EC Law in a Process of Development*, Kluwer Law International, Alphen aan den Rijn, 2008.

[27] Consider, e.g. ECJ 17 September 2002, Case C-413/99, *Baumbast and R v Secretary of State for the Home Department* [2002] ECR I-7091; ECJ 20 May 2008, Case C-352/06, *Brigitte Bosmann* [2008] ECR I-3827. Consider, along similar lines, the interaction between international agreements concluded by the Union and secondary legislation adopted by the Union legislature, e.g. ECJ 19 February 2009, Case C-228/06, *Soysal* [2009] ECR I-1031.

the other Union institutions but as regards situations deliberately excluded from the scope of the relevant secondary legislation.[28]

The fact that such important issues have been left so open-ended merely serves to emphasise the essentially selective and subjective nature of the judicial activism debate. Any given ruling addressing some controversial policy issue might well be isolated under a critical spotlight and convincingly portrayed as an instance of unilateralist judicial policymaking at the expense of the rightful prerogatives of the competent (national and / or Union) political institutions. But when exactly the same ruling is viewed from a longer term perspective and located within its broader legal context – one which acknowledges that the Union's current constitutional framework indeed offers a wide margin of discretion to the ECJ to determine for itself the terms of its interaction with the relevant (national and/or Union) political institutions – a very different impression can emerge. In negotiating the relationship between its own interpretation of the primary Treaty provisions and/or the general principles of Union law (on the one hand) and the existence of regulatory discretion conferred by or recognised under the Treaties (on the other hand), the Court is clearly capable of engaging in more multilateral and constructive processes of "constitutional dialogue" whereby judicial preferences respond to, stimulate and reshape legislative action.[29]

In that regard, many authors in various contexts have identified and discussed potential patterns of interaction between the judicial and political institutions in the development of Union law. Sometimes the Court appears to take an assertive lead in policymaking when the political authorities languish in a state of legislative sclerosis, and conversely to slip back into the shadows when the other Union institutions assume a more active and effective responsibility for addressing the relevant policy problem.[30] Such is the interpretation often attributed to the case law on the free movement of goods as it evolved from the ruling in *Cassis de Dijon* to the judgment in *Keck and Mithouard*;[31] and to the jurisprudence on effective

[28] Consider e.g. case law on various public contracts excluded from the Union's public procurement directives, e.g. ECJ 7 December 2000, Case C-324/98, *Telaustria Verlags GmbH and Telefonadress GmbH v Telekom Austria AG, joined party: Herold Business Data AG* [2000] ECR I-10745; ECJ 21 July 2005, Case C-231/03, *Coname* [2005] ECR I-7287; ECJ 13 October 2005, Case C-458/03, *Parking Brixen GmbH v Gemeinde Brixen and Stadtwerke Brixen AG* [2005] ECR I-8585; ECJ 14 June 2007, Case C-6/05, *Medipac-Kazantzidis AE v Venizeleio-Pananeio (PE.S.Y. KRITIS)* [2007] ECR I-4557. See further, e.g. B. Drijber and H. Stergiou, 'Public Procurement Law and Internal Market Law', (2009) 46 *CMLR* 805; M. Szydło, 'Contracts Beyond the Scope of the EC Public Procurement Directives: Who is bound by the requirement for transparency?', (2009) 34 *ELR* 720.

[29] Cp. K. Lenaerts, 'Some Thoughts About the Interaction Between Judges and Politicians in the European Community', (1992) 12 *YEL (Yearbook of European Law)* 1.

[30] See the influential analyses by J. Weiler, 'The Dual Character of Supranationalism', (1981) 1 *YEL* 267 and 'The Transformation of Europe', (1991) 100 *Yale Law Journal* 2403.

[31] ECJ 20 February 1979, Case 120/78, *Rewe-Zentral AG v Bundesmonopolverwaltung für Branntwein* [1979] ECR 649; ECJ 24 November 1993, Cases C-267–268/91, *Criminal proceedings*

judicial protection as it entered its most aggressive phase of development after the decision in *San Giorgio* only to retreat back again with the ruling in *Steenhorst-Neerings*.[32] Those same lines of case law have also been explained by the Court's sensitivity to the broader political context of judicial policymaking, especially as concerns the general direction and public reception of the European integration process – even if such diffuse perceptions and reactions are things more sensed than proven. Readers will no doubt recall academic discussion about the potential impact of the ratification problems surrounding the Maastricht Treaty upon the Court's short-term confidence precisely in the case law on the free movement of goods,[33] and effective judicial protection.[34]

Perhaps most interesting are those areas of Union law where the relationship between judicial and political institutions has resembled a direct conversation about how best to address a given regulatory dilemma. Consider, for example, the difficult problems once raised by the application of Regulation 1408/71 to so-called "hybrid benefits".[35] The Court in rulings such as *Newton* openly recognised that the Treaty's objective of eliminating obstacles to free movement resulting from the operation of the national social security systems needed to be balanced against the changing nature and fragile equilibrium of domestic welfare provision, whilst also explicitly acknowledging that any judicial policy choice in that regard should be made only in default of a legislative solution which (once adopted) would necessarily take priority over the previous case law.[36] True enough: once Regulation 1408/71 was amended so as to introduce a new regime on "special non-contributory benefits",[37] the Court in cases such as *Snares* found that the Union legislature was perfectly entitled to pursue a different solution to

---

*against Bernard Keck and Daniel Mithouard* [1993] ECR I-6097. See further, e.g. M. Maduro, *We, The Court: The European Court of Justice and the European Economic Constitution*, Hart Publishing, Oxford, 1998.

32 ECJ 9 November 1983, Case 199/82, *Amministrazione delle Finanze dello Stato v SpA San Giorgio* [1983] ECR 3595; ECJ 27 October 1993, Case C-338/91, *H. Steenhorst-Neerings v Bestuur van de Bedrijfsvereniging voor Detailhandel, Ambachten en Huisvrouwen* [1993] ECR I-5475. See further, e.g. M. Dougan, *National Remedies Before the Court of Justice: Issues of Harmonisation and Differentiation*, Hart Publishing, Oxford, 2004.

33 Further, e.g. N. Reich, 'The 'November Revolution' of the European Court of Justice: *Keck*, *Meng* and *Audi* Revisited', (1994) 31 *CMLR* 459.

34 Further, e.g. A. Ward, 'Effective Sanctions in EC Law: A Moving Boundary in the Division of Competence', (1995) 1 *ELJ* 205.

35 Last consolidated text published at [1997] OJ L28/1. See further, e.g. A.-P. van der Mei, 'Regulation 1408/71 and Coordination of Special Non-Contributory Benefits', (2002) 27 *ELR* 551.

36 ECJ 20 June 1991, Case C-356/89, *Roger Stanton Newton v Chief Adjudication Officer* [1991] ECR I-3017. Cp. ECJ 9 October 1974, Case 24/74, *Caisse régionale d'assurance maladie de Paris v Giuseppina Biason* [1974] ECR 999; ECJ 5 May 1983, Case 139/82, *Paola Piscitello v Istituto nazionale della previdenza sociale (INPS)* [1983] ECR 1427.

37 See Article 4(2a) Regulation 1408/71 (subsequently changed to "special non-contributory cash benefits" by Regulation 647/2005 [2005] OJ L117/1). See now Articles 3(3) and 70 Regulation 883/2004 [2004] OJ L200/1.

the problem of "hybrid benefits" from that previously advocated by the judges.[38] What could have been portrayed as an instance of improper judicial activism actually emerges as a positive engagement between judicial and political power, so as to articulate a common understanding of the relevant policy problem and work towards an effective solution.[39]

Those tensions in our interpretation of the Court's case law will now be explored in greater detail with specific reference to the jurisprudence on Union citizenship. In particular, it will be argued that that case law, as it developed in the ten years following the ground-breaking ruling in *Sala* in 1998,[40] attracted a considerable academic criticism: the Court was accused of embarking upon a unilateral process of transforming Union citizenship, particularly in the sphere of welfare provision, often to the cost of the political autonomy of the Member States and the regulatory discretion of the Union legislature. However, some of the more recent case law – particularly the *Förster* ruling from 2008[41] – suggests that the Court's confidence has been shaken and its vision for Union citizenship rendered more complex. Further reflection might lead one to accept that, viewed in its longer term and broader perspective, the case law on Union citizenship is less the product of judicial unilateralism than of an on-going process of constitutional dialogue between the ECJ and the competent political authorities about the true constitutional significance and precise legal content of EU free movement rights.

## 3. A CRITICAL READING OF THE CITIZENSHIP CASE LAW FROM 1998–2008

In the ten years following the ruling in *Sala*,[42] the Court – at first slowly and with hesitation, then particularly after the rulings in *Grzelczyk* and *Baumbast*,[43] more quickly and with increasing confidence – developed a clear, distinctive and consistent vision for Union citizenship, especially as regards the free move-

38 ECJ 4 November 1997, Case C-20/96, *Kelvin Albert Snares v Adjudication Officer* [1997] ECR I-6057. Cp. ECJ 11 June 1998, Case C-297/96, *Vera A. Partridge v Adjudication Officer* [1998] ECR I-3467; ECJ 6 July 2006, Case C-154/05, *J. J. Kersbergen-Lap and D. Dams-Schipper v Raad van Bestuur van het Uitvoeringsinstituut Werknemersverzekeringen* [2006] ECR I-6249.

39 However, note the impact of ECJ 11 September 2007, Case C-287/05, *D. P. W. Hendrix v Raad van Bestuur van het Uitvoeringsinstituut Werknemersverzekeringen* [2007] ECR I-6909 (see further the discussion below concerning Union citizenship and its impact on the social security coordination regime).

40 ECJ 12 May 1998, Case C-85/96, *María Martínez Sala* [1998] ECR I-2691.

41 ECJ 18 November 2008, Case C-158/07, *Jacqueline Förster v Hoofddirectie van de Informatie Beheer Groep* [2008] ECR I-8507.

42 ECJ 12 May 1998, Case C-85/96, *María Martínez Sala* [1998] ECR I-2691.

43 ECJ 20 September 2001, Case C-184/99, *Rudy Grzelczyk v Centre public d'aide sociale d'Ottignies-Louvain-la-Neuve* [2001] ECR I-6193; ECJ 17 September 2002, Case C-413/99, *Baumbast* [2002] ECR I-7091.

ment rights referred to in ex-Article 18 EC (now Article 21 TFEU), based upon its conviction that Union citizenship is destined to be the fundamental status of Member State nationals.[44] Rich and insightful accounts of that case law abound.[45] We shall content ourselves with identifying some of the key elements of the critical reception accorded to the Court's interpretation of Union citizenship, with specific reference to those concerned about an apparent tendency towards unilateral policymaking at the expense of the competent political authorities.[46]

To begin with, the Court's willingness to apply the Union citizen's rights of residency, equal treatment and freedom from "barriers to movement" with almost mechanical logic, to any and every national rule which actually or potentially crosses the individual migrant's path, has resulted in the creation out of the primary Treaty provisions of a remarkable series of second-order rights.[47] Those derived rights covers fields as diverse as the language in which criminal proceedings are conducted,[48] the individual's freedom of choice over his/her surname,[49] and the collection and retention of personal data for security purposes.[50] Most

44 ECJ 20 September 2001, Case C-184/99, *Grzelczyk* [2001] ECR I-6193, para 31. Repeated in many other cases since, e.g. ECJ 11 July 2002, Case C-224/98, *Marie-Nathalie D'Hoop v Office national de l'emploi* [2002] ECR I-6191, para 28; ECJ 2 October 2003, Case C-148/02, *Carlos Garcia Avello v Belgian State* [2003] ECR I-11613, para 22; ECJ 29 April 2004, Case C-224/02, *Heikki Antero Pusa v Osuuspankkien Keskinäinen Vakuutusyhtiö* [2004] ECR I-5763, para 16; ECJ 29 April 2004, Cases C-482 and 493/01, *Georgios Orfanopoulos and Others (C-482/01) and Raffaele Oliveri (C-493/01) v Land Baden-Württemberg* [2004] ECR I-5257, para 65; ECJ 12 July 2005, Case C-403/03, *Egon Schempp v Finanzamt München V* [2005] ECR I-6421, para 15; ECJ 9 November 2006, Case C-520/04, *Pirkko Marjatta Turpeinen* [2006] ECR I-10685, para 18; ECJ 7 June 2007, Case C-50/06, *Commission v Netherlands* [2007] ECR I-4383, para 32.

45 See further, e.g. C. Jacqueson, 'Union Citizenship and the Court of Justice: Something New Under the Sun? Towards Social Citizenship' (2002) 27 *ELR* 260; A.-P. van der Mei, *Free Movement of Persons within the European Community: Cross-Border Access to Public Benefits*, Hart Publishing, Oxford, 2003; E. Spaventa, *Free Movement of Persons in the European Union*, Kluwer Law International, Alphen aan den Rijn, 2007; H. Verschueren, 'European (Internal) Migration Law as an Instrument for Defining the Boundaries of National Solidarity Systems', (2007) 9 *European Journal of Migration and Law* 307; S. Giubboni, 'Free Movement of Persons and European Solidarity', (2007) 13 *ELJ* 360; A. Somek, 'Solidarity Decomposed: Being and Time in European Citizenship' (2007) 32 *ELR* 787; A. Iliopoulou, *Libre circulation et non-discrimination, éléments du statut de citoyen de l'Union européenne*, Bruylant, Brussels, 2007.

46 The following analysis draws upon certain ideas presented in greater detail in M. Dougan, 'The Spatial Restructuring of National Welfare States within the European Union: The Contribution of Union Citizenship and the Relevance of the Treaty of Lisbon' in U. Neergaard, R. Nielsen and L. Roseberry (eds), *Integrating Welfare Functions into EU Law: From Rome to Lisbon*, DJØF Publishing, København, 2009.

47 On the expanded personal and material scope of Union law in the light of Union citizenship, e.g. A. Epiney, 'The Scope of Article 12 EC: Some Remarks on the Influence of European Citizenship', (2007) 13 *ELJ* 611; E. Spaventa, 'Seeing the Wood Despite the Trees? On the Scope of Union Citizenship and Its Constitutional Effects', (2008) 45 *CMLR* 13; Y. Borgmann-Prebil, 'The Rule of Reason in European Citizenship', (2008) 14 *ELJ* 328.

48 E.g. ECJ 24 November 1998, Case C-274/96, *Bickel and Franz* [1998] ECR I-7637.

49 E.g. ECJ 2 October 2003, Case C-148/02, *Carlos Garcia Avello v Belgian State* [2003] ECR I-11613.

50 E.g. ECJ 16 December 2008, Case C-524/06, *Heinz Huber v Bundesrepublik Deutschland* [2008] ECR I-9705.

importantly, perhaps, the Court's second-order rights extend to the provision of welfare support by the host or home society for the benefit of economically inactive Union citizens who are not, or may not be entirely, capable of supporting themselves and their families.[51]

The content of those second-order rights appears to have been determined in large part by policy choices made by the Court itself. In the case of welfare provision, such policy choices are orientated around the assumption that the creation of Union citizenship by the Maastricht Treaty implied a willingness on the part of the Member States and their populations to accept a degree of mutual cross-border social solidarity. In particular, as regards relations between an economically inactive migrant and his / her host state, the inevitable compromise between (on the one hand) the desire to offer meaningful benefits to Union citizens regardless of their economic or financial status and (on the other hand) the need to respect the Member State's limited willingness to pay for the upkeep of foreign nationals who might otherwise present an unreasonable burden upon its public finances, has gradually manifested itself in the task of identifying a "real link" between migrant and host society.[52] The closer the bond between the individual claimant and the Member State, the more secure will be the claimant's right to reside within the territory, free from the fear of expulsion on economic or financial grounds;[53] and the more extensive his / her right to equal treatment within the host society, as regards welfare and other social benefits.[54]

---

51 ECJ 12 May 1998, Case C-85/96, *María Martínez Sala* [1998] ECR I-2691; ECJ 20 September 2001, Case C-184/99, *Grzelczyk* [2001] ECR I-6193; ECJ 17 September 2002, Case C-413/99 *Baumbast* [2002] ECR I-7091.

52 The concept was first employed by the ECJ in ECJ 11 July 2002, Case C-224/98, *D'Hoop* [2002] ECR I-6191. Its potential relevance is not restricted to migrant welfare rights, or even Union citizenship: consider, e.g. the rulings in ECJ 12 September 2006, Case C-145/04, *Spain v United Kingdom* [2006] ECR I-7917 on voting rights to the European Parliament for certain TCNs and ECJ 7 July 2008, Case C-66/08, *Proceedings concerning the execution of a European arrest warrant issued against Szymon Kozłowski* [2008] ECR I-6041 on grounds for non-execution of a European Arrest Warrant.

53 E.g. ECJ 20 September 2001, Case C-184/99, *Grzelczyk* [2001] ECR I-6193; ECJ 17 September 2002, Case C-413/99, *Baumbast* [2002] ECR I-7091; ECJ 7 September 2004, Case C-456/02, *Michel Trojani v Centre public d'aide sociale de Bruxelles (CPAS)* [2004] ECR I-7573.

54 E.g. ECJ 12 May 1998, Case C-85/96, *María Martínez Sala* [1998] ECR I-2691; Case C-184/99, *Grzelczyk* [2001] ECR I-6193; ECJ 11 July 2002, Case C-224/98, *D'Hoop* [2002] ECR I-6191; ECJ 23 March 2004, Case C-138/02, *Brian Francis Collins v Secretary of State for Work and Pensions* [2004] ECR I-2703; ECJ 15 March 2005, Case C-209/03, *The Queen, on the application of Dany Bidar v London Borough of Ealing and Secretary of State for Education and Skills* [2005] ECR I-2119; ECJ 15 September 2005, Case C-258/04, *Office national de l'emploi v Ioannis Ioannidis* [2005] ECR I-8275. Indeed, the Court considered that only migrants already either in possession of a residence permit, or able to demonstrate a certain period of residence, could be considered in a comparable position to established residents and thus entitled to equal treatment within the host state at all: see, e.g. Case C-456/02, *Michel Trojani v Centre public d'aide sociale de Bruxelles (CPAS)* [2004] ECR I-7573.

A similar approach emerged as regards relations between a migrant Union citizen and his / her home state.[55] The tension between (on the one hand) the desire not to hinder the movement of Union citizens who may be dependent upon some form of public support and (on the other hand) the political, financial and practical constraints that favour respect for the territorially bounded nature particularly of non-contributory welfare provision, has also been resolved through resort to a "real link" principle.[56] In this context, the stronger the relationship between a given welfare benefit and the domestic system of social solidarity, the weaker the force of the argument for severing the cord connecting payment of benefits to residence within the national territory.[57] In addition, however, the Court will examine the degree to which the individual claimant may assert membership of his / her home state's welfare community, even after having left the national territory, on the basis of past or present links other than continuing residence alone, which are nevertheless sufficient to warrant a right of access to the relevant benefits.[58]

Such judicial choices about the existence and extent of the migrant's second-order rights are then substituted quite readily for the views of the relevant Member State; and in some cases, even in place of the wishes expressed by the Union legislature itself. Against the Member State, the Court's chief weapon is the proportionality test. Even where it is legitimate in principle for the (host or home) authorities to

---

55 Either in tandem with (as in ECJ 8 July 2004, Cases C-502/01 and C-31/02, *Silke Gaumain-Cerri v Kaufmännische Krankenkasse – Pflegekasse and Maria Barth v Landesversicherungsanstalt Rheinprovinz*, [2004] ECR I-6483) or even in contradiction to (in rulings such as ECJ 11 September 2007, Case C-287/05, *D. P. W. Hendrix v Raad van Bestuur van het Uitvoerings-instituut Werknemersverzekeringen*, [2007] ECR I-6909) the coordination rules contained in Regulation 1408/71 and Regulation 883/2004: see further below.

56 See further, e.g. M. Dougan, 'Expanding the Frontiers of Union Citizenship by Dismantling the Territorial Boundaries of the National Welfare States?', in C. Barnard and O. Odudu (eds), *The Outer Limits of European Union Law*, Hart Publishing, Oxford, 2009. Note also the importance attached to monitoring non-resident benefit recipients, e.g. ECJ 18 July 2006, Case C-406/04, *Gérald De Cuyper v Office national de l'emploi* [2006] ECR I-6947; ECJ 4 December 2008, Case C-221/07, *Krystyna Zablocka-Weyhermüller v Land Baden-Württemberg* [2008] ECR I-9029.

57 Consider, e.g. ECJ 27 September 1988, Case 313/86, *O. Lenoir v Caisse d'allocations familiales des Alpes-Maritimes* [1988] ECR 5391; ECJ 31 May 2001, Case C-43/99, *Ghislain Leclere and Alina Deaconescu v Caisse nationale des prestations familiales* [2001] ECR I-4265; ECJ 18 December 2007, Cases C-396/05, C-419/05 and C-450/05, *Doris Habelt (C-396/05), Martha Möser (C-419/05) and Peter Wachter (C-450/05) v Deutsche Rentenversicherung Bund*, [2007] ECR I-11895; ECJ 15 May 2008, Case C-228/07, *Jörn Petersen v Landesgeschäftsstelle des Arbeitsmarktservice Niederösterreich* [2008] ECR I-6989.

58 Consider, e.g. ECJ 26 October 2006, Case C-192/05, *K. Tas-Hagen and R. A. Tas v Raadskamer WUBO van de Pensioen- en Uitkeringsraad*, [2006] ECR I-10451; ECJ 11 September 2007, Case C-287/05, *D.P.W. Hendrix v Raad van Bestuur van het Uitvoeringsinstituut Werknemersverzekeringen*, [2007] ECR I-6909; ECJ 23 October 2007, Cases C-11–12/06, *Rhiannon Morgan v Bezirksregierung Köln (C-11/06) and Iris Bucher v Landrat des Kreises Düren (C-12/06)* [2007] ECR I-9161; ECJ 22 May 2008, Case C-499/06, *Halina Nerkowska v Zakład Ubezpieczeń Społecznych Oddział w Koszalinie* [2008] ECR I-3993.

expect a "real link" between a given claimant and the relevant welfare community, evidence to support that "real link" cannot be gathered exclusively on the basis of generalised criteria (such as past or continuing residency). The Member State must also give due consideration to the "personal circumstances" of each individual claimant, even if this implies taking into account factors or circumstances not recognised as relevant or compelling under the applicable domestic legislation.[59] Against the Union legislature, the Court has relied upon the idea that secondary legislation which itself purports to restrict the migrant's opportunities for free movement is nevertheless amenable to a form of "indirect judicial review" intended to guarantee that it does not unduly prejudice the existence or exercise of the Union citizen's rights, i.e. whereby Member States are obliged to apply Union legislation which appears to limit the rights of Union citizens in accordance with the general principles of Union law, so that the relevant Union rules may not be enforced against an individual where that would exceed what is necessary to protect the Member State's legitimate interests.[60]

Moreover, the nature of the migrant Union citizen's second-order rights seems to be shaped by a structure and style of judicial reasoning which treats "free movement" as an overriding (Union) policy goal at the expense of other legitimate manifestations of the (national) public interest. Despite Marshall's influential categorisation of social rights alongside more traditional civil and political rights in the triptych of modern citizenship,[61] other scholars have argued that social – and especially welfare rights – are marked by an important difference: they are fundamentally about the redistribution of income between social groups, and imply a claim on resources and legitimisation of the redistributive role of the state.[62] Questions about entitlement to welfare engage not only the individual's

---

59 Consider the rulings in Case C-224/98, *D'Hoop* [2002] ECR I-6191; ECJ 23 March 2004, Case C-138/02, *Brian Francis Collins v Secretary of State for Work and Pensions* [2004] ECR I-2703; ECJ 15 March 2005, Case C-209/03, *Bidar* [2005] ECR I-2119; ECJ 15 September 2005, Case C-258/04, *Office national de l'emploi v Ioannis Ioannidis* [2005] ECR I-8275; ECJ 11 September 2007, Case C-287/05, *D.P.W. Hendrix v Raad van Bestuur van het Uitvoeringsinstituut Werknemersverzekeringen* [2007] ECR I-6909; ECJ 23 October 2007, Cases C-11–12/06, *Rhiannon Morgan v Bezirksregierung Köln (C-11/06) and Iris Bucher v Landrat des Kreises Düren (C-12/06),* [2007] ECR I-9161; ECJ 22 May 2008, Case C-499/06, *Halina Nerkowska v Zakład Ubezpieczeń Społecznych Oddział w Koszalinie,* [2008] ECR I-3993. See further, e.g. E. Spaventa, 'Seeing the Wood Despite the Trees? On the Scope of Union Citizenship and Its Constitutional Effects', (2008) 45 *CMLR* 13.

60 In particular: ECJ 20 September 2001, Case C-184/99, *Grzelczyk* [2001] ECR I-6193; ECJ 17 September 2002, Case C-413/99, *Baumbast* [2002] ECR I-7091. Consider also the rulings in Case C-406/04 *De Cuyper* [2006] ECR I-6947; ECJ 11 September 2007, Case C-287/05, *D.P.W. Hendrix v Raad van Bestuur van het Uitvoeringsinstituut Werknemersverzekeringen,* [2007] ECR I-6909; ECJ 11 September 2008, Case C-228/07, *Jörn Petersen v Landesgeschäftsstelle des Arbeitsmarktservice Niederösterreich* [2008] ECR I-6989. See further, e.g. M. Dougan, 'The Constitutional Dimension to the Case Law on Union Citizenship', (2006) 31 *ELR* 613.

61 T. H. Marshall, *Citizenship and Social Class,* Cambridge University Press, 1949, reprinted Pluto Press, London, 1991.

62 M. Kleinman, *A European Welfare State?,* Palgrave, Basingstoke, 2002, pp 194–195.

personal expectation of social support, but also the relevant society's choices about the allocation of its available resources, which in turn reflect collective moral judgments concerning the nature of its social solidarity: what risks to protect against, what levels of support to offer, and which individuals fall within the catchment area of collective responsibility.[63] Yet it is arguable that the Court's approach risks neglecting that crucial collective dimension to social solidarity.[64]

In that regard, one might begin with the observation that it has become so easy to trigger the application of the provisions on Union citizenship that the mere existence of a prima facie infringement of the Treaty has surely lost its ability to tell us anything meaningful about the balance of policy interests at stake in any given dispute. In other words, breaching the Treaty has become so commonplace that the relevant national rules should not *per se* be treated with antagonism, as if it can thenceforth be taken for granted that they have offended against some higher public interest.[65] That would be to elevate the simple principle of movement – and incidentally, all of the second-order rights derived from that movement, such as individual rights to welfare support from the host or home state – above all other manifestations of the general good. Yet that often appears to be exactly the nature and outcome of judicial reasoning in free movement cases: having triggered the application of the Treaty on the basis of an individual right connected to movement, the onus then falls upon the Member State to explain and defend its disputed national rules, in accordance with the constraints imposed by the principle of proportionality and other general principles of Union law. The very structure of legal argumentation before the Court of Justice therefore emphasises from the outset the importance of the individual and endorses his/her claim of entitlement to welfare support, whereas the collective aspects of social solidarity are put on the defensive and thereby at an inherent disadvantage.[66]

---

63 For a detailed analysis of the theoretical nature of social solidarity, including the relationship between individual and collective interests, see S. Stjernø, *Solidarity in Europe: The History of an Idea,* Cambridge University Press, Cambridge, 2005.

64 Similar allegations have been raised against the "individualistic" approach to social and welfare rights in the EU's Charter of Fundamental Rights: see, e.g. M. Berezin and M. Schain (eds), *Europe Without Borders: Remapping Territory, Citizenship and Identity in a Transnational Age,* John Hopkins University Press, Baltimore, 2003. See further, e.g. J. Tooze, 'Social Security and Social Assistance', in T. Hervey and J. Kenner (eds), *Economic and Social Rights Under the EU Charter of Fundamental Rights,* Hart Publishing, Oxford, 2003; D. Damjanovic and B. de Witte, 'Welfare Integration through EU Law: The Overall Picture in the Light of the Lisbon Treaty' in U. Neergaard, R. Nielsen and L. Roseberry (eds), *Integrating Welfare Functions into EU Law: From Rome to Lisbon,* DJØF Publishing, København, 2009.

65 See, in a similar sense, N. Nic Shuibhne Annotation of *Schwarz, Commission v Germany* and *Morgan and Bucher* (2008) 45 *CMLR* 771.

66 See further, e.g. M. Dougan and E. Spaventa, 'Wish You Weren't Here... New Models of Social Solidarity in the European Union' in M. Dougan and E. Spaventa (eds), *Social Welfare and EU Law,* Hart Publishing, Oxford, 2005.

That inherent disadvantage is aggravated by certain other features of adjudication before the Court of Justice. On one side, the Court does not allow the process of triggering the Treaty (for example, on the basis of unequal treatment by the host state or a barrier to movement by the home state) to be complicated by the need for the individual to demonstrate empirically that his/her movement has actually been deterred or impeded in any meaningful way. The Court relies on intuitive – sometimes even counter-intuitive – assessments which attribute the average citizen with both penetrating foresight and inordinate sensitivity, such that almost any inequality of treatment for migrants acts as a deterrent to their apparently boundless expectation of unimpeded mobility.[67] On the other side, the Court often insists that Member States fearful of the consequences that rights to free movement and / or equal treatment for individual Union citizens might inflict upon national policy choices, even those recognised as valid imperative requirements capable in principle of justifying an infringement of the Treaty, must nevertheless produce firm evidence to substantiate those fears.[68] In several cases, Member States have failed to defend their national policy choices simply because they were unable to present to the Court fully documented empirical analyses to substantiate their concerns.[69] In the battle between competing suppositions, it seems that those favouring the individual will often trump those designed to protect the public interest, so that the nature as well as the burden of proof in free movement cases conspires against the collective aspects of social solidarity.

The case law on Union citizenship also illustrates how the process of judicial policymaking through the medium of the primary Treaty provisions often stands at odds with the system of variegated Union competences which underpinned the old TEU and EC Treaties (and are now expressly enshrined in the post-Lisbon TEU and TFEU). In fields such as health, education and social security, the Treaties confer upon the Union legislature only limited powers to intervene in the national legal systems, strictly circumscribed by the terms of the applicable legal bases (which, in most cases, expressly rule out the possibility of harmonising domestic law).[70] Yet the Member State's duty to respect the obligations imposed

---

67 For a vivid example, consider ECJ 1 April 2008, Case C-212/06, *Government of the French Community and Walloon Government v Flemish Government*, [2008] ECR I-1683.

68 Though not in every dispute: consider, e.g. ECJ 12 July 2001, Case C-157/99, *B.S.M. Geraets-Smits v Stichting Ziekenfonds VGZ and H.T.M. Peerbooms v Stichting CZ Groep Zorgverzekeringen* [2001] ECR I-5473; ECJ 23 October 2007, Cases C-11–12/06, *Rhiannon Morgan v Bezirksregierung Köln (C-11/06) and Iris Bucher v Landrat des Kreises Düren (C-12/06)*, [2007] ECR I-9161.

69 Consider, e.g. ECJ 13 May 2003, Case C-385/99, *V.G. Müller-Fauré v Onderlinge Waarborgmaatschappij OZ Zorgverzekeringen UA and E.E.M. van Riet v Onderlinge Waarborgmaatschappij ZAO Zorgverzekeringen* [2003] ECR I-4509; ECJ 7 July 2005, Case C-147/03, *Commission v Austria* [2005] ECR I-5969; ECJ 10 September 2009, Case C-269/07, *Commission v Germany*, [2009] ECR I-07811.

70 On health: ex-Article 152 EC (now Article 168 TFEU). On education: ex-Articles 149–150 EC (now Articles 165–166 TFEU). On social security: ex-Articles 18 and 137 EC (now Articles

directly under the Treaty, as interpreted by the ECJ in its free movement case law, manages to exert an increasingly profound influence on the exercise of domestic prerogatives concerning the organisation and functioning of their healthcare, education and social protection systems.

It is true that the Court's case law pursues an admirable logic when it refuses to exclude *per se* such matters as health, education and social security from the impact of the primary Treaty provisions.[71] But logic can provide Union law with only so much legitimacy. After all, the social, economic, political and cultural sensitivities of interfering with national rules on health, educational or welfare policy are similar regardless of whether that interference emanates from the Union legislature or instead the judiciary. Indeed, it is arguable that judicial intervention – precisely because it lacks a clear mandate, bypasses deliberation by democratic institutions, and (especially in cases concerning the interpretation of primary Treaty provisions) is difficult to amend or reverse – raises even greater legitimacy problems in fields of marginal Union responsibility than action by the accountable political institutions.

This incongruous disjunction between the willingness of the Court to rely on the primary Treaty provisions as a means to interfere in all manner of domestic policy choices, and the apparent inability of the Union's political institutions to take the initiative in exercising any binding influence of their own over exactly the same range of issues, can give rise to further difficulties. In some situations, such disjunction may actually have the incidental effect of expanding the Union's regulatory powers beyond the limits intended by the Treaties, as matters previously considered to be of purely complementary competence become amenable to harmonisation pursuant to the Union's free movement legal bases.[72] In other situations, where recourse to such legal bases is either not possible or simply not likely, the result of the Court's policy-making under the primary Treaty provisions may be to privilege the assertion of judicial authority over the

21 and 153 TFEU – the former provision extending the Union institutions' competence over social security / social protection for migrant Union citizens).

71 See, e.g. ECJ 16 May 2006, Case C-372/04, *The Queen, on the application of Yvonne Watts v Bedford Primary Care Trust and Secretary of State for Health* [2006] ECR I-4325, para 92 (as regards healthcare); ECJ 11 September 2007, Case C-76/05, *Herbert Schwarz and Marga Gootjes-Schwarz v Finanzamt Bergisch Gladbach* [2007] ECR I-6849, para 70 (as regards education); ECJ 22 May 2008, Case C-499/06, *Halina Nerkowska v Zakład Ubezpieczeń Społecznych Oddział w Koszalinie* [2008] ECR I-3993, paras 23–24 (as regards welfare benefits).

72 Consider the Commission's proposal for a directive on the application of patients' rights in cross-border healthcare (based on ex-Article 95 EC (now Article 114 TFEU)): COM(2008) 414 Final. Further, e.g. W. Sauter, 'The Proposed Patients' Rights Directive and the Reform of (Cross-Border) Healthcare in the European Union', (2009) 36 *LIEI* 109. See also: D. Wyatt, 'Community Competence to Regulate Medical Services', in M. Dougan and E. Spaventa (eds), *Social Welfare and EU Law*, Hart Publishing, Oxford, 2005; G. Davies, 'The Community's Internal Market-Based Competence to Regulate Healthcare: Scope, Strategies and Consequences', (2007) 14 *MJ* 215.

exercise of political power: the Court is free to express certain regulatory choices, but the other Union institutions are simply unable to respond with (different) policy preferences of their own.[73]

To a degree, such a phenomenon is hardly new to the Union legal order. Indeed, the early spill-over effects of the primary Treaty provisions were often the subject of favourable academic comment: the judicial nurturing of embryonic policies towards (say) the protection of the environment, workers or consumers took place under the auspices of the free movement provisions, and was accompanied by the articulation of common social policy values by the political institutions in the exercise of their market-building competences, well before the introduction into the Treaties of any explicit regulatory powers in such fields.[74] But the relevant legal and political circumstances have since changed enormously. Legally, there are few policy fields left where the Treaties do not define explicitly the nature and limits of Union competences – and such definitions are phrased in more variegated and more precise terms than in earlier versions of the Treaties – making the process of spill-over more complex and contested than in the past.[75] Politically, the state of benign neglect from which the Court surely benefited in the pre-Maastricht era has given way to a closer and more critical scrutiny of the impact of judicial law-making on Member State competences and inter-institutional relations.[76] Similarly, as disputes such as *Tobacco Advertising* and *Environmental Crimes* show, the ability of the Union institutions to persuade the Court to endorse a broad construction of their existing competences now gives rise to acute concerns as regards the principle of attributed powers.[77]

In short: the case law on Union citizenship in the decade following *Sala* provided the basis for an extensive body of academic criticism focusing on allegations that the Court had embarked upon a process of social engineering through the top-down manufacture of novel welfare rights and obligations; embedded its own policy preferences into the primary Treaty provisions in a manner that

---

73 Consider, e.g. the limitations on internal market competence imposed under ex-Article 95(2) EC (now Article 114(2) TFEU).

74 Further, e.g. D. Chalmers, 'The Single Market: From Prima Donna to Journeyman' in J. Shaw and G. More (eds), *New Legal Dynamics of European Union,* Clarendon Press, Oxford, 1995; P. Craig, 'The Evolution of the Single Market', in C. Barnard and J. Scott (eds), *The Law of the Single European Market: Unpacking the Premises,* Hart Publishing, Oxford, 2002.

75 See, e.g. A. von Bogdandy and J. Bast, 'The Federal Order of Competences' in A. von Bogdandy and J. Bast (eds), *Principles of European Constitutional Law,* Hart Publishing, Oxford, 2nd ed, 2010. Further: R. Schütze, *From Dual to Cooperative Federalism: The Changing Structure of European Law,* Oxford University Press, 2009.

76 Further, e.g. J. Weiler, 'Journey to an Unknown Destination: A Retrospective and Prospective of the European Court of Justice in the Arena of Political Integration', (1993) 31 *JCMS* 417.

77 ECJ 5 October 2000, Case C-376/98, *Germany v Parliament and Council* [2000] ECR I-8419 and ECJ 13 September 2005, Case C-176/03, *Commission v Council,* [2005] ECR I-7879 (respectively). See further, e.g. S. Weatherill, 'Competence and Legitimacy' in C. Barnard and O. Odudu (eds), *The Outer Limits of European Union Law,* Hart Publishing, Oxford, 2009.

appreciably constricts the room for choosing to adopt a different policy choice, certainly of the Member States acting individually, and to some extent also of the Council and European Parliament in the exercise of the regulatory competences conferred upon them by the Treaties; tended to elevate free movement within the EU over all other manifestations of the general interest, in particular, by privileging individual welfare rights and expectations over the collective interests and priorities normally inherent in concepts of social solidarity; and risked aggravating such a state of "constitutional asymmetry" by the way in which the political institutions, even if minded to do so, might be hamstrung by their limited regulatory competences and thus unable to substitute a different assessment of how to balance the competing public goals.[78]

## 4. DEVELOPMENTS IN THE CITIZENSHIP CASE LAW SINCE 2008

Since 2008, however, the Court's previously clear and consistent case law on the free movement rights associated with Union citizenship has undergone a strikingly sudden change, becoming more confused and more unpredictable, which might well suggest a new mood of uncertainty about the appropriate direction of judicial policymaking and its constitutional relationship to the Union's political institutions. Such developments have concerned both the technique of "indirect judicial review" over regulatory choices of the Union legislature which restrict the rights enjoyed by Union citizens, and the obligation incumbent upon the Member States to undertake a "personal circumstances" assessment in order to comply with the proportionality principle.

Dealing first with indirect judicial review, two recent rulings have explored the Court's attitude towards the restrictive provisions now contained in Article 24(2) Directive 2004/38, which derogate from the general right of Union citizens to equal treatment on grounds of nationality, by providing that the Member State is not obliged to offer maintenance assistance to migrant students unless and until they qualify as permanent residents after living in the host territory for five years, or to provide social assistance to migrant workseekers throughout the period when they reside in the host state prior to becoming engaged in gainful employment.[79]

---

[78] Cp. F. Scharpf, 'The European Social Model: Coping With the Challenges of Diversity' (2002) 40 *JCMS* 645.

[79] [2004] OJ L158/77.

*Förster* concerned a German national who moved to the Netherlands in 2000 and began studying for a university degree there in 2001.[80] Upon completion of that degree in 2004, she entered employment as a social worker in the Netherlands. Throughout her studies, Förster had undertaken various kinds of paid employment, and also received maintenance assistance for her university studies from the Dutch authorities. However, an investigation into her employment record showed that Förster had in fact been out of work for a period of six months during 2003, and the Dutch authorities therefore sought recovery of that portion of her maintenance grant. Under Dutch law, migrant Union nationals who are not in employment are only entitled to student grants if they have been lawfully resident in the Netherlands for at least five years (no such requirement being imposed upon students of Dutch nationality). Förster challenged the Dutch rules relying on the Court's previous ruling in *Bidar*.[81] There, English rules on access to student loans requiring at least three years residency prior to attending university, and imposing a requirement that claimants be "settled" in the UK which in practice was virtually impossible for migrant EU students to satisfy, were declared incompatible with the right to equal treatment under ex-Article 12 EC (now Article 18 TFEU).[82]

In principle, the Court agreed that Förster was entitled to benefit from the principle of equal treatment as regards access to the Dutch maintenance grant. But in practice, the Court chose to distinguish *Bidar* and uphold the validity of the Dutch rules. According to the Court, the English rules at issue in *Bidar* were fatally flawed not so much by the three year residency requirement, but rather because of the condition that claimants had also to be "settled" in the UK, the latter being virtually impossible for any migrant student to fulfil, regardless of their actual degree of integration into the host society. Yet the ruling in *Bidar* also affirmed that the host state may ensure that the grant of maintenance assistance to foreign students does not become an unreasonable burden which could have consequences for the overall level of assistance granted by that Member State. It is legitimate for a Member State to grant maintenance assistance only to students who have demonstrated a certain degree of integration into the host society, evidenced by the fact that the student in question has resided in the host state for a certain length of time. Here, the Dutch requirement of five years residence within the Netherlands could be considered appropriate and proportionate to that objective (provided it was applied by the national authorities on the basis of clear criteria known in advance).

80 ECJ 18 November 2008, Case C-158/07, *Förster* [2008] ECR I-8507.
81 ECJ 15 March 2005, Case C-209/03, *Bidar* [2005] ECR I-2119.
82 See further, e.g. C. Barnard, Annotation of *Bidar* (2005) 42 *CMLR* 1465; O. Golynker, 'Student Loans: the European Concept of Social Justice According to *Bidar*', (2006) 31 *ELR* 390.

There are several doctrinal weaknesses in the Court's ruling in *Förster* – not least the idea that directly discriminatory national rules can be objectively justified by the "real link" imperative requirement.[83] But more important for present purposes is the fact that the Court apparently backtracked from the technique of indirect judicial review previously cultivated in its case law on Union citizenship. Many commentators had identified a direct tension between the *Bidar* ruling on equal treatment as regards maintenance assistance within the host state and the more restrictive provisions contained in Article 24(2) Directive 2004/38 as subsequently enacted by the Union legislature. It was further argued that that tension could be resolved precisely through recourse to indirect judicial review, i.e. requiring the Member States to offer equal treatment, despite the express provisions of Directive 2004/38, where required by the principle of proportionality.[84] Indeed, exactly such an approach was recommended to the Court in *Förster* by Advocate General Mazák.[85] The ECJ, however, refused to follow suit. On the contrary, even though Directive 2004/38 had not yet entered into force at the time of the dispute in *Förster*, the Court directly referred to Article 24(2) in support of its relatively accommodating approach towards the disputed Dutch residency requirement. *Förster* therefore implies that national rules on access to student financial assistance, adopted in compliance with the "five year test" contained in Article 24(2) Directive 2004/38, will be enforceable as such. In itself, that makes *Förster* a rather poor disciple of the principle enunciated by the Court only shortly before in *Metock*, to the effect that Directive 2004/38 is intended to strengthen the legal status of Union citizens and should not be interpreted so as to confer fewer rights than existed before its adoption.[86] But beyond that, how far does the Court's more conservative approach in *Förster* suggest that the technique of indirect judicial review will henceforth be restricted or even suppressed, to be replaced by greater judicial deference towards the parameters of welfare support for Union citizens set out by the political institutions?[87]

83 Further: M. Dougan, 'Legal Developments' in T. Haughton and N. Copsey (eds), *Journal of Common Market Studies: The European Union Annual Review 2008 / 2009*, Blackwell Publishing, Oxford, 2009; S. O'Leary, 'Equal Treatment and EU Citizens: A New Chapter on Cross-Border Educational Mobility and Access to Student Financial Assistance', (2009) 34 *ELR* 612.

84 E.g. M. Dougan, 'Fees, Grants, Loans and Dole Cheques: Who Covers the Costs of Migrant Education within the EU?', (2005) 42 *CMLR* 943; O. Golynker, 'Student Loans: the European Concept of Social Justice According to *Bidar*', (2006) 31 *ELR* 390.

85 ECJ 18 November 2008, Case C-158/07, *Förster* [2008] ECR I-8507, paras 128–133 Opinion.

86 ECJ 25 July 2008, Case C-127/08, *Blaise Baheten Metock and Others v Minister for Justice, Equality and Law Reform* [2008] ECR I-6241. Contrast also with ECJ 23 February 2010, Case C-480/08, *Maria Teixeira v London Borough of Lambeth and Secretary of State for the Home Department*, nyr; ECJ 23 February 2010, Case C-310/08, *London Borough of Harrow v Nimco Hassan Ibrahim and Secretary of State for the Home Department*, nyr.

87 Cp. O. Golynker, Annotation of *Förster* (2009) 46 *CMLR* 2021; S. O'Leary, 'Equal Treatment and EU Citizens: A New Chapter on Cross-Border Educational Mobility and Access to Student Financial Assistance', (2009) 34 *ELR* 612.

In that regard, one should consider the implications of the subsequent ruling in *Vatsouras*, concerning two Greek nationals working in Germany but in receipt of social benefits to top-up the relatively low income they derived from their employment.[88] When that employment came to an end, the claimant's benefits were also withdrawn by the German authorities, on the grounds that they no longer qualified for support as migrant Union workers. Working on the (questionable) assumption that the two claimants were to be classed merely as migrant workseekers, the nature of their rights under Union law seemed to be confused by a divergence between the Court's established case law and the Union legislature's subsequent regulatory choices. The ruling in *Collins* had held that migrant workseekers are entitled, thanks to Union citizenship, to claim equal treatment as regards social benefits intended to facilitate access to the national labour market (provided they can demonstrate a "real link" to the host society, in particular, by establishing that the claimant has, for a reasonable period of time, in fact genuinely sought work in the host state).[89] But *Collins* thereby seemed directly to contradict the approach preferred by the Union legislature, as manifested in Article 24(2) Directive 2004/38, of expressly ruling out any entitlement of migrant workseekers to social assistance within the host territory.

Before the judgment in *Vatsouras* was delivered, there seemed to be two main options for bridging that divergence between judges and legislators. In the first place, following its established case law on indirect judicial review, the Court could have ruled that Article 24(2) Directive 2004/38 may well be valid, but it is nevertheless a limitation on the rights of migrant workseekers as conferred by the Treaty itself, and must as such be applied by the Member States with due regard to the principle of proportionality.[90] In the second place, following the more recent precedent of *Förster*, the Court could have ruled that national rules which faithfully and literally transpose the provisions of Article 24(2) Directive 2004/38 are to be accepted per se as an enforceable limitation on the rights of migrant

88 ECJ 4 June 2009, Cases C-22/08 & C-23/08, *Athanasios Vatsouras (C-22/08) and Josif Koupatantze (C-23/08) v Arbeitsgemeinschaft (ARGE) Nürnberg 900*, [2009] ECR I-04585. Consider also various recent rulings concerning the interaction between the primary Treaty provisions and the secondary legislation on social security coordination, e.g. contrast ECJ 16 July 2009, Case C-208/07, *Petra von Chamier-Glisczinski v Deutsche Angestellten-Krankenkasse*, [2009] ECR I-06095; with ECJ 1 October 2009, Case C-3/08, *Ketty Leyman v Institut national d'assurance maladie-invalidité (INAMI)* [2009] ECR I-09085.

89 ECJ 23 March 2004, Case C-138/02, *Brian Francis Collins v Secretary of State for Work and Pensions* [2004] ECR I-2703. See also ECJ 15 September 2005, Case C-258/04, *Office national de l'emploi v Ioannis Ioannidis*, [2005] ECR I-8275. See further, e.g. J. Meulman and H. de Waele, 'Funding the Life of Brian: Jobseekers, Welfare Shopping and the Frontiers of European Citizenship', (2004) 31 *LIEI (Legal Issues of Economic Integration)* 275; H. Oosterom-Staples, Annotation of *Collins* (2005) 42 *CMLR* 205.

90 E.g. M. Dougan, 'The Court Helps Those Who Help Themselves... The Legal Status of Migrant Workseekers Under Community Law in the Light of the *Collins* Judgment', (2005) *EJSS (European Journal of Social Security)* 7; O. Golynker, 'Jobseekers' Rights in the European Union: Challenges of Changing the Paradigm of Social Solidarity', (2005) 30 *ELR* 111.

Union citizens – such provisions reflecting the need to demonstrate a "real link" to the host society, the criteria for which have now been determined exhaustively by the Union legislature.[91]

Yet in the end, the decision in *Vatsouras* follows neither of those options. The Court began by affirming its ruling in *Collins*: migrant workseekers who have established real links with the labour market of the host state are entitled to rely on the primary Treaty provisions in order to receive financial benefits which are intended to facilitate access to that labour market. It is for the competent national authorities and, where appropriate, the national courts not only to establish the existence of a real link with the host labour market, but also to assess the constituent elements of the relevant benefit, in particular, its purposes and the conditions subject to which it is granted. In any event, the derogation from the principle of equal treatment for Union citizens as provided for under Article 24(2) Directive 2004/38 must be construed in accordance with the Treaty itself. Financial benefits which, independently of their status under national law, are intended to facilitate access to the host labour market cannot be regarded as constituting "social assistance" within the meaning of Article 24(2) Directive 2004/38.

In other words, the Court in *Vatsouras* held that the reference to "social assistance" in Article 24(2) Directive 2004/38 does not include benefits which are intended to facilitate access to the national labour market; on that basis, the veracity of the ruling in *Collins* was not affected by the adoption of the new Directive, while the validity of the new Directive is not called into question by upholding the ruling in *Collins*. Such reasoning is not very persuasive: it was widely assumed that the reference in Article 24(2) Directive 2004/38 to "social assistance" was not meant in some narrow and technical sense, but should be construed broadly so as to cover any publicly funded financial benefit claimed by migrant workseekers, in keeping with the apparent desire of the Union legislature to absolve host states from an unfair burden towards that particular category of economically inactive Union citizen.[92] Furthermore, although the Court in *Vatsouras* identified one category of benefit which does not fall within the economy of Article 24(2), it has still not provided a positive definition of those benefits which do count as "social assistance".[93] In that regard, it should be borne in mind that the implications

[91] See further: AG Ruiz-Jarabo Colomer 12 March 2009 in Cases C-22/08 & C-23/08, *Athanasios Vatsouras (C-22/08) and Josif Koupatantze (C-23/08) v Arbeitsgemeinschaft (ARGE) Nürnberg 900* [2009] ECR I-04585.

[92] Further, e.g. M. Dougan and E. Spaventa, 'Wish You Weren't Here... New Models of Social Solidarity in the European Union', in M. Dougan and E. Spaventa (eds), *Social Welfare and EU Law*, Hart Publishing, Oxford, 2005.

[93] Consider the definition of social assistance under Regulation 1408/71 and Regulation 883/2004, e.g. ECJ 31 March 1977, Case 79/76, *Carlo Fossi v Bundesknappschaft* [1977] ECR 667. Consider also the ruling in ECJ 4 March 2010, Case C-578/08, *Rhimou Chakroun v Minister van*

of adopting a more restricted interpretation of that concept are not limited to the particular situation of migrant workseekers: "social assistance" is employed elsewhere in Directive 2004/38 to define the residency rights of economically inactive migrants, so that the narrow definition hinted at in *Vatsouras* might also have the incidental effect of confining further the circumstances in which Member States may consider such Union citizens to have become an "unreasonable burden" upon its resources.[94]

In any event, the Court's approach in *Vatsouras* confuses rather than clarifies the task of ascertaining the current status of the technique of indirect judicial review. If (on the one hand) the Court in *Vatsouras* had followed *Förster* and denied that the German rules were in breach of Union law, we would at least have had a clear signal that such indirect judicial review was in full-scale retreat. If (on the other hand) the Court in *Vatsouras* had simply applied its established case law and insisted on the proportionate application of Article 24(2), we could have assumed that the case law on Union citizenship was still generally on the march – with the possible exception of the rights enjoyed by migrant students vis-à-vis their host state, where *Förster* suggested an appreciable but specific and limited change in the Court's approach.[95] Instead, all we can take safely from the ruling in *Vatsouras* is that benefits intended to facilitate access to the labour market fall altogether outside the scope of Article 24(2) and remain subject to the "real link" assessment previously articulated in *Collins*. But as regards social assistance within the meaning of the Directive, *Vatsouras* gives no indication of whether such benefits will be exempted per se from the right to equal treatment in accordance with the letter of Article 24(2) and the spirit of *Förster*; or instead whether that provision remains amenable in the future to the technique of indirect judicial review, so that the national authorities might well be obliged to offer migrant workseekers access to social assistance, even in the technical sense of Article 24(2), where the principle of proportionality so requires.[96]

Turning secondly to the requirement for Member States to undertake a personal circumstances assessment of each individual migrant Union citizen, before refusing access to any given social benefit, the recent case law has if anything been even more confusing and incoherent. The *Förster* ruling again provides a

*Buitenlandse Zaken*, nyr. concerning the definition of "social assistance" for the purposes of the Family Reunification Directive 2003/86 [2003] OJ L251/12.

94 See, in particular, Articles 7 and 14 Directive 2004/38.

95 And possibly a shift of emphasis from the financial responsibilities of the host state to those of the home state: cp. ECJ 23 October 2007, Cases C-11–12/06, *Rhiannon Morgan v Bezirksregierung Köln (C-11/06) and Iris Bucher v Landrat des Kreises Düren (C-12/06),* [2007] ECR I-9161. See further, e.g. M. Dougan, 'Cross-border educational mobility and the exportation of student financial assistance', (2008) 33 *ELR* 723.

96 For a different perspective, see E. Fahey, 'Interpretive Legitimacy and the Distinction Between 'Social Assistance' and 'Workseekers Allowance', (2009) 34 *ELR* 933.

useful starting point. It is particularly striking that the Court in that case made no effort whatsoever to require the Dutch authorities to examine the claimant's personal circumstances, with a view to establishing whether her "real link" to Dutch society could be verified by reference to factors other than the generalised requirement of five years lawful residency within the national territory. Yet if her personal circumstances had indeed been taken into account, the claimant would surely have had a strong case for arguing that the blanket application of the disputed Dutch rule was entirely disproportionate in her case, since she had apparently become fully integrated into Dutch society at an educational, professional and personal level.[97] Does *Förster* therefore indicate that the Court has begun to retreat back, not just from the principle of indirect judicial review over Union secondary legislation, but also from an interventionist approach to the justification of national rules hindering the free movement or equal treatment rights of migrant Union citizens, based on the personal circumstances assessment?[98] If so, that would seem to vindicate O'Brien's argument that the Court's understanding of Union citizenship is more concerned with guaranteeing procedural fairness than with promoting any particular substantive vision of transnational solidarity – rendering academic concerns about intrusive judicial policymaking at the expense of vital Member State competences premature if not altogether exaggerated.[99]

Again, however, the judicial will might seem determined to remain inscrutable. On the one hand, the Court in other rulings following *Förster* has endorsed the use by Member States of entirely generalised criteria by which to restrict the free movement rights of migrant Union citizens, appearing to accept that such blanket rules protect the public interest in a proportionate manner, without imposing any additional obligation to undertake specific consideration also of the individual circumstances of any given claimant. Consider, for example, the judgment in *Wolzenburg*,[100] which concerned the principle of equal treatment as regards, not the provision of welfare support to migrant Union citizens, but rather national implementation of the European Arrest Warrant Framework Decision.[101] In particular, Dutch rules providing for the non-execution of a European Arrest

[97] Cp. AG Mazák 10 July 2008, Case C-158/07, *Förster* [2008] ECR I-8507, paras 128–133 Opinion.

[98] Cp. O. Golynker, Annotation of *Förster* (2009) 46 *CMLR* 2021; S. O'Leary, 'Equal Treatment and EU Citizens: A New Chapter on Cross-Border Educational Mobility and Access to Student Financial Assistance', (2009) 34 *ELR* 612.

[99] C. O'Brien, "Real links, abstract rights and false alarms: the relationship between the ECJ's 'real link' case law and national solidarity', (2008) 33 *ELR* 643. Cp. criticism of the vague and flexible nature of the "real link" concept by S. O'Leary, 'Solidarity and Citizenship Rights in the Charter of Fundamental Rights of the European Union', in G. de Búrca (ed), *EU Law and the Welfare State*, Oxford University Press, 2005; S. Besson and A. Utzinger, 'Future Challenges of European Citizenship: Facing a Wide-Open Pandora's Box', (2007) 13 *ELJ* 573.

[100] ECJ 6 October 2009, Case C-123/08, *Dominic Wolzenburg* [2009] ECR I-09621.

[101] Framework Decision 2002/584 [2002] OJ L190/1.

Warrant in the case of migrant Union citizens, with a view to the enforcement of a custodial sentence, only if they had been lawfully resident within the national territory for a continuous period of five years, were not considered incompatible with ex-Article 12 EC (now Article 18 TFEU): such a blanket requirement was judged both appropriate and necessary to its objective of reserving the possibility of non-execution to persons who could demonstrate a certain degree of integration into the host society. *Wolzenburg* thus shares with *Förster* not only the Court's willingness to justify apparently directly discriminatory rules by reference to an imperative requirement, but also its uncritical acceptance of a generalised and exclusive residency criterion for establishing the crucial "real link" between migrant citizen and host society.[102]

On the other hand, more light-touch rulings such as *Förster* and *Wolzenburg* live cheek-by-jowl with several decisions where the Court still insists that Member States undertake an assessment of each individual Union citizen's personal circumstances before restricting the exercise of his / her fundamental Treaty freedoms. Consider, for example, the rulings in *Nerkowska* and *Grunkin and Paul* (both delivered shortly before the judgment in *Förster*).[103] In the former case, Polish rules under which the payment of civilian war benefits was limited to resident nationals were found to breach the Union citizen's right to free movement, and could not be objectively justified where an overall assessment of the claimant's personal circumstances indicated that, despite being non-resident, he / she could nevertheless demonstrate a certain degree of connection to the relevant society. In the latter case, ex-Article 18 EC (now Article 21 TFEU) was held to preclude the German authorities from refusing to recognise an own national's surname as it had been determined and registered in another Member State, where the claimant had actually been born and since resided; however legitimate the Member State's objectives in regulating the use of surnames by its own nationals, those objectives were outweighed by considerations relating to the specific situation of this particular claimant.

If *Förster* really marked the Court's abandonment of its personal circumstances approach to Union citizenship, it would therefore have amounted to a remarkably sudden as well as silent *volte face*. But any such abandonment seems all the more unlikely given that, unlike in *Wolzenburg*, other post-*Förster* rulings have once more affirmed the importance of conducting a personal circumstances

102 It is worth noting that the ECJ in *Wolzenburg* referred explicitly to both the ruling in *Förster* and the period laid down in Directive 2004/38 for acquisition of the right to permanent residence.

103 ECJ 22 May 2008, Case C-499/06, *Halina Nerkowska v Zakład Ubezpieczeń Społecznych Oddział w Koszalinie* [2008] ECR I-3993; ECJ 14 October 2008, Case C-353/06, *Stefan Grunkin and Dorothee Regina Paul* [2008] ECR I-7639.

assessment.[104] For example, in *Gottwald*, Austrian rules restricting free travel on toll roads to disabled persons ordinarily resident in the national territory were judged compatible with ex-Article 12 EC (now Article 18 TFEU), taking into account the flexible manner in which the national authorities were prepared to recognise other factors (such as regular travel by a non-resident to the territory for professional or personal reasons) capable of demonstrating a certain degree of integration between the claimant and the host society.[105] Moreover, in *Rottmann*, German rules providing for the withdrawal of nationality acquired by naturalisation, on the grounds that the claimant had perpetrated a deception, and thus leading to the loss also of Union citizenship and its associated rights, fell within the scope of Union law and had to be objectively justified. For those purposes, the principle of proportionality required the competent national court to have regard to all relevant circumstances, including any adverse consequences for the claimant and his / her family, the gravity of the deception offence, the time elapsed since naturalisation, and the possibilities for recovering the claimant's original nationality.[106]

Overall, therefore, it would be inaccurate to assert that the ruling in *Förster* marks the death of the ECJ's creative, adventurous, even aggressive interpretation of Union citizenship. Viewed together with other decisions such as *Vatsouras* on indirect judicial review, and *Wolzenburg* or *Rottmann* on the personal circumstances assessment, the case law suggests not only the potential emergence of a significant differentiation in the quality of the rights enjoyed by various categories of Union citizens, but also an unhelpful fragmentation in the range of legal tools by which the Court reasons through the impact of Union citizenship upon both individual national policy choices and the complex political bargains struck by the other Union institutions.[107]

## 5. A MORE CONSTRUCTIVE READING OF THE CITIZENSHIP CASE LAW?

From a purely doctrinal viewpoint, the most recent case law on Union citizenship therefore appears increasingly confusing and unpredictable. It does nevertheless serve the valuable function of reminding us to keep allegations of judicial ac-

104 Note also the particular circumstances (even if they were not entirely personalised) taken into account in ECJ 23 April 2009, C-544/07, *Uwe Rüffler v Dyrektor Izby Skarbowej we Wrocławiu Ośrodek Zamiejscowy w Wałbrzychu* [2009] ECR I-03389.

105 ECJ 1 October 2009, Case C-103/08, *Arthur Gottwald v Bezirkshauptmannschaft Bregenz* [2009] ECR I-09117.

106 ECJ 2 March 2010, Case C-135/08, *Janko Rottman v Freistaat Bayern*, nyr.

107 Cp. E. Spaventa, 'The Constitutional Impact of Union Citizenship', in U. Neergaard, R. Nielsen and L. Roseberry (eds), *The Role of Courts in Developing a European Social Model: Theoretical and Methodological Perspectives*, DJØF Publishing, København, 2010.

tivism within their proper perspective and context. In particular, a (necessarily brief) retrospective on the Court's jurisprudence suggests that the judicial transformation of Union citizenship has in fact taken place within a long-term process of constitutional dialogue and may well have been decisively influenced by the evolving political environment of European integration.

To begin with, it is worth recalling that the Court's expansive definition of "worker" for the purposes of ex-Article 39 EC (now Article 45 TFEU),[108] and its equally generous interpretation of the social benefits attached to the status of economically active migrant,[109] meant that, by the 1980s, the right to free movement had already drifted away from its original and purely functional relationship to the construction of an Internal Market. Insofar as the Court's case law helped pave the way towards a more socially oriented conception of free movement, one could argue that it was perfectly in tune with the political leanings of the time. Since the early 1970s, and increasingly throughout the period building up to and following the Single European Act, the (then) Community institutions, as well as the European Council, had been encouraging a more balanced orientation in the EEC's activities and priorities so that economic integration and growth were not pursued to the total neglect of social protection and inclusion.[110] The political institutions also picked up where the Court's case law under ex-Article 39 EC (now Article 45 TFEU) had necessarily left off: the legislature enacted the three Residency Directives in 1990–1993, extending rights beyond the economically active also for the benefit of the financially independent;[111] for their part, the Member States in their capacity as "masters of the Treaties" created Union citizenship, and its associated right to free movement, under the Maastricht Treaty.[112]

---

108 E.g. ECJ 23 March 1982, Case 53/81, *D.M. Levin v Staatssecretaris van Justitie* [1982] ECR 1035; ECJ 3 June 1986, Case 139/85, *R. H. Kempf v Staatssecretaris van Justitie* [1986] ECR 1741; ECJ 26 February 1992, Case C-357/89, *V.J.M. Raulin v Minister van Onderwijs en Wetenschappen,* [1992] ECR I-1027.

109 E.g. ECJ 30 September 1975, Case 32/75, *Anita Cristini v Société nationale des chemins de fer français,* [1975] ECR 1085; ECJ 14 January 1982, Case 65/81, *Francesco Reina and Letizia Reina v Landeskreditbank Baden-Württemberg* [1982] ECR I-33; ECJ 10 March 1993, Case C-111/91, *Commission v Luxembourg,* [1993] ECR I-817; ECJ 23 May 1996, Case C-237/94, *John O'Flynn v Adjudication Officer,* [1996] ECR I-2617.

110 See further, e.g. M. Dougan, 'Free Movement: The Workseeker as Citizen', (2001) 4 *CYELS* 9. Note in particular: Declaration by the Heads of Government of the Member States meeting at Paris on 19–20 October 1972 (EC Bull 10–1972); Reports from the *ad hoc* Committee on "A People's Europe" (EC Bull Supp 7/85).

111 Directive 90/364 [1990] OJ L180/26; Directive 90/365 [1990] OJ L180/28; Directive 93/96 [1993] OJ L317/59.

112 For early analyses of Union citizenship after its introduction by the Maastricht Treaty, e.g. C. Closa, 'The Concept of Citizenship in the Treaty on European Union', (1992) 29 *CMLR* 1137; R. Kovar and D. Simon, 'La Citoyenneté Européenne' [1993] *Cahiers de Droit Européen* 285; S. Hall, *Nationality, Migration Rights and Citizenship of the Union,* Martinus Nijhoff, Dordrecht, 1995; S. O'Leary, *The Evolving Concept of Community Citizenship: From the Free Movement of Persons to Union Citizenship,* Kluwer Law, The Hague, 1996.

Even if there is a general sense that the Member States did not intend any substantive changes to result from the introduction of ex-Article 18 EC (now Article 21 TFEU), they could hardly have been surprised if the ECJ felt entitled to infuse that provision with new meaning for itself.[113] The real question was how far the Court would go in interpreting the new provisions on Union citizenship and thus in extending rights to residency, equal treatment and (more generally) freedom from "barriers to movement" beyond the existing categories of economically active persons under the primary Treaty provisions on workers and self-employed persons, and financially independent persons under the three Residency Directives. We have seen the Court's basic response in rulings such as *Sala*, *Grzelczyk* and *Baumbast*; then the flood of case law which followed and elaborated on them.[114] Adventurous and creative though those decisions undoubtedly were, it is worth making two observations.

In the first place, the underlying parameters for the Court's interpretation of Union citizenship continued to be provided by the provisions of the three Residency Directives as previously enacted by the legislature, and the qualified right to free movement under the Treaty as agreed upon by the Member States: ideas such as sufficient resources, comprehensive medical insurance and unreasonable burdens on the public finances still furnished the legal foundations upon which concepts such as real links, personal circumstances and indirect judicial review were then built by the Court (even if it became more difficult to see them, or at least easier to forget them, as the case law developed in more interesting ways). In the second place, it is tempting to speculate about the timing of the Court's rulings – particularly the long delay in delivering the *Sala* decision, followed by another significant gap before Union citizenship really took flight in *Grzelczyk* and *Baumbast*. Is it mere coincidence that the latter judgments were delivered in the early and essentially optimistic stages of the constitutional reform process begun in Nice and developed at Laeken?[115] Or did those decisions seem to the Court a timely and distinctive judicial contribution to the process of "bringing Europe closer to its citizens", in the midst of a major review of the Union's constitutional basis and constructive re-evaluation of its policy activities?

---

113 Cp. N. Nic Shuibhne, 'The Outer Limits of EU Citizenship: Displacing Economic Free Movement Rights?' in C. Barnard and O. Odudu (eds), *The Outer Limits of European Union Law*, Hart Publishing, Oxford, 2009.

114 ECJ 12 May 1998, Case C-85/96, *María Martínez Sala* [1998] ECR I-2691; ECJ 20 September 2001, Case C-184/99, *Grzelczyk* [2001] ECR I-6193; ECJ 17 September 2002, Case C-413/99 *Baumbast* [2002] ECR I-7091.

115 Nice European Council Presidency Conclusions of 8 December 2000; Laeken European Council Presidency Conclusions of 14 December 2001. *Grzelczyk* was delivered between the Nice and Laeken European Council meetings; *Baumbast* was decided during the deliberations of the Convention of the Future of Europe.

The latter hypothesis could go some way to explaining the Court's confident assertion in *Grzelczyk* that Union citizenship is destined to become the fundamental status of Member State nationals.[116] Indeed, without taking into account that broader political context, the normative basis for such an assertion would otherwise appear weak, and the allegation of activist and ambitious judicial policymaking all the more plausible to sustain. Certainly, the substantive legal content of the case law as it developed after *Grzelczyk* and *Baumbast* – and particularly the technique of indirect judicial review – attracted criticism on the grounds that the Court seemed to be usurping the role of the accountable political institutions, and extending rights to Union citizens beyond (and indeed despite) the clear limits negotiated and agreed by the Union legislature.[117] Yet it is striking how much of the Court's case law was to be effectively codified by the Council and European Parliament when they adopted Directive 2004/38: not only the key idea in *Grzelczyk* and *Baumbast* that recourse to social assistance should not justify automatic expulsion from the host state;[118] but also the emphasis on identifying a "real link" between claimant and host society, not least in the introduction of the right to permanent residency.[119] Much of what we once thought of as the Court's swaggering approach to cross-border social solidarity was thus effectively endorsed by the other Union institutions.[120]

It is true that not every aspect of the Court's case law on Union citizenship was adopted as its own by the Union legislature. Within Directive 2004/38 itself, as we have seen, the derogations from the principle of equal treatment in respect of students and workseekers seemed to directly contradict the rulings in *Bidar* and *Collins*.[121] Beyond that, the technique of indirect judicial review, and the requirement to assess each individual's personal circumstances, implied that application of the primary Treaty provisions on Union citizenship could wreak havoc with a whole range of Union secondary legislation capable of adversely affecting free movement rights. That was true not least as regards the social security coordination regime contained in Regulation 1408/71 (and now Regulation 883/2004),[122] which appeared positively to restrict or preclude the

---

116 ECJ 20 September 2001, Case C-184/99, *Grzelczyk* [2001] ECR I-6193, para 31.

117 In particular: K. Hailbronner, 'Union Citizenship and Access to Social Benefits' (2005) 42 *CMLR* 1245.

118 Article 14(3) Directive 2004/38.

119 Chapter IV Directive 2004/38. Note also the limited entitlement to equal treatment associated with the right to three months residency; arguably reflected in the ECJ's ruling in Case C-456/02, *Trojani* [2004] ECR I-7573 as regards the equal treatment rights of short-term economically inactive migrants.

120 See further, e.g. M. Dougan, 'The Constitutional Dimension to the Case Law on Union Citizenship' (2006) 31 *ELR* 613.

121 ECJ 15 March 2005, Case C-209/03, *Bidar* [2005] ECR I-2119; ECJ 23 March 2004, Case C-138/02, *Brian Francis Collins v Secretary of State for Work and Pensions* [2004] ECR I-2703.

122 Regulation 1408/71, last consolidated text published at [1997] OJ L28/1; Regulation 883/2004 [2004] OJ L200/1.

exportation of certain benefits (such as unemployment benefits and special non-contributory [cash] benefits) by non-resident claimants, and thus create barriers to movement from their home state by migrant Union citizens.[123]

If the Court had really been bent on a campaign of unilateral policymaking to enforce its own will regardless of, and if necessary despite, the preferences of the Union legislature as expressed in measures such as Directive 2004/38 and Regulation 1408/71 / 883/2004, then the clear and consistent case law developed between 1998 and 2008 could have provided it with the legal tools (indirect judicial review and personal circumstances assessment) to do so. To have stood by the assertion that Union citizenship is destined to be the fundamental status of Member States nationals would also have continued to furnish a respectable constitutional basis for elevating the relevant primary Treaty provisions to a special place within the Union's hierarchy of norms – justifying the Court's more rigorous examination of the impact of political choices by the national / Union authorities upon the exercise of the individual's fundamental freedoms.[124] But the Court has not proven so intransigent. Instead, the case law since 2008 can be seen as a new phase in an already well-established process of constitutional dialogue between judges and legislators; and also as a reflection of the changed political climate surrounding European integration since the negative French, Dutch and Irish referenda on constitutional reform.

In terms of constitutional dialogue, the case law since 2008 seems to reveal the Court struggling to reconcile its previous jurisprudence on indirect judicial review over Union secondary legislation, and on assessing the personal circumstances of individual claimants, with the fact that the Union legislature has since positively intervened in the legal framework governing the free movement rights of Union citizens. As regards Directive 2004/38 especially, rulings such as *Förster* and *Vatsouras* suggest that the Court remains unsure how to smoothen out the rough dovetails between Article 24(2) and its own case law on migrant

123 On the latter concept, as applied to Union citizenship, e.g. ECJ 11 July 2002, Case C-224/98, *D'Hoop* [2002] ECR I-6191; ECJ 11 December 2003, Case C-364/01, *The heirs of H. Barbier v Inspecteur van de Belastingdienst Particulieren/Ondernemingen buitenland te Heerlen* [2003] ECR I 15013; ECJ 29 April 2004, Case C-224/02, *Heikki Antero Pusa v Osuuspankkien Keskinäinen Vakuutusyhtiö* [2004] ECR I-5763; ECJ 26 October 2006, Case C-345/05, *Commission v Portugal* [2006] ECR I-10633; Case C-520/04, *Turpeinen* [2006] ECR I-10685; Case C-522/04, *Commission v Belgium* [2007] ECR I-5701; ECJ 11 September 2007, Case C-76/05, *Herbert Schwarz and Marga Gootjes-Schwarz v Finanzamt Bergisch Gladbach* [2007] ECR I-6849; ECJ 11 September 2007, Case C-318/05, *Commission v Germany* [2007] ECR I-6957; ECJ 17 January 2008, Case C-152/05, *Commission v Germany* [2008] ECR I-39. Cf. ECJ 16 September 2004, Case C-386/02, *Josef Baldinger v Pensionsversicherungsanstalt der Arbeiter* [2004] ECR I-8411; ECJ 12 July 2005, Case C-403/03, *Egon Schempp v Finanzamt München V* [2005] ECR I-6421.

124 In particular: M. Dougan, 'The Constitutional Dimension to the Case Law on Union Citizenship', (2006) 31 *ELR* 613.

students and workseekers. The picture is similarly messy as regards Regulation 1408/71 (and now Regulation 883/2004), where the parallel application of the primary Treaty provisions and the secondary coordination regime has also become standard practice.[125] On the one hand, the Court repeatedly invoked the legal tools developed in the context of Union citizenship so as to extend the right to exportation to persons and benefits deliberately excluded by the Union legislature from its coordination regime.[126] Furthermore, the Court in cases such as *Hendrix* was clearly willing to employ the primary Treaty provisions as a means of distorting the allocation of financial responsibilities intended by the Union legislature in respect of certain benefits (*in casu*, special non-contributory [cash] benefits) clearly included within and directly regulated by the coordination system.[127] On the other hand, rulings such as *Petersen* have hinted that, although parallel application of the Treaty and Regulation 1408/71 / 883/2004 will remain possible, and in particularly compelling circumstances may well result in divergent approaches, Member States whose social security legislation complies with the obligations imposed by the Union legislature will not be subject to a significantly more probing analysis by the Court on the basis of the Union citizenship provisions.[128]

That sense of confusion and contradiction is reinforced when one turns to consider the broader political context of the Court's case law since 2008. While the Union's generous approach to free movement by the economically active had always enjoyed an express mandate in the Treaty, benefited from a reasonably clear teleology to guide its development, and been furnished with the hard

[125] E.g. ECJ 8 July 2004, Cases C-502/01 and C-31/02, *Silke Gaumain-Cerri v Kaufmännische Krankenkasse – Pflegekasse and Maria Barth v Landesversicherungsanstalt Rheinprovinz* [2004] ECR I-6483; ECJ 16 July 2009, Case C-208/07, *Petra von Chamier-Glisczinski v Deutsche Angestellten-Krankenkasse* [2009] ECR I-06095.

[126] ECJ 26 October 2006, Case C-192/05, *K. Tas-Hagen and R. A. Tas v Raadskamer WUBO van de Pensioen- en Uitkeringsraad,* [2006] ECR I-10451; ECJ 18 July 2007, Case C-213/05, *Wendy Geven v Land Nordrhein-Westfalen* [2007] ECR I-6347; ECJ 18 July 2007, Case C-212/05, *Gertraud Hartmann v Freistaat Bayern* [2007] ECR I-6303; ECJ 23 October 2007, Cases C-11–12/06, *Rhiannon Morgan v Bezirksregierung Köln (C-11/06) and Iris Bucher v Landrat des Kreises Düren (C-12/06)* [2007] ECR I-9161; ECJ 22 May 2008, Case C-499/06, *Halina Nerkowska v Zakład Ubezpieczeń Społecznych Oddział w Koszalinie* [2008] ECR I-3993; ECJ 4 December 2008, Case C-221/07, *Krystyna Zablocka-Weyhermüller v Land Baden-Württemberg* [2008] ECR I-9029. Note the expanded list of excluded benefits now contained in Article 3(5) Regulation 883/2004 as amended by Regulation 988/2009 [2009] OJ L284/43.

[127] ECJ 11 September 2007, Case C-287/05, *D.P.W. Hendrix v Raad van Bestuur van het Uitvoeringsinstituut Werknemersverzekeringen* [2007] ECR I-6909.

[128] ECJ 11 September 2008, Case C-228/07, *Jörn Petersen v Landesgeschäftsstelle des Arbeitsmarktservice Niederösterreich* [2008] ECR I-6989. Cp. ECJ 18 July 2006, Case C-406/04 *Gérald De Cuyper v Office national de l'emploi* [2006] ECR I-6947. Consider also: ECJ 16 July 2009, Case C-208/07, *Petra von Chamier-Glisczinski v Deutsche Angestellten-Krankenkasse* [2009] ECR I-06095; but note ECJ 1 October 2009, Case C-3/08, *Ketty Leyman v Institut national d'assurance maladie-invalidité (INAMI)* [2009] ECR I-09085.

legal tools required to achieve its goals,[129] it must be admitted that the Court's bold conception of free movement by economically inactive Union citizens could call upon only an ambiguous mandate under the Treaty, and lacked any distinct teleology to direct its interpretation, while the legal armoury potentially available to the Union institutions was more limited in scope and strength. The Court's fragile normative basis for proceeding regardless – the idea that Union citizenship *really is* destined to be the fundamental status of all Member States nationals – therefore exposed a weak flank in the case law as the constitutional reform process began to unravel and its once-grand ambitions implode.[130]

It might be an interesting game to speculate about whether the smooth ratification and entry into force of the original Constitutional Treaty, as proposed by the Convention on the Future of Europe and adopted by the IGC in 2004, would have vindicated the Court's trailblazing vision of Union citizenship and emboldened the judges to push further their particular conception of supranational welfare solidarity.[131] But as events turned out, the crisis triggered by the negative referenda in France and the Netherlands in 2005, together with the fresh jolts from the Irish "no" vote in 2008, perhaps left dangerously exposed the main problems – allegations of social engineering and judicial activism – associated with the Court's case law on the welfare rights of Union citizens. Had the Court's adventurous interpretative approach to ex-Article 18 EC (now Article 21 TFEU) in fact been ahead of its time? Should the Court now retreat back towards a more restrained interpretation of Union citizenship, in which there was greater judicial deference towards political choices about how best to allocate a given society's available welfare resources? Recent rulings such as *Förster*, *Vatsouras*, *Wolzenburg* and *Rottmann* might suggest that the ECJ's vision has indeed become more complex, reflecting the political and social uncertainties of what it actually means to be a Union citizen, and of what the "fundamental destiny" of Union citizenship itself might be, in a world where the optimism expressed at Laeken appears to have borne (at best) only limited success.[132]

---

129 But note the argument that, in certain cases involving migrant workers (e.g. ECJ 18 July 2007, Case C-213/05, *Wendy Geven v Land Nordrhein-Westfalen* [2007] ECR I-6347; ECJ 18 July 2007, Case C-212/05, *Gertraud Hartmann v Freistaat Bayern* [2007] ECR I-6303), the "real link" as developed in the context of economically inactive citizens has actually triggered a contraction in the rights also of economically active individuals: see S. Currie, 'The Transformation of Union Citizenship', in M. Dougan and S. Currie (eds), *50 Years of the European Treaties: Looking Back and Thinking Forward*, Hart Publishing, Oxford, 2009; S. O'Leary, 'Developing an Ever Closer Union between the Peoples of Europe? A Reappraisal of the Case Law of the Court of Justice on the Free Movement of Persons and EU Citizenship', (2008) 27 *YEL* 167.

130 See further, e.g. M. Dougan, 'The Treaty of Lisbon 2007: Winning Minds, Not Hearts', (2008) 45 *CMLR* 617.

131 [2003] OJ C169 (draft Constitutional Treaty); [2004] OJ C310 (final Constitutional Treaty).

132 Other recent rulings deemed particularly controversial could also be located within the broader trajectory of the constitutional reform process, i.e. as examples of the Court anticipating certain reforms confident that they reflected the clear political will of the Member States (overlooking for present purposes whether such anticipation could be justified having regard

## 6. CONCLUDING REMARKS

Debates about judicial activism are always contingent upon unresolved questions concerning the proper nature of the judicial function within the Union legal order, and often depend upon a highly selective analysis of a small number of rulings, sometimes taken inappropriately out of their broader legal and political contexts, in a way that fails to offer a balanced and rounded portrait of the Court's vital contribution to the development of Union law. The case law on Union citizenship is no exception. On the one hand, that case law can indeed be portrayed as a case study in unilateral judicial policymaking, wherein the ECJ has spontaneously initiated an audacious process of social engineering, to the detriment of the political preferences of the Member States, as well as the regulatory prerogatives of the Union legislature itself. On the other hand, however, exactly the same jurisprudence can instead be interpreted as a more long-term, and more interactive, process of constitutional dialogue. In discharging the entirely proper but inherently difficult task of defining the relationship between its own interpretation of the primary Treaty provisions and / or the general principles of Union law (on the one hand) and the exercise of political discretion conferred by or recognised under the Treaties (on the other hand), the Court in its case law on free movement and Union citizenship has both prompted and accommodated the exercise of Union legislative power – in effect, a two-way dialogue between judges and politicians about how best to balance the construction of a meaningful form of Union citizenship, against the need to respect the social competences and financial concerns of the Member States – while at the same time remaining sensitive to significant changes in the broader landscape of European integration.

It would be foolhardy to predict the future direction of the case law on Union citizenship. But the constellation of a Union legislature which has taken a more proactive interest in regulating the free movement and welfare rights of Union citizens, together with a public discourse which seems (at least) as sceptical as it has ever been about the ends and means of the integration process, might lead us to expect two new trends in the Court's approach to free movement. First, the parallel application of primary law and secondary legislation will continue, but the technique of indirect judicial review might become more muted, so that scrutiny under the Treaty itself is more closely tied to the regulatory preferences expressed by the other Union institutions.[133] Secondly, the Court's approach to

to the ratification problems surrounding the Constitutional Treaty after the French and Dutch referenda). Consider caselaw on the legal value of the Charter of Fundamental Rights, e.g. ECJ 27 June 2006, Case C-540/03, *Parliament v Council* [2006] ECR I-5769. Consider also caselaw gradually breaking down the barrier between the old First and Third Pillars, e.g. ECJ 16 June 2005, Case C-105/03, *Criminal proceedings against Maria Pupino* [2005] ECR I-5285 and ECJ 13 September 2005, Case C-176/03, *Commission v Council* [2005] ECR I-7879.

133 Cf. C. Timmermans, '*Martínez Sala* and *Baumbast* Revisited', in M. Maduro and L. Azoulai (eds), *The Past and Future of EU Law*, Hart Publishing, Oxford, 2010.

the principle of proportionality may well prove more accommodating of national choices in particularly sensitive policy fields, especially those characterised by only complementary Union competence,[134] so that condemnation is reserved primarily for those rules which can be considered unfairly arbitrary or intolerably inconsistent.[135] Overall, one senses that the opportunity to effect a more profound transformation in relations between State, Union and Citizen either was squandered in the period after Laeken by the inept political salesmanship of the Member States and Union institutions alike; or that such an opportunity never really existed in the first place because it actually fell so far out of tune with the deeply-held wishes of the general European population.[136] The joint efforts of the Court and the legislature may well have delivered appreciable improvements in the rights enjoyed by certain categories of migrant, but perhaps we must now content ourselves with a period of consolidation and reflection,[137] awaiting the next "constitutional moment" before we can or should expect significant further advances in the legal construction of free movement and welfare rights for Union citizens.[138]

---

134 For a similar view, see F. Jacobs, 'Citizenship of the European Union: A Legal Analysis', (2007) 13 *ELJ* 591; M. Cousins, 'Citizenship, Residence and Social Security', (2007) 32 *ELR* 386.

135 Cf. the gambling case law under ex-Article 49 EC (now Article 56 TFEU). On the one hand: ECJ 24 March 1994, Case C-275/92, *Her Majesty's Customs and Excise v Gerhart Schindler and Jörg Schindler* [1994] ECR I-1039; ECJ 21 September 1999, Case C-124/97, *Markku Juhani Läärä, Cotswold Microsystems Ltd and Oy Transatlantic Software Ltd v Kihlakunnansyyttäjä (Jyväskylä) and Suomen valtio (Finnish State)* [1999] ECR I-6067; ECJ 8 September 2009, Case C-42/07, *Liga Portuguesa de Futebol Profissional and Bwin International Ltd v Departamento de Jogos da Santa Casa da Misericórdia de Lisboa,* [2009] ECR I-07633. On the other hand: ECJ 21 October 1999, Case C-67/98, *Questore di Verona v Diego Zenatti* [1999] ECR I-7289; ECJ 6 November 2003, Case C-243/01, *Criminal proceedings against Piergiorgio Gambelli and Others,* [2003] ECR I-13031; Cases C-338/04, C-359/04 and C-360/04, *Criminal proceedings against Massimiliano Placanica (C-338/04), Christian Palazzese (C-359/04) and Angelo Sorricchio (C-360/04)* [2007] ECR I-1891.

136 Cf. S. Besson and A. Utzinger, 'Future Challenges of European Citizenship: Facing a Wide-Open Pandora's Box', (2007) 13 *ELJ* 573; P. Magnette, 'How Can One be European? Reflections on the Pillars of European Civic Identity', (2007) 13 *ELJ* 664.

137 A sentiment echoing that of E. Spaventa, 'The Constitutional Impact of Union Citizenship', in U. Neergaard, R. Nielsen and L. Roseberry (eds), *The Role of Courts in Developing a European Social Model: Theoretical and Methodological Perspectives,* DJØF Publishing, København, 2010.

138 Though prospects for enhancing the political participation of Union citizens in the exercise of public power by the Union institutions might seem more fruitful: consider, e.g. Commission, *Green Paper on a European Citizens' Initiative,* COM(2009) 622 Final; and for discussion, e.g. Editorial, 'Direct Democracy and the European Union… Is that a threat or a promise?', (2008) 45 *CMLR* 929. See generally: J. Shaw, *The Transformation of Union Citizenship: Electoral Rights and the Restructuring of Political Space,* Cambridge University Press, Cambridge, 2007.

# "RESERVED AREAS" OF THE MEMBER STATES AND THE ECJ: THE CASE OF HIGHER EDUCATION

Dragana DAMJANOVIC

## 1. INTRODUCTION

### 1.1. ARTICLE 165 TFEU (EX ARTICLE 149 ECT): EDUCATION AS A "RESERVED AREA" OF THE MEMBER STATES AND THE BOLOGNA PROCESS

Higher education is a central element of a nation's culture and its identity, and within the EU, typically also a central part of the Member States' welfare regimes.[1] As such it is an excellent example of a policy area for which the Member States, within the European integration project, have always tried to retain and secure their autonomy. Initially, they did so by not mentioning the term education in the treaty at all. Together with the general rule of conferred powers[2] this should have meant – so went the widely held belief at that time – that the Community, in principle, was not allowed to interfere with educational policy.[3]

Later, with the Maastricht treaty revision in 1992, the Member States reinforced their competence in the area by expressly stating, by the introduction for the first time of an article on education (Articles 126 and 127 ECT), that the

---

1 Provided one takes the broad definition of social policy (the welfare state) as established by T.H. MARSHALL, *Social Policy in the Twentieth Century*, Hutchinson, London, 4th ed, 1975, 15: *"the use of political power to supersede, supplement or modify operations of economic systems in order to achieve results which the economic system would not achieve on its own... guided by values other than those determined by market forces."* For such a perspective on education as a welfare benefit, see also S. JORGENSEN, 'The Right to Cross-border Education in the European Union', (2009) 46 *CMLR (Common Market Law Review)* 1567, at 1567; note in this context also the increased importance of social issues (the social dimension of education) within the Bologna process (B. WÄCHTER, 'The Bologna Process: developments and prospects', (2004) 39 *European Journal of Education* 265, at 266–267).

2 According to which, the Community shall only act within the limits of the powers conferred upon it by the treaty. Originally: Article 4 EECT, now: Article 3 para 6 TEU.

3 See K. LENAERTS, 'Education in European Community law after "Maastricht"', (1994) 31 *CMLR* 7, at 9; and B. DE WITTE: 'Introduction', in B. DE WITTE (ed.) *European Community Law in Education* (1993), 9, referring to the Greek government's argumentation in the ECJ 6 December 1989, Case 147/86 *Commission v Greece* [1989] ECR 4119.

legislative competence for education shall in any case remain in their hands.[4] The inclusion of this article on education, for the first time, conferred a "true negative vertical competence"[5] with regard to a special policy field[6] to the Community, even though, or maybe exactly because the ECJ in the meantime had held in various cases that it is impossible to exclude education and in particular higher education altogether from the European integration project.[7]

Today, in the new Lisbon treaty, the Member States still adhere to this provision[8] and still expressly deny any legislative competences for the EU, even though in the last twenty years the ECJ case law has not only indirectly affected but rather substantially dealt with education (and in particular higher educational issues).[9] The European integration process in general has shown that the case law of the ECJ, when it reaches a certain dimension, typically also requires action by the EU legislator, otherwise a regulatory vacancy, and therewith regulatory and political uncertainties, results within the respective policy field.[10] What is even more bizarre in the case of higher education is that the Member States, while still reserving this area for their domain, simultaneously very clearly agree on the political necessity to move towards a coherent European system in this policy field, i.e. to create a "European Area of Higher Education". This is considered to be indispensable in answering the common problems the European higher education institutions face today (i.e. growth and diversification of education, employability of graduates, expansion of private and transnational education and global competitiveness) as well as, in the establishment of a more far reaching and complete Europe, which in particular also means a European Union which is more than a mere economic but a true political union.[11]

---

4 The text of this provision expressly obliged the Community to "*fully respect the responsibility of the Member States for the content of teaching and the organization of education systems and their cultural and linguistic diversity*".

5 As to this terminology: A. von Bogdandy and J. Bast, 'The European Union's Vertical Order of Competences: The Current Law and Proposals for its Reform', (2002) 39 *CMLR* 227, at 238. Today this type of competence provision is typically denominated 'a complementary competence of the EU': the competence to carry out actions to support, coordinate or supplement the actions of the Member States (Art 6 TEU).

6 Such a 'negative vertical competence' has been laid down for culture and health care (Article 128 ECT, Article 129 ECT); with the Nice treaty revisions it has been implicitly extended to other areas of the welfare state (social protection and the combating of social exclusion by social security and social assistance: Art 137 para 1(j) and (k) in combination with para 2(b) and para 4 ECT (in the version of Nice).

7 For an overview on the case law of the ECJ in (higher) education from the mid 80s to the Maastricht treaty, see K. Lenaerts, 'Education in European Community law after "Maastricht"', (1994) 31 *CMLR* 7, at 7 ss.

8 Art 165 TFEU.

9 On this case law see below.

10 Cf. e.g. the developments within the traditional SGEI sectors (the public utilities) where the application of the EU market rules to these sectors by the ECJ has triggered a number of secondary law measures on the liberalisation and de-regulation of these sectors.

11 See e.g. in the text of the Bologna Declaration and the explanation of the Bologna Declaration on the European space for higher education, at: http://ec.europa.eu/education/policies/educ/bologna/bologna.pdf.

It's exactly this paradox between, on the one hand, the desire of the Member States to remain as sovereign as possible in the field of higher education and, on the other hand, the political necessity to bring the European higher education systems in line with each other, which explains the evolvement of the Bologna Process, i.e. the process of European integration of higher education[12] actually outside the system of the EU utilizing mere soft law instruments within an intergovernmental and voluntary process.[13] This way of integrating higher education at the EU level allows the Member States, at least in a legally technical sense, to remain sovereign in the field of higher education, since the European integration has been reached through a mere intergovernmental and voluntary process, therefore not qualifying as harmonisation in the meaning of Article 165 TFEU.[14] Practically, however, the results achieved by the Bologna Process resemble very much what also could have been achieved by traditional harmonisation measures, not only with regard to their substance,[15] but also with regard to the reform pressure[16] they put on the Member States' systems and consequently also on their autonomy to organise their systems as they whish. At the same time, Bologna exhibits some deep-seated implementation problems,[17] which is why this way of integrating European higher education has been described by many as suboptimal, and from a European constitutional perspective – in particular in terms of democracy and transparency – as very problematic.[18] But Bologna and European integration through soft law is not the topic of this paper. In line with the general title of this book, the paper will rather focus on the role of the

---

12 Which is, at first, limited to structural comparability: comparable degrees, ECTS, three cycle architecture of Bach-Master-PhD, free circulation of students among others. It does not entail content harmonisation. See S. Garben, 'The Bologna Process from a European Law Perspective', 2008/12 *EUI Working Papers Law*, 5.

13 Officially, Bologna is not even part of the OMC. However, it strongly resembles the entire set up of OMC. S. Garben, 'The Bologna Process from a European Law Perspective', 2008/12 *EUI Working Papers Law*, 17. This is why some authors consider it as part of the OMC. See e.g. J. Lonbay, 'Reflections on Education and Culture in EC Law', in R. Craufurd Smith (ed) *Culture and European Community Law*, Oxford University Press, Oxford, 2004, p 253.

14 In the context of European Law, harmonisation generally means the approximation of national laws in order to create one European standard by means of legislation.

15 Cf. S. Garben, 'The Bologna Process from a European Law Perspective', 2008/12 *EUI Working Papers Law*, p 5.

16 This is just political and not legal pressure (as the soft informal processes are subject to the national veto of non action), but this is practically almost as powerful as legal pressure, see J. Lonbay, 'Reflections on Education and Culture in EC Law', in R. Craufurd Smith (ed) *Culture and European Community Law*, Oxford University Press, Oxford, 2004, p 253; in relation to the reform pressure in particular on the Austrian system, H. Pechar and A. Pellert: 'Austrian Universities Under Pressure From Bologna', (2004) 39 *EJE (European Journal of Education)* 317, at 317 ss.

17 In this regard see H. Pechar and A. Pellert: 'Austrian Universities Under Pressure From Bologna', (2004) 39 *EJE* 317.

18 See e.g. S. Garben, 'The Bologna Process from a European Law Perspective', 2008/12 *EUI Working Papers Law*, 18; J. Lonbay, 'Reflections on Education and Culture in EC Law', in R. Craufurd Smith (ed) *Culture and European Community Law*, Oxford University Press, Oxford, 2004, p 253 and 273.

ECJ in the Europeanisation process of higher education, which we will in the following denominate "the legal integration of higher education" in the EU – so as to contrast it to mere political integration by policy instruments (e.g. Bologna) and political integration through law (primary or secondary law measures).

## 1.2. THE 'IMPLIED POWERS DOCTRINE' AS THE BASIS OF EU LEGAL INTEGRATION WITHIN HIGHER EDUCATION

The process of legal integration of higher education by the ECJ rests on the so called 'implied powers doctrine'. According to this doctrine, education can also be relevant from the perspective of policy fields for which the EU has been attributed explicit powers, as e.g. the 'functional power' to build an internal market with free and fair competition.[19] On this basis, the EU has 'implied powers' for education, which cannot be limited by the fact that they encroach upon a substantive policy field for which the treaty lays down a special negative competence clause. More specifically, the existence of a special negative competence clause[20] for education does not mean that the Member States have an exclusive competence for education, i.e. that this policy field is hermetically sealed from EU influence. Rather, the Member States, when excercising these competences must also comply with European Union Law.[21]

It's not astonishing that on the basis of such a doctrine it is still quite unclear how far the competences of the EU in the field of education actually go, respectively, to what extent the competences of the Member States within the field of education are limited. In particular, it remains unsettled whether to differentiate between matters which merely lie within the treaty's scope of application – and as such fall under the jurisdictional competence of the EU – on the one hand and matters which fall under the legislative competence of the EU on the other hand;[22] or, does a certain correlation between jurisdictional and legislative competences derive from the EU legal system as such? For example, if the ECJ applies the general non-discrimination provision in combination with the union citizenship chapter to the matter of student mobility within the EU, can we consider that the EU

19 The same applies to the other areas of the MS' welfare regimes for which the treaty provides similar negative competence clauses (i.e. merely complementary competences).

20 Or before Maastricht: the fact that this policy field has not been mentioned in the treaty at all.

21 See lately ECJ 11 September 2007, Case C-76/05, *Herbert Schwarz and Marga Gootjes-Schwarz v Finanzamt Bergisch Gladbach* [2007] ECR I-06849, para 70 in analogy to ECJ 16 May 2006, C-372/04, *The Queen, on the application of Yvonne Watts v Bedford Primary Care Trust and Secretary of State for Health* [2006] ECR I-04325, para 92 and 147; in the literature see A. von Bogdandy and J. Bast, 'The European Union's Vertical Order of Competences: The Current Law and Proposals for its Reform', (2002) 39 *CMLR* 227, at 233.

22 So e.g. A. Dashwood, 'The Limits of Community Powers', (1996) 21 *EPL (European Public Law)* 113, at 113 ss.

legislator, in principle, might utilise these EU primary law provisions to also issue secondary law measures on this matter?[23]

### 1.3. AIM OF THIS PAPER

Against this background the aim of this paper is, basically, to provide an analysis of the various strands of ECJ case law within the field of higher education in a systematic and structured way. At a glance these comprise of the following issues: a) the mutual recognition of professional qualifications; b) mobility of students with respect to educational courses; c) mobility of students with respect to student grants (as e.g. maintenance aids); and finally, d) the establishment of an open European market with fair competition within the higher education arena. The focus of this analysis thereby lies on the ECJ case law on student mobility (with respect to educational courses and to student grants) as this is currently the most relevant one.

Overall, the analysis shall serve as a basis to demonstrate the level which the Europeanisation of higher education through ECJ case law has already reached, to what extent this ECJ case law, i.e. legal integration, has triggered political integration (through secondary law and soft law instruments) and finally, how these legal and political processes at the EU level have so far influenced the organisation of the higher education systems by the Member States.

## 2. THE VARIOUS STRANDS OF ECJ CASE LAW IN HIGHER EDUCATION

### 2.1. PROFESSIONAL RECOGNITION

Already in the 1970s, the ECJ established the rule that Member States have to recognise professional qualifications acquired in other Member States.[24] That the Court was legitimised to do so on the basis of the EU free movement of workers, establishment and services provisions (in order to facilitate the mobility of employed and self-employed union citizens as well as services within the EU internal market) has never been seriously questioned, since within the scope of the free movement of establishment provisions the Treaty itself had, already in its

23 This is basically the argument used to legitimise the patient's mobility directive [Directive 2011/24/EU, OJ 2011, L 28/45] on the basis of the EU's internal market competences. See in this context also the arguments provided by B. de Witte, 'Non-Market Values in Internal Market Legislation', in N. Nic Shuibhne (ed), *Regulating the Internal Market*, Edward Elgar, Cheltenham, 2006, p 61 ss.

24 For the foundational judgments of the first generation of ECJ case law on mutual recognition, see V. Hatzopoulos, 'A (More) Social Europe: A Political Crossroad or a Legal One-Way? Dialogues between Luxembourg and Lisbon', (2005) 42 *CMLR* 1599, at fn 93.

very original version, expressly empowered the Union to issue directives for the mutual recognition of diplomas, certificates and other evidence of formal qualifications, accepting that this might lead to certain incursions in the Member States' educational policies.[25]

In order to bring these incursions into line with the expressly codified reserved powers of the Member States for education (i.e. to explain how Article 57 EECT, now Article 53 TFEU and Articles 126–127 EECT, now Article 165 TFEU interact), the literature has developed the doctrinal differentiation between professional and academic recognition, according to which the EU rule on mutual recognition of professional qualifications based on Article 53 TFEU, in principle, only relates to Member States' provisions on the licensing of certain professions (the "regulated professions"), but not to Member States' provisions on the organisation of (higher) education and the academic status of obtained degrees and diplomas and, therewith related, the admission of migrant students. Such a purely "academic recognition" of diplomas is clearly the subject of Article 165 TFEU and therefore falls outside the scope of Article 53 TFEU – or at least so goes the standard argumentation, which is however far from being undisputed.[26]

Some authors argue that the differentiation established is artificial.[27] The EU system of professional recognition, as in the meantime manifested in secondary EU law[28] on the basis of the ECJ's jurisprudence, in fact shows some very deep incursions into the organisation of the national (higher) education policies. In particular, the sector-specific provisions applying to certain medical professions, lawyers and architects also directly affect the national organisation of (higher) education by (at least partly) harmonising the duration, the structure and even the content of the relevant training curricula in the Member States. But also the general system of recognition[29] puts high pressure on the Member States to bring their educational policies in line with each other, as it only functions if and when the readability and comparability of degrees is, at least to a certain extent, guaranteed. To achieve structural comparability amongst the European higher education systems to facilitate mutual recognition is also one of the overarching aims of the Bologna process. In this respect, Bologna constitutes a direct result of the precedent Europeanisation of higher education by case law and secondary legislation.

---

25 Article 57 EECT, providing that the Council shall issue directives for the mutual recognition of diplomas, certificates and other evidence of formal qualifications.

26 S. Garben, 'The Bologna Process from a European Law Perspective', 2008/12 *EUI Working Papers Law*, 6–7.

27 S. Garben, 'The Bologna Process from a European Law Perspective', 2008/12 *EUI Working Papers Law*, 7 (with further references).

28 And has finally been consolidated by one single directive: 2005/36/EC, OJ 2005, L 255/22. See recital 9 of Directive 2005/36 for the directives which were previously in force and repealed by 2005/36.

29 According to which a Member State, in which a profession is regulated, must take account of the qualifications obtained in another Member State and assess whether they correspond to those which it requires, recital 11 Directive 2005/36 (fn 28).

As the issue of mutual recognition of professional qualifications and the Europeanisation of higher education that follows from it are already dealt with in secondary legislation, and not anymore primarily by ECJ case law,[30] we will not deal with it in further detail here.[31] At this point, it suffices to summarise that the ECJ was the initial actor in establishing the main principles on professional recognition within Europe, which the legislator later transferred into an elaborated system consisting of sectoral and general provisions on mutual recognition, which in the meantime have been codified in one single directive. This Europeanisation process, even though it has been pursued inside the Community's institutional framework of the EU system (i.e. by legal not by mere soft law instruments) and even though it led to certain inroads into the MS' higher education policies, has remained quite uncontroversial, as the treaty itself from the beginning has explicitly provided for legislative competences of the Union in this field.

## 2.2. STUDENT MOBILITY: CROSS-BORDER ACCESS TO HIGHER EDUCATION COURSES

### *2.2.1. The issue of student mobility within the triangle of EU case law, EU hard law and European soft law (in particular, the Bologna process)*

Free mobility of students within Europe – which implies first and foremost the right of students to pursue their education in another Member State on a non-discriminatory basis,[32] (in particular also outside the Socrates/Erasmus programs)[33] – has evolved into an indispensable component of European integration. It is qualified as a central principle of EU law[34] and is seen as an essential precondition, not only for the effective realisation of the free movement of persons and labour and of the internal market as such,[35] but also to increase the internation-

---

30 The ECJ, however, still remains a factor in this process, by considerably extending the scope and enhancing the effectiveness of the mutual recognition directives, while still insisting on the parallel and complementary application of the rules of primary legislation. See V. Hatzopoulos, 'A (More) Social Europe: A Political Crossroad or a Legal One-Way? Dialogues between Luxembourg and Lisbon', (2005) 42 *CMLR* 1599, at 1618 ff.

31 But see in detail H. Schneider and S. Claessens, 'The Recognition of Diplomas and the free Movement of Professionals in the European Union', in. Schneider (ed.), *Migration, Integration and Citizenship, A Challenge for Europe's Future, Vol I* Forum Maastricht, Maastricht, 2005, p 123–167.

32 As to the right to access to student grants when studying in another Member State, see below at B.3.

33 For the Socrates/Erasmus programs, see in more detail on the Commission's website: http://ec.europa.eu/education/index_en.htm.

34 The Court refers to the 'principle of freedom of movement for students guaranteed by the Treaty', see ECJ 7 July 2005, C-147/03, *Commission v. Austria,* [2005] ECR I-05969 (repeated in many other cases).

35 See the argumentation of the ECJ in its very first judgement on student mobility: ECJ 13 February 1985, C-293/83, *Françoise Gravier v City of Liège* [1985] ECR 00593, para 23.

alisation of European universities to make them competitive on the global scale. As such, the goal of student mobility is not only widely accepted but in principle also expressly required within Europe, both by the responsible politicians of the Member States and the universities, themselves.[36] It remains a highly contested issue, though, how to achieve this goal.

So far, student mobility (outside Socrates/Erasmus) is merely a construct of ECJ jurisprudence.[37] That jurisprudence, however, is generally perceived through the various treaty amendments already approved by the Member States at the level of EU primary law (as *acquis communautaire*). In particular, the negative competence clause for education, introduced in 1992, some years after the ECJ had issued its first foundational judgment on student mobility (*Gravier* in 1986), is said to respect and built upon the jurisprudence of the ECJ.[38] In their role as members of the EU legislator, however, the national states so far have – with reference to their autonomy in this field[39] – refrained to lift that case law to the level of EU secondary law, i.e. to develop it into a more general and coherent EU legal framework, even if – and that is the paradox – they in principle acknowledge the necessity and importance of student mobility as construed by the ECJ.

Promotion of student mobility within Europe by political integration processes has at least become a central issue of Bologna, probably even the most consensual amongst the parties.[40] But yet, even within this merely voluntary setting the national states have so far not managed to produce any answers to the most crucial aspect of student mobility within the EU, i.e. to ensure that the financing of migrant education is fairly distributed amongst the Member States and that no single states which are 'net importers' of students have to bear a too great burden, which again might destabilise the funding mechanism of their own higher education systems.[41]

Since this issue is still unresolved at the Member States political level, the Court has already been called upon several times to judge on this very sensitive matter: how to handle student mobility in cases where great imbalances in student

---

36 See e.g. in the explanation of the Bologna declaration, prepared by the Confederation of EU's Rectors Conferences and the Association of European Universities (CRE), at 4.

37 Built on the basis of the treaty's general non-discrimination clause in combination with the EC's policy on vocational training, respectively lately in combination with the Union citizenship chapter. Case *Gravier* (Fn 35), para 30 and ECJ 13 April 2010, C-73/08, *Nicolas Bressol and Others and Céline Chaverot and Others v Gouvernement de la Communauté française* [2010] nyr, para 30 s.

38 See K. Lenaerts, 'Education in European Community law after "Maastricht"', (1994) 31 *CMLR* 7.

39 And by arguing that a legal basis for such a secondary law would be missing; but see S. Garben, 'The Bologna Process from a European Law Perspective', 2008/12 *EUI Working Papers Law*, 3s.

40 Cf. B. Wächter, 'The Bologna Process: developments and prospects', (2004) 39 *European Journal of Education* 265, at 266, at 268.

41 On that aspect in more detail, M. Dougan, 'Fees, Grants, Loans and Dole Cheques: Who covers the cost of migrant education within the EU?', (2005) 42 *CMLR* 943 and A.P Van der Mei, 'EU Law and Education: Promotion of Student Mobility versus Protection of Education Systems', in M. Dougan and E. Spaventa (eds), *Social Welfare and EU Law* (2005) 219 – 239, p 232 ss.

movements are to be expected. So far the Court has consistently recognised the right of student mobility,[42] and not accepted the arguments brought forward by the Member States that this might result in an overly excessive burden on the financing of their higher education systems. However, in its latest decision on this matter – *Bressol*[43] – the Court seems to be more permissive on this issue. In the following, we will look at these cases in more detail.

### 2.2.2. *The Austria v Commission and Belgium v Commission 'student mobility' cases*

The Member States particularly concerned by the problem of unbalanced student mobility within Europe are Belgium and Austria, two smaller members of the Union that both have a big neighbouring country (France and Germany respectively) with a much larger population,[44] but with the same language. Originally, i.e. before the ECJ issued its judgments in these cases, Belgium and Austria pursued an open access policy (unlimited free access to education). France and Germany, in contrast, run a restrictive access system.

Due to these structural peculiarities in the cross-border relationship between Austria and Germany and Belgium and France, Austria and Belgium feared[45] an influx of students from Germany and France (from those not admitted to higher education in their own home country), that – given the relatively high population in these countries – might be considerable and could thus pose a serious risk to the financial balance of their own higher education systems. So to maintain the financial equilibrium of migrant education, they established rules – one could say in analogy with the general "*mutual recognition principle*" as developed by the ECJ in the context of the free movement rules[46] – that allowed cross border access to their universities only to those foreign EU students who would also have been accepted to university in their own home country.[47] By doing so, they particularly intended to ensure that they would not have to provide and finance more educational services for a foreign EU student than its home country would have done.

As is well known, the ECJ qualified these measures, both in the case of Austria and Belgium, as incompatible with EU law. The legal reasoning it

---

42 See the cases *Gravier* (Fn 35), ECJ 1 July 2004, C-65/03, *Commission v Belgium* [2004] ECR I-6427, and *Commission v Austria* (Fn 34).

43 Fn 37.

44 In the case of Germany to Austria the ratio is about 10 to 1.

45 See the argumentation of Austria in *Commission v Austria* (Fn 34), para 25.

46 For an overview of this principle see C. Barnard, *The Substantive Law of the EU. The four freedoms*, Oxford University Press, Oxford, 2004, at 507-508.

47 In Belgium, foreign students not admitted to courses in their own home countries had to take and pass an additional aptitude test (Article 1b of the Royal Decree of 20. July 1971); in Austria they were simply not admitted to the courses (paragraph 36 UniStG, BGBl I 1997/48 version of BGBl I 2002/121 ['Law on University Studies']).

developed, more detailed for the Austrian case (as Belgium back then didn't even attempt to defend its measure),[48] can be summarised as follows: First, the measures qualify as indirect discrimination under Article 12 read in conjunction with Articles 149 and 150 ECT (now Article 18 read in conjunction with Articles 165 and 166 TFEU). With regard to the Austrian case, it concretely places holders of secondary education diplomas awarded in a Member State other than the Republic of Austria at a disadvantage, since they must not only produce that diploma (as the Austrians), but also prove that they fulfil the conditions of access to higher and university studies in the state where they obtained their diploma.[49] Second, that indirect discrimination is unjustifiable because – again in particular with regard to the Austrian case – "*excessive demand for access to specific courses could be also met by the adoption of specific non-discriminatory measures such as the establishment of an entry examination or the requirement of a minimum grade*".[50] In addition, Austria failed "*to demonstrate*[51] *that in the absence of the national legislation in question, the existence of the Austrian education system in general and the safeguarding of the homogeneity of higher education in particular would be jeopardized.*"[52]

### 2.2.3. *Criticism against the Court*

The judgments were strongly criticised both by the legal scholars and the politicians of the countries affected.[53] The central points of criticism have been the following:

- The Court does not accept the MS' policy choice for a higher education system based on open access
  First, in particular with regard to the Austrian case, it was broadly argued that the Court, by taking the view that "*excessive demand could be also met by the adoption of some sort of entry restriction system*", does not respect the nation state's policy choice for a higher education system based on free access, even if Article 149 para 1 ECT (now Article 165 para 1 TFEU) guarantees that MS have the primary responsibility for the content of teaching and the

48 But just amended the legislation in question and introduced for most of the courses a non-discriminatory entry restriction system.

49 *Commission v Austria* (Fn 34), para 42 and 46; and very similar in the Belgian case: *Commission vs Belgium* (Fn 42), para 29.

50 *Commission v. Austria* (Fn 34), para 63.

51 Austria presented figures according to which in the case of medical studies the expected number of applications from foreign (mainly German) secondary education diploma holders would exceed the places available fivefold.

52 *Commission v Austria* (Fn 34), para 66.

53 For Austria, see the interview with the then Federal Chancellor of Austria *Wolfgang Schüssel* in the German paper 'Süddeutsche Zeitung' from 31 December 2005/1 January 2006, at p. 14; and in particular S. Griller, 'Vom Diskriminierungsverbot zur Grundrechtsgemeinschaft?', in Akyürek/Baumgartner/Jahnel/Lienbacher/Stolzlechner (eds), *Staat und Recht in europäischer Perspektive, Festschrift Heinz Schäffer*, Mainz Verlag, Wien, 2006, p 203–239.

organisation of their education systems. It simply disregards Austria's policy choice by treating it as the instrument of the Austrian higher education system rather than its goal,[54] and by openly accepting that the effectuation of the non-discrimination principle in the special cases of Austria and Belgium will very probably force them to reform their higher education systems, in particular to assimilate them to those of their big neighbouring countries Germany and France.

The inconsistency of the Court's reasoning on this point becomes particularly obvious when comparing it with its jurisprudence in the field of the SGEI (services of general economic interest)[55] on the basis of Art 16, Article 86 para 2 ECT (now Articles 14 and 106 para 2 TFEU), where it continuously holds that the Member States are free to define the central policy aim pursued within these policy fields;[56] as to the policy aims, they are only subject to checks for 'manifest errors' and only the instruments used in reaching this policy aim shall be under closer EU law scrutiny. One could argue that if this is the case for a category of services of general interest (SGI) which are qualified as economic and for which the treaty even confers a shared power to the Union, it shall hold true even more for a category of SGI, which in principle qualifies as non-economic[57] and for which the treaty merely transfers a complementary competence to the Union, i.e. which is the primary responsibility of the Member States.[58]

- The Court applies different standards within the proportionality test in the cases of cross-border access to educational benefits, to social benefits and to health care benefits

In the patient mobility cases, which are comparable to the student mobility cases – insofar as in both cases Union citizens ask for access to welfare benefits[59] in a Member State other than their own – the Court recognises the right

54 See e.g. S. Griller, 'Vom Diskriminierungsverbot zur Grundrechtsgemeinschaft?', in Akyürek/Baumgartner/Jahnel/Lienbacher/Stolzlechner (eds), *Staat und Recht in europäischer Perspektive, Festschrift Heinz Schäffer*, Mainz Verlag, Wien, 2006, p 235 ss.

55 Traditionally public utilities: energy, traffic, telecommunication, broadcasting, etc.

56 See e.g. ECJ 27 April 1994, C-393/92, *Almelo* [1994] ECR I-1477, para 47–50. Cf. also H. Schweitzer, 'Die Daseinsvorsorge im Verfassungsentwurf des Europäischen Konvents – Ein europäischer "service public"'?, in Schwarze (ed.), *Der Verfassungsentwurf des Europäischen Konvents*, Nomos, Baden-Baden, 2004, p 273; the Commission's last Communication on SGIs, COM (2007) 725, at 9.

57 More on this differentation see below at 2.4.

58 From a structural perspective there is, though, one objection to this argument, namely that the referred case law in the field of SGEIs primarily addresses the application of the competition rules (Articles 81, 82 in combination with Article 86 para 2 EC) whereas the present case deals with the application of the non-discrimination principle; the application of the competition rules results in far more intense implications for the organisational structure of MS' welfare regimes and MS' public utilities (opening the system to a free market) than the application of the non-discrimination rule (opening the system 'just' to cross border access for the union citizens).

59 I.e. services, which are provided by MS' welfare regimes (Fn 1) outside the market system, essentially, financed by MS' public budgets.

to cross border access only under the conditions set in the foreign patient's country of origin. More precisely this means that the cross border treatment has to be financed by the patient's own home state welfare regime and only to the extent of a treatment provided within the national context.[60] This is similarly resolved when it comes to the issue of cross-border access to social assistance (e.g. maintenance grants for students,[61] family allowance, etc). In general, the Court only grants to Union citizens the right to export the social assistance provided by their home Member States. Access to social assistance in the host Member State is, on the other hand, in principle put under the condition that the foreign Union citizen has established a genuine link within the host Member State, which is usually the case when the Union citizen has resided legally for a continuous period of five years in the host Member State.[62] Both, as to health care and social assistance, the Court justifies these limits to cross border access with the need to ensure the financial equilibrium of the host Member States welfare regimes. Only in the case of public higher education the Court grants the access unconditionally. It does so without providing any explanations why the financial stability of the host MS' welfare regimes with regard to health care and social assistance is a relevant criterion when deciding under which conditions cross border access is to be provided, but is not with regard to education. Advocate General Jacobs' argumentation on this point[63] – that in the case of cross border access to social assistance the financial burden on state resources would be significant, but in the case of cross border access to the educational services it is not – is not convincing, particularly so in the case of Belgium and Austria where education is provided for free as a welfare benefit and financed by the public budget and especially in consideration of how resource intensive higher education is.[64]

---

60 ECJ 28 April 1998, Case C-158/96, *Raymond Kohll v Union des caisses de maladie* [1998] ECR I-01931 and ECJ 28 April 1998 C-120/95, *Nicolas Decker v Caisse de maladie des employés privés* [1998] ECR I-01831; ECJ 12 July 2001, C-157/99, *B.S.M. Geraets-Smits v Stichting Ziekenfonds VGZ and H.T.M. Peerbooms v Stichting CZ Groep Zorgverzekeringen* [2001] ECR I-05473; ECJ 13 May 2003, C-385/99, *V.G. Müller-Fauré v Onderlinge Waarborgmaatschappij OZ Zorgverzekeringen UA and E.E.M. van Riet v Onderlinge Waarborgmaatschappij ZAO Zorgverzekeringen* [2003] ECR I-04509 and ECJ 16 May 2006, C-372/04, *The Queen, on the application of Yvonne Watts v Bedford Primary Care Trust and Secretary of State for Health* [2006] ECR I-04325.

61 For more on this jurisprudence see below at 2.3.

62 This is now explicitly also enshrined in secondary law: see Article 16 para 1 and Article 24 Directive 2004/38/EC, OJ 2004, L 158/77. But see also the different approach by the ECJ when it comes to cross border access to unemployment benefits in ECJ 4 June 2009, Joined Cases C-22/08 and C-23/08, *Athanasios Vatsouras and Josif Koupatantze v Arbeitsgemeinschaft (ARGE) Nürnberg 900* [2009] ECR I-04585.

63 See the opinion in the case *Commission v Austria* (fn 34) at para 43.

64 See also M. Dougan, 'Fees, Grants, Loans and Dole Cheques: Who covers the cost of migrant education within the EU?', (2005) 42 *CMLR* 943, at 960, arguing that from the perspective of the budgetary resources of the national welfare States all these modes of support are of an essentially similar character.

- The Court applies a strict proportionality test
  According to the Court, the burden is on the national authorities to prove that the deviation from the general principle of free movement of students (i.e. the discriminatory measure) is necessary and proportionate. One could argue that such a strict proportionality test, which imposes the whole burden of proof on the Member States, is inappropriate when applying EU law to policy fields which are principally reserved to the Member States, in particular when considering the difficulties in proving ex ante how a situation might have developed without the deviation from EU law, i.e. if cross-border access was granted on a non-discriminatory basis. If it does not follow from Article 165 para 1 TFEU that the MS within the policy field of education can per se act outside the EU law framework, but has to comply with Community law when exercising that power,[65] then the special competence of the MS laid down in this provision should be taken into account at least when conducting the proportionality test. Otherwise the provision becomes empty of any meaning in the given context of student mobility.[66] Consequently, it should not be for the Member States alone to show that the national measure is proportionate and necessary, which again means that within the infringement proceedings, where the Commission sues a Member State for violation of EU law,[67] the Commission should also be obliged to substantiate its argument of violation of EU law, i.e. to prove that the policy aim pursued by the Member States (which they should be free to define)[68] can also be attained when abolishing the restrictive national measure (in the present case the requirement for the foreign students to show that they have been admitted to the studies in their country of origin). Or, at least it should suffice that the Member States can reasonably argue a serious probability of negative consequences for their higher education systems resulting from the application of the non-discrimination principle in this area. The Court has deployed such a more flexible proportionality test[69] over time also with regard to the SGEI (the public utilities) in order to guarantee the Member States sufficient discretionary power to pursue their policy aim of universal provision within these policy fields.[70]
- Non-discriminatory access for foreign students in Austria and Belgium leads to an under-provision of higher education services for their own nationals; it

65 See above 1.2. (the 'implied powers doctrine').

66 In fact, the arguments of the ECJ do not depend on whether the special negative competence clause exists or not. It would have reached the same result, if Article 165 TFEU was simply not included in the treaty.

67 In contrast, in the reference cases, it is the national courts that have to assume the task of conducting the proportionality test. See in the case *Bressol* (Fn 37) at para 64.

68 Fn 56.

69 Which it conducts under Article 106 para 2 TFEU.

70 For these developments see J. Maillo, 'Article 86. Services of General Interest and EC Competition Law', in G. Amato and C.D. Ehlermann (eds.), *EC Competition Law: A Critical Assessment,* Hart Publishing, Oxford, 2007, p 606 ss.

jeopardises the quality of higher education as well as the quality of the national public health care system, due to the possible future shortage of qualified medical personnel.

The strongest arguments against the Court's judgments at issue refer to the effects their implementation have had on the Austrian and Belgium higher education systems. After introducing a non-discriminatory and for certain studies[71] a restrictive access system, they experienced a disproportionally high rise of foreign students in these studies. Within the medical and paramedical studies the rise even went up to 80% (!) in the Belgian French Community.[72] Thus, the restrictive access system the Court proposed to introduce so as to avoid an excessive demand for access to specific courses could limit the number of students in total, but due to the particular characteristics of the cross-border relationship between Austria and Germany and respectively Belgium and France,[73] not the influx of the foreign students. It was argued that that influx, again, not only jeopardised the provision of high quality education services for their own nationals, but in particular also – because of the nature of the programs at issue – could pose a substantial risk to the stability of the nation's public health care system as a result of a potential shortage of health care professionals practicing in the country.

Above all, it was considered unfair that Austria and Belgium had to take over the funding of such high numbers of foreign students without receiving any equivalent consideration.[74] In this context, the discussion arose again about the establishment of a European wide reimbursement mechanism (some sort of a financial equalisation scheme) to ensure that the financial burdens resulting from cross border education are fairly distributed amongst the Member States.[75] But Europe is far away from implementing such a mechanism; for

---

71 Namely those, where the experiences of the last years have shown an excessive demand (in particular: the studies in human medicine, dentistry, veterinarian medicine and psychology).

72 See the figures presented in the judgment of the Belgium Cour Constitutionelle, l'Arrêt n° 12/2008 du 14 février 2008, Numéros du rôle: 4034 et 4093 and the opinion of AG Sharpston in the case *Bressol* (Fn 37), at para 20. In Austria they increased 50% according to information obtained by the Austrian Federal Ministry for Science and Research.

73 In short, a small MS with a free access system is confronted with a big MS (with a population about 10 times higher) with a restrictive access system.

74 Austria and Belgium welcome far more foreign students in comparison to the number of their own nationals who go abroad. Already under the 'discriminatory university entry rules" (as qualified by the Court), Austria was amongst the countries in Europe receiving the most foreign students (18.7%). See M. Dougan, 'Fees, Grants, Loans and Dole Cheques: Who covers the cost of migrant education within the EU?', (2005) 42 *CMLR* 943, at 956.

75 As to this discussion in Austria see e.g P. Hilpold, 'Hochschulzugang und Unionsbürgerschaft – Das Urteil das EuGH vom 7.7.2005 in der Rechtssache C-147/03, Kommission gegen Österreich', (2005) *EuZW* (*Europäische Zeitschrift für Wirtschaftsrecht*) 647, at 652. At the European level, the idea of such a reimbursement mechanism has been brought up by the European Commission already at the very beginning of the creation of the European higher education space. See the Commission's Memorandum on higher education in the EC, COM (91) 349 final.

various reasons this appears to be an extremely difficult task.[76] Attempts to find bilateral solutions in the cases at issue[77] have so far failed as well.

### 2.2.4. *Reaction to the Court's judgments: a quota regulation system for medical studies*

Due to these disproportional high numbers of foreign students in the medical studies, Austria and Belgium introduced a quota regulation system for the courses affected – in the Austrian case reserving 75% of the study places to applicants with a secondary education diploma awarded in Austria and in the Belgian case 70% of places were reserved for students who were resident in Belgium.[78]

Because of these quota regulations, the Commission again initiated infringement proceedings against Austria and Belgium in January 2007, but soon afterwards (in November 2007) suspended those for a period of five years. Unofficially it is said that the suspension was the result of political pressure exercised by Austria in the context of the Lisbon treaty negotiations. Officially, it shall give Austria and Belgium more time to submit additional data in the present case, in particular to collate evidence in support of the argument that without such quota systems their public health care systems might face serious problems in the future.[79]

### 2.2.5. *The Bressol judgment*

Parallel to the proceeding initiated by the Commission, in 2008 the Belgian *Cour Constitutionnelle* – due to a claim brought by French students against the Belgian quota regulation system – referred to the ECJ asking it to decide on the matter of cross-border access to higher education between France and Belgium again and thereby to answer in particular whether EU law (Articles 18 and 21, in conjunction with Article 165 TFEU) precludes such a quota regulation system even if unlimited cross border access could place an excessive burden on public finances, jeopardise the quality of the education provided and in the end lead to

---

76 "*The core problem is that such schemes compel States to repay the costs incurred by other States*", see A.P Van der Mei, 'EU Law and Education: Promotion of Student Mobility versus Protection of Education Systems', in M. Dougan and E. Spaventa (eds), *Social Welfare and EU Law*, Hart Publishing, Oxford, 2005, p 233.

77 As they for example exist between the European Nordic States (Denmark, Finland, Island, Norway and Sweden). See the multilateral agreement on access to higher education amongst these States from 3 September 1996, Kopenhagen (http://www.norden.or).

78 In Austria decided by the universities in self autonomy on the basis of Article 124 b(1) UG (BGBl I 120/2002 in the version of BGBl I 74/2006), which entitles the Austrian universities to establish an entry restriction system for those courses for which the German numerus clausus system applies. For the Belgian system in detail see the summary of the legal framework applicable to the case *Bressol* (Fn 37), para 8–16.

79 See S. Garben, 'The Bologna Process from a European Law Perspective', 2008/12 *EUI Working Papers Law*, para 12–14.

an insufficient number of qualified medical personnel in Belgium to ensure the quality of the public health system in that community.[80]

The Court's findings in *Bressol* are very much in line with its previous cases. The judgment seems just more moderate as it is based on a preliminary procedure, in contrast to the previous cases which were initiated by the Commission. The Court could thus confine itself to repeat general principles without the need to conduct the proportionality test, i.e. to make a definite decision on the matter at issue. This it devolved back again to the referring Court.

The judgment starts by recalling that the Member States might exercise their reserved powers only to the extent as this is in compliance with EU law. The ECJ therewith confirms that the special competence provision in higher education is subsidiary to other EU law.[81] From there, it then follows[82] that the Member States are free to opt for an open or restrictive access system in higher education as long as they ensure compliance with EU law, i.e. non-discriminatory treatment of the foreign students.

This conclusion is irritating, in particular before the background of the Belgian and Austrian higher education systems, which have clearly shown that because of financial reasons it is simply not possible to run an open access system while simultaneously maintaining non-discriminatory access to foreign students – at least without a functioning EU reimbursement mechanism. Even when giving up an open access and implementing a restrictive system, non-discriminatory treatment of foreign students and the guarantee of the MS' welfare systems cannot be accomplished at the same time. The Court's legal reasoning on the Member States' competences in the field of higher education insofar has no basis in reality.

What leaves even more open questions, is the Court's hint that the issue of cross-border access to education courses might not only fall under the union citizenship chapter and the non-discrimination clause of EU primary law, but in particular also under Article 24 para 1 of the Union Citizenship Directive from 2004,[83] which it leaves the referring Court to decide on. It is unclear whether this, if so, would involve a change of the EU legal framework on cross border access to higher education. One might argue that if the issue of higher education in fact falls under Article 24 para 1, then from para 2 it follows that it has to be granted without any limits. This is so, because first para 2 explicitly only excludes the entitlement to social assistance from the general equal treatment clause of para 1,

---

80 See case *Bressol* (fn 37), para 26; and the comment by S. Garben, 'Annotation of Case C-73/08 Nicolas Bressol and Others', (2010) 47 *CMLR* 1493.

81 Fn 37, para 28.

82 See the formulation in para 29: "The Member States are *thus* free ..."

83 See in para 38–39. Directive 2004/38/EC (Fn 62) holds in Article 24 para 1: "Subject to such specific provisions as are expressly provided for in the Treaty and secondary law, all Union citizens residing on the basis of this Directive in the territory of the host Member State shall enjoy equal treatment with the nationals of that Member State within the scope of the Treaty. The benefit of this right shall be extended to family members who are not nationals of a Member State and who have the right of residence or permanent residence."

and, secondly, established case law of the ECJ (with regard to the EU free movement provisions) holds that where a Community harmonisation measure already exists, Member States are not allowed to invoke public interest justifications on the basis of primary law.[84] However the next steps of the Court's argumentation in the *Bressol* case, in which it elaborates which reasons might qualify as objective justifications of the indirect discrimination at issue, speak against such a broad interpretation of Article 24 UC Directive. According to the ECJ all the reasons called on by the Belgian Constitutional Court – excessive burden on the financing of higher education, high quality of higher education and the stability of the Member States' public health care systems – are in principle legitimate reasons to justify indirect discrimination of the foreign students.[85] With this passage the ECJ above all makes clear, first that ensuring the financial stability of a Member States' welfare regime is not an 'aim of a purely economic nature', which according to settled case law may not be invoked (as has been intensively debated in the context of higher education)[86] and second, that the Belgium quota regulation system does not constitute direct discrimination, which can only be justified on the basis of explicit Treaty derogations (as AG Sharpston has tried to argue in her opinion).[87]

Starting from the point that the justifications put forward with regard to the protection of the public higher education system are the same as those linked with public health, the Court in the following just elaborates on the justification relating to the safeguarding of public health. Here, it provides guidance to the national Court on how to finally determine whether there are genuine risks to the protection of public health and if so, whether in light of the evidence provided by the national authorities, the legislation at issue can be regarded as appropriate for attaining the objective of protecting health. In doing so, it clearly shows, first that it still adheres to the strict proportionality test; and second, pursuant to which aspects it would review the national Court's final decision on the legitimacy of the Belgium quota regulation system in the case of an eventually succeeding infringement proceeding initiated by the Commission. In the given context, it is interesting to note that the ECJ in its remarks on the proportionality test, even though the decision is already based on the Lisbon treaty, does not mention the new social clause of the Lisbon treaty,[88] which obliges the Union to mainstream social policy issues (explicitly also comprising a high quality of higher education) in all its other policy areas.

---

84 See e.g. ECJ 23 May 1996, Case C-5/94, *The Queen v Ministry of Agriculture, Fisheries and Food, ex parte: Hedley Lomas (Ireland) Ltd.*, [1996] ECR I-02553, para 18.

85 See *Bressol* (fn 37), para 47–61.

86 See e.g. S. Griller, 'Vom Diskriminierungsverbot zur Grundrechtsgemeinschaft?', in Akyürek/Baumgartner/Jahnel/Lienbacher/Stolzlechner (eds), *Staat und Recht in europäischer Perspektive, Festschrift Heinz Schäffer*, Mainz Verlag, Wien, 2006, 231–233; N. Nic Shuibhne, 'Case law C-76/05, C-318/05 and joined cases C-11/06 and C-12/06', (2008) 45 *CMLR* 771, at 781–786; and in para 89 ff. of the case *Bressol* (fn 37).

87 See in para 64–76 and 128–131 of the Opinion of AG Sharpston in the case *Bressol* (fn 37).

88 Article 9 TFEU.

### 2.2.6. *Conclusion*

ECJ case law on student mobility shows that the competences of the Member States in higher education are clearly limited. As soon as they cannot prove, by demonstrating solid and consistent data, that the restriction of access for the foreign students is necessary to safeguard the functioning of their higher education system, and as a consequence thereof of their public health care system, the organisation of their higher education systems is to be regarded as incompatible with EU law and has thus to be adapted. By applying that strict proportionality test the Court puts itself in the comfortable position of arguing a violation of EU law simply by pointing out that the Member States have not provided enough evidence. In the past, this has led to situations where small Member States (such as Austria and Belgium) were, in the end, confronted with an 80% rise in the number of foreign students in certain courses, which again clearly indicates that EU-wide cross-border access can only work to its fullest extent under the condition of some sort of an EU wide compensation mechanism for the financing of cross-border higher education. The establishment of such a compensation mechanism within the EU is clearly the task of the EU political actors, i.e. at the bottom the Member States composing part of the EU secondary legislator. If the political actors refuse to do so, the Court, as a legal actor within the EU integration process, should respect that political decision and appropriately integrate it in its decision on the legitimacy of certain Member States to deviate from the non-discrimination principle by restricting access to higher education particularly for the foreign students in order to ensure that cross-border access does not become an unreasonable burden for their higher education systems.

## 2.3. STUDENT MOBILITY: CROSS-BORDER ACCESS TO FINANCIAL SUPPORT FOR EDUCATION

Besides cross-border access to the educational courses (as discussed above), the issue of cross-border access to financial support provided by the Member States for higher education is another distinctive factor in the promotion of student mobility and therewith the creation of a European wide area of higher education.[89] Different from the former issue, it is however not only a matter of the Member States' educational but also of their social policies,[90] in particular when the finan-

[89] See M. Dougan, 'Fees, Grants, Loans and Dole Cheques: Who covers the cost of migrant education within the EU?', (2005) 42 *CMLR* 943, at 952, referring to various Community policy documents highlighting this aspect of EU student mobility.

[90] Or, as the case ECJ 11 September 2007, Case C-76/05, *Herbert Schwarz and Marga Gootjes-Schwarz v Finanzamt Bergisch Gladbach* [2007] ECR I-06849 (concerning primary education) shows: it is also a matter of the MS' taxation policy, when the financial support is not provided by direct social assistance but indirectly by the possibility of deducting, from taxpayers income, part of the school fees.

cial support (in the form of grants, loans and other social assistance) is provided dependent upon the social needs of the scholars. The impetus of such measures is clearly of a social nature, namely to allow also pupils from lower classes of our society to enrol in higher education and so to create a truly meritocratic society.[91]

This slight difference of 'a matter not only of educational but also social policy' provided the Court, for a long time, a legitimate reason to treat the issues of cross-border access to education (including assistance provided to cover registration and tuition fees)[92] and cross-border access to maintenance assistance for students differently, holding that the latter (as part of the MS' social policies) in principle does not fall under the scope of EU law, so that migrant students could not claim cross-border access to student grants under the general non-discrimination principle.[93] Likewise, it refused a claim to export student grants on the basis of the free movement of services provisions,[94] holding that higher education financed, essentially, out of public funds does not constitute a 'service' within the meaning of the free movement of services provisions so that students cannot be regarded as recipients of services.[95]

By starting its broad reading of the Union citizenship chapter (beginning of this century)[96] the Court has changed its approach on the issue of cross-border access to maintenance assistance for students – in general on cross-border access to social benefits for non-economic union citizens – considerably. It regards these issues to now, in principle, fall under EU law (Article 18 read together with Article 21 TFEU) and therewith also under its jurisdiction. So far, the Court has however allowed the Member States under the proportionality test to broadly deviate from these rules when it comes to the question of granting maintenance assistance also to the foreign students on the same basis as to their national students. As first decided in *Bidar*[97] and repeated in some other cases, then codified in Article

91 The central aim of financial support which is provided on a universal basis (to all students who enrol) is, on the other hand, to increase the number of higher education graduates and therefore an educational policy matter. Social and educational policies are in this context however closely linked to each other.

92 See e.g. ECJ 21 June 1988, C-197/86, *Steven Malcolm Brown v The Secretary of State for Scotland* [1988] ECR 03205, para 17.

93 See e.g. ECJ 21 June 1988, C-197/86, *Steven Malcolm Brown v The Secretary of State for Scotland* [1988] ECR 03205, para 18.

94 The claim construed the students as recipients of higher education services who may not be restricted in their right to receive services from another Member State by granting social assistance only for higher education pursued in the home State. See the preliminary question 1 in ECJ December 1993, C-109/92, *Stephan Max Wirth v Landeshauptstadt Hannover* [1993] ECR I-06447, para 11.

95 ECJ December 1993, C-109/92, *Stephan Max Wirth v Landeshauptstadt Hannover* [1993] ECR I-06447, paras 15–19.

96 For an overview on this case law, see E. Spaventa, 'Seeing the wood despite the trees? On the scope of union citizenship and its constitutional effects', (2008) 45 *CMLR* 13.

97 ECJ 15 March 2005, C-209/03, *The Queen, on the application of Dany Bidar v London Borough of Ealing and Secretary of State for Education and Skills* [2005] ECR I-02119. See the comment on this judgment by C. Barnard, 'Case C-209/03', (2005) 42 *CMLR* 1465.

24 para 2 of the Union Citizenship Directive[98] and lately confirmed in the case *Förster*,[99] the Member States can make the grant of such social benefits to foreign students based on a condition of a five year residence requirement[100], in order to ensure that such grants to foreign students do not become an unreasonable burden to their welfare regime. The cross-border access of foreign students to social assistance in the host Member State in their capacity of Union citizens (i.e. on the basis of Articles 18 and 21 TFEU) is, thus, still quite limited. In this context, it must however be recalled that the ECJ by developing a very broad concept of the worker[101] has considerably opened up the possibility for foreign students to qualify as workers in the sense of Article 45 TFEU[102] and consequently to access as such the social benefits provided by the host Member States.[103]

Above, in the case *Morgan and Bucher*,[104] the Court indicated that it is willing to allow migrant students in their capacity of Union citizens (thus, on the basis of Articles 18 and 21 TFEU) to export student grants from their home Member States to pursue higher education in another Member State. When the higher education the migrant student wishes to pursue in the host Member State is provided by a private institution the exportability of students' grants can be also based, besides Article 18 TFEU, on the free movement of services provisions (Article 49 TFEU). In fact, the latter constitutes a specific expression of the rights guaranteed by the general non-discrimination principle (Article 18 TFEU) and thus applies primarily in relation to this.[105]

---

98 Cf. fn 62.

99 ECJ 18 November 2008, C-158/07, *Jacqueline Förster v Hoofddirectie van de Informatie Beheer Groep* [2008] ECR I-08507. See also the comment on this case by S. O'Leary, 'Case Comment: Equal Treatment and EU Citizens: A new chapter on cross-border educational mobility and access to student financial assistance', (2009) 34 *ELR (European Law Review)* 612.

100 Or to put it more generally: that the foreign union citizen can show that he/she has established a genuine link to the society of the host Member State. On this 'genuine link' doctrine, see M. Dougan, 'The Spatial Restructuring of National Welfare States within the European Union: the Contribution of Union Citizenship and the Relevance of the Treaty of Lissabon', in U. Neergard/R. Nielsen/L.M.Rosebery (eds), *Integrating Welfare Functions into EU law*, Djof Publishers, Copenhagen, 2009, 147.

101 For an overview of the Court's case law as to the concept of 'worker', see: E. Spaventa, *Free Movement of Persons in the European Union,* Kluwer, Alphen aan den Rijn, 2007, 1–32; C. Barnard, *EC Employment Law*, Oxford University Press, Oxford, 3rd ed, 2006, 171–294.

102 Already a part time job conducted for a rather short period of time can give a student the status of a worker, see ECJ 21 June 1988, C-39/86, *Sylvie Lair v Universität Hannover* [1988] ECR 03161; ECJ 6 November 2003, C-413/01, *Franca Ninni-Orasche v Bundesminister für Wissenschaft, Verkehr und Kunst* [2003] ECR I-13187.

103 As to the extensive body of case law with regard to social benefits provided to foreign nationals qualifying as workers, see M. Dougan, 'Fees, Grants, Loans and Dole Cheques: Who covers the cost of migrant education within the EU?', (2005) 42 *CMLR* 943, at 945.

104 ECJ 23 October 2007, C-11/06 and C-12/06, *Rhiannon Morgan v Bezirksregierung Köln (C-11/06) and Iris Bucher v Landrat des Kreises Düren (C-12/06)* [2007] ECR I-09161 commented by N. Nic Shuibhne, 'Case law C-76/05, C-318/05 and joined cases C-11/06 and C-12/06', (2008) 45 *CMLR* 771.

105 ECJ 11 September 2007, Case C-76/05, *Herbert Schwarz and Marga Gootjes-Schwarz v Finanzamt Bergisch Gladbach*, [2007] ECR I-06849, para 67, 81 and 34 (see also N. Nic

Overall, we can conclude that cross-border access to social assistance for migrant students as implemented by ECJ case law has already reached a quite substantial level, however different from the cases of cross border access to the educational courses not to be financed by the host Member State but the student's home Member State. As a consequence the migrant students are not provided with financial benefits to the same extent as the nationals in the host Member State but – in analogy to the ECJ case law in the health care sector – to the extent that they would have been provided within the national context.[106]

## 2.4. BUILDING THE EU INTERNAL MARKET BASED ON FREE COMPETITION FOR HIGHER EDUCATION

The ECJ, so far, has been very reluctant to qualify public institutions within the higher education sector financed, entirely or mainly, by public funds as undertakings in the sense of competition or state aid law (Articles 101–106 and 107–109 TFEU), respectively the educational courses they provide as services within the meaning of the free movement of services provision (Article 49 TFEU). The central argument for the non-application of these rules is that the Member States within this field typically do not intend to involve themselves in remunerated activities, but are carrying out a task in the social, cultural and educational fields towards its population.[107] The Court has thus so far in principle refrained from implementing the application of the EU market rules' open market principles within the public pillar of the European higher education area.

Private institutions, on the other hand, which within the Member States' dualist higher education systems provide, alongside to the public institutions, educational courses on a commercial basis, i.e. for remuneration, do qualify as undertakings (establishments which carry out an economic activity) and the educational courses they offer as services within the meaning of Article 49 EC.[108] The consequence of this is that private higher education institutions can, in principle, claim before the Court on the basis of the free movement rules to provide the educational services also within another Member State or to establish themselves within another Member State,[109] irrespective of whether the public higher education institutions within that other Member State are qualified to run

Shuibhne, 'Case law C-76/05, C-318/05 and joined cases C-11/06 and C-12/06', (2008) 45 *CMLR* 771, at 774).

106 The Court does not explicitly state this in the cases *Morgan/Bucher* (fn 104) and *Schwarz* (fn 105), but it can be read between the lines of these judgments.

107 See fundamentally in ECJ 27 September 1988, C-263/86, *Belgian State v René Humbel and Marie-Thérèse Edel* [1988] ECR 05365 para 2; repeated in many other judgments.

108 Most recently *Schwarz* (fn 105), para 40.

109 Cf. in this respect the case ECJ 10 March 2009, Case C- 169/07, *Hartlauer Handelsgesellschaft mbH v Wiener Landesregierung and Oberösterreichische Landesregierung*, [2009] ECR I-01721 (referring to the health care sector).

an economic activity or not.[110] The Member States again would have to prove, if they wanted to limit and control the provision of higher education services by (foreign) private institutions within their higher education system, that such limits are necessary and proportionate to attain a certain public interest, which e.g. could be to ensure the stability of the public pillar of their higher education system.[111] The Court so far applies a quite flexible proportionality test to this issue, accepting limitations by the Member States to set up private institutions as long as such limitations are also foreseen for the national private institutions, i.e. are non-discriminatory. With this approach the Court in principle respects the MS' discretion to decide to what extent they want to build up a dualist system in higher education. However, the Court's last judgment on this issue – relating particularly to the educational sector – is as far back as the 1980s and does not concern higher but rather primary education.[112] Therefore, it's not clear whether the Court nowadays would still be that permissive on this issue.[113]

As long as the public higher education institutions do not qualify as undertakings as intended by the competition rules, (foreign) private education providers cannot attack, on the basis of the competition rules, the special or exclusive rights granted to the public higher education institutions by the Member States. The organisation of the Member States' dualist systems within higher education is not yet subject of EU law. This will however very probably change in the coming years, considering that public universities throughout Europe, both in research and teaching, increasingly engage in economic activities (by e.g. providing post graduate programs at market prices or research for the industry).[114] We can in general witness a trend towards increased private funding of the public universities in Europe[115] due to the financial pressures the Member

---

110 See already ECJ 15 March 1988, Case C-147/86, *Commission v Greece* [1988] ECR 1637 (however not concerning the higher, but the primary education sector (to set up a private school and to provide teaching at home).

111 See the arguments put forward by the Austrian government in the *Hartlauer* case (Fn 109) to argue the necessity for the restriction of the establishment of private health care providers in Austria. The core aspects of this argumentation could be also applied to the higher education sector.

112 *Commission v Greece* (Fn 110), para 1: "*on the other hand, a prohibition on the setting up of private vocational training schools does not constitute a failure to fulfil those obligations since it applies to nationals of that state and to nationals of other Member States alike.*"

113 In the case *Hartlauer* (Fn 109), which relates to the health care sector, the ECJ was quite permissive. But it is difficult to draw, from this judgement only, conclusions for the higher education sector.

114 The Commission has already started, in some of its state aid decisions, to challenge the qualification of public higher institutions as non-undertakings. See M. Kleis and P. Nicolaides, 'The Concept of Undertaking in Education and Public Health Systems', (2006) *EStAL (European State Aid Law Quarterly)* 505, at 506–507.

115 Cf. S. Jorgensen, 'The Right to Cross-border Education in the European Union', (2009) 46 *CMLR* 1567, at 1587s. See in this context the Study on the financing of higher education in Europe completed by European Research Associates (EU-RA), commissioned by the European Commission (DG Education and Culture), 2004.

States have to face today – some of them[116] not at least because the Commission and the ECJ are pushing for student mobility within the EU even without the existence of an adequate European wide reimbursement mechanism to fairly distribute the costs for such student mobility amongst the Member States.

## 3. CONCLUSION

The European Court of Justice has, on the basis of its implied powers for higher education, over the last 30 years consistently worked on the creation of a European area of higher education and as a consequence thereof curtailed the Member States' 'reserved competences' within this policy field. It has promoted the system of mutual recognition of professional qualifications within the EU, first by developing, on the basis of EU primary law, case by case the central components of this system, and subsequently by extending the secondary law provisions that have been issued as a result of its jurisprudence in this field built on EU primary law. It has so far strictly enforced the right of cross-border access to higher education courses, even in very controversial cases like Austria and Belgium, for which it has been sharply criticised. Its new judgment in this matter, *Bressol*, does not necessarily indicate that it is willing to deviate in the future from the path it has so far followed on this matter. Finally, by allowing the exportability of student grants (and access to student grants in the host Member State after a genuine link has been established) it has extended the right to student mobility beyond mere access to educational courses, so as to cover also social assistance.

The Court has, however, thus far, been quite reluctant to introduce market principles (free movement of private actors and competition amongst the public and private higher education institutions) within the European area of higher education, which indicates that in principle it respects the Member States' decision to run higher education primarily as a public service and public responsibility. Given the trend to increase private funding in the higher education sector, which is a prevailing one throughout the EU today, the Court's perspective on that issue might, however, change in the future.

The European legislator has, so far, only partly followed these developments of a Europeanisation of higher education induced by the ECJ, in fact only within the field of mutual recognition of professional qualifications (for which an explicit primary law basis exists); and above to codify the limits to cross border access to student grants within the host Member State.[117] The creation of a European area of higher education rather, takes place outside the EU system, within the Bologna process. This has been, however, heavily criticised for democratic, constitutional

[116] The Member States which 'import' more students than they 'export'. For some numbers see M. Dougan, 'Fees, Grants, Loans and Dole Cheques: Who covers the cost of migrant education within the EU?', (2005) 42 *CMLR* 943, at 956.

[117] See Article 24 para 2 Union Citizenship Directive (Fn 62).

and efficiency reasons. Above that, Bologna, so far, has not provided answers to the most crucial question in the creation of a European area of higher education, namely how to fairly distribute the costs of student mobility within the EU amongst the Member States.

While it seems quite reasonable[118] to convey the burdens of student mobility in relation to student supports primarily on the student's Member State of origin, it is, on the other hand, not really comprehensible why, with regard to cross-border access to higher education, the host Member State shall assume the entire burden for the financing of foreign students. On the basis of ECJ case law, i.e. by mere legal integration, it is however difficult to think of other mechanisms of financing. In fact, the only option available to the Court is ruling that there has been an unfair distribution of the costs amongst the Member States, thus restricting student mobility (amongst certain Member States) and therewith the idea of a European area of higher education.

So, if student mobility is to function to the full extent within the EU, which in principle is the goal of all involved parties, the political actors have to become active, preferably – given the many objections against Bologna – through EU secondary law mechanisms.[119] Political and positive integration will certainly be necessary so as to ensure that the European area of higher education can also develop outside the internal market rationale (to which the ECJ is bound), i.e. to ensure that higher education can in the long-run remain, within the broader context of the EU, a primarily public good and public responsibility.

## REFERENCES

C. Barnard, *The Substantive Law of the EU. The four freedoms,* Oxford University Press, Oxford, 2004.

C. Barnard, *EC Employment Law*, Oxford University Press, Oxford, 3rd ed, 2006.

C. Barnard, 'Case C-209/03', (2005) 42 *CMLR (Common Market Law Review)* 1465.

A. von Bogdandy and J. Bast, 'The European Union's Vertical Order of Competences: The Current Law and Proposals for its Reform', (2002) 39 *CMLR* 227.

A. Dashwood, 'The Limits of Community Powers', (1996) 21 *European Public Law* 113.

---

[118] Following the logic that the home Member States would have had to pay anyway, also when the students would have remained within the home Member State; but see M. Dougan, 'Fees, Grants, Loans and Dole Cheques: Who covers the cost of migrant education within the EU?', (2005) 42 *CMLR* 943, at 981 ss.

[119] The Union citizenship chapter and the free movement of services provisions could serve, in the style as they are applied by the ECJ to the higher education area, as a legal base for such measures. On the assumption that (also public) higher education will in the future throughout the EU be increasingly provided on a commercial basis, the new Article 14 TFEU on the SGEI could also become relevant as such a legal base. For the existence of a legal base to issue positive measures in higher education, see also S. Garben, 'The Bologna Process from a European Law Perspective', 2008/12 *EUI Working Papers Law*, 3 ss.

B. De Witte, 'Introduction', in B. De Witte (ed.) *European Community Law in Education* (1993) 9–18.

B. De Witte, 'Non-Market Values in Internal Market Legislation', in N. Nic Shuibhne (ed.), *Regulating the Internal Market*, Cheltenham, Edward Elgar, 2006, 61–86.

M. Dougan, 'The Spatial Restructuring of National Welfare States within the European Union: the Contribution of Union Citizenship and the Relevance of the Treaty of Lissabon', in U. Neergard/R. Nielsen/L.M.Rosebery (eds.), *Integrating Welfare Functions into EU law*, Djof Publishers, Copenhagen, 2009, 147–187.

M. Dougan, 'Fees, Grants, Loans and Dole Cheques: Who covers the cost of migrant education within the EU?', (2005) 42 *CMLR* 943.

S. Garben, 'The Bologna Process from a European Law Perspective', (2008) 12 *EUI Working Papers.*

S. Garben, 'The Belgian/Austrian Education Saga', (2008) 01 *Harvard European Law Working Paper.*

S. Garben, 'Case 73/08', (2010) 47 *CMLR* 1493.

S. Griller, 'Vom Diskriminierungsverbot zur Grundrechtsgemeinschaft?', in Akyürek/ Baumgartner/Jahnel/Lienbacher/Stolzlechner (eds.), *Staat und Recht in europäischer Perspektive, Festschrift Heinz Schäffer*, Mainz Verlag, Wien, 2006.

V. Hatzopoulos, 'A (More) Social Europe: A Political Crossroad or a Legal One-Way? Dialogues between Luxembourg and Lisbon', (2005) 42 *CMLR* 1599.

P. Hilpold, 'Hochschulzugang und Unionsbürgerschaft - Das Urteil das EuGH vom 7.7.2005 in der Rechtssache C-147/03, Kommission gegen Österreich', (2005) *EuZW (Europäische Zeitschrift für Wirtschaftsrecht)* 647 - 652.

S. Jorgensen, 'The Right to Cross-border Education in the European Union', (2009) 46 *CMLR* 1567.

M. Kleis and P. Nicolaides, 'The Concept of Undertaking in Education and Public Health Systems', (2006) *EStAL (European State Aid Law Quarterly)* 505.

K. Lenaerts, 'Education in European Community law after "Maastricht"', (1994) 31 *CMLR* 7.

J. Lonbay, 'Reflections on Education and Culture in EC Law', in Craufurd Smith (ed.) *Culture and European Community Law*, Oxford University Press, Oxford, 2004.

J. Maillo, 'Article 86. Services of General Interest and EC Competition Law', in Amato and Ehlermann (eds.), *EC Competition Law: A Critical Assessment,* Hart Publishing, Oxford, 2007.

T.H. Marshall, *Social Policy in the Twentieth Century*, Hutchinson, London, 4th ed, 1975.

N. Nic Shuibhne, 'Case law C-76/05, C-318/05 and joined cases C-11/06 and C-12/06', (2008) 45 *CMLR* 771.

S. O'Leary, 'Case Comment: Equal Treatment and EU Citizens: A new chapter on cross-border educational mobility and access to student financial assistance', (2009) 34 *ELR (European Law Review)* 612–627.

H. Pechar and A. Pellert: 'Austrian Universities Under Pressure From Bologna', (2004) 39 *EJE (European Journal of Education)* 317–330.

H. Schneider and S. Claessens, 'The Recognition of Diplomas and the free Movement of Professionals in the European Union', in: Schneider (ed.), *Migration, Integration and Citizenship, A Challenge for Europe's Future, Vol I* Forum Maastricht, Maastricht, 2005.

H. Schweitzer, 'Die Daseinsvorsorge im Verfassungsentwurf des Europäischen Konvents – Ein europäischer "service public"'?, in Schwarze (ed.), *Der Verfassungsentwurf des Europäischen Konvents,* Nomos, Baden-Baden, 2004.

E. Spaventa, *Free Movement of Persons in the European Union,* Kluwer, Alphen aan der Rijn, 2007.

E. Spaventa, 'Seeing the wood despite the trees? On the scope of union citizenship and its constitutional effects', (2008) 45 *CMLR* 13.

A.P Van der Mei, 'EU Law and Education: Promotion of Student Mobility versus Protection of Education Systems', in M. Dougan and E. Spaventa (eds), *Social Welfare and EU Law,* Hart Publishing, Oxford, 2005, 219–239.

B. Wächter, 'The Bologna Process: developments and prospects', (2004) 39 *EJE* 265, at 266–267.

# THE EUROPEAN COURT OF JUSTICE, MEMBER STATE AUTONOMY AND EUROPEAN UNION CITIZENSHIP: CONJUNCTIONS AND DISJUNCTIONS[1]

Dora Kostakopoulou

## 1. INTRODUCTION[2]

Scholarship on the role of the European Court of Justice in shaping the polycentric European governance and the law and politics of 'sovereign' national authorities contains plenty of discords. Yet its role as a driving force of European integration is probably beyond dispute. Not only jurists but also political scientists have acknowledged its authoritative reasoning on issues of integration and principle, notwithstanding the existence of concerns about growing judicial power and the perennial disagreement over whether judicial processes are less legitimate than democratic ones.[3] Certainly, if the meaning of the latter is confined to majoritarian processes, then the assumption of a quasi-legislative role by courts, that is, their ability to bypass political and legislative processes, appears to be problematic. But since democratic systems are built upon majoritarian electoral processes as well as reflective values and rights, which place constraints on governments' powers, the judicial protection and advancement of these values and rights are normatively and empirically justified. Courts function as 'fora of principle'[4] and

---

1 The phrase is borrowed from Octavio Paz's collection of essays, entitled *Conjunctions and Disjunctions*, Arcade Publishing, New York, 1991. The 2007 edition has been published by Little, Brown and Company.

2 In this chapter the law is as stated on 1 December 2009.

3 See, for instance, H. Rasmussen, *On Law and Policy in the European Court of Justice*, Martinus Nijhoff, The Hague, 1986; U. Everling, 'The ECJ as a Decision-making Authority', (1994) 82 *Michigan Law Review* 1294; J.H.H. Weiler and N.J.S. Lockhart, '"Taking Rights Seriously" Seriously: the European Court of Justice and its Fundamental Rights Jurisprudence', (1995) 32 *CMLR (Common Market Law Review)* 51; T. Tridimas, 'The European Court of Justice and Judicial Activism', (1997) 22 *ELR (European Law Review)* 199; K. Alter, 'the European Union's Legal System and Domestic Policy', (2000) 54 *International Organisation* 489; et al.

4 R. Dworkin, 'The Forum of Principle', in *A Matter of Principle*, Harvard University Press, Cambridge, MA, 1985, p 91; *Taking Rights Seriously*, Harvard University Press, Cambridge, MA, 1977.

have been recognised as reliable agents for securing equitable settlements within and above the nation-state.

Seen from the perspective of achieving rights-enhancing and fairer settlements, ensuring non-discrimination and promoting human welfare, the role of the courts, be they national constitutional courts or the ECJ, is commendable. Seen from the (narrower) perspective of the actually existing world of majoritarian democracy, which entails the promotion of 'the right' and 'the good' through the exercise of governmental power, any institution which might call into question the 'undisputed' sovereign authority of the state, is bound to be seen as having an adverse effect on democratic decision-making. To some extent, this debate reveals contrasting conceptions of democracy held by political and legal scholars and the frequent identification of rulers with the people (the ruled). But it may also be seen to reflect contrasting perspectives depending on the question of 'who is looking at the ECJ'; that is, national executives or the members of their publics. At the heart of this question thus essentially lie different beliefs in how far and in what ways governance should be responsive to the governed, should pro-actively address their needs and enhance their welfare.

In this chapter, I seek to address the debate between judicial activism at the EU level and Member State autonomy by comparing and contrasting two dimensions of the same institution; namely, the judicialised material scope (section 2) and the non-judicialised personal scope of European Union citizenship (section 3). The latter institution was established by the Treaty on European Union in 1993 and its material scope has developed significantly owing to the European Court of Justice's interventions as well as the entry into force of Directive 2004/38 (the so called 'Citizenship Directive') on 1 May 2006.[5] To an extent, the maturation of European citizenship could be seen as a manifestation of 'governing with judges'.[6] But while the material scope of Union citizenship has been characterised by incremental, principled and transformative institutional change, its personal scope, that is, the question of who is entitled to be a member of the European citizenry, has by and large evaded a similar process of critical reflection and adaptation to changing conditions. In the subsequent discussion, I reflect on the consequences of governing with or without judges and the Member States' relative autonomy and argue that the political consequences as far as the rights of citizens and residents, substantive commitments to non-discrimination and equal treatment and the vision of an inclusive European public are concerned are too important to be left to self-regulation.

---

5 European Parliament and Council Directive 2004/38/EC, OJ 2004 L 157/77. The transposition of the Directive has not been effective according to the European Commission's 5th Report on EU Citizenship, COM (2008) 85 final, page 5.

6 The term is borrowed from A. Stone-Sweet, *Governing with Judges: Constitutional Politics in Europe*, Oxford University Press, Oxford, 2000.

## 2. EUROPEAN UNION CITIZENSHIP AS AN EXPERIMENTAL INSTITUTION

The adoption of the Directive *on the Right of Citizens and their Family Members to move and reside freely within the territory of the Member States*[7] remedied the sector-by-sector and fragmented approach to free movement rights by incorporating and revising the existing Directives and amending Council Regulation 1612/68.[8] It built on, and further extended, the rights-based approach characterising the rights of free movement since the 1960s and made Union citizenship a genuine mode of associated living by establishing an unconditional right of permanent residence for Union citizens and their families[9] who have resided in the host MS for a continuous period of five years. Permanent residence brings along a formal expectation for the elimination of the barrier of nationality; Union citizens are entitled to full equal treatment in the areas covered by the Treaty in the Member State of their residence. Below the apex of permanent residence there exist two other types of residence rights; namely, free circulation during short periods of residence not exceeding three months and longer periods of residence exceeding three months. The former type of residence rights enables Union citizens to exercise their rights without any conditions or any formalities other than the requirement to hold a valid identity card or passport, but does not carry an entitlement to social assistance for non-active economic actors. In *Oulane* the Court reiterated that a MS may not refuse to recognize a person's right of residence because she did not present one of these documents and that any document that could prove that the person concerned is a Community national would suffice.[10] This is not to say that third country nationals who are family members of Union citizens do not continue to encounter problems with respect to the authorization of their entry and the issue of residence cards in practice. Periods of residence exceeding three months, on the other hand, entail a right of residence for Union citizens and their family members provided that they are active contributors to the commonwealth or self-sufficient: they are workers or self-employed persons in the host MS; or have sufficient resources and comprehensive sickness insurance cover, if they are non-active economic actors; or they are students enrolled at a private or public establishment, have comprehensive sickness insurance cover and are self-sufficient in order to avoid becoming a burden on the social assistance

---

7 Directive 2004/38/EC, OJ 2004 L 158/77.

8 Articles 10 and 11 of Council Reg. 1612/68 were repealed with effect from 30 April 2006.

9 The definition of a 'family member' includes a registered partner if the legislation of the host MS treats registered partnership as equivalent to marriage.

10 ECJ 17 February 2005, Case C-215/03, *Oulane* [2005] ECR I-1215. In addition, in *Commission v the Netherlands* the Court ruled that national provisions which required non-active and retired persons to have adequate personal resources sufficient for at least a year's stay in the host MS contravened Community law (i.e., Dir 38/360 and Directives 90/364 and 90/365); Case C-398/06, Judgment of the Court of 10 April 2008.

system of the host MS.[11] The Directive also makes reference to the possibility to extend the period of time during which Union citizens and their family members may reside in the territory of the host MS without any conditions.[12] The rights of family members have also been reinforced by extending family reunification to registered partners and by giving spouses and partners who are non-EU nationals independent rights of residence in the event of divorce, annulment of marriage or termination of the registered partnership. In addition, by incorporating the Court's reasoning in *Grzelczyk,*[13] the Directive states that as long as the beneficiaries of the right of residence do not become an unreasonable burden on the social assistance system of the host MS they should not be expelled.[14]

On reflection, the provisions of the Directive reveal three important trends which correspond to the increasing political importance of European integration. Firstly, they attest to a reconfiguration of community membership in ways that attribute greater importance to the observable fact of residence than the habits of loyalty and ideology associated with nationality. The right to permanent residence is an offshoot of connexive citizenship, that is, the real links and genuine connections that a Union citizen develops in a MS other than that of its origin, rather than being the by-product of one's naturalization in the host MS.[15] As recital 17 in the preamble to the Citizenship Directive states: 'enjoyment of permanent residence by Union citizens who have chosen to settle long term in the host MS would strengthen the feeling of Union citizenship and is a key element in promoting social cohesion which is one of the fundamental objective of the Union'. Union citizenship thus gradually changes our understanding of community membership and fosters more inclusive forms of political association. In sum, the new Directive creates the institutional preconditions for a notion of citizenship that is more inclusive than nationality-based models of citizenship.[16] Secondly, Union citizenship has become a fundamental status of nationals of EU member states thereby endowing them with an increasing range of rights which are exercised not within the domain of a given national polity but within the wider context of a wide Europolity. In this way, the political and social constructivist aspects of European integration are realized; the so called 'market Europe'

11 Article 7 of Council Directive 2004/38.

12 Ibid, Chapter VII, Article 39.

13 Dir. 2004/38, note 26 above, Article 14.

14 Article 14(1) of Directive 2004/38.

15 D. Kostakopoulou, 'European Citizenship and Immigration After Amsterdam: Openings, Silences, Paradoxes', (1998) 24:4 *Journal of Ethnic and Migration Studies* 639–656; *The Future Governance of Citizenship*, Cambridge University Press, Cambridge, 2008.

16 However, egalitarian processes co-exist with the practice of exclusion of long-term resident third country nationals from the personal scope of Union citizenship. In addition, transitional arrangements with respect to the nationals of eight Central and Eastern European states which joined the EU on the 1 May 2004 and 1 of January 2007 have resulted in a hierarchical European citizenry.

is transformed into a peoples' Europe or a European society.[17] As Advocate General Maduro has stated, 'when the Court describes Union citizenship as 'the fundamental status' of nationals it is not making a political statement; it refers to Union citizenship as a legal concept that goes hand in hand with specific rights for Union citizens'.[18] And further, 'Citizenship of the Union must encourage Member States to no longer conceive of the legitimate link of integration only within the narrow bonds of the national community, but also within the wider context of the society of peoples of the Union'.[19]

It follows from both the preceding considerations that Union citizenship is not a simple, and weaker, corollary to national citizenship. True, the EU may lack the traditional state paraphernalia, but, as we shall see below, its supranational character rules out national sovereignty claims over the grant of migration rights to EU nationals and their family members, residence rights for them and their children enrolled at educational establishments[20] and regulatory autonomy in the granting of welfare assistance and the payment of war related pensions and allowances. And this, quite unavoidably, gives rise to reactions and criticisms. It has been argued, for example, that the Citizenship Directive weakens state autonomy in matters of passport controls, extends the definition of the EU citizen's family, threatens to increase social and financial burdens in the MS and prevents national executives from implementing proposals for the automatic expulsion of 'foreign criminals' who are sex offenders or are given custodial sentences.[21]

In assessing the merits of national anxieties about, and criticisms against, the scope and the pace of creating 'an ever closer Union among the peoples' of Europe' either by legislative fiat or judicial activism, it seems to me a prior reflection on both the appropriateness and legitimacy of the yardstick to be used is necessary. Although ideology, pragmatism, normative concerns or simply convenience, which is often manifested in a belief in the fixity of the status quo, all can impact

17 Compare the Opinion of Advocate General Jacobs in Case C-168/91 *Konstadinidis v Stadt Altensteig* [1993] ECR I-1191 and his reference to 'civis europeum'.

18 See the AG's Opinion 3 April 2008, in C-524/06, *H. Huber v Bundesrepublic Deutschland* [2008] ECR I-9705.

19 See point 23 of AG Maduro's Opinion 28 February 2008, Case C-499/06, *Nerkowska* [2008] ECR I-3993; see also the Opinion of AG Trstenjak 28 June 2007, Joined Cases C-396/05, C-419/05 and C-450/05, *Habelt and Others* [2007] ECR I-11895), para 82 to 84.

20 See ECJ 23 February 2010, Case C-310/08, *London Borrow of Harrow* v *Nimco Hassan Ibrahim and Secretary of State for the Home Department*, nyr, Opinion of AG Mazak delivered on 20 October 2009, Case C-480/08, *Maria Teixeira* v *London Borough of Lambeth and Secretary of State for the Home Department*, Opinion of Advocate General Kokott delivered on 20 October 2009, nyr.

21 It thus comes as no surprise that its transposition and correct implementation have been problematic. In June 2007 fifteen infringement procedures were open, four of which have been referred to the European Court of Justice and in December 2008 the Commission announced that only Cyprus, Greece, Finland, Portugal, Malta, Luxembourg and Spain had adopted more than 85% of provisions of the Directive; European Commission, 5th Report on Citizenship of the Union (1 May 2004–30 June 2007) COM(2008) 85 Final, page 5. Following this report, the Commission has recently had to adopt guidelines to ensure its transposition; COM(2009) 313.

on the choice of the yardstick, in my opinion what justifies and legitimates institutional structures at all levels, functions and policies is their capacity to recognize and fulfil human needs by removing barriers, be they unacceptable inequalities, unfair applications of rules of collective action, prejudice or simply wasteful struggles. J. Dewey has brilliantly outlined such a human needs-based yardstick in another context and with respect to another political organisation, namely, the state: he observed that 'a measure of the goodness of the state is the degree in which it relieves individuals from the waste of negative struggles and needless conflict and confers upon them positive assurance and reinforcement in what he undertakes'.[22] Such a yardstick stands in sharp contrast to both the deification of state power and the belief that the commands of sovereign authorities deserve unqualified respect by the European judges as well as the false identification of the interests of national executives with the interests of the citizens they claim to represent. It is on the account of its consequences on individuals and their life chances that the judicialisation of European Union citizenship will be approached and judged in this chapter.

## 2.1. EU CITIZENSHIP AS A FUNDAMENTAL STATUS

It is beyond doubt that the ECJ has contributed decisively to the developments of Article 18(1) EC which were in turn enshrined in the Citizenship Directive. Following an initial period of judicial minimalism (1993–1997)[23] and governmental reactions against the Court's influential integrationist approach which were manifested in concrete proposals to limit its power prior to the 1996 Intergovernmental conference, the Court enhanced the normative and political weight of Union citizenship by stating that 'it is destined to be the fundamental status of nationals of the Member States'.[24] As the Court put it, it enables 'those who find themselves in the same situation [as nationals of the host Member State] to enjoy the same treatment in law irrespective of their nationality, subject to such exceptions as are expressly provided for', thereby echoing and reinforcing Advocate General Leger's statement in *Boukhalfa*, 'taken to its ultimate conclusion, the concept should lead to Citizens of the Union being treated absolutely equally, irrespective of nationality. Such equal treatment should be manifested in the same way as among nationals of one and the same Member State'.[25]

---

22 J. Dewey, *The Public and Its Problems*, H. Holt, New York, 1927, reprinted by Swallow Press and Ohaio University Press, 1991, p 72.

23 D. Kostakopoulou, 'Ideas, Norms and European Citizenship: Explaining Institutional Change', (2005) 65:2 *Modern Law Review* 233–267, 244–245.

24 ECJ 20 September 2001, Case C-184/99, *Grzelczyk v Centre Public d'Aide Sociale d'Ottignies-Louvain-la-Neuve* [2001] ECR I-6193, para 31.

25 ECJ 30 April 1996, Case C-214/94, *Boukhalfa v Federal Republic of Germany* [1996] ECR I-2253; [1996] 3 *CMLR* 22 delivered on 14 November 1995.

A few years later, the Court stated that Article 18(1) EC creates a directly effective right (*Baumbast*)[26] despite the express reference to the 'limitations and conditions laid down in this Treaty and by the measures adopted to give it effect' in Article 18(1) EC. According to the Court, 'the application of the limitations and conditions acknowledged in Article 18(1) EC in respect of that right of residence is subject to judicial review. Consequently, any limitations and conditions imposed on that right do not prevent the provisions of Article 18(1) EC from conferring on individuals rights which are enforceable by them and which the national courts must protect'. Although this ruling led certain commentators to argue that the ECJ illegitimately rewrites the rules laid down in secondary Community law with the aid of Union citizenship and the principle of proportionality,[27] it, nevertheless, was the case that the attribution of direct effect to Article 18(1) EC (now Article 21(1) TFEU) had an empowering effect on individuals and a 'path dependent' effect on its subsequent jurisprudence.

In the years that followed, the Court proceeded to weaken the link between economic self-sufficiency and the exercise of free movement rights. The right to move and reside freely within the territory of the Member States thus became a fundamental right that all Union citizens should enjoy irrespective of their economic status. This was achieved by combining Article 18 EC with Article 12 EC, the non-discrimination clause, a combination that enabled Union citizens lawfully resident in the territory of a MS to rely on Article 12 in all situations that fell within the scope (*rationae materiae*) of Community law. Accordingly, in *Bidar*[28] the Court departed from earlier case law which excluded students from the grant social assistance, by ruling that, as Union citizens, students who have demonstrated 'a certain degree of integration into the society of the host state' can claim maintenance grants.[29] But the Member States are also entitled to ensure that 'the grant of assistance does not become an unreasonable burden'. Even though the requirement of demonstrating 'a certain degree of integration' was not sufficiently clear, the Court had, nevertheless, indicated that a reasonable period of lawful residence[30] and the ensuing immersion in a web of interactions in the host state[31] generates an entitlement to non-discrimination and equal treatment in the social field. The Court thus ruled in *Trojani* that a lawfully resident non active economic actor was entitled to a social assistance benefit on

26 ECJ 17 September 2002, Case C-413/99, *Baumbast and R v Secretary of State for the Home Department* [2002] ECR I-7091.

27 M. Dougan, 'The Constitutional Dimension to the Case Law on Union Citizenship', (2006) 31 *ELR* 613; E. Spaventa, 'Seeing the Wood despite the Trees?', (2008) 13 *CMLR* 29.

28 ECJ 15 March 2005, Case C-209/03, *Bidar v London Borough of Ealing* [2005] ECR I-2119.

29 In Bidar's case, a subsidised student loan.

30 Ibid. See also ECJ 7 September 2004, Case C-456/02, *Trojani v CPAS* [2004] ECR I-7573, para 43. The ECJ refers to 'lawful residence in the host MS for a certain time or the possession of a residence permit'.

31 Bidar had completed his secondary education in the UK.

the basis of Article 12 EC,[32] whereas in *Collins*, the absence of a genuine link between a jobseeker and the employment market of the host state invalidated an entitlement to a jobseeker's allowance.[33] In both cases, however, the principle of proportionality must be respected and the application of a residence requirement is open to judicial review. In the two tide-over allowance cases, namely *D'Hoop and Ioannidis*, the Court held that the place of completion of one's secondary education did not reflect the real and effective degree of connection between the individual concerned and the employment market of the MS. D'Hoop, a Belgian national and graduate who had obtained her baccalaureate in France, was denied the benefit which would give her access to special employment programmes by the MS of her origin. The Court in this case highlighted that Union citizenship forms the basis of rights to equal treatment irrespective of nationality[34] and noted that it would contravene EC law if a citizen received in her own Member State treatment less favourable than that she would otherwise enjoy had she not availed herself of the right to free movement. In *Ioannidis*, on the other hand, Belgium did not grant the tideover allowance to a Greek national resident in Belgium who had completed his secondary education in Greece, but who could be an active participant in the Belgian employment market.[35]

Although in the Court's 'real link' jurisprudence many detected a conscious attempt by the ECJ to create a form of transnational solidarity by undermining the exclusivity of national welfare systems,[36] O'Brien has convincingly argued that the 'real link implies a right to be assessed, but no more'.[37] General provisions and blanket exclusions of economically inactive (– not yet active) persons form access to social benefits such as those that pertained under *Lebon*, that is, equal access to employment and not with respect to social and tax advantages under Article 7(2) of Council Regulation 1612/68, were no longer consonant with the constitutionalisation of Union citizenship and its growing importance as

32 See fn 29 above.

33 ECJ 23 March 2004, Case C-138/02, *Brian Francis Collins* [2004] ECR I-2703. Similarly, the taking up of residence abroad is not a satisfactory indicator of a loss of connection with one's home Member State which is demonstrating its solidarity with the applicant by granting a civilian war benefit to him/her; ECJ 26 October 2006, Case C-192/05, *K. Tas-Hagen and R.A. Tas* [2006] ECR I-10451.

34 ECJ 11 July 2002, Case C-224/98, *Marie-Nathalie D'Hoop v Office national de l'emploi* [2002] ECR I-6191.

35 Compare also ECJ 15 September 2005, Case C-258/04, *Ioannidis* [2005] ECR I-8275. Ioannidis was denied a tideover allowance on the grounds that he had completed his secondary education in another Member State.

36 A. Somek, 'Solidarity Decomposed: Being and Time in European Citizenship', (2008) 32 *ELR* 787; H. Verschueren, 'European (internal) migration law as an instrument for defining the boundaries of national citizenship systems', (2007) 9:3, *European Journal of Migration Law* 307–346; O. Golynker, 'Jobseekers' rights in the European Union: challenges of changing the paradigm of solidarity', (2005) 30:1 *ELR* 111–122.

37 C. O'Brien, 'Real links, abstract rights and false alarms: the relationship between the ECJ's "real link" case law and national solidarity', (2008) 33:5 *ELR* p 643–665.

well as with growing citizen mobility.[38] Instead, a case-by-case approach and personalized assessments of the extent and weight of the connections that non –, or not yet –, active economic actors have established with the host MS either through residence or study or employment[39] or both appear to furnish a better ground for determining the boundaries of full community belonging.[40]

Although the Member States have complained against what they see as the gradual erosion of their national welfare schemes and the reduction of executive discretion in decisions on the award of social welfare assistance, it may be noted that the Court's reasoning is both reasonable and consonant with the fundamental status of Union citizenship.[41] Union citizenship in the new millennium could no longer be a privilege of 'the few' 'favoured EU nationals', that is, of active economic actors; instead, it had to obtain a more universal application in line with the concept of citizenship itself. Otherwise put, the promise of equal treatment irrespective of nationality,[42] which underpins Union citizenship, could not continue to be grounded in inequality in economic status; the latter had to be made less consequential. At the same time, however, pragmatic considerations about disparities in welfare across the EU dictated that the distinction between economically active and non-active economically Union citizens and the concomitant differential residency and welfare rights could not be completely

---

38 N. Reich, 'The Constitutional Relevance of Citizenship and Free Movement in an Enlarged Union', (2005) 11 *ELJ* 675–698; F. Jacobs, 'Citizenship of the EU-A Legal Analysis', (2007) 13:5 *ELJ* 591.

39 It is true that the migration of the real link reasoning to the realm of frontier workers has resulted in a more 'messy' approach, since in *Hartmann* (ECJ 18 July 2007, Case C-212/05 *Hartmann* [2007] ECR I-6303) the Court ruled that a child-raising allowance which had been made conditional on residence in Germany by law, should not be denied to a frontier worker who continue to be employed in Germany while residing in a neighboring Member States, but Ms Geven was denied the same child raising allowance because her employment in Germany was only 'minor' (ECJ 18 July 2007, Case C-213/05, *Geven v Land Nordrhein-Westfalen* [2007] 3 *CMLR* 45). And in *Hendrix* (ECJ 11 September 2007, Case C-287/05 [2007] 3 *CMLR* 46) the Court ruled that a wage supplementing benefit should be paid to Dutch national who had changed his place of residence from the Netherlands to the Belgium but continued to work in his state or origin, the Netherlands.

40 However, this does not mean that the Court will not embark upon balancing exercises. In *De Cupyer*, for example, the Court upheld the proportionality of Dutch measures which conditioned an entitlement to unemployment allowance on actual residence in the Netherlands on the ground that the effective monitoring of the employment and family situation of unemployed persons could not have been achieved by less restrictive measures, such as the production of documents or certificates; ECJ 18 July 2006, Case C-406/04, *G. De Cuyper v. Office national de l-emploi* [2006] ECR I-6947). Compare also ECJ 15 July 2004, Case C-365/02, *Lindfors* [2004] ECR I-7183 and ECJ 12 July 2005, Case C-403/03, *Schempp v Finanzamt Munchen V* [2005] ECR I-6421.

41 P. van der Mei, *Free Movement of Persons within the European Community*, Hart Publishing, Oxford, 2003, pp 43 et seq. For a different view, see K. Hailbronner, 'Union Citizenship and Access to Benefits', 42 (2005) *CMLR* 1245.

42 For a recent manifestation of this, see ECJ 5 June 2008, Case C-164/07, *James Wood v Fonds de garantie des victims des actes de terrorisme et d'autres infractions* [2008] ECR I-4143. The Court ruled in this case that EC law precludes national legislation which excludes resident EU nationals from the grant of compensation from a Member State fund intended to help the victims of crime.

eliminated.[43] Residence and access the social assistance had to be relaxed, but could not be wholly disentangled, from economic activity. Accordingly, 'the requirement of exhibiting a certain degree of financial solidarity with nationals of other Member States' (*Grzelczyk*) does not extend to situations where a person becomes an unreasonable burden on the welfare system of the host MS. In addition, the Member States retain discretion in determining the latter as well as in making the assessment of the existence of a certain degree of integration conditional on the fulfilment of appropriate residence requirements. In *Forster* the ECJ ruled that it is legitimate for Member States to make the grant of maintenance grants to students who are nationals of other Member States conditional on their sufficient integration into the host society, which, in turn, may be deduced by a finding that the student has resided in the host Member State for a certain length of time, such as, for instance, for five years.[44] Although this ruling stood in sharp contrast to the Advocate General's Opinion and the momentum to enhance students' rights with respect to maintenance grants and assistance generated by the previous case law, it is, nevertheless, consonant with secondary law. Article 24 of Council Dir. 2004/38 explicitly states that prior to the acquisition of the right of permanent residence, the Member States are not 'obliged to grant maintenance aid for studies, including vocational training, consisting in student grants or student loans to persons other than workers, self-employed persons, persons who retain such status and members of their families'.

The validity of Article 24(2) of Dir. 2004/38 in light of Article 12 EC (now Article 18 TFEU) read in conjunction with Article 39 EC (now Article 45 TFEU) was raised in preliminary reference proceedings in the joined cases of *Vatsouras* and *Koupatantze*.[45] Although both the Advocate General Colomer and the Court concluded that 'no factor capable of affecting the validity of Article 24(2) of Directive 2004/38 had been disclosed', the Court's ruling is, nevertheless, significant not only for confirming that excluding job-seekers from social assistance without a prior examination of the possible existence of a real link with the labour marker contravenes EU law, but also for clarifying that Article 24(2) of Dir. 2004/38 reflects the MS' competence to judge whether to a job-seeker is entitled to receive social assistance whilst (s)he is actively seeking for work and

---

43 For a defence of the opposite argument, see F. Wollenschlager, 'Union Citizenship, its Dynamics for Integration Beyond the Market', Paper Presented at the EUSA 11th Biennial International Conference, Los Angeles, USA, April 23–25 2009.

44 ECJ 18 November 2008, Case C-158/07, *Jacqueline Forster v Hoofddirectie van de Informatie Behher Groep* [2008] ECR I-8507; compare also Advocate General Mazak's Opinion delivered on 10 July 2008, points 142–144.

45 ECJ 4 June 2009, Joined Cases C-22/08 and C-23/08, *Athanasios Vatsouras v Arbeitsgemeinshcaft (ARGE) Nurnberg 900 and Josif Koupatantze v Alrbeitsgemeinschaft (ARGE) Nurnberg 900* [2009] ECR I-4585.

has a genuine change of finding employment in the host MS, the exercise of which is subject to review by the Court of Justice.[46]

Vatsouras and Koupatantze were Greek nationals who following a short spell of employment in Germany (one year and two months respectively) became involuntarily unemployed and had to rely on social assistance whilst actively seeking employment. Although the applicants could well be seen to fall within the scope of Article 39 EC since they engaged in activities which were neither marginal or ancillary and they retained the status of worker owing their involuntary unemployment, the ambivalence of the referring court as to whether they had attained the status of a worker owing to their 'brief and minor employment', led the Court to address the question whether jobseekers who do not enjoy worker status are entitled to social assistance. Applying its case law,[47] the Court ruled that that 'in view of the establishment of citizenship of the Union and the interpretation of the right to equal treatment enjoyed by citizens of the Union, it is no longer possible to exclude from the scope of Article 39(2) EC a benefit of a financial nature intended to facilitate access to employment in the labour market of a Member State' (para 37), provided that there is a real link between the jobseeker and the labour market of that MS. The existence of a real link can be inferred from the fact that a Union citizen has genuinely sought work in the territory of the MS for a reasonable period (para 39). Accordingly, the old maxim that non-active economic actors are entitled to equal treatment under Article 39(2) EC only with respect to access to employment and not with respect to enjoyment of social and tax advantages under Article 7(2) of Council Reg. 1612/68 had been firmly surpassed; job-seekers who have established a real link with the labour maker of the host MS could rely on Article 39(2) EC in order to receive a benefit of a financial nature intended to facilitate access to the labour market.

Interestingly, the Court then proceeded to state that that 'benefits of a financial nature which, independently of their status under national law, are intended to facilitate access to labour market cannot be regarding as constituting 'social assistance' within the meaning of Article 24(2) of Directive 2004/38' (para 45). The removal of jobseekers' allowances and benefits from the realm of social assistance may be analytically controversial, but in practice it will provide important pointers for national legislators who might be inclined to exclude jobseekers seeking employment following previous spells of employment from the receipt of such allowances. But one cannot also disregard the fact that the inclusion of paragraph 45 in the Court's judgment could also lead to a number of

46 Advocate General Colomer states that it is unlikely that institutions which adopted Dir 2004/38 were unaware of the Collins judgement and its implications and notes that the Citizenship directive 'leaves each national legislature free to find the appropriate balance'; point 55 of the Opinion delivered on 12 March 2009.

47 ECJ 23 March 2004, Case C-138/02, *Collins* [2004] ECR I-2703, para 63, and ECJ 15 September 2005, Case C-258/04, *Ioannidis* [2005] ECR I-8275, para 22.

permutations. Conceivably, MS concerned about the state of their public finances might use para 45 to argue that jobseekers are not entitled to other type of social assistance benefits, such as, for example, housing benefit, which fall within the scope of Article 24(2) of the Directive 2004/38, despite the fact that the ECJ's case law has confirmed the application of Article 18 TFEU in combination with Article 21 TFEU in favour of claimants who have established a link with the host MS. Conversely, one could interpret para 45 in an expansive way by arguing that jobseekers' allowances (– not social assistance in general) could be granted to jobseekers entering another MS for the purpose of seeking employment in the first three months of their residence, provided that they have managed to establish a sort of link, even a loose one, with the labour market of the host MS due to job-searching for two months, visiting job centres and being invited for job interviews, or to past periods of residence there. Of course, such an argument would presuppose a more fundamental reorientation of the way in which jobseekers are perceived and a shift in the perception of migration as capital or a resource. For if job seekers are seen as not yet fully active economic actors, as the Advocate General Colomer has noted in his Opinion – and not as non-active economic actors and burdens, the grant of any form of assistance that helps them join the labour market and promotes their employability is both desirable and legitimate under Article 39(2) EC. It thus remain to be seen whether para 45 will trigger more expansive interpretations of Union citizenship and the formation of an ethos of European solidarity or will be used to legitimate attempts to place a lid on such expansive interpretations by placing all those benefits which are not designed to facilitate access to employment and integration into the labour market beyond jobseekers' reach irrespective of whether they can demonstrate the existence of a link with the host MS during the first three months of residence or for longer periods under Article 24(2) of Dir. 2004/38.

## 2.2. FAMILY REUNIFICATION

The ECJ has also been very influential in the domain of family migration. Although since the 1960s derivative free movement and residence rights were granted to the spouse and other family members of Community workers, the European Court of Justice has played a central role in establishing a fundamental right to family reunification in Union law. The Court has also extended the net of protection to third country national spouses of EU nationals, thereby lifting them out of the regulative confines of national, and often restrictive, migration regimes. Commencing with a consequentialist perspective which viewed family unification as an important aid to intra-Community mobility and necessary for 'the integration of the worker and his family into the host MS without any difference in treatment in relation to nationals of that state', the ECJ proceeded to pronounce respect for family light (Article 8 ECHR) an integral part of the general principles of Community law.[48] In *Commission v Germany*, it ruled that a German provision which made the issuing of a residence permit for a family member of a Community worker conditional on the possession adequate accommodation for the whole duration of the family's stay in Germany contravened Article 10(2) of Council Regulation 1612/68, whereas in *Baumbast* and *Carpenter* it asserted the normative priority of the fundamental right of respect for family life enshrined in Article 8 of the ECHR over national migration laws.[49] More specifically, in *Carpenter* the Court inferred a right of residence for Mrs Carpenter, a national of the Philippine and spouse of a UK national who provided cross border services and who was threatened with deportation, from Mr Carpenter's status as service provider (Article 49 EC), thereby overriding restrictive national immigration rules.[50] It ruled that Mr Carpenter's right to provide and receive services in other Member States 'could not be fully effective if Mr Carpenter were to be deterred from exercising it by obstacles raised in his country of origin relating to the entry and residence of his spouse',[51] and hence Article 49 interpreted 'in light of the principle of respect for family life, which is recognised by Community law',[52] precluded Mrs Carpenter's deportation.

On 25 July 2002 when the legality of Belgium's restrictive measures on the movement and residence of third country national spouses of Union nationals was challenged by the Movement Against Racism, Anti-Semitism and Xenophobia ASBL (Mouvement contre le racisme, l'antisémitisme et la xénophobie ASBL, (MRAX)) the Court drew on *Carpenter* and emphasized that third country national spouses' residence rights do not derive from states' authorisation of their entry.[53] Instead, they are grounded in their family ties with Union citizens. Accordingly, MS should not send back to the border third country national spouses of EU nationals who do not possess the necessary entry documents (an identity document or visa) or deny them a residence permit or order their expulsion order on the grounds that they were 'illegal' entrants or residents. Nor should it impose additions conditions on the exercise of the rights of entry and residence of non-EU national family members of Union citizens which flow from

48 ECJ 18 May 1989, Case 249/86, *Commission v Germany* (Re Housing of Migrant Workers) [1989] ECR 1263, paras 10, 11.

49 ECJ 17 September 2002, Case C-413/99, *Baumbast, R v Secretary of State for the Home Department* [2002] ECR I-7091.

50 ECJ 11 July 2002, Case C-60/00, *M. Carpenter* [2002] ECR I-6279. I have discussed this more extensively in 'Ideas, Norms and European Citizenship: Explaining Institutional Change', (2005) 68:2 *Modern Law Review* 233–267, pp 54–55. See also G. Barrett, 'Family Matters: European Community Law and Third Country Family Members', (2003) 40 *CMLR* 369–421, 406.

51 Ibid at para 39.

52 On this, see the provisions of the Council Regulations and directives on the free movement of employed and self-employed persons as well as Article 8 ECHR.

53 ECJ 25 July 2002, Case C-459/99, *MRAX* [2002] ECR I-6591.

their family links.[54] The Court's ruling in *MRAX* led the Commission to amend Article 9 of the Draft Citizenship Directive by including the provision that 'family members may not be refused a residence card solely on the grounds that they have no visa or that their visa has expired prior to the submission of the application for a residence card.[55]

The Court reiterated the importance that Community law attributes to respect for family life in *Akrich*,[56] but it, nevertheless, gave the impression that Article 10 of Council Reg 1612/68 could only be invoked if the third country national spouse of an EU national seeking to move to a MS was lawfully resident in another MS.[57] The UK had resisted Mr Akrich's invocation of Community law in order secure residence rights in the UK following the return of his spouse, a UK national, to the country of origin, on the grounds of his past record as an undocumented migrant who had been deported twice to Algeria. Drawing in this ruling, the UK Home Office distinguished between the intra-Community movement of lawfully resident family members of Community nationals, which allegedly fell within the ambit of Community law, and the entry of such persons from outside the Community which was seen to fall within the sovereign prerogative of the UK. Accordingly, it was officially stated that national migration rules should apply to the latter case and that third country nationals 'who are illegally in the UK and marry British citizens should not be able to abuse EC law to remain here'.[58] The *Immigration (European Community Area) Regulations 2006* thus stated that third country national dependent relatives or members of a household of a Community national seeking to exercise rights of free movement in the UK must have previous lawful residence in another MS in order to be eligible for a resident permit. Denmark, Finland and Ireland also required prior lawful residence in another MS.[59]

In *Jia* the Court revisited, and distinguished, the factual underpinnings of *Akrich*, and ruled that Community law does not require prior lawful residence in a member state for the grant of a permanent residence permit to a family member

---

54 In *Commission v Spain*, the grant of a residence permit to a non-EU national family members of a UK national was conditional upon applying and obtaining a residence visa prior at the Spanish consulate in their last country of domicile. The Court ruled that Spanish law violated Directives 68/360, 90/365 and 73/147; C-157/03 [2005] ECR I-2911.

55 Article 9(2a) of the Draft Directive, COM (2003) 199 final, 15.4.2003.

56 ECJ 23 September 2003, Case C-109/01, *Secretary of State for the Home Department v Hacene Akrich* [2003] ECR I-9607.

57 At para 61. However, the Court also ruled that in genuine marriages the intentions of the parties in making use of the rights conferred by Community law is not relevant to an assessment of their legal situation by the competent migration authorities.

58 See the reply of Baroness Scotland of Asthal to the question by Lord Tebbit on 17 November 2003, HL Deb 17 November 2003 Vol 654 cc 252–3WA.

59 But following the Court's ruling in *Metock and Others*, which is discussed below, national regulations had to be amended, notwithstanding delays and legal challenges in some MS. See, for example, *R. on the application of Yaw Owusu v Secretary of State for the Home Department* (21 January 2009) [2009] EWHC 593 (Admin).

of a Community national who has exercised her right to free movement.[60] Mrs Jia, a Chinese national and the dependent relative (mother in law) of a German national living in Sweden, entered Sweden on a 90 day visit visa and before the visa's expiry she applied for permanent residence there. Her application was refused by the Swedish authorities, and on a preliminary reference from the Swedish Aliens Board, the ECJ held that there was no requirement for Mrs Jia to have resided in another MS before making the application and that the switch of status from visitor to resident did not pose any problems for Community law. Finally, in Metock and Others,[61] the ECJ outlawed national legislation making the right of residence of family members subject to prior lawful residence in another MS. It also stated that Article 3(1) of Directive 2004/38 must be interpreted as meaning that a national of a non-member country who is a spouse of a Union citizen residing in a MS whose nationality he does not possess and who accompanies or joins that Union citizen benefits from the provisions of that directive, irrespectively of when and where their marriage took place (whether the marriage took place before or after the citizen's exercise of his/her right to free movement) and of how the national of a non-member country entered the host MS (regularly or irregularly). Although the ruling is consistent with the ECJ's case law prior to *Akrich* and the secondary legislation adopted in the 1960s and 1970s, it was, nevertheless, viewed by Ireland and Denmark as an illegitimate judicial interference with national policies designed to combat undocumented migration and 'marriages of convenience'. The Danish Government pledged to seek amendment of the Citizenship Directive sidestepping the fact that Article 35 of the Citizenship Directive addresses 'the case of abuse of rights or fraud, such as marriages of convenience'. According to Article 35, the MS are free to refuse, terminate or withdraw any Directive right in such a case, provided that such decisions are proportionate and meet the procedural safeguards provided for in Articles 30 and 32 of Directive 2004/38. What they are not free to do, however, is to subjugate Union rules to their domestic political requirements and restrictive migration policies.[62]

The Court continued to strengthen the rights of third country national members of the Union citizens following their return in the country of origin. In *Eind*, it

---

60 ECJ 9 January 2007, Case C-1/05, *Jia v Migrationsverket* [2007] ECR I-1. See also the Commission's 5th Report on Citizenship of the Union, 15.2.2008, which mention's the need to interpret the right to free movement in the light of fundamental rights and in particular the right to respect for family life and the principle of proportionality.

61 ECJ 25 July 2008, Case C-127/08, *Metock* [2008] ECR I-6241.

62 The Court's decision in *Metock* has also important implications for the recently introduced 'integration abroad' requirements in the Netherlands, France and Germany. By requiring that third country national spouses of EU nationals seeking reunification must have adequate knowledge of the national language and society and its values and pass tests in the countries of origin in order to be granted a visa, MS have infringed the Citizenship Directive (2004/38), in so far as they make the family reunion dependent on their migration regulations and not on the existence of conjugal ties with EU citizens.

ruled that the Surinamese daughter of a Dutch national, who lived with him in the UK while he was working there, was entitled to reside in the Netherlands when her father returned there even though he did not exercise any effective and genuine economic activities.[63] The fact that the daughter did not have a right to reside in the Netherlands before residing in the UK under Dutch law was seen to have no bearing on the recognition of a right of entry and residence as a family member of a Community worker.[64] According to the Court, to assert otherwise would be tantamount to denying that the rights of residence of family members of Community nationals derive from Community law.

## 2.3. NON-DISCRIMINATORY RESTRICTIONS

The evolution of Union citizenship has brought also another dynamic; namely, the prohibition of measures which might be unfavourable to persons moving between Member States, thereby making a decision to remain at home more attractive or penalizing those who have exercised their European Union law rights. In *Pusa* Advocate General Jacobs stated that, far from being limited to a prohibition of direct or indirect discrimination, Article 18 EC applied to non-discriminatory restrictions, including unjustified burdens.[65] Non-discriminatory restrictions involve measures liable to hinder or make less attractive the exercise of fundamental freedoms guaranteed by the Treaty and can only be justified if they are based on overriding considerations of public interest and are proportionate to the legitimate aim of the national decisions.[66] In *Tas-Hagen* the Court utilised the non-discrimination model by stating that Dutch legislation on *benefits for civilian war victims 1940–1945* which required that beneficiaries were resident in the Netherlands at the time of the submission of their application was 'liable to dissuade Netherlands nationals' from exercising their rights under Article 18(1) EC and 'constituted a restriction'.[67] Indeed, 'the opportunities offered by the Treaty in relation to freedom of movement cannot be fully effective if a national of a Member State can be deterred from availing himself of them by obstacles raised to his residence in the host Member State by legislation of his State of origin penalising the fact that he has used them'.[68] And although the restriction can be justified on the ground that the obligation of solidarity could only apply to civilian war victims who had links with the population of the Netherlands dur-

---

63 ECJ 11 December 2007, Case C-291/05, *Eind* [2007] ECR I-10719, para 45.

64 Ibid, para 42.

65 ECJ 29 April 2004, Case C-224/02, *Heikki Antero Pusa v. Osuuspankkien Keskinainen Vakuutusyhio* [2004] ECR I-5763.

66 See ECJ 18 July 2006, Case C-406/04, G. *De Cuyper v. Office national de l-emploi* [2006] ECR I-6947.

67 ECJ 26 October 2006, Case C-192/05, *K. Tas-Hagen, R. A. Tas v. Raadskamer WUBO van de Pensioen- en Uitkeringsraad* [2006] ECR I-10451, para. 32.

68 Ibid, para 30.

ing and after the war, residence abroad was not a sufficient indicator of a person's disconnection from the Member State granting the benefit. The requirement of residence in the Netherlands therefore did not meet the test of proportionality.

A similar conclusion with respect to residence requirements enshrined in national legislation regulating the award of disability pensions to victims of war was reached in *Nerkowska* and *Zablocka-Weyhermuller.*[69] In the former case a disability pension compensating for the suffering endured by Ms Nerkowska, a Polish national, following her deportation to Siberia, was suspended because she changed her place of residence from Poland to Germany. In the latter case, Ms Zablocka-Weyhermuller, the surviving spouse of a German national victim of war, was denied the partial pension she received in Germany when she took residence in Poland. In both cases, the Polish and German governments, respectively, put forward justifications for the existence such a residence clause, which in effect limited the scope of potential beneficiaries of the benefits, such as, the need for the effective monitoring of the employment and social situation of the beneficiaries and for restricting the obligations of solidarity to those who retain a sufficient degree of connection with the national society. But these arguments failed to convince the Court. Quite rightly, in *Nerkowska* the ECJ concluded that a change of residence does not imply the shaking off of a necessary connection with the MS of origin. What mattered, instead, was that Ms Nerkowska was a national of the MS granting the benefit and had lived in that state for more than 20 years. Accordingly, 'the residence clause throughout the period of payment of the benefit concerned did not meet the test of proportionality'.[70] Similarly, the residence clause imposed by the German legislation was a restriction deterring Union citizens from taking advantage of their full rights to free movement and residence in the EU which did not comply with the principle of proportionality.[71] This is because the German legislation had confined the applicability of the residence requirement to certain MS only and not to others where the cost of living is lower that that in Germany and provided for the suspension of payment of benefits – and not for their adaptation in line with the cost of living in the state of residence or domicile. What is astonishing in these cases is not the ECJ's intervention in favour of Europe's war victims and the progressive interpretation of EU law in line of the changing landscape of the Union,[72] but the Member States'

[69] ECJ 22 May 2008, Case C-499/06, *Halina Nerkowska* v *Zaklad Ubezpieczen Spolecznych* [2008] ECR I-3993; ECJ 4 December 2008, Case C-221/07, *Krystyna Zablocka-Weyhermuller* v *Land Baden-Wurttembrg*, [2008] ECR I-9029.

[70] Ibid, paras 35, 37 and 39–47.

[71] Paras 36–44.

[72] As the ECJ stated in ECJ 18 December 2007, Joined Cases C-396/05, C-419/05 and C-450/05, *Doris Habelt and Others v Deutsche Rentenversicherung Bund* [2007] ECR I-11895 'To allow the competent MS to rely on grounds of integration into the social environment of the state in order to impose a residence clause would run directly counter to the fundamental objective of the Union which is to encourage the movement of persons within the Union and their integration into the society of other MS'; para 2.

appalling treatment of some of the most vulnerable members of their publics, namely, their elderly citizens and members of their families who have been exposed to unbelievable suffering.[73]

In the field of education, the Court ruled that national law which stipulates that education and training grants for studies in another MS can only be awarded for studies which are a continuation of education or training pursued for at least one year in the MS awarding the grant is liable to deter citizens of the Union from exercising their fundamental rights under Article 18(1) EC. In this respect, it constitutes an unjustified restriction on the free movement of Union citizens.[74] By moving beyond the discrimination model,[75] the Court has thus managed to provide effective protection to Union citizens who have taken advantage of the opportunities afforded by the Treaty but have been placed at a disadvantage by legislation of their state of origin.

## 2.4. INCREASED PROTECTION OF UNION CITIZENS IN THE MEMBER STATE OF RESIDENCE

The public security, public policy and public health derogations from free movement have been marked by the disjunction between governmental interests and sovereign power and Union regulation. Member States have been keen on maintaining the vestiges of their sovereignty. Under Union law, they have the power to restrict the free movement rights of Union citizens and their family members on public security, public policy and public health grounds (Article 45(3) TFEU), but the latter must be strictly interpreted and comply with the principle of proportionality.[76] These grounds cannot be invoked by a MS in order to serve economic ends. Instead, they have to be based exclusively on the personal conduct of the individual concerned and may never be imposed automatically.[77] MS must verify that a Union citizen's personal conduct poses 'a genuine and sufficiently serious threat to the requirements of public policy affecting one of the fundamental in-

[73] On this see C. Lyons' excellent analysis in 'A Door into the Dark; Doing Justice to History in the Courts of the European Union'. EUI Working Paper, 2008/11, EUI, Florence.

[74] ECJ 23 October 2007, Joined Cases C-11/06 and C-12/06, *Rhiannon Morgan v Bezirksregierung Köln and Iris Bucher v Landrat des Kreises Düren* [2007] ECR I-9161. See also ECJ 11 September 2007, Case C-76/05, *Schwarz and Gootjes-Schwarz* [2007] ECR I-6849.

[75] This also applies to matters other than the payment of financial benefits, such as the recognition of surnames; see ECJ 14 October 2008, Case C-353/06, *Grunkin and Paul* [2008] ECR I-7639. In this case, a refusal by the authorities of a MS to recognise the surname of a child as already determined and registered in another Member State in which the child was born and resident since birth was seen to hamper the exercise of the right to free movement and residence under Article 18(1) EC.

[76] ECJ 26 November 2002, Case C-100/01, *Ministre de l'Interieur v Aitor Oteiza Olazabal* [2002] ECR I-10981; ECJ 29 April 2004, Joined Cases C-482/01 and C-493/01, *Orfanopoulos and Oliveri v Land Baden-Wurttemberg* [2004] ECR I-5257.

[77] See the Opinion of Adv. General Mazak 14 February 2008, Case C-33/07, *Gheorghe Jipa* [2008] ECR I-5157 delivered on, para 23.

terests of society'.[78] This also applies to restrictions on the right of exit imposed by the MS of origin on one of its nationals. In *Jipa*, a reverse discrimination case since the applicant requested his state of origin to lift a restriction on his right to cross-border movement (Article 38 of Romanian Law 248/2005) in order to travel to Belgium which had repatriated him owing to his irregular residence there, the Court ruled that in the absence of a genuine threat to public policy or public security the MS of origin cannot restrict an EU national's right of exit.[79] The same assessment must take place with respect to third country national spouses of Union nationals who have been the subject of alerts entered in the Schengen Information System. The ECJ has stated that both the Member State issuing an alert and the Member State that consults the Schengen Information System state must first establish that the presence of a person constitutes a genuine, present and sufficiently serious threat affecting one of the fundamental interests of society.[80]

The ECJ's preference for a rights-based approach to the interpretation of the Treaty's derogations form the free movement provisions has attributed priority to the interests of the protected persons over the interests of states and has sedimented the requirement that policy or security risks are clearly personified before any action is taken by national authorities. By requiring concreteness, as opposed to abstract interpretations of threats or risks, and contextualism, that is, the identification of real and specific harms caused by individuals' actions as opposed to abstract harms and exaggerated risks flowing from the authorities' perceptions about certain individuals and their actions, Union nationals and their families have been shielded from utilitarian calculations and arbitrary state practices. Accordingly, a MS cannot order the expulsion of a Union citizen as a deterrent or a general preventive action.[81] Nor can exclusion or expulsion decisions be justified on the basis of governmental policy agendas, such as, for example, tackling pornography or organized crime. This also rules out the application of pre-emption or the precautionary principle which became salient in counter-terrorist law and policy post 9/11. And previous criminal convictions shall not in themselves constitute grounds for imposing limitations on cross-border movement.[82] As Article 27(2) of Council Directive 2004/38 states, 'justifications that are isolated from the particulars of the case or that rely on considerations of general prevention shall not be accepted'. According to Advocate General Mazak, 'it follows from the ruling of the Court in *Commission v Spain* that a MS, when limiting the rights granted to Union citizens pursuant to Article 18(1) EC,

78 ECJ 27 October 1977, Case 30/77, *R v Bouchereau* [1977] ECR 1999.

79 ECJ 10 July 2008, Case C-33/07, *Gheorghe Jipa* [2008] ECR I-5157. Romania had placed this restriction following a Readmission agreement it had signed with Belgium before its accession to the EU.

80 ECJ 31 January 2006, Case C-503/03, *Commission v Kingdom of Spain* [2006] ECR I-1097.

81 ECJ 26 February 1975, Case 67/74, *Bonsignore* [1975] ECR 297, para 6, and ECJ 28 October 1975, Case 36/75 *Rutili* [1975] ECR 1219, para 29.

82 Article 27(2) of Dir. 2004/38; ECJ 19 January 1999, Case C-348/96, *Calfa* [1999] ECR I-11, paras 22 to 24.

cannot rely on general non-specific assertions made, in relation to the conduct of a Union citizen, by another MS. A MS when limiting the fundamental freedoms of Union citizens must itself verify and confirm whether the exercise of those freedoms poses a genuine and sufficiently serious threat to the requirements of public policy affecting one of the fundamental interests of society'.[83] True, there is no isomorphomism in the definition of public policy across the EU – public policy and public security remain 'national concepts', that is, they are defined on the basis of national laws and traditions. However, the European Court of Justice has clearly stated for more than three decades that the Member States' discretion in this area is circumscribed by European law.[84]

Although the strict interpretation of the public policy derogations furnished by secondary legislation (Dir 64/221 initially and Dir 2004/38 from 30 April 2006) and the ECJ's jurisprudence have circumscribed the Member States' discretionary power, they, nevertheless, continue to deport Union citizens owing to enforceable criminal convictions. In *Calfa* automatic expulsion for life following a criminal conviction without consideration of the personal conduct of the offender or the danger (s)he represents for the requirement of public policy was seen to contravene Treaty provisions (Article 49 EC) and Dir 64//221 (now Dir 2004/38).[85] And Advocate General Stix-Hackl has stated in *Commission v Germany* that 'the German practice of automatic deportation, without regard for personal circumstances, justified on the ground of its deterrent effect on other foreigners and in breach of the fundamental right to family life breaches Community law'.[86] Recently, in *Huber* the ECJ took issue with the German Central Register of Foreign Nationals and ruled that the prohibition of discrimination on the ground of nationality laid down in Article 12(1) EC precluded the establishment of a system for processing personal data for the purpose of fighting crime specifically for Union citizens while no such similar system exists with respect to nationals of that Member State. But it reached the opposite conclusion with respect to the use of a central register for foreign nationals for the purpose of regulating their residential status.[87]

The Citizenship Directive (2004/38) has enhanced security of residence for Union citizens.[88] It stipulates that permanent residents can be ordered to leave only on 'serious grounds of public policy or public security' (Article 28(2)), and permanent resident Union citizens for the previous ten years and minors may not be ordered to leave the territory of a Member State, except on imperative grounds

83 ECJ 27 October 1977, Case 30/77, *R v Bouchereau* [1977] ECR 1999, para 43.

84 ECJ 4 December 1974, Case 41/74, *van Duyn* [1974] ECR 1337.

85 ECJ 19 January 1999, Case C-348/96, *Calfa* [1999] ECR I-11.

86 See the Advocate General's Opinion 2 June 2005, Case C-441/02, *Commission v Federal Republic of Germany* [2006] ECR I-3449.

87 ECJ 16 December 2008, Case C-524/06, *Heinz Huber v Bundesrepublik Deutschland* [2008] ECR I-9705.

88 Article 28(1) of Directive 2004/38.

of public security (Article 28(3)).[89] In addition, according to Article 33 of Dir 2004/38, an expulsion order cannot be issued by the host MS as a penalty or legal consequence of a custodial penalty unless the general requirements pertaining to the application of restrictions on entry and residence apply (Articles 27–29) and if it is issued, it should be subject to assessment after two years (Article 33).

Notwithstanding the ECJ's continued supervision of MS' compliance with Union law and the increasing weight and relevance of European Union citizenship, it may be argued that that the continuation of the practice of deportation on the grounds of security and public policy undermines the principle of equal treatment irrespective of nationality fostered by Union citizenship. For although the gradual relaxation of MS' coercive powers is noticeable enough and the public policy, public security and public health derogations have now become restrictions in the exercise of the European free movement rights, it, nevertheless, remains the case that, as far as security of residence is concerned, Union citizenship appears to be a lesser status than that of national citizenship. Essentially, it approximates third country national long-term residence status. The paradox here is that while EU citizenship has demonstrated that community belonging does not have to be based on organic-national qualities, cultural commonalities or individuals' conformity to national values, but can be built on de facto associative relations and connections brought about through residence and de jure equal membership as far as possible,[90] the deportation of Union citizens makes nationality the ultimate determinant of belonging.[91] The latter issue is further explored in the subsequent section which examines the relation between Member State nationality and Union citizenship.

## 3. EU CITIZENSHIP AND MEMBER STATE NATIONALITY: RETHINKING THE LINK?

That European Union citizenship remains an unfinished institution is beyond any doubt. Even its modest original content enshrined in the Treaty of European Union revealed this. Article 22 EC (now Article 25 TFEU) had always carried the promise of a future extension of the material scope of Union citizenship by a unanimous decision of the Council on a proposal from the Commission and following consultation with the European Parliament. Although this procedure has not been activated yet, the discussion in the previous section demonstrat-

89 Article 28(3) of Directive 2004/38.

90 D. Kostakopoulou, 'European Union Citizenship: Writing the Future' (2007) 13:5 *ELJ* 623–646.

91 By so doing, it facilitates the stigmatisation of EU citizens and the possible erosion of their special, citizen status in the host MS by official discourses on 'the deportation of foreign criminals. Such anti-migrant and xenophobic discourses have featured in the media in the UK, Italy and the Netherlands recently.

ed the evolutionary and experimental character of Union citizenship. For more than a decade, the ECJ has not hesitated to subject it to critical reflection and inquiry and to embark upon unknown and controversial terrains, thereby inviting both admiration and fierce criticism. European judges have taken quite seriously constitutionalisation of Union citizenship and sought to respond positively to citizens' needs and expectations. But as their decisions are guided by norms which often conflict with states' interest in unilateral migration control and the pursuit of power, governments have not hesitated to express their disapproval of what they perceive to be judicial policy-making.

Having said this, one must not overlook the fact that the ECJ's interventions have been uneven. While the material scope of Union citizenship has been adjusted in ways that are responsive to Union citizens' welfare needs and their concerns, its personal scope, that is, the question of how and under what conditions can EU citizenship be acquired and lost, has largely evaded critical reflection and adaptation. Access to EU citizenship was premised on the possession or acquisition of MS nationality (Article 17 EC) and any attempt to loosen the grip of the latter on the former is hastily taken to signal an external intrusion into the sovereign domain of MS (– the so called creeping Communitarisation) or a threat of an aggressive Community take over. Sovereignty concerns have thus marked off the field of determination of nationality, which falls within the exclusive competence of the MS but must nonetheless be exercised with due regard to Union law,[92] from review by the Union institutions.

And yet polarised positions and 'either/or dualisms' more often than not hide the complexity and potentialities inherent in relationships. For in relations of all sorts, not only does mutual dependence co-exist with mutual 'relative' autonomy, but also if the latter is denied or circumscribed within a very narrow margin then the relationship ceases to function properly. By analogy, although the relationship between EU citizenship and MS nationality is one of dependence, if it is dogmatically asserted that dependence rules out the existence of relative autonomy in domain of either EU citizenship or national citizenship then the relationship is bound to exhibit cracks. With respect to MS nationality, the ECJ has made it clear that the MS enjoy relative autonomy by upholding the international law maxim that determination of nationality falls within their exclusive jurisdiction, despite the anomalies that this creates in the field of application of EU law and its exclusionary implications with respect to the rights of long-term resident third country nationals.[93] In *Micheletti*, the ECJ confirmed

92 ECJ 7 July 1992, Case C-369/90, *Micheletti and Others v Delegacion del Gobierno en Catanbria* [1992] ECR I- 4329.

93 The debate on the position of long-term resident third country nationals has highlighted the exclusionary effects of Union citizenship. For proposals to disentangle Union citizenship from state nationality and to award it to all persons residing lawfully in the territories of the Union for a certain period of time, see European Parliament (1989) Resolution on the Declaration of Fundamental Rights and Freedoms, A2–0003/89; (1989) Resolution on the Joint Declaration Against Racism and Xenophobia and an Action Programme by the Council of Ministers, A2–

that determination of nationality falls within the exclusive competence of the Member States, but it went on to add that this competence must be exercised with due regard to the requirements of Community law,[94] and in *Kaur* it stated that 'it is for each Member State, having due regard to Community law, to lay down the conditions for the acquisition and loss of nationality.[95] Accordingly, nationals of a Member state should be able to exercise their rights to free movement without impediments imposed by additional regulations adopted by other Member States. In *Chen*, the European Court of Justice criticised the restrictive impact of such additional conditions for the recognition of nationality of a Member State. It ruled that the United Kingdom had an obligation to recognise a minor's (Catherine Zhu) Union citizenship status even though her MS nationality had been acquired in order to secure a right of residence for her mother Chen, a third country national, in the United Kingdom. Since Catherine had legally acquired Irish nationality under the ius soli principle enshrined in the Irish Nationality and Citizenship Act 1956 and had both sickness insurance and sufficient resources, provided by her mother, the limitations and conditions referred to in Article 18 EC and laid down by Directive 90/364 had been met thereby conferring on her an entitlement to reside for an indefinite period in the UK.[96]

261/88; (1990) Resolution on Freedom of Movement for Non-EEC Nationals, A3–175/90, OJ C175, 16.7.90; (1991) Resolution on the Free movement of Persons A3–0199/91, OJ C 159/12–15, 17.6.91; ECSC (1991) Opinion on the Status of Migrant Workers from Third Countries 91/C 159/05, OJ C 159/12, 17 June 1991. Early academic literature on this subject includes: A. Evans, Third Country Nationals and the Treaty on European Union', (1994) 5 *European Journal of International Law* 199–219; D. O'Keeffe, 'Union Citizenship' in D. O'Keeffe and P. Twomey (eds.), *Legal Issues of the Maastricht Treaty*, Wiley, Chichester, 1994; M. Martiniello, 'European Citizenship, European Identity and Migrants: Towards the Postnational State?' in R. Miles and D. Thranhardt (eds), *Migration and European Integration: The Politics of Inclusion and Exclusion in Europe*, Pinter, London, 1995, 37–52; D. Kostakopoulou, 'Towards a Theory of Constructive Citizenship in Europe', (1996) 4:4 *Journal of Political Philosophy* 337–358; H. Lardy, 'The Political Rights of Union Citizenship', (1996) 2 *European Public Law* 611–33; S. Peers, 'Towards Equality: Actual and Potential Rights of Third Country Nationals in the European Union, (1996) 33:1 *CMLR* 7–50; D Kostakopoulou, 'European Citizenship and Immigration After Amsterdam: Openings, Silences, Paradoxes', (1998) 24:4 *Journal of Ethnic and Migration Studies* 639–656; M. La Torre (ed.), *European Citizenship: An Institutional Challenge*, Kluwer Law International, The Hague, 1998 and in particular the essays written by R. de-Groot, J. Monar, A. Castro Oliveira, R. Rubio-Marin, M.-J. Garot, A. Evans and Antje Wiener; D Kostakopoulou, 'Nested 'Old' and 'New' Citizenships in the EU: Bringing Forth the Complexity', (1999) 5:3 *Columbia Journal of European Law* 389–413; E. Guild, *The Legal Framework and Social Consequences of Free Movement of Persons in the European Union*, Kluwer Law International, The Hague, 1999; H. Staples, *The Legal Status of Third Country Nationals Resident in the European Union*, Kluwer Law International, The Hague, 1999. For a recent account, see J. Shaw, *The Transformation of Citizenship in the European Union; Electoral Rights and the Restructuring of Political Space*, Cambridge University Press, Cambridge, 2007.

94 ECJ 7 July 1992, Case C-369/90, *Micheletti and Others v Delegacion del Gobierno en Catanbria* [1992] ECR I-4329.

95 ECJ 20 February 2001, Case C-192/99, *R v Secretary of State for the Home Department, ex parte Kaur* [2001] ECR I-1237, para 19.

96 ECJ 19 October 2004, Case C-200/02, *Kunqian Catherine Zhu and Man Lavette Chen v Secretary of State for the Home Department*, [2004] ECR I-9925.

But the 'relative autonomy' of the other party to this relationship, that is, of EU citizenship, has not been addressed in a systematic way yet. Does this mean that it should be ruled out a priori that EU citizenship may be relatively autonomous under certain conditions and within certain parameters even though it is activated by the possession of MS nationality? Could it be argued that the Member States' regulatory autonomy in nationality matters would be infringed, thereby leading to a violation of Article 17(1) EC, if EU citizenship were seen to survive if the MS nationality link which gave it rise in the first place ceased to exist? Such questions have recently arisen by virtue of the Rottmann case.[97]

Mr Rottmann, an Austrian national by birth, fearing arrest for suspected serious fraud, emigrated to Germany where he subsequently obtained citizenship by naturalization. He lost his Austrian nationality under Austrian nationality law, and, when the Austrian authorities revealed that he had been the subject of a criminal investigation for fraud and an arrest warrant, Germany revoked his naturalisation on the ground that he had received German citizenship fraudulently. Mr Rottman sought the annulment of this decision arguing that the deprivation of his German citizenship makes him stateless under public international law and that it would lead to loss of Union citizenship which is contrary to Union law. The preliminary ruling reference procedure was activated by the national court which required clarification on whether EU law prevented the loss of Union citizenship under the circumstances pertaining to the case in hand and whether either Germany or Austria had an obligation to comply with EU law. Advocate General Maduro made it clear that the case was not a purely internal matter falling outside the remit of application of Union law since it entailed the requisite cross-border dimension (points 9–13) and proceeded to elaborate on the scope of the Member States' obligation to comply with Union law in exercising their regulative autonomy in nationality matters (point 22 et seq). While the Advocate General eloquently pinpointed that EU citizenship and MS nationality are 'inextricably linked but also autonomous' (point 23), 'all rights and obligations attached to Union citizenship cannot be unreasonably limited' by the conditions pertaining to access to Union citizenship (point 23) and that national rules determining the acquisition and loss of nationality must be compatible with EU rules and respect the rights of EU citizens (point 23), he proceeded to state that inferring that the withdrawal of nationality is impossible if it entails loss of Union citizenship would violate MS autonomy in this area and thus contravene Article 17(1) EC as well as Article 6(3) EU concerning the EU's obligation to respect the national identities of the MS.[98]

Although the analysis provided by the Advocate General is significant and illuminating, it may be worthy to pause for a moment to reflect on his conclusion.

[97] Opinion of AG Maduro 30 September 2009, Case C-135/08, *Janko Rottmann v Freistaat Bayern*, nyr.

[98] Ibid, paras 24 and 25.

In examining closely his Opinion, it seems to me that there exist two lines of argumentation that are congruent with the analysis up to point 23. The first, which is encapsulated in point 24, is that a MS cannot revoke naturalisation or withdraw nationality, if this leads to a loss of Union citizenship. This, as the Advocate General has noted, would constrain MS autonomy in an area that falls within the MS exclusive jurisdiction. But the Advocate General overlooks a second possible argument; namely, that the MS can revoke naturalization or withdraw their nationality, provided, of course, that they comply with Union law, but Union law precludes the ensuring automatic loss of Union citizenship if a Union citizen is rendered stateless. In other words, loss of MS nationality would not automatically result in the forfeiture of Union citizenship, if the Union citizen concerned were rendered stateless. Indeed, given that EU citizenship is dynamic concept and institution and a fundamental status, a certain degree of autonomy as far as Union citizenship is concerned is required in order to preserve the link between the citizen and the Union and his/her place in the European community of citizens. Arguably, it is not fair that a Union citizen who has established a multitude of relations and connections in a MS other than his/her state or origin and a link directly with the Union (and its Treaties) from which directly effective rights and obligations flow, is automatically denied of social and political standing in the Union legal order because a MS decides to deprive him/her of nationality, however legitimate the reasons may be. After all, the EU law rights of free movement, residence and equal treatment do not come into view because one is a MS national (millions of MS nationals can not invoke these rights if their situations are purely internal, that is, they have not established links with Union law by engaging in activities with a cross-border dimension), but because a MS national has activated his Union law status. Accordingly, this status, which is not a status of subjection – as nationality is – but a status of participation in civil society, needs to be protected. This can be done by recognizing that each person holding the nationality of a Member State is a citizen of the Union, but this status shall be unaffected by a subsequent loss of state nationality which renders the individual stateless.

True, critics may be quick to observe that national governments are likely to react negatively against such a conclusion fearing that EU citizenship might take over national citizenship. Such fears have been expressed in the past but they lack empirical foundations. One may recall the Declaration on Nationality of a Member State, annexed to the Final Act of the Treaty on European Union, which expressly stated, 'the question whether an individual possesses the nationality of a Member State shall be settled solely by reference to the national law of the Member State concerned'.[99] Similar declarations were adopted by the European Council at Edinburgh and Birmingham. The Birmingham declaration confirmed that, in the eyes of national executives, Union citizenship constitutes an additional

99 OJ C 191, 29 July 1992.

tier of rights and protection which is not intended to replace national citizenship – a position that found concrete expression in the amended Article 17(1) at Amsterdam[100] and the Lisbon Treaty.[101]

On close reflection, however, the above mentioned possibility neither contravenes the Declaration on Nationality of a MS nor threatens to replace national citizenship. Nor does it in may way impinge upon state autonomy which is clearly manifested in the act of deprivation of citizenship. It merely maintains the legal effects of Union citizenship and safeguards the rights that individuals derive directly from EU law, thereby enabling a stateless EU citizen to continue to enjoy the freedoms guaranteed by the Treaty and the protection afforded to him/her by EU law, including security of residence, respect for family life and the maintenance of the relations (s)he has established. True, this would be of little use to persons holding two or more MS nationalities. But it would make a great deal of difference to mono-national EU citizens resident in another MS. It would also demonstrate in practice that EU citizenship is a fundamental status and that it matters. In what follows, I wish to defend such an argument on both analytical and legal grounds, namely, the fundamental status of Union citizenship (the EU citizenship norm) and the *effet utile* of Union law.

Analytically, the argument in favour of the independent legal effect of EU citizenship in the event of statelessness can be derived from the intersystemic relation between EU citizenship (A) and MS nationality (B) as well as the nature of their interaction. By the latter, I mean the perception of the interaction as process-driven and dynamic. In most relations of dependence where A can only be activated by B, it would be incorrect to conclude that all properties and effects of A are contained by B. B may be the triggering mechanism or the source of A, but it can bear little or no relation to other parts of A and their reconfiguration at any time. I take this to be the true meaning of 'additionality' or 'complemetarity' or 'existing alongside': it delineates a degree of relative autonomy and, by no means, implies that A and B cannot function apart. Additionality cannot entail a logic of complete subsumption of Union citizenship to the extent that it automatically disappears when MS nationality is lost. To assert the latter would be tantamount to distorting the relation of complementarity or additionality and replacing it with a relation of complete subjugation. Such a relation of subordination may please state-centrists, but it would not be congruent with the principle of the maintenance of the full effectiveness of Union law[102] and Union citizens' legal positions which are protected by it. It is recognized that an individual who has

[100] Bull. EC 10–1992 I 8.9. The Amsterdam Treaty added the statement that 'Union citizenship shall complement national citizenship' to Article 8(1) EC (Article 17(1) on renumbering).

[101] Article 9 of the Consolidated Version of the Treaty on European Union (TEU) states that 'Citizenship of the Union shall be additional to national citizenship and shall not replace it'.

[102] As the ECJ has stated in Joined Cases C-46 and 48/93, the full effectiveness of Community rules and the effective protection of the rights which they confer are principles inherent in the Community legal order; ECJ 5 March 1996, Joined Cases C-46 and 48/93, *Brasserie du Pecheur v Germany and R v Secretary of State for Transport ex parte Factortame* [1996] ECR I-1029.

activated Union law by crossing borders has the status of an EU citizen in addition to the status of a MS national. The former has been granted to him by virtue of EU law and authenticates all the rights (s)he derives in the host MS. A national decision depriving him/her of nationality interferes with his Union-based legal position and his/her free movement rights thereby depriving them of full force and legal effects. A Union citizen may thus find himself/herself stripped of all his/her rights overnight, totally unprotected in the territory of the host MS and bereft of Union citizenship.

In addition, all intersystemic relations are dynamic, that is, they entail a process-driven dimension in response to endogenous and exogenous pressures and possible discrepancies. As we have seen in the previous section, the relation between national citizenship and EU citizenship constitutes no exception. EU citizenship has become a fundamental status of Union citizens who have increasing expectations (and doubts) about the EU's capacity to deliver and to give meaning and depth to it. Accordingly, a system within which nested citizenships[103] overlap, interact, impact on each other, but also retain their relative autonomy and independent properties, would create the preconditions for citizens to develop their potential, enrich their life chances and to enjoy adequate protection.

The survival of EU citizenship following the break down of the link between an individual and a MS as a default option in cases of statelessness does not challenge the Member States' definitional monopoly over nationality and their autonomy to withdraw nationality on the ground of fraudulent naturalisation. It is thus consonant with the ECJ's rulings in *Michelletti* and *Kaur*. This tenet has no boundary-testing effects: it does not call into question the boundaries of national belonging. Nor does it undermine national identities. It merely ensures that the rights that Union law (Article 21 TFEU) has conferred on individuals remain fully effective thereby facilitating the attainment of the Community's objectives pursuant to the Community law doctrine of *effet utile* (the principles of effectiveness) and the fundamental status of Union citizenship.[104] For the full effectiveness of Community rules would be impaired and the protection of the

[103] D. Kostakopoulou, 'Nested 'Old' and 'New' Citizenships in the EU: Bringing Forth the Complexity', *Columbia Journal of European Law*, Vol. 5(3), 1999, 389–413; *Citizenship, Identity and Immigration in the European Union: Between Past and Future*, Manchester University Press, Manchester, 2001.

[104] AG Maduro has acknowledged that 'any standard of Community law may be invoked' – not only the general principles of Community law and human rights, in the exercise of state jurisdiction in matters of acquisition and loss of nationality (point 28). Relevant academic literature includes: S. Hall, 'Loss of Citizenship in Breach of Fundamental Rights', (1996) 21 *ELR* 129; *Nationality, Migration Rights and Citizenship of the Union*, Martinus Nijhoff, Dordrecht, 1995; G.-R. de Groot, 'The Relationship Between the Nationality Legislation of the Member States of the European Union and European Citizenship', in M. La Torre (ed.) *European Citizenship: An Institutional Challenge*, Kluwer, The Hague, 1998, 115–148; 'Towards a European Nationality Law', in H. Schneider (ed.), *Migration, Integration and Citizenship: Volume 1*, Maastricht, Forum Maastricht, 2006). Compare also ECJ 9 December 1997, Case C-265/95, *Commission v France* [1997] ECR I-6959; ECJ 15 May 2003, Case C-300/01 *Salzmann* [2003] ECR I-4899; ECJ 12 September 2006, Cases C-145/04, *Spain v UK* [2006] ECR I-7917

rights granted by Article 21 TFEU would be weakened, if in being an apatride and thus a person without 'the right to have rights', according to Arendt, one's Union citizen status were erased automatically. Conversely, as long as the fundamental status of Union citizenship and the *effet utile* of Union law are kept in the forefront of the analysis, a stateless person would continue to receive the protection of EU law, maintain his/her associative ties and be a participant in the European Union public. My main worry, here, is that if we look in the wrong place for European citizenship, it will become devoid of significance.

## 4. CONCLUSION

The foregoing discussion has examined the Court's contribution to enhancing the stature of Union citizenship and its perceived encroachment on Member State autonomy by comparing and contrasting developments in the material and personal scopes of Union citizenship. The discussion has shown that EU citizenship is an evolving, experimental institution set within a framework that is constantly in motion. As both observers of and participants in such a restless framework, we often struggle to comprehend how institutional change has taken place, how it affects domestic policies and the subsequent development of European norms and how it shapes actors' conduct. In this respect, it might be wise to eschew dogmas and political fixity and to maintain an open mind as to who advances citizens' rights, creates openings and unlocks potentialities which may be frustrated by unnecessary barriers. And we should not forget that 'national ways of doing things' and 'statal autonomy' have often disempowered citizens and helped to justify the raw force of restrictive and coercive practices. Accordingly, I deployed in this chapter the lens of 'the third party perspective', that is, the perspective of citizens, in order to reflect on judicial interventions in the domain of citizenship and migration. This has enabled the surmounting of the familiar supranationalism/intergovernmentalism dualism and concomitant debates about contestations of power and competition between supranational institutions and the Member States.

Bettering citizens' life chances, meeting their needs and enhancing their protection should not be perceived as a matter of accident or rebellion, praise or blame of the ECJ, defective exercise of jurisdiction and an anomalous bypassing of democratically elected legislatures. Instead, it has been the ECJ's working hypothesis consistently for decades. True, its preference for a rights-based approach to free movement of persons and Union citizenship has often conflicted with national governments' preference for the status quo, unilateral citizenship and migration control and a power-driven approach. However, as the preceding

and ECJ 12 September 2006, C-300/04, *Eman and Sevinger v College van burgemeester en wethouders van Den Haag* [2006] ECR I-8055.

discussion has shown, concrete advances have been made that have enhanced the interests of ordinary citizens and states have had to concede a number of important changes in their practices that bring renewed growth in associated action and promote non-discrimination. In this respect, there is nothing fundamentally wrong in the ECJ's testing of the limits of the European public or EU citizenship. After all, we cannot expect things to operate unchanged for years to come and, more importantly, the more we test the limits of the European citizenship, the broader its limits will be.

# PART IV

# FUNDAMENTAL RIGHTS

# THE CASE OF FUNDAMENTAL RIGHTS: A STATE OF AMBIVALENCE

Loïc Azoulai

## 1. INTRODUCTION. THE QUESTION HAS CHANGED

When the demands concerning the protection of fundamental rights appeared on the European stage, they were assumed to threaten the autonomy of the Community and its legal order. The protection of these rights was upheld by the German and Italian Courts and supported by domestic doctrines.[1] As additional damage, but somehow also as a purposeful goal, it weakened the integrity, the authority and the legitimacy of the new legal order edified by the European Court of Justice. The Court could no longer ignore these demands. However, instead of being paralysed by these effects, the Court turned them into useful "means of action", thereby realising the possibility of expanding its field of action. What could have been a defeat, the Court turned into a powerful instrument to enlarge its jurisdiction.[2]

How did this happen? Two well known series of processes occurred. First, that of incorporation and "immunisation". The Court had to take the Member States' fundamental requirements into consideration without surrendering the autonomy and the unity of EC law. Integrating the substance of fundamental rights was the answer, giving them a foundation apparently common to the Member States (the general principles of EC law derived from the "constitutional traditions common to the Member States") while simultaneously maintaining the formal neutrality of EC law regarding any foreign source, even if that source was constitutional. It also allowed the Court to conserve a significant freedom of appreciation when it came to the definition and the scope of these rights. The result of these processes converged and can be pinpointed in the formula elaborated in *Internationale Handelsgellschaft*: "*respect for fundamental rights forms an*

[1] See P. Pescatore, 'Les droits de l'homme et l'intégration européenne', *Cahiers de droit européen*, 1968, p 629.

[2] See B. de Witte, 'The Past and Future Role of the European Court of Justice in the Protection of Human Rights' in P. Alston (ed), *The European Union and Human Rights*, OUP, Oxford, 1999, p 859.

*integral part of the general principles of law protected by the Court of Justice. The protection of such rights, whilst inspired by the constitutional traditions common to the Member States, must be ensured within the framework of the structure and objectives of the Community".*[3]

The other series of processes consisted in projecting these requirements, as interpreted by the Court, into the enlarged field of application of EC and EU law. Since the decision of the Court in the *Wachauf* case, the addressees were not only the European institutions but also the national authorities.[4] As the Court states in *Advocaten voor de Wereld*: "*It must be noted at the outset that, by virtue of Article 6 EU, the Union is founded on the principle of the rule of law and it respects fundamental rights, as guaranteed by the European Convention for the Protection of Human Rights and Fundamental Freedoms, signed in Rome on 4 November 1950, and as they result from the constitutional provisions common to the Member States, as general principles of Community law. It follows that the institutions are subject to review of the conformity of their acts with the Treaties and the general principles of law, just like the Member States when they implement the law of the Union*".[5] As a consequence of these developments, the underlying question has changed over time. The potential constraint stemming from the application of fundamental rights no longer originates from the national courts and is no longer directed against the Community; rather it emanates from supranational law and is directed against the Member States.

To appreciate the reality of this threat, we must not concentrate on the general terms of the case-law. Quoting the judgments of the Court that provoked hostility from the Member States does not suffice. I shall rather attempt to present an analytical framework of the interpretations offered by the Court in this field. Three points are essential for understanding how EU protection of fundamental rights can be both consecutively and simultaneously reducers and vectors of autonomy for the Member States of the EU. At each point, a different prerogative of the state is at stake: its liberty (the condition of being free from any European control), its independence (the power to act as an autonomous authority) and its identity (the distinct legal features of the state).

## 2. PLAYING WITH THE SCOPE OF THE PROTECTION: THE LIBERTY OF THE STATE

EU fundamental rights do not apply universally. The fear of an unlimited extension of the application of EU law by the sole effect of the invocation of EU fundamental rights in every situation, even irrelevant to the objectives of the EU,

[3] ECJ 17 December 1970, Case 11/70, *Internationale Handelsgesellschaft* [1970] ECR 1125.
[4] ECJ 13 July 1989, *Wachauf v Federal Republic of Germany* Case C-5/88 [1989] ECR 2609.
[5] ECJ 3 May 2007, Case C-303/05 [2007] ECR I-3633, para. 45.

has culminated due to the Court's reliance on fundamental rights as general principles of EC law. The institutional answer to that fear is to be found in Article 6 of the Treaty on European Union as amended by the Lisbon Treaty: *"the provisions of the Charter [of Fundamental Rights of the European Union] shall not extend in any way the competences of the Union as defined in the Treaties"*. The judicial response is that *"the Court has no such jurisdiction with regard to national provisions outside the scope of Community [EU] law and when the subject-matter of the dispute is not connected in any way with any of the situations contemplated by the treaties"*.[6] EU fundamental rights do not produce their own conditions of applicability in the national sphere: they need to be 'carried' by other EU rules. Only national rules falling within the scope of application of EU law, or situations connected with situations contemplated by the EU Treaty, will be subjected to fundamental rights review.[7] In cases where no connecting factor can be established, EU fundamental rights are not applicable.

EU fundamental rights infiltrate via two common types of "vehicles": the internal market freedoms and secondary EU law. Firstly, fundamental rights can be applied in every cross-border situation in which the freedoms of movement can be invoked. Therefore, the scope of protection of fundamental rights is largely determined by the scope of application of the economic freedoms. As this scope of application is quite expansive, and expands well beyond the competences attributed to the European Union, no area is a priori excluded from the field of application of fundamental rights. This is the result of a simple and recurrent formula in the Court's rulings: *"even if, in the areas which fall outside the scope of the EU's competence [such as social protection, direct taxation, education, civil status of individuals, nationality law...], the Member States are still free, in principle, to lay down the conditions governing the domain in question, the fact remains that, when exercising that competence, the Member States must nevertheless comply with EU law"*, in particular the provisions on the economic freedoms.[8] Therefore, no 'reserved competences' of Member States can be said to be excluded from the empire of EU law and, consequently, from EU fundamental rights. The *K.B.* case is a good example of the expansion of fundamental rights review to a domestic regime of civil law.[9] Secondly, fundamental rights can be applied in every situation

6 ECJ 6 October 2005, Case C-328/04, *Criminal proceedings against Attila Vajnai* [2005] ECR I-8577, para 13.

7 See J. Temple Lang, 'The Sphere in which the Member States are obliged to comply with the General Principles of Law and Community Fundamental Rights Principles', *Legal Issues of European Integration*, 1991/2, p 23.

8 See e.g. ECJ 11 December 2007, Case C-438/05, *International Transport Worker's Federation, Finnish Seamen's Union* v. *Viking Line* [2007] ECR I-10779, para 40. K. Lenaerts, 'L'encadrement par le droit de l'Union européenne des compétences des Etats membres' in *Mélanges en l'honneur du Professeur Jean Paul Jacqué*, Dalloz, Paris, 2010.

9 ECJ 7 January 2004, Case C-117/01, *K.B. v National Health Service Pensions Agency and Secretary of State for Health* [2004] ECR I-541.

related to EU norms. Since there has been an increase in volume of EU legislation, which raises sensitive questions of civil liberties and social rights, the scope of the EU fundamental rights protection is potentially expanding. Legislation regarding non-discrimination adopted under Article 19 TFEU (Article 13 EC) and legislation adopted in the vast area of Freedom, Security and Justice form a new and large domain that is subject to fundamental rights.[10]

However, the fact remains that the ECJ has no universal jurisdiction on fundamental rights. The liberty of the State outside the scope of EU law is preserved. This is no longer the case when the Court takes the initiative to create itself the "connecting factor" with the sole objective of applying EU fundamental rights in mind. In some cases, this extension is appealed by national Courts.[11] More often, it is forced by the ECJ. In these cases, instead of subordinating the application of fundamental rights to the existence of a clearly applicable EU rule, the Court creates such a rule. It is as if the desire of the Court to apply fundamental rights required the existence of a connecting factor. Therefore, the protection of fundamental rights becomes a vehicle of its own. As a result, EU fundamental rights make their own way into the autonomous national legal sphere.

This can be observed in the two legal contexts mentioned. In some cases, the Court interprets broadly the conditions of applicability of the economic freedoms for the sole purpose of applying fundamental rights. In the *Carpenter* (C-60/00), *Akrich* (C-109/01) or *Parking Brixen* (C-458/03) cases, the link to a cross-border situation was far from clear; still, the Court insisted that fundamental rights and the principle of non-discrimination must be taken into account. In the *ERT* case, the Court goes even further by delineating that fundamental rights review is extended to national rules adopted on the basis of a derogation conferred by the Treaty freedoms.[12] A new regime is thus created, by which the constraint is transferred to national policies with only tiny or potential links with EC law.[13]

In the context of secondary law, two famous cases can be cited. In the *Karner* case, the national measure, classified as a 'selling arrangement', was deemed outside the field of application of the free movement of goods by application of the *Keck & Mithouard* case-law.[14] However, the Court obliged the national court to take into consideration Article 10 ECHR. In the reasoning of the Court, the

---

10 See ECJ 27 February 2007, Case C-354/04 P, *Gestoras Pro Amnistía and Others v Council* [2007] ECR I-1579 and ECJ 27 February 2007, Case C-355/04 P, *Segi and Others v Council* [2007] ECR I-1657. Note that the Lisbon treaty has enlarged the jurisdiction of the Court over the second pillar and part of the third. However, transitional provisions are in application during which the Court's jurisdiction remains unchanged (see protocol 36 on transitional provisions).

11 See ECJ 10 April 2003, Case C-276/01, *Joachim Steffensen* [2003] ECR I-3735.

12 ECJ 18 June 1991, Case C-260/89, *Elliniki Radiophonia Tiléorassi AE and Panellinia Omospondia Syllogon Prossopikou v Dimotiki Etairia Pliroforissis and Sotirios Kouvelas and Nicolaos Avdellas and others* [1991] ECR I-2925.

13 F. Jacobs, 'Human Rights in the EU: the Role of the Court of Justice', (2001) 26 *ELR (European Law Review)* 331.

14 ECJ 25 March 2004, Case C-71/02, *Herbert Karner Industrie-Auktionen GmbH v Troostwijk GmbH* [2004] ECR I-3025.

justification remains unclear. The only reasonable basis for the application of EU fundamental rights is to consider that the national legislation in question was connected to EU law as a measure of 'reinforced protection' in the meaning of the EC Directive on misleading advertising. In the *Mangold* case, the Court established the relevance of a general principle of non-discrimination on the ground of age whilst admitting that Directive 2000/78, to which the situation could have been connected, was not fully applicable.[15] How could this solution be justified? By the fact that the German law in question can be considered as a measure of "implementation" of another statute, the Directive concerning fixed-term work? Again, the connecting factor was tenuous.

In each of these cases, the model of fundamental rights as "secondary rules", dependent on the application of other EU rules, is maintained. But the connection is somewhat 'forced' and for this reason subject to contestation. Another model would be to autonomise the protection of fundamental rights as proposed by Advocate General Poiares Maduro in the *Centro Europa* case.[16] The idea is that some serious violations of fundamental rights in the Member States may amount to a violation of the rules of free movement, by making impossible in practice the exercise of the rights flowing from these rules. This proposal, to reverse the conditions of applicability of EU rules, is revolutionary: it has not yet however been accepted by the Court.

## 3. DESIGNING THE CONSTRAINTS: THE INDEPENDENCE OF THE STATE

Member States are required to observe fundamental rights when applying EU law. Fundamental rights are limits to their actions.[17] But they are limits of a special nature, which apply indirectly. The ECJ doctrine runs as follows: Respect for fundamental rights is a condition of the lawfulness of EU acts;[18] National law must be applied in conformity with EU law; Therefore, Member States must apply EU rules "in accordance" with the requirements of fundamental rights. In this way, the respect for fundamental rights is "transferred" to the national level, where they become part and a parameter of the consistent application of EU rules.

This appears clearly in the first case concerning the obligation of the Member States with regard to fundamental rights, the *Wachauf* case.[19] In this case, an EC

[15] ECJ 22 November 2005, Case C-144/04, *Werner Mangold v Rüdiger Helm* [2005] ECR I-9981.

[16] ECJ 31 January 2008, Case C-380/05, *Centro Europa 7 Srl v Ministero delle Comunicazioni e Autorità per le garanzie nelle comunicazioni and Direzione generale per le concessioni e le autorizzazioni del Ministero delle Comunicazioni* [2008] ECR I-349.

[17] O. Due & C. Gulmann, 'Community Fundamental Rights as Part of National Law' in *Scritti in Onore di G.F. Mancini*, vol. II, Giuffrè Editore, Milano, 1998, p 405.

[18] ECJ 28 March 1996, Opinion 2/94 *Accession by the Community to the Convention for the Protection of Human Rights and Fundamental Freedoms*, [1996] ECR I-1759, para 34.

[19] ECJ 13 July 1989, Case C-5/88, *Wachauf v Federal Republic of Germany*, [1989] ECR 2609.

legislation designed to reduce milk production was under scrutiny. It was this legislation which was questioned by the referring German court. However, the Court decided to transfer the test for compliance with fundamental rights: indeed, the requirements of the protection of fundamental rights *'are also binding on the Member States when they implement Community rules'*. The reason for this transfer is given by the Court in its decision: *"The Community regulations in question leave the competent national authorities a sufficiently wide margin of appreciation to enable them to apply those rules in a manner consistent with the requirements of the protection of fundamental rights"*. EC rules in question are incomplete, and therefore it is for the national authorities to ensure that the national rules completing the EC legislation are adopted in light of EC fundamental rights. In other words, the Court recognised the responsibility of the Member States for determining the concrete conditions of application of property rights in the case in hand. National authorities must respect fundamental rights to the full extent allowed by EU rules.

Fundamental rights are conditions of the lawfulness of EU provisions but, in fact, the effective constraint is borne by the Member states. The constraints referred to mainly concern balancing. The Court imposes on the national authorities the need to weigh, in each factual and specific situation, the competing rights and interests involved and to strike a balance between them. The fundamental rights review adds to the classical commitment of 'denationalisation' of national law induced by the application of the freedoms of movement, a requirement of 'concrete balancing'. Recently the Court had to deal with the difficult case of balancing between two conflicting rights.[20] In *Promusicae*, the Court stated that *"the Member States must, when transposing the directives, take care to rely on an interpretation of the directives which allows a fair balance to be struck between the various fundamental rights protected by the Community legal order"*.[21]

In the *Lindqvist* case, the Court went one step further. [22] Mrs Lindqvist submitted that the Directive on the protection of personal data, in so far as it prohibits processing of personal data of a sensitive nature, is contrary to the general principle of freedom of expression. The Court stated that *"in many respects, the Member States have a margin of manoeuvre in implementing the Directive"*, so that *"it is rather, at the stage of the application at national level of the legislation implementing the Directive in individual cases that a balance must be found between the rights and interests involved"*, *"including the fundamental rights protected by the Community legal order"*. This conception has been systematised in

20 See J.P.Jacqué, 'Vers une nouvelle étape dans la protection des droits fondamentaux dans l'Union européenne?' in *Mélanges en l'honneur de Jean Charpentier*, Ed. Pedone, Paris, 2008, p 345.

21 ECJ 29 January 2008, Case C-275/06, *Productores de Música de España (Promusicae) v Telefónica de España SAU* [2008] ECR I-279, para 68.

22 ECJ 6 November 2003, Case C-101/01, *Criminal proceedings against Bodil Lindqvist* [2003] ECR I-2971.

the *European Parliament v. Council* case on immigration policy. The Parliament contended that the provisions of the Directive on the right to family reunification do no respect fundamental rights, in particular the right to family life and the right to non-discrimination. The Court could not find any direct violation of fundamental rights in the provisions of the Directive. It is enough to conclude that *"while the Directive leaves the Member States a margin of appreciation, it is sufficiently wide to enable them to apply the Directive's rules in a manner consistent with the requirements flowing from the protection of fundamental rights"*.[23] The EU level is not the adequate level to ensure the protection of fundamental rights. At this level, rights are defined in a highly abstract way. A real protection must be concrete, substantive and effective; therefore, it is up to the national courts to provide for it. National courts have the power to design the appropriate practical modalities to ensure respect for fundamental rights, under the scrutiny of the ECJ.[24] In both cases, the binding character of the EU protection of fundamental rights is fading behind the recognition of the autonomy of the national authorities in ensuring this protection.

This case-law is ambivalent. The wording of the *Wachauf* judgment by which Member States must, *"as far as possible"* apply EU rules in accordance with fundamental rights assumes, in the subsequent case-law, two different meanings. On the one hand, and originally, it has the effect of protecting EU acts. These acts are sheltered from censure by the sole fact of their incompleteness. Any flexibility in the EU legislation is thus interpreted as an implicit commitment to respect for fundamental rights. Consequently, if the EU legislation as applied in a Member State conflicts with the requirement of protection of fundamental rights, it is the national measure which shall be blamed and must be set aside. On the other hand, it grants the national authorities a certain independence of action and interpretation. Ultimately, the transfer of constraint implies a transfer of power. Indeed, the national authorities must not only interpret its national law in a manner consistent with EU law but it must also interpret the implemented EU rules in a manner consistent with the fundamental rights protected by the EU legal order. The Court confers to the ordinary courts a true "European" power: *a power to interpret the EU rules in conformity with superior rules of EU law.*[25] This transfer of power is also internal to the Member States. What the Court gives to the ordinary courts, under its own scrutiny, is precisely what it took from the constitutional courts as a result of the *Nold* case (Case 4/73), that is the determination of the substance of the fundamental rights and the jurisdiction to

---

23 ECJ 27 June 2006, Case C-540/03, *European Parliament v Council of the European Union*, [2006] ECR I-5769.

24 See e.g. ECJ 13 March 2007, Case C-432/05, *Unibet (London) Ltd and Unibet (International) Ltd v Justitiekanslern*, [2007] ECR I-2271.

25 See ECJ 6 November 2003, Case C-101/01, *Criminal proceedings against Bodil Lindqvist*, [2003] ECR I-12971, para 87; ECJ 26 June 2007, Case C-305/05, *Ordre des barreaux francophones et germanophone and others* [2007] ECR I-5305, para 28; ECJ 16 June 2005, Case C-105/03, *Criminal proceedings against Maria Pupino* [2005] ECR I-5285, para 59–60.

control the compatibility of the applicable rules with fundamental rights. This amounts to a massive empowerment of the ordinary courts.

However, this transfer of power generates risks. National courts may be tempted to use the margin of appreciation recognised by the ECJ so as to impose its own conception of fundamental rights. Supreme and constitutional courts may be tempted to control themselves the validity of EU rules, using the requirement of the interpretation of EU law in conformity with fundamental rights. The Court's judgment in the "professional secrecy of lawyers" case gave rise to such temptations.[26]

## 4. CONCEPTUALISING THE RIGHTS: THE IDENTITY OF THE STATE

Traditional conceptions of rights view rights as the substantial protection of few privileged interests reflecting superior values. M. Kumm has shown that fundamental rights are structured in a totally different manner by the case-law of the Court.[27] The Court is prompt to classify as "a right" any sort of interest which conditions the *access* to those collective goods which are vectors of economic and social integration (markets, labour markets, professions, justice, systems of social protection, etc). Therefore, various types of interests can be protected as fundamental rights. Fundamental rights give capacities to the private parties to take advantage of the facilities given by the economic freedoms or the social legislation of the Union. One of the most extensive rights in EU law is certainly the right to non-discrimination.[28] But, as with all rights in EU law, the right to non-discrimination is subject to limitations and to a proportionality test.[29] Rights violations may be justified by weighty reasons of public policy. As a result, there is no clear and absolute hierarchy between the individual rights and the public interests protected as limitations to the rights. Rights and policy considerations compete on the same level in EU law.

---

26 ECJ 26 June 2007, Case C-305/05, *Ordre des barreaux francophones et germanophones and others* [2007], ECR I-5305, para 28. See, in Belgium, Cour constitutionnelle, 23 January 2008, n° 10/2008, *Moniteur belge* 11 février 2008, p. 8933 and P. Martens, 'Restaient les étrangers…' in J.-Y. Carlier (ed), *L'étranger face au droit*, Bruylant, Bruxelles, 2010, p 609; in France, Conseil d'Etat, CE, Sect., 10 April 2008, *Conseil national des barreaux e.a.*, n° 296845, 296907 and L. Azoulai, 'Le Conseil d'Etat, nouvelle autorité de droit européen', *Revue juridique de l'économie publique*, 2008, n° 655, p 19.

27 See M. Kumm, '*Internationale Handelsgesellschaft, Nold* and the New Human Rights Paradigm' in M. Poiares Maduro & L. Azoulai (eds), *The Past & Future of EU Law. The Classics of EU Law Revisited on the 50th Anniversary of the Rome Treaty*, Hart Publishing, Oxford, 2010.

28 See D. Schiek, in this volume.

29 This conception contradicts an approach which is commonly used in some Member States. In France, for example, it was common to state that a direct discrimination cannot be justified by any legitimate interest, since prohibition of discrimination protects a superior value: See G. Calvès, 'L'égalité' in J.-B. Auby (ed.), *L'influence du droit européen sur les categories du droit public*, Dalloz, Paris, 2010.

This conception has important consequences on the legal identity of the Member States. On the one hand, it allows for an extension of the protection of rights in the private sphere. A good example is provided by the *Kücükdeveci* case in which the Court reiterated the solution given in *Mangold*.[30] In this case, the Court was confronted with the impossibility of applying the provisions of Directive 2000/78 EC, establishing a general framework for equal treatment in employment and occupation, to private litigation. The Court chose to refer to the general principle of non-discrimination on the ground of age. As a superior expression of the specific provisions of the directive, this constitutional principle becomes a source of rights and obligations that the national court has the obligation to protect in any private litigation. This technique, rooted in *Defrenne* (Case 43/75), has the effect of subordinating the relations traditionally governed by private law and based on party autonomy to some obligations of justification. Alleging subjective preferences is not enough. The principle of non-discrimination requires that comparable situations must be treated alike and different situations must not be treated in the same way unless such treatment is *objectively* justified by the pursuit of a *legitimate aim* and provided that it is appropriate and necessary to achieve it. The private party may have a "public" responsibility under EU law. This is potentially disturbing for the social policy of the state but also for the structural features of the national system of private law.[31]

Conversely, the public authority may lose its privileges under EU law. In subjecting all the legitimate public interests to a proportionality test in every single situation, the ECJ can give the impression of privileging the private interest on the general interest: for example, the individual right to equal treatment prevailing over the national requirements of public security in the *Kreil* case.[32] Therefore, the ECJ may be perceived as being unaware of the problem of identity and collective action raised in the national contexts. States are subject to the continuous need to justify themselves, before European bodies and national courts, in view of the objectives of the Union and in front of the prerogatives given to the individuals. This model of reasoning is potentially threatening the traditional asymmetric relationship between the private individual defending his/her own interests and the public authority protecting the national values.

It is adaptable, however. With the same premises, it could be concluded that special importance should be given to the public interest against any competing private interest in some specific situations. The case-law initiated in the *Schmidberger* case and reproduced in *Omega* can be read as an adaptation of

---

30 ECJ 19 January 2010, Case C-555/07, *Seda Kücükdeveci v Swedex GmbH & Co. KG*, [2010], not yet published.

31 See N. Reich, 'The Public/Private Divide in European Law' in F. Cafaggi & H.W. Micklitz (eds), *European Private Law after the Common Framework of Reference*, Edward Elgar, Cheltenham, 2010.

32 ECJ 11 January 2000, Case C-285/98, *Tanja Kreil v Bundesrepublik Deutschland* [2000] ECR I-69.

the traditional features of the Court's analysis.[33] These judgments are based on the recognition of the Member States' national identities within the integration process.[34] The interests protected by the Court in these cases have been suggestively labelled as "*fundamental rights of the Member States*".[35] Indeed, the Court accepts and takes into account the importance of the fundamental rights protected by the respective Constitutions against the competing EU objectives. Instead of confining the public interest to a strict application of the proportionality principle, the Court acknowledges in *Schmidberger* that, in defining the right protected in the internal order (the right of freedom of expression and freedom of assembly) and in the balance of this right with the Treaty's economic freedoms, "*the competent authorities enjoy a wide margin of discretion*".[36] In fact, the Court restricts itself to submitting this assessment to a review of whether it is "reasonable". In *Omega*, the Court goes even further in that it grants the Member State broad discretion for the purpose of specifying the content and scope of human dignity according to the specific view the Member State has of the protection appropriate to that fundamental right on its territory. As a result, "*the fact that the view of the fundamental right held by a Member State is not shared by other Member States does not prevent that Member State from relying on it so as to justify a restriction of the freedom to provide services*".[37] This case-law clearly favours the constitutional autonomy of the Member States and, by the same token, the national autonomy of citizens. Moreover, it gives the national authorities a constitutional task, that of bringing fundamental national values into accordance with EU provisions, taking account of the specific features of the national state.

The elevation of certain interests to the rank of national values allows the Court to relax its standards of control on states policies. Now, any interest can be translated in terms of values and ethical issues. This approach can be easily extended to systems of private law[38] or to some sensitive parts of the social or economic regulation of the state.[39] There is only one reserve to this approach,

[33] ECJ 12 June 2003, Case C-112/00, *Eugen Schmidberger, Internationale Transporte und Planzüge v Republik Österreich* [2003] ECR I-5659 and ECJ 14 October 2004, Case C-36/02, *Omega Spielhallen- und Automatenaufstellungs-GmbH v Oberbürgermeisterin der Bundesstadt Bonn* [2004] ECR I-9609.

[34] See D. Ritleng, 'Le respect de l'identité constitutionnelle nationale des Etats membres' in *Vers un droit fondamental des Etats membres de l'Union ?* Bruylant, Bruxelles, 2010.

[35] See J.-D. Mouton, 'Vers une reconnaissance des droits fondamentaux aux Etats dans le système communautaire?' in *Les dynamiques du droit européen en début de siècle. Etudes en l'honneur de J.-C. Gautron*, Pedone, Paris, 2004, p 463.

[36] ECJ 12 June 2003, Case C-112/00, *Eugen Schmidberger, Internationale Transporte und Planzüge v Republik Österreich* [2003] ECR I-5659, para 82.

[37] Opinion of Advocate General Poiares Maduro 8 October 2008 in Case C-213/07, *Michaniki AE v Ethniko Symvoulio Radiotileorasis and Ypourgos Epikrateias* [2008] ECR I-9999, para 32.

[38] See Opinion of Advocate General Sharpston 24 April 2008 in Case C-353/06, *Stefan Grunkin and Dorothee Regina Paul* [2008] ECR I-7639.

[39] See e.g. ECJ 19 May 2009, Joined Cases C-171/07 and C-172/07, *Apothekerkammer des Saarlandes and others* [2009] ECR I-04171; ECJ 8 September 2009, Case C-42/07, *Liga Portuguesa*

revealed by the *Laval* case.[40] What the Court had previously granted to Member States, it then refused to trade unions that had been nevertheless placed under the same constraints.[41] The collective autonomy of citizens is not protected where it is based on a social organisation and not on State identity.

## 5. CONCLUSION

The analytical framework of the Court in the field of the protection of fundamental rights leads to ambivalent results. At each stage of this short analysis, it has been shown that the interpretations of the Court can be either reducers or vectors of autonomy for the Member States, depending on the context of interpretation. This creates a need for justification. What is lacking is a clear set of justifications for the constraints imposed upon the Member States. In the field of the fundamental freedoms of movement, the idea has been stated that the Court's case-law is governed by "the argument from transnational effects": conferring EU rights would be a way to force the Member States not to disregard the interests of those who are involved in cross-border situations.[42] In the field of the protection of fundamental rights, the work of justification has not yet been carried out. The teleology of the 'Social Market Economy' and the necessity to protect weak parties in litigation could possibly explain cases like *Mangold* and *Kücükdeveci*. The protection of individual rights and personal capacities is the underlying ideology for cases like *Kreil* and *K.B.* In other cases, imposing EU fundamental rights on national law has merely a "legalization" effect on EU law. It allows the Court to relax the pressure on the EU legal system by shifting the constraint on the implementing national law (*Lindqvist, European Parliament v. Council*). Providing justifications is certainly an important task which would allow a better assessment of the desirability and the reality of the alleged encroachments on Member States' autonomy in each particular case.

---

*de Futebol Profissional* [2009] ECR I-07633; ECJ 19 May 2009, Case C-531/06, *Commission v Italy* [2009] ECR I-04103.

40 ECJ 18 December 2007, Case C-341/05, *Laval un Partneri Ltd v Svenska Byggnadsarbetareförbundet, Svenska Byggnadsarbetareförbundets avdelning 1, Byggettan and Svenska Elektrikerförbundet* [2007] ECR I-11767.

41 See L. Azoulai, 'The Court of Justice and the Social Market Economy: The Emergence of an Ideal and the Conditions for its Realization', (2008) 45 *CMLR (Common Market Law Review) 1335*.

42 See C. Joerges & J. Neyer, 'Deliberative Supranationalism' Revisited', *EUI Working Paper Law*, 2006/20; M. Poiares Maduro, 'Reforming the Market or the State? Article 30 and the European Constitution: Economic Freedom and Political Rights', (1997) *ELJ (European Law Journal)*. For the critics, see A. Somek, 'The Argument From Transnational Effects I: Representing Outsiders Through Freedoms of Movement', The University of Iowa College of Law, Research Paper N° 9–23, May 2009 (available online at: http://ssrn.com).

# FUNDAMENTAL RIGHTS JURISPRUDENCE BETWEEN MEMBER STATES' PREROGATIVES AND CITIZENS' AUTONOMY

Dagmar SCHIEK[1]

## 1. INTRODUCTION

The title to which the editors originally invited me to work was "The ECJ and the Autonomy of Member States – Fundamental Rights". This heading seemed an enigma. Surely, fundamental rights are meant to impinge inter alia upon the prerogatives of governments in order to protect the autonomy of (human) individuals. Thus, if the Court's fundamental rights case law has the effect of restricting the prerogatives of Member States, this would not seem to be problematic in principle.

The apparent enigma resonates with a traditional view of fundamental rights, according to which "in principle, fundamental rights (...) are rights of defence enjoyed by the individual vis-à-vis public authority".[2] This function of fundamental rights certainly continues to be of relevance. However, in an era of globalisation and increasing private power the functions of human rights change. When states are no longer the sole governors of the world (if they ever were), fundamental rights would be of limited relevance if they were only binding on states. Accordingly, the above quote mentions "public authority", which includes the European Union as well as other conglomerates of states. But is public authority still the most relevant threat to actual enjoyment of fundamental rights? Do we need yet other layers of fundamental rights law? If one asks these questions seriously, the relation between the ECJ's fundamental rights case law, Member States' prerogatives and citizens' autonomy appears much less clear cut than sketched above initially. In particular, Member States (and other public

1 This chapter originated from a presentation in April 2009 and owes much to the critical remarks by the participants, as well as to valuable feedback by the editors. The draft was reworked for publication in March 2010.

2 AG TRSTENJAK, Opinion of 30 June 2009, Case C-101/08, *Audiolux and Others* [2009] ECR I-9823, para 77, rejecting any relevance of equality principles for private law for this reason.

authorities) may have positive roles as well as negative ones in achieving the true values of fundamental rights.

The primary aim of this paper is to analyse recent case law by the Court of Justice and to consider how it relates to Member States' prerogatives and citizens' autonomy. This question rests on a notion of fundamental rights which places autonomy at the centre. This notion will be sketched first. From this starting point, potentially positive and negative relations between the EU, Member States' prerogatives and citizens' rights will then be sketched, in order to contextualise the Court's fundamental rights case law. This will also enable us to re-read the doctrines usually presented as centrally underlying its fundamental rights doctrine. Following this, recent case law will be analysed. This part will have a quantitative appetizer, which will formalise some assumptions and test them on a total of 150 cases before the European judiciary.[3] It will then offer a more conceptual account of case law on fundamental rights to equality and non-discrimination on the one hand, and around fundamental rights of workers to actively shape employment and labour relations on the other hand. In conclusion, some suggestions will be made as to how the Court's fundamental rights doctrine could develop more positively in order to moderate diverging interests of different parts of the citizenry in protecting fundamental rights.

## 2. THE NOTION OF FUNDAMENTAL RIGHTS – AUTONOMY OF HUMAN BEINGS

In deliberating whether there is a European approach to human rights, Leben[4] reminds us that a European revolution stood at the bedrock of human rights, with one of its most radical ideas being that any man or woman is endowed with inalienable rights. These were rights, not liberties, irrespective of the fact that so called "liberal rights" are often seen as the first layer of human rights, while social rights are conventionally considered of somewhat later (and possibly lesser) origin. A right is bestowed on an individual, and the spirit of the French Revolution was – in line with European Enlightenment – very much concerned with freeing individuals from conventional bonds to land, aristocrats and so forth, while not leaving them isolated.

Without attempting to write a treatise on this question here, it is submitted that European human rights are based on the idea of autonomy,[5] which is at the

[3] Following the Treaty of Lisbon, the European judiciary includes the Court of Justice (ECJ) as well as the General Court (which used to be the Court of First Instance) and the Civil Service Tribunal.

[4] C. Leben, 'A European Approach to Human Rights?' in: F. Alston (ed), *The EU and Human Rights*, OUP, 1999, 69–97, at 74–75.

[5] See also K. Möller, 'Two Conceptions of Positive Liberty: Towards and Autonomy-based Theory of Constitutional Rights' (2009) 29 OJLS (*Oxford Journal of Legal Studies)* 757–786.

same time constitutive for the purpose of fundamental rights. Autonomy of human beings presupposes that they remain able to self-govern their lives. Of course, this self-governance must be approached against the background that humankind is a social species, and any individual life takes place against the background of being connected to others.[6] Would autonomy be considered in a merely formal way, this dimension of interconnectedness would be lost. A substantive notion of autonomy takes social reality into account. In social reality, individual autonomy must take account of the needs of others and be protected against claims of rule at the same time. Such claims continue to be made by public authority, which is, however, not the only source of such claims. In particular, market-based societies are structured to allow relations of economic dependency to develop. Thus, such private power needs to be considered.[7]

Fundamental rights protection can take different stands here. Proceeding from the notion of formal autonomy (and thus the self-contained self able to rely, inter alia, on his personal wealth for ruling his life) a liberal notion of fundamental rights protection focuses on containing a potentially ever usurping state (as in Jellinek's *status negativus*[8]). From a substantive notion of autonomy, the actual enjoyment of fundamental rights attains centre stage, and fundamental rights are no longer mainly perceived as liberating, but rather as enabling at the same time. To enable actual enjoyment of fundamental rights (which could be related to Jellinek's *status positivus*), two principal (state) activities seem necessary. First, citizens need to be endowed with basic facilities (or capabilities[9]) enabling them to actually enjoy rights. Such basic endowments include education, housing, employment as well as functioning communicative spheres and effective (court) systems for rights enforcement. Second, citizens need to be enabled to ward off private power. As a consequence of its ever increasing threats, horizontal effect of fundamental rights is being demanded,[10] for example through the medium of

6 See for a feminist perspective on human rights S.M. Okin, 'Equal Citizenship: Gender/Justice and Gender: An unfinished debate' (2004) 72 *Fordham Law Review* 1537.

7 Some even consider that the "most dangerous threats to human rights, today, originate from activities by private groups" (B. de Witte, 'The Past and Future Role of the European Court of Justice in the Protection of Human Rights', in: F. Alston (ed), *The EU and Human Rights*, OUP, 1999, 859–897, at 874).

8 See on the different "status" of fundamental rights Kühling 'Fundamental Rights' in A. Von Bogdandy & J. Bast (eds), *Principles of European Constitutional Law*, Hart, Oxford et al, 2nd revised ed, 2010, 479–514, at 492–496.

9 J. Browne J, S.F. Deakin and F. Wilkinson, *Capability, Social Rights and European Market Integration*, University of Cambridge CBR WP 253, December 2002, inaugurated a research design on the capabilities approach. S.F. Deakin ('The Capability Concept and the Evolution of the European Social Model' in *Social Welfare and EU Law* (M. Dougan & E. Spaventa (eds), Hart, Oxford, 2005, 3–24) elaborates the concept in relation to EU social policy, and the contributions in S.F. Deakin and A. Supiot (eds), *Capacitas: Re-examining the Legal Concept of Capacity*, OUP, Oxford, 2009 apply it to contract law.

10 See for a variety of approaches on this D. Oliver & J. Fedtke (eds.), *Human Rights and the Private Sphere*, Routledge-Cavendish, London et al, 2007.

private law.[11] Citizens will also need to be endowed with rights to defend their actual autonomy within societies (probably beyond Jellinek's status doctrine, as a *social status activus*). In this last reading, fundamental rights would indeed become collective rights for human beings who can only hope to ward off arbitrary rule by those in possession of economic power through collective organisation. [12]

Considering the last two, more substantive, layers of fundamental rights protection, states no longer appear exclusively as addressees of fundamental rights. Rather, positive state activities are needed to empower citizens.[13] In this perspective, case law intruding upon states' prerogatives may endanger effective protection of fundamental rights. The need for positive state activities should not overshadow the main purpose of fundamental rights, which remains strengthening the substantive autonomy of individuals. Thus, increasing prerogatives of states, supranational institutions or non-governmental organisations should always be assessed in relation to its effects on the individual and her substantive autonomy. In this perspective, rights to secure one's own income are preferable to rights to social welfare, for example, and rights to collective action in order to overcome structural imbalances in markets over statutory rights.

## 3. THE MULTI-LAYERED CONTEXT OF FUNDAMENTAL RIGHTS IN THE EUROPEAN UNION

The deliberations on substantive autonomy and fundamental rights protection offered so far could be made in relation to any national legal system. In a multilevel polity such as the EU, protecting and promoting fundamental rights becomes a multi-layered task, in which states and also the European Union will interact with each other and their citizens, who will in turn interact with each other. It is in this multi-polar context that the functions of fundamental rights in the EU legal order should be considered.

---

11 Often referred to as 'constitutionalisation' in writings of Dutch and German scholars (see T. Barkhuysen & S. D. Lindenbergh, *Constitutionalisation of Private Law,* Martinus Nijhoff, Leiden, 2006, for a European perspective see O.H. Gerstenberg, 'Private Law and the New European Constitutional Settlement', (2006) 10:6 *ELJ (European Law Journal)* 766–786.

12 For a grounding of European collective agreements in this see D. Schiek, 'Autonomous Collective Agreements as a Regulatory Device in European Labour Law: How to Read Article 139 EC', (2005) 34 *ILJ (Industrial Law Journal)* 23–56.

13 See on this in much detail S. Fredman, *Human Rights Transformed,* OUP, Oxford, 2008.

## 3.1. PROTECTING FUNDAMENTAL RIGHTS ALONGSIDE ECONOMIC INTEGRATION

EU law is part of "International Economic Law".[14] As such, it transforms economic integration and corresponding individual rights of economic actors into constitutional principles.[15] In developing the doctrines of direct effect and supremacy, the ECJ has created the condition to enforce market integration through individual claims. It has often been said that the Court transformed citizens and other economic actors[16] into advocates or prosecutors of European integration.[17] Such individual advocacy in favour of market integration may certainly impinge upon Member States' prerogatives. Rather than containing private power, the juridification of the fundamental freedoms has supported its transnational expansion. Considered from the substantive autonomy function of fundamental rights, this enhances the need of fundamental rights protection.

If the Court would use fundamental rights in similar ways as fundamental freedoms in order to contain Member States' policy choices, this would suggest an instrumental use (possibly an abuse) of fundamental rights by the Court.[18] Such accusations might gain weight if its fundamental rights case law would only rarely contain the European Union's powers,[19] or if it was mainly instrumental for maintaining the ECJ's institutional autonomy from other human rights courts'

---

14 See E.-U. Petersmann, 'Human Rights, International Economic Law and 'Constitutional Justice'', (2008) 19 *EJIL (European Journal of International Law)* 769–798.

15 O. Gerstenberg, 'Expanding the Constitution Beyond the Court', (2002) 8 *ELJ*, 172 192, at 179.

16 The notion of economic actors is obviously wider than the notion of citizen, the latter always being a human being. While many individual citizens are also economic actors, many economic actors are corporations. Depending on their specific organisation, the link between the real person engaging in his or her profession and the corporation can be quite loose.

17 This is even referred to as "extending constitutional rights of citizens" E.-U. Petersmann, 'Human Rights, International Economic Law and 'Constitutional Justice'', (2008) 19 *EJIL* 769–798, at 776.

18 It is well known that the ECJ has been so accused. (J. Coppel & A. O'Neill, 'The European Court of Justice: Taking Rights Seriously?', (1992) 12 *Legal Studies* 227–239 have coined the term of "offensive use" of human rights, when the ECJ only enounces them "in order to extend its jurisdiction into areas previously reserved to Member States' courts and to expand the influence of the Community over the activities of the Member States"). This has attracted some counter-critique at the time (J. Weiler & N. Lockhart, 'Taking Rights Seriously Seriously: The European Court of Justice and its Fundamental Rights Jurisprudence', (1995) 32 *CMLR (Common Market Law Review)* 51 and 579).

19 Harpaz criticises the ECJ for just that, maintaining that its standard of fundamental rights protection is below that required by the ECHR ('The European Court of Justice and its relations with the European Court of Human Rigths: The Quest for enhanced reliance, coherence and legitimacy', (2009) 46 *CMLR* 105–141, at p 116 with further references in footnote 73). Douglas-Scott, writing in 2006, states laconically "It was not until 28 years later in *Baustahlgewebe* (Case C-185/95 [1998] ECR I-8417) that the ECJ actually found an EU institution to have violated fundamental rights." ('A Tale of Two Courts: Luxembourg, Strasbourg and the growing European Human Rights Acquis', (2006) 43 *CMLR* 629–665, at 633).

case law.[20] If, on the other hand, the Court's fundamental rights case law would strengthen citizens' autonomy, this might disarm such criticism. Contributing to substantive autonomy of human individuals, fundamental rights EU style might even weaken claims of powerful economic actors for private rule that have often been based on the market freedoms. At the same time, the ECJ case law may gain in legitimacy.

Analysis of ECJ fundamental rights case law takes up the critique of ECJ "judicial activism" from the perspective of Member States' prerogatives.[21] The corresponding focus on the ECJ's role as a go-between between political and juridical institutions has also been the focus of scholarship at the margins between legal, political and sociological research.[22] Trans-nationalisation and globalisation of societies, economies and politics tends to strengthen juridical actors. The loss of governmental capacity by public authorities empowers non-state actors to an unprecedented extend.[23] The positive legal regimes created by states within and beyond their territory are increasingly dependent on the prudential use of elements that enable flexible development of legal regimes, such as open norms and procedural rather than substantive law. Along with societal and economic actors who possess the resources to effectively engage at a transnational or global level, international and supranational courts thus become one category of those empowered by globalisation. Thus, there is ample need to analyse courts' activities, taking due account of the political character of their role as adjudicators[24] without disregarding the realm of legal doctrine.[25] Doctrinal developments, often portrayed as value-neutral, may seem to reinforce themselves based on the honest conviction of ECJ judges and advocates generals that a certain kind of legal reasoning is compelling from a doctrinal point of view. The crux is to achieve a challenge of such seemingly compelling arguments that unmasks the political and socio-economic forces and, at the same time offers

---

20 T. Ahmed & I. de Jesus Butler, 'The European Union and Human Rights: An International Law Perspective', (2006) 17 *EJIL* 771. As a solution to these dilemmas, an integration of ECJ and ECHR jurisdictions has been demanded (see Harpaz, as cited above), while it is at the same time doubted whether this is sufficient or even realistic (F. Van den Berghe, 'The EU and Issues of Human Rights Protection: Same Solutions to more Acute Problems?', (2010) 16:2 *ELJ* 112–157).

21 See 'The Court of Justice in the limelight – again', (2008) 45 *CMLR* 1571–1579 (anonymous "Editorial Comments"), Herzog & Gerken, "Stoppt den Europäischen Gerichtshof" *FAZ (Frankfurter Allgemeine Zeitung)* of 8 September 2008.

22 See e.g. K. Alter, *The European Court's Political Power*, OUP, Oxford, 2009, and B. Rehder, *What is political about jurisprudence? Courts, Politics, Political Science, in Europe and the United States*, MPlfG Discussion Paper 05/5.

23 For one of the many examples of such accounts, see C. Cutler, *Private Power and Public Authority*, Cambridge University Press, Cambridge, 2003.

24 B. Rehder, *What is political about jurisprudence? Courts, Politics, Political Science, in Europe and the United States*, MPlfG Discussion Paper 05/5.

25 See the critique against the analysis by J. Coppel & A. O'Neill, 'The European Court of Justice: Taking Rights Seriously?', (1992) 12 *Legal Studies* 227–239 brought forward by J. Weiler & N. Lockhart, 'Taking Rights Seriously Seriously: The European Court of Justice and its Fundamental Rights Jurisprudence', (1995) 32 *CMLR* 51, at 54.

doctrinally convincing alternatives to lines of case law that seem less adequate for sustaining substantive autonomy of human beings.

## 3.2. FUNCTIONS OF THE COURT'S FUNDAMENTAL RIGHTS PROTECTION

Without retelling the whole story of development of the Court's fundamental rights doctrine,[26] it seems worthwhile to consider which different functions its fundamental rights jurisprudence can fulfil.

Generally, the beginning of the ECJ case law on fundamental rights protection is associated with combating the EEC's legitimacy deficit stemming from the lack of a fundamental rights catalogue.[27] In what has been termed a "defensive" move,[28] the Court began developing a doctrine of EU style fundamental rights with cases such as *Stauder, Internationale Handelsgesellschaft, Nold* and *Hauer.*[29] By relying on general principles of Community law (and now EU law), the Court also managed to maintain its own autonomy in the field of fundamental rights. By taking resort to any other source of human rights law only by way of "inspiration", its case law became independent from both national constitutional and international courts, such as the European Court of Human Rights.[30] Thus, maintaining the autonomy of EU law (and the court adjudicating it) may well be the overarching function of developing fundamental rights protection by the Court (rather than by national and international courts).

The question is whether ECJ case law can at the same time contribute to fulfilling the three functions ascribed to fundamental rights protection above, i.e. protection of citizens against claims of public authority, protection of citizens against claims of private power and maintaining the enabling function of states (and potentially the EU itself) in supporting preconditions for the actual enjoyment of fundamental rights.

---

26 See the references in footnotes 6, 17, 18 and 19; see also J. Weiler, 'Methods of Protection: Towards a Second and Third Generation Protection', in: A. Cassese et al (eds), *Human Rights and the European Community: Methods of Protection,* Baden-Baden, Nomos, 1991, p 555.

27 Also J. Weiler, 'Methods of Protection: Towards a Second and Third Generation Protection' in: A. Cassese et al (eds), *Human Rights and the European Community: Methods of Protection,* Baden-Baden, Nomos, 1991, p 581.

28 J. Coppel & A. O'Neill, 'The European Court of Justice: Taking Rights Seriously?', (1992) 12 *Legal Studies* 227–239, at 228.

29 ECJ 12 November 1969, Case 29/69 *Stauder* [1969] ECR 419, at 425; ECJ 17 December 1970, Case 11/70 *Internationale Handelsgesellschaft* [1970] ECR 1125, at 1134; ECJ 14 May 1974, Case 4/73 *Nold* [1974] ECR 491, at 507; ECJ 13 December 1979, Case 44/79 *Hauer* [1979 ] ECR 3727, at 3732.

30 S. Douglas-Scott, 'A Tale of Two Courts: Luxembourg, Strasbourg and the growing European Human Rights Acquis', (2006) 43 *CMLR* 629–665 and G. Harpaz, 'The European Court of Justice and its relations with the European Court of Human Rigths: The Quest for enhanced reliance, coherence and legitimacy', (2009) 46 *CMLR* 105–141.

In the early cases, the demands for fundamental rights protection were aimed at EU legislation, which was deemed to violate fundamental rights. In these cases, the Member States were partly held responsible for interpreting EU legislation in ways that enable safeguarding fundamental rights. Today, fundamental rights violation by EU legislation occurs mainly in the relatively new field of immigration law. Unsurprisingly, the Court has likewise held Member States responsible, for example when implementing the family reunification directive[31] or the directive on refugee status.[32] However, it also has invalidated decisions implementing UN resolutions that deprived persons deemed to be connected to terrorist activities of their personal liberties.[33] Curiously, this protection of third country nationals corresponded with claiming the EU's relative independence from the UN when protecting fundamental rights. Protecting citizens against arbitrary rule by EU institutions also remains relevant in the field of EU competition law, where the recipients of fundamental rights protection are typically economic actors, who tend to defend their rights to property and conducting business as well as procedural rights derived from Article 6 ECHR.[34]

Still fulfilling the function of containing claims of public rule, the ECJ has also held Member States bound by EU fundamental rights also when relying on exceptions from the economic freedoms provided by EU law.[35] If the Court was set to maintain the autonomy of EU law, it did not have much choice in the matter. It could not very well allow Member States to provide for fundamental rights protection through their national constitutions (written or unwritten), as this would have led to divergent interpretations of EU law in line with fundamental rights, and to divergent scopes of exceptions provided in EU law. The court could also not forego fundamental rights protection altogether, not least because fundamental rights rhetoric lends legitimacy to any legal order. Thus, what was termed the offensive use of fundamental rights[36] was unavoidable. It was even possibly needed in order to remedy a lack of fundamental rights protection of migrant EU citizens in Member States that accord protection of some political rights only to their citizens. The protection of the non-national EU citizen is a recurrent theme[37] also in younger case law, now in connection with Union citizenship rights.

---

31 ECJ 27 June 2006, Case C-540/03, *EP v Council and Parliament* [2006] ECR I-5769, para 63.

32 Case C-175/08, *Salahadin Abdullah* ECJ judgment 2 March 2010, nyr.

33 CFI (now GC) 30 September 2009, Case T-341/07, *Sison v Council* [2009] ECR II-3625.

34 On the "relatively minor importance" of these cases under the wider perspective of human rights protection see J. Weiler & N. Lockhart, 'Taking Rights Seriously' Seriously: The European Court of Justice and its Fundamental Rights Jurisprudence', (1995) 32 *CMLR* 51, at 84–89.

35 ECJ 18 June 1991, Case C-260/89, *Elliniki Radiofonia Tileorasi (ERT)* [1993] ECR I-2925.

36 J. Coppel & A. O'Neill, 'The European Court of Justice: Taking Rights Seriously?' (1992) 12 *Legal Studies* 227–239.

37 Examples include the cases ECJ 11 July 2002, Case C-60/00, *Carpenter* [2002] ECR I-6279; ECJ 29 April 2004, Case C-482/01 *Orfanopoulos* [2004] ECR I-5257.

The substantive protection of fundamental rights values by containing private power is less obvious in ECJ fundamental rights case law. Perhaps the rhetoric of interpreting primary and secondary EU law in line with fundamental rights can contribute to fulfilling this function. For example, in the field of gender equality rights, which have played an important role in supporting European integration, fundamental rights served to give more vigour to EU law rights, also when relied upon against private employers.[38] The function of fundamental rights as a supporting and expanding EU law concept has the potential to contain Member States' prerogatives. This will not always be directly related to violations of fundamental rights by the Member State. Often the enhanced breadth of application of primary or secondary legislation, or its horizontal effect, will contain autonomy of economic actors in favour of strengthening substantive autonomy of individual human beings. Thus, this function of fundamental rights will often work horizontally. Similarly, cases in which fundamental rights are deemed to potentially conflict with economic freedoms, may offer some potential for containing private power. Given the tendency of ECJ economic freedoms case law to expand transnational economic power, it would be a real achievement if overwhelming private power would also be contained. The question in how far the ECJ contributes to this achievement will be discussed below in more detail.

### 3.3. MULTI-POLAR DILEMMAS UNDERLYING THE COURT'S FUNDAMENTAL RIGHTS CASE LAW

In sum, the multi-polar system of protecting fundamental rights in the EU confronts its Court of Justice as human rights arbitrator with some typical dilemmas. It may find itself compelled to contain Member States' prerogatives in order to ensure that fundamental rights of non-citizens are protected adequately by these same Member States. It may also find itself containing Member States' policies promoting fundamental rights when enforcing the economic freedoms to the advantage of powerful economic actors. In empowering economic actors transnationally, the economic freedoms case law may endanger the national constitutional values of enabling less powerful citizens to defend their substantive autonomy. Whether and in how far the Court succeeds in solving these dilemmas and contributing to substantive enjoyment of fundamental rights is the question of the remainder of this article.

[38] The ECJ first enounced in the Defrenne cases that gender equality rights are human rights (ECJ 15 June 1978, Case 149/77, *Defrenne III* [1978] ECR 1365, para 27).

# 4. RECENT ECJ CASE LAW BETWEEN EU, CITIZENS AND MEMBER STATES

## 4.1. A QUANTITATIVE APPETIZER

Without being able to offer a full analysis of fundamental rights case law from 2001 in this contained space,[39] a quantitative analysis of 150 cases emerging as containing the catch word "fundamental rights" on the ECJ case law search machine shall be used to establish some tentative hypothesis. The most recent case law, from the 18th of March 2010 backwards, has been chosen in order to illusttrate recent trends. Of the 150 cases containing the catch word, only 120 substantively affected fundamental rights.[40]

The initial hypothesis would be that the Court exposes a certain degree of instrumentalism. One of the editors of this collection has rightly demanded that "one should not forget that the Court's case law has other important functions than the protection of rights per se, such as the promotion of European integration and (...) the supremacy of EC law before national courts."[41] The resulting hypothesis can be formalised quite nicely. One can evaluate whether Member States' prerogatives (or autonomy), the EU institutions' prerogatives or citizens' autonomy was effectively protected in the end.

In 28 cases, the relevant Court did not refer to fundamental rights explicitly, although these had been relied upon by one of the parties, or the AG had considered fundamental rights.[42] In 52 cases, the decision of the Court resulted in supporting one fundamental or other right in favour of a citizen, without impinging on fundamental rights of another citizen at the same time. 17 of these favoured citizens were undertakings or other economic actors, 10 were third country nationals and one an environmental NGO.

33 cases resulted from direct actions of citizens against acts of the EU, mainly Commission decisions. In these cases, there is no point of looking towards any violation of the autonomy of the Member States. In most of these cases,[43] economic

[39] 2001 would seem an adequate starting date because the Charter of Fundamental Rights in the European Union had been "solemnly declared" during the Nice IGC in December 2000, which can be seen as starting a new phase in fundamental rights policy

[40] Errors included an AG opinion containing "fundamental rights" in the English version where it should clearly have been fundamental freedoms, or cases where recitals or paragraphs of secondary legislation contained the phrase, although fundamental rights were not relevant to the question. The search function is also partly under-inclusive (see below fn 88). The case analysis, updated to March 2010, is summarized in an annex to this chapter.

[41] B. de Witte, 'The Past and Future Role of the European Court of Justice in the Protection of Human Rights', in: F. Alston (ed), *The EU and Human Rights*, OUP, 1999, 859–897, at 874.

[42] In one case each, the AG referred to EU citizens' right of free movement as fundamental rights (C-524/06) or to social fundamental rights (C-350/06). There was also one case where the ECJ relied on fundamental rights, but the AG did not (C-73/07).

[43] Atypical cases include a challenge by an MEP against recovering excess expenses, a challenge of criminal sanctions following the import of protected species and cases by Third Country Nationals against freezing their assets in the wake of UN anti-terrorism resolutions.

actors sought relief against decisions in the field of competition and state aid law. In 22 cases, the Commission won its case, and in 11 the citizen prevailed.

The remaining cases cover a very wide spectrum. These are references, annulment actions by Member States or infringement actions by the Commission. Especially in cases which were referred, competing rights of several citizens can be involved. Thus, if the court strengthens the rights of one citizen, it might weaken competing rights of other citizens. One might assume that it is different for Member States' prerogatives, but there are also 8 cases where the Court favours one national tradition over another.[44] Thus, the picture is really mixed. In 11 cases the Court weakened the rights of one group of citizens while strengthening the rights of others, including the much-discussed cases in Laval and Viking.[45] In 35 cases, the Court strengthened the rights of citizens at the expense of Member States' autonomy, and in 9 cases the Member States' prerogatives were supported at the expense of citizens' autonomy. In the recent field of EU immigration law, fundamental rights claims of Third Country Nationals were resolved at the expense of Member States' prerogatives no less than 6 times, whereas the EU institutions' prerogatives were impinged upon 3 times.[46] In 12 cases, the final decision was left to the national courts. However, it was always possible to make a judgment whether the court had ultimately strengthened one interest over the other.

This small sample does not allow far-reaching conclusions, but leads to the following hypothesis:

- If fundamental rights protection will strengthen citizens' autonomy at the expense of Member States' prerogatives, it is more likely to succeed than if it would impede the EU's prerogatives.
- Also, a certain supportive tendency towards economic actors prevails.

## 4.2. SUBSTANTIVE ASSESSMENT OF SOME NEURALGIC FIELDS

### *4.2.1. Assumptions and adequate fields*

On a more substantive level, more complex hypotheses are adequate. Rights from the status negativus, also referred to as civil rights, aim at preserving a personal sphere for citizens and economic actors that is free from interference by the state or other official institutions. These rights constitute the oldest layer of human

44 These include Laval and Viking, where arguably the weak industrial relation system in Estonia and Latvia was favoured over the strong industrial relation model in Sweden and Finland.

45 See below fn. 89 and 90.

46 This includes one case where also the Member States' prerogatives could be seen as infringed, as the restrictive interpretation of refugees' rights will need to be adapted after the ECJ judgment (see above fn. 32).

rights, going back to "habeas corpus," and at the same time they form the basis for rights to a fair trial. One would expect this layer of fundamental rights to be developed furthest, in particular given the fact that the EEC had an active competition law authority with repressive powers since 1957. However, these rights would mostly be enforced by individuals against the Union, thus leaving little room for a multipolar relation between the individual, the Union and the Member State.

Deriving from the general task of the Court to further European (economic) integration, one would expect it to be particularly inventive in developing such fundamental rights that support economic integration. Here, equality rights come to mind, as well as any rights to free movement, either for human beings or legal entities. As these rights are usually relevant within economy and society, relevant cases would also form a good background for investigating a multipolar relation as sketched above.

In stark contrast, there is a rather young layer of status positivus rights, also referred to as social rights.[47] These are less developed than civil and political rights internationally, and one would expect these to be least developed at Union level as well. National constitutional courts and also international human rights tribunals have been reluctant to judicially enforce rights of individuals to receive state funds or protection. They have been even more reluctant to acknowledge citizens' rights to protect themselves through collective action against infringements of rights by other citizens. Collective labour rights were only fully acknowledged in the 20th century against initial prohibitions in favour of employers' economic rights.[48] Thus, one would expect the ECJ case law on these rights to be still in its infancy, especially given the Court's tendency to favour the protection of rights of economic actors. These rights would also often involve horizontal relations, and thus a triangular relation between national and supranational authorities and the individual.

The fields to be explored in more detail have thus been identified. On the one hand, there is one field in which we can expect the tendency to support citizens' rights at the expense of Member States prerogatives to be prevalent: this is the field of EU equality law. While in other fields of employment law, fundamental rights arguments are only raised exceptionally,[49] in the field of equality law it is

[47] Often, the reference is also to "social and economic rights" in line with the title of the International Covenant on Economic, Social and Cultural Rights (see, for example, M. Tushnet, 'Comparative Constitutional Law', in: M. Reimann & R. Zimmermann (eds.), *Oxford Handbook on Comparative Law,* OUP, Oxford, 2008, 1225–1257, at 1231). For the European context, the notion of social rights seems more appropriate, as it mirrors the main Council of Europe instrument's title (European Social Charter) as well as the division between social and economic rights within EU law (see, for example, ECJ 10 February 2000, C-270/97 *Sievers & Schrage* [2000] ECR I-929, para 53).

[48] See M. Finkin, 'Comparative Labour Law', in M. Reimann & R. Zimmermann (eds.), *Oxford Handbook on Comparative Law,* OUP, Oxford, 2008, 1131–1160 pp 1142–49.

[49] In the sample analysed, only AG Trstenjak relied on the fundamental social right to rest and leisure in her opinion on the joined cases *Schultz-Hoff* (C-350/06) and *Stringer & others* (C-

quite usual to cite fundamental rights arguments. These have inter alia been used to achieve results that have prompted severe constitutional reactions in at least one Member State.

On the other hand, one field where we would expect the tendency to support economic actors to impinge on the autonomy of Member States and the autonomy of citizens at the same time is the potential conflict between fundamental freedoms and those fundamental rights that have only recently come to the attention of EU judges. Of course, the recent conflictual cases in the field of collective labour rights come to mind here. Doctrinally, these build on case law developed for conflicts between EU fundamental freedoms and fundamental rights underpinning the social status activus. Thus, an analysis of those cases seems promising.

#### *4.2.2. Non-discrimination and equality*

*Between EU legislation, primary law and fundamental right*

Equal treatment has been characterised as "the most longstanding and well established principle of the EU legal system".[50] The principle is relevant in a number of fields of EU law through positive legislation. The prohibition to discriminate on grounds of nationality (Article 18 TFEU = ex Article 12 EC) is also implicitly or explicitly contained in Articles 45 (2), 49 and 56 TFEU (ex Articles 39, 43 and 49 EC). Article 40(2) TFEU (ex Article 34 EC) contains a special prohibition to discriminate between producers or consumers in agricultural legislation,[51] and Article 102 TFEU (ex Article 82 EC) also contains a prohibition for undertakings in a dominant market position to discriminate between other undertakings.[52] In secondary law, the principle of equal treatment is embodied in directives on gender equality law[53] as well as on non-discrimination on grounds other than gender.[54]

---

520/06), based on the Charter of Fundamental Rights in the European Union, the ECS, ICESR and ILO Convention 132 (which was not taken up by the ECJ, although it followed her opinion in general)

50 Opinion of AG Colomer, 6 September 2007, Case C-267/06, *Tadao Maruko* [2008] ECR I-1757, para 83.

51 See Opinion of AG Trstenjak, 3 February 2009, Case C- 428/07, *Horvath* [2009] ECR I-6355 with extensive references to its use in the field of agricultural law in fn 51.

52 On this see ECJ 16 September 2008 in Joined Cases C-468/06 to C-478/06, *Sot. Lelos kai Sia* [2008] ECR I-7139, para 49, first used in Case 27/76, *United Brands and United Brands Continental* v *Commission* [1978] ECR 207, para 182.

53 Directive 2004/113/EC targets sex discrimination in provision of goods and services, but not in the field of education, thus falling short of the wide scope of application of Directive 2000/43/EC. Directive 2006/54/EC covers sex discrimination in employment and social security and equal pay.

54 Directives 2000/43/EC (equal treatment irrespective of race and ethnicity) and 2000/78/EC (equal treatment of persons in employment and occupation, covering the grounds of age, disability, sexual orientation and religion and belief) are a result of the Community action program cited above. A further directive targeting discrimination outside the employment field has been tabled (COM 2008 (426) fin).

The European Court of Justice has laid out a fundamental rights base for all these rights, in a more or less coherent fashion. Starting in the field of agriculture, it acknowledged the "general principle of equality which is one of the fundamental principles of Community[55] law" and "requires that similar situations shall not be treated differently unless different treatment is objectively justified"[56] This formula is used in other contexts, for example in assessing the legality of EU legislation combating "greenhouse gas"[57], or for assessing Spanish legislation implementing directive 80/987 on employers' insolvency.[58]

This fundamental right, also referred to as "equality before the law" in the Western constitutional tradition, has been criticised as not being a sound basis for non-discrimination law, i.e. the body of law that aims at combating societal discrimination against individuals and groups on specific grounds.[59] Non-discrimination law as a freestanding principle is for example mirrored in UN human rights law with its three non-discrimination covenants. These oblige signatory states to combat discrimination as a social phenomenon. In this combat, a prohibition of discrimination is but one instrument.[60] In European human rights law, Article 14 ECHR contains an open equality clause, which specifies a number of "discrimination grounds".

In contrast, the EU has its own body of non-discrimination legislation. As regards the exact content of a fundamental right to non-discrimination, ECJ case law seems contradictory. In its gender equality case law, the Court routinely

---

55 The Community has been superseded by the EU with the entry into force of the Treaty of Lisbon (Article 1 TEU). In quotes dating from before the 1st of December 2009, the term 'Community' will of course be preserved.

56 ECJ 19 October 1977, Joined Cases 117/76 and 16/77, *Ruckdeschel* [1977] ECR 1753, para 7, see also references in fn 51.

57 ECJ 16 December 2008, Case C-127/07, *Arcelor Atlantique and Lorraine and Others* [2008] ECR I-9895, para 23–57 (rejecting the claim of invalidity, due to the wide discretion the EU legislator enjoys).

58 ECJ 12 December 2002, Case C-442/00, *Rodriguez Caballero* [2002] ECR I-11915, para 31–39 (holding that differentiation between different groups of workers by the national legislator cannot be justified); ECJ 17 January 2008, Case C-246/06, *Velasco Navarro* [2008] ECR I-105, para 38 confirming that national courts are under an obligation to ensure that national legislation is interpreted and applied in line with the principle of "equality and non-discrimination" in EU law.

59 M. Bell, 'Walking in the Same Direction? The Contribution of the European Social Charter and the European Union to Combating Discrimination', in: De Burca & Witte (eds.), *Social Rights in Europe* (Oxford 2005) 261–278, at 263, referring to it being restricted to "equality as consistency". See also D. Schiek, L. Waddington & M. Bell, Introductory Chapter in D. Schiek, L. Waddington & M. Bell (eds), *Cases, Materials and Text on National, Supranational and International Non-Discrimination Law*, Hart, Oxford et al, 2007, p 25–31. For a distinction between the Aristotelian and a social equality principle D. Schiek, 'Torn between arithmetic and substantive equality? Perspectives on Equality in German Labour Law', (2002) *IJCLLIR* 137–153, at 158.

60 UN Convention for the Elimination of all forms of Discrimination against Women (CEDAW), UN Convention for the Elimination of all forms of Racial Discrimination (CERD), UN Convention for the Rights of People with Disabilities (CRPD). These conventions are referred to in the recitals of the Directives cited in footnote 53 (the CRPD is only cited in the draft directive, due to its late arrival on the international plane).

assumes that the right not to be discriminated against on grounds of sex is one of the fundamental human rights which it protects as general principles of EU law.[61] Characterising gender equality as a fundamental right seemed to signify a difference between gender equality and the prohibition of discrimination on grounds of nationality. In the latter field, the Court had only stressed the "fundamental nature" of equal treatment of workers. Also, a general "principle of equality of the sexes" is certainly distinct from the general principle of equality before the law. One would expect that the theme of a specific fundamental right to non-discrimination would have been taken up in case law on directives referring to other discrimination grounds. When the Court took up the theme in its (in) famous Mangold decision,[62] the constitutional principle of non-discrimination on grounds of age emerged with very little reasoning.[63] However, it was clear from the wording used ("The principle of non-discrimination on grounds of age must thus be regarded as a general principle of Community[64] law") that the Court did not follow AG Tizzano, who had proposed to derive a similar result from applying the principle of equality before the law as used in FOGASA.[65] In subsequent cases, no less than four Advocates General engaged with the Court ruling in Mangold. AG Mazak[66] and AG Geelhoed[67] criticised the Court for going too far, whereas AG Sharpston, in two opinions, urged the Court to follow the line AG Tizzano had proposed in his opinion: it should acknowledge more stringently the general principle of equality before the law.[68] AG Bot, in his opinion in the Küçükdeveci case, has supported the existence of a general principle of non-discrimination on grounds of age to be derived from the Charter of Fundamental Rights for the European Union.[69] In its decisions in *Palacios*[70] and *Chacon*,[71] the Court avoided to take a position on the question whether Directive 2000/78/EC was an

61 ECJ 15 June 1978, Case 149/77, *Defrenne III* [1978] ECR 1365, para 26 and 27; ECJ 20 March 1984, Joined Cases 75/82 and 117/82, *Razzouk and Beydoun* [1984] ECR 1509, para 16; ECJ 30 April 1996, Case C-13/94, *P. v S. and Cornwall County Council* [1996] ECR I-2143, para 19; ECJ 10 February 2000, Case C-270/97, *Sievers & Schrage* [2000] ECR I-929, para 56; in ECJ 11 September 2007, Case C-227/04 P, *Lindorfer* [2007] ECR I-6767, para 50 the court repeats that secondary and primary Community law on sex discrimination constitutes "specific expressions of the general principle of equality of the sexes".

62 ECJ 22 November 2005, Case C-144/04, *Mangold* [2005] ECR I-9981.

63 Para 74–77 of the judgment.

64 See above fn. 54.

65 Para 83–4 of his opinion. For more detail see D. Schiek, 'The ECJ decision in Mangold', (2006) 35 *ILJ* 329–341.

66 Opinion of AG Mazak, 15 February 2007, Case C-411/05, *Palacios de la Villa* [2007] ECR I-8531, para 79–100.

67 Opinion of AG Geelhoed, 16 March 2006, Case C-13/05, *Chacon Navas* [2006] ECR I-9981.

68 Opinion of AG Sharpston, 30 November 2006, Case C-227/04 P, *Lindorfer* [2007] ECR I-6767 and AG Sharpston, 22 May 2008, Case C-427/06, *Bartsch* 2008 ECR p. I-7245.

69 Opinion of AG Bot, 7 July 2009, Case C-555/07, *Kücükdeveci,* [2010] ECR I-365, para 77.

70 Above fn 65.

71 Above fn 66.

emanation of a fundamental right under EU law.[72] In its decision in *Bartsch*,[73] the Court finally confirmed the existence of a general principle of EU law containing a prohibition of age discrimination,[74] denying however, that the case before it fell within the scope of application of EU law. In its Küçükdeveci judgment, the Court confirms this, and for the first time accorded effects to the principle of non-discrimination on grounds of age.[75]

While an EU style fundamental right not to be discriminated against on grounds of age (and other grounds listed in Article 19 TFEU) has now been acknowledged, it remains to be seen whether this is but a variation of the principle of equality before the law or rather an emanation of a fundamental right to non-discrimination.

*Effects of the fundamental right of non-discrimination*

When the Court first acknowledged the human rights character of the principle of sex equality,[76] this did not have any effect on the case before the Court. The ECJ held that a general principle of EU law, even if it was supported by common traditions of Member States in the field of human rights, could not produce any effect in and of itself. In subsequent decisions on gender equality, the fundamental rights character was the basis for a wide reading of the notion of gender in favour of transsexual persons,[77] but this did not extend to protect homosexual persons.[78] The human rights character of gender equality also served as a basis for deciding that protecting equality enjoyed priority over economic aims[79] and for acknowledging a pension claim against the Commission, although the relevant directives did not apply to this institution.[80] In the field of gender equality as well as in other, more recent fields, the fundamental rights base of non-discrimination

72 The Court also avoided a position in its decisions in ECJ 18 April 2008, Case C-267/06, *Tadao Maruko* [2007] ECR I-1757 and ECJ 16 July 2008, Case C-54/07, *Feryn* [2008] ECR I-5837, which concerned Directive 2000/78/EC and 2000/43/EC respectively. The Court could focus in these decisions on the text of the directives rather than on general principles of EU law (see also below fn 80).

73 Above fn 67.

74 Para 25 ("(T)he answer to the first question must be that the application, which the courts of Member States must ensure, of the prohibition under Community law of discrimination on the ground of age is not mandatory where the allegedly discriminatory treatment contains no link with Community law").

75 ECJ 19 January 2010, Case C-555/07, *Seda Küçükdeveci,* [2010] ECR I-365.

76 ECJ 15 June 1978, Case 149/77, *Defrenne III* [1978] ECR 1365.

77 ECJ 30 April 1996, Case C-13/94, *P v S & Cornwall County* [1996] ECR I-2159; ECJ 7 January 2004, Case C-117/01, *K.B. / National Health Services Pension Agency* [2004] ECR I-541.

78 ECJ 17 February 1998, Case C-249/96, *Grant* [1998] ECR 621.

79 ECJ 10 February 2000, Case C-270/97, *Sievers & Schrage* [2000] ECR I-929.

80 Above fn 67.

law was also used in order to achieve a wider reading of provisions of secondary law, even if it was not referred to explicitly.[81]

Most of these consequences were felt outside the EU institutions, arguably restricting Member States' prerogatives and strengthening individual autonomy in highly personal issues such as seeking gender reassignment.[82] As all these cases occurred in the realm of employment law, they also had effects on the relation between the employees and employers in the Member States, with potentially far-reaching consequences.[83]

The same must be said for the *Mangold* decision.[84] The Court held fundamental rights EU style to bind national courts directly, which meant that they would have effects on the relation between employees and employers. To place this within the sphere of fundamental rights protection: cases such as Mangold not only strengthen the fundamental rights of one individual, they do this potentially at the expense of fundamental rights of other individuals. This is of course nothing special, if one acknowledges that fundamental rights aim at substantive autonomy of individuals rather than at formal autonomy warding off state interference in a narrow sense.[85]

For the *Mangold* case, this effect on employers' prerogatives is the reason why a constitutional complaint is presently pending before the German constitutional court. The Federal Labour Court has faithfully implemented the Mangold decision in its case law, and had reversed a decision by the Hamburg Labour court on the validity of a "Mangold type" fixed term contract.[86] Preceded by a vast number of condemning articles against the Court's decision,[87] this case was taken as a starting point for a constitutional complaint that aims at challenging the supremacy of EU law over fundamental rights protected by the German constitution.[88] The complaint considers the acknowledgment of a fundamental right to non-discrimination and its direct effect on national judicial proceedings

81 See ECJ 17 July 2008, Case C-303/06, *Coleman* [2008] ECR I- 5603, para 47 reading the non-discrimination principle widely, following AG Poiares Maduro, who relied on the fundamental rights quality of the principle of non-discrimination for this (para 8–11), ECJ 18 April 2008, Case C-267/06, *Tadao Maruko* [2008] ECR I-1757, para 60, reading the notion of pay in Directive 2000/78/EC widely, relying on AG Ruiz-Jarabo Colomer's opinion, who relied on the fundamental rights in support (paras 83 seq).

82 This was the theme of the cases *P.* and *K.B.*, ECJ 30 April 1996, Case C-13/94, *P v S & Cornwall County* [1996] ECR I-2159; ECJ 7 January 2004, Case C-117/01, *K.B. / National Health Services Pension Agency* [2004] ECR I-541.

83 For example, as a consequence of the decision in *Sievers & Schrage*, the Deutsche Post had to find funds for a huge number of occupational pensions, which led in turn to a rise in postage for letters, ECJ 10 February 2000, Case C-270/97, *Sievers & Schrage* [2000] ECR I-929.

84 Above fn 61.

85 See above text accompanying fn 1 and 6.

86 BAG 19th June 2007 – 7 AZR 396/06 AP Nr 179 zu Art. 9 GG.

87 See the faithful recount by AG Sharpston in her opinion on *Bartsch*, AG Sharpston 30 November 2006, Case C-227/04 P *Lindorfer* [2007] ECR I-6767, para 31.

88 In its decision of 6 July 2010 (2 BvR 2661/06, *NJW* 2010, 3422) the German Constitutional Court ruled that '*Mangold*' was not *ultra vires*.

and thus between parties of an employment contract as undue judicial activism, which is no longer authorised by the Treaties. The judgments in Küçükdeveci could be read as the affirmation by the Court that it intended to uphold effects of fundamental rights EU style also in the light of such a complaint.

*Puzzling results*

The result in this particular line of cases contradicts the expectations raised by the quantitative appetizer.[89] We are confronted with a field in which the Court positions itself between economically powerful and other citizens. The Court favours the substantive autonomy of employees and would-be employees over the formal autonomy of employers. This happens at the expense of Member States' prerogatives. Ultimately, the Court could demonstrate in this exemplary field how it contributes to social justice.

#### 4.2.3. *Collective labour rights between fundamental freedoms and fundamental rights*

This image seems to clash with the Court's recent case law on collective labour rights, the much debated decisions in *Laval*[90] and *Viking*.[91] These cases emerge from the doctrine of fundamental rights being used as "justifications" by Member States to defend "restrictions" of fundamental freedoms. Thus, a few lines on this case law seem necessary before analysing the disputed cases *Laval* and *Viking* with the approach used before. It should be said as a warning that there are a few cases concerning collective agreements, which do not refer to conflicts between fundamental freedoms and fundamental rights to collective action, although they have the potential to weaken national models of industrial relations.[92] Also, there are a number of issues that have been raised in relation to *Laval* and *Viking* which will not be covered here. These include the question whether European business will henceforth be able to choose the labour regime for their workers irrespective of the place of work[93] and the contentious issue whether the interpretation of Directive 96/71/EC forces Sweden to introduce a declaration of general application

89 Safe for *Bartsch* and *Küçükdeveci*, most of these judgments were too old to come up among the 150 latest cases on fundamental rights; the *Tadao Maruko* case did not contain the catchword "fundamental rights".

90 ECJ 18 December 2007, Case C-341/05, *Laval* [2007] ECR I-11717.

91 ECJ 11 December 2007, Case C-438/05, *International Transport Workers Federation and Finnish Seamen's Union v Viking Line ABP* [2007] ECR I-10779, commonly referred to as "Viking". See for a selection of reviews (2007–2008) 10 *CYELS (Cambridge Yearbook of European Legal Studies)*. Introduction by C. Barnard [pp 463–492], followed by a number of articles and a special issue of the (2008) 29 *Comparative Labor Law and Policy Journal*, p 547–604 (editorial introduction and articles by Eklund and Orlandini). See also B. Bercusson, 'The Trade Union Movement and the European Union: Judgment Day', (2007) 13 *ELJ* 279.

92 E.g. ECJ 3 April 2008, Case C-346/06, *Rüffert* [2008] ECR I-1989.

93 Deakin, 'Regulatory competition after Laval', (2008)10 *CYELS* 581–609.

of a collective agreement which would be in contrast with the constitutional protection of collective bargaining in that country. Here, the cases are only analysed as examples of the Court's conflict resolution between fundamental freedoms, arguably used in lieu of fundamental rights, and fundamental rights.

*Economic freedoms and fundamental rights – non-horizontal cases*

The doctrinal framework has been developed in the cases *Schmidberger*[94] and *Omega*.[95] Both these cases arose from conflicts between Member States and economic actors. In Schmidberger, the conflict originated from members of an environmental organisation expressing dismay about the amount of traffic on the Brenner Pass. These private actors initiated the hindrances about which the economic actor (in this case a small and medium enterprise) complained. Assuming that the facts of these cases are well known, I focus on the doctrinal developments they are said to represent.

Both cases are in part hailed as a new era in ECJ fundamental rights case law, because the ECJ is said to have developed a new doctrinal method to better accommodate fundamental rights on the one hand and fundamental freedoms on the other hand.[96] The ECJ "balanced" the conflict between economic freedoms and fundamental rights by the following formula, which was introduced in Schmidberger:

> (81) In those circumstances, the interests involved must be weighed having regard to all the circumstances of the case in order to determine whether a fair balance was struck between those interests. (82) The competent authorities enjoy a wide margin of discretion in that regard. Nevertheless, it is necessary to determine whether the restrictions placed upon intra-Community trade are proportionate in the light of the legitimate objective pursued, namely, in the present case, the protection of fundamental rights

The last sentence has been seen as signifier for the fact that the Court, while formally appraising the need to balance both fundamental freedoms and fundamental rights, only considers the question whether the restriction of the fundamental freedom in question is proportionate, and does not also appraise the proportionality of infringing a fundamental right in the name of protecting

[94] ECJ 12 June 2003, Case C-112/00 [2003] ECR I-5659.
[95] ECJ 14 October 2004, Case C-36/02 [2004] ECR I-9609.
[96] L. Azoulai, 'The Court of Justice and the Social Market Economy: The Emergence of an Ideal and the Conditions for its Realisation, (2008) 45 *CMLR* 1335–1356, at 1349; V. Skouris, 'Fundamental Rights and Fundamental Freedoms, *European Business Law Review* (2006), 225–236, see also M. Avbelj, *European Court of Justice and the Question of Value Choices*, Jean Monnet Working Paper 04/04, who assumes that the Court considers fundamental rights in principle as prevailing over free movement of goods at p 63 and 71.

economic freedoms.[97] In *Omega*, a further paragraph was added, to signal special respect for specific national traditions in constructing fundamental rights EU style. The test used in *Omega* also seems to clarify that the Court only requires justification of restricting fundamental freedoms, and does not scrutinise the corresponding infringement of fundamental rights for its proportionality.

> (35) (…) the protection of (fundamental) rights is a legitimate interest which in principle justifies a restriction of the obligations imposed by Community law, even under a fundamental freedom guaranteed by the Treaty (…)(36) However, measures which restrict the freedom to provide services may be justified on public policy grounds only if they are necessary (…) and in so far as those objectives cannot be attained by less restrictive measures (…) (37) It is not indispensable in that respect for the restrictive measure issued by the authorities of a Member State to correspond to a conception shared by all Member States as regards the precise way in which the fundamental right or legitimate interest in question is to be protected. (…)

The question remains whether fundamental rights – in these cases the right to assembly (Article 11 ECHR) and the protection of dignity under the German constitution – were sufficiently well balanced with competing rights. The Court considered the competing rights only in their capacity of fundamental freedoms. However, both cases concerned economic rights which may well have been protected by one of the national constitutions. Both Schmidberger and Omega were concerned that they could not conduct their undertaking in any way they wished. The Court has, in other contexts, acknowledged this interest as protected by fundamental rights, the right to property and the freedom to pursue a profession.[98] Thus, these were cases where fundamental rights of different citizens were in conflict with each other. This would seem to call even more for a balancing on an equal footing of both rights.

This line of case law seems contradictory. After announcing that the fundamental freedom and the fundamental right should be balanced, and that Member States have a wide discretion, the Court focuses on the question whether the restriction of the fundamental freedom is proportionate. In both cases the Court comes to the conclusion that this actually is not the case, although the final decision was left to the national court in Viking. What is apparent, however, and becomes damaging in the two cases of industrial conflict, is the absence

[97] J. Morijn, 'Balancing Fundamental Rights and Common Market Freedoms in Union Law: Schmidberger and Omega in the Light of an European Constitution', (2006) 12 *ELJ* 15–40 with further references, and AG Stix-Hackl in her opinion in Omega, decided shortly after Schmidberger (para 53 of her opinion, see for an adapted translation from the original German: Morijn, as above, p. 40).

[98] ECJ 9 September 2008, C-120/06 P, *FIAMM and FIAMM Technologies* [2008] ECR I-6513, para 183 with numerous further references.

of a counter test, should the proportionality test fail. Accordingly, there is no corrective deliberation as to whether the restriction of a fundamental right in the name of a fundamental freedom would be proportionate.

*Economic Freedoms and Fundamental Rights – Horizontal collective action cases and collective rights*

The two much discussed cases *Viking*[99] and *Laval*[100] arguably contained a combination of challenges that are not easy to master successfully for any court. Both were horizontal cases: one (or several) trade unions asserted rights that were in conflict with the rights of employers. The employers relied on their fundamental freedoms under the Treaty to protect their rights to pursue their profession unhindered from workers' actions. The trade unions asserted their right to collective action. This very right poses the second problem. It is a collective right, and a right to assert self-determination instead of claiming state protection. It has been claimed that the combination between social rights and collective rights is quite unique for collective labour rights, which is the very reason why courts may have difficulties dealing with resulting conflicts.[101] Of course, collective rights could have been asserted in other fields as well. But that has not happened,[102] leaving even highly learned EU lawyers to wonder why "specialists of labour law do not see this judgment as positive."[103]

The Court arguably attempted to recognise the right to collective action as a fundamental right. Thus, these cases can be praised for accepting that collective action is protected as a fundamental right under EU law.[104] The cases do not represent the return to 19th century doctrines of appraising collective action.[105] At that time, no court would have dreamt of according trade unions any rights, let alone collective labour rights. Even in the 20th century, national courts tended to approach the subject as a conflict between economic rights of employers and rights of workers under tort law. The ECJ, however, starts from the assumption that there is a human right to collective action. Its result, however, does resemble the results that courts achieved 200 years ago without any reference to the

99 See above fn 90.
100 See above fn 89.
101 T. Novitz, 'A Human Rights Analysis of the Viking and Laval Judgements', (2007–08) 10 *CYELS* 542–561, at 543–545.
102 For a critique of the lack of labour lawyers' attempts to change this L. Nogler, 'Why Do Labour Lawyers Ignore the Question of Social Justice in European Contract Law?', (2008) 14:4 *ELJ* 483–499, at 497.
103 Editorial CMLR (above fn 20) fn 27.
104 ECJ 18 December 2007, Case C-341/05, *Laval* [2007] ECR I-11717 para 90; ECJ 11 December 2007, Case C-438/05, *International Transport Workers Federation and Finnish Seamen's Union v Viking Line ABP* [2007] ECR I-10779, para 43, the latter explicitly referring to Article 6 ESC.
105 See on these F. Jacobs, 'Collective Self Regulation' in: Hepple (ed), *The Making of Labour Law in Europe: a Comparative Study of Nine Countries up to 1945*, Hart, Oxford, (reprint 2010), pp 134–156.

human rights dimension. After acknowledging the fundamental rights quality of collective labour rights, the Court goes on to state that these rights can be restricted. To acknowledge the right, it refers to a wide array of international agreements, inter alia the European Social Charter (ESC), which was also explicitly referenced in Article 151 TFEU (ex Article 136 EC). In order to define the restrictions, the court only refers to Article 28 EU Charter, which summarily explains that the rights are protected in accordance with EU law. The ESC seems a little stricter here, requiring in its Article 31 that any restriction of the right to collective action must be established by law, proportionate in itself and required in a democratic society. [106] The court then constructs in both cases the intent to influence collective bargaining by collective action as a restriction to the relevant fundamental freedom, which must be justified in any single event.

This view operates along the lines detected above in the *Schmidberger* and *Omega* decision: A fundamental right is acknowledged in principle, but the possibility to exercise it without undergoing a proportionality test is extremely remote. The parallel with *Schmidberger* and *Omega* is, however, limited. In these cases, there was a blockade of a road which made passing impossible, or an official order not to use the video animated game. Employees and their unions raising a strike threat are not in each case blocking the activity of the undertaking. The undertaking has a wide range of other opportunities, inter alia taking up negotiations, the outcome of which is not determined up front. This constellation raises the question whether subjecting an employer to collective action can already qualify as a restriction. Arguably, any restriction would only derive from a (legally or factually binding) collective agreement.[107]

The application of the proportionality principle arguably deviates from the approach taken in *Schmidberger*. Whereas in *Schmidberger* the right of assembly was acknowledged in itself, irrespective of the aim for which the assembly was organised, the strike action at stake in *Viking* and *Laval* was not protected in itself, but only after very close scrutiny of the aims pursued.[108]

As was to be expected after *Schmidberger* and *Omega*, a proportionality test is not applied to the restriction of the right to strike. The Court does not ask the question, whether the restriction imposed on the human right to collective action is justified by a legitimate aim. Nor does it consider whether it is necessary, in order

[106] A more thorough argument does not, in fact, necessarily lead to acknowledge any unlimited right to strike. For example, the German Labour Court, in (finally) acknowledging solidarity strikes under German law, cites its own case law as a legitimate restriction (BAG 19 June 2007 – 1 AZR 396/06 AP Nr. 179 zu Art. 9 GG).

[107] For example, in the Bosman case, which is cited in support by the ECJ in Viking, the Court had to address a fully established contractual framework, rather than the first steps towards establishing a contract.

[108] T. Novitz, 'A Human Rights Analysis of the Viking and Laval Judgements', (2007–08) 10 *CYELS* 542–561, at 554 with further references, see also C. Barnard, 'Employment Rights, Free Movement under the EC Treaty and the Services Directive' in: M. Rönnmar (ed), *EU Industrial Relations v National Industrial Relations*, Kluwer, Austin et al, 2008, 137–167, at 151 finding that this constitutes balance in name but not in substance.

to achieve that aim, to prohibit strikes aiming at maintaining a certain labour (law) regime (*Viking*) or at taking up negotiations about a collective agreement (*Laval*). Neither does the Court undertake any deliberations as to whether, if there is such a legitimate aim, the restriction of the right to strike is necessary to achieve it and does not go over and above what is necessary to achieve the aim. Such questions would indicate that there is indeed a balancing test.

Of course, one could go on to argue that the balancing between a mere economic freedom and a fundamental right might be expected to give more weight to the fundamental right. However, as the right to conduct one's business, contained in Article 16 Charter of Fundamental Rights for the European Union, may well have to be accepted as a fundamental right,[109] this conflict is also one between fundamental rights of powerful economic actors and individual human beings. The Court also refers to the social aims of the EU in both judgments. This would raise hopes that the reconciliation of fundamental rights on the part of the unions and their members and of fundamental freedoms (that could also be read as fundamental rights) on the part of the employers involves consideration for their different social power. If such reconciliation should take place under social considerations, the substantive autonomy of both sides of the trans-nationalised labour market should be considered before concluding the proportionality assessment.

*Puzzling result*

In the field of collective labour rights, the Court is not prepared to limit the rights claimed by economic actors in order to enhance workers' substantive equal freedom. As a result, employers' rights to pursue their profession (or to use their property) transnationally trump the workers' rights to achieve adequate earnings and working conditions through collective bargaining and collective action. This presents a stark contrast to the case law in equality matters, where the freedom to pursue one's business without hindrance is restricted quite drastically in order to protect the employee's substantive equal freedom.

In both cases, the weaker market position of employees could have been brought to the fore, substantiating the need to provide protection against discrimination as well as the need to provide for collective bargaining structures that necessarily must be supported by the potential threat of collective action. The ECJ does not engage explicitly with the conflict between fundamental rights on both side of the employment market. Thus, the reason behind this difference in position remains obscure.

---

109 This has been explicitly supported by Opinion of AG Kokott in her recent opinion of 17 September 2009, Case C-441/07 P *Arosa*, nyr, para 225 and AG Jacobs in his opinion in ECJ 26 November 1998, Case C-7/97 *Bronner* [1998] ECR I-7791, point 56. See also ECJ 9 September 2008, C-120/06 P, *FIAMM and FIAMM Technologies* [2008] ECR I-6513.

## 5. CONCLUSION

This chapter has brought to light more questions than answers. It has been demonstrated that the Court's case law on fundamental rights may fulfil different functions in the realm of legitimising substantially the EU legal order. It can provide protection against arbitrary rule by EU institutions, a domain which was not covered here except by the statistical exercise, as involvement of Member States prerogatives seems minimal. Fundamental rights can be used to interpret EU law and in fact expand its reach or substance. If applied to directives, this exercise will most likely lead to containing Member States' prerogatives in implementing them and the courts' prerogatives in applying them. Fundamental rights can also be used to contain Member States' prerogatives in using derogations from or justifying restrictions of fundamental freedoms. In both the latter cases, fundamental rights protection should lead to at least a minimal enhancement of substantive autonomy of citizens, be it individually or collectively.

From the general task of the Court of Justice to enhance European (economic) integration, an expectation derived that the Court would more often enhance substantive autonomy of citizens at the expense of Member States' prerogatives than at the expense of EU prerogatives. A sample of 120 court cases, chosen on the basis of the date of the ruling, led to a cautious conclusion that this might be the case. Considering the functions of fundamental rights discourse in EU adjudication, one would expect different outcomes for rights protecting equality and for rights protecting collective labour rights.

The short analysis of recent case law in these two fields did show the expected tendency, but at the same time also produced new questions. Focusing on the horizontal relation between claimants in court, it seems that both parties could rely on fundamental rights. The Court's case law did not provide for an adequate balancing of these fundamental rights. Rather the balancing took place with a certain preference for those rights supported by EU law in the field, if at all. Surprisingly, in the equality cases, balancing of equality rights against other rights did not occur.

The disrespect for one set of fundamental rights has led to challenges of the Court's case law and ultimately its authority.[110] It seems that the Court's legitimacy or at least its inherent authority in the field of fundamental rights could be enhanced by considering fundamental rights conflicts as what they are, instead of giving the fundamental right that is supported by EU law in each field priority.

The open questions thrown up by this are of course not negligible. What is required is a method of balancing fundamental rights whilst considering how substantive autonomy could be gained on both sides. Also, the question which

110 In the case of collective labour rights this may even lead to renewed divergences between European Union law as read by the Court and other fundamental rights supervision authorities, see K.D. Ewing & J. Hendy, 'The Dramatic Implications of Demir and Baykara', (2010) 39 (1) *ILJ* 2–51, at 47–51.

(aspects of) certain rights are best protected at national or even regional level or at EU level must be answered coherently in order to avoid undue limitations of the Member States' and the EU's prerogatives and citizens' autonomy.

# ANNEX: LIST OF CASES EVALUATED

| Case | | Date/ ECR | Parties | Parameter | | | | | | | |
|---|---|---|---|---|---|---|---|---|---|---|---|
| | | | | Member States' prerogatives | | Citizens' autonomy | | Community prerogatives | | Fundamental rights disregarded, or unusual notion of | Final judgement left to national court |
| | | | | Pro | Contra | Pro | Contra | Pro | Contra | | |
| C-317/08 | Judgment | [2010] ECR I-2213 | Alassini | x | | | **(eco act)**[1] | | | | |
| C-518/07 | Judgment | [2010] ECR I-1885 | Commission v Germany | | x | x | | | | | |
| AG differs | Mazak | 2009–11–12 | | x | | | | | | | |
| C-31/09 | Judgment | [2010] ECR I-1839 | Bolbol | x | | | **(TCN)**[2] | | | FR not referred to explicitly | |
| C-578/08 | Judgment | – | Chakroun | | x | **(TCN)** | | | | | |
| T-407/06 | Judgment | [2010] ECR II-747 | Zhejiang Aokang Shoes v Council | | | | **(eco act)** | x | | | |
| T-409/06 | Judgment | [2010] ECR II-807 | Sun Sang Kong Yuen Shoes Factory v Council | | | | **(eco act)** | x | | | |
| T-410/06 | Judgment | [2010] ECR II-879 | Foshan City Nanhai Golden Step Industrial v Council | | | | **(eco act)** | x | | | |
| C-175/08 | Judgment | [2010] ECR I-1443 | Salahadin Abdulla | | x | **(TCN)** | | | | | x |

[1] Economic actors.

| Case | | Date/ ECR | Parties | Parameter | | | | | | | |
|---|---|---|---|---|---|---|---|---|---|---|---|
| | | | | Member States' prerogatives | | Citizens' autonomy | | Community prerogatives | | Fundamental rights disregarded, or unusual notion of | Final judgement left to national court |
| | | | | Pro | Contra | Pro | Contra | Pro | Contra | | |
| T-16/04 | Judgment | [2010] ECR II-211 | Arcelor v Parliament and Council | | | | x | x | | | |
| C-480/08 | Judgment | [2010] ECR I-1107 | Teixeira | | x | x | | | | | |
| C-290/07 P | Opinion (Judgment | 2010–02–23 2010–01–02) | Commission v Scott | | | | **(eco act)** | x | | Only procedural fundamental rights | |
| C-409/06 | Opinion (Judgment | 2010–01–26 2010–04–08) | Winner Wetten | | | **(eco act)** | | | | Procedural rights | |
| C-555/07 | Judgment | [2010] ECR I-365 | Kücükdeveci | | x | **(employee)** | | | | | |
| C-340/08 | Judgment | [2010] ECR I-3913 | M (FC) and Others | | | **(TCN)** | | | | | |
| C-403/09 PPU | Judgment | [2009] ECR I-12193 | Detiček | **MS 1** | **MS 2** | **(child)** | | | | | |
| C-45/08 | Judgment | [2009] ECR I-12073 | Spector Photo Group and Van Raemdonck | | x | **(eco act)** | | | | Procedural rights (presumption innocence) | |
| C-323/08 | Judgment | [2009] ECR I-11621 | Rodríguez Mayor and Others | x | | | x | | | Referring court relates to FR, not ECJ | |
| C-392/08 | Judgment | [2010] ECR I-2537 | Commission v Spain | | x | | | x | | Right to good administration | |

| Case | | Date/ ECR | Parties | Parameter | | | | | | | |
|---|---|---|---|---|---|---|---|---|---|---|---|
| | | | | Member States' prerogatives | | Citizens' autonomy | | Community prerogatives | | Fundamental rights disregarded, or unusual notion of | Final judgement left to national court |
| | | | | Pro | Contra | Pro | Contra | Pro | Contra | | |
| C-399/06 P | Judgment | [2009] ECR I-11393 | Hassan v Council and Commission | | | **(TCN)** | | | **x** | | |
| C-171/08 | Opinion (Judgment | 2009–12–02 2010-07-08) | Commission v Portugal | | **x** | | | **x** | | Portugal relies on FR for itself | |
| C-357/09 P | Judgment | [2009] ECR I-11189 | Kadzoev | | **x** | **(TCN)** | | | | | |
| C-28/08 P | Opinion (Judgment | 2009–10–15 2010-06-25) | Commission v Bavarian Lager | | | **(1 eco act)** | **(other eco act)** | | **x** | | |
| T-390/08 | Judgment | [2009] ECR I-3967 | Bank Melli Iran v Council | | | | **TCN (eco act)** | **x** | | | |
| T-161/05 | Judgment | [2009] ECR II-3555 | Hoechst v Commission | | | | **(eco act)** | **x** | | | |
| T-341/07 | Judgment | 2009–09–30 | Sison v Council | | | **(TCN)** | | | **x** | FR not mentioned, although clearly relevant (refugee) | |
| C-441/07 P | Opinion (Judgment | 2009–09–17 2010–06–29) | Commission v Alrosa | | | | **(eco actor)** | **x** | | Freedom of contract as FR | |
| C-322/07 P | Judgment | [2009] ECR I-7191 | Papierfabrik August Koehler v Commission | | | **(eco act)** | | | **x** | | |

| Case | | Date/ ECR | Parties | Parameter | | | | | | | |
|---|---|---|---|---|---|---|---|---|---|---|---|
| | | | | Member States' prerogatives | | Citizens' autonomy | | Community prerogatives | | Fundamental rights disregarded, or unusual notion of | Final judgement left to national court |
| | | | | Pro | Contra | Pro | Contra | Pro | Contra | | |
| T-326/07 | Judgment | [2009] ECR II-2685 | Cheminova and Others v Commission | | | | (eco act) | x | | Procedural rights | |
| C-344/08 | Judgment | [2009] ECR I-7033 | Rubach | | x | x | | | | Presumption of innocence | |
| C-385/07 P | Judgment | [2009] ECR II-6156 | Duales System Deutschland | | | | (eco act) | x | | | |
| T-246/08 | Judgment | [2009] ECR II-2629 | Melli Bank v Council | | | | (eco act) | x | | | |
| C-101/08 | Judgment | [2009] ECR II-9823 | Audiolux and Others | | | | | x | | Claimants plead equal treatment, AG : doesn't apply to company law | |
| T-189/03 | Judgment | [2009] ECR II-7831 | ASM Brescia v Commission | | x | | (eco act) | x | | Procedural rights (41 Charter) | |
| T-292/02 | Judgment | [2009] ECR II-1659 | Confservizi v Commission | | x | | (eco act) | x | | (inadmissible) | |
| T-309/02 | Judgment | [2009] ECR II-1809 | Acegas v Commission | | x | | x | x | | (inadmissible) | |
| T-318/01 | Judgment | [2009] ECR II-1627 | Othman v Council and Commission | | | TCN | | | x | | |

| Case | | Date/ ECR | Parties | Parameter | | | | | | | |
|---|---|---|---|---|---|---|---|---|---|---|---|
| | | | | Member States' prerogatives | | Citizens' autonomy | | Community prerogatives | | Fundamental rights disregarded, or unusual notion of | Final judgement left to national court |
| | | | | Pro | Contra | Pro | Contra | Pro | Contra | | |
| C-553/07 | Judgment | [2009] ECR I-3889 | Rijkeboer | | x | x | | | | | |
| T-116/04 | Judgment | [2009] ECR II-1087 | Wieland-Werke v Commission | | | | (eco act) | x | | Procedural rights | |
| F-7/05 | Judgment | 2009-04-28 | Violetti and Others v Commission | | | x | | | x | | |
| C-394/07 | | [2009] ECR II-2563 | Gambazzi | **MS 1** | **MS 2** | **Citizen 1** | **Citizen2** | | | | x |
| C-421/07 | | [2009] ECR I-2629 | Damgaard | x | | | x | | | | |
| AG differs | Colomer[2] | 2008-11-18 | | | x | x | | | | | x |
| C-14/08 | Judgment | [2009] ECR I-5439 | Roda Golf & Beach Resort | | x | x | | | | ECJ did not consider FR, but AG qualified citizenship as FR | |
| C-125/07 P | Judgment | [2009] ECR I-5439 | Erste Bank der österreichischen Sparkassen v Commission | | | | | | | Fr not explicitly referred to by Court | |
| AG differs | Bot | 2009-03-26 | | | x | x | x (eco act) | x (COM) | | | |

[2] Names of AGs are only included when the Court did not endorse their opinion.

| Case | | Date/ ECR | Parties | Parameter | | | | | | | |
|---|---|---|---|---|---|---|---|---|---|---|---|
| | | | | Member States' prerogatives | | Citizens' autonomy | | Community prerogatives | | Fundamental rights disregarded, or unusual notion of | Final judgement left to national court |
| | | | | Pro | Contra | Pro | Contra | Pro | Contra | | |
| C-420/07 | Judgment | [2009] ECR I-3579 | Apostolides | x | x | x | | | | Procedural rights | x |
| C-22/08 | Judgment | [2009] ECR I-4585 | Vatsouras | | | | | | | ECJ does not consider FR | |
| AG differs | Colomer | 2009-03-12 | | | x | x | | | | citizenship rights as fundamental rights | |
| C-12/08 | Judgment | [2009] ECR I-6653 | Mono Car Styling | | x | x | | | | Procedural right | |
| C-427/07 | Judgment | [2009] ECR I-6277 | Commission v Ireland | x | | | x | | | Court disregards (procedural) FR | |
| C-511/06 P | Judgment | [2009] ECR I-5843 | Archer Daniels Midland v Commission | | | x (eco act) | | | x (COM) | Procedural rights (disregarded by AG) | |
| C-8/08 P | Judgment | [2009] ECR I-4529 | T-Mobile Netherlands and Others | | | | x (eco act) | x (COM) | | Court disregards FR | |
| C-75/08 | Judgment | [2009] ECR I-3799 | Mellor | | x | x | | | | Procedural FR (41 Charter) | |
| C-460/07 | Judgment | [2009] ECR I-3251 | Puffer | | | | x (eco. act) | x | | Equal treatment referred to as "principle" not right | |

| Case | | Date/ ECR | Parties | Parameter | | | | | | | |
|---|---|---|---|---|---|---|---|---|---|---|---|
| | | | | Member States' prerogatives | | Citizens' autonomy | | Community prerogatives | | Fundamental rights disregarded, or unusual notion of | Final judgement left to national court |
| | | | | Pro | Contra | Pro | Contra | Pro | Contra | | |
| C-388/07 | Judgment | [2009] ECR I-1569 | The Incorporated Trustees of the National Council for Ageing | x | | | x | | | Very slight reference to fundamental rights | |
| C-345/06 | Judgment (GC) | [2009] ECR I-1659 | Heinrich | | | x | | | x | Court disregards FR | |
| C-308/07 P | Judgment | [2009] ECR I-1059 | Gorostiaga Atxalandabaso v Parliament | | | | x | x | | | |
| C-465/07 | Judgment | [2009] ECR I-921 | Elgafaji | | x | x | | | | Court disregards fund. rights, AG acknowledges them | |
| C-185/07 | Judgment | [2009] ECR I-663 | Allianz (anciennement Riunione Adriatica di Sicurta) | **MS 1** | **MS 2** | **Citizen1** | **Citizen 2** | | | FR disregarded | |
| AG differs | Opinion Maduro | 2008-09-09 | | | x | | x | | | | |
| C-301/06 | Judgment (GC) | [2009] ECR I-593 | Ireland v Parliament and Council | | x | | | x | | IRL did not plead FR | |

| Case | | Date/ ECR | Parties | Parameter | | | | | | | |
|---|---|---|---|---|---|---|---|---|---|---|---|
| | | | | Member States' prerogatives | | Citizens' autonomy | | Community prerogatives | | Fundamental rights disregarded, or unusual notion of | Final judgement left to national court |
| | | | | Pro | Contra | Pro | Contra | Pro | Contra | | |
| C-19/08 | Judgment | [2009] ECR I-495 | Petrosian and Others | x | | | x | | | FR disregarded | |
| C-336/07 | Judgment | [2008] ECR I-10889 | Kabel Deutschland Vertrieb und Service | | x | x | | | | | x |
| C-349/07 | Judgment | [2008] ECR I-10369 | Sopropé | | x | | x | | | | x |
| C-47/07 P | Judgment (GC) | [2008] ECR I-9761 | Masdar (UK) v Commission | | | | x | x | | | |
| C-524/06 | Judgment (GC) | [2008] ECR I-9705 | Huber | | x | x | | | | FR (privacy, equality) not regarded | |
| AG differs | Maduro | | | | x | x | | | | citizenship as FR | |
| C-73/07 | Judgment (GC) | [2008] ECR I-9831 | Satakunnan Markkinapörssi and Satamedia | x | | | x | | | | x |
| AG differs | Kokott | | | | x | x | | | | AG disregards FR | x |

| Case | | Date/ ECR | Parties | Parameter | | | | | | | |
|---|---|---|---|---|---|---|---|---|---|---|---|
| | | | | Member States' prerogatives | | Citizens' autonomy | | Community prerogatives | | Fundamental rights disregarded, or unusual notion of | Final judgement left to national court |
| | | | | Pro | Contra | Pro | Contra | Pro | Contra | | |
| T-284/08 (appeal C-27/09) | Judgment | [2008] ECR II-3487 | People's Mojahedin Organization of Iran v council | | | **x (TCN)** | | | **x** | | |
| T-185/05 | Judgment | [2008] ECR II-3207 | Italy v Commission | **x** | | | | | **x** | FR disregarded | |
| T-69/04 | Judgment | [2008] ECR II-2567 | Schunk and Schunk Kohlenstoff-Technik v Commission | | | | **x (eco act)** | **x (COM)** | | | |
| C-120/06 P | Judgment | [2008] ECR-I-6513 | FIAMM and FIAMM Technologies v Council and Commission | | | | **x (eco act)** | **x (COM)** | | | |
| T-212/03 | Judgment | [2008] ECR II-1967 | MyTravel v Commission | | | | **x (eco act)** | **x (COM)** | | FR disregarded | |
| AG differs | Kokott | | | **MS1** | **MS 2** | **Citizen 1** | **Citizen 2** | | | judicial protection as FR | |
| C-402/05 P (et al) | Judgment | [2008] ECR I-6351 | Kadi v Council and Commission | | | **x (TCN)** | | | **x** | | |

| Case | | Date/ ECR | Parties | Parameter | | | | | | | |
|---|---|---|---|---|---|---|---|---|---|---|---|
| | | | | Member States' prerogatives | | Citizens' autonomy | | Community prerogatives | | Fundamental rights disregarded, or unusual notion of | Final judgement left to national court |
| | | | | Pro | Contra | Pro | Contra | Pro | Contra | | |
| C-127/08 | Judgment | [2008] ECR I-6241 | Metock and Others | | x | x (TCN) | | | | (FR only slightly mentioned) | |
| C-389/05 | Judgment | [2008] ECR I-5337 | Commission v France | | x | (x eco act) | | x (COM) | | FR disregarded | |
| C-195/08 PPU | Judgment | [2008] ECR I-5271 | Rinau | | | Citizen 1 | Citizen 2 | | | | |
| C-304/07 | Judgment | [2008] ECR I-7565 | Directmedia Publishing | | | Citizen 1 | Citizen 2 | | | Fr disregarded (privacy) | |
| T-221/05 | Judgment | [2008] ECR II-124* (sum) | Huvis v Council | | | x (eco act) | | | x | | |
| T-48/05 | Judgment | [2008] ECR II-1585 | Franchet and Byk v Commission | | | x | | | x | | |
| T-99/04 | Judgment | [2008] ECR II-1501 | AC-Treuhand v Commission | | | | x (eco act) | X (COM | | | |
| C-39/05 P | Judgment | [2008] ECR I-4723 | Sweden and Turco v Council | | | x (partly) | | | x (partly) | Court disregards FR | |
| AG differs | Maduro | | | | | x (partly) | | | x (partly) | considers access to doc's as FR | |
| T-276/04 | Judgment | [2008] ECR II-1277 | Compagnie maritime belge v Commission | | | | x (eco act) | x (COM) | | Court disregards FR | |

| Case | | Date/ ECR | Parties | Parameter | | | | | | | |
|---|---|---|---|---|---|---|---|---|---|---|---|
| | | | | Member States' prerogatives | | Citizens' autonomy | | Community prerogatives | | Fundamental rights disregarded, or unusual notion of | Final judgement left to national court |
| | | | | Pro | Contra | Pro | Contra | Pro | Contra | | |
| C-427/06 | judgment | [2008] ECR I-7245 | Bartsch | **x** | | **Citizen 1** | **Citizen2** | | | FR disregarded | |
| AG differs | Sharpstone | | | **x** | | **Citizen1** | **Citizen 2** | | | AG: Equal Treatment as FR | |
| C-127/07 | Judgment (GC) | [2008] ECR I-9895 | Arcelor Atlantique and Lorraine and Others | | | | **x (eco act)** | **x** | | | |
| C-228/07 | Judgment | [2008] ECR I-6989 | Petersen | | **x** | **x** | | | | Court disregards FR | |
| AG differs | Colomer | | | | **x** | **x** | | | | Citizenship rights as FR | |
| C-14/07 | Judgment | [2008] ECR I-3367 | Weiss und Partner | **MS 1** | **MS 2** | **Citizen 1** | **Citizen 2** | | | | **x** |
| C-353/06 | Judgment (GC) | [2008] ECR I-7639 | Grunkin and Paul | | **x** | **x** | | | | Court disregards FR | |
| AG differs | Kokott | | | | **x** | **x** | | | | Rights of child as FR | |
| C-345/06 | Judgment (GC) | 2009-03-10 | Heinrich (nyr) | | | | | | | Court disregards FR | |
| AG differs | Sharpstone | | | | | **x** | | | **x** | Legal certainty as FR | |

| Case | | Date/ ECR | Parties | Parameter | | | | | | | |
|---|---|---|---|---|---|---|---|---|---|---|---|
| | | | | Member States' prerogatives | | Citizens' autonomy | | Community prerogatives | | Fundamental rights disregarded, or unusual notion of | Final judgement left to national court |
| | | | | Pro | Contra | Pro | Contra | Pro | Contra | | |
| T-229/02 | Judgment | 2008–04–03 ([2008] ECR II-45 *) | PKK v Council | | | x | | | x | | |
| T-253/04 | Judgment | 2008–04–03 ([2008] ECR II-46 *- sum.) | Kongra-Gel and Others v Council | | | x (eco act) | | | x | | |
| C-244/06 | Judgment | [2008] ECR I-581 | Dynamic Medien | x | | | x | | | | |
| C-450/06 | Judgment | [2008] ECR I-581 | Varec | | x | x (eco act) | | | | | |
| C-303/06 | Judgment | [2008] ECR I-5603 | Coleman | | x | x | | | | Court disregards FR | |
| AG opinion differs | Maduro | | | | x | x | | | | Equality as FR widens notions of sec. law | |
| C-275/06 | Judgment | [2008] ECR I-271 | Promusicae | MS 1 | MS 2 | Citizen 1 | Citizen 2 | | | | x |
| C-350/06, C-520/06 | Judgment | [2009] ECR I-179 | Schultz-Hoff, Stringer et al | | Partly | partly | | | | Court disregards FR | |
| AG opinion differs | Trstenjak | | (Schultz-Hoff AND Stringer et al) | | Fully | fully | | | | Right to rest and leisure as FR | |
| C-55/07 | Judgment ( | [2008] ECR I-3135 | Michaeler and Subito | | x | x | | | | FR (social rights) disregarded | |

| Case | | Date/ ECR | Parties | Parameter | | | | | | | |
|---|---|---|---|---|---|---|---|---|---|---|---|
| | | | | Member States' prerogatives | | Citizens' autonomy | | Community prerogatives | | Fundamental rights disregarded, or unusual notion of | Final judgement left to national court |
| | | | | Pro | Contra | Pro | Contra | Pro | Contra | | |
| C-246/06 | Judgment | [2008] ECR I-105 | Velasco Navarro | x | | | | x | | | |
| C-268/06 | Judgment | [2008] ECR I-2483 | Impact | | x | x (eco act) | | | | FR disregarded | |
| AG opinion differs | Kokott | | | | x | x (eco act) | | | | Judicial protection as FR | |
| C-341/05 | Judgment | [2007] ECR I-11767 | Laval un Partneri | **MS1** | **MS2** | **Citizen1 (eco act)** | **Citizen2** | | | | |
| AG opinion differs | Mengozzi | | | **MS 2** | **MS 1** | **Citizen 2** | **Citizen 1 (eco act)** | | | | x |
| C-64/05 P | Judgment | [2007] ECR I-11389 | Sweden v Commission | | | x (NGO) | | | x | | |
| C-250/06 | Judgment | [2007] ECR I-11135 | United Pan-Europe Communications Belgium and Others | | x | x | | | | | x |
| C-309/06 | Judgment | [2008] ECR I-2283 | Marks & Spencer | | x | x | | | | | |

| Case | | Date/ ECR | Parties | Parameter | | | | | | | |
|---|---|---|---|---|---|---|---|---|---|---|---|
| | | | | Member States' prerogatives | | Citizens' autonomy | | Community prerogatives | | Fundamental rights disregarded, or unusual notion of | Final judgement left to national court |
| | | | | Pro | Contra | Pro | Contra | Pro | Contra | | |
| C-413/06 P | Judgment | [2008] ECR I-4951 | Bertelsmann and Sony Corporation of America v Impala | | | | **x (eco act)** | **x (COM)** | | Fr relevance minimal (formal equality) | |
| T-101/05 | Judgment | [2007] II-4949 | BASF v Commission | | | **x (eco act)** | | | **x (COM)** | | |
| C-161/06 | Judgment | [2007] ECR I-10848 | Skoma-Lux | | | **x (eco act)** | | | **x** | FR only relevant for temporal restriction of decision. Denied. | |
| C-438/05 ("Viking") | Judgment | [2007] ECR I-10779 | International Transport Workers' Federation and Finnish Seamen's Union | **MS 1** | **MS 2** | **Citizen 1 (eco act)** | **Citizen 2** | | | | **x** |
| C-341/06 P | Judgment | [2008] ECR I-4777 | Chronopost and La Poste v UFEX and Others | | | | **x (eco act)** | | | | |
| C-147/06 | Judgment | [2008] ECR I-3565 | SECAP | | **x** | **x (eco act)** | | | | Court Disregards FR | |

| Case | | Date/ ECR | Parties | Parameter | | | | | | | |
|---|---|---|---|---|---|---|---|---|---|---|---|
| | | | | Member States' prerogatives | | Citizens' autonomy | | Community prerogatives | | Fundamental rights disregarded, or unusual notion of | Final judgement left to national court |
| | | | | Pro | Contra | Pro | Contra | Pro | Contra | | |
| AG opinion differs | Colomer | | | | x | **X (eco act)** | | | | Right to be heard as FR | |
| T-3/00 | Judgment | [2007] ECR II-4779 | Pitsiorlas v Council and ECB | | | | **x (eco act)** | **x (COM** | | | |
| C-260/05 P | Judgment | [2007] ECR I-10005 | Sniace v Commission | | | | **x (eco act)** | **x (COM)** | | | |
| C-308/06 | Judgment | [2008] ECR I-14–57 | Intertanko and Others | | | **x** | | **x** | | interpretation of Directive in line with FR, guarding of FR when implementing Dir task of MS | |
| T-194/04 (app: C-28/08) | Judgment | [2007] ECR II-4523 | Bavarian Lager v Commission | | | **Citizen 1** | **Citizen 2** | | **x** | | |
| C-411/05 | Judgment | [2007] ECR I-8531 | Palacios de la Villa | **x** | | | **x** | | | | |
| T-474/04 | Judgment | [2007] ECR II-4225 | Pergan Hilfsstoffe für industrielle Prozesse v Commission | | | **x (eco act)** | | | **x (COM)** | | |

1 Economic actor (i.e. either a corporation or other legal person or a natural person)
2 Third Country National
3 Opinions for cases that have been decided are only included in the table if there is a discernible difference in result between AG and Court

# A PLURALISTIC EUROPE OF RIGHTS

Marta CARTABIA

## 1. INTRODUCTION

During the negotiation of the Lisbon Treaty a new set of controversial issues among the Member States emerged: from the stance taken by some Member States, it has become clear that even fundamental rights can be an obstacle to the process of integration and a reason for incrementing Member States' Euro-scepticism or Euro-resistance. So far, the most controversial among all the fundamental rights have been mainly the social ones: traditionally Europe is marked by a variety of social policies in different countries, and although a neoliberal approach to economic matters has been softened by welfare provisions in all European countries, each of them has its own social recipe, resulting from an original mix of the two components. With the Lisbon Treaty, the area concerning controversial fundamental rights has expanded. In particular the attitude maintained by the United Kingdom and Poland during the negotiation, and by Ireland during the ratification process, shows a sort of new distrust towards the 'Europe of rights' that should not be understated.

Unlike other aspects of European integration, the 'Europe of rights' has always been presented and perceived as a result of an existent common constitutional tradition, as opposed to the outcome of a political bargain. In the first steps of the European Court of Justice's case law on fundamental rights this was an explicit statement and the legitimacy of the judicial activism of the Court was grounded on the idea that it was 'just' interpreting some common and shared principles that needed only to be spelled out. Fundamental rights in Europe claim to be part of a *jus commune europaeum*, capable of unifying the different national constitutional identities, while at the same time distinguishing the European tradition from other western countries. Even the Charter of Fundamental Rights was presented as a 'restatement of law': the claim was made that the Charter was but a codification of unwritten principles implicit in the European system on which all the Member States agreed.

Recently, the action of the European institutions on fundamental rights – including the European Court of Justice – has been debated at the national level and the dissents of some countries have been rendered explicit.

Certainly, some national institutions have always been 'alert and vigilant' with regard to the activities of the European institutions on fundamental rights. Starting with the German '*Solange*' doctrine and the Italian '*controlimiti*' doctrine, a growing number of constitutional or supreme courts have maintained a cautious attitude towards European developments on the matter and have affirmed over and over again the possibility of contradicting the European interpretations of fundamental rights, if necessary. Those doctrines, however, have never been applied. Many scholars have detected the signs of a potential judicial conflict between the Courts in Europe,[1] but so far all open and direct conflicts between Courts have been avoided.

During the negotiation of the Treaty of Lisbon the dissent has broken out. Protocol no. 30 to the Treaty of Lisbon expresses some serious concerns on the part of the United Kingdom and Poland on the evolution of fundamental rights in Europe, and specific reference is made to the expanding role of the European Court of Justice. Despite the rather unclear wording of the Protocol, it is not difficult to deduce from it serious concern regarding the expanding scope of the European Court's scrutiny on national measures and regarding the inclination of national judges to give direct effect to the provisions of the Charter of Fundamental Rights, an inclination that will most likely take further hold with the ratification of the Lisbon Treaty in so far as it grants legally binding force to the Charter.[2] As to the substance, the British concerns regard, quite unsurprisingly, the entire chapter on social rights whereas the Polish ones seem to be rather addressed[3] towards rights involving ethical disputes, in particular those regarding family and the edges of life.

In the Irish case, the issue of fundamental rights was raised during the ratification stage. After the first referendum, resulting in a negative response to the Lisbon Treaty, the European Council, on 19 June 2009, attempted to remove all obstacles to Irish ratification, paving the way for a second referendum that was eventually held on 2 October 2009 resulting in a positive outcome. The European Council issued one decision and one declaration concerning all the problematic matters from the point of view of the Irish people. Among them a relevant place was occupied by some issues concerning fundamental rights such as the right to life, family and education.[4]

---

1 A. Torres Pérez, *Conflicts of Rights in the European Union*, Oxford University Press, Oxford, 2009, arguing that Europe has become a context of constitutional pluralism, where the protection of fundamental rights has been 'disaggregated' and for that reason there is a need for a reinforced dialogue among all the institutions involved.

2 Article 6.1 of the Treaty reads: "The Union recognizes the rights, freedom and principles set out in the Charter of Fundamental Rights of the European Union of 7 December 2000, as adapted at Strasbourg, on 12 December 2007, which shall have the same legal values as the Treaties".

3 See in particular Declaration nos. 61 and 62, where Poland restates its commitments to social rights, while claiming national autonomy in the fields of family law, and human dignity.

4 All the problems and possible solutions to the Irish crisis concerning the Lisbon Treaty are discussed in S. Kingston, 'Ireland's options after the Lisbon Referendum: Strategies, implica-

Why was there such a strong reaction on the part of these Member States on European fundamental rights? Are the concerns addressed to the innovation introduced by the Lisbon Treaty? Or are they rather due to an on-going expansion of fundamental rights activities started long before the Lisbon Treaty?

The Lisbon Treaty touches upon fundamental rights introducing two major changes: first and foremost it grants the Charter of Fundamental Rights legally binding status; the second change concerns the participation of the European Union as such to the European Convention of Human Rights.[5] Although relevant, these new principles would not suffice to explain the defensive reaction of some of the Member States. To better understand them, we are forced to inquire into the background of the Lisbon Treaty, looking into the case law of the European Court of Justice of the last decade.

In the domain of fundamental rights, the Member States can be said to display both common background elements and different traditions: social rights, family law, state and religion – just to mention some examples – are fields in which the 27 Member States have different legal regulations. The European Union is shaped by a pluralist framework,[6] a constitutional equilibrium made of 'contrapunctual'[7] elements, based on the principle of constitutional tolerance[8] and the mutual nourishment between the national and the European constitutions[9]. The tension between uniformity and diversity needs to be preserved in the European constitutional system and a fundamental antidote to the risk of judicial standardisation in the field of fundamental rights as well as the opposite risk of disaggregation is prevented by a lively judicial dialogue among the constitutional courts in Europe by means of the preliminary ruling. This is at present the most effective tool available in the European Union, permitting the national constitutional traditions to be conveyed before the European Court of Justice, especially in cases involving human rights. For this reason, this paper intends to

tions and competing visions of Europe', (2009) 34 *ELR (European Law Review)* 455. See also the British debate on the issue in House of Commons, *The Treaty of Lisbon: an uncertain future*, Research Paper 08/66 www.parliament.uk/commons/lib/research/rp2008/rp08-066.pdf, and The Treaty of Lisbon after the Second Irish Referendum, research Paper 09/75, www.parliament.uk/commons/lib/research/rp2009/rp09-075.pdf.

5 Article 6 TEU. For a general overview of the major changes introduced by the Lisbon Treaty see J. Ziller, *Il nuovo trattato europeo*, Il Mulino, Bologna, 2007, p 176; P. Craig, 'The Treaty of Lisbon, Process, Architecture and Substance', (2008) 33 *ELR* 173, in particular 161 ss.

6 On pluralism as the contemporary model of the relationship between Member States and the EU see N. MacCormick, *Questioning Sovereignty: Law, State and Nation in the European Commonwealth*, Oxford University Press, Oxford, 1999, p 120 and the rich debate triggered by this essay.

7 Recalling a famous definition by M. Poiares Maduro, 'Contrapunctual Law: Europe's Constitutional Pluralism in Action', in N. Walker (ed), *Sovereignty in Transition*, Hart Publishing, Oxford, 2003, p 501.

8 This reference recalls those authors who emphasise the pluralistic nature of the European Constitution, such as J.H.H. Weiler, who is the father of the idea of *constitutional tolerance*. See *The Constitution of Europe*, Cambridge University Press, Cambridge, 1999, at 238 ff.

9 I. Pernice, 'Multilevel Constitutionalism in the European Union', (2002) 27 *ELR*, 511 ss.

insist once again on the well-known issue of judicial dialogue[10] in the European Union. The paper recalls and shortly analyses some leading decisions of recent case-law of the European Court of Justice on human rights in order to appreciate the dramatic evolution of the European constitutional balance in the field of fundamental rights since the approval of the Charter in December 2000. The paper turns to the persistent refusal of many constitutional courts to enter into direct judicial dialogue with the European Court of Justice, a refusal which lacks justification. The European constitutional balance urges a plural constitutional dialogue: a strong and daring European Court concerned with fundamental rights needs to be surrounded by similar strong and daring interlocutors at the national level. This paper suggests that a step must be taken by both sides so as to favour an encounter of the actors in this European constitutional drama: the national Constitutional Courts should shake off their reticence to address directly the European Court; the latter, on its part, should strive to encourage judicial dialogue, which would in any case be in its own interest.

## 2. THE NEW MILLENNIUM AND THE FLOURISHING OF A 'EUROPE OF RIGHTS'...

Since the approval of the Charter in December 2000, fundamental rights have taken a place of honour on the European agenda. The Charter has survived the constitutional debacle of the beginning of the new century and has been endorsed by the Treaty of Lisbon despite the fact that it was meant to eliminate all constitutional language. Moreover, the Charter seems to have brought fresh constitutional fuel to the European Court of Justice's engine, which in many cases tends to act as a federal constitutional court, in particular in cases involving individual rights.[11] Whereas the European Union is not living the most auspicious moment as re-

10 Even though the legal literature on judicial dialogue is almost boundless, it is worth noting that some scholars criticise the idea of judicial dialogue in itself, contending that dialogue is a common practice within the political institutions, but is almost impossible among courts and judges. See B. De Witte, 'The Closest Thing to a Constitutional Conversation in Europe: The Semi-permanent Treaty Revision Process', in P. Beaumont, C. Lyons, N. Walker (ed), *Convergence and Divergence in European Public Law*, Hart Publishing, Oxford, 2002.

11 Most scholars think that the ECJ acts as a constitutional court at least in some cases, although they do not always support the proposal of transforming the ECJ into a special judge deciding only constitutional issues: O. Due, 'A Constitutional court for the European Communities', and F.G. Jacobs, 'Is the Court of Justice of the European Communities a Constitutional court?', in D. Curtin, D. O'Keeffe (eds), *Constitutional Adjudication in European Community and National Law*, Butterworth, Ireland, 1992, p 2 and p 25; B. Vesterdorf, 'A Constitutional Court for the EU', (2006) 4 *IJCL (International Journal of Constitutional Law)* 607. See however L. Favoreu, 'Les Constitutions nationales face au droit européen', (1996) 28 *RFDC (Revue française de droit constitutionnel)* 699, who affirms that at present the ECJ cannot be considered a constitutional court because it still lacks too many important elements, such as a veritable Constitution of the EU, an impartial appointment of judges and many others.

gards its political cohesion, the Europe of judges and rights is flourishing. As had been predicted,[12] a *Grunderechtsgemeinschaft* is quickly developing.

In a way this evolution is a *déjà-vu*: many other stages in the history of the European integration have been marked by the weakness of the political process and by the activism of the judicial branch. After all, it is quite common that political failures leave room for judicial activism. So, it is no wonder that since the political way to a fully-fledged European Constitution was closed, the European Court of Justice has yet again taken the centre stage of the constitutional arena.

What is more distinctive of the new wave of judicial constitutional activism is an intense activity in fields related to fundamental rights that is incrementally imposing a "European" understanding on national constitutions and traditions. A rich list of decisions regarding human rights corroborates this hypothesis. With a view to illustrating this, this paper now turns to outline some of the most distinguished case law examples, taking those cases which do not deal with social rights[13] as primary examples..

## 2.1. THE *TANJA KREIL* CASE

The starting point of the new dynasty of constitutional cases can be considered the *Tanja Kreil* decision in 2000,[14] a judgment pronounced before the approval of the Charter, but in the midst of the mood of constitutional euphoria that pervaded the European Union in those years. It is not necessary to recapitulate in detail such a famous case which has been discussed by many, but suffice to recall that all in all it presented the Court of Justice with a constitutional conflict, between a provision of the German Constitution, Article 12 of the *Grundgesetz*, which forbade women to carry out roles in the army which implied the use of arms, and a basic principle of Community law, namely the principle of non-discrimination

---

12 A. von Bogdandy, 'The European Union as a Human Right Organization?', (2000) 37 *CMLR (Common Market Law Review)* 1308. Soon after the solemn proclamation of the Charter of Rights by the European Union in Nice on 7th December 2000, Armin von Bogdandy sensed the first symptoms of an evolution destined to change the features of the European integration, from an *economic* community towards a *Grundrechtsgemeinschaft*, a community of fundamental rights. As the author had predicted, the Charter of Fundamental Rights actually marked a new era in the European integration process, displaying all its seductive power.

13 In the present paper I will give a few examples taken from the case law of the European Court of Justice, in fields other than social rights, although cases like C-438/05, *Viking*, and C-341/05, *Laval* are among the most relevant for a complete understanding of the ECJ's attitude towards fundamental rights. See on this point the contribution by D. Schieck in this book. ECJ 11 December 2007, C-438/05, *International Transport Workers' Federation and Finnish Seamen's Union v Viking Line ABP and OÜ Viking Line Eesti* [2007] ECR I-10779; ECJ 18 December 2007, C-341/05, *Laval un Partneri Ltd v Svenska Byggnadsarbetareförbundet, Svenska Byggnadsarbetareförbundets avdelning 1, Byggettan and Svenska Elektrikerförbundet* [2007] I-11767.

14 ECJ 11 January 2000, Case C-285/98, *Tanja Kreil v Bundesrepublik Deutschland* [2000] ECR I-00069.

on the basis of sex. Without beating about the bush, the Court of Justice states that the Community principle of non-discrimination 'precludes the application of national provisions, such as those of German law, which impose a general exclusion of women from military posts involving the use of arms and which allow them access only to medical and military music services'. Without insisting explicitly on the constitutional rank of the relevant German norms, the Court of Justice concludes by demanding a constitutional revision on the part of Germany, pointing out an irredeemable conflict between Community law and the national Constitution. So, while the Court of Justice up until then had prevented fanning a fire of conflict between national Constitutions and Community principles,[15] in the Kreil case it did not hesitate in obliging the Germans to come into line with the European principles by revising their Constitution. For this precise reason, Tanja Kreil can be considered as the forerunner of the new line of decisions of the European Court concerning human rights issues.

## 2.2. THE *SCHMIDBERGER* AND *OMEGA* CASES

From another viewpoint, important signs of novelty can be seen in some decisions regarding conflicts between the fundamental economic freedoms and human rights.

In the past, critics of the Court of Justice have repeatedly highlighted that it has exploited the rhetoric of human rights, aiming not so much at the protection of some basic values in themselves, but rather at strengthening economic integration.[16] In fact, for a long time, the Community protection of fundamental rights was highly conditioned by the general objectives of European economic integration and therefore, first and foremost, by the common market. Until very recently, the Court of Justice has shown great deference for the economic freedoms of the common market each time it has been necessary to set a balance between them and other fundamental rights. Indeed, the Court of Justice has never dealt with either fundamental freedoms or fundamental rights as absolute values and consequently has always been careful to maintain a balance between the reasons for economic freedom and those for fundamental rights. However, in this complex balance, often economic freedoms have had the upper hand.

[15] Suffice to recall the well known decisions of the ECJ concerning the Irish Constitution: ECJ 28 November 1989, Case C-379/87, *Anita Groener v Minister for Education and the City of Dublin Vocational Educational Committee* [1989] ECR 03967 on the protection of the Irish language and ECJ 4 October 1991, Case C-159/90, *The Society for the Protection of Unborn Children Ireland Ltd v Stephen Grogan and others* [1991] ECR I-04685 on the right to life and abortion.

[16] J. Coppel and A. O'Neill, 'The European Court of Justice: Taking Rights Seriously?', (1992) 29 *CMLR* 669.

And so, that explains why the *Schmidberger* case of 2003[17] was enthusiastically welcomed by many scholars and commentators. In that decision, the Court of Justice was called upon to resolve a controversy between a basic freedom of the market – in that case the free movement of goods – and some fundamental rights – the freedom of assembly and the freedom of speech – caused by a demonstration by an environmental association that blocked the Brenner motorway for thirty hours. Surprisingly, the Court gave prevalence to the latter, in a balanced decision in which for once the civil rights in question prevailed over the economic interests.

Even more astonishing, in many respects, was the *Omega* decision in 2004.[18]

Also in this case, the Court of Justice had to face a conflict between an economic freedom protected by the Treaty, specifically the free movement of services and to a lesser extent the free movement of goods, and the protection of fundamental rights, which in this specific case regarded human dignity in relation to a commercial service of entertainment offering games which simulate murders using toy laser guns.

The case could have been solved on different grounds, but the Court wanted to use the discourse of fundamental rights by affirming that human dignity is not only one of the basic values of the German Constitution, but it is also part of the values of the European system. The Court of Justice wanted to stress deliberately the commitment on the part of the European Union towards the respect for human dignity. When one reads the Omega decision, it is difficult not to perceive the subtle influence of the Charter of Fundamental Rights that opens precisely with the claim that the safeguarding of human dignity is an inviolable right. The efforts of the Court of Justice did not go unobserved. So in *Omega*, as in *Schmidberger*, fundamental rights prevailed over economic freedoms and justified the important restrictions placed on them.

## 2.3. *K.B.*, *RICHARDS* AND *TADAO MARUKO* CASES

From another point of view, it can be seen that in more recent years the Court of Justice tends to widen the scope of EU fundamental rights, going beyond the limits of the European Union competences that the doctrine of *incorporation* would permit.[19] This tendency is clearly visible in some cases regarding the rights of

---

17 ECJ 12 June 2003, Case C-112/00, *Eugen Schmidberger, Internationale Transporte und Planzüge v Republik Österreich* [2003] ECR I-05659. On this issue M. Avbelj, 'European Court of Justice and the Question of Value Choices', www.jeanmonnetprogram.org/papers/04/040601.pdf, visited 25 January 2009.

18 ECJ 14 October 2004, Case C-36/02, *Omega Spielhallen- und Automatenaufstellungs-GmbH v Oberbürgermeisterin der Bundesstadt Bonn* [2004] ECR I-09609.

19 More cases are read in this perspective of expanding the scope of the ECJ review on national measures in A. Torres Pérez, *Conflicts of Rights n the European Union,* Oxford University Press, Oxford, 2009, p 18 ss.

transsexuals: *K.B.*[20] and *Richards*.[21] Both cases originate in Great Britain, where at the time of the events a peculiar legal situation was in force, one which on the one hand permitted a change of sex, it even being funded by the national health service while on the other hand, however, the record of the change of sex in the registry office was prohibited, thus in effect preventing the transsexual from enjoying the status reserved to the person of the sex to which s/he belonged after the operation. In the cases brought to the attention of the Court of Justice, the impossibility to register the change of sex prevented the plaintiff from entering into marriage and thus from enjoying the survivor's pension, in one case, and from being able to retire at 60 – the age for women's retirement – in the second case. In both cases British law was judged incompatible with the principles of non-discrimination on the basis of sex and the United Kingdom, which had already on several occasions been censured by the Court of Luxemburg as well as by the Court of Strasbourg on the impossibility of correcting personal data recorded at birth in the case of sex change, ended up adapting its own legislation to meet the European principles on non-discrimination.

An interesting aspect regarding this jurisprudence is that in these cases the EU fundamental rights impinge upon the regime of British civil status, a subject certainly far from the Union's competence. The Court of Justice was asked to answer a question concerning the principle of non discrimination of sex in the entitlement of survivor's pension and the definition of retirement age, but its decision ends up dealing with a matter that the Member States certainly did not intend to transfer to the Community institutions, namely the legal status of transsexuals and the rules that govern the civil register.

As a matter of fact, in *K.B.* and *Richards* the European Court of Justice broadens the doctrine of *incorporation*. It is not necessary to insist here on this well known doctrine.[22] Suffice to recall that at the time *K.B.* and *Richards* were decided, the area of application of fundamental rights, apart from the acts of the Community institutions, was also extended to acts of the Member States that enter the field of European law, a rule that realised itself in two main hypotheses: when States' actions constitute an application of Community law – the Wachauf

20 ECJ 7 January 2004, Case C- 117/01, *K.B. v National Health Service Pensions Agency and Secretary of State for Health* [2004] ECR I-00541.

21 ECJ 26 April 2006, Case C-423/04, *Sarah Margaret Richards v Secretary of State for Work and Pensions* [2006] ECR I-03585.

22 The first and fundamental essay about the incorporation doctrine is J.H.H. Weiler, 'The European Court at a Crossroads: Community Human Rights and Member States Action', in F. Capotorti and others (eds), *Du droit international au droit de l'integration. Liber amicorum Pierre Pescatore,* Nomos, Baden-Baden, 1987, p 821 and on the recent evolutions of the incorporation principle see B. de Witte, 'The Past and Future Role of the European Court of Justice in the Protection of Human Rights', in P. Alston (ed), *The EU and Human Rights,* Oxford University Press, Oxford, 1999, p 873.

line of reasoning[23] – and when the State's action is an exception to one of the fundamental freedoms of the internal market – the ERT line.[24]

Now the *K.B.* and *Richards* cases obviously do not fall into either hypothesis. The censured British legislation did not implement or execute Community acts; nor did it constitute an exception to the fundamental economic freedoms. As the Court of Justice states unequivocally, British legislation on the registering of personal data does not directly jeopardise a right protected by Community law – the right to the survivor's pension, but it has a discriminatory impact on one of the conditions necessary to the entitlement thereof.

It is too soon to say if a new 'spin-off' of the doctrine of *incorporation* has been heralded. However it is clear that in cases involving the non-discrimination principle, European fundamental rights tend to break into the national legal orders, well beyond the limits of incorporation. This trend is evident for example in Tadao Maruko,[25] a decision that requests the amendment of German legislation on same sex partnerships in order to grant same sex partners the same rights of spouses, at least insofar as the right to pension is concerned. In many respects, this decision oversteps the boundaries between the national protection of fundamental rights and the European one. In fact, consequently to the decision, the *Bundesverfassungsgericht* as well as other German judges have reacted to the European Court's decision by refusing to apply its interpretation.[26]

If this trend were to continue, the impact of Union law on the fundamental rights guaranteed by the national Constitutions would be dramatically broadened, toppling the limits of jurisdiction which were so carefully established in the Charter of Fundamental Rights, in Article 51 and Article 53, according to the consolidated doctrine of incorporation. The risk involved in developing of a fully-fledged incorporation in Europe, based on the wave of the American experience, is to trigger sharp constitutional conflicts with some Member States and to transform Europe's constitutional richness and variety into a single constitutional monologue.

---

23 ECJ 13 July 1989, Case 5/88, *Hubert Wachauf v Bundesamt für Ernährung und Forstwirtschaft* [1989] ECR 02609.

24 ECJ 18 June 1991, Case 260/89, *Elliniki Radiophonia Tiléorassi AE and Panellinia Omospondia Syllogon Prossopikou v Dimotiki Etairia Pliroforissis and Sotirios Kouvelas and Nicolaos Avdellas and others* [1991] ECR I-02925.

25 ECJ 1 April 2008, C-267/06, *Tadao Maruko v Versorgungsanstalt der deutschen Bühnen* [2008] ECR I-01757 dealing with same sex marriage and the right to survivor's pension.

26 *BVerfG*, 6 May 2008, decision 2 BvR 1830/06. It has been argued that the Constitutional Courts of the new members of the EU are more reluctant to comply with the creative interpretations of the ECJ. See the interesting analysis by W. Sadurski, 'Solange, chapter 3: Constitutional Courts in Central Europe – Democracy – European Union', *EUI Working Papers Law*, n° 2006/40 in http://cadmus.eui.eu/dspace/bitstream/1814/6420/1/LAW-2006-40.pdf, visited 15 January 2009.

## 2.4. CASES ON TERRORISM

The Union's institutions have often been accused of using different standards of protection of fundamental rights, depending on the nature of the question under review: generally speaking the European Court of Justice seems to be much more demanding of the Member States (and even more so of third countries or States that are candidates for membership) and indulgent regarding the acts of the Union's institutions. In fact, the European Court of Justice's case law on fundamental rights is dotted with statements of principle but has rarely admitted a violation of rights on the part of the Union institutions concerning their actions, tending more frequently to ascertain violations on the part of the Member States.

If we keep this context in mind, the importance of some cases on terrorism is unmistakeable. The decisions on terrorism concern some European Union Council regulations which, in implementing UN resolutions, foresee important patrimonial restrictions for people and associations that are reputed to be connected to terrorist networks. In all these cases, a number of violations of fundamental rights were claimed by the plaintiffs, among which the violation of the right to property, the right to defence and the right to effective judicial remedy. The complaints originate from the fact that the lists of terrorists (or presumed terrorists) are compiled without permitting the subjects to explain their own reasons and thus refusing to allow them to refute the proof gathered against them.

The CFI faced this problematic area in several cases, such as *Yusuf and Kadi*,[27] *Ayadi and Hassan*[28] and in the *Modjahedines*[29] case providing different responses.

The first group of decisions caused some criticism, because they ultimately sacrificed completely the plaintiffs' fundamental rights.

Starting with the *Modjahedines* case, the European judges appear more 'rights-oriented': in *Modjahedines* the European Court declares the decision adopted by the European Union Council void for violation of fundamental rights such as the right to defence and of the right to an effective judicial remedy. The Court relies on the fact that the inclusion of the plaintiffs in the list of terrorists

---

[27] CFI (now GC) 21 September 2005, Case T-306/01, *Ahmed Ali Yusuf and Al Barakaat International Foundation v Council of the European Union and Commission of the European Communities* [2005] ECR II-03533; CFI 21 September 2005, Case T-315/01, *Yassin Abdullah Kadi v Council of the European Union and Commission of the European Communities* [2005] ECR II-03649. For a deep analysis and criticism of these decisions see P. Eeckhout, 'Community Terrorism Listing, Fundamental Rights, and UN Security Council Resolutions. In Search of the Right Fit', (2007) 3 *ECLR (European Constitutional Law Review)* 183 and C. Eckes, 'Judicial Review of European Anti-Terrorism Measures – The Yusuf and Kadi Judgements of the Court of First Instance', (2008) 14 *ELJ (European Law Journal)* 74. See also a criticism of the content of *jus cogens* as stated by the CFI in C. Tomuschat, 'Note on Kadi', (2005) 43 *CMLR* 537.

[28] CFI 12 June 2006, Case T-253/02, *Chafiq Ayadi v Council of the European Union* [2006] ECR II-02139; CFI 12 June 2006, Case T-49/04, *Faraj Hassan v Council of the European Union and Commission of the European Communities* [2006] ECR II-00052.

[29] CFI 12 December 2006, Case T-228/02, *Organisation des Modjahedines du peuple d'Iran v Council of the European Union* [2006] ECR II-04665.

was not done directly by the UN bodies but, on the contrary, by the European institutions, so that the *Organisation des Modjahedines* was harmed by virtue of a discretional choice of the European institutions.[30] More recently, in *Kadi*,[31] the European Court of Justice reversed a previous decision of the Court of First Instance and annulled some European Union Council regulations imposing restrictive measures against certain persons and entities associated with Usama Bin Laden, the Al-Qaeda network and the Taliban, for violation of fundamental rights – namely the right of defence – although the European regulations had been issued in execution of UN resolutions.

The choices made by the Union's judges are certainly very courageous. Not only did the Court use the sanction of annulment of the contested acts, something that occurs very rarely; but, of no lesser importance, the Union's judges tested their capacity to be rigorous in the guarantee of rights on one of the prickliest terrains, given that the seriousness of the international situation tends to mitigate the sensitivity towards the rights of suspected terrorists and generates a greater propensity towards the need for security rather that towards that of justice and freedom.[32]

## 2.5. A PANORAMIC OVERVIEW

If we consider the comprehensive result of this line of cases on fundamental rights, we cannot help remarking that something new has taken place in the European case law since 2000. This panoramic overview of the recent case law of the European Court of Justice on fundamental rights could continue ad infinitum, illustrating for example the consistent group of judgments regarding European citizenship or again illustrating the synergies which have over time been created with the protection of human rights guaranteed by the Court in Strasbourg and many others.[33]

Undoubtedly something is changing in the approach of the Court of Justice towards fundamental rights since 2000. Today many decisions issued by the EU's judges take fundamental rights extremely seriously. Since the approval of the

---

30 UN Security Council Resolution of 28 September 2001, 1373 (2001). Council Decision 2 May 2002, 2002/334/CE and Council Decision 17 June 2002, 2002/460/CE both containing the name of the plaintiffs in the list of the suspected terrorists.

31 ECJ (Grand Chamber) 3 September 2008, Case C-402/05P and C-415/05P, *Yassin Abdullah Kadi and Al Barakaat International Foundation v Council of the European Union and Commission of the European Communities*, [2008] ECR I-06351.

32 A thorough analysis of this case in the light of the position of the EU in the global context can be read in G. de Burca, 'The European Court of Justice and the International Legal Order after *Kadi*', *Jean Monnet Working Paper* 01/09, in www.jeanmonnetprogram.org/papers/09/090101.pdf at 21 *et seq.*

33 For a more complete analysis see M. Cartabia (ed.), *I diritti in azione*, (Bologna, Il Mulino, 2007). The problem is raised in L.B. and J.H.R, 'Editorial. The Relative Autonomy of the EU Human Rights Standard', (2008) 4 *ECLR* 199.

Charter, plaintiffs and their lawyers use human rights more and more often as crucial legal arguments in the proceedings before the European Court and they do not fail to speak the language of fundamental rights. Human rights, which in the past often seemed to be invoked as a mere rhetorical device, are beginning to affect the merits of the decisions of the European courts. In this development, one cannot but notice the powerful effect of the Charter of Fundamental Rights and the new 'visibility' of fundamental rights, which was precisely one of the purposes that the Charter intended to reach. Even before being granted official legal status, the Charter had had important judicial spin-off effects. One can reasonably expect that these effects will continue to appear after the Treaty of Lisbon.

Certainly, the European Court of Justice shows to be strongly committed to a specific selection of rights – in particular to the "new rights" which are developing on the ground of non discrimination and self determination principles – whereas its jurisprudence concerning other rights – and especially social rights – is generally considered as a disappointing one.[34] However, everything considered, after the approval of the Charter, the feared effects of freezing and paralysing jurisdictional activism on the subject of fundamental rights did not occur, rather, on the contrary, the result is the strengthening of the Court of Justice as a *Court of Rights*. It is probably for this reason that so many commentators now tend to define the European Court as a Constitutional Court.[35]

## 3. ... AND OF A 'EUROPEAN COURT OF RIGHTS'

The Charter of Fundamental Rights seems to have strengthened the position of the Court of Justice in two ways: on the one hand it has produced a *legitimising effect* and on the other a *hermeneutical effect*.

There is something paradoxical in the fact that the Charter has produced a legitimising effect on the Court long before having legal effect. However, the fact that immediately after its proclamation the Charter of Fundamental Rights has been invoked and applied by many national judges, including many national constitutional courts, and that it also appeared regularly in the decisions of the Court of First Instance as well as in the Conclusions of the Advocates General,

34 See for example L. Azoulai, 'Le rôle constitutionnel de la Cour de Justice des Communautés européennes tel qu'il se degage de sa jurisprudence', (2008) 44 *RTDE (Revue Trimestrielle de Droit Européen)* 29, who emphasises the constitutional role of the ECJ although criticising its jurisprudence on social rights, in particular after the decision of *Laval* and *Viking* ECJ 11 December 2007, C-438/05, *International Transport Workers' Federation and Finnish Seamen's Union v Viking Line ABP and OÜ Viking Line Eesti* [2007] ECR I-10779; ECJ 18 December 2007, C-341/05, *Laval un Partneri Ltd v Svenska Byggnadsarbetareförbundet, Svenska Byggnadsarbetareförbundets avdelning 1, Byggettan and Svenska Elektrikerförbundet* [2007] I-11767.

35 See *supra* note 3.

has created an aura of legality around the document, explaining the potential of legitimisation that it has produced also as regards the Court of Justice.

Moreover, also the Commission, the European Parliament and the Fundamental Rights Agency regularly refer to the Charter *as if* it were a legally binding document.

Even more striking are the hermeneutical effects of the Charter of Fundamental Rights.

Generally speaking every legal written text should serve to limit room for interpretation on the part of judges. This, at least, is the concept that has been spread by the multi-secular tradition of civil law countries since the French revolution. The legal systems in continental Europe, for right or for wrong, have been inspired by the idea that judges are the '*bouches de la loi*'[36] and that their mission is to say what the written law provides, and to apply it to the specific cases brought before them. And yet, the Charter does not seem to have coerced the creativity of the Court of Justice but rather seems to have produced quite the opposite result.

This paradoxical effect can be explained in several ways.

First and foremost, it needs to be considered that the goal of reducing the role of judicial power by means of the written law has not been achieved, not even in the national systems that follow the tradition of civil law. History has extensively shown that judicial activity cannot be reduced to the mechanical application of the law in the form of judicial syllogism, and in recent years the role of judges is becoming all the more relevant, in particular in fields related to fundamental rights.[37]

Moreover, it needs to be considered that the Charter of Fundamental Rights operates in a 'multi-level' system, where it is placed alongside many other 'bills of rights', such as the 27 national Constitutions, the European Convention of Human Rights, a wide range of unwritten constitutional principles elaborated by all the high courts that deal with human rights and especially by the Courts in Luxembourg and Strasbourg. As is well known, in the systems of *common law*[38] judges enjoy a wide discretionary power for the simple fact that in order to solve a case or controversy they can take into account many different sources of law. In fact, one of the main reasons that explains the extent of the discretionary power of judges in the systems of *common law* is the possibility that they are offered to refer to a multiplicity of competing sources of law in exercising the *judicial review*.

36 For a critical historical overview of this principle, see K.M. Schönfeld, 'Rex, Lex, Judex', (2008) 4 *ECLR* 274.

37 For the Italian experience see E. Lamarque, 'L'attuazione giudiziaria dei diritti costituzionali', (2008) *Quaderni costituzionali* at 266, who demonstrates the creation of an impressive number of new fundamental rights by means of judicial decisions concerning requests of compensation for damages.

38 See in particular on this point M. Rosenfeld, 'Constitutional adjudication in Europe and in the United States: paradoxes and contrasts', (2004) 2 *IJCL* 633, at 646.

The habit of judges to recall *foreign law* and *international law* in cases involving fundamental rights offers further options to their discretionary power.

Lastly, it must also be considered that the text of the Charter is, so to speak, loosely formulated. The language of the Charter is very general and consequently it does not provide strict guidelines for its interpreters. In order to find a satisfactory compromise for all the Member States, the Charter uses a very broad wording, limiting itself to codifying principles and basic values which are generally shared, postponing the more controversial issues to a more detailed legal regulation or to the discretionary power of judges. Let us consider some of the provisions of the Charter: 'Human dignity is inviolable. It must be respected and protected', 'Everyone has the right to life', 'Everyone has the right to his or her own physical and mental integrity', 'Everyone has the right to freedom and security', 'Everyone has the right to respect for his or her own private and family life'. Faced with such a text, all the interpretative options lie wide open and the discretionary power of the interpreter plays a most important part.

For all these reasons, far from paralysing jurisdictional creativity, the written nature of the Charter of Fundamental Rights is further increasing the power of European Union judges, who have always been a vital engine for the development of European integration.

## 4. 'UNITED IN DIVERSITY' AT RISK

As with every relevant change, even the new trend in the European Court of Justice's case law entails both advantages and disadvantages. In particular, judicial activism in the field of fundamental rights brings about some concern for the constitutional equilibrium between the European Union and the Member States, and – more importantly – for the survival of the diverse historical traditions entrenched in the national constitutions, which are part and parcel of European identity. I do not want to insist on the risk of the *gouvernement des juges*, although it is clearly implied in the present phase of European integration. I would rather draw attention to a different concern.

It could be easily predicted that the approval of the Charter of Fundamental Rights would produce a centralising effect, gradually drawing the protection of human rights to the European level and simultaneously sterilising the protection guaranteed by the national Constitutions and breaking the limits of jurisdiction in which the action of the Community institutions should be carried out.[39] In this centralising movement, the national constitutional traditions risk to be extinguished.

---

39 A. von Bogdandy, *The European Union as a Human Rights Organization?* cit. *supra* note 2, at 1316–1318. See also on this point A.C. Pereira-Menaut, 'A Plea for a compound res publica europea: proposal for increasing constitutionalism without increasing statism', (2003) 18 *Tulane European and Civil Law Forum* 75, at 97–98.

Cases like *K.B.*, *Richards*, and *Tadao Maruko* are unquestionable examples of the invasion of the Union's protection of fundamental rights into areas where responsibility should lie with the national Constitutions. Article 51 of the Charter and the principles of incorporation[40] limit European judicial review of national acts only to cases where "the Member States are implementing Union law". In the aforementioned cases, the Member States were not implementing EU law. All this considered, why should the Court of Justice concern itself with violations of transsexuals' rights in the British system? The problem was under control; in particular it was under the supervision of the British courts and the Strasbourg Court.[41] Cases like *K.B.*, *Richards* and *Tadao Maruko* widen the scope of the European Court of Justice's judicial review on states' legislation well beyond the limits of the doctrine of incorporation. Besides this, as the *Kreil* case shows, this expansion can also impinge upon the national Constitutions. The Charter was conceived with a limited scope, addressing essentially the Union's institutions and the national institutions only when they execute Union law. Nonetheless, the Charter tends to be treated as if it were to overcome the national constitutions.

The expansion of the scope of fundamental Union rights is not only a matter of jurisdiction – the role of the Court of Justice in assuming the responsibilities of national Courts – but also a question about the substance of the protection of fundamental rights, because it could happen that the Union's understanding of some rights does not correspond entirely to that of one or more Member States: after all, the European Union endorses an individualistic/libertarian interpretation, whereas some national constitutions are oriented towards a personalistic/dignitarian conception of fundamental rights[42] like, for example, the Italian Constitution which is inspired by the second line of thought, starting with its Article 2: 'The Republic recognises and guarantees the rights of each human being considered both as an individual and within the intermediate social bodies where his/her personality flourishes'. The expansion of the Union's protection of rights may end up having an impact on those fields where the national particularity is intentionally defended.

Most cases brought before the European Court of Justice concern weak subjects such as women and migrant workers and understandably the Court seeks to fulfil what it considers to be its constitutional duty towards those persons. However, in most Member States of the European Union problems related to sexual orientation, same sex marriage, abortion, bioethics issues, immigration and the like, mark deep cultural and political cleavages and are usually dealt with

---

40 See *supra* note 17.

41 After all the European Court of Human Rights of Strasbourg in Goodwin v. United Kingdom, 11 July 2002, 28957/1995 had already condemned the United Kingdom for its legislation on transsexuals.

42 On the interpretation of these two lines see M.A. Glendon, 'Human Rights at the Dawn of the Third Millennium', in L. Antonini (ed), *Il traffico dei diritti insaziabili* Rubbettino, Cosenza, 2007, p 45.

very carefully by the national institutions in order to find balanced solutions that reconcile the different points of view at stake. The European Court of Justice has taken over its own 'judicial policy' in favour of women, immigrants, homosexuals, transsexuals and in general all weak subjects. All this is commendable. What is more debatable is that this mission is always within the institutional limits of the European Court. Expanding the jurisdiction of the European Court of Justice produces a centralising effect, suffocates pluralism, diversity and disagreement and consequently the possibility of a more considerate decision making process.

The practical effects of the Charter of Fundamental Rights as interpreted by judges are supported by a widespread legal thought that fosters the development of common European values – a '*jus commune europaeum*'. [43] This implies the idea that the whole continent can be unified around universally shared values and that unification flows from the judges' pens.[44] Whereas the European Union is going through a phase of political and economical stagnation, the Europe of judges and rights looks vigorous and dynamic. The success of the Europe of judges and rights is at least partly due to the opinion that the European – and more generally – the international institutions seem to be located at a more suitable level for the protection of fundamental rights. Fundamental rights are pulled out of the local boundaries, because they have a universal core: human dignity. That is why the protection of fundamental rights seems to fit better on the international scene rather than in national or local communities. Given the universal nature of human rights, European law and international law are taking the place that used to be occupied by natural law, since they imply the idea of a core of values and rights common to all human beings.

We must not, however, forget that fundamental rights have an ambivalent nature. In the struggle for fundamental rights there is a longing for *universality* that justifies the need to go beyond the boundaries of the national legal systems; but there is also a *historical dimension* in which the traditions and deepest conscience of each people is reflected, of which the national constitutional charters are one of the salient expressions. Rooted in the value of human dignity, the idea of fundamental rights necessarily contains a *universal dimension*. Embedded in the historical, religious, moral, linguistic and political peculiarities of each people, such rights are fed by particularity and pluralism.[45]

---

43 In relation to the origin of this line of thought see I. Pernice, 'Multilevel Constitutionalism in the European Union', quoted *supra* note 7, at 511. In Italy see at least G. Silvestri, 'Verso uno ius comune europeo dei diritti fondamentali', (2006) *Quaderni costituzionali* at 7; A. Pizzorusso, *Il patrimonio costituzionale europeo*, Il Mulino, Bologna, 2002; V. Onida, 'Armonia tra diversi e problemi aperti', (2002) *Quaderni costituzionali* at 549.

44 For an insight on the American debate about the aristocratic and paternalistic character of judge-made law see A. Gutmann (ed.), *A Matter of Interpretation*, Princeton University Press, Princeton, 1997 in particular the Comment to Justice A. Scalia by M. A. Glendon, p 95.

45 P. G. Carozza, 'Uses and misuses of comparative law in international human rights', (1998) 74 *Notre Dame Law Review* at 1235.

The attraction for a European protection of human rights risks forfeiting the national historical and cultural traditions that characterise the pluralistic nature of Europe.

Even more serious: what happens if one of the fundamental rights protected at the European and international level belongs only to one or some specific traditions or cultures and does not reflect any common shared value? Who guarantees that the European and the international institutions stick to the protection of the common fundamental rights and are not tempted to impose a particular interpretation of them as if it were universal?

The role of the Court of Justice is crucial and extremely delicate. Its pronouncements on the subject of fundamental rights tend to establish *the* standard that must be respected throughout the 27 countries of the Union.[46] Once a fundamental right enters the jurisdiction of the Court of Justice it becomes a European fundamental right. The decisions taken by the Court of Justice are binding in all the Member States even if the case originated in a particular legal system.

As has been highlighted, the very nature of the European Union is that of a pluralistic, tolerant, multiple, 'contra-punctual' legal order,[47] where a plurality of voices tends to harmonisation. Should the European Union move towards a uniform standard in the field of fundamental rights, trampling on the plurality of national constitutional traditions, or impose one out of many understandings of each fundamental right then it would betray its own ontological structure.

## 5. LOOKING FOR AN ANTIDOTE

This risk needs to be coupled with an effective antidote. It is difficult to elaborate the complete formula of it, but some of its components can be singled out. First, every new fundamental right should be tested with a strict scrutiny and recognised only if is part of a common basic experience throughout the whole European continent; second, the common experience of the people of Europe cannot be defined once and forever in a dogmatic style, in abstract formulas or written principles: fundamental rights are living concepts that can only emerge from the dynamic of the *encounter* among different peoples, each one having its traditions and culture, in a bottom up movement, and for that reason are continually re-shaped. In a way, this proposal recalls the idea of a common basic floor of shared values throughout the continent. However, there is here a major difference, because, the common basic ground that I am proposing is supposed to emerge from the dynamic encounter and dialogue of different peoples and traditions.

---

46 This effect is clearly grasped in S. Panunzio, *I diritti fondamentali e le Corti in Europa*, Jovene, Napoli, 2005, p 58.

47 See *supra* note n. 7.

If we want to prevent the extinction of the existing constitutional traditions, it is necessary that the category of fundamental rights is not excessively widened and, what is more relevant, every 'new fundamental right' should be verified within the living experience of European peoples. The further away we get from the core of fundamental rights, the greater the historical and cultural divergence between the various legal systems. The proliferation of 'fundamental rights' may impair the constitutional balance of the whole Union. The *jus commune europaeum* or, if you like, the 'common constitutional traditions' are undoubtedly a reality recognisable around a consolidated and limited nucleus of values, even though it is a category that becomes uncertain and shaky the further one distances oneself from that essential nucleus of really common values. Great care must be taken when recognising 'new fundamental rights' at the European level. After all, the primary task of the Courts is to guarantee the existing fundamental rights rather than create new ones.

However, here a crucial problem arises and needs to be answered: how can those common rights be recognised? Here I would like only to make a methodological remark: the common core of different cultures and traditions can only emerge from the encounter among living subjects able to express them. The only way to identify the rights common to different traditions is a careful observation of the common experiences emerging from the encounter among peoples belonging to the different traditions. Comparing legal and judicial texts is necessary, but not enough. The texts of the declarations of rights around the world very often repeat similar formulas. However, the judicial experiences of peoples and societies show relevant diversities. Human rights reveal their meaning when they touch upon real problems and facts. They can only be recognised in the historical experience of peoples. That is why all the subjects that can express a specific tradition should be active players in the European constitutional construction: social groups, legislators, judges, public authorities. In a certain sense, the European motto could read 'unity *from living* diversity'.

Democratic institutions, agencies, NGOs, all sorts of social subjects are required to become effective agents of a living culture of fundamental rights in Europe. And indeed a distinguished task rests on judges and on their dialogues. All sorts of democratic and judicial dialogues need to be strengthened and all forms of participation highly valued: a Europe of rights is to be grounded on the polyphony of the voices and traditions that make themselves heard, and if one voice is missing the cultural patrimony of the whole of Europe would be diminished. The very nature of the European Constitution or – might I even dare to say – the very nature of Europe itself, requires a lively participation of all the plurality of voices, traditions and historical experiences which altogether are part and parcel of the European identity. It is not only in the interest of a particular national tradition that the constitutional conversation on European values and fundamental rights is to be kept alive. It is also of vital importance for the European Union to encourage and support the participation of all its components, in order to be faithful to its own origin and structure.

The attitude of the Polish, British and Irish peoples when faced with the Lisbon Treaty can be considered an unconventional attempt to make themselves heard in the construction of a pluralistic Europe of rights. Should their stance be downplayed by the European institutions, then the whole construction would be at risk. A Europe of rights is not susceptible to have different speeds: either it is the expression of common and shared experiences of all peoples in Europe, or sooner or later it will fall apart. In this perspective, the Lisbon Treaty contains important steps forward towards a Europe of rights, but also relevant claims on the part of some Member States that are now in the hands of the European institutions.

# PART V

# PROCEDURAL AUTONOMY OF THE STATES

# THE "PROCEDURAL AUTONOMY" OF MEMBER STATES AND THE CONSTRAINTS STEMMING FROM THE ECJ'S CASE LAW: IS JUDICIAL ACTIVISM STILL NECESSARY?

Adelina Adinolfi*

## 1. INTRODUCTION

The scrutiny of national procedural rules that ensure the judicial protection of rights conferred under the EU Treaties is a very revealing issue for exploring the constraints on the autonomy of Member States stemming from the case-law of the European Court of Justice. It also constitutes an excellent standpoint for observing the reaction provoked at the national level by the European Court's approach.

The principle of "procedural autonomy" of Member States is firmly grounded in the case-law of the Court of Justice. The well-known "stock phrase" used by the Court runs as follows: "in the absence of Community legislation, it is for the Member States to lay down the procedural rules for legal proceedings intended to protect the rights conferred to individuals by EC law".[1] This stance seems to give

* University of Florence.

1 See *inter alia* ECJ 16 December 1976, Case 33/76, *Rewe-Zentralfinanz eG and Rewe-Zentral AG v Landwirtschaftskammer für das Saarland,* [1976] ECR 1989, para. 5; ECJ 9 February 1999, Case C 343/96, *Dilexport Srl v Amministrazione delle Finanze dello Stato* [1999] ECR I-579, para. 25; ECJ 26 October 2006, Case C-168/05, *Elisa María Mostaza Claro v Centro Móvil Milenium SL* [2006] ECR I-10421, para. 24; ECJ 12 December 2006, Case C-446/04, *Test Claimants in the FII Group Litigation v Commissioners of Inland Revenue* [2006] ECR I-11753, para. 203; ECJ 19 September 2006, Joined Cases C-392/04 and C-422/04, *i-21 Germany GmbH (C-392/04) and Arcor AG & Co. KG (C-422/04) v Bundesrepublik Deutschland* [2006] ECR I-8559, para. 57; ECJ 24 March 2009, Case C-445/06, *Danske Slagterier v Bundesrepublik Deutschland* [2009] ECR I-02119, para. 31; ECJ 6 May 2010, Joined Cases C-145/08 and 149/08, *Club Hotel Loutraki AE and Others v Ethnico Symvoulio Radiotileorasis and Ypourgos Epikrateias (C-145/08) and Aktor Anonymi Techniki Etaireia (Aktor ATE) v Ethnico Symvoulio Radiotileorasis (C-149/08)* [2010] ECR I-4165, para 74; ECJ 8 July 2010, Case 246/09, *Susanne Bulicke v Deutsche Büro Service GmbH*, nyr, para 25.

full support to the autonomy of Member States, and appears consistent with the present position of EU political institutions which is not in favour of harmonising national procedural rules.

In spite of the crystal-clear wording quoted above, the Court's case-law has indeed a significant impact on the "procedural autonomy" of the Member States, by imposing important constraints both on the law-maker and on national courts.[2] The Court often makes an in-depth review of national rules of procedure in order to assess whether they comply with the principles of "equivalence" and of "effectiveness", principles that the Court itself has long since decided to adopt as parameters for appraising the suitability of domestic procedural rules to enforce the rights conferred by EC law. Under these principles, the national procedures available to obtain judicial protection of such rights must "be no less favourable than those governing similar domestic claims nor render virtually impossible or excessively difficult the exercise of rights conferred by Community law".[3] Moreover, some general principles of EU law – such as legal certainty, proportionality, or the right of defence[4] –, are sometimes used by the Court in the scrutiny of domestic procedural rules or considered within the framework of the principle of effective protection.[5] More recently, the ECJ case-law also stated effects that directly impinge on judgments of national courts: some novel trends affect the principle of *res judicata* by requiring, under certain circumstances, a fresh examination of national measures that are final because of their inconsistency with EU law.

Pursuant to the reform of Lisbon, the modified TEU seems to offer some support to the Court's case-law by imposing on Member States the obligation to "provide remedies sufficient to ensure effective legal protection in the fields

---

2 Among the huge volume of literature on the subject see A.P. Tash, 'Remedies for European Community Law Claims in Member State Courts: towards a European Standard' (1993) 34 *Columbia Journal of Transnational Law* 377; G. Tesauro, 'The Effectiveness of judicial Protection and Co-operation Between the Court of Justice and the National Courts' (1994) 14 *Yearbook of European Law* 1; F.G. Jacobs, 'Enforcing Community Rights and Obligations in national Courts: Striking the balance' in J. Lonbay and A. Biondi (eds.), *Remedies for Breach of EC Law*, Chichester, 1997, 25; C.N. Kakouris, 'Do the Member States possess judicial procedural 'autonomy'?' (1997) 34 *CMLR* 1389; J. Temple Lang, 'The Duties of National Courts under Community Constitutional Law' (1997) 22 *ELR (European Law Review)* 3; G. Anagnostaras, 'The quest for en effective remedy and the measure of judicial protection afforded to putative Community law rights' (2007) 33 *ELR* 727.

3 ECJ 2 December 1997, Case C-188/95, *Fantask A/S e.a. v Industriministeriet (Erhvervministeriet)* [1997] ECR I-6703. Cf. S. Prechal, 'EC Requirements for an Effective Remedy' in J. Lonbay and A. Biondi (eds), *Remedies for Breach of EC Law*, Chichester 1997, 3; J. S. Delicostopoulos, 'Towards European Procedural Primacy in National Legal Systems' (2003) 9 *ELJ* 599.

4 Cf. ECJ 14 December 1995, Case C-312/93, *Peterbroeck, Van Campenhout & Cie SCS v Belgian State*, [1995] ECR I-4599, para 14. In administrative proceedings further principles – such as that of reasonable diligence – may have significance.

5 In striking the balance between the need for respect of Member States' "procedural autonomy" and the requirement that enforcement of EU law is effectively ensured, the general principles of the European legal system play a crucial role. The scheme applied by the Court aims at ascertaining if a restriction to the principle of effectiveness may be justified under different principles, e.g. that of legal certainty.

covered by Union law" (Art. 19). Such provision may be understood as requiring, *inter alia*, that national procedures are available to ensure effective judicial protection of the rights conferred by EU law; thus it gives overt expression to a principle which was previously derived from the general duty of cooperation with the Union, imposed on Member States under Article 10 of the EC Treaty.

The scrutiny of national procedural rules implies a wide discretionary power on the part of the ECJ, especially in ascertaining whether the condition of effectiveness of protection is fulfilled, and thus leaves room for criticism based on an allegedly excessive judicial activism of the Court. Indeed the Court's assessment may require that national rules of procedure are modified even under important aspects. Further criticism is raised by the approach followed by the Court: the attainment of a fair balance between the asserted procedural autonomy of the Member States and the duty to ensure effective application of EU law by means of national procedures leads to changeable appraisals, giving rise to inconsistent outcomes in the case-law of the Court. The call for a thorough consideration of the national legal context makes the results of the scrutiny carried out by the Court even more doubtful.

In light of the foregoing framework, this paper aims firstly to assess the scope of application of the constraints resulting from the need to ensure effective judicial protection of the rights conferred by EU law, and secondly to ascertain, through a brief survey of the Court's case-law,[6] the arguments which may give ground to the impingement of EU principles on national judicial procedures. On the basis of such an analysis the paper will consequently aim to verify to what extent those arguments may help to explain some of the inconsistencies resulting from the ECJ approach. An analysis of the constraints imposed on Member States from the perspective of judicial protection would arguably contribute to a better understanding of the general issue of restriction on Member States' autonomy which stems from the case-law of the Court. The paper will finally consider – without going into detail on possible technical solutions – the advantages that might be offered by the adoption of EU legislation aimed at fixing a minimum standard for judicial protection of the rights conferred by EU law.

The basic idea underlying this paper is that effective enforcement of EU law necessarily requires that a certain standard of protection be ensured by national rules of procedure. The role of the Court has so far compensated for the lack of EU legislation: the Court balanced the need for adequate standards of procedural rules with the autonomy of the Member States, deriving its stance from the fact that there is no EU legislation adopted in this area. With the persistence of legislative inertia, judicial activism is arguably needed to ensure effective enforcement of EU law, and to avoid that Member States, when infringing their obligation under the

[6] For the purpose of this paper, there is no need to review in detail the significant volume of case-law of the Court that has already been widely explored in literature; attention will be paid only to the most recent case-law with the aim of detecting possible new directions in the Court's stance.

Treaties, take advantage from a less protective judicial system to the detriment of the rights of individuals and of the uniform application of EU law.

## 2. THE CONSTRAINTS ON "PROCEDURAL AUTONOMY" OF THE MEMBER STATES: THE EXTENT OF THE DISCRETIONARY POWER OF THE COURT IN THE ASSESSMENT OF THE ADEQUACY OF NATIONAL PROCEDURES

In the absence of a thorough harmonisation of national judicial procedures,[7] the appraisal made by the Court of Justice aims, first of all, at considering whether the rules applied to protect rights conferred by EU law are less favourable than those governing similar domestic procedures. The paradigm used to that effect is quite familiar under the ECJ's case-law, as it consists of the application to the procedural national rules of a scheme not different in its essence from that employed for assessing whether substantive domestic provisions comply with the EU principle of non-discrimination.

In making such assessment the discretionary power of the Court is not very extensive: it is simply aimed at ascertaining whether a certain judicial action is "similar" to another one, and at comparing requirements imposed by national procedural laws. However, the appraisal as to what exactly a "similar action", made available for the protection of the rights conferred by domestic law, is, may occasionally be difficult.[8] The Court usually states some broad criteria to that

[7] A growing body of EU legislation imposes specific requirements that national procedural rules have to satisfy; see e.g. Directive 2006/54/EC of the European Parliament and of the Council of 5 July 2006 (OJ 2006, L 204/23) which, with regard to the burden of proof in anti-discrimination cases, establishes that, under certain conditions, "it shall be for the respondent to prove that there has been no breach of the principle of equal treatment". Cf. also Directive 2007/66/EC of the European Parliament and of the Council of 11 December 2007 amending Council Directives 89/665/EEC and 92/13/EEC (OJ 2007, L 335/31) with regard to improving the effectiveness of review procedures concerning the award of public contracts; this requires Member States to take the measures necessary to ensure that "as regards contracts falling within the scope of Directive 2004/11/EC, decisions taken by the contracting authorities may be reviewed effectively and, in particular, as rapidly as possible in accordance with the conditions set out in Articles 2 to 2f of this Directive, on the grounds that such decisions have infringed Community law in the field of public procurement or national rules transposing that law" (Article 1, para. 1). To that effect, the Directive specifies the requirements that the review body should satisfy (even when it is not judicial in character) and the powers that such a body should be provided with, laying down some minimum standards of protection as to the standstill period and the time limit for starting the review procedure, and indicating the consequences (i.e. ineffectiveness or alternative penalties) in cases where a contract is concluded in violation of EU law. For further references cf. S. Prechal, 'Community law in national courts: The lessons from van Schijndel', (1998) 35 *CMLR* 681, at note 4.

[8] E.g. ECJ 8 July 2010, Case 246/09, *Susanne Bulicke v Deutsche Büro Service GmbH*, nyr. Cf. Prechal, *supra* note 7, 688.

effect, and declares that it is for the referring court to make such a comparison. Sometimes the Court prefers making a direct appraisal, as in the recent judgment in the case of *Transportes Urbanos y Servicios Generales*:[9] the Court verified whether the claim for damages alleging breach of EU law brought by the plaintiff in the main proceeding, on the one hand, and the claim that the same company could have brought in the case of a possible breach of the Spanish Constitution, on the other, could be regarded as similar. To make this assessment the Court examined in detail the features of the claim brought before it and that of a hypothetical action for violation of the Constitution, drawing the conclusion that "the only difference between the two actions [...] is the fact that the breaches of law on which they are based are established, in respect of one, by the Court in a judgment given pursuant to article 226 EC and, in respect of the other, by a judgment of the Tribunal Constitucional" (para. 43). According to the Court, this fact alone "cannot suffice to establish a distinction between those two actions in the light of the principle of equivalence": thus they may be regarded as similar. Arguably the Court prefers making a direct assessment when the domestic rule at issue has constitutional significance under the EU legal system; in the case referred to above the actual application of the principle of liability of Member States, which under the case-law of the Court is regarded as "inherent in the system of the Treaty",[10] was made rather difficult because of the strict requirements for bringing an action for damages alleging breach of EU law.

The Court appears to enjoy wider discretion when reviewing national procedures in the light of the principle of effectiveness. Under the most recent wording, in the absence of EU rules governing the matter, it is for the domestic legal system to designate the courts having jurisdiction and to lay down the detailed procedural rules governing actions for safeguarding rights conferred on individuals by EU law; however, "the Member States are nevertheless responsible for ensuring that those rights are effectively protected in each case".[11] In order to verify whether a procedural rule makes the exercise of a right impossible or too difficult, the Court often carries out a rather "intrusive" control of national legal systems, assessing, for instance, whether a national statute establishing

---

9 ECJ 26 January 2010, Case C-118/08, *Transportes Urbanos y Servicios Generales SAL v Administración del Estado* [2010] ECR I-635.

10 ECJ 19 November 1991, Joined Cases 6/90 and 9/90, *Andrea Francovich and Danila Bonifaci and others v Italian Republic* [1991] ECR 5357, para. 35.

11 Cf. ECJ 18 March 2010, Joined Cases C-317/08, C-318/08, C-319/08, and C-320/08, *Rosalba Alassini v Telecom Italia SpA (C-317/08), Filomena Califano v Wind SpA (C-318/08), Lucia Anna Giorgia Iacono v Telecom Italia SpA (C-319/08) and Multiservice Srl v Telecom Italia SpA (C-320/08)* [2010] ECR I-2213, para 47. Cf. also ECJ 15 April 2008, Case C-268/06, *Impact v Minister for Agriculture and Food and Others*, [2008] ECR I-2483 paras 44 and 45, and ECJ 16 July 2009, Case C-12/08, *Mono Car Styling SA, in liquidation v Dervis Odemis and Others* [2009] ECR I-6653, para 48.

time-limits for bringing an action, or requiring documentary evidence to obtain repayment of a unduly paid sum,[12] can provide adequate judicial protection.

The discretionary power exerted by the Court is particularly wide when it relies on the principle of reasonableness: actually, the Court may verify whether a limitation period seems to be "reasonable" by just relying on its completely discretional appraisal. The Court may further ascertain if a procedure limiting the protection of rights can "reasonably be regarded as justified" for the sake of a certain general principle, such as the principle of legal certainty.[13] Reasonableness acts in this role to provide the Court with the discretion to ascertain whether a national procedure can adequately ensure the protection of rights conferred on individuals under EU legislation or under the Treaty.[14]

## 3. THE CRITICAL REACTIONS CAUSED BY THE JUDICIAL LIMITATION OF "PROCEDURAL AUTONOMY" OF MEMBER STATES

Because of the extensive scrutiny made in the EU case-law, it is no surprise that whenever the Court declares that a national procedure cannot provide adequate judicial protection, this ruling is likely to produce a critical response in the concerned Member State (or even in other Member States). Arguably, the domain of procedural rules is a very sensitive area in spite of its highly technical aspect. One should consider that these rules are deemed to be tightly linked with national legal traditions, and they usually are embodied in long-standing codes or deeply rooted in settled case-law. Furthermore, they often give expression to general principles of law recognised in each Member State, and sometimes to the rule of law. Thus, when the Court assesses whether national rules comply with the principle of effectiveness one could express the view that through such an assessment

---

12 As in the leading ECJ 9 November 1983, Case 199/82, *Amministrazione delle Finanze dello Stato v SpA San Giorgio*, [1983] ECR 3595, where the Court found that a Member State cannot make the repayment of national charges levied in breach of Community law conditional upon the proof that the charge has not been passed on to consumers "if the repayment is subject to rules of evidence which render the exercise of that right virtually impossible, even where the repayment of other taxes, charges or duties levied in breach of national law is subject to the same restrictive conditions" (para 18). On the same issue cf. Case ECJ 9 February 1999, C-343/96, *Dilexport Srl v Amministrazione delle Finanze dello Stato* [1999] ECR 579, where the Court held that the same national provision would infringe the principle of effectiveness had the burden of proof been on the plaintiff rather than on the administration (paras. 52–54).

13 ECJ 3 September 2009, Case 2/08, *Amministrazione dell'Economia e delle Finanze and Agenzia delle entrate v Fallimento Olimpiclub Srl* [2009] ECR I-07501, where the Court assess whether a procedure constituting an "extensive obstacles to the effective application of the Community rules on VAT" might reasonably be justified in the interest of legal certainty.

14 I examined elsewhere the issue concerning the role that reasonableness plays in the ECJ's case-law as a means for extending the Court's discretionary power: A. Adinolfi, 'The Principle of Reasonableness in European Law' in *Reasonableness and Law*, G. Bongiovanni, G. Sartor, C. Valentini (eds), Springer, Dordrecht, 2009, 400–401.

the Court gives a political appraisal which overlaps the discretionary power of the national law-maker, or even completely replaces it.

These remarks may help to explain the strong criticism – or even the astonishment – caused by some decisions of the ECJ that impinge on national procedural rules. Suffice it to recall the reaction provoked by *Lucchini*,[15] since the Court required the referring court to discard the principle of *res judicata* embodied in the Italian civil code because it prevented the recovery of a State aid granted in breach of Community law; or by the ruling in *Traghetti del Mediterraneo*,[16] where the Court declared that the Italian statute aimed at guaranteeing the independence of the judiciary had to be set aside insofar as it precluded the application of the principle of liability of a Member State for breach of EU law as stated in *Köbler*.[17]

One cannot deny that in such cases the Court's decision clearly seemed to collide with the core of national legal systems.

Further criticism is likely to break out when the concrete consequences of the Court's rulings, which restrain procedural autonomy of Member States, become manifest: national procedural statutes have to be shaped or re-shaped by the law-maker so as to ensure a degree of protection of the rights conferred by EU law that is capable of satisfying the Court's appraisal of effectiveness. Sometimes these amendments produce a "domino effect" requiring further legislative revision in order to avoid the possibility of "reverse discrimination", which could violate the principle of equality laid down by national Constitutions: thus, the need for a more favourable standard of protection regarding the rights conferred by EU law may imply that the procedural rules applied to "national rights" should be aligned to such a standard. Under this perspective, the role that the Court has

---

15 Among the many comments see P. Biavati, 'La sentenza Lucchini: il giudicato nazionale cede al diritto comunitario' (2007) 30 *Rassegna tributaria* 1591; A. Biondi, 'Case Lucchini' (2008) 45 *CMLR* 1459; P. Briza, 'Lucchini SpA – is There Anything Left of Res Judicata Principle?' (2008) 27 *Civil Justice Quarterly* 1, 40; C. Consolo, 'La sentenza *Lucchini* della Corte di Giustizia: quale possibile adattamento degli ordinamenti processuali interni e in specie del nostro?' (2008) *Rivista di diritto processuale* 225; E. Fontana, 'Qualche osservazione in margine al caso *Lucchini*. Un tentativo di spiegazione', *Diritto del commercio internazionale* (2008) 193; F. Lajolo Di Cossano, 'L'Europa abbatte un mito: il giudicato' (2007) *Diritto del commercio internazionale* 724; G. Mari, 'La forza del giudicato delle decisioni dei giudici nazionali di ultima istanza nella giurisprudenza comunitaria' (2004) *Rivista italiana di diritto Pubblico comunitario* 1007; N. Picardi, 'Eventuali conflitti fra principio del giudicato e principio della superiorità del diritto comunitario' (2008) *Giustizia civile*, I, 559; E. Scoditti, 'Giudicato nazionale e diritto comunitario' (2007) *Foro italiano* 533; M. T. Stile, 'La sentenza *Lucchini* sui limiti del giudicato: un traguardo inaspettato?' (2007) *Diritto comunitario e degli scambi internazionali* 733; A. Hatje, 'Gemeinschaftsrechtliche Grenzen der Rechtskraft gerichtlicher Entscheidungen – zur Entscheidung des EuGH in der Rs. C-119/05 (Lucchini) vom 18. Juli 2007' (2007) 42 *Europarecht* 654; B. Zuffi, 'Il caso Lucchini infrange l'autorità del giudicato nazionale nel campo degli aiuti statali' (2008) *Giurisprudenza italiana* 382.

16 ECJ 13 June 2006, Case C-173/03, *Traghetti del Mediterraneo SpA v Repubblica italiana* [2006] ECR I-5177.

17 ECJ 30 September 2003, Case C-224/01, *Gerhard Köbler v Republik Österreich* [2003] ECR I-10239.

been playing might be regarded as an encroachment on the discretionary power of the Member States to regulate the exercise of the judicial function.

Important constraints may directly affect the role of national courts. These may be required to make "adjustments" – sometimes quite significant – to national procedural rules, either by setting aside certain provisions or by construing a rule so that it may satisfy the standard of protection fixed by the ECJ. National courts should even have to figure out remedies that would otherwise be unknown in their respective legal systems; this may at times require the exercise of a rather "inventive" interpretation of domestic rules.

A further criticism towards the prevailing judicial trend is that the ECJ, when ascertaining whether national procedural rules are adequate, follows a case by case approach which renders the outcome of its assessment rather unpredictable. The method applied by the Court, which consists in the finding of a fair balance among different principles – e.g. *res judicata* or legal certainty, on the one side, and supremacy or effective application of EU law on the other – may lead to an unexpected outcome. Indeed, in analysing the case-law concerning national procedural rules one may often find solutions that are expressly linked to the particular cases at issue. The Court usually employs wording clarifying that the solution adopted in a certain ruling "was justified by the particular circumstances of the case…":[18] e.g. in *Olimpiclub* the Court, referring to *Lucchini*,[19] declared that the latter judgment "concerned a highly specific situation, in which the matters at issue were principles governing the division of powers between the Member States and the Community in the area of State aid", whilst "issues of that nature, relating to the division of powers, do not arise in the present case" (par. 25). Sometimes the Court specifies that a certain appraisal applies in "circumstances such as those which arise in the main proceedings";[20] this reasoning links the ruling to a specific national framework, making it rather difficult to transpose the principle in question to a different national context. Furthermore, the way in which different principles are weighed against each other also depends on the specific circumstances of the case.

The completion of an in-depth scrutiny of national procedural rules necessarily requires a thorough analysis of the circumstances of the main proceeding and of the national legislation at stake, something that is indeed, often made by the Court. For instance, in *Kühne & Heitz* the Court described in detail the national law conferring on administrative bodies, under certain circumstances, the competence to reopen a decision which has become final

18 ECJ 25 July 1991, Case C-208/90, *Theresa Emmott v Minister for Social Welfare and Attorney General* [1991] ECR I-4269.

19 *Olimpiclub, supra* note 13.

20 ECJ 7 June 2007, Joined Cases C-222/05 to C-225/05, *J. van der Weerd and Others (C-222/05), H. de Rooy sr. and H. de Rooy jr. (C-223/05), Maatschap H. en J. van 't Oever and Others (C-224/05) and B. J. van Middendorp (C-225/05) v Minister van Landbouw, Natuur en Voedselkwaliteit* [2007] ECR I-4233.

as a result of a judgment of a national court against whose decisions there was no judicial remedy (paras. 25–26). This analysis was aimed at declaring that a similar pattern had to be applied when the administrative decision that became final was based on an interpretation of Community law which proved incorrect in the light of a subsequent judgment of the Court. The need to consider the particular circumstances of the national legal context is well illustrated by the recent judgment in *Olimpiclub:* the Court remarked that the review of a national provision under the principle of effectiveness has to be conducted "by reference to the role of that provision in the procedure, its progress and its special features, viewed as a whole, before the various national bodies", and that for this purpose "account must be taken, where appropriate, of the basic principles of the domestic judicial system, such as protection of the rights of the defence, the principle of legal certainty and the proper conduct of procedure" (para. 27).

When a national rule of procedure is considered in the framework of a preliminary ruling, the need for a thorough appraisal may imply a special duty on the national court to describe in detail the domestic provisions at stake.[21] However the framework given by national courts in their preliminary references may reveal inadequate to cope with interpretative issues which may subsequently emerge in the proceedings before the Court. In order to apply the test of equivalence and/or effectiveness, the Court necessarily has to interpret the national legislation at issue: possible divergence of interpretation showed by the parties in the main proceedings or by the Governments intervening before the Court may cause uncertainties in the Court's decision. Thus, the tight link with the circumstances of the case may at times induce the Court to adopt a vague solution that has to be further adapted according to the clarification of the legal context carried out by the national court.[22] On the contrary, the assessment of national legislation may

21 The general duty of national courts to "set out the tenor of any applicable national provisions and identify, where necessary, the relevant national case-law giving in each case precise references" (Informative Note on Preliminary Rulings, para. 22) may sometimes imply a more detailed description of the national legal context or the need for supplementary information; e.g. the Court recalled in ECJ 26 January 1993, Joined Cases C-320/90, C-321/90 and C-322/90, *Telemarsicabruzzo SpA and Others v Circostel, Ministero delle Poste e Telecomunicazioni and Ministero della Difesa* [1993] ECR I-393, that " it is necessary that the national court define the factual and legislative context of the questions it is asking or, at the very least, explain the factual circumstances on which those questions are based", and added that "those requirements are of particular importance in the field of competition, which is characterized by complex factual and legal situations" (paras 5–6).

22 Also illustrated by the case *Dilexport* (*supra* note 1): since the national legal context was unclear, the Court declared that "if, as the national court considers, there is a presumption that the duties and charges unlawfully levied or collected when not due have been passed on to third parties and the plaintiff is required to rebut that presumption in order to secure repayment of the charge, the provision in question must be regarded as contrary to Community law. If, on the other hand, as the Italian Government maintains, it is for the administration to show, by any form of evidence generally accepted by national law, that the charge was passed on to other persons, the provisions in question are not to be considered contrary to Community law" (paras. 52–53). By adopting that approach, the Court leaves in substance to the referring

sometimes result in a very specific outcome, as in the recent case of *Alassini*:[23] the Court decided that a mandatory out-of-court settlement procedure complied with the principle of effectiveness since electronic means were not the only means by which the settlement procedure could be accessed.

On the basis of the case-by-case approach described above, it may be difficult at first sight to explain why in seemingly similar legal contexts the outcome was different. A striking example is that concerning time-limits respectively in *Emmott*[24] and in *Fantask*. In *Emmott* the Court declared that the authorities of a Member State cannot rely on "national procedural rules relating to time-limits for bringing proceedings so long as that Member State has not properly transposed that directive into its domestic legal system" (para. 24). In *Fantask*[25] the Court completely reversed that approach by holding that EC law does not prevent a Member State which has not implemented a Directive "from resisting actions for the repayment of charges levied in breach thereof by relying on a limitation period under national law which runs from the date on which the charges in question became payable" (para. 52); the Court emphasised that the solution adopted in *Emmott* "was justified by the particular circumstances of that case" (para. 51). However, one may observe that the principle stated in *Fantask* had precisely the effect which the Court had decided to avoid in *Emmott*, that is the risk that the enforcement of rights conferred by EC law would be jeopardised.[26]

One may also wonder why in one case the principle of *res judicata* has to be overcome, while in another it has to be fully respected. Or why at times the European Court leaves to national courts the task of ascertaining whether a certain national legislation gives adequate protection, while occasionally it "substitutes" its own assessment to that of the referring court. Actually, in some cases the Court gives sound guidance to national courts or even declares the clear-cut solution that they have to take, whilst in others the principle of procedural autonomy is given priority, leaving the assessment fully, or to a large extent, to national courts. An emblematic case that assigned to national courts a very wide discretion was that of *Sopropé*; the core of the appraisal was left to the national

court the duty to clarify the legal context, while limiting the discretion of such a court the appraisal of conformity with EU law of the national provision at issue.

23 ECJ 18 March 2010, Joined Cases C-317/08, C-318/08, C-319/08 and C-320/08, *Rosalba Alassini v Telecom Italia SpA (C-317/08), Filomena Califano v Wind SpA (C-318/08), Lucia Anna Giorgia Iacono v Telecom Italia SpA (C-319/08) and Multiservice Srl v Telecom Italia SpA (C-320/08)* [2010] ECR I-2213, para 60.

24 ECJ 25 July 1991, Case C-208/90, *Theresa Emmott v Minister for Social Welfare and Attorney General* [1991] ECR I-4269.

25 ECJ 2 December 1997, Case C-188/95, *Fantask A/S e.a. v Industriministeriet (Erhvervministeriet)* [1997] ECR I-6703.

26 Another well-known example may be that of *Van Schijndel* (ECJ 14 December 1995, Joined Cases C-430 and 431/93, *Jeroen van Schijndel and Johannes Nicolaas Cornelis van Veen v Stichting Pensioenfonds voor Fysiotherapeuten* [1995] ECR I-4705) and *Peterbroeck* (ECJ 14 December 1995, Case C-312/93, *Peterbroeck, Van Campenhout & Cie SCS v Belgian State* [1995] ECR I-4599), cases that "are hard to reconcile": A. Arnull, 'Note on Unibet' (2007) 44 *CMLR* 1779.

referring court, while the Court enounced just very loose criteria.[27] When the appraisal is left to national courts, the Court only declares that certain general principles have to be respected because they are recognised in the EU legal system, whilst the task of reaching a fair balance among such principles is handed over to the national court.[28] An opposite approach was followed in *Manfredi*,[29] where the referring court was given a very limited discretion in assessing whether a national rule (which provided a time-limit for seeking compensation for damages caused by anti-competitive practice) rendered it practically impossible or excessively difficult to obtain compensation.

The unsteady approach described above may produce disconcert among national courts, and implies that previous ECJ case-law may be of little help to the national courts. Thus, a further consequence of this judicial attitude may be that of increasing the need to obtain a Court's appraisal through preliminary references.

## 4. WHY LIMIT THE "PROCEDURAL AUTONOMY" OF MEMBER STATES?

### 4.1. SUPREMACY OF EU LAW

In spite of the lack of EU legislation concerning national rules of procedure one cannot deny that these have crucial importance for ensuring the enforcement of EU law:[30] the effective application of EU law actually depends on the degree of

---

27 ECJ 18 December 2008, Case C-349/07, *Sopropé – Organizações de Calçado Lda v Fazenda Pública* [2008] ECR I-10369. The referring court asked whether a certain period granted to an undertaking to submit its observations on an administrative decision complies with the principle of effectiveness. The Court stated that it is for the national court to assess whether, having due regard to the facts specific to the case, the time range assigned for collecting the observations of the parties concerned made it "possible for them to exercise their rights of defence in accordance with the principle of effectiveness" (para. 44).

28 E.g. ECJ 21 June 2007, Case C-158/06, *Stichting ROM-projecten v Staatssecretaris van Economische Zaken* [2007] ECR I-5103, where the Court declared that "it is not contrary to Community law to apply the principle of legal certainty so as to preclude repayment by that beneficiary of the amounts wrongly paid, provided that it is possible to establish the beneficiary's good faith." (para 34). Cf. also ECJ 19 September 2002, Case C-336/00, *Republik Österreich v Martin Huber* [2002] ECR I-7699 where the Court held that "Community law does not preclude the application of the principles of the protection of legitimate expectations and legal certainty in order to prevent the recovery of aid part-financed by the Community which has been wrongly paid, provided that the interest of the Community is also taken into consideration." (para. 59).

29 ECJ 13 July 2006, Joined Cases from C-295/04 to C-298/04, *Vincenzo Manfredi v Lloyd Adriatico Assicurazioni SpA (C-295/04), Antonio Cannito v Fondiaria Sai SpA (C-296/04) and Nicolò Tricarico (C-297/04) and Pasqualina Murgolo (C-298/04) v Assitalia SpA* [2006] ECR I-6619.

30 As K. Lenaerts puts it, "... each Member State contributes its own judicial system for the sake of ensuring the effective application and enforcement of Community law, which is indeed in line with the deeper philosophy of unity and diversity underlying the Union itself" in 'The

protection given by national procedural rules. As the Court held, "it is for all the authorities of the Member States to ensure observance of the rules of Community law within the sphere of their competence".[31] If national rules give poor protection – e.g. because of short time-limits – the rights conferred under the Treaties will be scarcely protected and the effective application of EU law will be endangered. Indeed there is a close link between the quality of the judicial protection offered in national legal systems and the correct application of EU law. The simplistic view originally taken by the founding fathers of the EC Treaty – according to which EU legislation is adopted by European institutions whilst applied by national authorities under their respective procedural rules – shows in practice some important shortcomings. One cannot disregard that substantial provisions are likely to be ineffective in the absence of an adequate procedural mechanism aimed at ensuring their application. As referred to above, under the reform established by the Treaty of Lisbon such a need is expressed by the new provision according to which Member States have to guarantee effective legal protection in the fields covered by Union law (Art. 19 TEU); this obligation may be understood as aimed at requiring Member States to provide for an efficient judiciary system, including the application of procedural rules capable of ensuring effective judicial protection.

Thus, the procedural autonomy of the Member States may have to be restrained based on the need that procedural rules give proper protection to EU rights.[32] The way the Court has tried to balance the procedural autonomy of the Member States, on the one hand, with the duty of correct application of EU law, on the other, is that of scrutinising national rules according to a minimum standard of protection. Under this perspective, monitoring the adequacy of national procedural rules is part of the control on compliance with EU obligation by Member States.

A first reason that may arguably influence the Court's approach in limiting the procedural autonomy of Member States is closely linked with the principle of supremacy of EU law: in short, sound procedural rules are a crucial guarantee

Rule of Law and the Coherence of the Judicial System of the European Union' (2007) 44 *CMLR* 1625. On the interplay between the principles of supremacy, effectiveness, equivalence and autonomy cf. M. Hoskins, 'Tilting the balance: Supremacy and National Procedural Rules' (1996) 21 *ELR* 370; F. Becker, 'Application of Community Law by Member States' public authorities: Between autonomy and effectiveness' (2007) 44 *CMLR* 1035.

31 Cf. *inter alia* ECJ 13 January 2004, Case C-453/00, *Kühne & Heitz NV v Produktschap voor Pluimvee en Eieren* [2004] ECR I-837, para 20.

32 The *ratio* of supremacy also emerges in cases declaring that national procedural rules cannot be applied since they would limit the power of the national courts to refer preliminary rulings: cf. ECJ 14 December 1995, Case C-312/93, *Peterbroeck, Van Campenhout & Cie SCS v Belgian State* [1995] ECR I-4599 where the Court declared that under certain conditions Community law precludes the application of a national procedural rule the effect of which is to prevent the national court from considering on its own motion whether a measure of domestic law is compatible with a provision of Community law when the latter provision has not been invoked by the litigant within a certain period.

for providing full compliance with an obligation under EU law. A Member State may take advantage of its violation of the obligations under the Treaty whenever judicial protection is limited or impossible, as is the case when a very short time-limit is established for obtaining reimbursement of tax requested by a Member State in violation of EU law.

The assessment by the Court of the effectiveness of procedural rules is perfectly coherent with the principle of supremacy of EU law, and is its natural follow-up in the domain of judicial procedure. This was already shown by less recent case-law; for instance, in *San Giorgio* the Court stated that "entitlement to the repayment of charges levied by a Member State contrary to the rules of Community law is a consequence of, and an adjunct to, the rights conferred on individuals by the Community provisions prohibiting charges having an effect equivalent to customs duties..." (para 12). The same link emerged in *Oleificio Borelli* in respect of remedies: the need to ensure judicial protection caused the Court to declare that national courts have an obligation to "regard an action [...] as admissible even if the domestic rules of procedure do not provide for this in such a case".[33]

In striking the balance along the lines indicated above, the prevailing aim is to ensure the supremacy of Community law. This was expressly stated in *Lucchini*,[34] in which it was held that a national final judgment could not prevent the recovery of State aid granted in breach of Community law. The Court – well aware that this stance may conflict with the principle of *res judicata* – clarified that the *res judicata* must be set aside only in so far as the State aid has been found to be incompatible with the common market by a decision of the European Commission that has become final. Hence, while, on the one hand, the *Lucchini* judgment seemed to mark a significant departure from the softer stance outlined above, on the other, it has to be considered in light of the very particular circumstances of the case, rather than offsetting a different – and more rigorous – approach. This resulted overtly by the subsequent ruling in *Olimpiclub*[35] where the Court clarified, as previously stated, that in *Lucchini* the matters at issue "were principles governing the division of powers between the Member States and the Community in the area of State aid, the Commission of the European Communities having exclusive competence to assess the compatibility with the common market of a national state aid measure" (para. 25).

The Court aims at balancing the need to respect *res judicata*, in accordance with a well-established principle in all national legal systems, with the obligation to comply with EU law even where a breach thereof arises from a national

[33] ECJ 3 December 1992, Case C-97/91, *Oleificio Borelli SpA v Commission of the European Communities* [1992] ECR I-6313, para 13.

[34] ECJ 18 July 2007, Case C-119/05, *Ministero dell'Industria, del Commercio e dell'Artigianato v Lucchini SpA* [2007] ECR I-6199.

[35] ECJ 3 September 2009, Case C-2/08, *Amministrazione dell'Economia e delle Finanze and Agenzia delle entrate v Fallimento Olimpiclub Srl, supra* note 13.

judgment. The most recent developments in the Court's case-law are therefore directed to striking the right balance between these two conflicting needs: on the one hand, the Court affirms that "Community law does not require that administrative bodies be placed under the obligation, in principle, to reopen an administrative decision which has become final",[36] and overtly acknowledges "the importance, both for the Community legal order and national legal systems, of the principle of *res judicata*".[37] On the other hand, the Court states that, when administrative authorities "are required to withdraw an administrative decision which become final if that decision is manifestly incompatible with domestic law, that same obligation must exist if the decision is manifestly incompatible with Community law".[38] National courts should be empowered "to review and set aside a final decision if that decision should be contrary to Community law" when they are "empowered under national law to reopen that decision".[39] Under this fresh approach the supremacy of EU law is ensured only when the national legal system allows, under certain circumstances, *res judicata* to be overcome. Thus, one may observe that the Court, in the end, admits that supremacy may be undermined to avoid the upset of a well-established principle of a national legal system.

## 4.2. UNIFORM APPLICATION OF EU LAW

A further ground which implies constraints to the procedural autonomy of the Member States stems from the need to attain uniform or harmonised protection of rights conferred by EU law in the national legal systems.[40] For instance, the objective of harmonisation pursued by a Directive could be undermined if weak protection was given to rights conferred under such legislation. All the more so when EU legislation establishes uniform rules, as usually occurs with Regulations. The Court said that Member States should provide for criminal penalties to punish breaches of the rights conferred by a Directive when this is necessary to ensure its effective application.[41] Similarly, procedural rules should guarantee

---

36 ECJ 19 September 2006, Joined Cases C-392/04 and C-422/04, *i-21 Germany GmbH (C-392/04) and Arcor AG & Co. KG (C-422/04) v Bundesrepublik Deutschland* [2006] ECR I-8559.

37 ECJ 16 March 2006, Case C-234/04, *Rosmarie Kapferer v Schlank & Schick GmbH* [2006] ECR I-2585, para. 20.

38 Joined Cases C-392/04 and C-422/04, *i-Germany and Arcor, supra* note 36, para. 69.

39 Case C-234/04, *Kapferer, supra* note 37, paras 23–24.

40 As expressed by former Advocate General Van Gerven, the need for harmonisation of procedural rules "is inherent in the concept of uniformity: in the absence of (sufficiently) harmonised legal remedies, uniform rights cannot be adequately secured throughout the Community": W. Van Gerven, 'Bridging the Gap between Community and National Laws: towards a Principle of Homogeneity in the Field of Legal Remedies?', (1995) 32 *CMLR* 690.

41 Cf., *inter alia*, ECJ 18 October 2001, Case C-354/99, *Commission* v *Ireland* [2001] ECR I-7657, para 46: "it should be noted that where a Community regulation does not specifically provide for any penalty for an infringement or refers for that purpose to national laws, regulations and administrative provisions, Article 5 of the Treaty requires the Member States to take all measures necessary to guarantee the application and effectiveness of Community law. For that

an effective protection of the rights conferred by a Directive so that the result pursued by the Directive is attained.

The link between effectiveness of procedural rules and effective implementation of Directives is clearly shown by the case of *Alassini*:[42] the Court observed that "it is admittedly true that making the admissibility of legal proceedings conditional upon the prior implementation of an out-of-court settlement procedure affects the exercise of rights conferred on individuals by the Universal Service Directive" (para. 52). According to this perspective, the duty to apply procedural rules which conform to the principle of effectiveness may be regarded as falling within the general obligation of Member States to comply with EU Treaties.

The lack of uniform application of EU law, for the reason that procedural rules in a given legal system preclude or hinder judicial protection, may first of all, as remarked above, give an undue advantage *vis-à-vis* the other Member States to the Member State which infringed its obligation.[43] In any case, the duty to implement a Directive cannot be regarded as fully complied with when effective judicial protection of the rights conferred under the same Directive is lacking. This reasoning arguably lies at the basis of the new Treaty provision referred to above (Article 19, para. 1, TEU).

Furthermore, the lack of uniform or harmonised procedural rules may undermine the protection of citizens causing discrimination on the basis of the dissimilar standards provided in the legal systems of the Member States,[44] and

purpose, while the choice of penalties remains within their discretion, they must ensure in particular that infringements of Community law are penalised under conditions, both procedural and substantive, which are analogous to those applicable to infringements of national law of a similar nature and importance and which, in any event, make the penalty effective, proportionate and dissuasive". Cf. also ECJ 21 September 1989, Case 68/88, *Commission* v *Greece* [1989] ECR 2965, paragraphs 23 and 24; ECJ 7 December 2000, Case C-213/99, *José Teodoro de Andrade v Director da Alfândega de Leixões, intervener: Ministério Público* [2000] ECR I-11083, para 19. For a similar reason the Court subsequently recognised that "when the application of effective, proportionate and dissuasive criminal penalties by the competent national authorities is an essential measure for combating serious environmental offences, the Community legislature may require the Member States to introduce such penalties in order to ensure that the rules which it lays down in that field are fully effective": ECJ 23 October 2007, Case C-440/05, *Commission* v *Council* [2007] ECR I-9097.

42 ECJ 18 March 2010, Joined Cases C-317/08, C-318/08, C-319/08 and C-320/08, *Rosalba Alassini v Telecom Italia SpA (C-317/08), Filomena Califano v Wind SpA (C-318/08), Lucia Anna Giorgia Iacono v Telecom Italia SpA (C-319/08) and Multiservice Srl v Telecom Italia SpA (C-320/08)*, *supra* note 23.

43 This was plainly held in the dated case *Commission* v *Italy* of 1973: in an infringement proceeding against Italy for non-implementation of the EC Regulation aimed at eliminating surpluses of certain products, the Court declared that "the Member State which omits to take, within the requisite time limits and simultaneously with the other Member States, the measures which it ought to take, undermines the efficacy of the provision decided upon in common, while at the same time *taking an undue advantage to the detriment of its partners* in view of the free circulation of goods": ECJ 7 February 1973, Case 39/72, *Commission* v *Italy* [1973] ECR 101, para 21 (emphasis added).

44 Compliance with the principle of effectiveness is seen also in light of the need for certainty to the benefit of the citizens: "a situation marked by significant legal uncertainty may involve a breach of the principle of effectiveness, because reparation of the loss or damage caused to

may even produce alteration in the functioning of the common market. One cannot exclude a sort of "forum shopping" on the part of companies, considering that the standards of protection provided in the Member States may be influential when choosing the place of investment. Indeed, one of the reasons for the harmonisation of procedural rules is that natural or legal persons should benefit from a uniform or similar judicial protection in different Member States. The opportunity to bring action in whatever Member State under uniform or similar procedural rules would certainly facilitate the judicial protection of natural and legal persons.[45]

## 4.3. THE FUNDAMENTAL RIGHT TO OBTAIN JUDICIAL PROTECTION

The fundamental right to effective judicial protection implies not only the availability of a judicial remedy (i.e. access to justice), but also that a certain degree of protection (i.e. *effective* protection) is guaranteed. The Court declared that the requirements of equivalence and effectiveness "embody the general obligation on the Member States to ensure judicial protection of an individual's rights under Community law. They apply both as regards the designation of the courts and tribunals having jurisdiction to hear and determine actions based on Community law and as regards the definition of detailed procedural rules".[46] Under the European Charter of Fundamental Rights, "Everyone whose rights and freedoms guaranteed by the law of the Union are violated has the right to an effective remedy before a tribunal in compliance with the conditions laid down in this Article" (Article 47).

Under both its meanings – that is access to justice and effectiveness of judicial protection – the fundamental right to obtain judicial protection may have a significant impact on national procedures. In reviewing national law under such a right, the Court not only requires that access to justice be ensured but also that certain qualitative standards of judicial protection be respected. Thus, a further reason that can help to explain the Court's approach, aimed at restraining the procedural autonomy of Member States, pertains to the need to ensure respect of a fundamental right in a domain falling within EU law.

This approach assumes that fundamental rights under EU law may at times confer a higher protection than that granted on the basis of national provisions.

individuals by breaches of Community law for which a Member State can be held responsible could be rendered excessively difficult in practice if the individuals were unable to determine the applicable limitation period with a reasonable degree of certainty": ECJ 24 March 2009, Case C-445/06, *Danske Slagterier* [2009] ECR I-2119, para 33.

45 Cf. J. Normand, 'Le rapprochement des procedures civiles dans l'Union européenne' (1998) 6 *European Private Law* 388.

46 ECJ 29 October 2009, Case C-63/08, *Virginie Pontin v T-Comalux SA* ECR I-10467, para 44.

A procedural rule which complies with national standards of protection could be inadequate to satisfy the requirements imposed by a fundamental right which is protected as a general principle of EU law. Yet in principle, the right to obtain judicial protection under the Charter of Fundamental Rights should have the same meaning as that in national legal systems. Actually, one should first consider that the Charter "contains rights and fundamental freedoms, the meaning and scope of those rights shall be the same as those laid down by the" European Convention on Human Rights (Article 52, para. 3); furthermore, all Member States are bound by this Convention. However, the Charter permits a more favourable treatment to be conferred in the EU legal system since the provision quoted above "shall not prevent Union law providing more extensive protection" (Article 52, para. 3). Thus, one cannot exclude that a different level of protection of a fundamental right may be required under domestic rules as opposed to under EU law, whether on the basis of the Charter or as a general principle enounced by the Court.

Member States are required to comply with general principles as construed by the Court when applying or implementing EU law and even in respect of national legislation falling within the scope of the Treaties. When national legislation implements EU law, the *ratio* for application of the European principles is hardly questionable; in contrast the criterion based on impingement of a national statute upon the scope of EU law leaves a very wide discretion to the ECJ. The link with the scope of EU law may sometimes appear rather thin, for example where a national provision indirectly restrains a fundamental freedom established by the Treaty. Furthermore, the scope of the Charter of Fundamental Rights may not cover such a hypothesis since under its Article 51 para. 1 the Charter is applied "to the Member States only when they are implementing Union Law".

The stance adopted by the Court after the entry into force of the Treaty of Lisbon is well illustrated by the recent decision in *Kücükdeveci*.[47] The Court decided that the fact that national legislation concerned an issue (i.e. conditions of dismissal) that was already touched upon by a Directive implied that such legislation had to be reviewed in light of European law principles.[48] In some previous cases the impact on the application of a Treaty provision (in the absence of an EC act) had been considered by the Court as a sufficient link for justifying the scrutiny of a national legislation under EU general principles. The assessment of such a link clearly implies an appraisal that may considerably vary according to the particular case in point. One may further consider that the Court would probably prefer to rely on principles rather than on the Charter because of the limitation stemming from Protocol No 30, according to which the Charter "does not extend the ability of the Court of Justice of the European Union or any Court or Tribunal of Poland or of the United Kingdom, to find that the laws, regulation

---

47 ECJ 19 January 2010, Case C-555/07, *Seda Kücükdeveci v Swedex GmbH & Co. KG* [2010] ECR I-365.

48 Cf. G. Thüsing and S. Horler, 'Case C-555/07 Seda Kücükdeveci v. Swedex Judgment of the Court of Justice (Grand Chamber) of 19 January 2010 nyr' (2010) 47 *CMLR* 1161.

or administrative provision, practices or action of Poland or of the United Kingdom are inconsistent with the fundamental rights freedoms and principle that it reaffirms". A similar solution was subsequently agreed in respect of Ireland and the Czech Republic.[49]

In order to ensure respect of the fundamental right to judicial protection, Member States may also be required to compensate, through national remedies, for the lack of remedies under the Treaties. The Court stated that, in order to ensure that this fundamental right is respected, a Member State should allow the review of national measures even when this would not otherwise be admitted in the given legal system.[50] As the Court declared in *Unibet*, although the EC Treaty "was not intended to create new remedies in the national courts to ensure the observance of Community law other than those already laid down by national law", nevertheless it "requires that the national legislation does not undermine the right to effective judicial protection".[51] The relationship between national remedies and those available under EU law was emphasised in *Unión de Pequeños Agricultores*[52] where the Court declared that "it is for the Member States to establish a system of legal remedies and procedures which ensure respect for the right to effective judicial protection" (para. 41); thus "national courts are required, so far as possible, to interpret and apply national procedural rules governing the exercise of rights of action in a way that enables natural and legal persons to challenge before the courts the legality of any decision or other national measure relative to the application to them of a Community act of general application, by pleading the invalidity of such an act" (para. 42).

The new criterion for bringing an annulment action established under the Treaty of Lisbon may apparently be framed in the pattern traced by the Court. The TFUE gives private applicants the *locus standi* to bring an action against "a regulatory act which is of direct concern to them and does not entail implementing measures"; therefore any natural or legal person may institute proceedings against such an act irrespective of the severe criterion of "individual concern". This entails that national remedies are implicitly recognised with some priority, assuming that when a redress is not available in national courts there should be greater *locus standi* to bring an action before the Court of Justice of the European Union. Thus, the new Treaty might give some support to the idea that respect of the fundamental right to judicial protection *vis-à-vis* EU legislation should be ascertained considering both national and EU legal systems. This solution may appear to be coherent with the approach taken by the Court which was referred

49 Cf. the Presidency conclusions of the European Council of 19 June 2009 and of 30 October 2009.

50 ECJ 3 December 1992, Case C-97/91, *Oleificio Borelli SpA v Commission of the European Communities* [1992] ECR I-6313.

51 ECJ 13 March 2007, Case C-432/05, *Unibet (London) Ltd and Unibet (International) Ltd v Justitiekanslern* [2007] ECR I-2271, paragraphs 40–42.

52 ECJ 25 July 2002, Case C-50/00, *Unión de Pequeños Agricultores v Council of the European Union* [2002] ECR I-6677.

to above; however, one should consider that in the Court's view the need for compensating the rigorous conditions to challenge EU legislation before the Court of Justice was aimed at avoiding the violation of a fundamental right in the absence of a reform of the Treaty. Instead, under the TFEU, a greater opportunity to challenge acts before EU Courts would be reasonable, considering that when a redress is sought from a national court the uniform application of EU law may be undermined because of different standards of protection provided by domestic procedural rules.

In the Court's appraisal, a further degree of discretion derives from the balancing test usually applied when reviewing national laws in light of protection of fundamental rights. These rights are not regarded as "unfettered prerogatives"[53] but they may be restricted for the sake of objectives of general interest pursued by a given measure. So, when a national measure prejudices the respect of the principle of effective judicial protection the Court ascertains whether the measure may be justified, and if it is, verifies whether it conforms to the principle of proportionality. This scheme was recently applied to an Italian statute which made judicial review concerning the rights, conferred by the Universal Service Directive, conditional upon an attempt to settle the dispute out of court.[54] Such a measure restricted the principle of effective judicial protection but was regarded as justified because it pursued legitimate objectives in the general interest – namely, the need to provide quicker and less expensive settlement – and wasn't disproportionate in relation to the objective pursued.

## 5. A TENTATIVE PARADIGM TO EXPLAIN THE COURT'S UNSTEADY APPROACH IN ASSESSING ADEQUACY OF NATIONAL PROCEDURAL LAW

On the basis of the foregoing survey, one may note that the different *ratios* of the Court's rulings which led to a restriction of the procedural autonomy of Member States can help in explaining why, as remarked above, non-uniform approaches were often held in the ECJ case-law.

One may first of all observe that the Court's approach is shaped by the degree of substantive harmonisation that is attained in a certain area on the basis of EU legislation. The Court's view arguably seems more influenced by the degree of harmonisation actually achieved in a given sector than by the area of competence that is affected.[55] The fact that national rules of procedure are applied to ensure enforcement of EU legislation falling in a domain of concurrent competence or

53 *Alassini*, *supra* note 11, para. 63.

54 Ibidem.

55 Furthermore one may submit that the approach followed by the Court may be influenced by the area of EU law that is concerned. For instance, the Court seems to adopt a more severe stance in certain areas, such as competition law. I do not enter into details on such analysis

in an area of exclusive competence is not significant in that respect: the degree of harmonisation attained by EU legislation may indeed be very high also in areas of concurrent competence.[56] A minimum standard of protection by national procedural rules cannot be adequate to ensure application of EU legislation when this latter is aimed at attaining uniform or strongly harmonised solutions.[57] Furthermore the Court's attitude may evolve as EU legislation is adopted: national procedural rules may be required to satisfy more severe requirements when a higher level of substantive harmonisation is pursued by the EU law-maker. Thus, whenever the constraints on procedural autonomy of Member States reflect the need for uniform application of EU legislation one may expect a rather "intrusive" ruling by the Court, providing for a direct appraisal of adequacy of national procedural rules or giving sound guide to the referring court.

Furthermore, the Court arguably seems more rigorous when the supremacy of EU law is at stake, and does not hesitate in restraining even considerably the procedural autonomy of Member States. This is clearly shown by the rulings that actually lead to the principle of *res judicata* being overcome, so as to avoid the disregard of EU law. On the contrary the Court usually leaves to the national courts the task of assessing whether domestic procedures comply with EU principles – providing just general criteria – when only the *level* of judicial protection of legal or natural persons is at stake (as in *Sopropé*, referred to above). In these kinds of cases the Court seems satisfied with just a minimum standard, provided that protection is not completely excluded.[58] Such a stance may possibly be based

---

that is extensively conducted in this book by H.W. Micklitz, 'A judge-made European Law on Remedies? A plea for a more active ECJ'.

56 As firstly showed by the leading Case ECJ 5 April 1979, *Criminal proceedings against Tullio Ratti* 148/78 [1979] ECR 1629 where the Court emphasised that in an area of concurrent competence (free movement of goods) Member States could not enjoy any residual competence: "it is a consequence of the system introduced by Directive No 73/173 that a Member State may not introduce into its national legislation conditions which are more restrictive than those laid down in the Directive in question, or which are even more detailed or in any event different, as regards the classification, packaging and labelling of solvents...".

57 As was observed, whereas the rights conferred by EU law "are by definition uniform in substance" their enforcement should be "as efficient as possible and also as uniform as possible throughout the Community": W. van Gerven, 'On Rights, Remedies and Procedures' (2000) 37 *CMLR* 530.

58 E.g. the Court just required that a time-limit be fixed in advance and held that "Community law does not preclude the limitation period applicable to an action for damages against the State for incorrect transposition of a directive from beginning to run on the date on which the first injurious effects of the incorrect transposition have been produced and the further injurious effects thereof are foreseeable, even if that date is prior to the correct transposition of the directive"(*Danske Slagterier, supra* note 1, para. 56). The Court also declared that a total exclusion of loss of profit as a head of damage for which compensation may be awarded in the case of a breach of Community law cannot be accepted (ECJ 17 April 2007, Case C-470/03, *A.G.M.-COS.MET Srl v Suomen valtio and Tarmo Lehtinen* [2007] ECR I-2749, para 95); and held in *Ecotrade* that the principle of effectiveness is not infringed "merely because the tax authority has a longer period in which to recover unpaid value added tax than the period granted to taxable persons for the exercise of their right to deduct" (ECJ 8 May 2008, Joined Cases C-95/07 and C-96/07, *Ecotrade SpA v Agenzia delle Entrate – Ufficio di Genova 3* [2008] ECR 3457).

on the assumption that national provisions can adequately ensure respect of the fundamental right to effective judicial protection. One may suggest that in substance a constraint on national procedures operates when required, i.e. so that EU law is properly applied as opposed to guaranteeing a standard of protection higher than that established in a given Member State.

In principle, this suggestion gives support to the idea that fundamental rights are sometimes used as an instrument for containing the autonomy of Member States rather than for enhancing citizens' rights.[59] However, it may sometimes be difficult to detect what the actual purpose of a certain principle is and what are its effects. In guessing, one may figure out when a certain approach which produces enhancement of judicial protection is determined by the need to grant supremacy to EU law or is rather the effect of a higher standard of protection of a fundamental right. There is no sharp distinction between the rulings inspired by one or the other consideration: supremacy of EU law and the fundamental right to judicial protection often coexist in the case-law, and converge in requiring a certain standard of procedural law. In any event, one may argue that more often, it is the principle of supremacy of EU law that requires an enhancement of judicial protection rather than vice-versa. According to a pragmatic view, one may suggest that the aim of ensuring full compliance with EU obligations indirectly implies an enhancement of judicial protection: e.g. judicial protection would be improved where a national statute, one providing a restrictive i.e. a too short time-limit, be discarded in order to avoid a Member State taking advantage by its non fulfilment of EU law.

In spite of the strong reasons mentioned above justifying the Court's review of national procedural rules, in recent case-law the Court seems to more frequently leave the assessment to national courts, and is seemingly exploring techniques to ease the impact of EU law on national procedural rules. As referred above,[60] from *Kühne & Heitz* onwards[61] the Court has found a "softer" solution, declaring that the revision of a final act which violates EC (now EU) law is required only in the case that under national law the domestic bodies have competence to review a decision infringing national law.

This new approach may be construed as a consequence of the principle of equivalence and clearly offers the advantage of avoiding an upset of procedural rules under the national legal systems. It respects the balance between different principles currently in play in the national legal system in question. In the absence of a legislative framework, the recourse to the said solution, in refraining from "forcing" the national legal systems too much, may arguably prevent criticism concerning excessive judicial activism of the Court. However, the solution

---

59 Cf. in this book D. Schieck, 'The European Court of Justice and the Autonomy of Member States – Fundamental Rights'. Cf. also J. Coppel and A. O'Neill, 'The European Court of Justice: Taking Rights Seriously' (1992) 29 *CMLR* 669.

60 See para 5 above.

61 A similar stance results from *i-21 Germany and Arcor, supra* note 1.

is unsatisfactory in so far as it leads to a non-uniform protection of the rights conferred by EU law, when different procedural rules are applied in the various Member States. One might thus argue that this approach counters the aim of ensuring a certain homogeneity among the procedural rules applied in Member States as it precludes the attainment of a "uniform" protection of the rights conferred on citizens by EU law. Therefore, this stance may be regarded as an expression of an attitude of judicial self-restraint by the Court.[62]

## 6. CONCLUSION

The approach taken by the Court in restricting the procedural autonomy of Member States has led to the avoidance of major differences in the protection of EU rights throughout the European Union, and has also resulted in a certain degree of convergence of national judicial provisions, despite the absence of EU legislation aimed at harmonising national rules of procedure. Thus, the old pattern, according to which judicial activism aims at compensating for legislative inertia, seems to still be alive insofar as national rules of procedure are concerned. Indeed one may argue that judicial activism has compensated for the absence of legislation ensuring effective and uniform application of EU law, as well as respect of fundamental rights in the EU legal system. However, as suggested above, judicial activism cannot ensure certainty because of the limits embedded in the judicial function, in spite of the efforts often made by the Court to state in general terms the requirements that procedural rules should comply with. This effort is well illustrated in *Kühne & Heitz* where the Court tried to set forth all the conditions that may justify the overcoming of the principle of *res judicata* by establishing a detailed set of requirements. These efforts risk to produce poor results in presence of national procedural rules that show very significant differences, since the judicial outcome concerning a certain national system is unlikely to be transposed to another.[63]

In any case, the review of national procedural rules in light of the principle of effectiveness undoubtedly produces a minimum level of indirect harmonisation. The case-law of the Court gives support to the emerging of a "common procedure", by favouring indirect and spontaneous harmonisation of national rules through the means of minimum standards of protection. This effect may be increased because of the need, referred to above, to prevent reverse discrimination or, under

[62] X. Groussot and T. Minssen, 'Res judicata in the Court of Justice Case-Law: Balancing Legal Certainty with Legality?' (2007) 3 *European Constitutional Law Review* 401.

[63] As Advocate General Tizzano considered in his conclusions in *Kapferer* the solution reached in *Kühne & Heitz* could not simply be transposed to the different situation of *Kapferer* since the principle held in *Kühne & Heitz* was concerned only with the reviewability of a final administrative decision adopted in breach of Community law while in *Kapferer* the different issue involving the principle of *res judicata* was at stake (Opinion delivered on 10 November 2005, Case C-234/04, *Rosmarie Kapferer v Schlank & Schick GmbH* [2006] ECR I-2585, para 25).

a more general perspective, to avoid practical disadvantages stemming from a two-tier system.[64]

Finally, the Court has smoothed the way for the EU legislator,[65] favouring, through the shaping of minimum standards of protection, possible attempts to harmonise national procedural rules as far as this is needed to ensure enforcement of EU law.[66] More than thirty years ago, in *Rewe-Zentralfinanz,* the Court urged the Member States to adopt EC procedural legislation, and even specified the legal basis that should have been used.[67] The revised Treaties could give a more solid foundation for such an attempt.[68]

64 The shortcomings stemming from the existence of different sets of procedural rules as to administrative authorities are pointed out by J. Schwarze, *European Administrative Law*, Sweet & Maxwell, London, 2006.

65 Cf. on that issue see C.N. Kakouris (*supra* note 2, 1395) who drew from the case law of the Court an implicit support for the adoption of a "harmonised system of procedural law by means of secondary law" based on the EC Treaty pre-Amsterdam.

66 Pursuant to a request of the Commission, a group of jurists presented in 1994 a draft European Judicial Code: M. Storme (ed.), *Approximation of Judiciary Law in the European Union*, Kluwer, Dordrecht, 1994. However an attempt to accomplish a comprehensive codification of procedural rules seems a very difficult task; whilst the harmonisation of the procedural rules which are most significant for the enforcement of EU law would seem a more feasible purpose. Furthermore, a comprehensive codification would not be a decisive solution with regard to effective enforcement of EU law: as remarked by Kakouris (*supra* note 2, 1411–1412) "Community law has its own particular needs", thus "even after harmonisation has been introduced there will still be procedural rules requiring to be adapted to the needs of substantive Community law".

67 The Court, implicitly regretting the absence of EC legislation, has paved the way declaring that "Where necessary, articles 100 to 102 and 235 of the Treaty, enable appropriate measures to be taken to remedy differences between the provisions laid down by law, regulation or administrative action in Member States if they are likely to distort or harm the functioning of the common market" (para 5).

68 One might construe an EU implied power founded on the argument that harmonisation of certain domestic rules of procedure is instrumental to the enforcement of EU legislation: in short, the competence to harmonise procedural rules may be regarded as implied by the need to ensure that EU law is correctly applied. A similar reasoning led the Court to establish an EC competence to adopt criminal penalties (ECJ 13 September 2005, Case C-176/03, *Commission v Council* [2005] ECR I-7879). The new Article 19, para. 1, TEU, quoted above, may be regarded as the first codified expression of this need: it does not provide for a legal basis but would certainly contribute in justifying an action based on Article 352 TFUE. Furthermore, the new wording of Article 352 (that abandons the reference to the attainment of the common market used in the former Article 308 EC Treaty) may strengthen such a possibility as it allows the adoption of an action provided that this "should prove necessary within the framework of the policies defined in the Treaties".

# WHY THERE IS NO PRINCIPLE OF "PROCEDURAL AUTONOMY" OF THE MEMBER STATES

Michal Bobek

## 1. INTRODUCTION

This article offers a critical look at the dual requirement of equivalence and effectiveness and at the notion of "procedural autonomy" of the Member States in the area of procedures and remedies for the enforcement of EU law based rights before the Member States′ courts. The first part of this article (points 2, 3 and 4) gives a short introduction into the case law and into some doctrinal views concerning the requirements of equivalence and effectiveness. The second part of the article (points 5 and 6) critically examines these requirements, arguing that their simultaneous use is illogical, unpredictable and misleading and that it should be reconsidered. Finally, it is explained why, in the current state of EU law, there is no such principle as "procedural autonomy" of the Member States in the area of enforcement of EU law based rights on the national level.

## 2. THE ORTHODOXY

In the absence of EU law provisions, the enforcement of EU law on the national level is governed by the institutional and procedural rules of the Member States. The EU reliance on the national procedures is, however, made subject to two conditions: equivalence and effectiveness. *Equivalence* requires that the Member State shall not discriminate between claims based on national law and claims arising out of EU law: the judicial or legislative treatment of the latter shall not be less favourable than the treatment of the former. *Effectiveness* seeks to prevent the situation in which the national procedural rules would make the enforcement of EU law based rights impossible or excessively difficult. In such cases, the Court of Justice asks the national courts to go beyond simple equivalence and to make a particular type of procedure or remedy available. The combination of the absence of EU law procedural provisions and the dual requirement of equivalence and effectiveness are often labelled as the principle of "procedural autonomy" of the

Member States, which governs, as a certain default rule, the enforcement of EU law before national courts.

A classic statement of these requirements can be found in the *Rewe* and *Comet* cases from December 1976: "*[...] in the absence of Community rules on this subject, it is for the domestic legal system of each Member State to designate the courts having jurisdiction and to determine the procedural conditions governing actions at law intended to ensure the protection of the rights which citizens have from the direct effect of Community law, it being understood that such conditions cannot be less favourable than those relating to similar actions of a domestic nature [...] the position would be different only if the conditions and time-limits made it impossible in practice to exercise the rights which the national courts are obliged to protect.*"[1]

In later case law, the second requirement of effectiveness was extended as not to include just situations where the enforcement of EU law would be merely impossible, but as to cover also situations in which national procedural rules would make the enforcement of EU law based rights more difficult. Such a "consolidated" statement of the requirements can be found for instance in the *Brasserie* decision: "*In the absence of relevant Community provisions, it is for the domestic legal system of each Member State to set the criteria for determining the extent of reparation. However, those criteria must not be less favourable than those applying to similar claims based on domestic law and must not be such as in practice to make it impossible or excessively difficult to obtain reparation.*"[2]

---

1 ECJ 16 December 1976, Case 33/76, *Rewe-Zentralfinanz eG and Rewe-Zentral AG v. Landwirtschaftskammer für das Saarland* [1976] ECR 1989, para 5, since then repeated in dozens of cases, e.g. ECJ 16 December 1976, Case 45/76, *Comet BV v Produktschap voor Siergewassen* [1976] ECR 2043, para 13; ECJ 28 September 1994, Case C-128/93, *Geertruida Catharina Fisscher v Voorhuis Hengelo BV and Stichting Bedrijfspensioenfonds voor de Detailhandel* [1994] ECR I-4583, para 39; ECJ 6 December 1994, Case C-410/92, *Elsie Rita Johnson v Chief Adjudication Officer* [1994] ECR I-5483, para 21; ECJ 23 November 1995, Case C-394/93, *Gabriel Alonso-Pérez v Bundesanstalt für Arbeit* [1995] ECR I-4101, para 28; ECJ 11 December 1997, Case C-246/96, *Mary Teresa Magorrian and Irene Patricia Cunningham v Eastern Health and Social Services Board and Department of Health and Social Services* [1997] ECR I-7153, para 37; ECJ 16 May 2000, Case C-78/98, *Preston* [2000] ECR I-3201, para 31; ECJ 22 February 2001, Joined Cases C-52/99 and C-53/99, *Office national des pensions (ONP) v Gioconda Camarotto (C-52/99) and Giuseppina Vignone (C-53/99)* [2001] ECR I-1395, para 21; ECJ 13 March 2007, Case C-432/05, *Unibet (London) Ltd and Unibet (International) Ltd v Justitiekanslern* [2007] ECR I-2271, para 39; ECJ 15 April 2008, Case C-268/06, *Impact v Minister for Agriculture and Food and Others* [2008] ECR I-2483, para 44; ECJ 6 October 2009, Case C-40/08, *Asturcom Telecomunicaciones SL v Cristina Rodríguez Nogueira* [2009] ECR I-09579, para 41.

2 ECJ 5 March 1996, Joined Cases C-46/93 and C-48/93, *Brasserie du Pêcheur SA v. Bundesrepublik Deutschland and the Queen v Secretary of State for Transport, ex parte: Factortame Ltd and others* [1996] ECR I-1029, para 83.

## 3. THE CASES

The test to which national procedural rules are made subject, i.e. the dual requirement of equivalence and effectiveness, has been repeated in a mantra-like style for the last thirty years or so. In spite of the fact that the test remained the same, the results that the Court of Justice reached while (at least facially) applying the same test diverged considerably over time.

As far as the scope of the principle was concerned, the Court held in 1981 that "*[...] although the EEC Treaty has made it possible in a number of instances for private persons to bring a direct action, where appropriate, before the Court of Justice, it was not intended to create new remedies in the national courts to ensure the observance of Community law other than those already laid down by national law.*"[3] In 1990, however, the full effectiveness of EU law required that a new remedy must be created in national law, namely the power to grant an interim relief.[4]

Similarly in 1973, state liability for infringement of EU law was made dependent exclusively on the relevant national provisions of each of the Member States.[5] In 1991, the full effectiveness of EU law required there to be a harmonised set of conditions for state liability triggered by the failure to implement EU law.[6]

In 1991, EU law did not require Member States' courts to raise points of EU law of their own motion; it just stated that EU law does not preclude a national court from doing so if it chooses to.[7] In 1995, in some cases, EU law still did not require Member States' courts to abandon their passive position,[8] in others it did.[9] In 1999, in matters of competition law,[10] national courts became obliged to raise EU law points of their own motion, even if national law does not allow for this. Since

---

3 ECJ 7 July 1981, Case 158/80, *Rewe-Handelsgesellschaft Nord mbH and Rewe-Markt Steffen v. Hauptzollamt Kiel* [1981] ECR 1805, para 44.

4 ECJ 19 June 1990, Case C-213/89, *The Queen v. Secretary of State for Transport, ex parte: Factortame Ltd and others* [1990] ECR I-2433, paras 19 – 23.

5 Case 60/75, *Carmine Antonio Russo v. Azienda di Stato per gli interventi sul mercato agricolo* [1976] ECR 45, para 9.

6 Joined Cases C-6/90 and C-9/90, *Andrea Francovich and Danila Bonifaci and others v. Italian Republic* [1991] ECR I-5357, para 33.

7 Joined Cases C-87/90, C-88/90 and C-89/90, *A. Verholen and others v. Sociale Verzekeringsbank Amsterdam* [1991] ECR I-3757, paras 15 and 16.

8 ECJ 14 December 1995, Joined Cases C-430/93 and C-431/93, *Jeroen van Schijndel and Johannes Nicolaas Cornelis van Veen v. Stichting Pensioenfonds voor Fysiotherapeuten* [1995] ECR I-4705. See also ECJ 24 October 1996, Case C-72/95, *Aannemersbedrijf P.K. Kraaijeveld BV e.a. v. Gedeputeerde Staten van Zuid-Holland* [1996] ECR I-5403 and Joined Cases C-222/05 to C-225/05, *J. van der Weerd and others* [2007] ECR I-4233.

9 ECJ 14 December 1995, Case C-312/93, *Peterbroeck, Van Campenhout & Cie SCS v. Belgian State* [1995] ECR I-4599.

10 ECJ 1 June 1999, Case C-126/97, *Eco Swiss China Time Ltd v. Benetton International NV* [1999] ECR I-3055, para 36.

2000, the same duty applies in consumer matters,[11] recently expanding also into enforcement proceedings.[12]

As far as the duty to revisit final decisions incompatible with EU law is concerned, in 1999, there was no such duty. National administrative authorities were just obliged to disapply, for the future, previously adopted administrative acts which later turned out to be incompatible with EU law.[13] In 2004, the requirement of effective protection of individual rights amounted to the duty to reopen final national decisions provided that the administrative authority had such powers under national law.[14] In 2006, the principle was interpreted as not requiring from national courts to reopen final judicial decisions incompatible with EC law.[15] Just a year later, in 2007, the same principle meant the opposite.[16] In 2008, the Court of Justice appears to be retreating somewhat, perhaps heading back to the position originally announced in 2004.[17]

A great number of other examples from the case law of the Court of Justice could be mentioned here, concerning standing, burden of proof, time limits and their lapse and other issues in civil, administrative or criminal procedures.[18] Similar trends can also be found in other areas of national procedures, which do not directly concern the dual requirement of equivalence and effectiveness. One

---

11 ECJ 27 June 2000, Joined Cases C-240/98 to C-244/98, *Océano Grupo Editorial SA v. Roció Murciano Quintero and others* [2000] ECR I-4941; ECJ 21 November 2002, Case C-473/00, *Cofidis SA v. Jean-Louis Fredout* [2002] ECR I-10875; ECJ 26 October 2006, Case C-168/05, *Elisa María Mostaza Claro v. Centro Móvil Milenium SL* [2006] ECR I-10421; ECJ 4 June 2009, Case C-243/08, *Pannon GSM Zrt. v Erzsébet Sustikné Győrfi* [2009] ECR I-04713.

12 ECJ 6 October 2009, Case C-40/08, *Asturcom Telecomunicaciones SL v Cristina Rodríguez Nogueira* [2009] ECR I-09579.

13 See, e. g. ECJ 29 April 1999, Case C-224/97, *Erich Ciola v. Land Vorarlberg* [1999] ECR I-2517; ECJ 7 January 2004, Case C-201/02, *The Queen on the application of Delena Wells and Secretary of State for Transport, Local Government and the Regions* [2004] ECR I-723.

14 ECJ 13 January 2004, Case C-453/00, *Kühne & Heitz NV and Productschap voor Pluimvee en Eieren* [2004] ECR I-837.

15 ECJ 16 March 2006, Case C-234/04, *Rosmarie Kapferer v. Schlank & Schick GmbH* [2006] ECR I-2585.

16 ECJ 18 July 2007, Case C-119/05, *Ministero dell'Industria, del Commercio e dell'Artigianato v. Lucchini SpA* [2007] ECR I-6199.

17 ECJ 12 February 2008, Case C-2/06, *Willy Kempter KG v. Hauptzollamt Hamburg-Jonas* [2008] ECR I-411 and ECJ 3 September 2009, Case C-2/08, *Amministrazione dell'Economia e delle Finanze and Agenzia delle entrate v. Fallimento Olimpiclub Srl* [2009] ECR I-07501.

18 See e.g. M. Eliantonio, *Europeanization of Administrative Justice? The Influence of the ECJ's Case Law in Italy, Germany and England*, Europa Law Publishing, Groningen, 2009; J. H. Jans, R. de Lange, S. Prechal, R. Widdershoven, *Europeanisation of Public Law*, Europa Law Publishing, Groningen, 2007; T. Tridimas, *The General Principles of EC Law*, 2nd Ed, Oxford University Press, Oxford, 2006; M. Dougan, *National Remedies Before the Court of Justice*, Hart, Oxford, 2004; J. Lonbay, A. Biondi (eds.), *Remedies for Breach of EC Law*, John Wiley & Sons, Chichester, 1997; M. Tonne, *Effektiver Rechtsschutz durch staatliche Gerichte als Forderung des Europäischen Gemeinschaftsrechts*, Carl Heymanns Verlag, Köln, 1997; T. Von Danwitz, *Verwaltungsrechtliches System und Europäische Integration*, Mohr (Paul Siebeck), Tübingen, 1996.

of the recent examples is the national procedural framework for preliminary rulings, more precisely the national rules on appeals against a decision to submit a request for a preliminary ruling. In 1962[19] as well as in 1974,[20] EU law did not raise any objections to the order for a preliminary ruling submitted to the Court of Justice by the referring national court from remaining subject to the remedies normally available under national law, typically to an appeal to a higher court. In 2008,[21] however, without any change in the Treaties or any other procedural framework in EU law itself, the referring judge can no longer be bound by the issue of a possible appeal against an order to refer, as this would impede the effective communication between the Court of Justice and lower national courts.[22]

## 4. THE THEORIES

There is no shortage of theories which seek to conceptualise what the Court of Justice has been doing in the area of review of national procedures and remedies. Some of them focus on the general evolution of the law in the area of remedies, others more concretely on the test(s) the Court of Justice should be using when reviewing national procedural rules. Some of them are descriptive, other more prescriptive. To mention just a few:

M. Dougan suggested that there are three periods in the case law of the Court of Justice reviewing national procedures and remedies: the initial deference to the national remedies in 1970 and 1980 was followed a middle period in 1990 which was characterised by a more assertive approach by the Court as far as the Community remedial competence was concerned. The case law in the new millennium would retreat somewhat back to the (limited) negative approximation.[23] T. Tridimas[24] concurred in dividing the case law of the Court in the three periods, with noticing, however, that the most recent case law of the Court[25] may suggest another resurgence of interventionism.

---

19 ECJ 6 April 1962, Case 13/61, *De Geus v. Bosch* [1962] ECR 45.

20 ECJ 27 March 1974, Case 127/73, *Belgische Radio en Televisie v SV SABAM and NV Fonior* [1974] ECR 251 and ECJ 12 February 1974, Case 146/73, *Rheinmühlen-Düsseldorf v. Einfuhr- und Vorratsstelle für Getreide und Futtermittel* [1974] ECR 139.

21 ECJ 16 December 2008, Case C-210/06, *Cartesio Oktató és Szolgálbató bt* [2008] ECR I-09641.

22 Critically see M. Bobek, Cartesio – 'Appeals Against an Order to Refer under Article 234(2) EC Treaty revisited', (2010) 29 *Civil Justice Quarterly* 307.

23 M. Dougan, *National Remedies Before the Court of Justice*, Hart, Oxford, 2004, pp 227–233.

24 T. Tridimas, *The General Principles of EC Law*, Oxford University Press, Oxford, 2nd ed, 2006, pp 420–422.

25 Quoting in this respect ECJ 9 December 2003, Case C-129/00, *Commission v. Italy* [2003] ECR I-14637 and ECJ 30 September 2003, Case C-224/01, *Gerhard Köbler v. Republik Österreich* [2003] ECR I-10239.

It was especially in the "middle" period following the Court's decision in *Van Schijndel* that the case law of the Court in this area came under closer scrutiny and a number of conceptions what the Court is doing in terms of the actual test emerged. *Van Schijndel* was hailed as the introduction of the "procedural rule of reason",[26] which would allow for institutionalised balancing between the interests of the Community and the procedural interests of the Member States. The balancing would involve a type of proportionality argument, which would institutionalise the balancing of the need for effective application of Community law on the national level on the one hand and various legitimate Member States′ interest on the other.[27]

There would be also no shortage of normative visions, arguing either that the Court of Justice would be going too far and thus upsetting the "relationship of cooperation" between itself and the national courts[28] or, conversely, that it is doing too little and that it should adopt a fully-fledged harmonisation agenda in the area of national procedural laws. [29]

Unfortunately, the case law of the Court of Justice in this area resists any conceptualisation. The area is vast and its various segments move at different speed. One may agree that the beginning of the nineties was the dawn of a more assertive approach by the Court of Justice towards national procedures. The Court started to harmonise positively some areas of remedies, replacing possible national regimes with a unified EU one. It is hard, however, to detect any genuine "retreat" in the case law of the Court ever since.

The changes in case law in the area of procedures and remedies tend to be spasmodic; there would typically be the first case announcing a broad and bold new principle. Some commentators would greet the new principle as yet another evidence of the strong integrative drive by the Court; others would be shocked and fear yet another inroad into the Member States' "procedural autonomy". The real important cases are, however, the second and third "wave" ones, which qualify and lay down the genuinely applicable principles. They tend to be more moderate,

---

26 S. Prechal, 'Community Law in National Court: the Lessons from Van Schijndel', (1998) 35 *CMLR (Common Market Law Review)* 681, at p 690 and 691.

27 G. De Búrca, 'National Procedural Rules and Remedies: the Changing Approach of the Court of Justice', in J. Lonbay and A. Biondi (eds.) *Remedies for Breach of EC Law,* John Wiley & Sons, Chichester, 1997, pp 37–46.

28 E.g. A. Biondi, 'The European Court of Justice and Certain National Procedural Limitations: Not such a tough Relationship', (1999) 36 *CMLR* 1271.

29 Writings of W. van Gerven represent an illustrious example of the latter approach. See, most notably, W. Van Gerven, 'On Rights, Remedies and Procedures', (2000) 37 *CMLR* 501, where the author suggested a differentiated approach by the Court of Justice depending on the fact whether the case would concern remedies, rights or procedures. But see also W. van Gerven, 'Bridging the Gap Between Community and National Law: Towards a Principle of Homogeneity in the Field of Legal Remedies?', (1995) 32 *CMLR* 679.

qualifying and narrowing the previous potentially too broad a principle. Looking into the second waves, one would realise, for instance, that despite the bold decision in *Francovich*,[30] Mr Francovich in the end never received any damages from the Italian government;[31] that *Emmott*[32] is a very narrow case applicable only when the government misleads or deceits the individual;[33] so is *Levez*[34] in private law relationships; and that *Lucchini*[35] is actually about misuse of powers and gross illegality on the part of the government, not about any destruction of the *res iudicata* principle[36] etc.

The fact that, for a few years, there would be no such "great" head-case which would break the news does not mean that the Court became less active. A lot is happening in the second and third waves, which may not only narrow, but also enlarge the scope of the previous case law. However, as these appear to be already "explored" areas, they may not stir that much attention, even though their impact might be greater than that one of the original case. Additionally, the case law on domestic procedures keeps spilling over into new areas and questions, previously untouched by EU law; the above mentioned issues of the duty to reopen final decisions incompatible with EU law and the extension of the duty to raise EU law issues of own motion being the most recent examples, where the case law has been created over the last few years. This could hardly be interpreted as any "retreat" and return to occasional negative harmonisation only.

Ever since the beginning of 1990, the case law can thus be said to be more or less constantly "progressive". What has been more problematic to decipher was the actual test the Court of Justice would be using in approaching the issues of national procedures and remedies. The above mentioned approaches, suggested by the doctrine, are all conceptually very sound; they just don't appear to be employed in

30 ECJ 19 November 1991, Joined Cases C-6/90 and C-9/90, *Andrea Francovich and Danila Bonifaci and others v. Italian Republic* [1991] ECR I-5357.

31 In subsequent litigation, it was found out that Mr. Francovich himself was actually not covered by the Directive. The EU law norm breached thus gave him no rights (the first condition of the *Francovich* liability) and he was therefore not entitled to any damages – see ECJ 9 November 1995, Case C-479/93, *Andrea Francovich v. Italian Republic* [1995] ECR I-3843.

32 ECJ 25 July 1991, C-208/90, *Theresa Emmott v. Minister for Social Welfare and Attorney General* [1991] ECR I-4269.

33 See ECJ 27 October 1993, Case C-338/91, *H. Steenhorst-Neerings v. Bestuur van de Bedrijfsvereniging voor Detailhandel, Ambachten en Huisvrouwen* [1993] ECR I-5475; ECJ 6 December 1994, Case C-410/92, *Elsie Rita Johnson v. Chief Adjudication Officer* [1994] ECR I-5483; ECJ 2 December 1997, Case C-188/95, *Fantask A/S and others v. Industriministeriet (Erhvervministeriet)* [1997] ECR I-6783.

34 ECJ 1 December 1998, Case C-326/96, *B.S. Levez v. T.H. Jennings (Harlow Pools) Ltd.* [1998] ECR I-7835.

35 ECJ 18 July 2007, Case C-119/05, *Ministero dell'Industria, del Commercio e dell'Artigianato v. Lucchini SpA* [2007] ECR I-6199.

36 Case ECJ 3 September 2009, C-2/08, *Amministrazione dell'Economia e delle Finanze and Agenzia delle entrate v. Fallimento Olimpiclub Srl* [2009] ECR I-07501, para 25.

the judicial practice of the Court. The "balancing" or "proportionality" test which could be inferred from paragraph 19 in *Van Schijndel*,[37] would actually introduce a test different from the dual requirement of equivalence and effectiveness. The question would no longer be whether national procedural rules in question are equivalent and/or effective, but whether reasonable balance is struck between the (recognised and identified) legitimate interests of the European Union on the one hand and those of the Member State(s) on the other.[38]

The Court did not take this route; instead, it keeps employing, at least facially, the "standard" test of equivalence and effectiveness. One of the many problems of this test is that it internally contradicts itself and is almost impossible to conduct. Consequently, the Court is not really using it and the genuine test carried out is a sort of "I-know-it-when-I-see-it" effectiveness test, which, depending on the drafting of the question, other materials before the Court and the composition of the respective chamber, can result in declaring a time limit of 2 years incompatible with EU law one day and, in quite similar factual circumstances, in approving of a 1 year time limit two weeks later.

## 5. THE REQUIREMENTS

Let us explain why the dual test of equivalence and effectiveness is internally inconsistent. For doing so, we will first look at each of the "prongs" of the test separately and then meditate on what their internal relationship might be.

### 5.1. EQUIVALENCE

The principle of equivalence is essentially a prohibition of discrimination between national law claims and European Union law claims; the treatment of the latter shall not be less favourable than that of the former as far as procedures are concerned. Direct as well as indirect discrimination would be covered, i.e. not just situations where the fact that a claim is an EU law based claim would be the reason for different treatment but also cases, in which another, facially neutral criterion for differentiated treatment would be used, which would, however, as applied, disproportionately disadvantage EU law based claims.

---

[37] And paragraph 14 in *Peterbroeck*, albeit one may wonder whether in *Peterbroeck*, such considerations were actually really employed, ECJ 14 December 1995, *Peterbroeck, Van Campenhout & Cie SCS v Belgian State* [1995] ECR I-04599.

[38] As actually suggested by AG Jacobs in his Opinion to *Van Schijndel* case (Opinion of 15 June 1995, *Jeroen van Schijndel and Johannes Nicolaas Cornelis van Veen v Stichting Pensioenfonds voor Fysiotherapeuten* [1995] I-04705) and also in an extra-judicial piece 'Enforcing Community Rights and Obligations in National Courts: Striking the Balance', in J. Lonbay, A. Biondi (eds.), *Remedies for Breach of EC Law*, John Wiley & Sons, Chichester, 1997, pp 25–36.

In order to carry out such a test of equivalence, one must compare. What is needed is a comparison between an EU law claim procedural regime and a procedural regime for a similar domestic claim(s). These are the points of comparison: the purely national and the EU law regime. The aim of comparison is to contrast the procedural feasibility of both or more of these procedural regimes.

There are at least three issues which make such comparative exercise by the Court of Justice problematic.

Firstly, any comparison involves a value judgment about what is comparable. The choice of points of comparison is by its very nature subjective;[39] some common elements are highlighted, other are suppressed in order to carry out the comparison. This means, for the Court of Justice, to make choices about national law and, by its very nature, also interpret national law, a competence the Court of Justice does not have, at least facially.

The traditional division of work between the Court of Justice and the national courts was that the Court of Justice is not competent to interpret national laws: that is the matter for the national courts. This would be for instance also captured in the formulation of the preliminary rulings questions submitted to the Court: the question is not supposed to ask whether or not provision X of national statute Y is compatible with EU law, but rather whether a provision of EU law would allow for a generic national legislative scheme having such and such characteristics.[40] To a great extent, this is obviously just a façade. The national law of such and such characteristics is nothing else than the national statute in question. It is, however, a helpful façade. Not only does it enforce the impression of keeping the division of

39 For an introduction into these problems from theory of comparative law, see e.g. G.-R. de Groot, H. Schneider, 'Das Werturteil in der Rechtsvergleichung' in K. Boele-Woelki, et al (ed), *Comparability and Evaluation*, Martinus Nijhoff, Dordrecht, 1994, pp 53–68 and the references to literature contained therein.

40 A national court, which would submit a question concerning the interpretation of national law, would either see its question rephrased or, in the more unlucky scenario, rejected as inadmissible *ratione materiae*. An example of the first, more common scenario, in which the Court of Justice would rephrase the question, could for instance be provided already by the ECJ 5 February 1963, Case 26/62, *NV Algemene Transport- en Expeditie Onderneming van Gend & Loos v. Netherlands Inland Revenue Administration* [1963] ECR (English Special Edition) p 1, in which the second question originally submitted by the Dutch court read: "*Whether the application of an import duty of 8% to the import into the Netherlands by the applicant in the main action of ureaformaldehyde originating in the Federal Republic of Germany represented an unlawful increase within the meaning of article 12 of the EEC Treaty [...]*". The Court of Justice observed that it was not competent to answer such question, as it clearly concerns the interpretation of Dutch customs legislation and not the Treaty. It however went on and stated that "*However, the real meaning of the question put by the Tariefcommissie is whether, in law, an effective increase in customs duties charged on a given product as a result not of an increase in the rate but of a new classification of the product arising from a change of its tariff description contravenes the prohibition in article 12 of the Treaty.*", a question which the Court is entitled to answer.

work provided for by the Treaties. It also helps the pronouncements of the Court of Justice to be universally relevant: if stated in generic terms, they are not just limited to the legal situation in one Member State.

However, it is virtually impossible to stick to such a "generic" phrasing convention also when assessing the equivalence of the national procedural regime for enforcing EU law based claims with other national regimes. It would require conjuring a number of additional generic parallel "national" regimes, which would have such and such characteristics, an argumentative exercise which borders on the absurd. Alternatively, the Court of Justice is required to enter national laws and their interpretation, because before comparing, one must necessarily interpret first.

Secondly, the process of comparison requires there to be a suitable comparator on the national level, one which remains more or less at the same level of abstraction. With progressive harmonisation of various areas of national laws by the European Union, there are more and more legal regimes where the only claims made will be on the basis of EU law and a suitable national comparator is altogether missing. This would typically be the case of regimes which were newly created in the national legal system following the implementation of EU directives and where there was no similar national legislation before. The problem which arises is that there is no purely national claim with which the EU law one could be compared.

An example of such "missing comparator" is for instance a recent case[41] which concerned the question whether or not a time limit of 15 days from the date on which a working contract was terminated for bringing an action for annulment by a pregnant worker is compatible with EU law. The protection enjoyed by pregnant workers is, however, by now a harmonised field of law, having its national origins in the Pregnant Workers Directive.[42] The protection of pregnant workers in cases of dismissal is thus exclusively "European": there are no pregnant workers "according to national law" on the one hand and pregnant workers "according to European Union law" on the other. Should one wish to look for a potential comparator on the national level, one would have to leave the specific legal regime for pregnant workers altogether and to look, for instance, for similar regimes in other areas of anti-discrimination laws. The problem with these might, however, be just the same, as most of them would again be nothing else than harmonised EU legal regimes. The only remaining logical step would thus be to go many levels up in the abstraction, looking for general time limits in the national civil or

[41] ECJ 29 October 2009, Case C-63/08, *Virginie Pontin v. T-Comalux SA* [2009] ECR I-10467.

[42] Council Directive 92/85/EEC of 19 October 1992 on the introduction of measures to encourage improvements in the safety and health at work of pregnant workers and workers who have recently given birth or are breastfeeding, OJ L 348/1 of 28 November 1992.

labour law procedure, which in turn may be too far from the special regime and therefore hardly comparable with the specific protection for pregnant workers.[43]

Thirdly, the perhaps greatest problems for the Court of Justice in assessing the equivalence of national procedural rules are of practical nature. To carry out similar comparisons, one must have a very detailed knowledge of the national law, its various procedural regimes and their functioning. With all due respect to the Court, this will normally not be the case. The information on the national legal system in question will normally be framed by the preliminary ruling in question, which sometimes contains more, sometimes however less information on the national law, normally however limited to the case at hand. A horizontal or diagonal comparison of different legal regimes in the national law would require quantitatively more time and information.

To carry out detailed studies of Member States′ laws is finally hardly a task for the Court of Justice, not just from the practical, but also theoretical point of view. It serves to be mindful that once the yardstick is the equivalence with a comparable national procedural regime, the Court of Justice is in a way adjudicating within up to 27 parallel worlds. Should the Court therefore engage in the study of equivalence, for which it has, as a matter of fact, no mandate, no knowledge and which is, at the end of the day, only able to create 27 different disparate "standards"?

In view of the number of practical as well as conceptual problems with the principle of equivalence, it is perhaps not surprising that the Court of Justice only scarcely carries out such type of comparisons. In those cases, where comparisons are attempted, it will be because of an express invitation to this effect by the referring court. No real conceptual framework or test for such comparisons can be, however, found in the case law of the Court. There are few Opinions of Advocate Generals,[44] in which they sought to elaborate some general guidelines as to how to approach the application of the principle of equivalence. On the whole, however, if invoked, the principle of equivalence in the area of procedures

43 For other examples of the same problems, see e.g. ECJ 10 July 1997, Case C-261/95, *Rosalba Palmisani v. Istituto nazionale della previdenza sociale* [1997] ECR I-4025 or ECJ 1 December 1998, Case C-326/96, *B.S. Levez v. T.H. Jennings (Harlow Pools) Ltd.* [1998] ECR I-7835 and especially the Opinions of AGs in both cases.

44 See, *inter alia*, Opinion of AG Mancini, 27 September 1983, Case 199/82, *Amministrazione delle Finanze dello Stato v. SpA San Giorgio* [1983] ECR 3595; Opinion of AG Jacobs, 9 March 1995, Case C-62/93, *BP Soupergaz Anonimos Etairia Geniki Emporiki-Viomichaniki kai Antiprossopeion v. Greek State* [1995] ECR I-1883; Opinion of AG Cosmas, 10 July 1997, Case C-261/95, *Rosalba Palmisani v. Istituto nazionale della previdenza sociale* [1997] ECR I-4025; and Opinion of AG Léger, 1 December 1998, Case C-326/96, *B.S. Levez v. T.H. Jennings (Harlow Pools) Ltd.* [1998] ECR I-7835.

and remedies serves rather as a type of a shorthand message "I don't wish to deal with this (now)" and for referring the decision back onto the national level.

## 5.2. EFFECTIVENESS

The problem with the requirement of effectiveness is that it is not a legal "principle", as it has no internal limits. To be more precise: the "impossibility" reservation, which was originally the content of the effectiveness requirement, could be said to have certain shape. "Impossible" means impossible, i.e. a situation in which there is no standing, there is no claim, there is a zero time-limit. Once, however, the effectiveness was extended as to contain also situations in which the enforcement of EU law would be made excessively difficult or have a too dissuasive effect on the claimant, any internal limit within "effectiveness" fell. The above described suggestions for various balancing tests were in fact efforts to re-establish at least some internal limit to the shapeless "effectiveness", making it subject to the weighing with other interests, be it on European or national level. The full effectiveness of EU law is, unfortunately, an intolerant God, who does not have any sympathy with polytheists.

There are perhaps some limits to the claims made in the name of full effectiveness of EU law, but these are not of legal nature. They cannot be put in boxes of test or judicial algorithms. They are of political nature, constraining an institution only by what it believes might be permissible at a given moment and, eventually, by the acceptance of its decision by their addressees.

In the context of review of national procedural rules, it is not always evident what the requirement of effectiveness means in the particular case. Is effectiveness measured according to the protection guaranteed to an individual in a particular case, i.e. is it about the fate of the individual? Or is effectiveness a code name for a harmonised level of protection within the European Union, where only the same level of protection for all individuals within the Union can guarantee "effective" protection?

Both dimensions may overlap, they may, however, also part. They would part in cases of negative judicial harmonisation, where the Court would only state that, for instance, a 2 years time-limit in a Member State for bringing an action is ineffective and thus incompatible with EU law. Without giving much of further guidance, such decisions might provide justice in the individual case; they leave, however, a much differentiated level of protection in other Member States within the Union. Both dimensions may overlap in cases of positive harmonisation, i.e. where the Court would provide justice in the individual case and, at the same time, set a unified set of criteria for all Member States. There is, however, also a third scenario, in which the Court would positively harmonise but leave the individual without a remedy. These would be typically cases in which a grand new principle is announced and, at the same time or immediately afterwards, the principle is found not to be actually applicable to the individual who brought the action.[45]

In all of the scenarios described above, the requirement of (full) effectiveness of EU law would be used in order to justify the results reached; in each of the scenarios, effectiveness means a different thing.

## 5.3. THEIR RELATIONSHIP

The traditional perception[46] of the relationship between the two requirements would be one of a successive, two prong test. The Court of Justice would firstly ascertain whether or not the national law makes any distinction between the claims based on national and on EU law. Provided it does not make any such distinction, it would assess whether, additionally, the national procedural rules are not framed in the way as to render virtually impossible or excessively difficult the exercise of rights conferred by EU law. The effectiveness requirement would thus serve as a certain additional requirement, which may correct the outcome in cases where the national procedural regime for EU law based rights would be equal to that one for national claims, which would however mean equally deficient.[47]

The already mentioned *Factortame I*[48] case could serve as an example here: applied to this case, equivalence would mean the absence of any interim relief, as no one would be entitled to interim relief against the Crown in purely national cases before the English courts. It was the requirement of effectiveness which asked the Member State to go beyond mere equivalence and to create a new legal remedy.

Should such a vision of the relationship between both requirements be correct, then their relationship in terms of formal logic would be one-sided inclusion. The requirement of effectiveness would be a subset of equivalence, or, more precisely,

45 Apart from the *Francovich II* case quoted above (fn 31), another example of such scenario would be the *Köbler* decision (ECJ 30 September 2003, Case C-224/01, *Gerhard Köbler v. Republik Österreich* [2003] ECR I-10239), in which the principle of state liability is extended as to cover judicial breaches as well, but Mr. Köbler himself is not entitled to anything, as the breach was not "sufficiently serious".

46 See e.g. H. G. Schermers, D. F. Waelbroeck, *Judicial Protection in the European Union*, 6th ed, Kluwer Law International, The Hague, 2001, at p 199 and ff.

47 Thus preventing the classical problem of formal equality as just consistency without any substantive underpinning, which may results into "equally" meaning "equally bad". Further see e.g. S. Fredman, *Discrimination Law*, Oxford University Press, Oxford, 2002, at p 8 and f.

48 ECJ 19 June 1990, Case C-213/89, *The Queen v. Secretary of State for Transport, ex parte: Factortame Ltd and others* [1990] ECR I-2433.

the default set of equivalence would include a subset with the qualification of "ineffectiveness". If and only if a national rule is equivalent but ineffective, the requirement of effectiveness will be raised and the Member State will be asked to go beyond equivalence.

The case law of the Court of Justice cannot be, however, squeezed into such a mental image. In a growing number of cases, the Court does not deal with equivalence at all. It only asks itself whether the national rule is effective, i.e. whether it provides individuals with effective judicial protection of their EU law derived rights. This would in logical terms mean that there is a free standing set of "effectiveness" outside of the set of equivalence. This would in turn be confirmed by the already mentioned gradual extension of effectiveness, which includes not just situation of impossibility, but also growing number of cases where it is just "difficult", without there to be any reference to the national law.

The relationship between both requirements is thus different: it is no "and", as stated by the Court in the traditional formula, but rather "or", i.e. the logical relationship is no conjunction, but (inclusive) disjunction. The national rule may be found incompatible in cases when it is either not equivalent or it is not efficient or it is not equivalent as well as not efficient.

Such reading (and especially such practice) considerably expands the scope of review of national procedural rules.[49] However, the practice of the Court of Justice can only be reasonably conceptualised in these terms. More and more often, the Court would no longer address any issues of equivalence at all and would go directly to argue on the basis of effectiveness. Such approach can be said to be understandable; for various reasons explained above, the Court is ill-suited to assess the equivalence of EU law enforcement procedures with purely domestic procedures.

The problem is, however, that for such mental exercise the Court still uses a formula devised some thirty years ago, which not only contains internal contradictions, but by now no longer reflects the type of review the Court is actually carrying out at all. The striking difference between what the Court claims it is doing and what it actually is doing in turns invites more and more criticism against the Court for creating an inconsistent mass of case law, which does not respect the "procedural autonomy" of the Member States.

---

[49] Which, in a way, is not that surprising; as in other areas of the case law, language and formal logic cannot withstand the full effectiveness of EU law – cfr. for instance the interpretation of "or" as in "*lump sum or penalty payment*" into an "and" in the context of Article 228 EC [Article 260 TFEU] in ECJ 12 July 2005, Case C-304/02, *Commission v. France* [2005] ECR I-6263. Such an exercise is, in terms of formal logic at least, relatively easy, as an unspecified "or" might be an exclusive as well as inclusive disjunction.

# 6. THE MISUNDERSTANDING

Much of the critique against the Court for what it has been doing in the area of national procedures and remedies is based on a misunderstanding. The reasons for it are varied.

One reason is on the side of the Court of Justice. As we have already seen, in the area of remedies and procedures, it is actually doing something else than it claims to be doing. While using the above analysed standard formula of equivalence and effectiveness, it tends more and more just to review only whether or not national rules are effective or more likely adequate. Equivalence is little employed. However, both criteria are still connected by an "and" and appear that they are to be used every time.

This creates internal contradictions in the test, renders its use very unpredictable in the practice and creates false impressions. The contradiction is what S. Prechal aptly called the "*Rewe/Simmenthal contradiction*".[50] The initial deferential approach, which would favour equivalence and which was announced in *Rewe*, is still part of the test. However, the intrusive *Simmenthal* effectiveness vision was also added and gradually expanded: from impossibility to difficulty. If one would take the test on the face value and claim that the relationship between both requirements is a conjunction, than it is indeed contradictory, as both prongs of the test cannot be employed at the same time without pushing into completely different directions: equivalence towards the Member States′ national regime, effectiveness towards an harmonised Euro-standard.

The ensuing judicial practice is, unfortunately, a mess. Even a specialist in the area has no idea which one of the two requirements will the Court pull out of the hat: will it be "just" equivalence, which would typically mean that the national measure will "survive" the test, or will it be effectiveness, which in turn typically means that it will not.

On the other hand, it is fair to admit that the uncertainty as to the standard employed is only short- or middle-term one. In the long term, the tendency is quite clear; as can be seen from the few examples listed by way of passing reference above, in part 3, the overall harmonising tendency is evident. It may not progress in all areas at the same speed; there might also be instances of three steps ahead and two steps back. Gradually, the requirement of effectiveness takes nonetheless over in all areas.

---

[50] S. Prechal, 'Community Law in National Court: the Lessons from Van Schijndel' (1998) 35 *CMLR* 681, at 687.

The misunderstanding is also due to a part of the doctrine, which maintains that there is "procedural autonomy" of the Member States and, regularly after a new decisions of the Court where it leaned greater towards the requirement of effectiveness in detriment of a Member States′ procedural rule, starts asking itself whether there actually is anything left of the "procedural autonomy" of the Member States.

There is no such thing as "procedural autonomy" of Member States. An Oxford Dictionary defines the word "autonomy" as "*the ability to act and make decisions without being controlled by anyone else*".[51] The use of the term "autonomy" would thus imply that there are areas of procedural law in which the Member States are "free" from any EU law constraints, uncontrolled by the Court of Justice.

There are no such areas. Firstly, in the current constitutional set-up, there is no area of procedural law which would be a "*domaine réservé*" of the Member States, into which EU law could not reach. There is of course the constitutional principle of attributed competence of the European Union;[52] this principle, however, conditions only Union's legislative or administrative power of initial law-making. The way EU law reaches into national procedural rules is, however, very different: the (incidental) authority to reach into domestic procedure is dependent of the existence of EU substantive law or rights on the national level. Once this condition is satisfied, its reach is limitless. In other words, once there is a EU law based right which is to be enforced on the national level, its equivalent or effective enforcement covers all possible aspects of national procedure: from court fees, time-limits and standing via representation, burden of proof to appeals, enforcement and finality of the decision.

Secondly, the dual requirement of equivalence and effectiveness is omnipresent in all areas of national procedure, provided, as the Court of Justice mentions every time, that there are no relevant Community provisions on the subject. Whether, in the individual case, anyone bothers to ask herself whether or not, in the presence of EU law based claims, a national procedural rule actually is equivalent and/or efficient is a different question, which does not invalidate the normative vision of EU law requirements covering the entire space of domestic procedural rules in cases with EU law aspects.

To use, in such conditions, the term "procedural autonomy" creates a false impression, namely that in procedural matters, Member States are "autonomous" and that any judicial activity of the Court of Justice in this field is actually a "trespass" onto the autonomy of the Member States. Quite the opposite is actually

51 *Oxford Advanced Learner's Dictionary*, Oxford University Press, Oxford, 2005, p 85.
52 Newly fleshed out in a greater detail in Articles 2–6 TFEU.

true: in the areas of domestic enforcement of EU law, the area is either harmonised or the Member States are obliged to ensure the enforcement is equivalent and/or effective. In this area, there is no autonomous space of the Member States.

A lot obviously depends on how one defines "autonomy". It could suggest that the above use of a dictionary definition is unduly narrow and that one could also employ the term "procedural autonomy" in a more "softer" sense, just as a convenient nickname for the default rule that the primary shaping of the procedures is in the hands of the Member States, while being fully aware of the limits set on the "autonomy" by the Court of Justice. But that is precisely the problem: names are not just convenience labels, but also symbols, sometimes quite powerful symbols, especially once they and their use leave the circle of few lawyers specialising in EU law and procedure and are picked up in the broader legal and political discourse. It is no accident that for instance the Court of Justice itself has not been using, up until very recently, the term "procedural autonomy of the Member States".[53] In this case, the name shapes the way the rose smells.[54]

Finally, the misunderstanding is also nourished by a deeper divergence in opinions as to what are the Court of Justice's functions and what it should actually be doing. Over the last years, a number of dissatisfied voices appeared, suggesting that the case law of the Court is going beyond the attributed competence, that it does not respect the competence of the Member States and that all that is done with poor, sloppy or no reasoning at all.[55]

The critique of the Court is legitimate and should be voiced; a professional critique is the only way of controlling supreme institutions. Part of the critique, however, is based on diverging assumptions about what is the institutional role of the Court, assumptions which have little or no support in the Treaties or the up-to-date practice. Thus, for instance, R. Herzog and L. Gerken suggested that

53 See the review and argument provided by C.N. Kakouris, Do the Member States Possess Judicial Procedural "Autonomy"? (1997) 34 CMLR 1389, at 1405, who suggested, in 1997, that the term "procedural autonomy" does not appear in the case law of the Court of Justice. About a decade later, however, the term started being used in the reasoning of the Court of Justice – see, eg: ECJ 7 January 2004, Case C-201/02, *The Queen on the application of Delena Wells and Secretary of State for Transport, Local Government and the Regions* [2004] ECR I-723, paras 65, 67 and 70, or ECJ 6 October 2009, Case C-40/08, *Asturcom Telecomunicaciones SL v Cristina Rodríguez Nogueira* [2009] ECR I-9579, para 38. This is thus an intriguing example of how the language of the Court of Justice is being influenced by academic writings, from where the notion was taken over.

54 Romeo and Juliet (Act II, scene ii, 1–2).

55 Strongly and with considerable political impact (not just in Germany) voiced by Roman Herzog and Lüder Gerken in their joint article entitled "*Stoppt den Europäischen Gerichtshof*", published in the *Frankfurter Allgemeine Zeitung* of 8 September 2008, accessible also online at http://www.cep.eu. For a review of more critical voices, see the Editorial Comments 'The Court of Justice in the limelight – again' (2008) 45 *CMLR* 1571.

*"The ECJ was created with the expectation of being also an arbitrator between the interest of the EU and those of the Member States".*[56]

The Court of Justice is a child and later one of the motors of the European integration. That is its institutional design and mission, partly defined in the Treaties, mostly, however, in its past decisions and institutional self-perception. The preservation of the Member States′ competence was really not anything the Court would be traditionally strong at, quite to the contrary. Should now anyone wish the Court to defer more greatly to the Member States, it must first redefine its mission first; it is, however, problematic to scorn an institution not fulfilling one's believes which do not correspond with those of the institution and also not with its past tradition.[57]

The "procedural autonomy" is then just one of the concrete examples of this broader phenomenon: from time to time, the Court is criticised for not safeguarding the "procedural autonomy" of the Member States. As the rules of the game now stand, however, there really is not anything it could safeguard. If anything were to change in order to favour the Member States′ competence, then it is the rules of the game themselves …

## 7. CONCLUSION

The arguments developed in this article attempted to be descriptive and analytical, not articulating any opinion on whether what the Court of Justice is doing is right or wrong and whether there should be more or less judicial harmonisation of national procedural rules. The only normative vision voiced did not concern the issue *what* the Court is doing, but just *how* it is doing it.

Within the "how" question, it was argued that the thirty years old test of equivalence and effectiveness should be reconsidered, as it really does not reflect what the Court of Justice is doing in this area. The test causes considerable uncertainty as to the applicable standard and only creates false impressions and expectations. The first prong of the test, the requirement of equivalence, should be discarded. Not only is the Court not able to carry out such examination, the effectuation of the test gets also more and more problematic as more and more areas of national law get harmonised, thus depriving the test of any suitable comparator. The test

56 *"Der EuGH ist in der Erwartung geschaffen worden, einen Schiedsrichter gerade auch zwischen den Interessen der EU und jenen der Mitgliedstaaten zu haben."*

57 To do justice to the arguments presented by R. Herzog and L. Gerken, they are (well) aware that the preservation of Member States competence is not on the Court's agenda. That is actually why they suggested the creation of a new independent court for issues of competence ("*vom EuGH unabhängigen Gerichtshofes für Kompetenzfragen*").

the Court is genuinely carrying out is one of effectiveness and adequacy of the national procedure or remedy. The requirement of effectiveness or adequacy would, however, need some internal limits. In this perspective, the (unfortunately somewhat still-born) approach announced in *Van Schijndel* was not a bad start at all.

# NATIONAL VOICE AND EUROPEAN LOYALTY

## Member State Autonomy, European Remedies and Constitutional Pluralism in EU Law

Daniel SARMIENTO*

This chapter explores the relationship between national institutional autonomy, European remedies and the European Court of Justice's role as the watchdog of constitutional identity and individual rights. It will be argued that a specific form of discourse has developed in the context of judicial review of national law before the European Court of Justice (hereinafter ECJ), granting voice to both Member States and individuals, but also imposing obligations upon them. The case will be made for a reconsideration of the present state of European remedies before national courts and the ECJ, and the main weaknesses of the present status will be developed. Finally, I advance a new conception of *Voice* for Member States, one which entails an active role for the individual before the ECJ and a discursive approach to constitutional issues. This proposal will be made with constitutional pluralism as a conceptual reference, but with the aim of also improving its current doctrinal development. Overall, it will be submitted that the authority of EU law and the autonomy of Member States can co-exist. It is the *framework* that needs adjusting, combining a proper measure of *Voice* for Member States with a necessary amount of *Loyalty* on their part as well.

In Part II the place of Member State autonomy will be identified by depicting three different conflicting contexts. The main weaknesses of the ECJ's judicial review will be explored when the scrutiny concerns national legislative provisions, judicial decisions from courts of last instance and constitutional norms. Part III will deal with the difficult position of individual litigants before the ECJ and the role played by European remedies in protecting their legal status. It will be

* Référendaire (ECJ), Professor of Administrative and EU Law (Universidad Complutense de Madrid). All opinions are strictly personal. Many thanks to David Baez-Seara and to all the participants of the Workshop organised by Bruno de Witte and Hans-W. Micklitz on "The European Court of Justice and the Autonomy of the Member States" for their useful comments. The usual disclaimer applies.

argued that the weakness of Member State *Voice* before the ECJ is intimately intertwined with the drawbacks faced by individuals in the same forum. In Part IV, a normative proposal will be made combining *Voice* and *Loyalty* in a context of constitutional pluralism.

## 1. EXIT, VOICE, LOYALTY AND THE LEGITIMACY OF THE EUROPEAN COURT OF JUSTICE

Albert Hirschman's classic critique of liberalism introduced a conceptual trio under the name of *Exit*, *Voice* and *Loyalty*, that portrays the interplay between consumer or social demand and their response to economic or political output.[1] Hirschman's work supported the idea that simple binary responses of either *Exit* or *Voice* were insufficient, and lacked explanatory accuracy in portraying the workings of the market or the political process. Consumer or citizen response is also conditioned by *Loyalty*, which may appear as a form of brand loyalty in the case of consumers, or patriotism in the case of citizens. The role of *Loyalty* explains why *Exit* strategies may be reduced when options are not appealing, and why, in those circumstances, actors keep exerting *Voice* in an effort to provide greater opportunity for feedback and criticism. Hirschman's argument is therefore useful in complex institutional frameworks, explaining how interactions result in net outcomes of legitimacy.

In this paper, *Exit*, *Voice* and *Loyalty* will be portrayed as methodological categories, the aim of which is to explain the interaction between Member States, individuals, national courts and the European Court of Justice, in the overall context of EU law and the attribution of legitimacy to the ECJ in specific conflicting scenarios. Through *Voice*, Member States and individuals can participate in the process of determining the proper interpretation and application of EU law, using *channels* that make their involvement *effective and efficient*. On the other hand, individuals and Member States can *Exit* and thus withdraw from the process, a result that will be avoided as a consequence of the interplay of *Loyalty*, a conduct involving commitment despite a lack of incentives.

It will be argued that in specific contexts the ECJ's source of legitimacy is not grounded on the Treaties, but in a more subtle institutional interplay that grants or deprives authority to and from the Court. Such contexts can occur in procedures before the ECJ that entail judicial review of national parliamentary laws, and even more vigorously when judicial review involves issues of constitutional pedigree. This scenario poses conceptual problems, and more particularly issues relevant to

[1] A.O. Hirschmann, *Exit, Voice, and Loyalty: Responses to Decline in Firms, Organizations and States*, Harvard University Press, Cambridge, 1970.

Member State autonomy: by scrutinising the conformity of national law with EU law, the ECJ may be employing procedures that do not guarantee a proper channel to exert *Voice*, or the way to do so effectively and efficiently. Therefore, *Voice* becomes an essential criterion in determining how the ECJ enables individuals and Member States, either through the Executive, the Legislature or the Judiciary, to exercise the means to preserve and articulate their autonomy in the course of a procedure of judicial review before the Luxembourg Court.

## 2. MEMBER STATE VOICE

Challenging Member State autonomy before the ECJ entails a restriction of national decision-making procedures. By judicially reviewing national decisions, the ECJ's case law conditions the way in which national decisions will ultimately be rendered. This result introduces democratic constraints that become difficult to accept by Member States when they touch upon national legislative processes, the judicial process or the paradigm of democratic expression: the *pouvoir constituant*, the *We the People*, that fleshes out each Member State's claim of existence and ultimately the core of national identity. These three conflicting contexts will be analysed through examples in the ECJ's case law.

### 2.1. JUDICIAL REVIEW OF NATIONAL LEGISLATION

In EU law, judicial review can become an odd creature when faced with national rules, namely national parliamentary legislation. European courts have no authority under the Treaties to supervise the conformity of domestic law with European provisions, and it is therefore surprising to witness how, in the past fifty years, the ECJ has succeeded in accomplishing exactly the opposite result to what the Treaties express. As is well known, the preliminary reference procedure of interpretation has contributed decisively to this purpose, enabling national courts to set aside inconsistent national rules with the aid of the ECJ.[2]

Due to the weak foundations underlying judicial review of national legislation, the democratic credentials of the ECJ come under fire when facing highly consensual normative decisions made at the national level. Also, the procedural rules of the ECJ, originally drafted with a consultative procedure in mind, are not designed for private parties and national authorities, but for European Institutions and

2 See K. Lenaerts, 'Form and Substance of the Preliminary Rulings Procedure', in D. Curtin and T. Heukels (eds), *Institutional Dynamics of European Integration. Essays in Honour of Henry G. Schermers v. 2*, Kluwer Academic Publishers, the Hague, 1994, p 364 et seq and C. Barnard and E. Sharpston, 'The Changing Face of Article 177 References', (1997) 34 *CMLR (Common Market Law Review)*, p 1116.

traditional sovereign States acting in an international capacity.[3] Private parties do not always stand on an equal footing with national authorities or Member States, and they may find themselves litigating against several governments and EU Institutions, all of which are foreign to the main proceedings in the Member State. The process also depends on the goodwill of national courts, which enjoy a wide margin of discretion when making references to the ECJ and can sometimes be instrumentalised by a party or parties to the case.

The weaknesses of the current status are graphically portrayed in *Mangold,*[4] a case which raises a number of interesting issues, ranging from aspects of procedure over the interpretation of the Framework Agreement on Fixed-Term Employment (put into effect by Directive 1999/70[5]) to the application of the Anti-Discrimination Directive 2000/78[6] and its temporal effects during its transposition period. German employment law provided for a general prohibition of fixed-term employment. Fixed-term employment contracts could validly be entered into only if there were objective grounds justifying the fixed period. Employment contracts with older employees could, however, be concluded on a fixed-term basis even without any objective justification. The purpose of this exception was to promote the vocational integration of unemployed older workers. The relevant age-limit was 60 until the end of 2000. As of 2003, the age-limit was reduced to 58. Between 2003 and the end of 2006, the age-limit was again reduced to 52. The questions referred to the Court of Justice asked whether these provisions were compatible with the Framework Agreement on Fixed Term Employment and the Anti-Discrimination Directive 2000/78.

Rüdiger Helm, the defendant employer in the main proceedings, had already opposed the provisions on fixed-term employment of older employees in the legislative process, ultimately without success. He then hired Werner Mangold, apparently for the sole purpose of proving the incompatibility of the said provisions with EU Law. In fact, there appears to be substantial evidence supporting the fact that – contrary to the presumed interests of the parties – it was he, Mr Helm, who brought the present case before the ECJ.

---

3 See Article 23, paragraph 2 of the Statute of the Court, according to which "within two months of this notification, the parties, the Member States, the Commission and, where appropriate, the institution, body, office or agency which adopted the act the validity or interpretation of which is in dispute, shall be entitled to submit statements of case or written observations to the Court."

4 ECJ 22 November 2005, Case C-144/04, *Mangold* [2005] ECR I-9981.

5 Council Directive 1999/70/EC of 28 June 1999 concerning the framework agreement on fixed-term work concluded by ETUC, UNICE and CEEP (OJ 1999 L 175, p 43).

6 Council Directive 2000/78/EC of 27 November 2000 establishing a general framework for equal treatment in employment and occupation (OJ 2000 L 303, p 16).

In its judgment, the ECJ argued that Directive 2000/78 does not contain a prohibition of discrimination (merely a framework) but determined that such prohibition was a general principle of Community Law.[7] The Court also found that the national provision had to be set aside, disregarding the fact that the period prescribed for the implementation of Directive 2000/78 into domestic law had not expired when the fixed-term employment contract was concluded nor when the decision was handed down.[8] In doing so, the ECJ was, firstly, questioning its own case law on admissibility of fabricated litigation, although it was cautious enough not to quote it even once;[9] secondly, recognising the existence of a principle of European law which found hardly any recognition in national legal traditions (discrimination on the grounds of age, only to be found in the Finnish and Portuguese legal orders); and thirdly, putting aside its case law on horizontal and temporary effects of Directives, through recourse to general principles of EU Law.[10]

The loud reaction provoked by the Mangold decision in Germany is a clear example of how European judicial review exerts democratic pressures that are difficult to assume by Member States.[11] First, the German provisions under scrutiny were the outcome of a wide national consensus, in the context of an ambitious reform to fight a stagnant national economy and labour market. Second, it is probable that Mr. Mangold and Mr Helm fabricated the case, and despite this fact the ECJ was, contrary to its past case law, willing to make a ruling on the substance of the case. Third, there was an evident problem of applicability of EU provisions, and that would have been enough to decide the case in favour of the German rules.

---

7 See ECJ 22 November 2005, Case C-144/04, *Mangold* [2005] ECR I-9981, para 75.

8 In para 76 of the judgment the Court stated that "observance of the general principle of equal treatment, in particular in respect of age, cannot as such be conditional upon the expiry of the period allowed the Member States for the transposition of a directive intended to lay down a general framework for combating discrimination on the grounds of age, in particular so far as the organisation of appropriate legal remedies, the burden of proof, protection against victimisation, social dialogue, affirmative action and other specific measures to implement such a directive are concerned."

9 Reading paras 32 to 39, it is surprising to see how the Court's case-law on fictitious references (see Case 244/80 Foglia [1981] ECR 3045, paragraph 21; Case C-83/91, *Meilicke* [1992] ECR I-4871, paragraph 23; Case C-379/98, *PreussenElektra* [2001] ECR I-2099, paragraph 39; or C-390/99, *Canal Satélite Digital* [2002] ECR I-607, paragraph 19) does not appear even once.

10 See, inter alia, ECJ 10 April 1984, Case 14/83, *von Colson and Kamann* [1984] ECR 1891, para 26; ECJ 13 November 1990, Case C-106/89, *Marleasing* [1990] ECR I-4135, para 8; ECJ 14 July 1994, *Faccini Dori* [1994] ECR I-3325, para 26; ECJ 18 December 1997, Case C-129/96, *Inter-Environnement Wallonie* [1997] ECR I-7411, para 40; ECJ 5 October 2004, C-397/01 to C-403/01, *Pfeiffer and Others* [2004] ECR I-8835, para 110; and ECJ 23 April 2009, Joined Cases C-378/07 to C-380/07, *Angelidaki and Others* [2009] ECR I-3071, para 106.

11 See the brief elaboration by L. Gerken *et al*, '"Mangold" als ausbrechender Rechtsakt" 2009, as well as the article published by R. Herzog and L. Gerken, Stop the European Court of Justice (available at www.cep.eu/fileadmin/user_upload/Pressemappe/CEP_in_den_Medien/Herzog-EuGH-Webseite_eng.pdf) and, inter alia, M. Höpner, 'Spitzen gegen Brüssel', *Frankfurter Rundschau*, 02 July 2009, p 2.

The *Mangold* judgment is therefore an example of how the ECJ can strike the questionalble chord when articulating national *Voice* before the Union's courts. European judicial review of national provisions requires a specific practice under clear rules with fixed conditions, among which the requisites of admissibility stand out. It is settled case law that the ECJ is not competent to decide on purely hypothetical or fabricated questions of law raised by national courts. According to the German government in its written submissions, that is exactly what Rüdiger Helm and Werner Mangold were doing: they constructed a fictitious case with the aim of challenging a German provision. Furthermore, the grounds on which such a provision could be questioned under EU Law could not yet be invoked: Directive 2000/78 was still in the process of being incorporated into German law, and it was also questionable whether it was applicable in a horizontal, *inter privatos*, relationship.[12] The overall result of the *Mangold* judgement sat uncomfortably with previous case law by stating that the case was admissible and invoking a general principle to avoid the issue of applicability of Directives. The ECJ's willingness to decide dramatically contrasted with the Member State's concern about the ECJ's authority to rule at a specific time and place. The result of this tension was solved by the Court's controversial decision to set aside all issues of admissibility and applicability, which amounts to a ruling that disregarded the arguments of the Member State claiming that the proper forum for this discussion lay elsewhere. The *Mangold* judgement therefore proves that Member State *Voice* must be exerted at the right time and place, and the ECJ's inability to do so entails running the risk of a further exercise of *Voice*: institutional disobedience.

The complexities underlying European judicial review of national laws should, however, be explored in its overall framework, which does not only include the national provisions under examination, but also judicial decisions and constitutional rules.

## 2.2. JUDICIAL REVIEW OF NATIONAL JUDICIAL ACTION

Judicial review of national parliamentary decisions raises democratic issues, whilst the scrutiny of national judicial decisions involves the rule of law, separation of powers and legal certainty. When the ECJ declares the incompatibility of a Supreme Court's judgment with EU Law, it is stating that a national judiciary has failed in the fulfilment of its European obligations. When courts breach such duties, the very essence of a national legal order comes into question: since courts

[12] It could have been argued if the Court's case law in ECJ 18 December 1997, Case C-129/96 *Inter-Environnement Wallonie* [1997] ECR I-7411 was applicable to the facts, but the Court decided not to approach the case in this direction.

are entrusted with the ultimate interpretation of the Law, the failure of the system to reach such goals in an appropriate fashion is also the failure of the rule of law. This delicate context has forced the ECJ to become very cautious when facing national case law of Courts of last instance, as the *Köbler* case proved.[13] After all, issues of *Voice* appear time and again: who is to grant damages when the infringement of EU Law is the result of a Supreme Court decision? How is a Member State to react once the breach has been declared by the ECJ? What is the real margin of action of a Member State when bargaining with the Commission in the course of the administrative proceedings of Article 258 TFEU? And how is a Member State government going to defend its position, if the questioned judgment becomes *res iudicata* under domestic law?

It appears that not only the ECJ is aware of the intricacies of this conflict, but also the Commission, that has traditionally been reluctant to bring before the Court an infringement procedure against a Member State as a result of a judicial decision of last instance. In fact, the leading (and sole) precedent in this regard, *Commission v Italy*,[14] was the result of a careful balance that led the ECJ to declare the infringement as a result of the Italian legislation, which eventually led the Italian Corte di Cassazione to develop case law contrary to the ECJ's decisions.[15] The *entente cordiale* came definitively to an end in 2009, or so it appears from the Commission's decision to bring proceedings against Spain, as a result of a Spanish Supreme Court's judgment of 2003, an obscure indirect taxation case concerning the application of VAT obligations to real estate registrars.[16]

For many years, real estate registrars in Spain were subject to VAT for the services they provided to regional authorities in the liquidation of regional taxes. A regional court ruled that the said obligation was wrong, and the Spanish government appealed before the Supreme Court using a special procedure, the *recurso en interés de ley*, specifically designed to declare authoritative precedents binding for all Courts. The Supreme Court upheld the regional Court's decision, and the Commission immediately launched an infringement action against Spain, claiming that the Supreme Court judgment was in breach of Directive

13 See ECJ 30 September 2003, Case C-224/01, *Köbler* [2003] ECR I-10239. On the context and the role Köbler plays in the Court's State liability case law, see K.M. Scherr, *The principle of State liability for judicial breaches: the case Gerhard Köbler v. Austria under European Community law and from a comparative national law perspective*, EUI PhD, Florence, 2008.

14 ECJ 9 December 2003, Case C-129/00, *Commission v Italy* [2003] ECR I-14637. On this case law, see C. Naômé, *Le renvoi préjudiciel en droit européen*, Larcier, Brussels, 2007, pp 47 and 48.

15 The Commission's file was lodged claiming that "by maintaining in force Article 29(2) of Law No 428 of 29 December 1990, which, as interpreted and applied by the administrative and judicial authorities, allows rules of evidence in relation to the repayment of taxes levied in breach of Community provisions which make the exercise of the right to repayment of such taxes impossible or in any event excessively difficult for the taxpayer, the Italian Republic has failed to fulfil its obligations under the EC Treaty."

16 ECJ 12 November 2009, Case C-154/08, *Commission v Spain* [2009], unpublished.

77/388/EEC.[17] Revisiting its case law in Commission v Italy, the ECJ stated, once again, that for the purposes of an infringement action under Article 258 TFEU, "isolated or numerically insignificant judicial decisions in the context of case-law taking a different direction, or still more a construction disowned by the national Supreme Court, cannot be taken into account. That is not true of a widely-held judicial construction which has not been disowned by the Supreme Court, but rather confirmed by it".[18] In sharp contrast with the result of Commission v Italy, the Court stated that Spain had breached its obligations under Directive 77/388/EEC, making it clear that the domestic decision under fire was the Supreme Court judgment.

A preliminary analysis of Commission v Spain should not surprise the reader. Indeed, nothing should stop the ECJ from declaring a breach by a Member State when the officials under scrutiny are national courts: a national jurisdiction is obviously a part of the State and it exerts public powers as granted by the Constitution or Parliament. However, there are important aspects to take into account when dealing with this peculiar form of institutional litigation.

First, the ECJ will be scrutinising *in Law* the conduct of a national court of last instance. Judicial action is ultimately an interpretative task involving the application of the Law, so in the present case an Article 258 TFEU procedure will eventually transform itself into a pseudo-appeal before the ECJ against decisions of national courts of last instance.[19] This pseudo-appeal is available only to the Commission and Member States (Articles 258 and 259 TFEU), and it enables the two to initiate procedures against a decision rendered by a national court of last instance. The "objective" character of the infringement procedure ties the ECJ to a strict analysis of conformity between a Community provision and the questioned national judgment, and the final decision will be given in terms of breach or non-breach of EU Law by the domestic court of last instance. It is questionable whether the drafters of the Treaties envisioned this type of procedure, especially in a system substantially based on the principle of national institutional autonomy, which applies with specific intensity to the judiciary. The logic behind the European system of remedies grants a specific role to national courts, and relies on them when the time comes to remove rebellious or unfortunate judicial decisions from the domestic legal order. By introducing a "new" course of action that directly

---

17 Sixth Council Directive 77/388/EEC of 17 May 1977 on the harmonisation of the laws of the Member States relating to turnover taxes – Common system of value added tax: uniform basis of assessment (OJ 1977 L 145, p. 1), as amended by Council Directive 95/7/EC of 10 April 1995 (OJ 1995 L 102, p 18).

18 ECJ 12 November 2009, Case C-154/08, *Commission v Spain* [2009], unpublished, para 32.

19 On the possibility of an appeal before the Court against decisions of national courts, see J. Baquero, 'La procédure préjudicielle suffit-elle à garantir l'efficacité et l'uniformité du droit de l'Union européenne ?' in L. Azoulai, and L. Burgorgue-Larsen (dir), *L'autorité de l'Union Européenne*, Bruylant, Brussels, 2006.

concerns national judgments that put an end to internal proceedings, the ECJ is setting limits to the said relationship between itself and national courts. That is: the scope of national institutional autonomy is reconsidered to the benefit of the EU, restricting thus the range of national *Voice*.

Second, the fact that *Köbler* enabled individuals to sue Member States for damages as a result of national judicial decisions contrary to EU Law does not automatically imply that Member States are in the same position in an Article 258 TFEU procedure. Quite the contrary, while damages require specific conditions and specific behaviour by the officials who inflict the loss, infringements are mere declarations of incompatibility of national action in the light of EU provisions. In fact, the standard of review appears to be stricter in the context of a "judicial infringement". Whilst the ECJ stated in *Köbler* that "State liability for an infringement of Community law by a decision of a national court adjudicating at last instance can be incurred only in the exceptional case where the court has manifestly infringed the applicable law",[20] the dictum in Commission v Italy and Commission v Spain does not sound so exceptional: although "isolated or numerically insignificant judicial decisions in the context of case-law taking a different direction, or still more a construction disowned by the national supreme court, cannot be taken into account" for the purposes of declaring a breach *ex* Articles 258 or 259 TFEU, "that is not true of a widely-held judicial construction which has not been disowned by the supreme court, but rather confirmed by it".[21] In Commission v Spain, only one regional court judgement, confirmed by a sole judgement of the Supreme Court, appeared to be enough to declare the breach.[22] It therefore appears that the standard of scrutiny is different and stricter in the context of an infringement procedure, restricting Member State autonomy not only in procedural terms, but in substantial terms as well.

Third, there are important procedural difficulties in dealing with "judicial infringements": Member States have no margin of manoeuvre before the Commission, unless legislative reforms can be undertaken (which may not always be the case) and it will be inevitable that constitutional tensions would arise between the executive and the judiciary; parties are left aside and will have to litigate again, if the Commission proves successful, in a long and costly procedure claiming damages, and with no certainty as to the outcome. Also, it is possible that the infringement is rendered at a time in which further domestic procedures are still pending, and doubts arise concerning the role of lower domestic courts that have to apply their Supreme Court's case law *and/or* a conflicting ECJ decision openly declaring a higher court's case law illegal. This situation poses important

[20] ECJ 30 September 2003, Case C-224/01, *Köbler* [2003] ECR I-10239, para 53.
[21] ECJ 9 December 2003, Case C-129/00, *Commission v Italy* [2003] ECR I-14637, para 32.
[22] Paras 125 to 127 of ECJ 12 November 2009, Case C-154/08, *Commission v Spain* [2009], unpublished.

issues of national judicial autonomy, touching particularly on the relationship between inferior and superior domestic courts. The fact that the ECJ is willing to interfere in this rapport is significant proof of its readiness to restrict national autonomy for the sake of the proper application of EU Law in domestic courts. This is exactly the tension underlying the recent *Cartesio* case law.

In *Cartesio,*[23] the ECJ introduced further pressure on national supreme courts, by recognising the ability of inferior courts to disregard appeals against referring orders. This clear call for judicial insurrection within the national hierarchies is an impressive restriction upon national autonomy that deserves further attention. The procedural circumstances surrounding Cartesio were the following: a Hungarian judge questioned whether a national rule, that allowed a separate appeal against a decision making a reference, was compatible with Article 267 TFEU. According to the provisions under scrutiny, the appellate court had the power to overrule that decision, to set aside the reference for a preliminary ruling and to order the first court to resume the domestic law proceedings. When confronted with this supervisory role of appellate courts over inferior judges who make a reference pursuant to Article 267 TFEU, the ECJ gave powerful support to the latter by claiming that "it is for the referring court to draw the proper inferences from a judgment delivered on an appeal against its decision to refer and, in particular, to come to a conclusion as to whether it is appropriate to maintain the reference for a preliminary ruling, or to amend it or to withdraw it".[24] For the sake of clarity, the judgement goes even further and states that the ECJ must "abide by the decision to make a reference for a preliminary ruling, which must have its full effect so long as it has not been revoked or amended by the referring court, *such revocation or amendment being matters on which that court alone is able to take a decision*".[25]

*Cartesio* raises questions about the degree of interference that the ECJ is willing to inflict on Member State judicial autonomy, but it is clear from its wording that national courts engaging in a preliminary discourse with the Luxembourg Court are protected from most appellate intrusions of superior domestic courts.[26] When the ECJ states that a revocation or an amendment from the appellate jurisdiction is a matter that the inferior court "alone is able to take a decision on", it is conferring on the said court a power to disregard a judgement delivered by

23 ECJ 16 December 2008, Case C-210/06, *Cartesio* [2008] ECR I-9641.
24 ECJ 16 December 2008, Case C-210/06, *Cartesio* [2008] ECR I-9641, para 96.
25 ECJ 16 December 2008, Case C-210/06, *Cartesio* [2008] ECR I-9641, para 97.
26 See J.-C. Barbato, 'Le droit communautaire et les recours internes exercés contre les ordonnances de renvoi', (2009) *Revue Trimestrielle de droit européen*, p 280; R. Alonso, 'Cuestión prejudicial comunitaria y autonomía procesal nacional: a propósito del asunto Cartesio', (2009) 30 *Revista Española de Derecho Europeo*, pp 209–211 and M. Bobek, 'Cartesio – Appeals Against an Order to Refer Under Article 234(2) EC Treaty Revisited', (2010) 29 *Civil Justice Quarterly*.

an appellate court, on a case that will eventually return to that same jurisdiction after the judgements of the ECJ and the referring court are dictated.

The judgment in *Cartesio*, which sits uncomfortably with *Rheinmühlen II*,[27] is still open to further developments in the Court's case law. For example, the way in which the ruling is drafted allows a certain margin of manoeuvre to national courts, as has been recently proved in *Nationale Loterij*.[28] Thus, the referring judge will be free to decide on the consequences of the appellate decision only "if the main proceedings remain pending before the referring court in their entirety".[29] This condition allowed the ECJ to remove from the docket the reference made by the Hasselt local court which had been quashed by the Court of Appeal of Antwerp, but which, at the same time, had been solved on the substance of the case. Also, it is still open to discussion whether the powers granted to national inferior courts are only in their hands when the appeal has been lodged on the grounds of EU Law, or whether it is an unlimited faculty that precludes the effects of the appeal whatever the motives were.[30] Due regard should also be had in the future to the opposite circumstance from the one in *Cartesio*: an appeal against a *refusal* to make a preliminary reference. Will the appellate Court's decision to quash the inferior judge's decision be also a "matter on which [the latter] court alone is able to take a decision"?[31]

Issues of *Voice* appear here in a specific context: that of judicial discourse. However, the underlying problems in circumstances that restrict the ability of Member States to exert legitimate claims are present here as well. Judicial infringements leave a member State in a zero-sum situation in terms of authority, in that an internal constitutional conflict will take place, the EU system of remedies is altered, and the practical outcome of a negative judgment from the ECJ leaves the domestic judiciary in an unstable position regarding authority and legal certainty. The Cartesio case-law poses similar conflicting issues, particularly from the national judiciary's perspective: the autonomous and exclusive power of an inferior court "to take a decision" on its superior court's stance and to "draw the proper inferences", although it is an impressive empowerment of national judges, appears also as a restriction on a Supreme Court's authority, to be applied only when issues of EU Law have been defectively handled by the latter. Issues of *Voice* appear here in an internal and an external dimension: first, limiting the ability of a superior court to state the law within its jurisdictional domain following a

27 ECJ 12 February 1974, Case 146/73, *Rheinmühlen-Düsseldorf* [1974] ECR 139.

28 ECJ Order 24 March 2009, Case 525/06, *Nationale Loterij* [2008] ECR I-2197.

29 ECJ Order 24 March 2009, Case 525/06, *Nationale Loterij* [2008] ECR I-2197, para 98.

30 See also, following the path of *Nationale Loterij*, ECJ 10 June 2010, Case 395/08 Bruno et Pettini [2010] nyr.

31 See R. Alonso, 'Cuestión prejudicial comunitaria y autonomía procesal nacional: a propósito del asunto Cartesio', (2009) 30 *Revista Española de Derecho Europeo*, p 217.

hierarchical chain or command that protects legal certainty; second, turning any possible defence before the ECJ into a diabolical trap for any government, who must choose not between competing legal answers, but competing legal claims of authority within the Member State's constitutional framework.

## 2.3. JUDICIAL REVIEW OF THE POUVOIR CONSTITUANT

A further example of how judicial review of national law exerts pressure upon Member State authority appears when it affects national constitutional provisions. In fact, it could be doubted whether this form of scrutiny is judicial review at all, inasmuch as the ECJ is indirectly judging on the validity of the normative framework (the Constitution) on which Member State legitimacy is grounded, including the State's authority to participate in European affairs. Issues of *Voice* assume here an even more profound meaning in the safeguarding of Member State autonomy. The ECJ can thus be driven into a terrain that stands somewhere between constitutional review and judicial review, but in procedures that are not designed to handle a conflict of this nature.

The way in which the ECJ can review national constitutional provisions is an old story many times told. For example, the development of EU fundamental rights is significant proof of the tensions between the Treaties, the Court's case law and fundamental rights provisions in national Constitutions. Furthermore, the recent past has witnessed important events in this area that deserve closer attention. Two main strands can be perceived in the Court's decisions, shockingly divergent but with a *prima facie* coherent rationale: a hands-on approach, whereby the Court declares the compatibility or incompatibility of a constitutional provision with EU Law; and a hands-off approach, stating general guidelines that are to be eventually followed (and completed) by the national referring court. The first strand can be found in *Kreil* [32]and *Michaniki*, [33] two judgements with spectacular results that unashamedly point at the incompatibility of German and Greek constitutional provisions with EU Directives. The second strand appears in cases such as *UGT-Rioja* [34]and *Viking* and *Laval*, [35] where a more subtle approach from the Court is perceived, and the final decision is deposited in the hands of the national court.

32 ECJ 11 January 2000, Case C-285/98, *Kreil* [2000] ECR I-69.

33 ECJ 16 December 2008, Case C-213/07, *Michaniki* [2008] ECR I-9999.

34 ECJ 1 September 2008, Case C-428/06, *Unión General de Trabajadores de La Rioja* [2008] ECR I-6747.

35 ECJ 11 December 2007, Case C-438/05, *International Transport Workers Federation (ITF) and Finnish Seaman's Union (FSU) v. Viking Line* [2007] ECR I-10779 and ECJ 18 December 2007, Case C-341/05, *Laval un Partneri Ltd v Bygnadds et al.* [2007] ECR I-11767.

It is open to discussion why the Court acts in such a way, or whether there is an underlying rationale in this apparently contradicting case law. The answer might be found in the fact that both *Michaniki* and *Kreil* concerned the implementation of secondary legislation. Member States negotiate in the Council and have the opportunity to express their constitutional concerns. Also, amending secondary Community legislation is a considerably easier process than amending the Treaties. This explanation could of course be questioned by referring to cases such as *Ordre des Barreaux*, [36] where the ECJ ruled on the conformity of a Directive that questioned the Belgian constitutional protection of privacy in the area of professional secrecy. However, the context of *Ordre des Barreaux* is certainly different from the one raised in cases previously mentioned: preliminary references of interpretation allow the ECJ to render "silent judgements", open-ended replies that grant national courts a wide margin of discretion, whilst references of validity are procedures that leave the Court with a binary *yes-no* type of answer. All in all, references of interpretation hide the inner workings of judicial review of national law; references of validity deal with judicial review of EU Law.

Member States can be driven into scrutinising their constitutional provisions in the light of EU Law by different procedural means, but the main course of action is the preliminary reference of interpretation. This means that the procedure of Article 267 TFEU has to adapt itself to the traits of procedures of review of constitutionality similar to the ones enshrined in most Member States before constitutional courts, or before superior courts with powers of constitutional review. However, the ECJ's case law proves that the effort of adaptation has been absent in the past, and that the Court's approach in procedural and substantial terms is not very different to the one used in ordinary references. This fact proves to be problematic for several reasons. First, the reason why the referring judge will make a reference may be to avoid constitutional review by the national Constitutional court, imposing thus a way to exert pressure upon the latter by means of a judgment of the ECJ.[37] Second, preliminary references leave the ECJ with only the facts and legal arguments raised by the referring court and the parties, which are sometimes clearly insufficient in helping the Court to set

---

36 ECJ 26 June 2007, Case C 305/05, *Ordre des barreaux francophones et germanophone and Others* [2007] ECR I-5305.

37 See the reference raised by the Audiencia Provicinal of Tarragona, questioning the Spanish Law on the Prevention of Violence on the grounds of sex in the light of EU Law, while at the same time the issue had been brought before the Spanish Constitutional Court (Cases C-483/09 and C-1/10, *Gueye & Salmerón Sánchez*, pending). Also, see the Belgian saga on the priority of preliminary references vis-à-vis questions of constitutionality, particularly Case C-457/09, *Chartry*, pending. The Belgian debate has an indirect reflection in the recent constitutional reform undertaken in France, which has introduced for a first time the question of constitutionality before the Conseil Constitutionnel. For the consequences of this reform for the EU and its impact on Article 267 TFEU, see F.-X. Millet, 'L'exception d'inconstitutionnalité en France ou l'impossibilité du souhaitable', (2008) 5 *Revue du droit public* 1305.

the proper context in which it will deliver its judgment. Third, articulating a discourse in terms of constitutionality is not always easy for Member States in the course of an EU legal dispute. For example, the rigid nature of the Greek Constitution or the political consequences of reforming the peculiar financial regime of the Basque Country are considerations that can hardly be used as a solid argument when discussing public procurement or state aid cases before the ECJ. Overall, Member States can see how a major domestic constitutional issue arrives at the ECJ whilst the context of discussion in Luxembourg ignores the underlying debate. *Voice* is abridged for the sake of EU Law, and Member State *constitutional* autonomy declines.

## 2.4. CONSTITUTIONAL VOICE AND NON-CONSTITUTIONAL CLAIMS

It is important at this point to call to attention the fact that judicial review of national law entails a constitutional dimension that renders the ECJ's task difficult to evaluate. However, not all cases of judicial review of national law have a constitutional "pedigree". Why does the Court get away with reviewing national VAT provisions, but not Germany's rules on fixed-term contracts? After all, the foundations upon which both types of review stand are the very same (*Costa v Enel* and *Simmenthal*[38]). If judicial review is not always a problematic device, the explanation can be found in the constitutional nature of the *issues* at hand. Therefore, it is only in a constitutional context where *Voice* becomes a source of legitimacy for EU Law. It is important, thus, to develop a series of criteria that flesh out what elements contribute to build, as of today, a constitutional case when litigating before the ECJ.[39]

Briefly, such cases will arise when the query posed before the Court touches upon fundamental rights, competences and the distribution of power within a Member State. In Part IV of this paper it will be claimed that constitutional issues require a specific methodological approach that finds its roots in a pluralist conception of the law. For present purposes, it must be noted that Member State *Voice* becomes an imperative normative claim when judicial review of national law touches upon any of the three elements that transform a case into a constitutional affair.

---

[38] ECJ 15 July 1964, Case 6/64, *Costa/ENEL* [1964] ECR 585, at 592 and ECJ 9 March 1978, Case 106/77, *Simmenthal* [1978] ECR 629.

[39] I have developed this argument in detail in *Poder Judicial e Integración Europea*, Civitas, Madrid, 2004, p 331 et seq.

## 3. INDIVIDUAL VOICE

EU remedies are a procedural means through which individuals exert *Voice* in the course of a judicial dispute with an EU link. Remedies guarantee a course of legal protection, their efficiency and equivalence, as an accessory to the substantial content of individual rights as granted by EU Law to private parties. The complete picture of European remedies must be depicted in its two-tiered structure: remedies before national courts and remedies before Community courts. This distinction is not only necessary for the purposes of assigning tasks to different institutional actors, but also for conceptual reasons: the underlying rationale and the scope of legal protection vary depending on which level we stand. It goes without saying that the lack of uniform procedural rules throughout Europe, as well as the need to safeguard national institutional autonomy, make the national level an infinitely more delicate area to handle.

The development of EU remedies before national courts is a familiar process that does not need to be portrayed here.[40] However, it is important to insist on how these mechanisms work within their broader framework while focusing our eyes upon the individual. The genetic feature of European remedies is its subsidiary character. As developed by the ECJ, European remedies are tools in the hands of the individual with the aim of correcting systemic failures. Graphically put, European remedies are *emergency responses* and are only put into action when national provisions do not give EU Law its due procedural course of protection. It is therefore important to note that European remedies are not a starting point, a guarantee of access to national courts, but a last recourse in case of systemic failure. Having said that, individuals enjoy remedies as a subsidiary form of legal protection, repairing the damage inflicted by the national system mostly *ex post facto*.

Are European remedies a proper mechanism in the attribution of *Voice* to individuals? The retrospective logic behind European remedies, mostly concerned with repairing procedural defaults of national law, does not necessarily appear as a protective mechanism when giving an active role to individuals in the exercise of their rights. Quite the contrary, the emphasis should be put on access and preventive remedies. By granting the individual the possibility to claim his or her Community rights from the very outset before national courts, the *ex post facto* role of State liability (*Köbler*), or of judicial or administrative revocations (*Kühne*), should assume their proper place as remedies of last resort. *Access* is, therefore, the appropriate expression of *Voice* for the individual, and the procedure

[40] See, inter alia, J. Lonbay and A. Biondi (eds), *Remedies for Breach of EC Law*, John Wiley & Sons, Chichester, 1997; C. Kilpatrick, T. Novitz, and P. Skidmore, *The Future of Remedies in Europe*, Hart, Oxford, 2000 and M. Dougan, *National Remedies Before the Court of Justice: Issues of Harmonisation and Differentiation*, Hart, Oxford, 2004.

that canalises this access should be Article 267 TFEU.[41] Preventive access is a combination of expediency and rights protection that the preliminary reference procedure assures. It gives an authoritative answer *before* the national court renders its decision, and it avoids interpretative doubts to both national courts and parties. Also, preliminary references combine individual protection with national autonomy, granting national courts a margin of action in the context of a cooperative relationship that safeguards domestic specificity.

But is it simply enough to promote the role of Article 267 TFEU as the sole solution to individual *Voice*? In light of how the preliminary reference procedure stands today, there are important weaknesses in both its design and praxis. Besides the procedural obstacles that it poses for individuals, its main drawbacks are to be found in the national forum: courts of first instance are not familiar with Article 267 TFEU, and those of last instance, under the obligation to make a reference, have substantially abused the *CILFIT* doctrine and appear instead to be *too familiar* with the procedure. From a conceptual point of view, Article 267 TFEU could be the source of future developments if its approach is to change. The procedure certainly needs reforms, but in its foundations it could undergo further transformations.

A possible way forward would be to consider Article 267 TFEU as part of the European fundamental right of access to justice. Following the path of *Johnston*[42] and of a series of national Constitutional Courts, Article 267 TFEU could be introduced within the margins of the said fundamental right; not as part of national fundamental rights of due process, but rather as part of the Union's fundamental right. In his Opinion in *La Roda Golf*,[43] the late Advocate General Ruiz-Jarabo Colomer raised this point and purported an interpretation of the provisions governing the preliminary reference procedure in light of this fundamental right.[44] Such an approach would bring about two important

41 See, inter alia, ECJ 15 May 1986, Cases 222/84, *Johnston* [1986] ECR 1651, paras 18 and 19; ECJ 15 October 1987, Case 222/86, *Heylens and Others* [1987] ECR 4097, para 14; ECJ 27 November 2001, Case C-424/99, *Commission v Austria* [2001] ECR I-9285, para 45; and ECJ 19 June 2003, Case C-467/01, *Eribrand* [2003] ECR I-6471, para 61.

42 ECJ 15 May 1986, Cases 222/84, *Johnston* [1986] ECR 1651.

43 ECJ 25 June 2009, Case C-14/08, *Roda Golf & Beach Resort* [2009] ECR I-5439.

44 "Access to justice is a fundamental pillar of western legal culture. 'To no one will we sell, to no one will we deny or delay right or justice' proclaimed the Magna Carta in 1215, expressing an axiom which has remained in force in Europe to the extent that it features in the European Convention on Human Rights, the Charter of Fundamental Rights of the European Union and the case-law of the Court. Therefore, the right to effective legal protection is one of the general principles of Community law, in accordance with which access to justice is organised. In a number of Member States, such as Germany and Spain, that fundamental right is framed in such a way that it also includes the preliminary ruling procedure under Article [267 TFEU]. The present reference is doubly crucial with regard to safeguarding the procedural rights of individuals at both Community and national level. Access to justice entails not only the commencement of legal proceedings but also the requirement that the competent court

consequences: first, a spill-over effect over national fundamental rights that will eventually host Article 267 TFEU among their own constitutional repertoire; and second, a tendency to approach *CILFIT* and its criteria in a more rigorous manner by national courts of last instance.[45]

Remedies before national courts are substantially different to those provided by the Treaties before Community courts. The latter respond to a different rationale, and the principled justifications of access and individual *Voice* have the mission of giving a jurisdictional course of scrutiny to Community action, not national action. However, inasmuch as direct remedies before Community courts are coherent with the requirements of individual *Voice*, remedies before national courts will not come under pressure. As was proved in *UPA* and *Segi*,[46] when the ECJ declined to create more generous standing requirements before Community courts, the course of action has been left in the hands of national jurisdictions. It is unclear whether Member States can fully guarantee this alternative, and it is even more doubtful whether the institutional autonomy of Member States can assume Community procedural failure at all times and in all circumstances. It appears that Member States have realised this, and the Lisbon Treaty has finally given an appropriate response to the extraordinarily restrictive standing conditions previously posed by the Treaties to individuals willing to appeal against general regulatory Community provisions.[47] However, the burden still rests on the shoulders of individual litigants when challenging EU legislative acts. These provisions have been left outside the scope of protection of Lisbon,[48] leaving

must be seized of those proceedings. Furthermore, from a procedural point of view, references for a preliminary ruling are subject to the principles of the uniformity and consistency of Community law, from which it follows that any national court must have competence to seek assistance from the Court of Justice. Any barrier preventing a national court from making a reference undermines that fundamental right" (paragraph 29 of the Opinion).

45 Judgment of the German Bundesverfassungsgericht of 9 January 2001; judgment of the Austrian Constitutional Court of 11 December 1995; judgment of the Spanish Tribunal Constitucional 58/2004 of 19 April 2004; judgment of the Czech Constitutional Court of 8 January 2009 and judgment of the Slovak Constitutional Court of 3 July 2008. See F. Arndt, 'The German Federal Constitutional Court at the Intersection of National and European Law: Two Recent Decisions', (2001) 11 *German Law Journal*; M. Bobek, 'The Duty to Submit a Request for a Preliminary Ruling as a Constitutional Issue – A Discreet remedy being born?', not yet published, and R. Alonso García, 'Comment of judgment 58/2004', (2005) 42 *CMLR (Common Market Law Review).*

46 ECJ 25 July 2002, Case C-50/00 *P*, *Unión de Pequeños Agricultores v Council* [2002] ECR I-6677 and ECJ 27 February 2007, Case C-355/04 *P*, *Segi and Others v Council* [2007] ECR I-1657. Analysing both decisions, see the contributions of K. Lenaerts, and A. Alemanno, in M. Maduro, and L. Azoulaï (eds), *The Past and Future of EU Law: The Classics of EU Law Revisited on the 50th Anniversary of the Rome Treaty*, Hart Publishers, Oxford, 2010.

47 H. Hofmann, 'Legislation, Delegation and Implementation under the Treaty of Lisbon: Typology Meets Reality', (2009) 15 *ELJ (European Law Journal).*

48 See the Order of the General Court of 6 September 2011, Case T-18/10, *Inuit Tapiriit Kanatami* [2011], not yet reported.

claimants once again in the hands of national courts and the normatively strong, but pragmatically weak, system of European-made remedies.

## 4. AUTONOMY THROUGH PLURALISM

At this point, it must be noted that Member State and individual *Voice* are forms of engagement that enhance the legitimacy of the ECJ's decisions. They do so in a mutually dependant manner: Member State *Voice* enriches values akin to democracy and the rule of law; individual *Voice* articulates the fundamental right of access to justice, and therefore opens the gates for individual protection in a Union governed by the rule of law.[49] The ways in which the ECJ has developed its case law prove that it has been careful not to entangle itself in areas of constitutional relevance, and the practice of European judicial review shows how this subtle balance has been attempted, albeit not always in a successful manner. The reason why the Court has not always achieved the desired outcome could be explained by the need to develop a more articulated and pragmatic conception of constitutional pluralism. While cases foreign to constitutional issues are well safeguarded from the risks of Member State or individual critique, it is in the terrain of constitutionally sensitive matters that pluralism appears as a well-suited conceptual tool, in both its descriptive and normative form.

Constitutional pluralism is a methodology that explains why and how legitimacy in the European Union is a shared enterprise, the result of the pooled sovereignty that the Union shares with Member States. In judicial terms, constitutional pluralism portrays why, under certain conditions, a *Grundnorm* can shift and within which limits.[50] For our present purposes, the way in which Member State and individual *Voice* are currently shaped justify why constitutional pluralism is a proper methodology in explaining and purporting issues of legitimacy in EU Law. However, constitutional pluralism is the result of a long process, and

---

49 J.H.H. Weiler, 'The European Community in Change: Exit, Voice and Loyalty', (1990) 3 *Irish Studies of International Affairs*.

50 N. Walker, 'The Idea of Constitutional Pluralism', (2002) 65 *Modern Law Review*; M. Maduro, 'Contrapunctual law: Europe's constitutional pluralism in action', in N. Walker (ed), *Sovereignty in Transition*, Hart, Oxford, 2003; N. Walker, 'Late Sovereignty in the European Union' in N. Walker (ed), *Sovereignty in Transition*, Hart, Oxford, 2003; M. Kumm, 'The jurisprudence of constitutional conflict. Constitutional supremacy in Europe before and after the constitutional Treaty', (2005) 11 *ELJ*; N. Barber 'Legal Pluralism and the European Union', (2006) 12 *EJL*, 306; J. Komárek, 'European constitutionalism and the European Arrest Warrant: in search of the limits of 'contrapunctual principles', (2007) 44 *CMLR*; M. Rosenfeld, 'Rethinking constitutional ordering in an era of legal and ideological pluralism', (2008) 6 *I-CON (International Journal of Constitutional Law)*; A. von Bogdandy, 'Pluralism, direct effect, and the ultimate say: On the relationship between international and domestic constitutional law' (2008) 6 *I-CON*; J. Baquero, 'The Legacy of the Maastricht – Urteil and the Pluralist Movement', (2008) 14 *EJL*, 389, at 391.

several theoretical variants have developed over the course of time. The history of EU Law is, in a way, a history of pluralism as a jurisprudential account of this legal order. It is precisely for this reason that constitutional pluralism is a more sophisticated and therefore advanced approach for integrating legal orders, and that it is particularly well suited as a descriptive and normative tool for EU Law.

Briefly put, pluralism has undergone three stages that are inherently linked to the evolution of EU Law. In a first stage, *discursive pluralism* was the theory that paved the way for the first articulation and more primitive expression of EU Law. Direct effect, as stated in *Van Gend & Loos*[51] was a development of international law by an international court; a *new* legal order, but definitely not a federal nor a state-based one. Primacy was a conflict rule, to be included in the arsenal of national conflicts of laws. The preliminary reference procedure was a cooperative tool that portrayed a very crude reality: the ECJ's inability to scrutinise national provisions or actions. In this context, discursive pluralism portrayed the reality of a new legal order that communicated with, but did not integrate itself with, national legal orders. It was something *more* than international law, but definitely *less* than national law; its trademark being the way in which it *communicated* with domestic provisions and courts.

The development of the EU into a complex and bureaucratic organisation took its legal order into new terrains of deeper sophistication, opening the gates of *institutional pluralism* as an explanatory tool that expressed why the Commission, the ECJ and Member States interacted in such a fashion, why national courts played a stick and carrot game with the ECJ, and why strategic litigation became a crucial piece in the development of the new legal order. The ECJ developed the procedural courses through which direct effect and primacy were to be articulated, and its main result was *Simmenthal*[52] and the inception of a decentralised system of judicial review.[53] On the other hand, the ECJ also inaugurated a preventive case-law with the aim of avoiding judicial review of Community acts by national courts: *Internationale Handelsgesellschaft*[54] and the fundamental rights saga with the German Constitutional Court gave the Union a normative and procedural priority to this effect. The ECJ also began to develop ways of institutional impulse to the political process in its *Cassis de Dijon* case-law,[55] sending a clear message to the Council with the aim of enhancing legislative harmonisation if Member States wanted to avoid judicial harmonisation by way of mutual recognition. As can be seen, institutional pluralism developed with the purpose of facilitating, in

51 ECJ 5 February 1963, Case 26/62, *Van Gend en Loos* [1963] ECR 1.
52 ECJ 9 March 1978, Case 106/77, *Simmenthal* [1978] ECR 629.
53 V. Ferreres Comella, *Constitutional Courts and Democratic Values*, Yale University Press, New Haven, 2009, p 122 et seq.
54 ECJ 17 December 1970, Case 11/70, *Internationale Handelsgesellschaft* [1970] ECR 1125.
55 ECJ 20 February 1979, Case 120/78, *Rewe Zentral* [1979] ECR 649.

procedural terms (and more discretely in substantial terms as well), a dynamic rapport among the Commission, ECJ and Member States (including national courts here) that would help to interiorise the foundations of this new legal order.

Both discursive and institutional pluralism were overcome by the events of the late eighties and early nineties. The constitutional drive that transformed the Community into the Union, the creation of citizenship, the active role of the European Parliament, the new competences and the consolidation of an expanding case law by the ECJ, made these expressions of pluralism insufficient as descriptive and normative materials. At this point, a third strand, that of *constitutional pluralism,* acquires a new and more poignant face, recognising traditional dogmas of European legal integration together with the attribution to national institutions of the ability to discard European obligations. The reason why constitutional pluralism is a more sophisticated version of discursive and institutional pluralism lies in the fact that it takes these two variants seriously, but discards them when issues assume a constitutional dimension. For these purposes, constitutional pluralism finds its roots in the *nature* of cases before courts, and develops a methodology for the resolution of the conflict, particularly when it entails a normative clash and judicial review must be put into action.

At the current stage of legal integration, the search for legitimacy can be put forward by articulating Member State and individual *Voice* in their proper institutional framework and with constitutional pluralism as its theoretical backdrop. Since constitutional pluralism involves the ability and duty of all institutions concerned to engage in a constructive discourse with the aim of allocating conflicting value claims, it also entails that such a process must be developed in good faith and that all interpretative and communicative efforts will be exhausted. Through this effort to engage, *Loyalty* becomes the trademark of constitutional pluralism. It is therefore through *Loyalty*, and by constructing its theoretical and pragmatic content, that European Law is now building its own normative foundation vis-à-vis national legal orders. *Loyalty* appears as that form of brand loyalty binding contending claims that on occasions may have no rational solution, as Hirschmann famously claimed when portraying consumer loyalty or patriotism.

In substantial terms, the development of *Loyalty* has recently appeared as a logical result of constitutional pluralism. In judicial terms, the recent Lisbon decision of the German Constitutional Court is a developed expression of *Loyalty* in a contentious scenario of conflicting value claims. After portraying the red lines that the German Fundamental Law sets to European integration, the Court openly claimed its willingness to interpret the Constitution in light of its openness to European Law (*Grundsatz der Europarechtsfreundlichkeit*).[56] This assertion entails a European-oriented interpretation of conflicting scenarios on the part of the German court; whilst it should imply, as a coherent response thereto, the ECJ's willingness to engage in national-oriented interpretations of Union Law when facing constitutional clashes.[57] The recent *Audiolux* [58] judgment is significant proof of such an approach on the part of the ECJ. In this decision the ECJ stated that only principles of constitutional pedigree are to be taken into account when developing its case law on general principles. The backdrop of the *Mangold* judgement and the loud German reaction to this judgment seem to be justifying this new approach, in an effort to adjust national claims of autonomy with the EU's need to count as a complete legal order that leaves space to non-written principles.

In a context in which all members strive to achieve a more perfect Union, *Exit* is not the alternative to *Voice*, but *Loyalty*. When such a perfect Union reaches a point in which it decides to make a claim of constitutional authority, the alternative to *Voice* comes only by articulating a form of expression that will not always be accountable on a rational basis. European remedies therefore appear not only as litigating tools, but also as the path through which *Loyalty* develops and ultimately grants legitimacy to the EU's legal order; an order which looks so very different today from how it looked on the day it was born.

56 2 BvE 2/08, 2 BvE 5/08, 2 BvR 1010/08, 2 BvR 1022/08, 2 BvR 1259/08, 2 BvR 182/09, of 30 June 2009 (the *Lisbon* judgment), para 225; and implementing the principle in a constructive pro-integration approach, see 2 BvR 2661/06 (the *Honeywell* judgment).

57 A. Vosskühle, *Der Europäische Verfassungsgerichtsverbund*, Trans State Working Papers no. 106, p 12 to 14, confirmed in the *Honeywell* judgment of the Federal Constitutional Court, previously quoted.

58 ECJ 15 October 2009, Case C-101/08, *Audiolux and Others* [2009] ECR I-9823.

# PART VI

# CONCLUDING REMARKS – THE RIGHT'S DIMENSION

# THE ECJ BETWEEN THE INDIVIDUAL CITIZEN AND THE MEMBER STATES – A PLEA FOR A JUDGE-MADE EUROPEAN LAW ON REMEDIES[1]

Hans-W. Micklitz

## 1. THE ECJ BETWEEN THE INDIVIDUAL CITIZEN AND THE AUTONOMY OF THE MEMBER STATES

It is a well known phenomenon that the ECJ strengthened the position of the individual citizen in what was designed to be a Treaty under international public law between sovereign states. This form of judicial governance[2] met with sympathy in particular from the business side as the ECJ helped to tear down statutory national barriers to trade thereby enlarging economic freedoms. Consumers from all over Europe silently or explicitly supported the opening up of markets as they benefitted from greater choice. Things became more complicated when the European integration process changed its outlook in the aftermath of the Single European Act. The completion of the Internal Market came at a price – the gradual strengthening of policies that reached beyond the market such as environmental, consumer, health and social protection. The ECJ had to face the challenge of how to integrate and transform the 'Social',[3] which gradually found its way into the Treaty, in a judge-made legal order which was constructed on individually enforceable rights. The difficulties increased even further when the Treaty of Amsterdam introduced the concept of European Union citizenship which reaches beyond the original economic design of the European *Economic* Union as it was originally called. There is an abundant literature on the way in which

1 I would like to thank Loïc Azoulai, Bruno de Witte, Norbert Reich and Hanna Schebesta for their comments, which helped to improve the paper. The usual disclaimer applies.

2 S. Frerichs, *Judicial Governance in der europäischen Rechtsgemeinschaft, Integration durch Recht jenseits des Staates*, Nomos, Baden-Baden, 2008.

3 D. Kennedy, 'Three Globalizations of Law and Legal Thought: 1850–2000' in D.M. Trubek / A. Santos, *The New Law and Economic Development*, Cambridge University Press, Cambridge, 2006, p 19.

the ECJ transformed all sorts of collective interests bearing a social dimension or even EU citizenship into individually enforceable rights. The ever stronger intrusion of the ECJ into the shaping of market freedoms, of social policies and of citizenship raised increasingly deep concerns in the Member States. The critique is nourished by one and the same concern – the weakening of the autonomy of the Member States through expansive and activist European courts that are blamed for the destruction of the national social welfare state – *Viking*[4] and *Laval*,[5] but also *Mangold*[6] and *Kücükdevici*[7] – and for undermining the autonomy and the sovereignty of the nation state via the creation of European Union citizenship – *Carpenter*[8] and *Metock*.[9] The critique has gained impetus and the language is getting harder. The ECJ is time and again attacked for overstepping its adjudicatory powers, for acting *ultra vires*, for claiming Kompetenz-Kompetenz, i.e. constituent power, *pouvoir constituent*.[10]

The purpose of the conference held in Florence in April 2009 openly addressed the tension between an invasive ECJ which uses its 'rights' rhetoric to expand the reach of the European legal order and the Member States which are more and more concerned by their gradually reduced autonomy. In light of these concerns, my plea for an even more invasive ECJ in promoting the development of a genuine European system of rights, remedies and procedures (RRP) might come as a surprise (see *Amtenbrink*). The legal-political and legal-academic mainstream seems to point in a different direction, maybe not to reducing the role and function of the ECJ as the driving force of European integration, but advocating for a kind of 'stand-still' agreement leaving room for more political co-ordination. This might be even more so in the aftermath of the failed European Constitution and the painstaking process which finally led to the adoption of the Lisbon Treaty. The Florence conference brought academics from all over Europe together, many of them outstanding scholars and leading experts in their respective fields. The original idea was to use a selection of areas of European law, such as competence, internal market, fundamental rights, citizenship, social rights, remedies – see the table of contents – to demonstrate the contrast between the pros and cons, the critics and the supporters of the ECJ. Whilst this attempt more or less failed, it is

4 ECJ 18 December 2007, Case C-341/05, *Laval un Partneri Ltd v Bygnadds et al.* [2007] ECR I-11767.

5 ECJ 11 December 2007, Case C-438/05, *International Transport Workers Federation (ITF) and Finnish Seaman's Union (FSU) v. Viking Line* [2007] ECR I-10779.

6 ECJ 22 November 2005, Case C-144/04, *Mangold v Helm* [2005] ECR I-9981.

7 ECJ 19 January 2010, Case C-555/07, *Seda Kücükdevici v Swedex*, nyr.

8 ECJ 11 July 2002, Case C-60/00, *Mary Carpenter v Secretary of State for the Home Department* [2002] ECR I-6279

9 ECJ 25 July 2008, Case C-127/08, *Metock* [2008] ECR I-6241.

10 This is the key argument of R. Herzog, published in *Frankfurter Allgemeine Zeitung*, 24. July 2008; see for a sound analysis of how these highly debated judgments fit into the existing European legal order, K. Lenaerts/J. A. Gutiérrez-Fons, 'The Constitutional Allocation of Powers and General Principles of EU Law', (2010) 47 *CMLR* 1629.

still sizable in the various contributions. My personal impression from two days of discussions and from re-reading the contributions is that the 'ECJ managed it quite well to strike a balance between extension of the EU law and autonomy of the Member States'.

I will develop my argument in four steps, thereby using the various contributions to the conference as building blocks. I will first underline where I take the legitimacy for my plea from – the genuine and autonomous European legal order (2). I will then try to sketch out how far the consensus in RRP reaches and where the dissent begins (3). The next two chapters are an attempt to give shape to the *institutional* framework of a judge-made European law on remedies (4), which reaches beyond individual subjective rights and which relates the different sources of the Treaty and its multi-faceted character as a legal order, a constitutional charter and a European Economic Constitution to a more developed and sophisticated system of rights, remedies and procedures. The final part (5) outlines how a judge-made European law on remedies *de lege lata* could and should look like *in concreto*, particularly focussing on how it would reach beyond consensus and allow for strengthening the particularities of a 'genuine' and 'autonomous' legal order. Judicial protection could and should not be limited to economic integration; rather it should be understood as a means of social integration, where the civil status and the economic status are merging. What I am presenting here are preliminary thoughts which take the findings of the conference into consideration, thoughts which need to be discussed and which need to be further sharpened.

## 2. RRP IN A 'NEW' EUROPEAN LEGAL ORDER HAVING ITS 'OWN' LEGAL SYSTEM

Let me first recall the oft-quoted references in the landmark judgments of the ECJ, where the ECJ transformed the Treaty into a European legal order and then later into a constitutional charter governed by supremacy and direct effect. I will put in bold letters what I believe to be decisive in the context of my argument. The question raised by *Adinolfi*[11] with reference to *Kakouris*[12] is whether the fact that 'EU law had its own particular needs' entails the development of community law specific RRPs. This implies the need to look closer into the character of the European legal order, whether and to what extent it must be seen as an integral part of the national legal orders or whether it remains distinct and even separated from the national legal orders. My overall argument is that judicial protection forms an integral part of the constitutionalisation process of the EU.

11 The 'procedural autonomy' of Member States and the constraints stemming from the ECJ's case-law: is judicial activism still necessary?, in this volume.

12 C.N. Kakouris, 'Do the Member States possess judicial procedural 'autonomy'?', (1997) 34 *CMLR* 1389, at 1411–1412.

## 2.1. THE EU LEGAL ORDER AUTONOMOUS AND/OR INTEGRATED

The first series of judgments in the early 1960's underlined the innovative character of EEC. The second series in the 1980's transformed the legal order into a constitutional charter thereby pursuing a twofold purpose: a progressive one when reading into the Treaty that the ECJ is equally competent to control the Parliament; and a defensive one in that the constitutional charter needs to be protected against political attempts to re-transform it into an international treaty. The most recent series then tackled the relationship between the European legal order and the national legal orders, which is crucial for our context.

In *Van Gend en Loos*,[13] the ECJ invented the formula which has dominated the debate over the legal character of the Treaty for almost 50 years:

> The objective of the EEC Treaty, which is to establish a common market, the functioning of which is of direct concern to interested parties in the Community, implies that this treaty is more than an agreement which merely creates mutual obligations between the Contracting States… The conclusion to be drawn from this is that the Community constitutes *a new legal order of international law* for the benefit of which the States have limited their sovereign rights, albeit within limited fields, and the subjects of which comprise not only member states but also their nationals. *Independently* of the legislation of Member States, Community law therefore not only imposes obligations on individuals but is also intended to *confer upon them rights* which become part of their legal heritage.

The 'new' legal order is different from any other legal order, but it is one which is designed under international law, one which grants directly enforceable rights to individuals. In the light of the arguments brought forward by the Member States in the proceedings, the ECJ was well aware of the fact that it had no blueprint against which the 'new' legal order could be designed and that it led the European Economic Union, as it then was, into rough political and legal waters.[14] The new legal order was 'new' in the true sense of the word. The European legal order was no longer regarded as a Treaty under international public law, nor was it seen

---

13 ECJ 5 February 1962, Case 26/62, *Van Gend en Loos* [1963] ECR-3.

14 F.C. Mayer, 'The Foundation of a Community of Law' in M. Poiares Maduro/L. Azoulai (eds) *The Past and The Future of EU Law, The Classics of EU Law Revisited on the 50th Anniversary of the Treaty of Rome*, Hart Publishing, Oxford, 2010, 16, at 18 'The Member States: A Double No', but see also the rather positive reaction from the head of the German delegation that negotiated the EEC Treaty at 22. For a reconstruction of the history of *van Gend en Loos* and *Costa Enel*, M. Rasmussen, 'From *Costa v. Enel* to the Treaties of Rome: A brief history of a Legal Revolution', in M. Poiares Maduro/L. Azoulai (eds) *The Past and The Future of EU Law, The Classics of EU Law Revisited on the 50th Anniversary of the Treaty of Rome*, Hart Publishing, Oxford, 2010, 69.

as a 'European nation' or 'a European state' similar to the Member States: the European legal order was identified as being 'different' and 'distinct' from all other national and international orders. The content of the 'new' order remains rather vague, though. All that we learn is that the new order is one which is based on a competence division and on rights conferred to individuals – and that it is for the ECJ alone to decide which of the rules of the Treaty are given direct effect.[15] In *Costa Enel*[16] the ECJ established the supremacy of the European law inside the legal systems of the Member States and thereby completed what *M. Rasmussen*[17] calls 'a revolution in European law'.[18] Here, contrary to *van Gend en Loos*, the ECJ was forced to take a position on the relationship between the two legal orders – the 'new' international one and the Member States' domestic legal systems. It referred to EEC Treaty as being governed by its 'own' legal system, but integrated into the Member States legal systems:

> By contrast with ordinary international treaties, the EEC treaty has created *its own legal system* which, on the entry into force of the Treaty, became *an integral part of the legal systems of the Member States* and which their courts are bound to apply.

In *Les Verts*[19] the ECJ called the Treaty for the first time a constitutional charter (with a small 'c'[20]), thereby strengthening the system of remedies provided to Member States and the EU for reviewing the legality of EU measures. It is here were we find for the first time the notion of 'a complete system of legal remedies and procedures'. This is a crucial message in the context of the paper as the doctrine affects the further shaping of RRPs as well as the constitutional character of RRPs:[21]

---

15 Which is said to be the 'crucial doctrinal contribution', B. de Witte, The Continuous Significance of *van Gend en Loos'* in M. Poiares Maduro/L. Azoulai (eds) *The Past and The Future of EU Law, The Classics of EU Law Revisited on the 50th Anniversary of the Treaty of Rome*, Hart Publishing, Oxford, 2010, 9, at 10.

16 ECJ 15 July 1964, Case 6/64, *Costa Enel* [1964] ECR 585.

17 M. Rasmussen, 'From *Costa v. Enel* to the Treaties of Rome: A brief history of a Legal Revolution', in M. Poiares Maduro/L. Azoulai (eds) *The Past and The Future of EU Law, The Classics of EU Law Revisited on the 50th Anniversary of the Treaty of Rome*, Hart Publishing, Oxford, 2010, 69.

18 See also the seminal article of E. Stein, 'Lawyers, Judges and the Making of a Transnational Constitution', (1981) 75 *AJIL* 1.

19 ECJ 26 September 1984, Case 294/83, *Les Verts* [1986] ECR 1339, at 23, for a deeper reading, N. Walker, 'Opening or Closure? The Constitutional Intimation of the ECJ', in M. Poiares Maduro/ L. Azoulai (eds) *The Past and The Future of EU Law, The Classics of EU Law Revisited on the 50th Anniversary of the Treaty of Rome*, Hart Publishing, Oxford, 2010, 333.

20 N. Walker, 'Big 'C' or small 'c'', (2006) 12 *ELJ* 12–14.

21 In later cases the ECJ was more reluctant on whether the system of the Treaty is to be regarded as 'complete', K. Lenaerts, 'A Community Based on a 'Constitutional Charter' Community Law as a Complete and Coherent Constitution System' in M. Poiares Maduro/L. Azoulai (eds) *The Past and The Future of EU Law, The Classics of EU Law Revisited on the 50th Anniversary of the Treaty of Rome*, Hart Publishing, Oxford, 2010, 298, at 307 with reference to 'Pupino';

(23) It must first be emphasized in this regard that the European Economic Community is a community based *on the rule of law, inasmuch as neither its Member States* nor its institutions can avoid a review of the question whether the measures adopted by them are in conformity with the *basic constitutional charter*, the Treaty. In particular, in Articles 173 (Now Article 230) and 184 (now Article 241), on the one hand, and in Article 177 (now Article 234) on the other, the Treaty established *a complete legal system of legal remedies and procedures* designed to permit the Court of Justice to review the legality of measures adopted by institutions.

In *Opinion 1/91*,[22] in which the ECJ rejects the compatibility of the EEA Treaty with the EU Treaty, the ECJ is even more outspoken on the reach of the constitutional charter which is no longer 'basic' and which not only includes a system of remedies, but is explicitly said to be dominated by 'supremacy' and 'direct effect':

(21) (The) EEC Treaty, albeit concluded in the form of an international agreement, none the less constitutes the *constitutional charter* of a Community based on the rule of law. As the Court of Justice has consistently held, the Community treaties established a new legal order for the benefit of which the States have limited their sovereign rights, in ever wider fields, and the *subjects* of which comprise not only Member States, but also their nationals (see, in particular the judgment in Case 26/62 Van Gend en Loos (1963) ECR 1). The essential characteristic of the Community legal order which has thus been established are in particular its *primacy* over the law of the Member States and the *direct effect of a whole series of provisions which are applicable to their nationals and to the Member States themselves.*

The latest in the series of judgments to be mentioned here is *Kadi*,[23] where the ECJ first recalled the formula found in *Les Verts*, but then added a new facet to the oscillating concept of a European Constitution:

(81) Being thus called upon, in the second place, to determine the scope of the review of legality, especially in the light of fundamental rights, that it must carry out concerning Community measures giving effect to resolutions of the Security Council, such as the contested regulation, the Court of First Instance

even harder A. Alemanno, 'What Has Been, and What Could Be, Thirty Years after Les Verts/ European/Parliament' in M. Poiares Maduro/L. Azoulai (eds) *The Past and The Future of EU Law, The Classics of EU Law Revisited on the 50th Anniversary of the Treaty of Rome*, Hart Publishing, Oxford, 2010, 324, at 326 referring to Case C-314/85, *Foto-Frost*, Case C-222/84 *Johnston*, Case C-188/92, *TWD Textilwerke Deggendorf*, which have completed the 'complete system'; and later in the text V.1.

22 ECJ 14 December 1991, *Opinion 1/91*, [1991] ECR I-6079, at 21.

23 ECJ 3 September 2008, Joined Cases C-402/05 P and C-415/05 P, *Kadi and Al Barakaat International Foundation v Council and Commission*, [2008] ECR I-6351.

> first recalled ... that ... the European Community is based on the rule of law, inasmuch as neither its Member States nor its institutions can avoid review of the question whether their acts are in conformity with the *basic constitutional charter*, the EC Treaty, which established a *complete system of legal remedies and procedures* designed to enable the Court of Justice to review the legality of acts of the institutions.
> (202) Furthermore, *the coexistence of the Union and the Community as integrated but separate legal orders, and the constitutional architecture of the pillars*, as intended by the framers of the Treaties now in force ... constitute considerations of an institutional kind militating against any extension of the bridge to articles of the EC Treaty other than those with which it explicitly creates a link.

Right from the beginning of what was later termed the 'constitutionalisation process of the European Union', two different strains of arguments can be clearly distinguished: (1) one which insists on the distinct nature of the European Treaty, encapsulated in references to a 'new' legal order which establishes 'rights' 'independent' from national legal orders (*van Gend en Loos*), enshrined in a constitutional charter (*Opinion 1/91*) and (2) one which underlines the strong link between the new European legal order, i.e. the constitutional charter, and its national counterparts by putting emphasis on the European legal order being an 'integral part of the national legal systems' (*Costa Enel*), being measured against the constitutional requirements inherent in national legal orders (*Les Verts*) or stressing explicitly the parallel nature of the Member States' and the Community's 'integrated but separated legal orders' (*Kadi*).

There is much room for interpretation of what exactly the latest shift in *Kadi* means and whether it contradicts the former concept. ECJ has not given a clear answer yet. One might, however, deduce from the landmark cases that the European legal order is both unique and separate, as well as being interrelated with – to the point of even being integrated into – the national legal orders. This distinction, however, is questioned by the well established practice of the ECJ to strive for an autonomous interpretation[24] of EU law, independently of whether it comes under the first or second category. Autonomous interpretation could therefore lead to differences even in areas where the EU law is integrated into the national law.

There is a first lesson to be learnt from the double function of the Treaty with regard to RRP – rights, remedies and procedures. There may be fields in which EU law and national law are congruent, but there might also be areas where the European legal order is specific in the sense that national legal orders do not contain a blueprint for action. The point then is not only where to draw the line

[24] ECJ 6 October 1982, Case C-283/81, *CILFIT and Lanificio di Gavardo SPA v Ministry of Health* [1982] ECR 3415.

between the two different situations but how to handle the doctrine established in *Les Verts* and confirmed in *Opinion 1/91* that the treaties provide for a 'complete system of remedies and procedures'.

## 2.2. THREE EUROPEAN LEGAL ORDERS – ECONOMIC, SOCIAL AND CITIZEN?

It is a truism that the European legal order is based on rights and that the ECJ has been and still is the driving force behind this development ever since. The credo of the ECJ has already been laid down in *van Gend en Loos*:[25]

> Independently of the legislation of Member States, Community law therefore not only imposes obligations on individuals but is also intended *to confer upon them rights which become part of their legal heritage*. These rights arise not only where they are expressly granted by the Treaty, but also by reason of obligations which the Treaty imposes in a clearly defined way upon individuals as well as upon the Member States and upon the institutions of the Community.

When the ECJ coined that formula Europe was still called European *Economic* Community. So what the ECJ had implicitly in mind was the creation of economic rights to the benefit of business. Under the strong influence of German ordo-liberal thinking the European Economic Union was conceived as a *European Economic Constitution*.[26] The constitutional order of the EEC, the four freedoms and the competition rules, should shield business against statutory regulatory interventions in the market order by which all sorts of non-market related policies could be promoted. The directly applicable rights which the ECJ deduced from the Treaty were turned into a tool to eliminate any national statutory regulatory measures regarded as unduly and illegitimately hindering the free flow of goods and services. The mechanism established by the ECJ mainly under the preliminary reference procedure is certainly unique and has no counterpart in national or other supranational regional legal orders. At most, national legal orders allow nationals to invoke rights against statutory measures. What makes the EU mechanism unique is that it allows for the striking down of national statutory measures by reference to a superior legal order.

---

25 ECJ 5 February 1962, Case 26/62, *Van Gend en Loos* [1963] ECR-3.

26 E.-J. Mestmäcker, *Wirtschaft und Verfassung in der Europäischen Union, Beiträge zu Recht, Theorie und Politik der Europäischen Integration*, Nomos, Baden-Baden, (2nd ed), 2006; Ch. Joerges, 'A Renaissance of the European Economic Constitution' in U. Neergard/ R. Nielsen/L. M. Roseberry (eds), *Integrating Welfare Functions into EU Law – From Rome to Lisbon*, Djof Publishers, Copenhagen, 2009, 29; J. Drexl, 'Wettbewerbsverfassung' in A. von Bogdandy/J. Bast (Eds), *Europäisches Verfassungsrecht*, Springer, Dordrecht etc, 2009, p 905.

In Germany ordo-liberal thinking came under pressure with the rise of the social welfare state where 'law' became widely used to implant into the market order social policy concerns, enhanced protection of workers, as well as the newly discovered devices to protect the environment and the consumer. Similar tendencies could be observed in the European Union in the aftermath of the Single European Act. *Craig*[27] analyses how the extension of social competences in the broadest sense affected the autonomy of the Member States and changed the outlook of the European Union. Some go as far as arguing that the adoption of the Maastricht Treaty in 1991 constituted the end of the ordo-liberal European Economic Constitution.[28] Be that as it may, the Lisbon Treaty not only makes the Charter of Fundamental Rights an integral part of the European legal order, it also introduces under pressure from France the new paradigm of a 'social market economy'. Whether the new paradigm must be read as the official end of the ordo-liberal version of the European Economic Constitution[29] or whether it is to be seen as mere window dressing,[30] remains to be seen.

What has undoubtedly changed is the character of the European legal order. The European economic order and the emerging European social order are standing side-by-side. I will not embark on the debate of whether the European Economic Constitution has now been complemented by a European Social Constitution, which would bring me to discuss the 'Many Constitutions of Europe'.[31] I would like, however, to raise the question whether and to what extent the so-called *European social order* could or should be regarded as a distinct legal order separate from the economic order governed by a proper understanding of RRPs. The major differences between the economic order on the one hand and the social order on the other is that the Treaty even in its most developed form does not establish self-executing social rights, but merely formulates policy objectives which can only be achieved by way of secondary community law measures.[32]

27 Competence and Member State Autonomy: Causality, Consequence and Legitimacy, in this volume.

28 Ch. Joerges, 'A Renaissance of the European Economic Constitution', in U. Neergard/R. Nielsen/L. M. Roseberry (eds), *Integrating Welfare Functions into EU Law – From Rome to Lisbon*, Djof Publishing, Copenhagen, 2009, p 29.

29 In this direction L. Azoulai, 'The Court of Justice and the Social Market Economy: The Emergence of an Ideal and the Conditions for its Realisation', (2008) 45 *CMLR* 1335.

30 J. Drexl, 'Wettbewerbsverfassung' in A. von Bogdandy/J. Bast (Eds) *Europäisches Verfassungsrecht*, Springer, Dordrecht etc, 2009, p 905.

31 K. Tuori/S. Sankari (eds), *The Many Constitutions of Europe*, Ashgate Publishing, Farnham/Burlington, 2010.

32 The ECJ is quite generous in recognising 'rights' either as individually enforceable rights or as 'interests', which have to be taken into account, M. Kumm, '*Internationale Handelsgesellschaft, Nold* and the New Human Rights Paradigm' in M. Poiares Maduro/L. Azoulai (eds) *The Past and The Future of EU Law, The Classics of EU Law Revisited on the 50th Anniversary of the Treaty of Rome*, Hart Publishing, Oxford, 2010, 106.

The social field is not homogenous. That is why the situation differs considerably in the various areas of 'The Social', in regard to the transfer of competences, in scope and in depth. The Member States were prepared to delegate powers to the EU in the field of environmental, consumer protection and anti-discrimination, but were much more reluctant in core areas of social security and employment law.[33] There is another major difference between the European economic order and the European social order. The former is inherently based on the idea that uniform standards apply all over Europe, while the latter draws on a distinction between minimum and maximum standards. The social dimension developed incrementally, step by step, and was designed to conceive a market based on a limited set of social guarantees. Originally social standards were regarded as being conceived as minimum standards per se, as the EU did not compete with the Member States over the design of the social welfare state. The deeper the EU intervened into 'The Social', the more the European Commission started advocating for maximum standards, at times alone but sometimes supported by the ECJ.[34] At the time of writing, it seems as if the heyday of maximum harmonisation policy is over and that a European social order will mainly be based on minimum standards or, to put it differently, the European social order based on minimum standards defines a framework which might be completed by higher national social standards.

Any shaping of RRPs has to face the challenges of the minimax debate and the overarching degree of compliance between the European social order and the national social order. This means that there will remain few areas where the European social order is distinct from the national legal order. Distinct differences might show up where European social measures embark upon new areas within the respective policy field, such as e.g. the anti-discrimination law or where they deal with particular trans-border issues that do not emerge in a purely national legal environment e.g. posted workers. RRPs should be the same whether the underlying social standards are fully or partially harmonised. It does not make sense to distinguish RRPs in fully harmonised areas from those where harmonisation lays down only minimum standards. However, one might consider the availability of distinct RRPs in social areas that bear a genuine European character and remain outside the Member States' ambit.

I wonder whether there is a third legal order in the offing which again bears a particular European connotation – a European *citizen rights order*, although here the *trans-border* dimension is much more dominant than in the social legal

---

33 F. Rödl, 'Europäische Arbeitsverfassung' in A. von Bogdandy/J. Bast (Eds) *Europäisches Verfassungsrecht*, Springer, Dordrecht etc, 2009.

34 See ECJ 16 December 2008, Case C-205/07, *Gysbrechts* [2008] ECR I-9947; comment W.-H. Roth, (2010) 47 *CMLR* 509.

order.[35] Union citizenship was introduced in 1991 in the Treaty of Maastricht. *Kostakopulou*[36]and *Dougan*[37] discuss the development European Citizenship and the particular role of the ECJ. There is overall agreement in the legal doctrine that the ECJ has freed Union citizenship from the economic foundations of the European Union. This means that citizenship issues must not be related to economic activities. Citizenship rights are protected independent of whether the nationals (or to a certain extent the non-nationals) exercises a profession or is at least a passive recipient of the four market freedoms. *Kostakopoulou*[38] distinguishes three areas: citizenship as status, family reunification and non discriminatory restrictions. A whole series of bold judgments – *Grzelczyk*[39] and *Baumbast*[40] defining the status of citizenship, *Carpenter, Metock* and *Chen*[41] providing for a broad understanding of family reunification, just to name a few, have raised strong concerns in the respective Member States. There are at least two reasons which justify the reluctance of the Member States and which at the same time demonstrate the potential which lies in the development of a particular European citizen rights order. The first reason is that in *Baumbast* the ECJ understood Article 21 TFEU as creating directly effective rights; the second that the ECJ deduced European Union citizenship directly from the nature of the EU legal order which seems to favour a reading under which the ECJ might be prepared to disconnect national from European Union citizenship.[42] However, in *Rottmann*[43] the ECJ clarified that there is no such thing as a European Union Citizenship which exists independent from national citizenship. In so far the ECJ interpreted Union citizenship as being an integral part of the national legal order.

What does this imply with regard to RRPs? Referring back to the basic distinction already enshrined in *van Gend en Loos* and *Costa Enel*, the European citizen rights order could be understood as a stand-alone order, widely disconnected though

35 The transborder dimension dominates the case law of the ECJ as well as the conception of European citizenship, F. Jacobs, 'Citizenship of the European Union – A Legal Analysis', (2007) 13 *ELJ*, 59; also L. Azoulai, 'La Citoyenneté Européenne, un Statut d'Integration Social' in *Mélange en l'honneur du Professeur Jean Paul Jacqué*, Dalloz, Paris, 2010, forthcoming.

36 'The European Court of Justice, Member State Autonomy and European Citizenship: Conjunctions and Disjunctions', in this volume.

37 'Judicial Activism or Constitutional Interaction? Policymaking by the ECJ in the field of Union Citizenship' in this volume.

38 In this volume.

39 ECJ 20 September 2001, Case C-184/99, *Grzelczyk v Centre Public d'Aide Sociale d'Ottignies-Louvain-la-Neuve* [2001] ECR I-6193.

40 ECJ 17 September 2002, Case C-413/99, *Baumbast and R v Secretary of State for the Home Department* [2002] ECR I-7091.

41 ECJ 19 October 2004, Case C-200/02, *Kunqian Catherine Zhu and Man Lavette Chen v Secretary of State for the Home Department* [2004] ECR I-9925.

42 At least this is the understanding of Kostakopoulou taken in this volume.

43 ECJ 2 March 2010, Case C-135/08, *Rottmann*, nyr. See for an attempt to separating nationality and citizenship M.J. Garot, *La Citoyenneté de l'Union Européenne*, 1999, as quoted in N. Reich, *Understanding EU Law*, Intersentia, Antwerp, 2nd ed, 2005, at 86.

not independent from the Member States legal order. Contrary to social rights, the ECJ designed Union citizenship as a directly enforceable right enshrined in the Treaty itself. It is plain that there is no similar article in the Treaty which grants a particular status to consumers or workers. However, one might wonder whether the citizenship case-law could not be used to upgrade the position of the consumer and the worker in the Treaty. The European Commission has already introduced the citizen-consumer, a concept which gains ground in the academic discussion although its legal content remains to be spelt out.[44] Why should there not be a citizen-worker then?[45] My starting hypothesis is that the European citizen rights order could strengthen the status of workers, consumers and environmentalists in the European social order, and thereby under the European Economic Constitution by extension. The rather independent and largely autonomous concept of European citizenship facilitates such a transfer of arguments and status from the European civil rights order to the social order. The European citizen rights order could serve as a bridge between the European economic order and the European social order – albeit a fragile bridge, however, as the two dimensions cannot so easily be merged.[46] The flip-side of the coin is the citizen-businessman. The citizenship dimension cannot be limited to the social order as it would equally affect the economic order. I will return to these implications later on.

## 2.3. A RIGHTS BASED ORDER – ECONOMIC, FUNDAMENTAL, SOCIAL, HUMAN, CITIZEN RIGHTS

The threefold distinction between the economic, the social and the citizen rights order suggests a clear-cut distribution between the respective categories of rights. Such an understanding is not very helpful, however. There would not seem to be any common understanding of how these different rights might be separated from one another, and if so what for. From my German background I would argue that distinguishing between economic, social and citizen rights is prima vista self-explanatory. Fundamental rights (Grundrechte)[47] cover all three dimensions,

---

[44] See J. Davies, 'Entrenchment of New Governance in Consumer Policy Formulation: A Platform for European Consumer Citizenship Practice?', (2010) 32 *JCP* 201.

[45] M. Dougan, 'Free Movement: The Workseeker as Citizen 2001', (2001) 93 *CYELS*, at 9; M. Bell/R. Whittle, 'Between Social Policy and Union Citizenship, The Framework Directive on Equal Treatment in Employment', (2002) 27 *ELRev* 677.

[46] A. J. Menéndez, 'European Citizenship after Martinez Sala and Bambast: Has European Law Become more Human and Less Social?' in M. Poiares Maduro/L. Azoulai (eds) *The Past and The Future of EU Law, The Classics of EU Law Revisited on the 50th Anniversary of the Treaty of Rome*, Hart Publishing, Oxford, 2010, 363.

[47] A.V. Bogdandy, 'The European Union as a Human Rights Organization?', (2000) 37 *CMLR*, 1308.

just as human rights do, at least if one takes the three generations of human rights into account. The difficulties are more subtle. The border line between economic and social rights is far from being clear. Many social rights bear a strong economic connotation, as came clear in *Viking* and *Laval*. Citizen rights reach into social rights, when combined in concepts like the citizen-consumer and citizen worker. Fundamental rights have no clear meaning. The ECJ sometimes qualifies economic rights as fundamental rights.[48] The EU Charter on Fundamental Rights sets out mostly social and citizen rights, but from a German understanding a number of these rights overlap with economic rights. *Azoulai*[49] and *Cartabia*[50] start from the premise that the Charter on Fundamental Rights, or even more specifically the notion of fundamental rights, does not deal with economic rights. Human rights – in particular via their interpretation through the European Court of Human Rights – are more and more economised which makes the envisaged integration of the European Human Rights Convention into the EU legal order more problematic.

RRPs show up as a human right in Articles 6 and 13 ECHR and as a fundamental right in Article 47 EU Charter. The ECJ has referred to Articles 6 and 13 ECHR in all sorts of cases notwithstanding the nature of the right, be it economic, social and citizen. The same holds true with regard to the case-law in which the ECJ also referred to Article 47 EU.[51] One might therefore wonder whether any attempt to classify the rights according to their origin or nature is helpful at all.

Similar confusion exists with regard to the right holder. The general understanding might be to associate rights, whatever they are and wherever they come from with a right holder, be it a natural or a legal person, a national, an EU national or a non-EU national. However, in *Schmidberger*[52] and *Omega*[53] the ECJ seems to understand the Member State as the right holder.[54] The question then arises as to whether Member States can hold fundamental rights,[55] as AG *Maduro*[56] seems to suggest when he writes: "the fact that the view of the fundamental rights held by a

48 ECJ 13 December 1989, Case C-49/89, *Corsica Ferries France* [1989] ECR 4441, at 8, in this context L. Azoulai, 'The Court of Justice and the Social Market Economy: The Emergence of an Ideal and the Conditions for its Realization', (2008) 45 *CMLR* 1335.

49 'The ECJ and the Autonomy of the Member States: The case of Fundamental Rights: A State of Ambivalence', in this volume.

50 'A pluralistic Europe of Rights', in this volume.

51 ECJ 16 July 2009, Case C-12/08, *Mono Car Styling* [2009] ECR I-6653, at 47.

52 ECJ 12 June 2003, Case C-112/00, *Eugen Schmidberger v Austria* [2003] ECR I-5659.

53 ECJ 14 October 2004, Case C-36/02, *Omega* [2004] ECR I-9609.

54 See for a critical assessment of such an understanding, N. Reich, 'How proportionate is the proportionality principle in the internal market case law of the ECJ', in this volume.

55 See the suggestive title of J.-D. Mouton, 'Vers une reconnaissance des droits fondamentaux aux Etats dans le système communautaire ?' in *Les Dynamiques du droit européen en début du siècle. Etudes en l'honneur de J.-C. Goutron*, Paris, Pedone, 2004, 463.

56 ECJ 16 December 2008, Case C-213/07, *Michaniki* [2008] ECR I-9999, at 32.

Member State is not shared by other Member States does not prevent that Member State from relying on it so as to justify a restriction of the freedom to provide services". The deeper question is whether and to what extent Member States may defend public interests against competing private economic interests, which leads directly to the next complicated question of what might be understood by public interests or public policy (policies) at the European level, as can easily be demonstrated by reference to the ECJ case law in the social (consumer protection) field.[57] *Claro*[58] adds a new dimension to the uncertainty in that it queries the proper classification of RRPs as individual rights or public policy. AG *Tizziano*[59] seeks the solution in the violation of the individual right to be heard, whereas the ECJ[60] seems prepared to understand certain mandatory consumer protection rules as public policy.

My search for a tentative explanation to the terminological and conceptual confusion directs me to what is termed 'constitutionalisation' of legal orders. The process of constitutionalisation is initiated and driven by the 'rights revolution'. It covers all fields of law and, to the dismay of a large number of civil lawyers, also encompasses the national and the European private law regimes.[61] Economic rights are constitutionalised – not only via the concept of the European Economic Constitution but in particular via the impact of non-economic (mainly social) rights on economic rights. This happened in *Viking* and *Laval*. Social rights are going to be constitutionalised via the Treaty and via the Charter on Fundamental Rights – *Kücükdevici* and the majority of the anti-discrimination cases might serve as examples. Civil rights may be regarded as constitutional rights per se, but in the framework of the Treaty they could serve a bridging function to social–constitutional rights (consumer protection) or economic–constitutional rights (the four freedoms).

---

57 E.g. whether consumer protection, being part of social protection, can be regarded as an integral part of public policy, ECJ 26 October 2006, Case C-168/05, *Elisa María Mostaza Claro v. Centro Móvil Milenium SL* [2006] ECR I-10421; ECJ 6 October 2009, Case C-40/08, *Asturcom Telecomunicaciones SL* [2009] ECR I-9579; ECJ 4 June 2009, Case C-243/08, *Pannon GSM Zrt. v Erzsébet Sustikné Győrfi*, [2009] ECR I-4713.

58 ECJ 26 October 2006, Case C-168/05, *Elisa María Mostaza Claro v. Centro Móvil Milenium SL* [2006] ECR I-10421.

59 Opinion of 27 April 2006, Case C-168/05, *Mostaza Claro* [2006] ECR I-10421, at 58.

60 ECJ 26 October 2006, Case C-168/05, *Mostaza Claro* [2006] ECR I-10421, at 36.

61 See for a discussion S. Grundmann (ed), *Constitutional Values and European Contract Law*, Wolters Kluwer, Alphen, 2008; O.O. Cherednychenko, *Fundamental Rights, Contract Law and the Protection of the Weaker Party, A Comparative Analysis of the Constitutionalisation of the Contract Law with Emphasis on Risky Financial Transactions*, Sellier, Munich, 2007; A.C. Ciachhi/G. Brüggemeier/G. Commandé (eds), *Fundamental Rights and Private Law in the European Union, Volume II, Comparative Analysis of Selected Case Patterns*, Cambridge University Press, Cambridge, 2010; C. Mak, *Fundamental Rights in European Contract Law, A Comparison of the Impact of Fundamental Rights on Contractual Relationships in Germany, the Netherlands, Italy and England*, Kluwer Law International, Alphen, 2008.

The constitutionalisation process yields two major effects as stressed by *Azoulai*:[62] the potential threat of EU fundamental rights to national legal orders and the need to balance out conflicting values, i.e. conflicting rights at the EU level. *Azoulai* demonstrates how the fundamental rights issue turned from a threat of national (constitutional) law to EU law into a threat posed by EU fundamental rights to national (inter alia constitutional) laws. The latter aspect is spelt also out in detail by *Cartabia*. I would add that the need for constitutional balancing will necessarily arise as seemingly each and every conflict and litigation today is claimed to bear a constitutional dimension. Such a finding implies that conflicts around RRPs are perceived as constitutional conflicts regarding divergent values and that the extension of European RRPs threatens the national legal orders. When each and every right bears a constitutional dimension as it enshrines constitutional values, then every right-holder also bears a constitutional responsibility.[63]

RRPs *could* have a constitutional dimension. Any recognition of a new right under the Treaty bears a constitutional dimension – but is this equally true with regard to rights enshrined in secondary law, i.e. in the field of social protection? Remedies might contain a constitutional dimension when they affect the 'particularities' of the legal order of the European Union, as in *Francovich*. But the same cannot be said for each and every remedy in the field of consumer and labour law, although one might wonder from what point onwards does the non-availability of appropriate remedies gain a constitutional dimension. Procedures could have a constitutional dimension, but how does one distinguish more technical rules from those with a human or fundamental rights impact? I will come back to that distinction later in my paper. The 'threat' can also take different forms. *Azoulai* uses the paradigm in order to analyse the liberty, the independence and the identity of the State. He stresses the institutional implications between the ECJ and the Member States, but he does not look into the implications for an individual seeking 'justice' before and through the ECJ. Plaintiffs behind preliminary reference procedures feel threatened by the insufficiency, or even absence, of national RRPs. They put their faith in the ECJ to improve their legal situation beyond the national level. In its rights-based approach to the European legal order the ECJ has itself set these expectations into motion, rather successfully with regard to the setting aside of national laws constituting barriers to trade, but much less successfully in the area of social regulation.

62 In this volume.

63 In this vein, L. Azoulai, 'The Court of Justice and the Social Market Economy: The Emergence of an Ideal and the Conditions for its Realization', (2008) 45 *CMLR* 1335, at 1350 et seq, see on the possible consequences for the shaping of RRPs under IV.3. b).

## 3. RRP – FIRST, SECOND, THIRD... HOW MANY GENERATIONS?

The majority of the voluminous literature dealing with RRP analyses the ECJ case-law *from within*, thereby trying to define a more or less clear demarcation of what shall be put in the hands of EU law and what shall remain for the Member States (courts). There is, however, a strong need to analyse the judge-made European legal order *from without*, i.e. from a constitutional perspective which starts from the premise that constitutionally a line must be drawn between EU and Member States competences in the application and enforcement of EU law. I will restrict myself to highlighting the difficulties which are enshrined in the concept of conferred or attributed powers when it comes down to shaping RRPs, before I try to show how far the consensus in RRP might reach and where dissent will probably begin. This is a difficult task in light of the inconsistent case-law in the area of RRP, which *Bobek* calls a 'mess'. My task is somewhat facilitated in that I do not intend to define a common denominator in the legal doctrine, but a common denominator in the case-law of the ECJ.

### 3.1. THE AMBIGUITIES OF THE CONCEPT OF CONFERRED OR ATTRIBUTED COMPETENCES

*Koen Lenaerts*, an active judge of the ECJ, wrote in 2007:[64]

> By virtue of the principle of conferred or attributed competences, the Court of Justice of the European Communities exercises only the jurisdiction conferred on it by the Treaties. Otherwise, it falls to the courts of the Member States to adjudicate cases involving community law. In other words, each Member States contributes its own judicial system for the sake of ensuring the effective application and enforcement of Community law, which is indeed in line with the deeper philosophy of unity and diversity underlying the Union itself.

This statement reproduces in a highly condensed form the general self-understanding of the ECJ which is obviously in line with what the founding fathers of the Treaty had in mind, setting aside the rather opaque formula of 'integrated but separated' the ECJ found in *Kadi*. The thinking departs from a sense of the European and the national courts being institutionally parallel. Though they are deemed to be interlinked by the principle of conferred and attributed powers, the quotation suggests that it is possible to draw a clear demarcation line between national and European competences, between national and European

[64] 'The Rule of Law and the Coherence of the Judicial System of the European Union', (2007) 44 *CMLR* 1625.

jurisdiction, and so between national and European Courts. With all due respect to such a nicely and well balanced statement which correctly reflects the political and legal common-sense, the question might be allowed whether it is factually and normatively correct. *Azoulai*, *Basedow*[65] and *Bobek*[66] are united in the conviction that the key problem of the principle of conferred and attributed powers is that it does *not* define clear borderlines which could and should be respected by the ECJ in order to safeguard the autonomy of the Member States and that, in particular, the preliminary reference procedure paved the way for the Court's activism which raised concern in the Member States. The competences rules are linked to the dynamic of completing the Internal Market and creating an ever closer Union: in short to a process which logically entails that there should be no boundaries at all. How close is close enough, how integrated is integrated enough? Already *E. Steindorff* has underlined that the European market is far from being fully integrated, at least in comparison to the US market. Whilst *Basedow* focuses on the open texture of the Internal Market logic as promoted by the preliminary reference procedure, *Bobek*[67] stresses that 'once there is an EU law based right which is to be enforced at the national level, its equivalent or effective enforcement covers all aspects of national procedure", which is in strong contradiction to *Lenaerts'* quotation.

My hypothesis is that it is exactly this open-textured judge-made legal order that, in the absence of a constitutional Treaty, explains the ever deeper incursions of the RRPs case-law into national autonomy. Due to the lack of political will amongst the Member States to adopt a European Constitution deserving of the name, which does not revolve around economic integration but develops a genuine European social outlook and shapes the boundaries of the EU and the Member States levels in the application and enforcement of EU law, the ECJ or more precisely the European courts simply have no choice other than to continue along the path they have followed since *van Gend & Loos* as well as *Costa Enel* if they do not want to jeopardize the European integration project as a whole. The ECJ is not in a position to shape these boundaries. Like in so many other fields of EU law, the ECJ's activism in RRP is inherently linked to the different functions the ECJ has to play. *Basedow* distinguishes between the review, the impulse and the uniformity function. In the field of RRPs the latter two are at the forefront of what the ECJ has been doing and are key in the context of this paper. This does not mean that the review function is not equally important. It comes to bear when the ECJ has to assess whether Member States RRPs suffice to meet the standard formula enshrined in secondary law.[68]

65 The Judge's Role in European Integration – The Court of Justice and its Critics, in this volume.

66 'Why there is no principle of "Procedural Autonomy" of the Member States?', in this volume.

67 At p. 320 of this contribution.

68 The post *Heininger* case-law of the ECJ might serve as a paradigmatic though rather sad example of judicial review in the field of consumer law, see under IV. 3. a).

## 3.2. A SHAKY CONSENSUS – THE COMPETENCE DIVIDE IN RRPs

There is a steadily growing case law on RRP – rights (subjective rights), remedies (compensation, restitution and injunctive relief/injunction) and procedure – and an equally growing voluminous literature. Advocates general and academics alike have been trying to structure the case law and sometimes to label its contents. First (initial deference to national remedies), second (assertive period of judicial activism) and third generation (retreat to the limited negative approximation) talk has become common, though the meaning and the selection criteria might differ.[69] The language is telling. The development of RRP is understood as a process which, although not never-ending, will be gradual and contain ups and downs, with activist and receptive phases. All in all, one might concur that RRP is creeping forward steadily but much less spectacularly than in other areas of substantive EU law, perhaps with the exception of the landmark decisions in which the ECJ 'invented' new remedies – interim relief in *Factortame*,[70] state liability in *Francovich*,[71] compensation for anti-discrimination in *Raccanelli*[72] and for antitrust injuries to the benefit of any person in *Courage*[73] and *Manfredi*,[74] as well as the somewhat less spectacular actions for injunction against discrimination in *Feryn*[75] and (individual) representative actions in environmental matters in *Janecek*.[76]

I will start by summing up where we are currently in what I call a 'judge-made Law on Remedies'. The ECJ, according to my hypothesis, is developing a genuine European Law on Remedies by drawing on the Treaty, secondary Union law and general principles.[77] One might argue that the ECJ is filling a 'gap' left in the Treaty and only partially covered by secondary Union law. This gap results from the absence of rules on a European procedural law.[78] Contrary to the United

---

69 M. Dougan, *National Remedies before the Court of Justice*, Hart, Oxford, 2004, 227–233; T. Tridimas, *The General Principles of EC Law*, 2nd ed., Oxford University Press, Oxford, 2006, 420–422.

70 ECJ 19 June 1990, Case C-213/89, *The Queen v. Secretary of State for Transport, ex parte: Factortame Ltd and others* [1990] ECR I-2433.

71 ECJ 19 November 1991, Joined Cases C-6/90 and C-9/90, *Francovich* [1991] ECR I-5357.

72 ECJ 17 July 2008, Case C-94/07, *Raccanelli* [2008] ECR I-5939.

73 ECJ 20 September 2001, Case C-453/99, *Courage* [2001] ECR I-7079.

74 ECJ 13 July 2006, Case C-295/04, *Manfredi* [2006] ECR I-6619.

75 ECJ 16 July 2008, Case C-54/07, *Feryn* [2008] ECR I-5187.

76 ECJ 25 July 2008, Case C-237/07, *Janecek* [2008] ECR I-6221.

77 K. Lenaerts/K. Gutman, Federal Common Law in the European Union: A comparative perspective from the United States, *AJCL* 2006, 1.

78 B. Hess, *Europäisches Zivilprozessrecht*, 2009, who argues that the bits and pieces are to become a consistent body of law, at least in the field of civil law. With regard to public procedural law, see J. Jans/R de Lange/S. Prechal/R.J.G.M. Widdershoven, *Europeanisation of Public Law*, Europea Law Publishing, Groningen, 2007 and J. Kokott, 'Europäisierung des Verwaltungsprozessrechts', (1998) 31 *Verw* 335.

States, which often serves as a comparator, primary and secondary community law has to be enforced through national procedural rules, setting aside the patchy provisions enshrined in a given context or subject-related secondary rules. Under the Treaty the Member States remain competent for the enforcement and application of EU law. The Treaty is based on the concept of '*Vollzugsföderalismus*' (literally 'enforcement federalism') – whereby the EU lays down the rules and the Member States apply them. It is from the institutional framework of the Treaty that the notion of 'procedural autonomy' of the Member States derives. Both concepts are interlinked but they should clearly be kept separated. *Azoulai* uses 'autonomy' as device to look deeper into what remains for the stateness of Member States in the on-going European integration, while *Sarmiento* places emphasis on national institutional autonomy in order to argue that the authority of the EU law and the autonomy of the Member States can co-exist. Both emphasize the relationship between two different institutions, the EU and the Member States. This should not be confounded with 'procedural autonomy' which results from European 'Vollzugsföderalismus'.

In the original perspective taken by the Treaty – and maintained in the various Treaty amendments, there is no room for the development of a judge-made European Law on Remedies. Be that as it may, as early as 1976 in *Rewe*,[79] the ECJ set into motion a process which, depending on the perspective, might be regarded as either integrationist – i.e. with a positive connotation – or interventionist i.e. with a negative connotation. The result of more than five decades of development[80] in the meantime is relatively clear and widely recognised. Since then, the ECJ has constantly stressed the 'procedural autonomy' of the Member States. At the same time, however, the ECJ is restricting and shaping that very same autonomy through the principle of equivalence – a variation of the anti-discrimination principle – the principle of effectiveness and occasionally the principle of proportionality. A striking example is the *ex officio* case-law where the ECJ struggles with the requirements under which Member States courts are obliged to investigate a possible infringement of EU law upon their own motion.[81] This development is perfectly characterised in the two contributions of *Adinolfi* and *Bobek*. If there is no such thing as procedural autonomy (*Bobek*), one might consider giving up the concept of 'procedural autonomy' and replacing it by 'procedural competence'. The idea behind such thinking is that the EU should follow the US where procedural matters are regarded as constitutional matters

[79] ECJ 16 December 1976, Case 33/76, *Rewe* [1989] ECR 176.

[80] See in particular the four contributions on Francovich in M. Poiares Maduro/L. Azoulai (eds) *The Past and The Future of EU Law, The Classics of EU Law Revisited on the 50th Anniversary of the Treaty of Rome*, Hart Publishing, Oxford, 2010, 403.

[81] H. Schebesta, 'Does the national court know European Law?' in S. Geschwandtner, V. Kosta, H. Schebesta, P. Verbrüggen, *The Impact of the Internal Market on Private Law of the Member Countries*, EUI Working Paper 22/2009, p 47 = 'Does the National Court Know European Law? A Note on *Ex Officio* Application after *Asturcom*' (2010) 18 *ERPL* 847.

as they cut across federal and state competence, whereas in the EU procedural autonomy is linked to the principles of efficiency and equivalence and so to the respective rights and remedies at stake.[82]

| | **Member States level**<br>**Autonomy** | **EU level – ECJ**<br>**EU Procedural law** |
|---|---|---|
| Rights | | Derived from the EU Treaty and from Secondary Law |
| Remedies | – Competence of the Member States | – Interim relief (*Factortame*)<br>– State liability (*Francovich*)<br>– Compensation for antitrust injuries (*Courage* and *Manfredi*)<br>– Reserve for additional remedies (*Unibet*)[83]<br>– Injunction in anti-discrimination law (*Feryn*)<br>– Representative action in environmental law (*Janecek*)<br>– Sector or subject related secondary law |
| Procedure | – Procedural autonomy of the Member States strictu senso[84]<br>– Duty to investigate infringements of EU law ex officio (*Eco Swiss,*[85] *Claro, van der Weerd,*[86] *Asturcom,*[87] *Pannon*[88]) | – Principle of effectiveness and equivalence (*Petersbroeck,*[89] *Palmisani,*[90] *San Giorgio*[91])<br>– Principle of Proportionality, rule of reason (*van Schijndel*[92])<br>– Policy related procedures in secondary law |

In defining the status quo in line with *W. van Gerven's* seminal article[93] 'on rights, remedies and procedure' I will use RRPs as a synonym for the emerging European Law on Remedies. The above chart is intended to outline a common(ly) agreed/

---

82 This is the conclusion of J. LINDHOLM, 'State Procedure and Union Rights – A Comparison between the European Union and the United States'; PhD Umäa, Iustus, 2007.

83 ECJ 13 March 2007, Case C-432/05, *Unibet (London) Ltd and Unibet (International) Ltd.* [2007] ECR I-2271.

84 VAN GERVEN, (2000) 37 *CMLR* 524.

85 ECJ 1 June 1999, Case C-126/97, *Eco Swiss China Time Ltd v. Benetton International NV* [1999] ECR I-3055.

86 ECJ 7 June 2007, Joined Cases C-222/05 to C-225/05, *J. van der Weerd and others* [2007] ECR I-4233.

87 ECJ 6 October 2009, Case C-40/08, *Asturcom Telecomunicaciones SL* [2009] ECR I-9579.

88 ECJ 4 June 2009, Case C-243/08, *Pannon GSM Zrt. v Erzsébet Sustikné Győrfi* [2009] ECR I-4713.

89 ECJ 14 December 1995, Case C-312/93, *Peterbroeck, Van Campenhout & Cie SCS v. Belgian State* [1995] ECR I-4599.

90 ECJ 10 July 1997, Case C-261/95, *Palmisani / INPS* [1997] ECR I-4025.

91 ECJ 9 November 1983, Case 199/82, *San Giorgio* [1983] ECR 3595.

92 ECJ 14 December 1995, Joined Cases C-430/93 and C-431/93, *Jeroen van Schijndel and Johannes Nicolaas Cornelis van Veen v. Stichting Pensioenfonds voor Fysiotherapeuten* [1995] ECR I-4705.

93 'Of Rights, Remedies and Procedures', (2000) 37 *CMLR* 501.

agreeable platform for further analysis. It takes a 'constitutional' perspective and relies on the distribution of competences between Member States and the EU as the starting point, despite concerns raised against the use of this paradigm in mapping the boundaries between EU and national law, thereby setting aside the public/private law divide[94] as well as possible differences resulting from primary/ secondary Union law and/or subjects/actors.

## 3.3. BEYOND CONSENSUS – THE HORIZONTAL IMPLICATIONS OF RRPs

The (assumed) harmony diminishes rapidly should the RRP be viewed from a different angle: one which turns the vertical state-based perspective into a horizontal one and where it is the relationship between individuals themselves rather than between the state and the individual that matters. By shifting from a vertical to a horizontal perspective the potential differences between the three legal orders, i.e. the economic, social and citizen rights order, as well as their implications come into clearer focus.[95]

Though somewhat oversimplified, it might be argued that RRP in primary Union law mainly serves economic market integration goals via the elimination of statutory national barriers to trade. This is a vertical relationship, clearly demonstrated when businesses challenge national statutory laws via EU economic rights, remedies and procedures. Competition law is different as there the horizontal dimension dominates. Problems have arisen as a result of private parties seeking to strike down statutory rules which restrict competition (*Meng*).[96] The ECJ has strengthened the horizontal dimension of the economic freedoms in two directions, namely by recognising the rights of recipients of market freedoms (*Cowan*)[97] and by placing statutory regulations and private collective agreements on an equal footing (*Bosman*,[98] *Angnose*,[99] *Viking*, *Laval*, but note *Wouters*[100]), thereby granting a limited horizontal direct effect to economic freedoms.

---

94 N. Reich, 'The public/private law divide in European Law', in H.-W. Micklitz/F. Cafaggi (ed), 'European Private Law After the Common Frame of Reference', Elgar, Cheltenham, 2010, 56; L. Azoulai, 'Sur un sens de la distinction public/privé dans le droit de l'union européenne', (2010) 48 *RTDeur* 853.

95 L. Niglia, 'Form and substance in European Constitutional Law: the 'Social' Character of Indirect Effect', (2010) 16 *ELJ* 439.

96 ECJ 17 November 1993, Case C-2/91, *Criminal proceedings against Meng* [1993] ECR I-5751.

97 ECJ 2 February 1989, Case C-186/87, *Cowan / Trésor public* [1995] ECR I-195.

98 ECJ 15 December 1995, Case C-415/93, *ASBL v Bosman* [1995] ECR I-4921.

99 ECJ 6 June 2000, Case C-281/98, *Angonese* [1995] ECR I-4139.

100 ECJ 19 February 2002, Case C-309/99, *Wouters and others* [1995] ECR I-1577.

RRP in secondary Union law may *grosso modo* be associated with social regulation. The emerging European social order is designed mostly through secondary law measures, as the primary law's role is in granting the powers needed to realise social policy objectives, as is developed more clearly in the contributions of *Craig*, *Schiek*[101]and *Damjanovic*.[102] Social regulation is enacted via public authorities, adopted by the EU and implemented and enforced by the Member States. Its effects may be vertical and/or horizontal depending on whether the contracting partner, or the wrongdoer in tort law cases, is a public authority or a private party. The ECJ was prepared to recognise the vertical direct effect of directives (*van Duyn*[103]), but it has rejected horizontal direct effects (*Dori*[104]). The consequence is that private parties are in a better position – at least with regard to EU law – when the contracting partner is a public employer or a state monopoly. The only means of reaching even a quasi-horizontal effect of secondary Union law measures in contract and tort law results from case-law requiring them to be interpreted in line with the community rules (*Marleasing*,[105] *Pfeiffer*,[106] *Adelener*[107]). Due to an active court, primary Union law may occasionally contain a social horizontal dimension, which is most clearly visible in directly applicable anti-discrimination cases (*Defrenne II*,[108] *Mangold*, *Kücükdevici*).[109] The second major area regards the recognition of patients' rights as an integral part of the freedom to choose trans-border health care services (*Kohll*,[110] *Decker*,[111] *Watts*,[112] but *Commission vs. France*[113]). However, the addressee of the right to choose is again a public health care institution.

I have already made clear that the case law on citizenship reaches beyond economic integration and disconnects individually enforceable rights from the market logic. In the area of citizen rights, the substance of primary Union law

[101] D. Schiek, 'ECJ Fundamental Rights jurisprudence between Member States' prerogatives and citizens' autonomy', in this volume.

[102] D. Damjanovic, "Reserved Areas' of the Member States and the ECJ: The Case of Higher Education', in this volume.

[103] ECJ 4 December 1974, Case C-41/74, *Van Duyn / Home Office* [1995] ECR 1337.

[104] ECJ 14 July 1994, C-91/92, *Faccini Dori / Recreb* [1994] ECR I-3325.

[105] ECJ 13 November 1990, Case C-106/89, *Marleasing / Comercial Internacional de Alimentación* [1990] ECR I-4135.

[106] ECJ 5 October 2004, Case C-397/01, *Pfeiffer and others* [2004] ECR I-8835.

[107] ECJ 4 July 2006, Case C-212/04, *Adeneler and others* [2006] ECR I-6057.

[108] ECJ 8 April 1976, Case 43/75, *Defrenne v. SABENA (Defrenne II)* [1976] ECR 455.

[109] L. Azoulai, 'Sur un sens de la distinction public/privé dans le droit de l'union européenne', (2010) 48 *RTD eur* 842, at 853.

[110] ECJ 28 April 1998, Case C-158/96, *Kohll / Union des caisses de maladie* [1998] I-1931.

[111] ECJ 28 April 1998, Case C-120/95, *Decker / Caisse de maladie des employés privés* [1998] I-1831.

[112] ECJ 16 May 2006, Case C-372/04, *The Queen, on the application of: Yvonne Watts v Bedford Primary Care Trust, Secretary of State for Health*, [1995] I-4325.

[113] Where AG Sharpston rejects the attempt of the European Commission to achieve via primary Community law what it failed to realise by the stalled patient rights directive, AG Sharpston 15 July 2010, Case C-512/08, *Commission / France*, nyr.

and Directive 2004/38 (the so-called citizenship directive)[114] might be read and interpreted as a homogeneous whole, at least with regard to the ECJ's vision of Union citizenship, and especially as regards the free movement rights conferred to in Article 21 TFEU (former Article 18). This is how I understand the analysis of the case-law of the ECJ undertaken by *Kostakopoulou* and *Dougan*. However, since 2008, and in particular with regard to the scope and content of Directive 2004/38, the ECJ's straightforward approach has lost its impetus and contours (*Förster*,[115] *Bidar*,[116] *Vatsouras*[117]). The ECJ has not yet had the opportunity to decide over the horizontal directive effect of Directive 2004/38. Setting aside the recognition of a directly applicable right under Article 21 TFEU in *Baumbast*, the existing case law does not, as far as I know, provide any substantial additional input to RRP.[118] Thus, it remains to be seen whether and how the citizen rights order may contribute to the further development of RRP in the European legal order as a whole. At the end of this paper, I will try to demonstrate what this impact might look like.[119]

The chart below condenses the existing case law and highlights the different stages of RRP in two areas: firstly, market integration via primary Union law and, secondly, in social regulation through secondary Union law, as is reflected in the distinction drawn between negative (market integration) and positive integration (social regulation). The parameters of analysis are the triad of rights, remedies and procedures in the way they have been given shape by the ECJ. The distinction between primary and secondary community law is crucial for a deeper understanding of the interplay between positive and negative integration as well as the concrete shaping of RRPs in all three of the chosen parameters. There are some directives, most notably in consumer, labour and anti-discrimination law, that contain more specific rights, more detailed remedies and more concrete procedural rules. For the sake of argument, sector specific particularities are set aside and the emphasis is instead put on the general formula.

---

114 OJ 2004 L 157/77. The Commission is quite critical on the effectiveness of the Directive, COM (2008) 85 final, at 5.

115 ECJ 18 November 2008, Case C-158/07, *Förster* [2008] ECR I-8507.

116 ECJ 15 March 2005, Case C-209/03, *Bidar* [2005] ECR I-2119.

117 ECJ 4 June 2009, Cases C-22/08 & C-23/08, *Vatsouras* [2009] ECR I-4585.

118 See the account of F. Jacobs, 'Citzenship of the European Union – A Legal Analysis', (2007) 13 *ELJ* 59 who does not devote particular attention to the RRP dimension, obviously because it does not play such an important role in the case-law.

119 See under 4.3 and 5.

| | **Individual vs. state Vertical** | **Individual vs. individual Horizontal** |
|---|---|---|
| (1) Rights under *primary* Union law<br>– negative integration –<br>– but *Johnston*[122] and *Heylens*[123]<br>– but *Kohll, Dekker, Watts* | – Market freedoms<br>– Competition law (*Meng*)<br>– Non-discrimination (*Johnston* and *Heylens)*<br>– Transborder health care (*Kohll, Dekker, Watts, Commission vs. France*) | – Market freedoms as far as collective regulations (*Bosman, Wouters, Angonse, Viking, Laval*)<br>– Competition law (*Courage* and *Manfredi*)<br>– Non-discrimination (*Defrenne II, Manfredi, Kücükdevici, Raccanelli*) |
| (1) Rights under *secondary* EU law<br>– positive integration – | – Vertical direct effect of directives (*van Duyn*) | – No horizontal direct effect (*Dori*)<br>– EU conforming interpretation (*Marleasing, Pfeiffer, Adelener*) |
| (2) Remedies under *primary* EU law<br>– negative integration –<br>– but *Carpenter* and citizenship cases | – Interim relief (*Factortame*)<br>– State liability (*Brasserie*[124]) | – Compensation for antitrust injuries (*Courage* and *Manfredi*)<br>– Compensation for violation of market freedoms (*Bosman, Laval via national courts,*[125] *Raccanelli*) |
| (2) Remedies under *secondary* EU law<br>– positive integration – | – State liability (executive) (*Dillenkofer,*[126] *Rechberger*[127])<br>– State liability (judiciary) *Commission vs. Spain*[128])<br>– Representative action in environmental law (*Janecek*) | – Injunctions against discriminations (*Feryn*)<br>– Injunctions in consumer law (no case law) |
| (3) Procedure under *primary* EU law<br>– negative integration – | – virtually impossible or excessively difficult (*Francovich formula*) | – |
| (4) Procedure under *secondary* EU law<br>– positive integration – | – State liability for violation of EU procedural rules (*COS.MET*[129])<br>– Stand still procedure (*CIA-Security*[130]) | – Standard formula 'effective, proportionate and dissuasive'[131]<br>– Consumer law (*Claro, Cofidis, Asturcom, Pannon*)<br>– Labour law and IP law |

120 ECJ 15 May 1986, Case 222/84, *Johnston / Chief Constable of the Royal Ulster Constabulary* [1986] ECR I-1651.

121 ECJ 15 October 1987, Case 222/86, *Unectef / Heylens* [1987] ECR I-4097.

122 ECJ 5 March 1996, Joined Cases C-46/93 and C-48/93, *Brasserie du Pêcheur SA v. Bundesrepublik Deutschland and the Queen v Secretary of State for Transport, ex parte: Factortame Ltd and others* [1996] ECR I-1029.

123 N. Reich, 'Laval, Vierter Akt', (2010) *EuZW* 454.

124 ECJ 8 October 1996, Case C-178/94, *Dillenkofer and others / Bundesrepublik Deutschland* [1996] I-4845.

125 ECJ 12 February 1998, Case C-139/97, *Rechberger and others* [1996] ECR I-3499.

126 ECJ 12 November 2009, Case C-154/08, *Commission / Spain* [2009] I-nyr. The Spanish Supreme Court judgment is blamed to be in breach of Directive 77/388/EC (common value added taxes).

127 ECJ 17 April 2007, Case C-470/03, *AGM-COS.MET* [2007] ECR I-2749.

128 ECJ 30 April 1996, Case C- 194/94, *CIA Security International / Signalson and Securitel* [1996] I-2201.

129 The formula slightly varies, but in substance it is composed of these three elements.

The differences between primary and secondary Union law as transposed into the distinction between vertical and horizontal relationships in the handling of RRPs are striking and often neglected in legal doctrine. On the whole, one might distinguish three different layers: (1) The ECJ is most vigorous and most intrusive when it comes to enforcing primary EU law rules in the vertical, i.e. individual vs. state relationship; (2) The ECJ seems ready to grant appropriate rights and develop corresponding remedies in horizontal situations as long as business relations are at stake; (3) The ECJ is most reluctant in matters relating to the shaping of horizontal relations under the European social order. A disclaimer applies, however. One might detect tendencies in the case law of the ECJ of a desire to overcome these layers and to develop a more coherent and consistent legal order, thereby strengthening the horizontal dimension of RRPs. Article 47 will have a key role to play. Since 2000 the ECJ has regularly referred to Article 47, often in tandem with Articles 6 and 13,[130] but it seems that *Alassini*[131] was the first occasion where the ECJ was ready to give Article 47 more weight in strengthening the role and function of ADR mechanisms as a means of access to justice.

All in all, the Charter might be read so as to confirm the high degree of autonomy Member States benefit from in shaping RRPs within social regulation. This results from the standard formula under which Member States are obliged to take efficient, proportionate and dissuasive measures to enforce a given directive.

## 4. THE INSTITUTIONAL FRAMEWORK OF JUDGE-MADE EUROPEAN LAW ON REMEDIES

I have explored elsewhere how the judge-made European legal order, which later came to be seen as a Constitutional Charter (*van Gend en Loos, Costa Enel, Les Verts, Opinion 1/91, Kadi*), is based on three pillars: judicial co-operation between the European courts and the national referring courts under the preliminary reference procedure, organised law enforcement via the systematic use of individually enforceable rights, and the political legitimacy of the judgments.[132] Such a preconception explains, to my mind, the key role of RRP in the development of the European law on remedies. This is the first matter explored below.

RRPs are built on the existence of *individual* rights whatever the qualifications and capabilities of the person at stake are. The ECJ has enhanced what

130 See ECJ 16 July 2009, C-12/08, *Mono Car Styling* [2009] ECR I-6653, at 27 with further references.
131 ECJ 18 March 2010, Case C-317/08, *Alassini and others* [2010], nyr at 61.
132 The Politics of Judicial Co-operation in the EU 2005, at 11.

*Durkheim*[133] called the 'cult of the individual', which was so paradigmatic for the developments seen the 20th century. The collective side of the society – solidarity between individuals and the realisation of solidarity through collective rights – largely falls by the wayside. Hence, the Procrustean bed of subjective rights forms the basis of my second point.[134]

RRPs have to be placed within the constitutional boundaries of the Treaty. This statement needs a short clarification of what constitutional boundaries in the Treaty are. I will refer here to a kind of a common sense found in the legal doctrine, and then transfer the constitutional boundaries to RRPs in order to test the possible impact on the distinction between primary and secondary EU law. Similarly, this will help in trying to define the line between constitutional and non-constitutional RRPs. Together, these discussions form my third point.

## 4.1. THE PARAMETERS: JUDICIAL CO-OPERATION, ORGANISED LAW ENFORCEMENT AND LEGITIMACY IN RRPS

This is not the place to go much deeper into the ways in which European courts and national courts co-operate in the RRP issues.[135] However, implicitly or explicitly, all contributors share the same conviction. The current debate around the autonomy of the Member States has, by and large, been triggered by the ECJ's approach to institutional shaping under the Treaty's preliminary reference procedure, which has remained unaffected since 1957. Two of the authors, *Reich* and *Sarmiento*, go even further and criticise the insufficient factual and normative basis on which the ECJ has to base its judgment. *Sarmiento* especially disapproves of the fact that individuals have no access to the preliminary reference procedure, an issue which deserves further exploration.[136]

Organised law enforcement was not really an explicit subject of the conference. Implicitly all those dealing with economic (*Basedow, Reich*), fundamental (*Azoulai, Cartabia*), social (*Schiek, Damjanovic*), citizen rights (*Dougan, Kostakopolou*) as well as those dealing with RRP (*Adinolfi, Bobek, Sarmiento*) rely on natural or legal persons, workers, migrants, citizens and consumers who are ready to fight

133 See on this R. Münch, *Die Konstruktion der Europäischen Gesellschaft*, Campus Verlag, Frankfurt, 2008, at 71 and 141.

134 P. Bobbitt, *Terror and Consent*, Allen Lane, London, 2008, at p 487 and D. Patterson/ A. Afilalo, *The New Global Trading Order, The Evolving State and the Future of Trade*, Cambridge University Press, Cambridge, 2008, argue both that the turn to the individual is the result of the transformation of the nation state after World War Two. In such a perspective the individualisation is the result of a process that cannot be turned back.

135 See on a deeper analysis of the kind of co-operation, L. Corrias, *The Passivity of Law: Competence and Constitution in the European Court of Justice*, PhD 2010, at 138 and 141.

136 See in more detail, under V. 1.

before both national courts and the ECJ through preliminary references for the rights they have been granted via primary or secondary EU law and now even via the Charter of Fundamental Rights.

The legitimacy issue appears again in the guise of the competence conflict between the intruding ECJ and the autonomy-defending Member States – which was the theme of the conference. Indeed, the legitimacy issue seemed to constitute an ever-present silent observer of the overall debate as to whether the ECJ has gone too far in the ever more expansive European legal order. A number of contributions shed new light on old questions, be they institutional or subject-related.

*Craig* highlights how the Member States themselves have, over the course of the more than fifty years since its signing, extended the regulatory frame of the Treaty to their own detriment and without ever setting outer boundaries on the jurisdiction of the ECJ, as highlighted by *Azoulai*, *Basedow* and *Bobek*. *Sarmiento* touches upon the democratic legitimacy of the preliminary reference procedure which has as its source the strong reliance on organised law enforcement that is, in principle, open not only to business, but also to workers, consumers and citizens. *Azoulai* confronts the well established legitimacy of the ECJ in building an economic order with the shaky one in the social order. He argues that in the field of economic rights the Court's case law is governed by 'the argument of transnational effects' which Member States have to take into account.[137] He claims that such a justification is still missing with regard to the trans-border reach of fundament rights (he refers mostly to social rights), although the newly introduced reference to the 'Social Market Economy' might fill that gap. I wonder whether the justification can be found in the need for member states to take the social rights of non-nationals and non-citizens into account when they seek justifications for national social standards.[138]

Beyond the more institutional patterns, the lesson to be learnt from the contributions is that legitimacy is connected to the issues at stake. *Dougan* takes a sharp critical stand against the ECJ case law on citizen rights and migration issues, which is said to set reduce Member States' room to manoeuvre when drafting policies. *Damjanovic* is concerned by the ECJ's massive intervention to

---

137 M. Poiares Maduro, 'Reforming the Market or the State? Art. 30 and the European Constitution: Economic Freedom and Political Rights', (1997) 3 *ELJ* 55, A. Menon/St. Weatherill, 'Legitimacy, Accountability, and Delegation in the European Union', in A. Arnull/D. Wincott (eds), *Accountability and Legitimacy in the European Union*, Oxford University Press, Oxford, 2002, 113.

138 AG Maduro made this argument in his opinion of 23 May 2007, Case C-438/05, *International Transport Workers Federation (ITF) and Finnish Seaman's Union (FSU) v. Viking Line* [2007] ECR I-10779, at 70, whereas L. Azoulai, 'The Court of Justice and the Social Market Economy: The Emergence of an Ideal and the Conditions for its Realisation', (2008) 45 *CMLR*, 1350 rejects that argument.

the benefit of students' mobility, in particular for those going from Germany to Austria and from France to Belgium. *Reich* pleads for more cautious use of the proportionality principle in what he terms the 'quasi-legislative approach' where the ECJ is charged with acting as a legislator.

## 4.2. IS THE CONCEPT OF SUBJECTIVE RIGHTS A PROCRUSTEAN BED?

Subjective rights are status-related. One must have an economic, social or civil status in order to be able to benefit from rights as businessmen, as consumers, customers, tourists, patients, workers, environmentalists, as citizens, migrants or students. The list could easily be extended. What the ECJ has been doing ever since its inception is defining a particular status for nationals as individuals and to link that status to the existence of a particular right, sometimes a remedy and then, last but not least, to the guarantee of minimum procedural requirements. The concept of subjective status-related rights leads to what *Luhmann* calls 'Ausdifferenzierung der Gesellschaft'. This is possible because the individual right holders defend not only their interests but also those of the public at large. In fact, these individual rights may be regarded as '*public*' individual rights.[139] In more practical and more doctrinal terms: one needs to have a status in order to have an enforceable right. I have demonstrated that the ECJ has developed a European legal order which is composed of three constitutive elements, the economic, the social and the citizen rights order. Each order is perceived and legally constructed through the lenses of the individual: the economic order is based on the ideology that individualism fosters economic success and economic integration; the social order relies on the individual in her particular status (consumer, customer, tourist, patient, etc) to foster and finally achieve equality and justice; the citizen rights order is not a political order as such, rather it is an order where the citizen only exists with regard to particular EU relevant activities, family reunification or migration.

One may easily squeeze the legal construction of the judge-made European legal order into such a scenario. In granting direct effect to the Treaty and later to the directives the ECJ relied on the self interest of individuals, private persons and legal entities to foster the integration process. The consistently high rate of preliminary reference procedures, about 50% of all cases, testifies to the success of the ECJ judges' 'realism and passion'. However, the whole concept of subjective (public) rights depends on those who are able and willing to file a law suit. Since

[139] See AG Trstenjak 4 September 2008, C-445/06, *Danske Slagterier* [2009] ECR I-2119, at 75, for a deeper analysis of individual public rights, L. Azoulai, 'Sur un sens de la distinction public/privé dans le droit de l'union européenne', (2010) 48 *RTD eur* at 851 with reference to N. Foulquier, *Les droits publics subjectifs des administrés*, Dalloz, Paris, 2003.

*Galanter*[140] we have become aware of the different chances of repeat players and single players. The ECJ mainly relies on the market for litigation which structurally favours business. The success of the judge-made legal order comes at a double price: the individualisation of society via status related rights – which, in turn, tilts the balance between the economic and the social.

#### *4.2.1. Prevalence of EU economic rights over social rights*

The Treaty even in its current form does not seem to counterbalance the dominant market rational of the European integration process. Translated into the logic of RRP, the Treaty does still not contain individually enforceable social rights. Here the difference between rights and interests matter. Social interests play a role, not least via the Charter of Fundamental Rights, and they may even gain constitutional relevance but they are not condensed into 'individually enforceable rights'.[141] One might even go further and raise the questions as to what extent 'the Social' can be broken down into individual rights at all. At the very least 'The Social' might change its outlook.[142] It is true that since *Cowan (tourists), Kohll* and *Watts (patients), Defrenne II (workers)* and *Viking (labour unions)* the recipients of the market freedoms may equally benefit from RRP to improve their legal position. The status as a recipient, however, is linked to the prior existence of economic freedoms as a reference point for taking action. *Viking* demonstrates that the recognition of a social right (the right to strike) via economic freedoms (Article 43 EU, now Article 49 TFEU) does not automatically lead to the legalisation of the collective activities. My point is not to challenge the need to balance conflicting rights (see on this aspect *Reich*), rather is that it matters whether a social right is derived from the social order or is derived from the economic freedoms. There are limits to construing a social order out of economic freedoms, limits which may also have to do with the methodology that the ECJ applies. *Azoulai*[143] has amply demonstrated that the ECJ uses the argumentation it developed in the shaping of economic freedoms to handle social and citizen rights.

With the outlook of the European Union gradually changing by way mainly of secondary legislation, the ECJ was faced with the challenge of whether and

140 M. Galanter, 'Why the 'Haves' Come Out Ahead: Speculations on the Limits of Legal Change' (1974) 9 *Law and Society Review* 95.

141 See M. Kumm, '*Internationale Handelsgesellschaft, Nold* and the New Human Rights Paradigm', in M. Poiares Maduro/L. Azoulai (eds) *The Past and The Future of EU Law, The Classics of EU Law Revisited on the 50th Anniversary of the Treaty of Rome*, Hart Publishing, Oxford, 2010, 106.

142 I have coined the term of 'access justice' which is characteristic for the model of justice dominating the European law, see Social Justice and Access Justice in Private Law, Working Paper EUI 2011.

143 As demonstrated in the way the ECJ decided *Viking* thereby turning *Defrenne* upside down, L. Azoulai, 'The Court of Justice and the Social Market Economy: The Emergence of an Ideal and the Conditions for its Realisation', (2008) 45 *CMLR* 1350–1351.

to what extent the concept of subject rights could be extended to market based (consumer law, company law, labour law) social regulation. The recognition of vertical direct effect (*van Dyn*) constituted a major step in the development of RRP, as did the discovery of state liability (*Francovich*) as a means of sanctioning the non- or incomplete implementation of directives by the Member States. However, the ECJ did not grant horizontal direct effect to directives. One might argue that the ECJ developed, or is going to recognise, a negative horizontal direct effect of directives (*Quelle, Mangold, Kücükdevici*) and that the obligation of EU conforming interpretation could operate as a functional equivalent to the missing horizontal direct effect of directives.

What is more important is that by denying horizontal direct effect the ECJ sent, possibly unintentionally, a rather problematic message to the Member States, their courts and to the EU citizens: We the Court are not responsible for striking a *structural* balance between the economic and social order. Social matters are instead for the Member States and their courts to decide. I will not deny that the ECJ may take favourable decisions to protect the weaker parties in individual cases, but it is not ready to free the protective device of secondary community law rules from its individualistic outlook and to transform it into a structural rule, like the German Constitutional Court did in the *Bürgschaftsurteil*.[144] The emerging European social order which establishes a kind of a framework of protections for consumers and workers could serve as a generally agreeable minimum standard of a 'European Social Market Economy'. In this vein, the 'constitutional division of power' (*Lenaerts*) and the transformation of the national social welfare state (*Bobbitt and Patterson/Afilalo*), which puts much more emphasis on individual public rights, could be united in a new supranational concept. So why not accept horizontal direct effect?[145] In *Kücükdevici* the ECJ has prepared the ground for such an understanding, at least with regard to the application of the non-discrimination principle.

In sum, thus far secondary community law that can often be equated with market based social regulation does not seem to benefit from the same weighty appreciation as do the four economic freedoms. One might glean from the case law that the application and enforcement of the market freedoms belongs (much more) to the core of the ECJ jurisdiction, compared to the application and enforcement of market based social regulation where Member States and their courts have to take the lead. Where the ECJ is ready to get involved in social regulation, it is accused of subjugating national social rights to the prevalence of EU economic freedoms (*Schiek*). Secondly, in differentiating between the

[144] Federal German Constitutional Court, BVerG, Beschl. v. 19 October 1993–1 BvR 567/89 u.a. in: NJW 1994, S. 36 ff.

[145] See for a summary of the arguments AG has done this perfectly in C-91/92, *Faccini Dori / Recreb* [1994] ECR I-3325; deeper L. Niglia, 'Form and substance in European Constitutional Law: the 'Social' Character of Indirect Effect', *ELJ* 2010 439.

potential horizontal direct effects of the market freedoms and the widely rejected horizontal direct effect of socially biased directives, the ECJ has created a model of individual 'rights without duties',[146] a legal system where the infringement of subject rights results in some form of state liability, if any. The addressees of the rights, i.e. those who have to meet the EU obligations, remain largely outside the ambit of EU law, perhaps with the exception of those who benefit from the broad interpretation of the anti-discrimination principle.

The judge-made European legal order looks more 'human'[147] if one takes the ECJ case law on citizen rights into account, at least in the view of those who hail the ground-breaking progress made by the ECJ in *Martinez Sala* and *Baumbast.*[148] However, both decisions have a 'dark' side, as they import a non-solidaristic logic into areas of the legal system which had previously been protected from economic pressure. It suffices to refer to the position the ECJ has taken with regard to student mobility. The individual advantage for the lucky ones may lead to a collapse of the whole institutional framework of higher education in Belgium and Austria (*Damjanovic*).[149] The 'transnational effects' that *Azoulai*[150] argues for, have not been taken into account by the ECJ. So there more is needed than simply linking the different orders together and then using citizen rights as a tool to 'upgrade' social (citizen-consumer) and maybe even economic (citizen-businessman) rights. In a nutshell, *Bosman*, *Agnose* and *Laval* may allow for a new understanding of the responsibilities imposed on private parties. If private parties are also the holders of the 'public interests' then they bear a responsibility which extends beyond seeking individual or collective economic advantage. The degradation of the state as the unique holder of social rights goes appears to hearld an increase in responsibilities for private parties.[151] This is in essence what the citizen dimension is all about.

---

146 N. Reich, 'Rights without Duties', forthcoming.

147 A.J. Menéndez, 'European Citizenship after Martinez Sala and Baumbast: Has European Law Become more Human and Less Social?', M. Poiares Maduro/L. Azoulai (eds) *The Past and The Future of EU Law, The Classics of EU Law Revisited on the 50th Anniversary of the Treaty of Rome*, Hart Publishing, Oxford, 2010, 363, at 364.

148 See the analysis of F. Jacobs, F. Jacobs, 'Citzenship of the European Union – A Legal Analysis', *ELJ* 2007 59.

149 ECJ 13 April 2010, Case C-73/08, *Bressol* [2010], nyr.

150 See also from the same author also L. Azoulai, 'La Citoyenneté Européenne, un Statut d'Integration Social', in *Mélange en l'honneur du Professeur Jean Paul Jacqué*, Dalloz, Paris, 2010, forthcoming, where he conceptualizes European citizenship as a form and means of social integration, thereby crossing the borderline between economic, social and citizen rights.

151 L. Azoulai, 'Sur un sens de la distinction public/privé dans le droit de l'union européenne', (2010) 48 *RTD eur* 842, the same, L. Azoulai, 'The Court of Justice and the Social Market Economy: The Emergence of an Ideal and the Conditions for its Realisation', (2008) 45 *CMLR*, 1350.

#### 4.2.2. *The missing EU collective rights*

A legal order based on individually enforceable rights is not in a position to cope with the collective dimension of social conflicts. The Lisbon Treaty and the Charter of Fundamental Rights have upgraded solidarity and made it into a value-guiding principle. However, the ECJ has neither managed to cope with solidarity and to transform it into a building block of the European Social Order, nor tried to build a link between the EU concept of solidarity and collective rights.[152] That is why collective conflicts have to be turned into individual rights to make them heard in the European right concert. This transformation matters in particular in the different fields of social regulation. Trade Unions, women's organisations and environmental organisations have all developed quite successful strategies of organised law enforcement in order to implement the doctrine of equal treatment.[153] Consumer organisations, meanwhile, have also followed suit but in a much less organised way and with less visible results. *Quelle*, however, may represent a creative attempt to use collective actions under national law to bring a consumer case to the ECJ via the preliminary reference procedure. The ECJ has been innovative in granting individuals standing where their actions produce collective effects. In *Janecek*[154] it obliged the Member States authorities to set up action plans against air pollution to protect the individual rights of EU citizens. The logic behind this could easily be transferred to the field of financial services.[155]

The Treaty does not deal with collective rights, with the exception of Article 263(4) TFEU. Notwithstanding, the question of under which exact conditions these articles grant NGOs standing to sue has been subject of a major controversy even between the CFI and the ECJ. In *UPA*[156] and *Jégo-Quéré*[157]the ECJ held – contrary to AG *Jacobs* – as inadmissible two actions for the annulment of community regulations because the respective applicants did not satisfy the condition of individual concern under the then Art. 230 EU. The ECJ delegated the question

---

[152] A. Wunder, *The Usage of Solidarity in the Jurisdiction of the ECJ: Symbolism or a European Legal Concept*, LLM thesis EUI, Florence, 2008.

[153] C. Kilpatrick, 'Gender Equality: A Fundamental Dialogue' in S. Sciarra (ed.), *Labour Law in the Courts: National Judges and the European Court of Justice*, Hart, Oxford et al, 2001, 31.

[154] ECJ 25 July 2008, C-237/07, *Janecek v. Freistaat Bayern* [2008] ECR I-6221.

[155] J. Keßler/H.-W. Micklitz/N. Reich (eds.), *Institutionelle Finanzmarktaufsicht und Verbraucherschutz, Eine rechtsvergleichende Untersuchung der Regelungssysteme in Deutschland, Italien, Schweden, dem Vereinigten Königreich und der Europäischen Gemeinschaft, unter Mitarbeit von Valentina Calderai/K. Purnhagen/P. Verbruggen*, Nomos, Baden-Baden, 2010, p 278, 279.

[156] ECJ 25 July 2002, Case C-50/00 P, *Union de Pequeños Agricultores (UPA) v. Council* [2002] ECR I-6677, affirming GC 23 November 1999, Case T-173/98, *Union de Pequeños Agricultores (UPA) v. Council* [1999] ECR II-3357.

[157] ECJ 1 April 2004, Case C-263/02 P, *Commission v. Jégo-Quéré & Cie SA* [2004] ECR I-3245, setting aside GC 3 May 2002, Case T-177/01, *Commission v. Jégo-Quéré & Cie SA* [2002] ECR II-2365.

of who should have standing to the Member States. In *Lesoochranárske VLK*[158] the ECJ will have to decide over an interesting variant of the collective standing issue or, in terms of the 'Les Verts' decision, whether or not the system of judicial protection under the Treaty is indeed 'complete'.[159] The Aarhus Convention is quite outspoken on the existence of collective rights in environmental matters. The European Commission presented a Draft[160] which was meant to implement the Aarhus Convention and which would have introduced common standards on collective actions European wide. However, the initiative failed and the Draft fell into oblivion. AG *Sharpston* rejected attempts by Slovakian environmental organisations to construe a right to standing in administrative procedures (access to courts) by reference to Article 9(3) Arhus Convention, thereby using the lack of the EU implementation measures as the key argument for delegating final decisions on locus standi claims to the Member States and, eventually, to national courts. This is very much in line with *UPA* and *Jego*-Quéré as well as the rejection of direct effect of the WTO Treaty.[161] I would not be surprised if the ECJ would fully confirm her reasoning.

In its case law on Article 263(4) TFEU, the ECJ has set the tone for the role and function NGOs could and should play in the building of the European legal order. In practice, they have effectively been excluded from the development of a judge-made legal order, as they have no direct access to the ECJ. Their role and function is left to the discretion of national courts and national legislators. To this extent, *UPA* and *Jégo Quéré* may be seen as equivalent to the denial of horizontal direct effect of directives.

What holds true for Article 263(4) TFEU is equally correct with regard to the role and function of NGOs in market-based social regulation. Their position depends entirely on the degree to which Member States are willing to introduce collective remedies, initiated via secondary EU law or not as the case may be. In consumer law the collective action of injunction in the hands of public authorities or consumer

158 Case C-240/09, pending.

159 K. Lenaerts, A Community Based on a 'Constititutional Charter' Community Law as a Complete and Coherent Constitution System, in M. Poiares Maduro/L. Azoulai (eds) *The Past and The Future of EU Law, The Classics of EU Law Revisited on the 50th Anniversary of the Treaty of Rome*, Hart Publishing, Oxford, 2010, 295, at 304.

160 COM (2003) 624 final, thereto H.-W. Micklitz, 'Collective action in European Consumer and European Environmental Law – A mutual learning Process', in R. Macory (ed.) *Reflections on 30 Years of EU Environmental Law A High Level of Protection, (Festschrift für Ludwig Krämer)*, European Law Publishing, Groningen, 2005, 451–473.

161 See for a recent case ECJ 22 January 2009, Case C-377/07, *Van Parys v. Belgische Interventie- en Restituiebureau* [2005] ECR I-1465. However, the ECJ has granted indirect effect in ECJ 22 June 1989, Case 70/87, *Fediol* [1989] ECR 1781 and ECJ 7 May 1991, Case C-69/89, *Nakajima* [1991] ECR I-2069.

organisations belongs to the minimum standard of collective actions.[162] The addressees of the actions for injunction, however, are Member States institutions. The consumer directives do not foresee that EU institutions could elaborate consumer rules which come under the scope of the different directives. A good example are the technical standards in the field of services which are, legally speaking, standard contract terms elaborated by the European standards bodies (CEN/CENELEC) within the framework of the Service Directive.[163] No case has ever reached the ECJ so far. Labour law and even anti-discrimination law remains behind consumer law. The respective directives do not provide for collective actions, not even for an action of injunction. In *Feryn,*[164] however, the ECJ, in line with Advocate General *Maduro,* developed a collective right to injunction in order to guarantee effective legal protection out of the individual right to be protected against discriminatory job selection criteria. Such reasoning seems in line with the reserve voiced in *Unibet* regarding the possibility of introducing new European remedies in cases of urgent need (*Sarmiento*).[165] Thus, *Unibet* might be understood as a cautious correction of *Les Verts* and *Opinion 1/91*, where the ECJ insisted on a 'complete system of remedies and procedures',[166] although it still seeks the roots for any new remedies in the national legal systems.[167]

The Treaty of Lisbon contains major changes which might facilitate access to the ECJ. It gives natural and legal persons locus standi to bring an action against "a regulatory act which is of direct concern to them and does not entail implementing measures". Therefore any natural or legal person may institute proceedings against such an act irrespective of the severe criterion of "individual concern" which was

---

162 See N. Reich/H.-W. Micklitz, *Europäisches Verbraucherrecht*, 4th ed, Nomos, Baden-Baden, 2006, § 29.15.

163 See H.-W. Micklitz, 'The Service Directive – The making of consumer contract law via standardisation, the example of the Service Directive', in *Festschrift für G. Brüggemeier*, 2009, 483; Ch. Busch, DIN-Normen für Dienstleistungen – Das Europäische Normungskomitee produziert Musterverträge, (2010) *NJW* 3061.

164 ECJ 10 July 2008, Case C-54/07, *Centrum voor gelijkheid van kansen en voor racismebestrijding/Firma Feryn NV* [2008] ECR I-5187.

165 For a more reluctant reading N. Reich, *Understanding EU Law*, 3rd edition, forthcoming 2011, who stresses the role of national law.

166 See ECJ 23 April 1986, Case 294/83, *Les Verts* [1986] ECR 1339, at 23; In later cases the ECJ was more reluctant on whether the system of the Treaty is to be regarded as 'complete', K. Lenaerts, 'A Community Based on a 'Constititutional Charter' Community Law as a Complete and Coherent Constitution System', in M. Poiares Maduro/L. Azoulai (eds) *The Past and The Future of EU Law, The Classics of EU Law Revisited on the 50th Anniversary of the Treaty of Rome*, Hart Publishing, Oxford, 2010, 298, at 307 under reference to 'Pupino'; even harder A. Alemanno, 'What Has Been, and What Could Be, Thirty Years after Les Verts/ European/Parliament', in M. Poiares Maduro/L. Azoulai (eds), *The Past and The Future of EU Law, The Classics of EU Law Revisited on the 50th Anniversary of the Treaty of Rome*, Hart Publishing, Oxford, 2010, 324, at 326 referring to Case C-314/85, *Foto-Frost*, Case C-222/84, *Johnston*, Case C-188/92, *TWD Textilwerke Deggendorf*, which have completed the 'complete system'.

167 ECJ 13 March 2007, Case C-432/05, *Unibet (London) Ltd and Unibet (International) Ltd.* [2007] ECR I-2271, at 64 and 72.

so hard to overcome in the past. *Adinolfi* argues that the new formula allows for the ECJ to overcome remaining barriers to national courts by facilitating access to the ECJ and bringing the national and European jurisdictions closer together in the uniform application of EU law.[168] Such a positive understanding would close the gap resulting from the narrow reading of the former Article 263(4) TFEU, thereby paving the way for natural and legal persons to challenge the legality of European acts, but even the Treaty amendment cannot compensative for the collective deficiencies in the design of the European social order. One might therefore wonder whether and to what extent the ECJ should not 'invent' a collective action along the line of *Feryn*, in order to make the action for injunction a universal tool applicable in all sorts of social relations to stop illegal activities. Article 47 Charter of Fundamental Rights is of little direct help in that respect, as it addresses only individual national persons. I will come back to the access question later on.

## 4.3. COMPETENCE (CONSTITUTIONAL) BOUNDARIES IN THE DEVELOPMENT OF AN EU LAW ON REMEDIES

The subjective rights rhetoric which was/is so effectively used to build and shape the European legal order turns rather a blind eye to the *constitutional* implications of the ever deeper intrusion of RRP into the Member States autonomy. On the surface this becomes clear with the notorious insistence on the 'procedural autonomy' of the Member States, which, however, is not unlimited. In the absence of EU rules national RRPs '*must not be less favourable than those relating to similar domestic claims and must not be so framed as to make it virtually impossible or excessively difficult to obtain (reparation)*'.[169] So what do 'constitutional boundaries' mean in light of the theoretically endless process of European integration, which does not have clear demarcation lines and which makes the handling of RRPs so difficult?[170]

I will not go deeper into what 'constitution' might mean,[171] but take a more doctrinal view under which the following parameters are usually attributed to the

---

168 In the same direction, K. Lenaerts, 'A Community Based on a 'Constitutional Charter' Community Law as a Complete and Coherent Constitution System', in M. Poiares Maduro/ L. Azoulai (eds), *The Past and The Future of EU Law, The Classics of EU Law Revisited on the 50th Anniversary of the Treaty of Rome*, Hart Publishing, Oxford, 2010, at 298 stressing also the importance of Article 19 EU 'Member States shall provide remedies, sufficient to ensure legal protection in the fields covered by Union Law'.

169 ECJ 19 November 1991, Joined Cases C-6/90 and C-9/90, *Francovich* [1991] ECR I-5357, at 43.

170 As explained under 5.1.

171 See N. Walker, 'Opening or Closure? The Constitutional Intimation of the ECJ', in M. Poiares Maduro/L. Azoulai (eds) *The Past and The Future of EU Law, The Classics of EU Law Revisited on the 50th Anniversary of the Treaty of Rome*, Oxford, Hart Publishing, 2010, 333, at 335 'status' and 'value'.

'constitutional charter' (*Sarmiento*):[172] horizontal division of powers (institutional balance between the different European institutions), vertical division of powers (institutional balance between the Union and the Member States), protection of fundamental rights, and the rule of law (complete and coherent system of judicial protection). These four parameters have been enshrined, though to differing degrees, in the constitutionalisation process right from the beginning, as initiated in *van Gend en Loos* and *Costa Enel*. In the early stage of constitutionalisation fundamental rights, however, show up as economic rights or economic freedoms only.

The dynamic of the constitutionalisation process can be brought into clearer focus by linking the four constitutional parameters to the three distinct orders, i.e. the economic, the social and the citizen rights order, in a RRP perspective. All three orders, but in particular the social order and to some extent the citizen rights order, were developed by way of secondary legislation. The vast amount of directives and regulations which have been adopted in the last fifty years affect the constitutional architecture of the European Union. The law making has changed the horizontal balance of power somewhat, but has had had a much more acute impact on the vertical balance. The social order is by and large a product of secondary community law, resulting from the transfer of powers from the Member States to the EU (*Craig*). Translated into constitutional language, the question then is whether and to what extent these second order rules benefit from constitutional standing and what the implications of such a classification would eventually be. It is here that supremacy (*Costa Enel, Simmenthal*) and direct effect of primary (*van Gend en Loos*) and (!) secondary EU law (*van Dyn, Dori*) ties in. By means of these legal tools, secondary EU law gains a quasi constitutional character as it is put on a more or less equal footing with the Treaties. The possible implications seem somewhat under-researched, most prominently with regard to RRPs. Only *Reich* stresses the need to differentiate in the application of the proportionality principle in the shaping of the Internal Market, however, without discussing its applicability with regard to RRPs, where the ECJ uses the equivalence and the effectiveness principle, with the exception of *van Schijndel* (*Bobek*).

In a constitutional perspective I will put emphasis on two parameters which are claimed to determine the elaboration of a judge-made European law on remedies: a) the implications of the distinction between primary and secondary EU law in RRPs and b) the implications of the different functions the ECJ has to fulfil with regard to RRP enshrined in primary and secondary EU law. I am aware that the

---

172 See e.g. K. Lenaerts, 'A Community Based on a 'Constititutional Charter' Community Law as a Complete and Coherent Constitution System', in M. Poiares Maduro/L. Azoulai (eds) *The Past and The Future of EU Law, The Classics of EU Law Revisited on the 50th Anniversary of the Treaty of Rome*, Hart Publishing, Oxford, 2010, 298.

question is huge. That is why I will limit myself to outlining a selection of the several lines for discussion, which deserve further investigation.

### 4.3.1. *The impact of the distinction between primary vs. secondary EU law on RRPs*

In RRP the ECJ starts from the premise that the EU law constitutes a unity. The ECJ uses identical criteria for the decision of whether EU law grants subjective enforceable rights or not. The origin of the subjective rights, whether they can be derived from the Treaty directly or are found in secondary EU law, is principally of no importance for the shaping of remedies and procedural rules provided that secondary law does not provide for more specific ones. This is witnessed by the transferability of remedies from the Treaty to secondary law and vice versa. However, the result is not the same with regard to state liability (*Francovich*), interim relief (*Factortame*) and compensation for antitrust injuries (*Courage* and *Manfredi*). Whereas transferability is fully realised in state liability (*Francovich* and *Brasserie de Pêcheur*), it is absent with regard to interim relief, as the ECJ made clear in *Unibet*.[173] Whether and to what extent horizontal liability can be transferred within primary EU law, in concreto from competition law to the directly applicable market freedoms has not yet been decided by the ECJ. In *Bosman*, the ECJ was not asked about compensation, unlike in *Raccanelli*,[174] where the ECJ insisted on the direct effect of Article 39 EU *vis-à-vis* an association under private law (Max Planck Gesellschaft eV). However, compensation for damage arising out of an alleged discrimination of the claimant must be assessed 'in the light of national legislation applicable to non-contractual liability'. This is exactly what happened in *Laval* through the Swedish Labour Court (Arbetsdomstolen).[175] In *Courage* the ECJ refers to *Factortame* to justify compensation. Horizontal liability in primary EU law has become a topical issue in academia,[176] but horizontal liability in directly applicable articles of the Treaty in the introduction of compensation claims under the standard formula of 'effective, proportionate and dissuasive' RRPs in national legal systems is a long way down the road. In the field of 'procedure' the ECJ uses its own case law for cross references in both directions from primary to secondary EU law and vice versa – and so do the academics. However, this does not mean that the results must be same. The obligation of national courts to investigate *ex officio* the compliance of the parties with EU

173 At 80: "Therefore, in the absence of Community rules governing the matter, it is for the domestic legal system of each Member State to determine the conditions under which interim relief is to be granted for safeguarding an individual's rights under Community law."

174 ECJ 17 July 2008, Case C-94/07, *Raccanelli*, [2008] ECR I-5939, at 52.

175 N. Reich, 'Laval ‚Vierter Akt'', *EuZW* 2010, 454; U. Bernitz/N. Reich, 'Comment Case No. A 268/04, The Labour Court Sweden Judgment No. 89/09 of 2 December 2009, Laval un Partneri', *CMLR* 2011 forthcoming.

176 N. Reich, 'Horizontal liability in EC law: Hybridization of remedies for compensation in case of breaches of EC rights', (2007) *CMLR* 705.

law obligations might serve as an example. There is no uniformity in *Eco Suisse*, *Claro*, *Asturcom*, *Pannon* and *van der Weerd*.[177] What is missing is a more systematic approach to possible differences between primary and secondary EU law and the implications on RRPs.

I would argue that there is a difference between the two sources of law which has to be more openly addressed. The starting point is the different understanding of *effectiveness*. In primary EU law, *effective application and enforcement* bears a *negative* connotation, independent of whether the ECJ deals with first, second or third generation RRPs. Negative here refers to the purpose of the effectiveness. The overall objective is to take away national statutory barriers to trade. This becomes clear in the formula the ECJ first used in *Rewe* and then expanded in *Francovich*. In secondary EU law the EU legislator uses a different formula which varies according to context and history. The overall message is that Member States are obliged to introduce effective, adequate and proportionate means to implement any given directive. Such wording implies a *positive* forward looking perspective. RRPs shall help to promote the realisation of social objectives. National measures must be shaped so as to allow for the realisation of the *effet utile* of the directive.[178] The open ended formula – when does effective become effective enough – raises much concern in academia and also explains why national courts tend to delegate allegedly insufficient national RRPs to Luxembourg (*Schulze*,[179] *Crailshaimer*,[180] *E. Friz*[181]).

Provided the distinction between negative and positive effectiveness holds true, the ECJ would in principle benefit from much broader leeway in secondary law than in primary law. However, reality seems different. *Adinolfi* argues that the ECJ is most rigorous, and most ready to intrude into Member States autonomy, when the supremacy of the European legal order is jeopardised. She refers to the case law on *res judicata*, but her understanding is in line with *Francovich*,

177 H. Schebesta, Does the national court know European Law? in S. Geschwandtner, V. Kosta, H. Schebesta, P. Verbrüggen, The Impact of the Internal Market on Private Law of the Member Countries, EUI Working Paper 22/2009, p 47 = 'Does the National Court Know European Law? A Note on *Ex Officio* Application after *Asturcom*' (2010) 18 *ERPL* 847.

178 H.-P. Schwintowski, 'Informationspflichten und effet utile – Auf der Sache nach einem effektiven und effizienten europäischen Sanktionssystem', in R. Schulze/M. Ebers/H.Ch. Grigoleit (eds), *Informationspflichten und Vertragsschluss im Acquis commautaire*, Mohr Siebeck, Tübingen, 2003, 267 demonstrated the power of the effet utile doctrine in the field of European private law.

179 ECJ 9 November 2006, Case C-120/05, *Heinrich Schulze* [2006] I-10745.

180 ECJ 25 October 2005, Case C- 229/04, *Crailsheimer Volksbank* [2005] I-9273.

181 ECJ 15 April 2010, Case C-215/08 [2010], nyr; F. Podewils, 'Haustürwiderrufsrichtlinie: Anwendung auf Personengesellschaften – Fortgeltung der Grundsätze der fehlerhaften Gesellschaft', (2010) *EuZW*, 265.

*Factortame* and *Courage*, *Manfredi*, *Unibet* where the ECJ seems more inclined to introduce new legal remedies.[182]

Quite to the contrary, the ECJ is rather reluctant in the field of secondary EU law, in particular when RRPs in the social order are at stake. *Adinolfi* and *Sarmiento* draw a distinction between constitutional claims (supremacy, horizontal and vertical competences) and those where 'only' the 'level of judicial protection' (these are the words from *Adinolfi*; *Sarmiento* speaks of access to justice) has to be defined. This assessment touches upon the relationship between RRPs and the social order, represented by environmental, labour, anti-discrimination and consumer law. Environmental law issues have reached the ECJ in particular via attempts of NGO's to obtain 'by force' access to the ECJ under Article 230(4) EU before its amendment via Article 263(4) TFEU. Labour law issues and anti-discrimination issues cannot be put in the same box. The ECJ is rather active when anti-discrimination issues are at stake (*Mangold*, *Kücükdevici*), whereas labour law does not provide a clear picture (*Schiek*). Consumer law suffers more and more from a rather strange bias. The ECJ is ready to confer rights to consumers under the various directives, but it is not ready to recognise a right to appropriate remedies and procedures associated with consumer rights based on EU law. The counter-productive effects of *Schulze*, *Crailshaimer*, *E. Friz* highlight what I mean. The ECJ grants a comprehensive right to withdrawal, thereby extending the scope of application of secondary EU law, but refused to guarantee via EU law – even using the pre-existing general formula of effective, proportionate and dissuasive protection – that the consumer is not worse off after having executed his right. The recognition of an individually enforceable EU right thus remains highly symbolic. Social rights are rather used to defend national autonomy than for enhancing the rights of workers (*Schiek*)[183] or consumers. Through such an interpretation of RRPs the ECJ sets the imbalance between economic and social rights in the European constitutional charter (*Les Verts*, *Opinion 1/91*) in stone. Constitutional concerns (division of vertical power) prevail over the right to effective judicial protection. This highlights the fact that judicial protection and access to justice does not form part of the 'complete system of remedies and procedures'.

182 ECJ 3 March 2007, Case C-432/05, *Unibet* [2007] ECR I-2271, at 40 "Although the EC Treaty has made it possible in a number of instances for private persons to bring a direct action, where appropriate, before the Community Court, it was not intended to create new remedies in the national courts to ensure the observance of Community law other than those already laid down by national law (Case 158/80, *Rewe* [1981] ECR 1805, paragraph 44);" at 41 "It would be otherwise only if it were apparent from the overall scheme of the national legal system in question that no legal remedy existed which made it possible to ensure, even indirectly, respect for an individual's rights under Community law (see, to that effect, Case 33/76, *Rewe*, paragraph 5; *Comet*, paragraph 16; and *Factortame*, paragraphs 19 to 23)."

183 J. Coppel/A. O'Neill, 'The European Court of Justice: Taking Rights Seriously', (1993) 29 *CMLR* 669.

### 4.3.2. *The line between constitutional and non-constitutional RRPs*

| | **Horizontal division of powers (institutional balance between the different European institutions)** | **Vertical division of powers (institutional balance between the EU and the Member States)** | **Rule of law (complete and coherent system of judicial protection)** | **Protection of fundamental rights** |
|---|---|---|---|---|
| Subjective rights Natural and legal persons | Art. 263(4) environmental and consumer organisations, trade unions | recognition of EU (fundamental-social) rights tilts the balance | access to preliminary procedure (?) | right to effective judicial protection, Art. 47 TFEU, Art. 17 EU |
| remedies | Annulment (Art. 263(4) injunction | against the state – compensation or positive action against contracting partner/ wrongdoer - (execution, restoration, compensation) | going beyond the existing system (*Unibet*) If: no remedy available in the national legal system | Art. 47 (?) Art. 17 EU (?) |
| Procedure | EU procedural rules | ECJ plea in *Rewe:*[184] European procedural law | *Van Schijndel*[185] (rule of reason) "role of that provision in the procedure, its progress and its special features, viewed as a whole, before the various national instances ... basic principles ... such as protection of the rights of the defence, the principle of legal certainty and the proper conduct of procedure" | Art. 47 (?) Art. 17 EU (?) |

[184] ECJ 16 December 1976, Case 33/76, *Rewe* [1989] ECR 176, at 5. With regard to the implicit message of the ECJ see ADINOLFI in this volume.

[185] ECJ 14 December 1995, Joined Cases C-430/93 and C-431/93, *Jeroen van Schijndel and Johannes Nicolaas Cornelis van Veen v. Stichting Pensioenfonds voor Fysiotherapeuten* [1995] ECR I-4705, at 19: "For the purposes of applying those principles, each case which raises the question whether a national procedural provision renders application of Community law im-

I am using the above-mentioned four parameters of what is to be understood as the content of the constitutional charter of the EU in order to demonstrate the relationship between these four parameters and rights, remedies and procedures. It will have to be shown that the third and the fourth category are closely interlinked. One might even argue that fundamental rights are just a means to give the 'complete and coherent system of judicial protection' a new outlook, one where the rights of individuals (and maybe in the long run collective entities) are given more consideration in shaping the future of the European legal order. The overall purpose is to find a reasonable line between the constitutional and the non-constitutional implications of RRPs.

The ECJ has to fulfil a manifold function; it operates as a constitutional and supreme court overlooking administrative, civil and even penal law matters. The chart shows the dominant constitutional dimension even under a RRP perspective.

The recognition of subjective enforceable rights affects the division of power – horizontally as far as new rights touch upon the balance between the European institutions, and vertically to the extent that new rights tilt the balance towards the prevalence of EU law over national law. The Lisbon Treaty opens the door for a more proactive stance in the development of subjective rights, individual and collective rights against legal acts of the European Union. Article 263(4) might serve to find a new balance at the EU level, a balance where the voice (*Sarmiento*) of the European citizen might be better heard. In this light, Article 263(4) reflects the understanding that the future European legal order can no longer be represented and shaped by the institutional actors. The ECJ has to integrate individual and collective action into its system of power. The amendment of the Treaty provides the ECJ with a unique opportunity to rethink the individualistic and anti-solidaristic outlook of the Treaty and to positively define the role and function of NGOs in society, and more theoretically of societal constitutional bodies generally.[186] So far the ECJ treats societal constitutional bodies (such as trade unions (*Viking*) or sport associations (*Bosman*)) like states, which may result from the limits enshrined into the market freedoms even in a horizontal perspective. They aim at setting aside statutory barriers to trade. The implications are far reaching as societal constitutional bodies are not granted the same margin

possible or excessively difficult must be analysed by reference to the role of that provision in the procedure, its progress and its special features, viewed as a whole, before the various national instances. In the light of that analysis the basic principles of the domestic judicial system, such as protection of the rights of the defence, the principle of legal certainty and the proper conduct of procedure, must, where appropriate, be taken into consideration."

186 M.C. Dorf/Ch. F. Sabel, 'A Constitution of Democratic Experimentalism', (1998) 98 *Columbia Law Review* 267; O. Gerstenberg/Ch. Sabel, 'Directly-Deliberate Polyarchy: An Institutional Ideal for Europe' in C. Joerges/R. Dehousse (eds), *Good Governance in Europe's Integrated Market*, Oxford University Press, Oxford, 2002, 289.

of discretion states have. They lack self-determination.[187] Granting them standing under Article 263(4) would constitute a first step in upgrading the role and function of such societal constitutional bodies.

Subjective rights in the vertical division of power have a different role to play. The Treaty as it stands even after Lisbon does not provide much room for the recognition of additional subjective rights, although the ECJ might always come up with a surprising new solution such as it did in *Sala* and *Baumbast*. What might change, however, are the character and understanding of the role and function of subjective rights. The constitutionalisation of values, not least via the Charter on Fundamental Rights, leads to an understanding whereby right holders also bear a constitutional responsibility.[188] They do not hold an individual right alone, as the right enshrines values that bear a public policy dimension. Whether such a development will lead to the recognition of new rights depends on how the ECJ will approach the declaration laid down in Article 51(2) of the Charter of Fundamental Rights. As is already clear in *Kücükdevici* or *Promusicae*,[189] the Charter will play a key role in the interpretation of secondary EU law. The EU itself is actively promoting such a development by referring in the recitals to the Charter of Fundamental Rights. Such a perspective might shed new light on the upcoming litigation in the field of the social legal order. The right of access to the preliminary procedure is a possible candidate for a new stand alone subjective right, which could be anchored in the Charter.

The recognition of new remedies can take two forms: the scope of application of established remedies could be extended – from the vertical into the horizontal perspective – from one field of EU law (competition) to another (market freedoms), or 'new' remedies could be introduced into the Treaty which do not yet belong to the *acquis communautaire*. Most scholars would agree that the ECJ did not strictly apply the doctrine developed in *Les Verts* and *Opinion 1/91*. A more difficult question arises when 'the national legal system does not provide for a remedy' (*Unibet*)? I would argue that a distinction should be made whether the question comes up in areas of the European legal order, (1) where the national legal order cannot serve as a blueprint because the question behind the search for a remedy is 'genuinely European' and (2) where the European legal order is clearly reaching beyond the

187 L. Azoulai, 'The Court of Justice and the Social Market Economy: The Emergence of an Ideal and the Conditions for its Realisation', (2008) 45 *CMLR* 1335, at 1350.

188 See on responsibilities enshrined in individual and collective rights, L. Azoulai, 'The Court of Justice and the Social Market Economy: The Emergence of an Ideal and the Conditions for its Realisation', (2008) 45 *CMLR* 1335, at 1350.

189 V. Kosta, 'Internal Market Law and the Private Law of the Member States. The Impact of Fundamental Rights' in S. Geschwandtner, V. Kosta, H. Schebesta, P. Verbrüggen, *The Impact of the Internal Market on Private Law of the Member Countries*, EUI Working Paper 22/2009, 25 = (2010) 6 *ERCL*, 409.

national legal orders in establishing new values which need to preserved. A striking example for the second variant is the anti-discrimination principle.

The horizontal division of power is governed by proper EU procedural rules and today also by inter-institutional agreements. These are missing in the vertical dimension where the ECJ as early as in *Rewe* cautiously advocated for the development of European procedural rules (*Adinolfi*). The constant reiteration of the reference to the principles of equivalence and effectiveness has not prevented the ECJ from heavily intervening in national procedure rules, mainly to break down barriers to trade – so-called negative effectiveness. The ECJ has not further developed the rule of reason doctrine enshrined in *van Schijndel (Bobek)*,[190] which might serve as a tool for fostering positive effectiveness. Whether or not the principles of equivalence and effectiveness will suffice to shape procedural rules remains to be seen. Just as in the field of remedies, it might be helpful to more clearly distinguish between areas where the European legal order and the national legal orders are interlinked in a comparable way from areas where the particularity of the European legal order requires solutions reaching beyond the national procedural rules.

If all RRP bear a constitutional dimension, what then remains for the ECJ acting as a Supreme Court?[191] One might feel tempted to seek a solution in the different types of remedies foreseen in the Treaty. It seems as if distinctions of this kind are not really helpful in finding out whether RRP is a matter for the ECJ as a constitutional court or whether it can also be regarded as a matter for the ECJ as a supreme court. It seems much more important to look into the substance of RRP and then to decide what are the questions that should be upgraded to the constitutional level and those which could be downgraded to the substantive level. Even if such an undertaking leads to feasible results, the overall effort is only worthwhile if the distinction between the constitutional level and the substantive level of RRP entails different legal consequences. What springs to mind is the conviction that a constitutional court will have to decide only on the very basics of the RRP and that it will be for a Supreme Court to go much more into the details of the respective rights, the respective remedies and the respective procedural rules. It is then only one step further to open the debate on where the CFI should precede the ECJ. The preliminary reference procedure seems to be one of the possible candidates for an enlarged body of CFIs.

190 Under reference to S. Prechal, 'Community Law in National Courts: The Lessons from van Schijndel', (1998) 35 *CMLR* 681, at 690.

191 With regard to private law, C. Schmid, 'The ECJ as a Constitutional and a Private Law Court', ZERP *DP* 4/2006.

## 5. THOUGHTS ON THE FUTURE FOR THE EU LAW ON REMEDIES *DE LEGE LATA*

In *Goethe*'s poem of the 'Sorcerers Apprentice' (Zauberlehrling) we can find the following quotation:[192]

> "From the spirits that I call, Sir, deliver me! (Die ich rief, die Geister werd ich nun nicht los)"

The ECJ remains bound to the spirit of the Treaty of Rome which has remained unchanged despite the major Treaty revisions through the Single European Act, the Maastricht and the Lisbon Treaty. European integration is a process, an open ended process which makes it difficult to define a clear line between the constituted and the constituent power of the ECJ. *L. Corrias*[193] concludes after analysing the relationship between constituent and constituted powers, both theoretically and legally, in selected areas of EU law: "Paradoxically 'ensuring that the law is observed' can only be done by going beyond a simple textual explanation of the Treaty. So the ECJ can only ensure the observance of the EU legal order by truly creative acts, acts of chiastic constitution. That is what constitutionalisation ultimately boils down to. Yet this is only half of the story. The ECJ can only bind others to the law while being bound by the law. It stands on trial while sitting on trial'.

In essence I am arguing for an active court, a court which takes the imbalance between the three orders seriously and which is ready to develop RRPs in the social legal order. So what is requested is a stronger 'impulse' (*Basedow*) and a 'quasi-legislative approach' (*Reich*) which urges the ECJ to 'invent' (*Bobek*) new RRPs – as an integral part of the European legal order. Article 47 of the Charter of Fundamental Rights will have to play a key role in that respect. The immediate question in the context of the conference is nevertheless from where such a claim for judicial activism or judicial governance could take its legitimacy. It took the ECJ decades before its concept of 'a genuine legal order' gained political and social acceptance. I am wondering why the legitimacy is so forcefully claimed when it comes to giving judicial shape to the European legal order. Maybe the reason can be found in the anxieties of the Member States that, having lost control over the national 'economic' order, they may also lose control over 'The Social'. If such a reading is correct it is necessary to go much deeper into the changing role of the

---

192 http://german.about.com/library/blgzauberl.htm.

193 *The Passivity of Law: Competence and Constitution in the European Court of Justice*, PhD 2010, at p 171.

national state, of the national welfare state and even of 'The Social' as such. Any answer, however, goes far beyond the purpose of this article.[194]

## 5.1. CONSTITUTIONAL IMPLICATIONS: A RIGHT TO ACCESS IN THE PRELIMINARY REFERENCE PROCEDURE

Let me start with a quotation from the late *Pierre Pescatore*, one of the grand old men of the European legal integration project, a former judge of the ECJ who joined the Court in 1967 and left us with the following legacy:[195]

> The court held that the vigilance of individuals concerned to protect their rights amounts to an effective supervision in addition to the supervision entrusted by Art. 169 and 170 in the diligence of the Commission and the Member States. This formulate is prophetic, since we would see later on that the preliminary reference procedure ... – will effectively become the infringement procedure for the European citizen.

Undoubtedly the ECJ was prophetic, but has the prophecy become reality? I do not think so, as the position of the citizen depends on the preparedness of the national court to refer her case to Luxembourg. One might construc arguments under the national legal systems which compel the national court to refer the case to Luxembourg, but even such a right cannot replace the chance of directly invoking the preliminary reference procedure. *Sarmiento* argues in favour of establishing a fundament right of access to the preliminary reference procedure in referring to the Opinion of the late Advocate General *Ruiz-Jarabo Colomer* in *La Roda Golf*,[196] who raised this point and purported an interpretation of the provisions governing preliminary references in light of this fundamental right:

> (29) Access to justice is a fundamental pillar of western legal culture. 'To no one will we sell, to no one will we deny or delay right or justice' proclaimed the Magna Carta in 1215, expressing an axiom which has remained in force in Europe to the extent that it features in the European Convention on Human Rights, the Charter of Fundamental Rights of the European Union and the case-law of the Court. Therefore, the right to effective legal protection is one of the general principles

---

[194] I have given a first account in *Social Justice and Access Justice in Private Law*, EUI WP 2011 forthcoming; see also The *Many Faces of Social Justice in Private Law* (ed), Elgar Publishing, forthcoming.

[195] P. Pescatore, '*Van Gend en Loos*, 3 February 1963 – A view from within' in M. Poiares Maduro/L. Azoulai (eds) *The Past and The Future of EU Law, The Classics of EU Law Revisited on the 50th Anniversary of the Treaty of Rome*, Hart Publishing, Oxford, 2010, 3, at 7.

[196] ECJ 25 June 2009, Case C-14/08, *La Roda Golf* [2009] ECR I-5439.

> of Community law, in accordance with which access to justice is organised. In a number of Member States, such as Germany and Spain, that fundamental right is framed in such a way that it also includes the preliminary ruling procedure under Article [267 TFEU]. The present reference is doubly crucial with regard to safeguarding the procedural rights of individuals at both Community and national level. Access to justice entails not only the commencement of legal proceedings but also the requirement that the competent court must be seized of those proceedings. Furthermore, from a procedural point of view, references for a preliminary ruling are subject to the principles of the uniformity and consistency of Community law, from which it follows that any national court must have competence to seek assistance from the Court of Justice. Any barrier preventing a national court from making a reference undermines that fundamental right".

In the forefront of the discussion over the content of a European Constitution, *N. Reich*[197] argued in favour of introducing into the revised legal system of the EU a *Europäische Grundrechtsbeschwerde* (a European fundamental right on access). Such a possibility has never been seriously taken into consideration. True, citizens in Europe may refer claims directly to the European Court of Human Rights and once the EU has joined the ECHR the role of citizens might even be further strengthened. Reading the TFEU, the Charter of Fundamental Rights and the ECHR together might even enhance the idea proposed here that the EU legal order embraces a constitutional right of access to justice.

There are convincing arguments in favour of establishing such a right of access to justice. It would reflect the increasing importance of citizen rights in the European constitutional charter, it would bring light into the black box of the preliminary reference procedure (*Reich*) and it would strengthen the democratic outlook of the EU. In *Unibet* the ECJ opened the door for completing the existing system of remedies and procedures. A right of access to justice, i.e. to the ECJ directly not only for individuals but also for collective entities, would be 'new' in the sense that direct access to the ECJ cannot have a counterpart in the Member States legal orders. Time seems ripe for a bold step forward in the development of the European legal order that finalises *Pescatore's* prophecy.

[197] Zur Notwendigkeit einer Europäische Grundrechtsbeschwerde, ZRP 2000, 375; also B. Hansel, *Effektiver Rechtsschutz in Grundrechtsfragen durch Vorlagepflicht oberster Bundesgerichte oder Europäische Verfassungsgerichte*, Walter Hallstein Institut, Berlin, 2003.

## 5.2. SUBSTANTIVE IMPLICATIONS: RRPs TO COUNTERBALANCE THE EUROPEAN ECONOMIC ORDER

The crux in the current state of RRPs in Europe is the standard formula of the principle of effectiveness and the principle of equivalence which the ECJ constantly reiterates – gebetsmühlenartig wiederholt – despite the unclear meaning of the two principles; despite the unsettled relationship between the two principles which have led to an inconsistent and often hard to understand case-law (*Bobek*); and despite its clear sometimes explicit, sometimes implicit focus on Member States RRPs as a yardstick even where the rights, remedies and procedures do not fit with the particularities of the European legal order.

I started this paper by reference to *Walter van Gerven's* seminal article and I will conclude this paper by again referring to his plea to transform the principle of equivalent and effective protection into a *principle of adequate and effective protection. Van Schijndel* points in this direction,[198] but the Court has not developed this path any further, despite numerous references in key judgments such as *Asturcom*, *Feryn*, *van der Weerd* and *Eco Suisse*, just to name those which are of relevance in our context.

I will sketch out three different possibilities for developing RRPs within the dominant paradigms, beginning with the doctrine of uniform application, shifting to the principle of effectiveness and concluding with a new reading of the principle of equivalence.

### 5.2.1. *From uniform application to uniform enforcement*

The principle of uniformity is a central theme in all decisions by the ECJ, which aims to ensure that the application and interpretation of EU laws does not differ between member states. *Basedow* calls this the uniformity function of the ECJ. There is a strong link between the ECJ's insistence on autonomous interpretation and the doctrine of uniform and effective application of EU law.[199] Uniform application of EU law cannot be equated with uniform enforcement. *However, is there a way to move from uniform application to uniform enforcement?*

Uniform enforcement seems to contradict the principle of procedural autonomy (*Adinolfi*) and the vertical division of power between the EU and the Member States. On the one hand, it must be overlooked that rights cannot be enforced

[198] See my attempt to use it for striking down highly doubtful time limits in investor protection rules, H.-W. Micklitz, 'Vereinbarkeit der Verjährungsregelung § 37 a) WpHG mit dem Gemeinschaftsrecht', (2005) *Zeitschrift für Wirtschafts- und Bankrecht* 536.

[199] ECJ 6 October 1982, Case C-283/81, *C.I.L.F.I.T.* [1982] ECR 3415, para. 7.

in compliance with the principle of uniformity without common standards on remedies and procedures.[200] On the other hand, uniform enforcement cannot mean that the Member States must establish identical rules on RRP. There is a second line of argumentation which enhances the pressure on more uniform standards of enforcement. Secondary law which is subject to RRP is regulatory law. Most of the directives are status-related. They tie the envisaged protection to the status of a worker, consumer or indeed a citizen, i.e. citizen consumer. It is precisely here that the European Commission is going to change its policy, admittedly more or less successfully. Minimum harmonisation shall be replaced by maximum harmonisation. The standard formula of the need for 'effective, proportionate and dissuasive' protection is still the same. However, maximum harmonisation can only yield the expected results if the development of enforcement mechanisms keeps pace with the intensity of harmonisation. Strangely enough, the highly questionable policy of maximum harmonisation[201] may lead to better and more harmonised RRPs.

A possible balance between the two conflicting rules may be found by distinguishing two sets of enforcement issues:[202] (1) the serious infringements that bear a trans-border connotation and (2) the less serious infringements that are more closely connected to a mere national legal environment. A similar distinction has been proposed by AG *Maduro* in *Centro Europa 7 Srl*:[203]

> 18. Since the adoption of the Treaty of Amsterdam, respect for fundamental rights is a formal legal requirement for membership of the European Union. Article 6 EU, as amended by that Treaty, now firmly proclaims that the Union is founded on the principles of liberty, democracy, respect for human rights and fundamental freedoms, and the rule of law, principles which are common to the Member States. Article 7 EU sets out a mechanism for imposing sanctions on a Member State where there is a clear risk of a *serious breach of those principles*, thus confirming that respect for fundamental rights is an indispensable condition of EU membership.
> 20. Against this background, the Court fulfils its function of ensuring the observance, by the Member States, of fundamental rights as general principles of law. *In*

200 I refer to *Adinolfi* (fn. 40): As expressed by former Advocate General *Van Gerven*, the need for harmonisation of procedural rules "is inherent in the concept of uniformity: in the absence of (sufficiently) harmonized legal remedies, uniform rights cannot be adequately secured throughout the Community": 'Bridging the Gap between Community and National Laws: towards a Principle of Homogeneity in the Field of Legal Remedies?', (1995) 32 *CMLR* 690.

201 B. Gsell/C. Herresthal (Hrsg.), *Vollharmonisierung im Privatrecht*, Mohr Siebeck, Tübingen, 2009.

202 See H.-W. Micklitz, 'Collective private enforcement in antitrust law – what is going wrong in the debate?', to be published in L. Tichy/J. Terhechte (eds), forthcoming = EUI Working Paper 00/2010.

203 AG Maduro 12 September 2009, Case C-380/05, *Centro Europa 7 Srl* [2009] I-349. The Court has not discussed this proposal yet.

> *this respect, a distinction must be drawn between, on the one hand, jurisdiction to review any national measure in the light of fundamental rights and, on the other hand, jurisdiction to examine whether Member States provide the necessary level of protection in relation to fundamental rights in order to be able adequately to fulfil their other obligations as members of the Union.* The first type of review does not yet exist and is not within the Union's current competences. However, the second type of review flows logically from the nature of the process of European integration. It serves to guarantee that the basic conditions are in place for the proper functioning of the EU legal order and for the effective exercise of many of the rights granted to European citizens. Though the degree of protection of fundamental rights at national level does not have to be exactly the same as the degree of protection of fundamental rights at the level of the European Union, there must be some measure of equivalence in order to ensure that the law of the Union can operate effectively within the national legal order.
> 21. The scenario may seem unlikely at first sight, but I do not discount, offhand, the idea that a serious and persistent breach of fundamental rights might occur in a Member State, making it impossible for that State to comply with many of its EU obligations and effectively limiting the possibility for individuals to benefit fully from the rights granted to them by EU law. For instance, it would be difficult to envisage citizens of the Union exercising their rights of free movement in a Member State where there are systemic shortcomings in the protection of fundamental rights. Such systemic shortcomings would, in effect, amount to a violation of the rules on free movement.

The Advocate himself made clear that the case at issue could be solved within the standard framework of rules. Thus it is not surprising that the court does not take the distinction into consideration. What matters in our context, however, is the plea for the identification of breaches where it is not possible to leave the level of judicial protection to the Member States but where common rules are needed – in particular to protect fundamental rights. This is exactly in line with the argument put forward throughout this paper.

### *5.2.2. The principle of effectiveness and the doctrine of economic efficiency*

The principle of effectiveness is not a normative concept as there is no normative yardstick available beyond or below the non-existence of appropriate RRPs or, in the terms of *Rewe*, making 'it impossible in practice to exercise the rights which the national courts are obliged to protect' (*Bobek*). On further reflection one might even doubt whether the impossibility doctrine has a normative nucleus, as the ECJ makes the impossibility depend on 'practice'. By downgrading the level of intervention to 'excessively difficult' (*Francovich*) the ECJ opened up a huge amount of leeway in instrumentalising the principle of effectiveness in both directions – in establishing a low level of enforcement or in requiring a high level of enforcement. Therefore the principle of effectiveness is technically an empirical concept which would, in theory, require the ECJ to investigate the existence of RRPs in the respective Member States, maybe even in a comparative perspective. The way the ECJ is using the principle, i.e. as a kind of jack-in-the-box instrument,[204] allows the Court to justify – within the limits of the impossibility doctrine – almost every result. The weakness of the concept is the reason behind the inconsistency of the current case-law in the field of RRP.

I see two ways out of this dilemma: to give up on the principle and to substitute it via a truly normative concept or else to take the factual implications seriously. The first variant would bring us back to *van Schijndel* which might be read as a 'rule of reason' formula against which Member States' RRPs could be measured. I would not put the rule of reason formula on an equal footing with the proportionality principle. *Reich* has shown that the proportionality principle needs to be revisited in order to avoid arbitrary results. He distinguishes between autonomous balancing (public policy choices or equally justified opposing state interests), state margins of appreciation (where law and facts do not give a clear answer), a fundamental rights approach (continuation of the division of work between EU and national jurisdictions), and a quasi-legislative approach. A transfer of these four categories to RRP would certainly not contribute to increasing legal certainty or to making the case-law of the ECJ more predictable.

So what remains is putting emphasis on the factual side. Since 2002, since the beginning of the governance debate,[205] the European Commission has put more and more emphasis on measuring EU regulation against the doctrine of economic efficiency. The technical means of doing so is enshrined in the ever more sophisticated apparatus of impact assessments.[206] So far the methodology has been used in order to test the probable effects of an EU measure that the European Commission intends to adopt, – with sometimes highly doubtful results[207] – but it has not yet been applied to evaluate the (economic) efficiency of national RRPs. In a methodologically-revised form the Impact Assessment Procedure might provide guidance to the ECJ on the situation in the Member States with regard to the effectiveness of RRPs. It seems therefore fair to assume

204 I borrow this metaphor from T. Wilhelmsson, 'Jack-in-the-box theory of European Community Law' in L. Krämer/H.-W. Micklitz/K. Tonner (eds./Hrsg.), *Law and diffuse Interests in the European Legal Order/Recht und diffuse Interessen in der in der Europäischen Rechtsordnung, Liber amicorum Norbert Reich*, Band 3 der VIEW Schriftenreihe, Nomos, Baden-Baden, 1997, p 177.

205 http://ec.europa.eu/governance/index_en.htm.

206 http://ec.europa.eu/governance/impact/index_en.htm.

207 See for a methodological critique R. Monday, 'In the Wake of Good Governance: 'Impact Assessments and the Politicisation of Statutory Interpretation', (2008) 71 *Modern Law Review* 385; for a demonstration of politically guided impact assessments, H.-W. Micklitz, 'The Targeted Full Harmonisation Approach: Looking behind the Curtain' in Howells/Schulze (eds), *Modernising and Harmonising Consumer Contract Law*, Sellier, Munich, 2009, 47.

that the principle of effective application and enforcement could be turned into a more efficient regulatory tool. However, it cannot overcome the uncertainties which result from a case-law whose outcome depends on non-normative criteria. But this is a methodological question which brings us too far away from the scope of the paper.

### *5.2.3. Materialising the principle of equivalence*

The principle of equivalence is *in nuce* a variant of the anti-discrimination principle. The national rules on RRP may pass the equivalence test if they do not discriminate against the enforcement of EU law rules. Even stronger and even more explicitly than the principle of effectiveness, the principle of equivalence uses national RRPs as reference points. This means that the ECJ has to find and to define a 'comparator' against which the RRPs needed to enforce the respective EU rules can be measured. It should be recalled that the ECJ cannot and does not compare European RRPs and national RRPs; rather it compares the feasibility of national RRPs being designed for a particular national purpose with their transferability to the relevant EU rules. More clearly, the ECJ compares substantive rules not procedural rules (RRPs). *Bobek* demonstrates the difficulties and, in a way, the arbitrariness of this selection process.[208] The experience the ECJ has gained over recent decades in finding the appropriate comparator in indirect discrimination cases should help to challenge the feasibility of the concept.

The first and most important step would be to more carefully look into the substance of the rules in order to find out whether and to what extent the EU rules complement national rules or whether the EU rules introduce regulatory elements which reach beyond the existing national frame and are designed to meet the particularities of the European legal order. So far the ECJ draws the distinction only implicitly, in that it does not apply the principles jointly but uses whichever one is more suitable in the case at issue. It would be worth analysing the abundant case-law to test the hypothesis that the ECJ tends to apply the principle of effectiveness when there are no comparable EU rules due to the particularities of the EU legal order. It would equally be worth analysing what kind of criteria the ECJ used to define the parameter. *Bobek* has already shown that the choice of the parameter depends on the level of abstraction. I would insist that the academic discourse on the ECJ case-law in RRPs does not take sufficiently into account the factual and the legal context of the cases. Even a more sophisticated contextual analysis, drawing a clearer border line between the cases which are apt for the equivalence test and those which are not, would still not overcome the inherent difficulties enshrined in the test.

---

208 W. Micklitz, 'Vereinbarkeit der Verjährungsregelung § 37 a) WpHG mit dem Gemeinschaftsrecht', (2005) *Zeitschrift für Wirtschafts- und Bankrecht* 536.

It is hard to imagine the ECJ giving up the equivalence test. The Court might be ready to upgrade the effectiveness test to an adequacy test, but it will and it must – in the light of the vertical division of power – stick with the equivalence test. The anti-discrimination test is in essence a *negative* one. In EU law, anti-discrimination and equal treatment are used interchangeably, although equal treatment bears a *positive* forward looking connotation. A promising starting point might therefore be to use equal treatment as the guiding principle, which comes also nearer to the wording of the principle of equivalence. *Mangold* and *Kücükdevici* provide evidence that the ECJ is going to materialise the anti-discrimination principle in labour law relations. The growing positive connotation of anti-discrimination could be used to reshape the principle of equivalence. I would plead for the development of a kind of materialised access test[209] which is not restricted to the already difficult comparison of whether Member States apply the same standards for the enforceability of similar national rules, but rather whether the existing RRPs in the Member States, beyond comparability, provide for adequate access to RRPs. Such an understanding could gradually merge the two principles of equivalence and effectiveness in the new formula of adequate judicial protection.

To be continued…

[209] See on the background to this argument, H.-W. Micklitz, *Social Justice and Access Justice in Private Law*, EUI Working Paper 2011, forthcoming.

# INDEX


abusive contract terms 76
access to justice 340, 342
annulment action 298
autonomy 305, 320, 321, 325, 327, 332, 333, 334, 336, 338, 339, 340, 341, 342, 345

balancing 310, 312, 316
Bologna process 73, 149, 151, 154, 155, 172
Bressol 156, 157, 161, 162, 163, 164, 165, 171

causality 11
collective action 26
collective labour law 239
company law 74
comparator 314, 322
competence 11, 12, 14, 15, 16, 18, 19, 20, 21, 23, 24, 25, 26, 30, 31, 34, 350, 353, 358, 364, 366, 375, 383
- complementary 150, 152, 159
- negative vertical 150
Constitution
- identity 40, 47, 48, 51, 52
- integrative function 38, 39, 40, 41, 42, 43, 44, 45, 46, 47, 48, 49, 50, 51, 60, 61, 62, 63
- legal traditions 56, 59, 62
- organizational function 43, 51
constitutional pluralism 260, 261
Court of Justice of the European Union 35, 49, 60

damages 311
declaration on nationality of a Member State 199, 200
direct effect 36, 38, 53
directives, implementation 295
discrimination 312, 314
economic freedoms and fundamental rights 237, 239, 264, 265, 267
economic integration 223, 230
effectiveness 305, 306, 307, 308, 312, 316, 317, 318, 319, 320, 322
effet utile 200–202
enforcement 283, 291, 303, 305, 306, 331–333, 335, 364, 365, 367, 373, 374, 375, 378, 380, 386, 395, 396, 397, 398
equivalence 305, 307, 308, 312, 313, 314, 315, 317, 318, 319, 320, 322
European economic order 357, 358, 360, 395
ex officio application of EU law 367, 368
externalities 27

family reunification 186, 189
free movement rights 122, 131, 137, 142, 143
fundamental rights 37, 38, 39, 40, 46, 47, 50, 53, 56, 57, 61, 219, 220, 221, 259, 260, 261, 262, 263, 264, 265, 266, 267, 268, 269, 270, 271, 272, 273, 274, 275, 276, 296

harmonisation 299, 300–302, 310, 311, 314, 316, 322
Herzog (German ex-president) 66
higher education 149–172
horizontal effect 370
human dignity 260, 265, 272, 274

implied powers 152, 171
impulse function of ECJ 69, 72–75
incorporation 265, 266, 267, 273
indirect judicial review 126, 131, 133, 134, 136, 137, 139, 141, 142, 143, 146
input legitimacy 31, 34
insurance market 73–74
integration
- legal 152, 153, 172
- political 152, 153, 156, 172
internal market 44, 55, 60, 62

Jellinek 221, 222
judicial protection 296, 300, 301

Kompetenz-Kompetenz 37

legal traditions 60
legitimacy 11, 16, 18, 25, 26, 27, 28, 31, 33

mandatory requirements 60
Mangold judgement 78, 328, 329, 330, 345

national courts 325, 326, 327, 328, 330, 332, 333, 334, 335, 337, 339, 340, 341, 342, 343, 344
national highest (constitutional) courts 62
negative harmonisation 56, 311
non-discrimination 137, 159, 161, 166, 167, 169, 230, 231, 232, 263, 264, 266, 267

output legitimacy 26, 27, 28, 29, 30, 31, 34

personal circumstances test 126, 131, 136, 137, 141, 142, 143
preliminary references 337, 340
preliminary ruling (role of national courts) 287, 288, 289
primacy of EU law 35, 36, 37, 38, 46, 47, 48, 52, 53, 56, 59, 60, 61, 63, 291–294, 300–301
principle of conferral 50, 55, 56
principles of EU law 286, 296, 297, 299, 300, 301
procedural autonomy 281–323
procedure 349–400
proportionality 55, 61, 127, 133, 134, 136, 139, 147, 159, 160, 161, 164, 165, 166, 167, 170, 310, 312
public policy and public security restrictions 192–195
public power 36, 38, 39, 41, 42, 43, 44, 52, 56, 62

quantitative appetizer 220, 228

real link 182, 185
real link test 124, 125, 126, 133, 134, 135, 136, 137, 138, 142
recognition
– academic 154
– professional 155
reimbursement mechanism 162, 164, 171
relative autonomy of Union citizenship 196, 199–200
remedies 349–400
residency rights 136
res judicata 287, 293
review function of ECJ 69, 70–71, 79
rights 8, 349, 350, 351, 352, 353, 354, 355, 356, 360, 361, 371, 389
right to access 393
Rottmann 198

Schüssel (Austrian ex-chancellor) 65
social rights 220, 230
social status activus 222
sovereignty 48, 50, 52, 54, 63
standing 341
State liability for breach of EU law 333, 339
student mobility 152, 153, 155, 156, 157, 159, 161, 166, 171, 172
subsidiarity 55
substantive autonomy 222, 223, 224, 225, 227, 235, 236, 241, 242

temporal perspective 12
terrorism 268
time-limits 306, 320

uniform application of EU law 294–295, 302
uniformity function of ECJ 69, 76–79
Union citizenship 113–147, 175–203

vertical effect 370, 378

welfare support 124, 127, 133, 137

www.ingramcontent.com/pod-product-compliance
Ingram Content Group UK Ltd.
Pitfield, Milton Keynes, MK11 3LW, UK
UKHW051919100926
8556IPUK00021B/1258